Oracle Database 10g Express Edition PHP Web Programming

Michael McLaughlin

New York   Chicago   San Francisco
Lisbon   London   Madrid   Mexico City   Milan
New Delhi   San Juan   Seoul   Singapore   Sydney   Toronto

The McGraw·Hill Companies

McGraw-Hill books are available at special quantity discounts to use as premiums and sales promotions, or for use in corporate training programs. For more information, please write to the Director of Special Sales, Professional Publishing, McGraw-Hill, Two Penn Plaza, New York, NY 10121-2298. Or contact your local bookstore.

Oracle Database 10*g* Express Edition PHP Web Programming

1234567890 CUS CUS 019876

ISBN-13:   978-0-07-226325-1
ISBN-10:   0-07-226325-3

ISBN-13: Book P/N 978-0-07-226330-5 and CD P/N 978-0-07-226326-8
of set 978-0-07-226325-1

ISBN-10: Book P/N 0-07-226330-X and CD P/N 0-07-226326-1
of set 0-07-226325-3

Sponsoring Editor Lisa McClain	**Proofreader** Paul Tyler
Editorial Supervisor Patty Mon	**Production Supervisor** George Anderson
Project Editor Claire Splan	**Composition** International Typesetting and Composition
Acquisitions Coordinator Alex McDonald Mandy Canales	**Illustration** International Typesetting and Composition
Technical Editor A. Scott Mikolaitis	**Cover Designer** Jeff Weeks
Copy Editor Robert Campbell	

To Lisa—my sweetheart, my inspiration, my wife and best friend; and Sarah, Joseph, Elise, Ian, Ariel, Callie, Nathan, Spencer, and Christianne—our terrific heaven-sent children. Thank you for your constant support, patience, and sacrifice that made writing this book possible.

About the Author

Michael McLaughlin is a professor at BYU – Idaho in the Computer Information Technology Department of the Business and Communication School. He is founder of Techtinker.com, a company focused on application development and development technologies. He worked at Oracle Corporation for over eight years in consulting, development, and support. He worked with the core technology stack and release engineering for the Oracle E-Business Suite. Prior to his tenure at Oracle Corporation, he worked as an Oracle developer, systems and business analyst, and DBA beginning with Oracle 6. He is coauthor of *Oracle Database 10g Programming* and *Expert Oracle PL/SQL*.

About the Technical Editor

A. Scott Mikolaitis is a Senior Principal Support Engineer at Oracle Corporation and has worked at Oracle for over nine years. He works as the Oracle Application ATG Bug Diagnostics and Escalation specialist, triaging bugs and performing advanced analysis in third-tier support. Scott enjoys working in Perl and web development technologies and has been working on Jabber technology and Oracle Application Framework diagnostics.

Contents at a Glance

PART IV
PHP and Oracle Express Development

PART V
Appendixes

Contents

PART I
PHP Fundamentals

PART II
PHP Programming

PART III
PHP Application Development

PART IV
PHP and Oracle Express Development

PART V
Appendixes

Acknowledgments

Many thanks go to Lisa McClain and Alex McDonald at McGraw-Hill/Osborne for their tireless work on this project; Claire Splan who efficiently moved this text through copyedit to production; and A. Scott Mikolaitis, a key Oracle Technology Resource, who provided invaluable feedback in his technical edit and review of the text.

Thanks to Luxi Chidambaran, Srinath Krishnaswamy, Christopher Jones, Shoaib Lari, and Richard Rendell from Oracle Development, who ran down OCI issues and provided answers to questions. Special thanks to Christopher Jones for reviewing and suggesting ideas while outlining the book.

Special thanks to Joseph McLaughlin who wrote Appendix A, "HTML Tag Index," and the first draft for Appendix E, "POSIX File Functions."

Thanks to BYU – Idaho Computer Information Technology Department faculty, and students who took an interest in the book and programming language—Craig Haessig, Benjamin Howard, and Brian Vance.

Finally, no acknowledgement would be complete without thanking the production department. Thanks to the production department for their conscientious attention to detail and hard work in putting all the pieces together.

Introduction

The book is designed to be read from beginning to end by those new to both PHP and the Oracle database. Those new to PHP 5 can benefit from reviewing Part I, which covers the installation, configuration and fundamentals of the language before they begin reading Part II. Experienced PHP programming language developers who are new to the Oracle database can read Chapter 2 to set up the environment and then start reading in Part IV.

Appendixes A through F provide support for HTML tags, programming concepts, and exploration of libraries discussed in the book. Oracle SQL*Plus, SQL, and PL/SQL primers are in Appendix G, H, and I respectively, while Appendix J contains the SQL and PL/SQL code required to build the database models used in Chapters 13, 14, and 15.

Part I: PHP Fundamentals

Part I introduces you to the book, the product installation, the process of writing web pages, the details of language data types, and the control structures that support the language.

- *Chapter 1: Overview of PHP and Oracle Web Programming*   Introduces the book and provides a thumbnail sketch about PHP programming and the Oracle database.

- *Chapter 2: Installing and Configuring Oracle Express, Apache, and PHP*   Explains how to install, configure, and test Apache, Oracle, and PHP products and the combined environment.

- *Chapter 3: Writing Web Pages*   Introduces the concept of server-side scripting and demonstrates how to use PHP syntax to write basic web pages.

- *Chapter 4: Variables, Operators, Data Types, and File Inclusion*   Examines how to declare, define, assign, compare, and process PHP variables.

- *Chapter 5: Control Structures*   Examines how to use conditional and iterative structures in your PHP programs.

Part II: PHP Programming

Part II discusses arrays, functions, objects, errors, and file operations. It works exclusively with the approaches used in PHP 5.

- *Chapter 6: Arrays*   Examines how to define, declare, assign, compare, and process arrays.

- *Chapter 7: Functions*   Examines how to define and use functions, and explores the new pass-by-reference model in PHP 5.

- *Chapter 8: Objects*   Examines how to define, initialize, and use objects, and explores new PHP 5 object reflection operations.

- *Chapter 9: Error Management and Exception Handling*   Examines how to manage runtime error and error suppression, and the concurrent PHP 5 exception handling process.

- *Chapter 10: File I/O*   Examines how to read, write, and upload files.

Part III: PHP Application Development

Part III discusses and demonstrates the RPC nature of server-side include programming environments, like PHP, and covers the concepts of HTTP Basic Authentication, and management of server-side sessions and client-side cookies.

- *Chapter 11: Basic HTTP Authentication and Forms*   Examines how to write and deploy interactive PHP forms using Basic HTTP Authentication.

- *Chapter 12: Cookies and Sessions*   Examines how to write and deploy interactive PHP forms using cookies, URL rewriting, and sessions.

Part IV: PHP and Oracle Express Development

Part IV discusses and demonstrates Oracle's OCI8 libraries, and how to connect and transact against scalar and composite variable data types.

- *Chapter 13: Oracle SQL Queries and Transactions*   Examines how to connect to the Oracle database, and both query and transact against records using SQL statements.

- *Chapter 14: Oracle PL/SQL Transactions*   Examines how to both query and transact against records using PL/SQL statements and stored procedures.

- *Chapter 15: Oracle Large Object Transactions*   Examines how to both query and transact against CLOB and BFILE LOB column values, using both SQL and PL/SQL statements and stored procedures.

Part V: Appendixes

Part V contains six appendixes that support how you use HTML tags, programming concepts, and library exploration and object reflection. It also has SQL*Plus environment, SQL, and PL/SQL primers for those new to the Oracle 10*g* family of products. The last appendix provides the SQL and PL/SQL source code to build the testing environment that supports Chapters 13, 14 and 15.

- *Appendix A: HTML Tag Index*   A summary review of major HTML and XHTML tags to support embedded HTML in the book chapters.

- *Appendix B: Strings, Tools, and Techniques*   A summary of basic string manipulation functions and applied techniques.

- *Appendix C: PHP Environment Constants*   A summary of sample environment constants.

- *Appendix D: Environment Interfaces and Object Types*   A summary of interfaces, objects, and extensions, with a program to query your environment settings.

- *Appendix E: POSIX File Functions*   A summary review of POSIX functions to support product use on Linux AS 3/4.

- *Appendix F: Date Functions*   A review of available data management functions, with examples of commonly used functions.

- *Appendix G: Oracle Database Primer*   A summary of working with the SQL*Plus environment, starting up and shutting down the database listener and server.

- *Appendix H: SQL Primer*   An explanation and demonstration of Oracle's implementation of SQL, covering standard and user-defined type definitions, Data Definition Language, Data Query Language, Data Manipulation Language, and Data Control Language examples.

- *Appendix I: PL/SQL Primer*   An explanation and demonstration of Oracle's implementation of PL/SQL covering the block structure, variables, assignments, operators, control structures, stored functions/procedures/packages, database triggers, collections, and the DBMS_LOB package.

- *Appendix J: Database Setup Scripts*   A listing of source code to configure and seed the sample database that supports examples in Chapters 13, 14 and 15.

What's on the Enclosed CD?

The enclosed CD-ROM includes

- The Oracle Database 10*g* Express Edition for Linux and Microsoft Windows and the Oracle documentation on the product

- The Apache 2.0.55 MSI file for Microsoft Windows

- Zend Core for Oracle, version 1.4.1

- A generic copy of the GNU PHP 5.1.4 files and the source code for all the examples in this book

PART
I

PHP Fundamentals

CHAPTER
1

Overview of PHP and Oracle Web Programming

his chapter introduces you to PHP programming, Apache HTTP server, and the Oracle database web development environments. It also discusses the advantages and challenges of developing web applications using the PHP programming language and Oracle Database 10*g* Express Edition.

This book is designed to enable you to develop PHP web applications using an Oracle database, and to provide you with working code and concepts that jump-start your productivity and fast-track your solution development time whether you're new to Oracle, PHP programming, or both.

This chapter discusses the following topics:

- History and background
  - What is PHP?
  - What is Oracle?
  - What is Zend?
- Developing web programming solutions
  - What goes where and why?
  - What does Oracle offer PHP?
  - Why is PHP 5 important?

The key question if you're browsing this chapter is: *Who should read this book and why?*

The answer is: *Everyone should read it who has or who will have a role in designing, developing, and administering PHP web applications using the Oracle database.*

Designers should read the book to understand how they can leverage both the PHP programming language and the Oracle database server. Web application developers should read this book because it teaches how to write PHP programs against the Oracle Database 10*g* family of products. PL/SQL programmers should read it to understand how they can best organize and write stored functions, procedures, and packages in the Oracle Database 10*g* family of products. Administrators should read it to understand the organization, flow of control, and configuration options that will make this solution scalable to your Internet or intranet customer base.

The book is designed to be an enabling reference but not a comprehensive treatment of the PHP 5 programming language. The book was written from a PHP 5 perspective but does provide a mapping of backward-compatible OCI function aliases to the new OCI8 library functions, as discussed in Chapter 13.

History and Background

The history and background of programming languages and software products can help you find and interpret old code snippets or administrative guidelines found on the Internet. This section discusses the history and background of the PHP engine and programming model; the Oracle Database 10*g* features and opportunities; and the Zend Technologies role, tools, and support for the PHP and Oracle combination.

What Is PHP?

Today PHP is a recursive acronym for PHP: Hypertext Preprocessor. In 1995, it stood for Personal Home Page and named a bunch of utilities that evolved from some Perl scripts. It was originally developed to display the résumé of the original author, Rasmus Lerdorf. The first major release was PHP 3 in 1997, and it was based on a new engine written by Zeev Suraski and Andi Gutmans. Zeev and Andi then formed Zend Technologies Ltd., rewrote the engine again as the Zend Engine 1.0, and released PHP 4 in 2000. A second major rewrite led to Zend Engine 2.0 and the release of PHP 5 in 2004. Each change in the engine has brought enhanced scalability, greater speed, and more features.

PHP is a weakly typed language, though some prefer to label it a dynamically typed language. It has a similar syntax to Perl in many respects, including variables preceded by dollar signs— `$variable`. PHP is also a server-side-include type of programming environment, deployable as a CGI or Apache module working with the Apache or Microsoft IIS server. It is an interpreted language, not a compiled one.

The language is flexible in two important ways: It is tightly integrated between PHP and HTML, and it has the ability to work with virtually all commercial databases. The language enables you to embed PHP in an HTML document and to embed HTML inside a PHP script. You can also use PHP as a server-side scripting language, but it has limited file I/O characteristics.

Critics assail PHP because it is weakly typed, has a single name space for functions, and is not thread safe. However, it is a flexible language that supports thousands of web applications around the world. It is also a fun-to-use programming language that is effective at solving complex problems and provides a quick prototyping solution for web applications.

What Is Oracle?

Oracle is a database produced by Oracle Corporation, headquartered in Redwood Shores, California. The Oracle Database 10*g* Express Edition is one of a family of database products. It is slightly restricted to a maximum size of 4GB of disk space and to 1GB of RAM, but all the features in it are found throughout the Oracle Database 10*g* family of products, and the concepts in this book work for *all* versions of Oracle Database 10*g* Release 2.

Oracle Corporation was founded in 1977 by Lawrence J. Ellison as Software Development Laboratories, renamed Relational Software Incorporated (RSI) in 1979, and finally named Oracle in 1983 to align the company name with the product. The Oracle Database 10*g* product leads the database market because it supports such advanced features as object types; collections; large objects; and a robust stored function, procedure, and package engine, known as PL/SQL: Procedural Language/Structured Query Language. Oracle also provides the Oracle Call Interface (OCI) that lets developers extend functionality into libraries written in C, C++, C#, Java, PHP, and so on.

The Oracle database has been marketed as unbreakable, until hackers ripped into it in 2002. However, overall the Oracle database is one of the most secure and stable database products on the market. At the time of writing, the Oracle database enjoys 50 percent market share.

The Oracle Database 10*g* is an ANSI SQL:2003 compliant database. It concurrently supports both relational and object relational models, a host of data warehousing functions, and a full regular expression search engine. In short, it is an awesome product that is constantly evolving.

What Is Zend?

Zeev Suraski and Andi Gutmans formed Zend Technologies Ltd. when they rewrote the PHP 4.0 engine as the Zend Engine 1.0. PHP 4.0 was released in 2000. Zend Corporation rewrote the PHP engine again as the Zend Engine 2.0, which was released as PHP 5 in 2004. Each change in the engine has brought greater scalability, speed, and features.

Zend Technologies is the magic behind the part of the GNU movement that brought the PHP language into the light. They provide licensing and support contracts for the Zend Engine, which contains features not found on the freely downloadable www.php.net site. The implementation of GNU software often finds resistance until a company provides support and a distribution model. Zend Technologies is doing that, and as a result the language is seeing even wider adoption by major corporations and government entities.

You must be a licensed customer using the Zend Core for Oracle and the Zend Engine 2.0 to receive support on your PHP and Oracle web applications. This also means that you are running PHP 5.1.4 or higher. This book code was tested using this combination.

Developing Web Programming Solutions

Web programming solutions are typically composed of an Apache or IIS HTTPD server, a server-side include (CGI or Apache module), and a database. The selection of the products is often hotly contested in many IT shops. For the moment, it is assumed that you have chosen Apache 2.0.55, PHP 5.1.4, and the Oracle Database 10*g* Release 2.

What Goes Where and Why?

There are many ways to deploy these architectural components, and the choice often depends on a number of factors. These factors can include the number or frequency of web hits, the volume of data in the database, and the acceptable response time window.

In the simplest architecture, you place the Apache server, PHP engine, and Oracle database on a single platform. Assuming this simple model, the customer request goes to the Apache server, which hands off dynamic calls to the PHP engine. The PHP engine supports the scope of execution of the PHP script, which can call the Oracle database server. The call from the PHP script is made through the Oracle Call Interface 8 (OCI8), as described in Chapter 13. When the database finishes processing the request, the PHP script then writes a temporary document that is served back to the original client.

The scalable architecture of PHP is devoid of standalone processes, like the Java Virtual Machine (JVM) supporting Java Server Pages (JSPs). Each PHP program acts as a standalone process, which makes the web-server tier very scalable by horizontally expanding the number of web servers. Large volume sites use a metric server to load balance across a series of web servers that are also known as a middle tier. This is depicted in Figure 1-1.

Each web server machine requires an Apache or IIS server, PHP server, and Oracle client or database server software. (Note: The instructions for installing the Oracle client software appear as a sidebar in Chapter 11.) You can deploy Service-Oriented Architecture (SOA) components on the web server to template forms from PHP libraries or on the database tier.

The distributed nature of PHP and Oracle web applications lets you position components close to the data or page rendering engine. You can replicate your PHP templates and business logic libraries across all instances of the web server or internally in the Oracle database. You put your code nearest the rendering engine when you place your templates, form rendering logic, and SOA components on the web-server tiers. You further distribute the web application by placing core business logic, transaction processing models, and data-specific SOA components on the database server. This increases the integration and reuse of coding components. Likewise, extended shared libraries can be placed on either the web-server or database-server tier, based on their

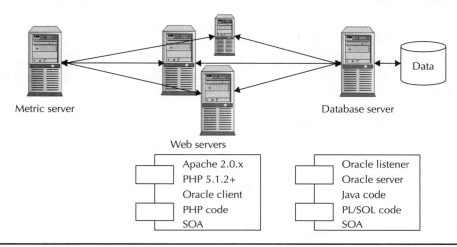

FIGURE 1-1. *Oracle, PHP, and Zend architecture*

most effective relationship. Stored database server functions and procedures have high utilization within the Oracle database shared memory realm.

The distribution of components is illustrated in Table 1-1, which represents directory (dir), host name (hn), domain name (dn), and file name (fn).

The architecture also lets you share the database-server tier PL/SQL code between both PHP and JSP program units. SOA can also be exploited by deploying Oracle 10*g* XMLType columns on the database tier.

What Does Oracle Contribute to PHP?

The Oracle Database 10*g* is deployed in half of all businesses, which present a nice market to Zend Technologies. The current OCI8 version now enables PHP developers to use several advanced features, such as

- Querying and transacting with collections data types
- Querying and transacting with reference cursors from stored procedures

Component	Web-Server Tier	Database-Server Tier
HTML Pages	http://*<hn>*.*<dn>*/*<fn>*.php	
Templates	*<dir>*/*<fn>*.inc	
Business Logic	*<dir>*/*<fn>*.inc	*<dir>*/php/*<fn>*.<so | dll>
C/C++/C# Code	*<dir>*/lib/*<fn>*.<so | dll>	*<dir>*/lib/*<fn>*.<so | dll>
Java	*<dir>*/lib/java/*<fn>*.<jar | zip>	*<dir>*/lib/java/*<fn>*.<jar | zip>

TABLE 1-1. *Distribution Matrix for PHP Web Application Coding Components*

■ Querying and transacting with BLOB, CLOB, and NCLOB data types

■ Querying CFILE and BFILE column values from internally referenced locators and returning externally stored files

Oracle has tentatively committed to extend the OCI8 to support object relational types and structures, but no *firm* date has been provided. Oracle offers PHP a robust database that works well with PHP programs.

Why Is PHP 5 Important?

The addition of refactored OCI8 code components into PHP 5.1.4 means that PHP and Oracle now natively support the new PHP 5 reference and object models. These were introduced by the Zend Engine 2 and are a stumbling block for many PHP 4 sites adopting the newest version of PHP. The PHP 5 object model is explained in Chapter 8.

PHP 5 supports traditional and persistent connections to the database. It also supports concurrent traditional and persistent connections from the same script. This extends PHP in a similar way to how Java Server Pages leverage a JServlet that maintains a connection pool.

The object model in PHP 5 is necessary to map Oracle collection and LOB data types to local PHP variables. It is demonstrated in Chapters 14 and 15. The PHP reference and object mode is a natural fit to the OCI architecture because it simplifies how developers gain access to composite data types in the Oracle database.

Summary

You have learned what components let you develop PHP web applications against the Oracle Database 10*g* family of products, and reviewed the architecture of PHP web applications. Hopefully, you have also learned how you can benefit from reading or referencing the book.

CHAPTER
2

Installing and Configuring Oracle Express, Apache, and PHP

he architecture of PHP applications using Oracle Database Express Edition requires three components be installed on the server machine: Oracle Database Express Edition, Apache HTTPD, and PHP. They are small enough that they may also be installed on a developer's laptop. This chapter describes the installation and configuration for the Red Hat Advanced Server and Windows XP Professional operating systems.

The installation programs work differently between Linux and Windows. For example, you can make a text-based menu-driven installation using Zend Core for Oracle on Linux, while a Microsoft Windows Installer is provided for Windows XP. Choices follow more or less the same sequence in both installations. Naturally, you may opt to install PHP manually from www.php.net rather than install Zend Core for Oracle, or you may substitute Microsoft Internet Information Server (IIS) for Apache HTTPD.

This chapter examines the installation and configuration of all three components; it covers the installations in the following order:

- Linux platform installation
  - Apache HTTPD
  - Oracle Database Express Edition
  - PHP engine
- Windows XP platform installation
  - Apache HTTPD
  - Oracle Database Express Edition
  - PHP engine

If you are working on a Linux system, you should read the Linux platform installation section. Alternatively, Windows XP Professional users should read the Windows XP platform installation section.

Linux Platform Installation

The Red Hat Linux Advanced Server (AS) versions 3.0 and 4.0 were used to develop these installation notes. Other Linux or Unix variants should follow more or less the same patterns, but you should check the release notes for any differences. You should install Apache or another HTTPD (for HTTP daemon—a daemon is a background process) and Oracle Express before installing the PHP engine because they are dependencies for the PHP engine.

Apache HTTPD

The Red Hat Linux AS operating system provides you an option to install Apache with the operating system. Some other Linux and Unix variants do not provide you with an option but simply install Apache for you as part of their operating system.

If you did not choose to install Apache when you built the operating system, it is recommended that you download the current source from the http://httpd.apache.org web site. You can then install Apache HTTPD on your Linux server.

If you installed the vendor-modified Apache version when you built the operating system, you can use the default port 80 or reconfigure the listening port. You can edit the listener port found in the httpd.conf file, which is in the /etc/httpd/conf directory:

```
# Listen: Allows you to bind Apache to specific IP addresses and/or
# ports, instead of the default. See also the <VirtualHost>
# directive.
#
# Change this to Listen on specific IP addresses as shown below to
# prevent Apache from glomming onto all bound IP addresses (0.0.0.0)
#
#Listen 12.34.56.78:80
Listen 80
```

If you change the listening port in the httpd.conf file while Apache is running, you will need to stop and restart the Apache HTTPD process. You may do this by using the restart option or running the utility with the stop and then start options. If it was not running, you can start the Apache HTTPD process as the root user. You do this by using the following utility, with restart as the recommended option:

```
# /usr/sbin/apachectl start | stop | restart
```

The httpd.conf file is found in the /etc/httpd/conf directory on Red Hat Linux AS. After you have stopped and started or restarted the Apache HTTPD, you can verify that it is working by using the following type of URL:

```
http://<host name>:<port number>/
```

If you configured the Apache HTTPD with the default listener port of 80, then you can use the following URL from the same machine because 80 is the assumed default port for all URLs when one is not provided:

```
http://localhost/
```

You will see the standard Red Hat Apache HTTPD static HTML file as the screen image in your web browser, as shown in Figure 2-1.

You have now installed, configured, or tested the Apache HTTPD on your server or workstation. If you encountered problems, you should check /var/log/httpd to see what may be causing the problem. Next, you will configure the Oracle Database Express Edition.

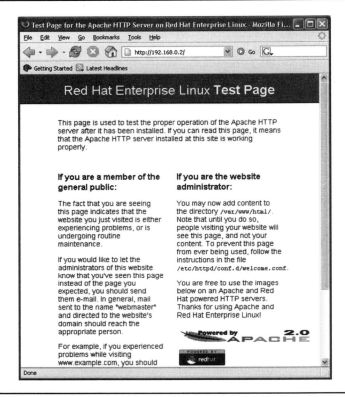

FIGURE 2-1. *Red Hat Linux Advanced Server Apache default HTML page*

Oracle Database Express Edition

The system requirements for Oracle Database Express Edition are as follows:

Requirement	Value
Operating system	One of the following operating systems: Red Hat Enterprise Linux RHEL3 or RHEL4 SUSE SLES-9 Fedora Core 4
Network protocol	TCP/IP
RAM	256MB minimum, 512MB recommended
Disk space	1.5GB minimum
Packages	Both of these libraries: glibc-2.32 gibaio-0.3.96
Permissions	Superuser (or root) privileges are required to install Oracle Database Express Edition

The Linux kernel parameters must be set to certain minimums to support the installation and operation of the Oracle Database Express Edition. You need to set the following values in the /etc/sysctl.conf file:

Kernel Parameter	Setting
semmsl	250
semmns	32000
semopm	100
semmni	128
shmmax	536870912
shmmni	4096
shmall	2097152
file-max	65536
ip_local_port_range	1024-65000

The following code illustrates how you should configure your sysctl.conf file in Red Hat AS 3.0:

```
# Set the default local port range
net.ipv4.ip_local_port_range = 1024 65000

# kernel.sem = semmsl semmns semopm semmni
kernel.sem = 430 129000 430 4000

# Set shared memory rules.
kernel.shmall = 2097152
kernel.shmmni = 300
kernel.shmmax = 2147483648

# Set the file management limits.
fs.file-max=65536
```

The Oracle Database Express Edition for Linux comes in a Red Hat Package Manager oracle-xe-10.2.0.1-0.1.i386.rpm file. As noted previously, you must be the superuser or root account to install the product. It will use an existing dba group and creates an oraclexe user account. However, you should create a dba group before running the installation. The default location for Oracle Database Express Edition is the /usr/lib/oracle/xe directory as the oraclexe user.

After you download the product, change your directory to that download directory and install Oracle Database Express Edition as the root user with the following syntax:

```
# rpm -ivh ./oracle-xe-10.2.0-1.i386.rpm
```

The installation program will illustrate progression and then notify you to run this command next:

```
/etc/init.d/oracle-xe configure
```

When you run the command, you will be asked to accept the default values for the HTML DB and Oracle listener ports. By default, HTML DB listens on port 8080 and Oracle Database Express Edition listener on port 1521. You may override these default port assignments if they conflict with your preference or other application use. The last question you will be asked is whether you want the database started when the system starts. The default is to enable this feature. You should disable it if you want to start and stop the database manually. These are the configuration steps you will see:

```
-- This is the screen display to a Linux Oracle XE install.

Oracle Database 10g Express Edition Configuration
-------------------------------------------------
This will configure on-boot properties of Oracle Database 10g Express
Edition.  The following questions will determine whether the database
should be starting upon system boot, the ports it will use, and the
passwords that will be used for database accounts.  Press <Enter> to
accept the defaults.
Ctrl-C will abort.

Specify the HTTP port that will be used for HTML DB [8080]:8181

Specify a port that will be used for the database listener [1521]:1621

Specify a password to be used for database accounts.  Note that the
same password will be used for SYS, SYSTEM and FLOWS_020100.  Oracle
recommends the use of different passwords for each database account.
This can be done after initial configuration:
Confirm the password:

Do you want Oracle Database 10g Express Edition to be started on
boot (y/n) [y]:y

Configuring Database...
Starting Oracle Net Listener.
Starting Oracle Database 10g Express Edition Instance.
```

As you see, in this example the default HTML DB and listener ports have been overridden and the database enabled to start on boot. If you change your mind about how the database should be set up, you can reconfigure it by rerunning the utility:

```
# /etc/init.d/oracle-xe configure
```

If you choose to manually start and stop the database, the utilities will be available in the GNOME or KDE menu selection for the root user. You can also start or stop the Oracle Database Express Edition using the root account at the command line with the following syntax and a start or stop argument:

```
# /etc/init.d/oracle-xe start | stop
```

Any user may then access the database by sourcing the appropriate environment files. They are found in the following directory:

```
/usr/lib/oracle/xe/app/oracle/product/10.2.0/server/bin
```

You use the `oracle_env.csh` file for C or tcsh shell environments and the `oracle_env.sh` file for Bourne, Bash, or Korn shell environments. You source environment files to set environment variables such as path statements. For example, you source a C or tsch file in the present working directory by running this command:

```
$ source oracle_env.csh
```

You source a Bourne, Bash, or Korn shell by using a period in lieu of the word "source" and another period to state the present working directory, as in this example:

```
$ . ./oracle_env.sh
```

After you install Oracle Database Express Edition, the database will be running and you can test the installation by opening a web browser on the server and entering the following type of URL:

```
http://<host name>:<port number>/htmldb
```

If you have installed Oracle Database Express Edition with the default HTML DB listener port of `8080`, then you can use the following URL from the same machine:

```
http://localhost:8080/htmldb
```

You will see the login screen shown in Figure 2-2 in your web browser.

FIGURE 2-2. *Oracle Express Edition Login page*

External users can access the machine provided you have no firewall on the server. Otherwise, you can open the default port 8080 or whichever port you specified during configuration. If you need to change your selected port, you can rerun the configuration utility. The same holds for SQL*Plus remote access, which will require you to enable the default port 1521 or your overriding port number.

If you log in to the database, you will find that you have four principal web navigation paths: administration, object browser, SQL, and utilities. You can do quite a lot in Oracle Express Edition without knowing much about SQL. The initial screen display is shown in Figure 2-3.

You have now installed and verified the installation of the Oracle Database Express Edition. Next, you will install the PHP engine.

PHP

You may install Zend Core for Oracle or manually install and configure PHP on your server. Zend Core for Oracle will detect all Apache HTTPD applications on your server and is the recommended approach if you have multiple Apache HTTPD installations configured on your system. Likewise, Zend Core will automatically configure the httpd.conf file and php.ini files during your installation of the product.

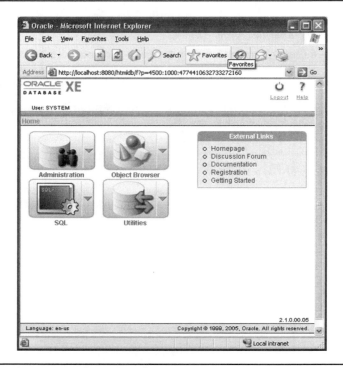

FIGURE 2-3. *Oracle Express Edition Portal page*

If you opt to run Zend Core for Oracle, you must have a supported operating system and must have installed the Apache 1.3.*x* or 2.0.*x* web server. These are the supported operating systems for Zend Core for Oracle:

- Linux (i386 and AMD64)
- SUSE Linux Enterprise Server (SLES) 9
- Red Hat Enterprise Linux (RHEL) 3
- IBM AIX 5.2 and later

Zend Studio 4.0 (or higher) is required to enable Zend Core for Oracle's interface with the Studio client. After downloading the current version of the Zend Core for Oracle file, you should unzip the file with the following command as the superuser:

```
# gunzip -c <package_name> | tar xvf -
```

This will unzip the file into the present working directory and create a new directory having the same name as the file. Next, as the root user, change your active directory to the newly created Zend Core directory and start the installation with the following command:

```
./install
```

The Zend Core for Oracle installation will present the following steps:

1. At the text-based Installation Wizard's welcome screen, press ENTER to begin.

2. At the license agreement screen, choose to continue by pressing ENTER.

3. At the acceptance agreement, select <Yes> to continue or <No> to exit the installation. You may press TAB to move between the choices.

4. You are prompted to enter an installation directory or accept the default /usr/local/ Zend/Core installation path. Press ENTER to continue the installation.

5. You are next prompted for a password to access the Zend Core for Oracle GUI. Select <Yes> to continue or <No> to exit the installation.

6. You are then prompted to enter the Zend network. Select <Yes> to continue or <No> to exit the installation. If you choose <Yes>, it will provide several additional screens not covered here.

7. You see a list of available web servers. You should select a web server from the list. Select <OK> to continue or <Cancel> to exit the installation. If you fail to select a web server, the installation will abort.

8. You are asked to choose from three different methods of installation. The fastest PHP installation method is Apache Module. However, you may select less common versions of Apache or else Fast CGI or CGI methods. It is recommended that you select an Apache module as the installation method. Select <OK> to continue or <Cancel> to exit the installation.

9. You see a list of virtual servers. Select the `Main server` to run the Zend Core for Oracle GUI on the server. You may choose not to install a virtual server, which means the Zend benchmarking and accessibility statistics will be unavailable. If you choose to install the virtual server, it may be installed on the main or other virtual servers. Select `<OK>` to continue or `<Cancel>` to exit the installation.

NOTE
Virtual web servers are very popular because they provide low-cost web hosting services. You may install multiple virtual web servers and configure PHP to run on all of them.

10. You see a screen acknowledging the successful installation of Zend Core for Oracle and the `httpd.conf` file that was modified. Select `<OK>` to end the installation.

NOTE
After the installation, you need to stop and restart the Apache HTTPD process for these changes to take place. This is required any time you make changes to the `httpd.conf` file. Zend Core will do this if you install anything but CGI.

Alternatively, you can download PHP from www.php.net and manually install and configure it. If you install it manually, you should follow the configuration steps. They are found in the INSTALL document that will be in the `php-5.1.1` directory created when you run the following command:

 `# gunzip php-5.1.1.tar.gz | tar xvf -`

There are several steps to configuring the generic PHP library and engine to run on your Linux machine:

1. Assuming you have installed Apache2 manually to the `/usr/local/apache2` directory, configure PHP to work with Apache 2.0 by using the following command in the directory where you have expanded the compressed file:

   `./configure -with-apxs2=/usr/local/apache2/bin/apxs`

   Alternatively, you can choose to configure PHP with an overriding directory for the `php.ini` file. You can do this with the following option flag to the `configure` executable:

   `-with-config-file-path=/<another path>`

   In this case, next proceed to Step 4.

2. Run the following commands to make the files and install them:

   ```
   make
   make install
   ```

3. Copy either the `php.ini-dist` or `php.ini-recommended` file from the directory where you have installed PHP to the `/usr/local/lib` directory. Use the following command:

   `cp php.ini-recommended /usr/local/lib/php.ini`

4. You should verify that the `make install` command noted previously placed the following line in your `httpd.conf` file:

    ```
    LoadModule php5_module modules/libphp5.so
    ```

    If this line is not in your `httpd.conf` file, add it below the other `LoadModule` lines. It is possible that you may have an `"Include conf.d/*.conf"` directive in your `httpd.conf` file, which means you should put it in the `/etc/httpd/conf.d/php.conf` file instead.

5. Add the following AddType statement to your `httpd.conf` file:

    ```
    AddType application/x-httpd-php .php .phps .phtml
    ```

6. Add the following configured path to your PHP installation directory in your `httpd.conf` file or, alternatively, the `/etc/httpd/conf.d/php.conf` file:

    ```
    PHPIniDir "/etc"
    ```

7. You should now stop and restart your Apache HTTPD process.

You have now reviewed how to install Zend Core for Oracle and generic PHP on Linux. Now that all the components are installed, you should verify that they work as a collective group. You can test your PHP configuration with the following program, which you should put into your HTTPD server document root directory, `C:\Program Files\Apache Group\Apache2\htdocs`:

`-- This is found in TestPHP.php on the enclosed CD.`

```
<html>
<head>
<title>
  PHPInfo Test Page
</title>
</head>
<body>
<?php phpInfo(); ?>
</body>
</html>
```

The `phpInfo()` function is a predefined PHP function that returns a web page with the PHP environment variables and values. Chapters 3 and 4 will cover the syntax and semantics for embedding PHP in your web pages. After creating the `TestPHP.php` file or copying from the online source, you can see the output by typing in a URL that follows the following pattern into a web browser of your choice:

`http://<hostname>.<domain name>:<port>/<virtual directory>/<file name>.php`

You may also substitute `<localhost>` for the `<hostname>.<domain name>`, and if you have configured the HTTPD server to listen on port `80`, you may exclude it from the URL because it is the assumed default for URL statements. Therefore, these are all valid URL statements if run from the server machine:

```
http://mclaughlin-dev.techtinker.com:80/TestPHP.php
http://localhost:80/TestPHP.php
```

If the default port is used, these are equivalent statements:

```
http://mclaughlin-dev.techtinker.com/TestPHP.php
http://localhost/TestPHP.php
```

If you want to localize various scripts, you create folders or directories beneath your document root directory. For example, if you were to put all your PHP files in a folder in your document root directory named `php`, you would use one of the following URLs to access the scripts through the HTTPD server:

```
http://mclaughlin-dev.techtinker.com/php/TestPHP.php
http://localhost/php/TestPHP.php
```

It is important to explain that the directory in your URL is a virtual path and that your virtual path is mapped through the `httpd.conf` file. The mapping takes the document root and appends the nested subdirectory. The book will use a `php` subdirectory, and all URL statements will reflect that `php` virtual path. The browser screenshot shown in Figure 2-4 demonstrates the `TestPHP.php` script file.

If this worked, then you have configured PHP successfully. The next step is to test whether or not you can get to Oracle. The next script makes some assumptions about your Oracle installation. It assumes that you have named your database XE and that you have built a `PHP` schema in the Oracle database. If you have a different name for your database instance, you may simply change it in the file from XE to your database name. Likewise, you may do the same for your user schema. If you would like to mirror the example in the book, you can create a `PHP` schema by logging in to Oracle as the `SYSTEM` user and running the following commands:

```
SQL> CREATE USER php IDENTIFIED BY php;
SQL> GRANT resource,connect TO php;
```

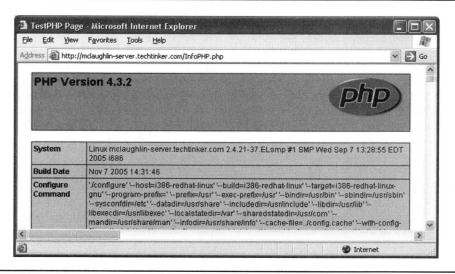

FIGURE 2-4. *TestPHP.php display of phpInfo() function*

After you have modified the script or built the mirroring environment, you may use the following script to test your ability to connect to the Oracle database:

-- **This is found in TestOraclePHP.php on the enclosed CD.**

```html
<html>
<head>
<title>
  Test Oracle PHP Connection.
</title>
</head>
<body>
<?php
    /*
     Attempt to connect to the database.
     ---------------------------------
     OCILogon Argument #1: Oracle user schema.
     OCILogon Argument #2: Oracle user password.
     OCILogon Argument #3: Oracle database name.
    */
    if ($c = OCILogon("php", "php", "xe"))
    {
      // Print successful message to web page.
      echo "Successfully connected to Oracle.<br>";

      // Log off the database.
      OCILogoff($c);
    }
    else
    {
      // Assign the OCI error.
      $errorMessage = OCIError();

      // Print failure message to web page.
      echo "Oracle Connect Error.<br>" . $errorMessage[text];
    }
?>
</body>
</html>
```

The PHP syntax is explained in Chapters 3 and 4. The PHP database connectivity components are explained in Chapter 11. Assuming you have built a php subdirectory in your HTTPD document root directory, use the following URL in your web browser to test the TestOraclePHP.php script:

```
http://localhost/php/TestOraclePHP.php
```

If everything is configured properly, you will see the following:

```
Successfully connected to Oracle.
```

If you did not connect, here are the best steps to look for errors:

■ Verify that you have the correct filename and extension for the file.

■ Verify that you have the file in the root document folder or a virtual path that is a subdirectory of the root document folder.

■ Verify that you have `PHPIniDir` in your `httpd.conf` file and that it points to the folder where you have the `php.ini` file and complete PHP environment.

■ Verify that you have uncommented `extension=php_oci8.dll` and put the subdirectory `ext` before the dynamic link library as

```
extension=ext/php_oci8.dll
```

NOTE
If you make any changes, don't forget to restart your Apache2 HTTPD service so that they can take effect.

You have learned how to install either Zend Core for Oracle or the generic PHP library and engine on Linux.

Windows XP Platform Installation

The Microsoft Windows XP Professional operating system was used to develop these installation notes. While there is no magic to the ordering of installation, you should install Apache or another HTTP daemon and Oracle Express before installing the PHP engine. If you are installing Oracle 10*g* Enterprise Edition, you should install Apache after you install Oracle. A natural extension is to use the Oracle 10*g* iAS product in lieu of a generic Apache installation.

NOTE
*Use of Oracle 10*g* iAS is recommended if you install Oracle 10*g* Enterprise Edition, which will install the Oracle 10*g* Enterprise Manager Agent on port 80. The Apache Microsoft Windows Installer default port is 80, which conflicts with the Oracle 10*g* Enterprise Manager Agent on port 80.*

TIP
Zend Core for Oracle and Oracle products have mutual dependencies on shared libraries or DLL files. It is critical that you ensure you have certified components of these products before attempting an install. Incompatible versions may cause SQL*Plus to fail.

You must be running Microsoft Windows XP Professional with at least Service Pack 1 or you will be subject to random corruption, for instance, to the cache of buffered file pages.

It is recommended to install Service Pack 2 but not required at the time of writing. Also, you may encounter problems running Apache2, such as corrupted or incomplete file downloads. You may eliminate those problems by setting the following directives in the `httpd.conf` file:

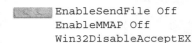
```
EnableSendFile Off
EnableMMAP Off
Win32DisableAcceptEX
```

NOTE
The EnableSendFile and Enable MMAP directives are provided as stubs in the Apache `httpd.conf` file. You simply remove the # character to set these off. The Win32DisableAcceptEX directive is not included in the `httpd.conf` file. You will need to add it to the file. It disables AcceptEX, which is enabled by default.

The Windows XP installation review will demonstrate Apache HTTPD, Oracle XE, and PHP installations. The PHP installation will be presented using a Zend Core for Oracle install and a generic PHP install from the www.php.net web site.

Apache HTTPD

You download the current source for Apache HTTPD from the http://httpd.apache.org web site. You can then install Apache HTTPD on your Windows XP operating system by running the Microsoft Installer (MSI). These steps will guide you through the installation sequence:

1. When you launch the Apache HTTPD MSI, the following welcome screen will appear. Choose Next to continue the install:

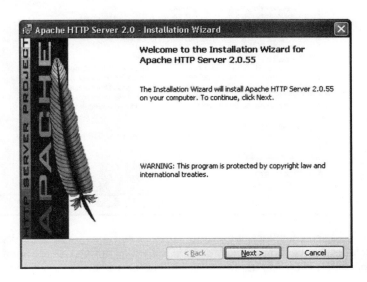

2. The next screen requires you to accept the license agreement. Then choose Next to proceed.

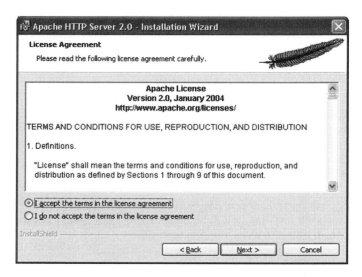

3. The next screen provides some release and product information about the installation. After you have read it, click Next to continue.

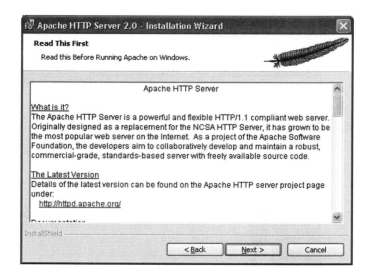

4. The next screen collects information about your server, desktop, or laptop machine. This includes the machine name, domain, and e-mail address for the administrator of the Apache HTTPD. You use this screen to choose whether you will restrict access to the

Apache HTTPD service. While this example grants all users permissions, a real installation would restrict this to a single user. In either case, you choose Next to continue.

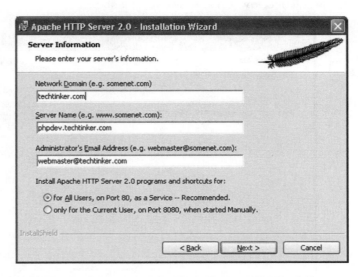

5. The next screen asks you whether you want a typical or custom installation. If you are new to Apache HTTPD, the typical choice is generally fine. These steps assume that you will choose the typical configuration. Click Next to continue.

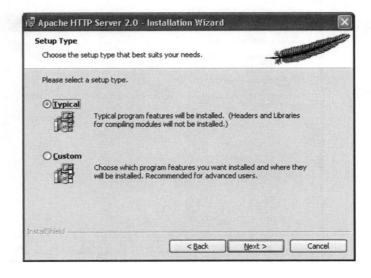

6. The next screen asks you whether you want to use the default `C:\Program Files\Apache Group` directory or choose a different directory. It is recommended that you use the default directory. Choose Next to continue.

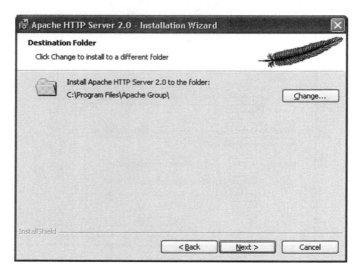

7. The next screen asks you whether to install the product or not. You should choose Install to continue.

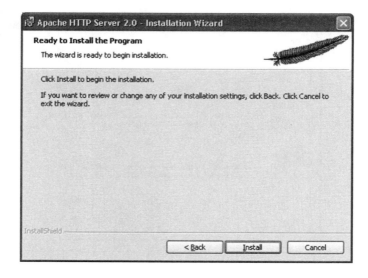

8.   The next screen displays a progress bar during the installation. When the bar completes, click Next to continue.

9.   The final screen displays the message that you have successfully installed Apache 2.0 on your machine. Click Finish to end the installation.

After you have stopped and started or restarted the Apache HTTPD, you can verify that it is working by using the following type of URL:

```
http://<host name>:<port number>/
```

If you configured the Apache HTTPD with the default listener port of 80, then you can use the following URL from the same machine because 80 is the assumed default port for all URLs when one is not provided:

```
http://localhost/
```

You will see the default HTML page as shown in Figure 2-5.

You have now installed Apache on your Windows XP operating system. Now you will install Oracle Express Edition.

Oracle Express

The Oracle Express installation does not require preinstallation steps. You can begin the installation provided you do so with a privileged account with administrator privileges. The system requirements for Oracle Database Express Edition are as follows:

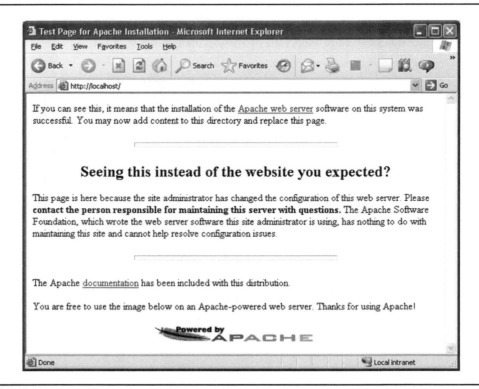

FIGURE 2-5. *Default Apache HTTPD page*

Requirement	Value
Operating system	One of the following 32-bit Windows operating systems: Windows 2000 with Service Pack 4 or later Windows Server 2003 Windows XP Professional Service Pack 1 or later
Network protocol	TCP/IP
RAM	256MB minimum, 512MB recommended
Disk space	1.2GB minimum
Packages	MSI version 2.0 or later, which you can download from http://msdn .microsoft.com
Permissions	The installer must have administrator privileges
.NET development	Runtime requires .NET Framework 1.x only

Oracle Database Express Edition installer uses a Microsoft MSI installation process. You will now step through the installation. Launch the Oracle XE icon in Windows Explorer and follow these steps:

1. When you launch the Oracle XE MSI Install Wizard, it will provide a progress bar to tell you that it is preparing for the installation. It completes and transits to the Oracle Express Edition Welcome page. Click Next to continue.

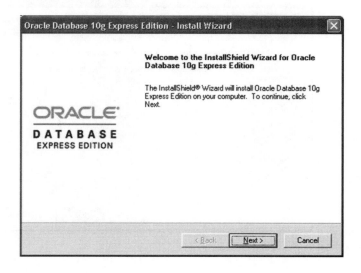

2. The next screen requires you to accept the license agreement and then choose Next to proceed. The screen shown is the beta license agreement.

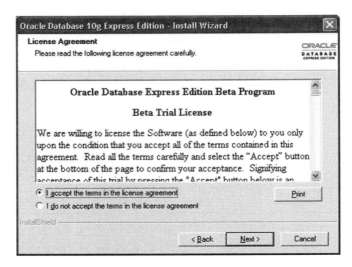

3. The next screen asks if you want to accept the C:\oraclexe default directory or choose another. It is recommended that you accept the default directory. Choose Next to continue.

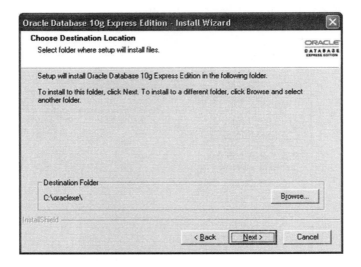

4.   The next screen requires you to enter a database password for the `SYS` and `SYSTEM` schemas. Make sure your entries match and click Next to continue with the install.

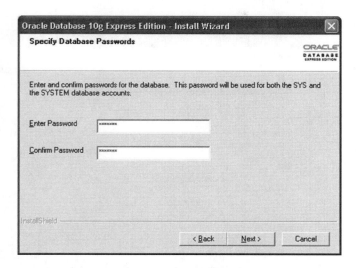

5.   The next screen shows you the default settings that will be used during the Oracle Express Edition installation. Note these port numbers and click Next to continue.

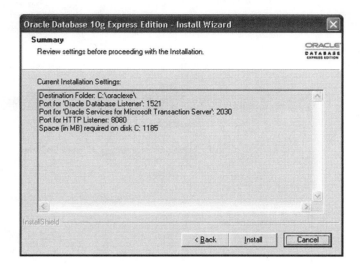

6. The next screen advises you that the installation is copying files. It will automatically conduct the copying process and move forward to configuration steps. This process will run for several minutes.

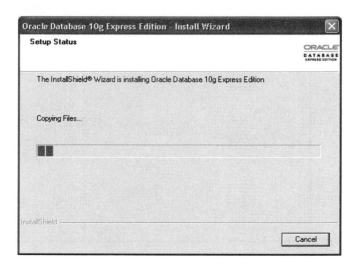

7. The next five screens will be progress bars like the one shown here. Only the last progress message is shown.

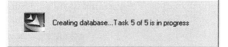

8. Finally, you will get the page telling you that you have successfully installed Oracle Express Edition and asking if you want to start it now. Leave the check box selected and click Finish.

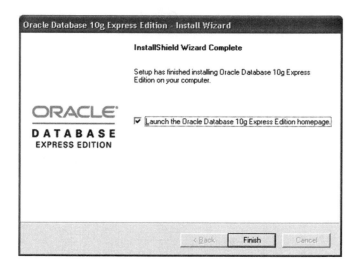

9. You have now successfully installed Oracle Express Edition. You can log in by going to the login page at http://localhost:8080/htmldb/, as shown in the following illustration:

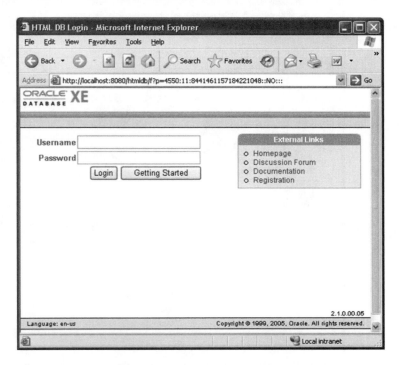

Others can access the machine, provided you have no firewall on the server. Otherwise, you can open the default port, 8080, or whichever port you specified during configuration. If you need to change your selected port, you can rerun the configuration utility. The same holds for SQL*Plus remote access, which will require you to enable the default port, 1521, or your overriding port number.

If you log in to the database, you will find that you have four principal web navigation paths—administration, object browser, SQL, and utilities. You can do quite a lot in Oracle Express Edition without knowing much about SQL. Figure 2-6 shows the initial screen display.

You have now installed Oracle Express Edition on Windows XP. In the next section you will see how to install Zend Core for Oracle or the generic PHP library and engine.

PHP

You may install Zend Core for Oracle or manually install and configure PHP on your server. Zend Core for Oracle will detect all Apache HTTPD applications on your server and is the recommended

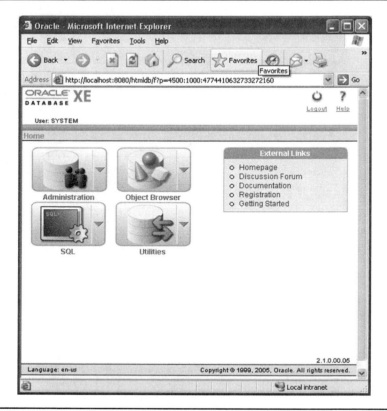

FIGURE 2-6. *Oracle Express Edition Portal page*

approach if you have multiple Apache HTTPD applications configured on your system. Likewise, Zend Core will configure the `httpd.conf` file and `php.ini` files for your installation.

The first installation will be demonstrated using Zend Core for Oracle, and the second will be a manual installation of generic PHP 5.1. It should be noted that Zend requires a local client to use many of the development engine features.

You can download Zend Core for Oracle from the http://otn.oracle.com web site, which will direct you to the Zend download page. You will need to fill in the license information before beginning the install. Here are the steps to install Zend Core for Oracle using the MSI:

1. When you launch the Zend XE MSI Install Wizard, it will first present the following welcome screen. Click Next to proceed with the install.

2. The next screen requires you to accept the license agreement and then choose Next to proceed. The screen shown is the beta license agreement.

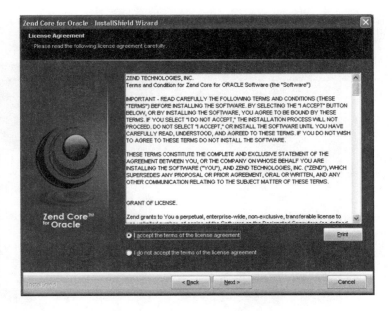

3. The next screen asks you to choose between a complete or custom installation of Zend Core for Oracle. You should choose a complete installation. Click Next to continue.

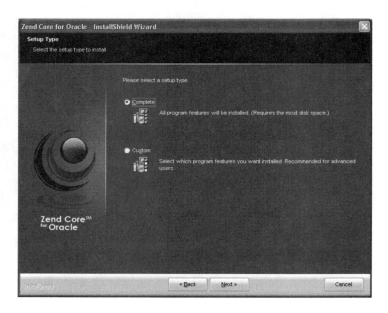

4. The next screen will provide you a list of discovered HTTPD listeners. You need to choose the one you want to configure and click Next to continue.

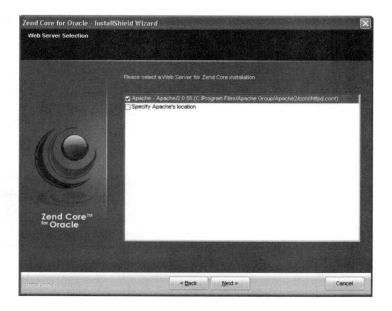

5. The next screen will show you the web server that you have chosen. Click Next to continue.

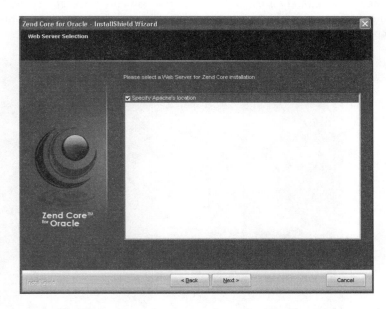

6. The next screen will ask you to choose a web server API. The choices are between an Apache module, a copy of Zend WinEnabler, and a CGI interface. It is recommended that you select an Apache module. Click Next to continue.

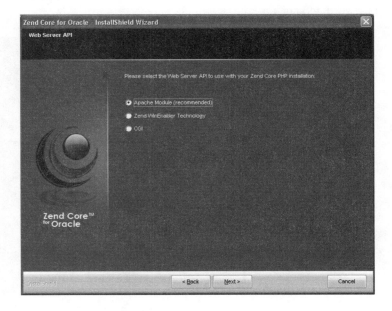

7. The next screen will ask you to choose from a list of possible PHP file extensions that you want enabled for the web server. You can add types later to the `httpd.conf` file if you change your mind. You should at a minimum choose `.php`. Click Next to continue the install.

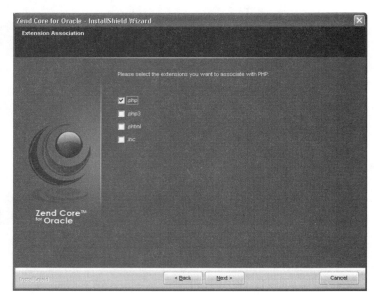

8. The next two screens will prompt you for the Zend Core GUI password. You should enter a password and click Next to continue.

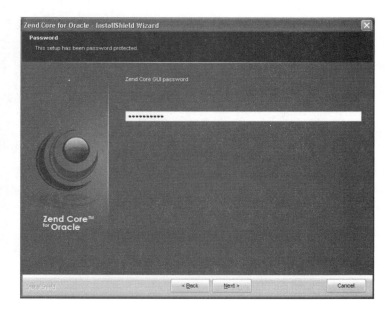

9. The next screen inquires if you want to sign up for a Zend support agreement. For simplicity, no is the choice shown here. However, if you want a Zend support agreement, the choices appeared rather straightforward. Click Next when you've opted for or against a support agreement.

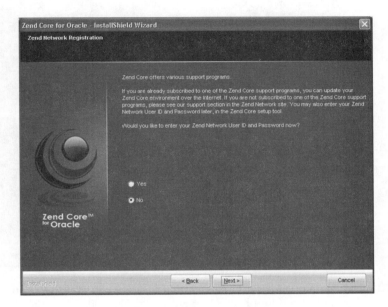

10. The next screen is the installation screen. Click Install to continue.

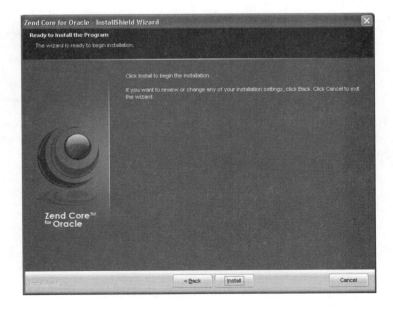

11. The next screen is the installation progress bar screen. When it has completed, a Next button will appear, which you should click to proceed.

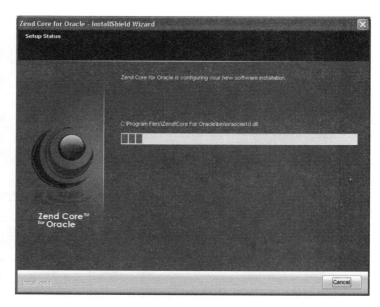

12. The next screen is an alert message that informs you that the Zend Core for Oracle installation has modified your `httpd.conf` file in the `C:\Program Files\ Apache Group\Apache2\conf` directory. You have no choice but to click OK and proceed.

13. The last screen announces that the installation is complete and prompts you to reboot your machine. You should choose the option to reboot and click Finish to end the installation.

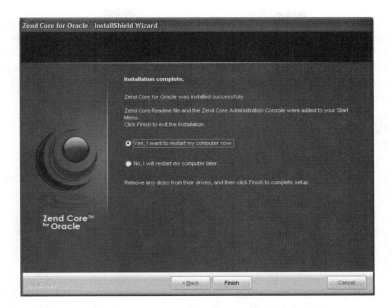

If you opt to install the generic PHP library and engine, you should continue through this section. You can download the generic PHP library and engine from www.php.net. The following instructions configure Apache2 to support PHP 5.1 as an Apache module. Other installation instructions for Apache 1.3 and CGI installations are found in the `install.txt` file, which is part of the `php-5.1.0-Win32.zip` download file. These are the manual configuration steps for generic PHP:

1. Download the current version Zip file of the PHP library and engine.

2. Unzip it into the `C:\PHP` directory.

3. Copy the `php.ini-recommended` file to `php.ini` in the `C:\PHP` directory and edit the file to include the following replacement to the `doc_root` line:

   ```
   doc_root = "c:\Program Files\Apache Group\Apache2\htdocs"
   ```

4. Add the `C:\PHP` directory to your Windows XP path, which can be done in this way:

   a. Open your Control Panel.

   b. Launch your System Properties window and choose the Advanced tab as shown here.

   c. Click the environment button, append the `C:\PHP` directory to your system `%PATH%` environment variable in the environment variables window, and click OK to set it. You will need to close any command windows open prior to the change because their `%PATH%` environment variable will not contain the modification.

5. Add the following lines at the ends of their respective sections in your `httpd.conf` file. For example, you will find a section where there are `LoadModule` directives in the `httpd.conf` file. You should make sure that the one below is added after all the others. The `PHPIniDir` should follow immediately below the `LoadModule` directive section. The `AddType` section contains recognized MIME types and these should go at the end of that group of directives.

```
LoadModule php5_module "c:/php/php5apache.dll"
PHPIniDir "C:/php"
AddType application/x-httpd-php .php
AddType application/x-httpd-php-source .phps
```

6. For PHP 4, uncomment and modify the following line in your `php.ini` file:

```
extension=php_oci8.dll
```

In PHP 5 or 5.1, the dynamic link libraries are no longer in the `C:\php` directory. They are now in the `C:\php\ext` subdirectory. You should include the following line to enable connecting to an Oracle database:

```
extension=ext/php_oci8.dll
```

After installing and configuring the server, you should start and stop the Apache2 Windows service. You can do this by navigating to Start | Run, typing **services.msc**, and clicking OK. You may also find services in the Control Panel. The precise location will depend on whether you are using the newer category view or the classic view. If you are using the category view, you select Performance and Maintenance, Administrative Tools and Services. The classic view allows you to directly choose Administrative Tools and then double-click the Services icon.

In the Services window, you click the Apache2 service name. When selected, the left portion of the frame will display Stop The Service and Restart The Service. You should stop the service and then start the service or restart. If it starts successfully, you have edited the `httpd.conf` file successfully. If it fails, however, you have an error that must be fixed. You will need to evaluate your event messages to determine what caused the Apache2 HTTPD service to start.

Fortunately, the Windows Event Viewer is also in the Administrative Tools window of your Control Panel. Alternatively, you can navigate to Start | Run and type **eventvwr.msc** to launch the Windows Event Viewer. In the left or right panel, click the Application icon that will display application events. A failure event will have a red circle with an X in it and state Error. You can double-click the icon to see the error, which generally will point to a specific line number in the `httpd.conf` file that is incorrect. You will need to fix the `httpd.conf` file and retry starting the Apache2 service until you have a valid `httpd.conf` file and the service starts.

You have now reviewed how to install Zend Core for Oracle and generic PHP on Windows XP. Now that all the components are installed, you should verify that they work as a collective group. You can test your PHP configuration with the following program, which you should put

into your HTTPD server document root—`C:\Program Files\Apache Group\Apache2\`
`htdocs` directory:

`-- This is found in TestPHP.php in the online source code.`

```
<html>
<head>
<title>
  PHPInfo Test Page
</title>
</head>
<body>
<?php phpInfo(); ?>
</body>
</html>
```

The `phpInfo()` function is a predefined PHP function that returns a web page with the PHP
environment variables and values. Chapters 3 and 4 will cover the syntax and semantics for
embedding PHP in your web pages. After creating the `TestPHP.php` file or copying from the
online source, you can see the output by typing a URL that follows the following pattern into a
web browser of your choice:

`http://<hostname>.<domain name>:<port>/<virtual directory>/<filename>.php`

You may also substitute `<localhost>` for the `<hostname>.<domain name>`, and if you
have configured the HTTPD server to listen on port `80`, you may exclude it from the URL because
it is the assumed default for URL statements. Therefore, these are all valid URL statements if run
from the server machine:

```
http://mclaughlin-dev.techtinker.com:80/TestPHP.php
http://localhost:80/TestPHP.php
```

If the default port is used, these are equivalent statements:

```
http://mclaughlin-dev.techtinker.com/TestPHP.php
http://localhost/TestPHP.php
```

If you want to localize various scripts, you create folders or directories beneath your document
root directory. For example, if you were to put all your PHP files in a folder in your document root
directory named `php`, you would use one of the following URLs to access the scripts through the
HTTPD server:

```
http://mclaughlin-dev.techtinker.com/php/TestPHP.php
http://localhost/php/TestPHP.php
```

It is important to understand that the directory in your URL is a virtual path and that your
virtual path is mapped through the `httpd.conf` file. The mapping takes the document root and
appends the nested subdirectory. This book will use a `php` subdirectory, and all URL statements

will reflect that `php` virtual path. The following browser screenshot demonstrates the `TestPHP.php` script file:

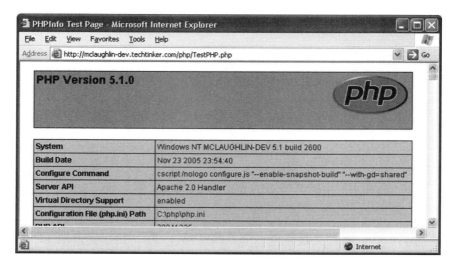

If this works, then you have configured PHP successfully. Testing whether or not you can get to Oracle is the next step. The next script makes some assumptions about your Oracle installation. It assumes that you have named your database XE and that you have built a PHP schema in the Oracle database. If you have a different name for your database instance, you may simply change it in the file from XE to your database name. Likewise, you may do the same for your user schema. If you would like to mirror the example in the book, you can create a PHP schema by logging in to Oracle as the SYSTEM user and running the following commands:

```
SQL> CREATE USER php IDENTIFIED BY php;
SQL> GRANT resource,connect TO php;
```

After you have modified the script or built the mirroring environment, you may use the following script to test your ability to connect to the Oracle database:

```
-- This is found in TestOraclePHP.php in the online source code.


<html>
<head>
<title>
  Test Oracle PHP Connection.
</title>
</head>
<body>
<?php
    /*
     Attempt to connect to the database.
     ---------------------------------
```

```
    OCILogon Argument #1: Oracle user schema.
    OCILogon Argument #2: Oracle user password.
    OCILogon Argument #3: Oracle database name.
*/
if ($c = OCILogon("php", "php", "xe"))
{
  // Print successful message to web page.
  echo "Successfully connected to Oracle.<br>";

  // Log off the database.
  OCILogoff($c);
}
else
{
  // Assign the OCI error.
  $errorMessage = OCIError();

  // Print failure message to web page.
  echo "Oracle Connect Error.<br>" . $errorMessage[text];
}
?>
</body>
</html>
```

The PHP syntax is explained in Chapters 3 and 4. The PHP database connectivity components are explained in Chapter 11. Assuming you have built a `php` subdirectory in your HTTPD document root directory, use the following URL in your web browser to test the `TestOraclePHP.php` script:

```
http://localhost/php/TestOraclePHP.php
```

If everything is configured properly, you will see this message:

```
Successfully connected to Oracle.
```

If you did not connect, the best steps to look for errors are to

- Verify that you have the correct filename and extension for the file.

- Verify that you have the file in the root document folder or a virtual path that is a subdirectory of the root document folder.

- Verify that you have `PHPIniDir` in your `httpd.conf` file and that it points to the folder where you have the `php.ini` file and complete PHP environment.

- Verify that you have uncommented `extension=php_oci8.dll` and put the subdirectory `ext` before the dynamic link library as:

  ```
  extension=ext/php_oci8.dll
  ```

NOTE
If you make any changes, don't forget to restart your Apache2 HTTPD service so that they can take effect.

There are more details about various setup patterns in the PHP and Apache documentation. If you're using Apache 1.3 or want PHP to work in the context of CGI, you should consult the base documents.

Summary

You have now installed and configured the components to work with PHP applications and Oracle Express. Chapter 3 will discuss writing PHP web pages and understanding how PHP is rendered in web pages.

CHAPTER
3

Writing Web Pages

HP is a server-side scripting or programming language. The primary purpose of server-side programming languages is to generate HTML web pages. PHP excels at generating HTML web pages because while it began as a small set of modules, it is now a powerful language that is easy to use and deploy. This language can be used to generate a complete web page but is generally used as part of a static or dynamic web page. PHP typically manages dynamic content display, which may include a server-side connection to a database like an instance of the Oracle Database XE. Two other benefits also make it very popular today: it is free, and it runs very fast on the server.

This chapter examines how you build web pages with the PHP programming language; it covers the following topics:

- Delimiting PHP program units
- Displaying output to web pages
- Putting comments in PHP programs

You will learn how to use PHP in your static HTML pages and display data using the PHP programming language. Chapter 4 will then cover PHP programming basics, including variables; statements; assignment, equality, and comparison operators; conditional statements; iteration; and reserved words.

Delimiting PHP Program Units

You have four possible styles to use for embedding PHP in your web pages: the default style (using the tags `<?php` and `?>`), HTML-style script delimiters (`<script language="PHP">` and `</script>`), short tags (`<?` and `?>`), and ASP-style tags (`<%` and `%>`). Among these styles short tags and ASP-style tags are discouraged. Using these two tag styles saves very little and presents more issues than benefits. The default syntax for embedding PHP programming units in your web page is the `<?php` and `?>` tags, as shown here:

`-- This is found in TestPHP.php on the enclosed CD.`

```
<html>
<head>
<title>
  PHPInfo Test Page
</title>
</head>
<body>
<?php phpInfo(); ?>
</body>
</html>
```

The sample program provides the HTML tags necessary to format a web page as well as the default delimiting `<?php` and `?>` tags to run a PHP program. The PHP program consists of a single statement followed by a semicolon. The `phpInfo()` function is a predefined function.

PHP also supports a script delimiter, something you are probably very familiar with if you have been developing web pages that include JavaScript programming units. The scripting syntax for

embedding PHP programming units in your web page consists of the `<script language="php">`
and `</script>` tags, as shown next:

-- **This is found in TestScriptPHP.php on the enclosed CD.**

```
<html>
<head>
<title>
  PHPInfo Test Page
</title>
</head>
<body>
<script language=php>
  phpInfo();
</script>
</body>
</html>
```

The sample program provides the HTML tags necessary to format a web page and the HTML scripting
tag syntax. While this delimiting syntax is possible, it is rarely seen.

PHP supports short tags provided you enable them in the `php.ini` configuration file. If you
installed Zend Core, this will be enabled. However, if you installed from the www.php.net web
site, you will need to manually enable the `short_open_tag` directive as follows:

short_open_tag = on

Short tags are disabled in the `php.ini-recommended` configuration file by default. They
have little advantage and can lead to confusion, but if you want to use them, the scripting syntax
uses `<?` and `?>` tags, as shown next:

-- **This is found in TestShortTagPHP.php on the enclosed CD.**

```
<html>
<head>
<title>
  PHPInfo Short-tag Test Page
</title>
</head>
<body>
<? phpInfo(); ?>
</body>
</html>
```

This sample program provides the HTML tags necessary to format a web page and the default
delimiting `<?` and `?>` tags to run a PHP program. Many developers like short tags, but these tags
lack an explicit descriptor of the scripting language. You may want to consider what benefits are
presented by short tags before choosing that development direction.

PHP supports Microsoft ASP page syntax, provided you enable it in the `php.ini` configuration
script by editing the `asp_tags` directive as follows:

asp_tags = on

ASP-style tags are disabled in the `php.ini-recommended` configuration file by default. They have the advantage of being familiar if you have been writing ASPs. If you want to use them, the scripting syntax uses `<%` and `%>` tags, as shown here:

 `-- This is found in TestASPTagPHP.php on the enclosed CD.`

```
<html>
<head>
<title>
   PHPInfo Short-tag Test Page
</title>
</head>
<body>
<% phpInfo(); %>
</body>
</html>
```

This example provides the HTML tags necessary to format a web page and the default delimiting `<%` and `%>` tags to run a PHP program. The potential downside of using the ASP-style tags is that developers expect them to appear with ASPs, not PHP programs.

NOTE
If you chose to enable `short_open_tag` or `asp_tags` in your `php.ini` file, you will need to restart your HTTPD for those changes to take effect.

You have learned the four delimiting styles supported by the PHP programming language. Short tags and ASP-style tags require resetting the recommended `php.ini` settings as discussed. The default syntax is the recommended approach and will be used in all of the example programs in the book. In the next section you will learn how to display information to web pages inside the PHP source page component.

Displaying Output to Web Pages

Two predefined PHP constructs and two predefined PHP functions are used to display output to web pages. They will be covered in this section along with another function that can convert variables to a formatted output string.

The first construct is the `echo()` statement. The difference between a function and a construct is that the parentheses are unnecessary in a construct. Moreover, if you want to pass multiple arguments to the `echo` command, parentheses cannot be used. The echo statement has the following formal definition:

`void echo(string arg1 [, string arg2 … ])`

The limitation of the `echo()` construct is that it returns nothing and therefore cannot be used in a complex expression. Each line that uses the `echo()` construct must be terminated by a semicolon, which makes the lines statements of execution. The following `TestEcho.php` program shows how to use the `echo()` construct to print a single argument with and without the parentheses and multiple arguments without the parentheses:

-- This is found in TestEcho.php on the enclosed CD.

```
<html>
<head>
<title>
  PHP echo() Construct Test Page
</title>
</head>
<body>
<?php
  echo("Hello One!<br>");
  echo "Hello Two!<br>";
  echo "Hello Three!<br>", "Hello Four!<br>";
?>
</body>
</html>
```

The sample program demonstrates using the echo() construct to print to a single string output to a web page with or without parentheses. The program also shows that you can submit multiple arguments to the echo structure in a single statement. The strings are delimited by double quotes, but you can also use single quotes. Each statement is terminated by a semicolon.

There are several recognized escape sequences that may likewise be included in the argument or argument list to the echo() construct. Those escape sequences that act as back-quoting operators are very useful, because they enable displaying reserved characters as ordinary text. The following file demonstrates back-quoting in PHP programming along with some escape sequences, such as a newline and a carriage return:

-- This is found in TestBackQuote.php on the enclosed CD.

```
<html>
<head>
<title>
  PHP echo() Construct &amp; Back Quoting Test Page
</title>
</head>
<body>
<?php
  echo "Print a backslash:\t[\\]<br>\n";
  echo "Print a dollar sign:\t[\$]<br>\r";
  echo "Print a double quote:\t[\"]<br>\n";
?>
</body>
</html>
```

The sample program uses an echo() construct to print a series of single lines. The first backslash back-quotes; that is, it tells PHP to render the next character as an ordinary character and not a special character. The embedded
 HTML tag instructs the web browser to perform a line break. The \t is the escape sequence for a tab, the \n is the escape sequence for a new line, and the \r is the escape sequence for a carriage return. None of these will have any impact on the rendered web page, but they are useful in the viewed source.

The sample program uses an echo() construct to then print a $, a backslash, and double quote symbols, which are reserved characters in the PHP programming language. The $ symbol is used to designate variables, the backslash is used to back-quote, and double quotes are used to delimit string values. As mentioned previously, these are not rendered in the web page.

NOTE
The \n, \r, and \t escape sequences are useful in debugging your PHP rendering issues because they enable you to manage the page source formatting. However, they are sometimes considered extra bytes in production environments.

The second construct is the print() statement. The difference between the print() and echo() constructs is that the print() construct does not support multiple arguments with or without the parentheses. The print() statement has the following formal definition:

```
int print(string arg)
```

The benefit of the print() construct is that it always returns an int value of 1. This means that it can be used in complex expressions. The following TestPrint.php program shows how to use the print() construct to print a single argument with and without the parentheses:

-- This is found in TestPrint.php on the enclosed CD.

```html
<html>
<head>
<title>
  PHP print() Construct Test Page
</title>
</head>
<body>
<?php
  print("Hello One!<br>");
  print "Hello Two!<br>";
?>
</body>
</html>
```

The sample program uses a print() construct to print a single line. The embedded
 HTML tag instructs the web browser to perform a line break. If it were not included, the next print() construct would begin at the end of the last line and not on a separate line.

Both the echo() and print() constructs have an important multiple line feature when combined with the PHP here document syntax. The here document syntax enables you to insert a large block of HTML code into your web page within the embedded PHP tags. The following script illustrates the insertion of JavaScript with comments and HTML text and button inputs within a PHP tag:

-- This is found in TestHereDoc.php on the enclosed CD.

```html
<html>
<head>
```

```
<meta http-equiv=Content-Type content=text/html;
      http-equiv=Content-Script-Type text/javascript charset=iso-8859-1>
<title>
  Test HereDoc Utility
</title>
</head>
<body>
<?php
print <<<HERE
  <script>
    function checkText(source,button,e)
    {
      // If e is true check it or assign window.event.
      e = (e) ? e : event;

      // Convert event value to a number.
      var charCode = (e.charCode) ? e.charCode :
                     ((e.keyCode) ? e.keyCode :
                     ((e.which) ? e.which : 0));

      // Enable the reset button if a character entry.
      if (charCode > 31)
        document.getElementById(button).disabled = false;
      else
        document.getElementById(source.id).value = "";

      return true;
    }

    // Define client side JavaScript resetText function.
    function resetText(buttonId,elementId)
    {
      // Reset text to null value.
      document.getElementById(elementId).value = "";

      // Disable button.
      document.getElementById(buttonId).disabled = true;
    }
  </script>
  <form id="sampleForm">
  Enter Text:
  <input type="text"
         id="text"
         onkeypress="return checkText(this,'reset',event)"><br>
  <input type="button"
         disabled="true"
         id="reset"
         value="Reset Text"
             onclick="resetText(this.id,text.id);"
  </form>
HERE;
?>
</body>
</html>
```

The sample program uses a `print <<<HERE ... HERE;` here document syntax to print a large part of a web page within the scope of a single command. The embedded web component within the `here` document tag provides two JavaScript functions with comments and two HTML input elements with multiple event listeners.

NOTE
While you can use any word in place of HERE, you must make sure that the ending word starts at the beginning of a line. If there is a single white space before the closing word used to delimit the `here` document, an error will occur rendering the web page. The `php.ini` configuration file's `display_errors` directive determines whether or not an error message will be displayed. If the `display_errors` directive is enabled, you will receive a parse error that will point to the closing line of the `here` document tag.

TIP
The `here` document syntax is a convenient way to insert code that will be formatted from the perspective of viewing the source.

Having covered the two predefined PHP constructs, you will now examine the two predefined PHP functions. They are the `printf()` and `vprintf()` functions. The former enables formatting a single string, and the latter formats an array of strings. The `printf()` function is very similar to the C programming language `printf()` function and has the following formal definition:

```
boolean printf(string format [, mixed args [, mixed ...]])
```

The format may contain optional padding, alignment, width, and/or precision arguments, as well as a type argument. The possible type arguments are noted in Table 3-1.

Type	Description
%b	Integer argument presented as a binary number
%c	Integer argument presented as an ASCII value character
%d	Integer argument presented as a signed decimal number
%f	Floating-point argument presented as a floating-point number
%o	Integer argument presented as an octal number
%s	String argument presented as a string
%u	Integer argument presented as an unsigned decimal number
%x	Integer argument presented as a lowercase hexadecimal number
%X	Integer argument presented as an uppercase hexadecimal number

TABLE 3-1.   *The `printf()` Formatting Values*

The benefit of the `printf()` function is that it returns an `int` value that may be treated as a Boolean value because PHP is a weakly typed language. The use of an `int` return data type supports conditional logic and complex expressions because PHP evaluates zero or a null string as false and any nonzero number or nonempty string as true. Some PHP programmers believe the `printf()` returns a Boolean because of this weakly typed behavior, which works as a type of implicit type casting. (More about variable types is found in Chapter 4.) The following `TestPrintf.php` program shows how to use the `printf()` function to print a single string and set of string arguments:

-- This is found in TestPrintf.php on the enclosed CD.

```
<html>
<head>
<title>
  PHP printf() Function Test Page
</title>
</head>
<body>
<?php
  printf("The [%s]<br>","String 1");
  printf("The [%1s] &amp; [%2s]<br>","String 1","String 2");
?>
</body>
</html>
```

The sample program uses an `printf()` construct to print a single line that substitutes the second argument into the position of the `%s` formatting specification. The embedded `<br>` HTML tag in the formatting output string instructs the web browser to perform a line break. If that tag were not included, the next thing printed would begin at the end of the last line and not on a separate line.

NOTE
You have broader formatting available using the `printf()` function, but the formatting will have impact only in your rendering source, not your rendered page.

Having covered the `printf()` function, you will notice that the `vprintf()` function has some similar behaviors. Like the former, `vprintf()` enables formatting strings and uses the same previously discussed formatting types. The `vprintf()` acts on arrays, not single strings. The following `TestVPrintf.php` program demonstrates using the `vprintf()` function:

-- This is found in TestVPrintf.php on the enclosed CD.

```
<html>
<head>
<title>
  PHP vprintf() Function Test Page
</title>
</head>
<body>
```

```
<?php
  $states = array('New Jersey','New Mexico','New York');
  vprintf("[%s]<br>
          [%s]<br>
          [%s]<br>",$states);
?>
</body>
</html>
```

The sample `program` uses a `vprintf()` function to print the three components of a string array. The embedded `<br>` HTML tag in the formatting output string instructs the web browser to perform a line break.

You have learned how to use the two predefined PHP constructs and two predefined PHP functions that display output to web pages. They will become second nature as you develop further skills in writing PHP programs. The next section covers how you can include comments in your PHP programs.

Putting Comments in PHP Programs

The PHP programming language supports three styles of writing comments. They should look familiar if you have worked in C, C++, C#, Java, JavaScript, or Linux/Unix shell scripting. The following types of commenting are supported in PHP:

- The single-line C++, C#, Java, or JavaScript comment syntax
- The multiple-line C++, C#, Java, or JavaScript comment syntax
- The Linux or Unix shell comment syntax

The next sections will demonstrate the various commenting syntaxes supported by the PHP programming language.

Single-Line PHP C++, C#, or Java-Style Comments

You may use a single-line comment to begin a line or to append a comment to a line. Single-line comments may be two forward slashes with no intervening white space. Both of these styles of using two forward slashes are demonstrated here:

```
<?php
  // This is a single-line comment.
  phpInfo(); // This calls the predefined phpInfo() function.
?>
```

Multiple-Line PHP C++, C#, or Java-Style Comments

You may use multiple-line comments anywhere in your file. They may start anywhere in a given line and end anywhere in another line. All text between the beginning and ending comment notation will be ignored as text at run time. The multiple-line style is demonstrated here:

```php
<?php
/*
    This is a multiple-line comment, which was required because
    the meaningful comment was too long to fit on one line.
*/
phpInfo();
?>
```

Single-Line PHP Linux or Unix Shell–Style Comments

You may use the # symbol to designate a single-line comment. It may begin a line or append a comment to a line. Both of these styles are demonstrated here:

```php
<?php
# This is a single-line comment.
phpInfo(); # This calls the predefined phpInfo() function.
?>
```

You have learned how to comment your PHP programs using two single-line styles and the multiple-line style. Use whichever style you prefer, but you should try to be consistent in the style you use to make your code more readable to programmers who may be responsible for its future maintenance.

Summary

You have learned how to use PHP in your HTML pages, display data using the PHP programming language, and comment your PHP programs. In the next chapter, you will cover PHP programming basics—including variables; statements; assignment, equality, and comparison operators; conditional statements; iteration; and reserved words.

CHAPTER
4

Variables, Operators, Data Types, and File Inclusion

his chapter examines how you define, declare, assign, compare, and process variables. It covers the following topics:

- Variables
  - User-defined variables
  - Operators
  - Data types
  - Global variables
  - Predefined variables
- Library file inclusion
- Reserved words and system constants

By the end of this chapter, you will understand how variables, operators, and data types work. You will also understand how to define global variables and be aware of the predefined variables available in PHP. At the end of the chapter you will find a list of reserved words and a tool to find your defined environment constants.

The chapter sections are organized sequentially and assume you have read the prior sections. Before skipping a section, you should consider browsing it even if you feel comfortable with the general concept.

Variables

Variables are structures in computer programming languages. Variables are also described as containers for things, like numbers, strings, and objects. A key aspect of the PHP programming language is that it is a loosely typed language. Loosely typed programming languages enable a variable to hold a number at one moment and a string or other data type at another. This means that you need to be careful with how you use, identify, and assign types.

The ability to change the data type of a variable is important in any programming language. The process of changing a variable from one type to another is called *typecasting.* In languages like Java, there are wrapper class files to enable you to explicitly change the data types of variables. While PHP doesn't provide you with a set of wrapper classes, you can explicitly cast PHP variables, like Java primitives. The details of how you do so are covered later in the chapter.

Beyond explicitly casting variable data types, PHP is a robust language that implicitly casts variables at run time according to a well-defined set of assumptions. Explicit and implicit casting works best when the programmer tests the behaviors of casts during unit testing.

User-Defined Variables

PHP variables are defined by a set of lower- and uppercase alphanumeric names that can start with or contain underscores. PHP variable names are case sensitive, which means a variable name `example` is different from `Example`. Variable names must start with an underscore or an alphabetical character. Underscores start most predefined PHP variables, so starting user-defined variables with an alphabetical character is a good idea. If you opt to start your user-defined variable names with underscores, you may find some future PHP predefined variable renders your variable name obsolete.

One variable naming convention uses a lowercase first word and title case for subsequent words. This pattern is commonly used in PHP programs; for instance, a variable that contains an individual's first name may be `firstName`. An alternative variable naming convention is separating words by underscores, which is a common practice in case-insensitive languages, such as SQL. PHP object type names infrequently follow any convention, but object-oriented languages typically use title case words. This means that all words start with capital letters and then use lowercase letters. When two or more words name an object type, each word uses title case. For example, an animal object type would be named `Animal` and an instance of the object type `$animal`.

PHP variables were once always assigned by value. Beginning with PHP 4, you can assign variables by value or by reference. This is a powerful tool, which is covered later in this chapter.

Defining variables typically requires the selection of a variable name and a data type. Loosely typed languages, like PHP, do not require you to identify a type when you define the variable, because the type is implicit with the value assigned. You define a variable in PHP by prefacing the variable name with a $ symbol, as shown by the following variable definitions:

```
$_MINE;           // A variable starting with an underscore.
$myVariable;      // A variable starting with an alphabetical character.
$my1234;          // A variable including numeric values.
```

Variables may be scalar or compound. Scalar variables can only hold one thing at a time, while compound variables may hold more than one thing. Scalar variables are considered more precise when they convey more information, so types that manage real numbers are more precise than types that manage integers. The data types section later in this chapter will explain what types are supported in PHP and how to work with them.

When you define and assign a value to a variable in one step, this is called *declaring* a variable. Type assignment is implicitly done for you in PHP, but you can explicitly typecast scalar variables during assignment operations. While this is often called assignment by value, you can assign variables by reference to other variables. Assignment also has another meaning when you initialize an instance of an object type. The specialized object-oriented programming assignment process is covered in Chapter 8.

Assignment by value is done using a binary assignment operator, which is the equal (=) symbol between two operands. The left operand is the target variable, and the right operand is a source value or reference. Assignment statements are typically terminated by a semicolon to complete the expressions.

As mentioned, during the assignment process, you can explicitly change a variable type by typecasting it. While most operators are covered in another section, the typecasting operators are presented here to support the user-defined variable example programs. The typecasting operators in PHP are shown in Table 4-1.

The default practice is to assign by value, but you can assign by reference. You assign by reference using a combination of an assignment operator and an ampersand (&) preceding the source variable name, like `&$variableName`. Only the source variable or *right* operand can be addressed by reference.

The difference between assignment by value and assignment by reference is not hard but can be confusing. For an analogy, a variable name is the key by which you access the contents of a variable, like opening a locked door. When all variables are assigned by value, they all contain

Cast Operator	Conversion Description
(array)	This changes the right operand into an array data type during assignment or use.
(bool) or (boolean)	This changes the right operand into a Boolean data type during assignment or use.
(int) or (integer)	This changes the right operand into an integer data type during assignment or use.
(object)	This changes the right operand into an object data type during assignment or use.
(real) or (double) or (float)	This changes the right operand into a float data type during assignment or use. The gettype() function will return the type as a double, which is a legacy operation in PHP 5.
(string)	This changes the right operand into a string data type during assignment or use. String data types are typically enclosed, or delimited, by single or double quotes. A null string can be represented as two single or double quotes, like ' ' or " ".

TABLE 4-1.   *Typecasting Operators*

only one key to setting and getting the variable value, or opening and closing the door. When variables are assigned by reference, the second variable acts like a copy of the original key or a master key to the same door. This means that both keys open the same door, and there are two keys that may change the content of a variable.

The VariableAssignment1.php program illustrates variable declaration by both value and reference. The program demonstrates how two variables can share and change the same content. The period or dot is the concatenation operator in PHP. The concatenation operator puts string literal square brackets around the string variable values in the program.

NOTE
If you type the program in manually, don't forget that the single or double quote marks must be in pairs or they will raise a fatal parsing error.

The following VariableAssignment1.php and future programs dispense with formal HTML tags where they do not add value:

-- This is found in VariableAssignment1.php on the enclosed CD.

```php
<?php
  // Declare variables by assigning a value.
  $myVar1 = 1;
  $myVar2 = 2;

  // Declare a variable by assigning a reference to another variable.
```

```
$myVar3 = &$myVar2;

// Print and format variables to the web page.
print "\$myVar1 [".$myVar1."]<br>";
print "\$myVar2 [".$myVar2."]<br>";
print "\$myVar3 [".$myVar3."]<br><p>";

// Print a line break;
print "<hr>";

// Reassign value to variable held by value and reference.
$myVar3 = "Three";

// Print and format variables to the web page.
print "\$myVar1 [".$myVar1."]<br>";
print "\$myVar2 [".$myVar2."]<br>";
print "\$myVar3 [".$myVar3."]<br>";
?>
```

The `VariableAssignment1.php` program declares two variables, $myVar1 and $myVar2, assigning them 1 and 2 respectively. The program then declares $myVar3 by reference, pointing to &$myVar2, which creates a second variable that points to the contents of $myVar2. When $myVar3 is updated by assigning the value "Three", the contents of both $myVar2 and $myVar3 change because the variable names point to the same content.

The program first prints the original assigned variable values:

```
$myVar1 [1]
$myVar2 [2]
$myVar3 [2]
```

After the assignment to $myVar3, the program then prints the modified contents, which demonstrates that both variables are keys opening the same door to the data:

```
$myVar1 [1]
$myVar2 [Three]
$myVar3 [Three]
```

The `VariableAssignment1.php` program demonstrates three concepts. First, a variable declared as an integer data type can be redefined by implicit casting during the assignment of a string. Second, a variable assigned by value can be altered through another variable defined by reference because they both point to the original content. Third, a reference assignment inherits the data type and can reset the data type of the referenced variable by indirect assignment of a different new type.

Operators

You have seen earlier in this chapter how to use assignment operators to assign by value, reference, and indirection. Earlier in this chapter, you learned how to use the string concatenation operator, which is a period. This section examines the list of possible assignment operators. These operators include unary, binary, and ternary operators that perform arithmetic, comparison, logical, and bitwise operations. In this section, you will learn the importance of operator type, associativity, and operation precedence.

Unary operators work with one operand or variable at any time. Unary operators typically increment or decrement values by 1 before or after their current use.

Binary operators work with two operands and perform some arithmetic, comparison, logical, or bitwise operations between them. How binary operators work varies according to a principle called *associativity*. Associativity governs which operand receives precedence of operation. When an operator uses left associativity, it evaluates the left operand before the right, and vice versa.

Ternary operators take three operands and have the benefit of writing if-then-else expressions. When the first operand evaluates as true, the second operand is returned or performed; and when the first evaluates as false, the third operand is returned or performed.

Array and type operators will be covered in Chapter 6. Error control operators will be covered in Chapter 9. In the following sections, you will cover operation assignment, arithmetic, bitwise, and logical operators. Then, you will cover operator precedence.

Operation Assignment Operators

Operation assignment operators are both binary and unary operators. They both assign and operate on one or more variables. Unary operation assignment operators take one operand and act on it, typically by incrementing or decrementing the operand's value. Binary operation assignment operators take two operands and use one as the target variable and the other as the source variable.

Table 4-2 provides a summary of operation assignment operators. It describes the available operators before demonstrating their use in an example program.

The following `VariableAssignment2.php` program illustrates how operation assignment operators work:

-- This is found in VariableAssignment2.php on the enclosed CD.

```php
<?php
  // Declare variables by assigning a value.
  $myVar1 = 1;
  $myVar2 = 1;
  $myVar3 = 1;
  $myVar4 = 1;
  $myVar5 = 1;
  $myVar6 = 1;
  $myVar7 = 1;

  // Print result of addition assignment operator.
  print "\$myVar1 [".($myVar1 += 10)."] [".gettype($myVar1)."]<br>";

  // Print result of subtraction assignment operator.
  print "\$myVar2 [".($myVar2 -= 10.1)."] [".gettype($myVar2)."]<br>";

  // Print result of concatenation assignment operator.
  print "\$myVar3 [".($myVar3 .= 10)."] [".gettype($myVar3)."]<br>";

  // Print result of preincrement/predecrement operator.
  print "\$myVar4 [".(++$myVar4)."] [".gettype($myVar4)."]<br>";
  print "\$myVar6 [".(--$myVar5)."] [".gettype($myVar6)."]<br>";
```

```
    // Print result of postincrement/decrement operator.
    print "\$myVar5 [".($myVar6++)."] [".gettype($myVar5)."]<br>";
    print "\$myVar7 [".($myVar7--)."] [".gettype($myVar7)."]<br><p>";
?>
```

The program uses increment and assign, decrement and assign, and concatenate and assign binary operators in conjunction with the `gettype()` function to illustrate implicit casting changes. The first operation demonstrates that you can assign and increment without a data type change when both left and right operands are the same scalar type. The second operation demonstrates you can assign and increment with a more precise variable, like a `float` data type. The assignment of a `float` to an `int` causes an implicit data type change to the left operand.

Operator	Behavior Description
+=	The increment and assign, or +=, operator is a binary operator that adds the right operand to the variable value contained in the left operand. The increment and assign operator can implicitly cast the data type of the left operand. Alternatively, you can explicitly cast the right operand to match the data type of the assignment target or left operand.
-=	The decrement and assign, or -=, operator is a binary operator that subtracts the right operand from the value contained in the left operand. The decrement and assign operator can implicitly cast the data type of the left operand. Alternatively, you can explicitly cast the right operand to match the data type of the assignment target or left operand.
.=	The concatenate and assign, or .=, operator is a binary operator that concatenates the right operand to the left operand. If the left operand is not a string, it is implicitly cast to a string and the right operand is concatenated to it as a string. *There is no way to avoid this string type casting behavior* with the concatenate and assign operator.
--	The decrement, or --, operator is a unary operator that decrements the contents of a variable by a value of 1. If the decrement unary operator precedes the variable name, it decrements the variable before using it. If the decrement unary operator follows the variable name, it decrements the variable after using the variable. The position before or after the variable determines whether the variable is decremented before or after variable use.
++	The increment, or ++, operator is a unary operator that increments the contents of a variable by a value of 1. If the increment unary operator precedes the variable name, it increments the variable before using it. If the increment unary operator follows the variable name, it increments the variable after using the variable. The position before or after the variable determines whether the variable is incremented before or after variable use.

TABLE 4-2. *Operation Assignment Operators*

The third operation demonstrates that you can concatenate and assign any value and implicitly cast the left operand to a string.

The `VariableAssignment2.php` program outputs the left operands after applying the referenced operators:

```
$myVar1 [11] [integer]
$myVar2 [-9.1] [double]
$myVar3 [110] [string]
```

Unary operations demonstrate behaviors before and after their current use. The increment and decrement unary operators first change the contents before returning the variable as an actual parameter to the print structure. In these cases the number is higher or lower than the original value. The postunary operations then demonstrate that the value is unchanged as an actual parameter to the print structure because they are incremented after the current variable use.

The preincrement and predecrement unary operators output the following:

```
$myVar4 [2] [integer]
$myVar5 [0] [integer]
```

The remaining postincrement and postdecrement output is

```
$myVar6 [1] [integer]
$myVar7 [1] [integer]
```

This previous example covered the implicit casting of $myVar2 and $myVar3. $myVar2 is cast from a less precise `int` to a `float`, and $myVar2 is cast from an `int` to a `string`. Understanding the impact of casting is a critical aspect of writing good programs. *Operators assume that you want them to manage things* when you don't do so explicitly in your code. A program can fail to perform the way you intended when you neglect implicit casting behaviors.

Arithmetic Operators

In this section, you will examine arithmetic operators. Like operation assignment operators, arithmetic operators can perform implicit casting. They cast the result of the operation to the more precise scalar operand type. This means when you work with an `int` and a `float`, the result will be a `float`. Table 4-3 lists the arithmetic operations; they will then be demonstrated in example programs.

The `MathAdd.php` program enables you to examine the properties of implicit and explicit casting using arithmetic operators. It provides the following examples:

- Adding two integers
- Adding two integers when one of the operands is explicitly cast as a float
- Adding an integer and a float

The example leverages a function to format and display results. The function is included at run time from the same relative directory as the `MathAdd.php` file. The concept of including files is covered later in this chapter. Functions are described in Chapter 7 if you want to explore the formatting function used in this section.

Name	Example	Description
Addition	`$c = $a + $b;`	The plus sign enables you to add two numbers. The result is cast to the more precise of the two operands. For example, a `float` added to an `int` will return a `float`.
Division	`$c = $a / $b;`	The forward slash enables you to divide the left value by the right value. If you divide two numbers and the operation returns a `float`, the result will be managed as a `float`. For example, dividing an `int` by an `int` will return an `int` *only when the division result is a whole number.*
Modulus	`$c = $a % $b;`	The percent sign enables you to do modulo mathematics and returns the modulus, which is an positive integer or zero. It is a positive integer when the quotient is not an integer but a real number, and zero when the quotient is an integer.
Multiplication	`$c = $a * $b;`	The asterisk enables you to multiply two numbers. The result of the multiplication is cast to the more precise operand type.
Negation	`$c = -$a;`	The minus sign as a unary operator enables you to negate a value. This turns a positive number to a negative and vice versa.
Subtraction	`$c = $a - $b;`	The minus sign as a binary operator enables you to subtract one number from another. The result of the subtraction is cast to the more precise operand type.

TABLE 4-3. *Arithmetic Operators*

The `MathAdd.php` program follows:

-- **This is found in the MathAdd.php on the enclosed CD.**

```php
<?php
   // Include the arithmetic display library.
   include("DisplayLibrary.php");

   // Declare int variables.
   $myIntVar1 = 17;
   $myIntVar2 = 23;

   // Declare float variable Pi.
   $myFloatVar = 22/7;

   // Define two variables without type definition.
   $myInteger;
   $myFloat;
```

```
// Get an integer by adding two integers.
$myInteger = $myIntVar1 + $myIntVar2;

// Display math operation.
display_add_results('$myInteger',$myInteger
                  ,'$myIntVar1',$myIntVar1
                  ,'$myIntVar2',$myIntVar2);

// Get a float when one integer is cast as a float.
$myInteger = $myIntVar1 + (float) $myIntVar2;

// Display math operation.
display_add_results('$myInteger',$myInteger
                  ,'$myIntVar1',$myIntVar1
                  ,'(float) $myIntVar2',(float) $myIntVar2);

// Get a float when one integer is cast as a float.
$myInteger = $myIntVar1 + $myFloatVar;

// Display math operation.
display_add_results('$myInteger',$myInteger
                  ,'$myIntVar1',$myIntVar1
                  ,'$myFloatVar',$myFloatVar);
?>
```

As demonstrated in the program, when you add, subtract, multiply, or divide with different data types, the result is cast to the more precise scalar type. When you are working in PHP you have a choice between two numeric types—integers and floats. Oddly enough, floats are reported as doubles by the gettype() function in PHP 5 incorrectly.

The output result of adding two integers is

PHP formula	**$myInteger = $myIntVar1 + $myIntVar2;**
PHP substitution	[40] = [17] + [23]
PHP data types	**[integer] = [integer] + [integer]**

The output result of adding two integers when one of the operands is explicitly cast as a float data type is

PHP formula	**$myInteger = $myIntVar1 + (float) $myIntVar2;**
PHP substitution	[40] = [17] + [23]
PHP data types	**[double] = [integer] + [double]**

The output result of adding integer and float operands is

PHP formula	**$myInteger = $myIntVar1 + $myFloatVar;**
PHP substitution	[20.142857142857] = [17] + [3.1428571428571]
PHP data types	**[double] = [integer] + [double]**

The multiplication assignment and subtraction assignment operators have the same behavioral characteristic as the addition operator. The negation arithmetic operator is a negative sign before any variable or numeric literal. It multiplies the variable or numeric literal by a negative 1.

This leaves you with one last arithmetic operator, the modulus operator. The modulus operator is useful when you want to check if a division operation produces an integer quotient as opposed to a real number. When the numerator is divided by the denominator and there is a zero remainder value from the operation, the quotient is an integer. However, the data type for the quotient will only be an `int` provided both the numerator and denominator are `int` types.

The following `Modulo.php` program demonstrates zero and nonzero modulus returns that would result from an integer division operation:

-- **This is found in Modulo.php on the enclosed CD.**

```php
<?php
  // Include the arithmetic display library.
  include("DisplayLibrary.php");

  // Declare int variables.
  $numerator1 = 16;
  $numerator2 = 17;
  $denominator = 2;

  // Define two variables without type definition.
  $modulus;

  // Get an integer by adding two integers.
  $modulus = $numerator1 % $denominator;

  // Display math operation.
  display_modulo_results('$modulus',$modulus
                         ,'$numerator1',$numerator1
                         ,'$denominator',$denominator);

  // Get a float when one integer is cast as a float.
  $modulus = $numerator2 % $denominator;

  // Display math operation.
  display_modulo_results('$modulus',$modulus
                         ,'$numerator2',$numerator2
                         ,'$denominator',$denominator);
?>
```

When the result of dividing an `int` by an `int` returns an `int`; the modulus operator returns a zero. This behavior is shown in the following `Modulo.php` program:

PHP formula	**$result_label = $numerator1 % $denominator;**
PHP substitution	[0] = [16] % [2]
PHP data types	**[integer] = [integer] % [integer]**

The Modulo.php program produces a nonzero result when dividing an int by an int that is not an integer but a real number, as shown here:

PHP formula	**$result_label = $numerator2 % $denominator;**
PHP substitution	[1] = [17] % [2]
PHP data types	**[integer] = [integer] % [integer]**

Bitwise Operators

The next set of operators enables you to work with bits instead of bytes. Bitwise operators allow you to logically examine the relationship of bits within variables. The behaviors of logical bitwise operations differ from logical variable comparisons. Table 4-4 describes the behavior of PHP bitwise operators.

Bitwise comparisons are useful when manipulating bits, but in general most web page programmers use logical operators. A caveat about bit comparisons in PHP is that bitwise comparisons differ from Perl. The difference is that PHP uses integers by default while Perl uses floats—the latter provides more accurate results than the former.

Logical Operators

Logical operators are frequently used by web programmers. They compare multiple truth expressions and determine whether one, one or the other, or both are true or false. These truth expressions can validate bool, int, float, and string variables as expressions in PHP. Table 4-5 describes PHP's logical operators.

Comparison Operators

Like the JavaScript programming language and a couple others, PHP provides an identity operator among its comparison operators. The identity operator is critical in a weakly typed language because it enables comparison of value and type in one command. Table 4-6 describes the comparison operators.

Name	Example	Description
And	`$c = $a & $b;`	The single ampersand sign verifies that both bits are on.
Not	`$c = ~$a;`	The tilde sign acts as a unary operator, enabling you to negate a bit and vice versa.
Or	`$c = $a | $b;`	The single pipe sign compares two bits to determine if one or the other is set.
Shift right	`$c = $a << $b;`	Two less-than symbols shift the bit in $b to bit $a.
Shift left	`$c = $a >> $b;`	Two greater-than symbols shift the bit in $a to bit $b.
Xor	`$c = $a ^ $b;`	The single circumflex sign compares two bits to determine if one is set and the other unset.

TABLE 4-4.   *Bitwise Logical Operators*

Name	Example	Description

And	`$c = $a and $b;`
	or
	`$c = $a && b;`
		The reserved word and or *two ampersand signs* enable you to verify if both variables are true.

Or	`$c = $a or $b;`
	or
	`$c = $a || $b;`
		The reserved word or or *two pipes* enable you to verify if one or another variable is true.

Xor	`$c = $a xor $b;`	The reserved word xor enables you to verify if one or variable is true and the other is false.
Not	`$c = !$a;`	The *exclamation mark,* also known in scripting and other programming languages as bang, *negates the truth of a variable.* When the variable evaluates as true, a bang in front of it makes it not true, or false. Alternatively, when the value is false, it is read as not false, or true.

TABLE 4-5.   *Logical Operators*

Name	Example	Description
Equals	`$a == $b`	The two equal signs together return true if the values are the same regardless of data type.
Identical	`$a === $b`	The three equal signs together return true if the values and data type are the same.

Not equal	`$a != $b`
	or
	`$a <> $b`
		The exclamation or bang operator and an equal sign or the less-than and greater-than symbols together return true if the values are different regardless of data type.

Not identical	`$a !== $b`	The combination of an exclamation mark and two equal signs together returns true if the values and data type are not the same.
Less than	`$a < $b`	The less-than sign returns true if the left operand contains a value less than the right operand.
Greater than	`$a > $b`	The greater-than sign returns true if the left operand contains a value greater than the right operand.
Less than or equal to	`$a <= $b`	The combination of the less-than and equal signs returns true if the left operand contains a value less than or equal to the right operand.
Greater than or equal to	`$a >= $b`	The greater-than sign returns true if the left operand contains a value greater than or equal to the right operand.

TABLE 4-6.   *Comparison Operators*

Operator Precedence

All unary, binary, and ternary operators work on established orders of precedence. Order of precedence governs whether an operator takes the operand on the left or right first before acting. Table 4-7 describes operator associativity by listing the operators, the direction of association (or use), and a description of their behaviors.

Operators	Associativity	Description
`and`	Left	This is a logical operator that compares the left operand against the right operand to determine if both are true.
`new`	Nonassociative	This is an object instance constructor and acts like a unary operator by signaling the construction of an instance of an object.
`or`	Left	This is a logical operator that compares the left operand against the right operand to determine if one or both are true.
`xor`	Left	This is a logical operator that compares the left operand against the right operand to determine *if only one or the other* is true.
`! ~ (int) (float) (string) (array) (object) @`	Nonassociative	These are for negation and typecasting.
`[`	Left	This is used in an `array()` type to delimit element indexes, followed by a number or string and closed by a right square bracket (]). These will be covered in Chapter 5, where `array()` data types are covered.
`,`	Left	This has many uses as a delimiter throughout the PHP language.
`+ - * / %`	Left	These are arithmetic operators.
`.`	Left	This is a string concatenation operator.
`<< >>`	Left	The *guillemet* operations, both << and >>, do bitwise shifts, which are left or right respectively.
`< <= > >=`	Nonassociative	These are operators for inequalities comparisons.
`== != === !==`	Nonassociative	These are operators for equalities and identity comparisons.
`&`	Left	This is used for bitwise and operations and to assign a variable by reference.

TABLE 4-7. *Operator Precedence*

Operators	Associativity	Description
^	Left	This is used for bitwise or operations.
|	Left	This is a logical operator for bitwise; one or the other is set but not both.
&&	Left	This is a logical operator that compares whether two variables are true or not.
||	Left	This is a logical operator that compares whether one or another variable is true or not.
= += -= *= /= .= %= &= != ^= <<= >>=	Right	These are assignment operators. The equal sign by itself assigns a right operand to a left operand variable. The others perform an operation in conjunction with the assignment. The *guillemet* operations, both << and >>, do bitwise shifts.
? :	Left	This is a ternary operator, which means it takes three operands. It will be covered in Chapter 5, when you examine conditional expressions.

TABLE 4-7. *Operator Precedence* (continued)

You have now covered the major operators in the PHP programming language. The next section will explore the data types in the language.

Data Types

PHP 5 supports three classes of variables: scalar, compound, and special. Four of the nine supported data types—bool, int, float, and string—are scalar. Scalar variables can only hold one value at any time. The compound variables are arrays and objects, while the special types are functions, resources, and nulls.

This chapter covers the four scalar variables and the special null type. Chapter 6 covers arrays, Chapter 7 covers functions, Chapter 8 covers objects, Chapter 10 covers file resources, and Chapter 13 covers database resources. A resource in PHP holds an external resource, like files and database connections.

The range of an int is 2^{32}; and the range for a float is 2^{64}. You should note that floats in PHP are 64-bit IEEE-compliant numbers, but working with large numbers requires leveraging libraries to ensure computational accuracy. The range of the scalar variables is found in Table 4-8.

The scalar variables have undergone changes as PHP matured. There is an older syntax supported for backward compatibility purposes, but the book will focus on the PHP 5 syntax. More or less, the differences lie in whether PHP sees an int or integer keyword as an integer and in how PHP manages a float data type, which is supported as a double prior to PHP 4.2. However, a variable cast as a float is returned as a double by the gettype() function in PHP 5.1 even though the double is deprecated. Table 4-9 explains the definition of variable types.

Scalar Data Type	Lower Limit	Upper Limit
bool	False is a zero or null value	True is anything other than a zero or null value
int	-2^{31}, or -2147483648	2^{31} or 2147483647
double	-2^{63}	2^{63}
string	Zero character	No practical limit

TABLE 4-8. *Scalar Data Limits*

It is important that implicit or explicit casting of variables may remove precision for variables. For example, if you assign a value of 2.123 to a variable and explicitly cast that variable to a Boolean data type, the new value will be 1; likewise, assigning a value of 2.123 and casting the variable to an integer will yield a new value of 2. The latter behavior rounded to the nearest lower whole number by removing the remainder.

Implicit casting occurs in PHP when the right operand of an assignment operator is a different type than the left operand. The left operand inherits the type of the right operand when it is more precise. Explicit casting requires the programmer to acknowledge the potential loss of precision; it is done by prefacing the right operand with a scalar data type enclosed in parentheses.

Data Type	Behavior
bool	The weakly typed behavior of a Boolean variable in PHP returns true for any nonzero number or nonempty string and false for zero or an empty string. This weakly typed behavior lets you to use int, float, and string types as Boolean values without casting them. Casting the scalar types diminishes their scalar precision.
int	The int (integer) type contains negative, positive, or zero whole numbers. If you assign a number like a float to an int, it will truncate all values to the right of the decimal point and round to the last whole number.
float	The float (double) type contains numbers that can have a value on both sides of the decimal point.
string	The string type contains a set of characters and is treated as a variable-length text string. String literals are delimited by single or double quotes. Appendix B contains a primer on predefined functions that enables you to manage string data types.
null	The null is a case-insensitive keyword that indicates a variable has been (a) assigned a null value, (b) not assigned a value, or (c) unset by the unset() function.

TABLE 4-9. *Primitive Variables and the Null Special Variable*

The following `ScalarVariables.php` program illustrates explicit casting at assignment in PHP 5:

-- This is found in ScalarVariables.php on the enclosed CD.

```php
<?php

    // Declare variables by assigning a value.
    $myVar1 = (boolean) 2.123;  // Explicit cast to boolean.
    $myVar2 = (int) 2.123;      // Explicit cast to integer.
    $myVar3 = (float) 2.123;    // Implicit cast to double.
    $myVar4 = (double) 2.123;   // Explicit cast to double.
    $myVar5 = (string) 2.123;   // Explicit cast to string.

    // Print and format variables to the web page with explicit casting.
    print "<font class=normal>";
    print "\$myVar1 [".gettype($myVar1)."] [".$myVar1."]<br>";
    print "\$myVar2 [".gettype($myVar2)."] [".$myVar2."]<br>";
    print "\$myVar3 [".gettype($myVar3)."] [".$myVar3."]<br>";
    print "\$myVar4 [".gettype($myVar4)."] [".$myVar4."]<br>";
    print "\$myVar5 [".gettype($myVar5)."] [".$myVar5."]<br><p>";
    print "</font>";
? >
```

The sample program demonstrates explicit casting, which illustrates the loss of precision that can occur when a more precise type is cast to a less precise type. The `ScalarVariables.php` program prints the following output demonstrating the data loss:

```
$myVar1 [boolean] [1]
$myVar2 [integer] [2]
$myVar3 [double] [2.123]
$myVar4 [double] [2.123]
$myVar5 [string] [2.123]
```

The loss of precision is demonstrated by reducing an `int` with a value of 2.123 to 1 by casting it as a `bool` and truncating it to 2 by casting it as an integer. Using the `settype()` function to reset the value cannot return the precision or roll back the change. The value of the original assignment is lost by the explicit casting of the data type. However, when you add another variable, assigned by reference, and change its data type to a less precise value with the `settype()` function, it will change the referenced variable too.

You can test the `settype()` function behavior on referenced variables by appending the following lines to the `ScalarVariables.php` program to demonstrate the behavior:

```php
// Declare a variable by reference to an existing variable.
$myVar6 = &$myVar5;

// Reset the data type of the referencing variable.
settype($myVar6,"boolean");

// Print the data type and value of the referenced variable.
print "\$myVar5 [".gettype($myVar5)."] [".$myVar5."]<br>";
```

The code will render the following to a web page:

 `$myVar5 [boolean] [1]`

> **NOTE**
> *It is not possible to explicitly typecast at the same time that you assign a variable by reference. If you attempt to do so, the page will not be rendered or it will raise a parsing error.*

There is one other data type assignment. It is used to support variable variables in PHP, which enable you to build dynamic or run-time variable names. You assign variable variables by using two dollar symbols on the left operand, which is read as a variable of a variable. Variable variables act like indirection assignments. The first dollar symbol indicates a variable, and the second dollar symbol identifies a variable within a variable.

The assigned value of the nested variable becomes a variable name that can contain a data value. Figure 4-1 shows a `$myVar` variable that contains a string literal of `"varName"`. Then, `$$myVar` is defined by pointing to the contents of `$myVar`. When you assign a string to `$$myVar`, you have defined a new variable named `$varName`. You can access the contents of `$varName` directly or indirectly through `$$myVar`, as shown in Figure 4-1.

The concept of using variable variables may seem odd at first glance, but it provides a tool to dynamically build variable names at program run time. For example, if you build a function that works differently according to a known list of values in a database, variable variables enable you to use those values as run-time variable names. This can make your program more meaningful than substituting other variable names because it enables the business logic to mimic more closely the concepts and choices that reflect user interactions.

You could accomplish this by defining a lookup list in a database table. For example, the lookup list might contain two values for gender—male and female. When you query the database, you could return those values from the database and then use them as run-time variables. Moreover, using variables like `$male` and `$female` can increase the readability of your code. Variable variables enable you to employ this technique.

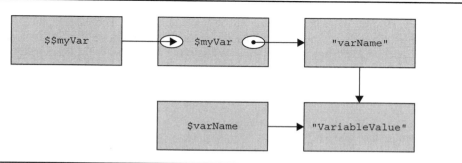

FIGURE 4-1. *Indirect variable variable assignments*

The following `VariableVariables.php` program illustrates this technique by using the same variable names as the preceding illustration:

⬛⬛ **-- This is found in `VariableVariables.php` on the enclosed CD.**

```php
<?php
   // Declare variables by assigning a value.
   $myVar = "varName";

   // Declare a variable variable by assigning the value of $myVar
   // as the name of variable in a variable.
   $$myVar = "Variable Value";

   // Print the variable names and contents.
   print "\$myVar [" . $myVar . "]<br>";

   // Print the variable variable by using two $ reference.
   print "\${\$myVar} [" . ${$myVar} . "]<br>";

   // Print the base variable name and the variable in a variable.
   print "\$varName [" . $varName . "]<br>";

?>
```

The `VariableVariables.php` program prints the contents of the initial `$myVar` variable assigned by value:

⬛ `$myVar [varName]`

The program then prints a newly assigned value through indirect reference to the base variable name and direct reference to the contents of the base variable:

⬛ `${$myVar} [Variable Value]`
`$varName [Variable Value]`

You have now covered the `bool`, `int`, `float`, and `string` data types and how to use them in user-defined variables. Likewise, you have covered the special case of the insensitive null data type. In the next section you will examine how to define and use global variables.

Global Variables

Global variables have two varieties, which have different scopes in your programs. Global variables can be built as environment-level or script-level variables. *Environment-level* global variables act as user-defined constants and can contain only scalar variable values. They are available anywhere in your PHP programs once defined. *Script-level* global variables are available only externally to functions unless you pass them to a function as an actual parameter. You can find more on the nuances of script-level variables in Chapter 7.

You define global variables by using the `define()` function. After you define them, you can't redefine them in your currently called program, which includes the primary file and any included files. You can redefine them at each call to the server, but generally constants are defined in libraries that are frequently used but infrequently changed.

Unlike true environment variables set by the PHP shared libraries, user-defined global environment-level variables last only for the duration of your server-side execution cycle. The convention is to label user-defined constants as uppercase strings, but you can define them in uppercase, lowercase, or mixed case. While there is no reason to do so, many programmers use single quotes to delimit the constant label and double quotes to delimit the string when defining constants. You can use either single or double quotes for both.

The Constants.php program demonstrates how you define and access a constant in your programs:

-- This is found in the Constants.php on the enclosed CD.

```php
<?php
  // Define a global constant.
  define('MY_GLOBAL_VARIABLE',"Enter Narnia by the wardrobe!");

  // Print the contents.
  print "[MY_GLOBAL_VARIABLE] = [".MY_GLOBAL_VARIABLE."]<br>";
?>
```

Alternatively, you can define a script-level variable by preceding the variable name with the GLOBAL keyword. When the variable is defined at the script level, the addition of the GLOBAL keyword does nothing, but inside a function, it makes the variable available outside of the function without having to return it. As mentioned previously, this is explained in more detail in Chapter 7.

You have now learned how to define global environment-level and script-level variables in your programs. The next section will introduce you to the PHP predefined variables.

Predefined Variables

PHP predefined variables are also known as superglobal variables. These variables provide a powerful set of features, which you will explore in different parts of the book. Later in the chapter you will see how to examine the contents of predefined variables beyond what you've seen using the phpInfo() function introduced in Chapter 2. Table 4-10 describes the PHP predefined or superglobal variables.

You have been introduced to user-defined and predefined variables. In Chapter 5 you will begin to discover the benefits of conditional and iterative structures to explore the contents of

Variable Name	Description
$GLOBALS	The variable contains a reference to every variable within the global scope of the script. The keys for these values are the names of the global variables.
$_COOKIE	The variable contains all HTTP cookies. It replaces the deprecated $HTTP_COOKIE_VARS array.
$_ENV	The variable contains all inherited environment variables or those directly set within the script. It replaces the deprecated $HTTP_ENV_VARS array.

TABLE 4-10. *Predefined Variables*

Variable Name	Description
$_FILES	The variable contains all variables provided by HTTP POST file uploads. It replaces the deprecated $HTTP_POST_FILES array.
$_GET	The variable contains all URL query string values. It replaces the $HTTP_GET_VARS array.
$_POST	The variable contains all variables provided by HTTP POST. It replaces the deprecated $HTTP_POST_VARS array.
$_REQUEST	The variable contains all variables provided by GET, POST, and COOKIE inputs. The order of the variable is set by the PHP variable order configuration parameter. *The values in this variable are a security risk* because it makes a man-in-the-middle attack more likely, since $_GET is insecure. You should use the $_POST in lieu of the $_REQUEST predefined variable.
$_SERVER	The variable contains variables set by the execution environment of the web server and current running scripts. It replaces the deprecated $HTTP_SERVER_VARS array.
$_SESSION	The variable contains variables bound to the current session. It replaces the deprecated $HTTP_SESSION_VARS array.

TABLE 4-10. *Predefined Variables* (continued)

these variables. The next chapter will explore the conditional and iterative structures necessary to any programming language.

Library File Inclusion

File inclusion is a wonderful concept that enables you to write library files and reuse them when you need to in other programs. Table 4-11 covers the four functions that enable you include PHP library files.

The include() and require() statements behave identically except for error management as noted in Table 4-11. Likewise, the include_once() and require_once() statements behave the same. It is really a matter of preference as to which one you choose to use. However, there is a definite choice when you pick between a blind inclusion and a one-time inclusion. A bad choice can cause your PHP libraries to fail—in a worst-case scenario, at the hands of your user community. You should always use the include_once() or require_once() statement in preference to the include() or require() statement because the risk of the latter outweighs any benefit.

NOTE
If you are using the Microsoft Windows operating system, you should know that these include *statements are case sensitive despite the case insensitivity of the operation system. This means both the directory path and the filename must be treated as case sensitive.*

Statement Name	Description
`include("path/name");`	The `include()` statement takes a single argument, which needs to be a string containing an absolute or relative path statement and file. The file needs to contain a working PHP program unit that is delimited by `<?php` and `?>` tags. The `include()` statement should only occur once per file, or you will inherit multiple copies of the library. The `include()` statement will raise a nonfatal warning if the file is unavailable.
`include_once("path/name");`	The `include_once()` statement takes a single argument, which needs to be a string containing an absolute or relative path statement and file. The file needs to contain a working PHP program unit that is delimited by `<?php` and `?>` tags. The `include_once()` statement will include only one copy of the file no matter how many statements call the file. This is nice because you may have a core library file called by many library files, and this makes sure you'll never have two copies of it.
`require("path/name");`	The `require()` statement takes a single argument, which needs to be a string containing an absolute or relative path statement and file. The file needs to contain a working PHP program unit that is delimited by `<?php` and `?>` tags. The `require()` statement should only occur once per file, or you will inherit multiple copies of the library. The `require()` statement will raise a fatal warning if the file is unavailable.
`require_once("path/name");`	The `require_once()` statement takes a single argument, which needs to be a string containing an absolute or relative path statement and file. The file needs to contain a working PHP program unit that is delimited by `<?php` and `?>` tags. The `require_once()` statement will include only one copy of the file no matter how many statements call the file. This is nice because you may have a core library file called by many library files, and this makes sure you'll never have two copies of it.

TABLE 4-11. *File Inclusion Statements*

The following `Include.php`, `Library1.php`, `Library2.php`, and `Included.php` programs demonstrate the process of PHP file inclusion. You should ensure that all these files are placed in the same directory because they depend on the present working directory for the path and provide only a filename as an actual parameter.

The `Include.php` file includes two theoretically high-level libraries:

-- **This is found in Include.php on the enclosed CD.**

```php
<?php
  // Include two high-level libraries.
  include_once("Library1.php");
  include_once("Library2.php");
?>
```

The `Library1.php` and `Library2.php` files are identical except in filename and contain the following:

-- **This is found in Library1.php and Library2.php on the enclosed CD.**

```php
<?php
  // Include a low-level library file.
  include_once("Included.php");
?>
```

The next program displays the sample low-level library that is called by both of the high-level libraries. As you can see in the following, only a string is printed to the console, which enables you to see that using the `include_once()` statement works:

-- **This is found in Included.php on the enclosed CD.**

```php
<?php
  // Prints the name of the file.
  print "This is the [Included.php] file.";
?>
```

If you were to substitute the `include()` statement in the high-level library files, you would see two lines rendered to the web page because it would include the file twice.

Another way to include standard header and footer files is to set them in the `auto_prepend_file` and `auto_append_file` directives in your `php.ini` file. These work well if you *always* require a specific header and footer. They eliminate the need for you to explicitly include them in your program's files because they'll always be there.

You have learned how to include your PHP libraries in your executable programs in this section. The next section will cover reserved words and system constants.

Reserved Words and System Constants

You have learned the basics about writing PHP programs, but a comprehensive list of reserved words is always helpful. Table 4-12 contains the PHP reserved word list (the number following the reserved word indicates the release when it became available).

And	else	include_once()	php_user_filter
or	elseif	isset()	interface 5
xor	empty()	list()	implements 5
__FILE__	enddeclare	new	extends
exception 5	endfor	print()	public 5
__LINE__	endforeach	require()	private 5
array()	endif	require_once()	protected 5
as	endswitch	return()	abstract 5
break	endwhile	static	clone 5
case	eval()	switch	try 5
class	exit()	unset()	catch 5
const	extends	use	throw 5
continue	for	var	cfunction 4
declare	foreach	while	old_function 4
default	function	__FUNCTION__	this 5
die()	global	__CLASS__	
do	if	__METHOD__	
echo()	include()	final	

TABLE 4-12.   *Reserved Word List*

You should also know that there is a long list of standard constants that changes with point releases of the PHP engine, like moving from 5.1.0 to 5.1.4. They are contributed by the PHP community Zend Corporation and SAPI modules. There are also variations based on the modules used in your server environment.

You can find the defined constants in your environment by using the get_defined_constants() function, but it does not render them in a user-friendly way. Sorting the returned array is a bit tricky too because it will require a user-defined sort function. You can find more about the array sorting options by checking the uksort() function definition in Chapter 6; functions in general are covered in Chapter 7.

The GetConstants.php program demonstrates how you can discover your environment constants. The program formats the output into an HTML table that uses cascading style sheet definitions. The following are used in the program to render the table:

```
<style>
.e {background-color: #ccccff; font-weight: bold; color: #000000;}
.h {background-color: #9999cc; font-weight: bold; color: #000000;}
.v {background-color: #cccccc; color: #000000;}
</style>
```

You should include the preceding style tag if you type the next program as opposed to using the copy on the enclosed CD. The following GetConstants.php program sets and sorts your server environment constants:

```php
<?php
  // Declare an array of environment constants.
  $constants = get_defined_constants();

  // Sort by promoting the keys to uppercase.
  uksort($constants,'uppercase_sort');

  // Print the table with column labels.
  print to_table($constants,'Constant Names','Constant Values');

  // -----------------------------------------------------------

  // A function to render a table.
  function to_table($array_in,$column_1,$column_2)
  {
    // Declare variable with table start.
    $output = "<table border=0 cellpadding=0 cellspacing=0>";
    $output .= "<tr><td class=h>".$index."</td>";
    $output .= "<td class=h>".$data."</td></tr>";

    // Read and add array keys and values to a string.
    foreach ($array_in as $hashName => $hashValue)
    {
      // Append row tag and first column value.
      $output .= "<tr><td class=e valign=top>[".$hashName."]</td>";

        // Append non-array value with cell tags.
        $output .= "<td class=v>[".$hashValue."]</td></tr>";
    }

    // Close HTML table.
    $output .= "</table>";

    // Return the HTML table.
    return $output;
  }

  // -----------------------------------------------------------
  // Define a comparison function.
  function uppercase_sort($a,$b)
  {
    // Promote all keys to uppercase.
    $a = strtoupper($a);
    $b = strtoupper($b);

    // Check if one is greater than the other.
    return ($a > $b) ? 1 : -1;
  }
?>
```

The return set is too large for this chapter, but it is included as Appendix C. The sort function promotes the keys to uppercase because the `asort()` fails to do so correctly. It appears that the sort failure is linked to a magic constant, `__FUNCTION__`, and its ability to display functions in their case-sensitive declaration format. Regardless of the reason, it gives you an opportunity to forward-reference array sorting operations that are covered in Chapter 7.

This section has covered the reserved words and available environment constants. You also have a tool to determine all of your system constants, which will depend on your installed shared libraries.

Summary

You have learned the basics of writing PHP programs in this chapter. The section "Variables" has shown you how to define user-defined variables, operators, data types, global variables, and predefined variables. You have also learned how to include library files, encountered the reserved word list, and learned how to find your PHP environment constants. These skills will support your exploration of any part of this book, but tackling Chapters 5–10 in order will round out your fundamental knowledge of the language.

CHAPTER
5

Control Structures

his chapter examines how you define, declare, assign, compare, and process variables in conditional and iterative structures. It covers the following topics:

- Conditional structures
  - If statement
  - Switch statement
- Iterative control structures
  - Do-While loop
  - For loop
  - Foreach loop
  - While loop

By the end of this chapter, you will have completed your introduction to PHP and can begin writing larger and more complex programs.

While you now understand primitive variable definition and assignment, variables require conditional and iterative structures to become useful. This section will examine conditional structures and then iterative structures available in PHP.

Conditional Structures

Conditional structures describe the if-then, if-then-else, if-then-else-if-then-else, and switch statements. These structures enable you to make decisions based on single variables or collections of variables.

It is important to note that PHP provides conditional structured Boolean statements with a great deal of flexibility and power, which can be used well or poorly. As discussed previously, a Boolean evaluation returns true for any nonzero number or nonempty string and false for zero or an empty string. If you cast a variable to a Boolean data type, it will have a value of 0 for false or 1 for true.

If Statement

If statements evaluate an expression or set of expressions to determine whether the expression is true or false. When only one execution statement is linked to an if-then, the pattern is

```
if (expression) statement;
```

With two or more execution statements linked to an if-then, the prototype requires curly braces like those used in C, C++, C#, Java, or JavaScript programming. Whether represented as a single statement without curly braces or a set of statements enclosed by curly braces, the statements are considered an `if` block. The following pattern illustrates the use of curly braces with a set of conditional statements:

```
if (expression)
{
  statement1;
  statement2;
}
```

The expression in the if-then statement can have variations. One variation is a single variable that is evaluated to determine whether it is true or false. Another expression is a single variable compared against another variable, or a numeric or string literal, to evaluate whether it is true or false. Both of these expression types are considered single expression evaluations.

You can also link multiple expressions by using logical comparison operators. When you combine expressions, the result is known as a *compound expression,* like the following prototype that evaluates if only one or the other expression is true:

```
if ((expression) xor (expression))
{
  statement1;
  statement2;
}
```

A major advantage of writing PHP programs is leveraging the flexibility of a weakly typed language. In strongly typed languages, you can use a Boolean variable by itself as an expression. The weakly typed nature of PHP lets you evaluate any type of variable as true or false according to the previously discussed rule.

The following IfThen1.php program demonstrates an if-then statement that uses an integer in place of Boolean variables:

-- **This is found in IfThen1.php on the enclosed CD**.

```php
<?php
  // Declare a variable by assigning a value.
  $myVar = -1.234;

  // Print and format variables to the web page.
  print "Before the if-statement, ";
  print "\$myVar is [".$myVar."] and a double data type.<br />\n";

  // Check if only one of two expression is true.
  if (($myVar) xor (1 == 2))
  {
    // Print the output as three statements.
    print "After the if-statement, \$myVar is: ";
    print "[".$myVar."] and a [".gettype($myVar)."] data type.<br />\n";
  }
?>
```

The IfThen1.php program PHP script demonstrates a combination conditional expression join by an either/or logical operator, xor. The $myVar variable contains a value and is therefore found true as an expression. Since one is not equal to two, the second expression is false, and the combined expression is true. The program also shows that the `$myVar` variable data type is unchanged by an implicit Boolean evaluation.

The `IfThen1.php` program prints the following output:

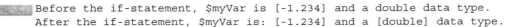
```
Before the if-statement, $myVar is [-1.234] and a double data type.
After the if-statement, $myVar is: [-1.234] and a [double] data type.
```

NOTE
The reasons `integer`, `float`, *and* `string` *data types are frequently used in conditional evaluations are: (1) They may be easily used by leveraging the benefits of a weakly typed language; and (2) they are not implicitly cast with a loss of utility or precision when evaluated against the rules for truth.*

TIP
If you leave out parentheses in conditional evaluations, you will return a fatal parsing error or fail to render the page.

The if-then also supports an `else` clause. As with the `if` block, when a conditional evaluation is false, the statements processed are those in the `else` block. The following prototype demonstrates the `else` clause, which also uses multiple statement lines and curly braces:

```
if (expression)
{
  statement1;
  statement2;
}
else
{
  statement1;
  statement2;
}
```

The next example extends the previous one by making a change to the second of the two logically compared expressions. This change will make nested expressions independently true and the compound expression false, which will trigger the `else` block in the following code:

-- This is found in IfThen2.php on the enclosed CD.

```
<?php
  // Declare a variable by assigning a value.
  $myVar = -1.234;

  // Check if only one of two expression is true.
  if (($myVar) xor (1 == 1))
```

```
{
  // Print the output as one statement.
  print "This is impossible to reach.";
}
else
{
  // Print a failure message.
  print "The \$myVar variable is [".$myVar."] and 1 does equal 1.";
}
?>
```

The `IfThen2.php` program prints the following statement from the `else` clause:

The $myVar variable is [-1.234] and 1 does equal 1.

Many business problems aren't as simple as whether or not a single variable or set of variables is collectively true or false. Some require complex conditional evaluations to determine which code block to execute. Others examine alternative expressions involving a single variable or set of variables.

In the case of alternative expressions, a series of evaluations are made before choosing which code block to execute. The evaluation expressions should ensure that no data can meet more than one condition. When two or more conditional expressions overlap, only the first one in execution sequence can be met.

There are two solutions to evaluating a series of conditional expressions. The most general solution to this type of problem is the if-then-else-if-then-else statement, which has the following prototype:

```
if (expression)
{
  statement1;
  statement2;
}
else if (expression)
{
  statement1;
  statement2;
}
else
{
  statement1;
  statement2;
}
```

The next program demonstrates an example of the if-then-else-if-then pattern by extending the prior if-then-else example:

-- **This is found in IfThen3.php on the enclosed CD.**

```
<?php
  // Declare variables by assigning a value.
```

```
$myVar = 0.234;

// Check if variable is greater than or equal to 1.
if ($myVar >= 1)
{
  // Print desired message.
  print "\$myVar is a positive number 1 or greater.";
}
// Check if variable is equal to zero.
else if ($myVar == 0)
{
  // Print desired message.
  print "\$myVar is zero.";
}
// Check if variable less than zero.
else if ($myVar < 0)
{
  // Print desired message.
  print "\$myVar is a negative number.";
}
// The only thing left is a real number between 0 and 1.
else
{
  // Print desired message.
  print "\$myVar is a real number between 0 and 1.";
}
?>
```

The `IfThen3.php` program checks the condition of the `$myVar` variable against a condition in the `if` statement and two other conditions in the `else-if` clauses. When none of those conditions are met, the program performs the `else` clause. In this case, the value of the variable fails all conditions because it is less than one and greater than zero, and so the program prints the following output:

`$myVar is a real number between 0 and 1.`

While the if-then-else-if-then-else syntax solves many problems, there is an alternative syntax for conditional statement evaluations. Called a `switch` statement, it is particularly effective when you want to evaluate a single variable against multiple result values.

Switch Statement

The `switch` statement accepts one formal parameter, which should be either an `integer`, `float`, or `string` primitive variable. The `switch` statement evaluates a single variable against a set of results in sequence. When none of the results match, the code block in the optional default case is selected. The `switch` statement has the following prototypes:

Integer/Float Variable	**String Variable**

```
switch (variable)                  switch (variable)
{                                  {
  case 0:                            case 'string0':
    statement;                         statement;
    break;                             break;
  case 1:                            case 'string1':
    statement;                         statement;
    break;                             break;
  default:                           default:
    statement;                         statement1;
}                                  }
```

The break statement is required in each case statement to signal that the evaluation has found a match and should exit the switch statement. If there is no break statement in a case, the program will *fall through* once it has found a match until it runs the default case statements. You may replace the break statement when the switch statement runs within a loop by using the continue statement. The continue statement, like the break statement, stops execution in the switch by passing control back to the containing loop structure.

As a rule, you will probably want to use break statements in your switch statements. However, later in the chapter you will examine a useful purpose for fall-through.

The Switch1.php program illustrates a switch statement with an integer:

-- **This is found in Switch1.php on the enclosed CD**.

```php
<?php
  // Declare a variable by assigning a value.
  $myVar = 2;

  switch ($myVar)
  {
    case 0:
      print "\$myVar is a [".$myVar."].";
      break;
    case 1:
      print "\$myVar is a [".$myVar."].";
      break;
    case 2:
      print "\$myVar is a [".$myVar."].";
      break;
    default:
      print "\$myVar is a [".$myVar."].";
      break;
  }
?>
```

The Switch1.php program uses a switch statement to check against a set of numeric literals. It evaluates cases until a match is found and exits when it encounters a break statement. The Switch1.php program produces the following output:

```
$myVar is a [2].
```

Now that you have examined the basic semantics of a switch statement, it is time to consider another approach. You may use this one when you want to evaluate complex expressions by their Boolean outcomes rather than a series of integer, float, and string value comparisons. This approach enables you to use inequality comparisons in a switch statement.

The Switch2.php program shows a simple example of this approach:

-- This is found in Switch2.php on the enclosed CD.

```php
<?php
  // Declare a variable by assigning a value.
  $myVar = 1.34;

  switch (true)
  {
    case ($myVar <= 1):
      print "\$myVar [".$myVar."] is less than [1].";
      break;
    case ($myVar > 2):
      print "\$myVar [".$myVar."] is greater than [2].";
      break;
    default:
      print "\$myVar is a [".$myVar."].";
      break;
  }
?>
```

The Switch2.php program uses a case statement to evaluate whether a variable has an inequality relationship to a constant. The program renders the following output:

```
$myVar is a [1.34].
```

The Switch2.php program presents an interesting logical problem *when these specific inequalities statements are reversed* because a number that is greater than one can also be less than two. When there is no break statement in the first case and the inequalities are reversed, the program will run the statements for the first two cases. This result would tell us that the number is both greater than one and less than two or equal to two.

You may define these Boolean evaluations to include compound statements. The compound statements can solve tricky problems by leveraging the switch statement, which can make your code more readable than complex if-then-else-if-then statements. Extending the prior example, you can substitute a variable for the numeric literal to make the case statement behavior more dynamically. When you substitute the variable for the literal value, the dynamic behavior produces a solution that is more elegant and algorithmic.

TIP
Extending switch *statements to use complex Boolean logic should be done with great care. You should consider mapping the logic through a truth table to ensure you don't code yourself into an undesired and intermittent code feature, that is, a bug.*

You have now examined the basic conditional statement structures used in PHP, except one. The remaining structure enables you to do if-then-else logic by the use of a single expression. This structure is the ternary operator introduced in Chapter 4. Like many things in modern programming languages, it has its origins in mathematics. The syntax for the ternary operator comes from the C programming language. This operator is used in many other languages, like C++, Java, and JavaScript. The ternary operator has the following prototype:

```
expression ? true statement : false statement
```

The absence of parentheses is recognized by the PHP parser, which is convenient. The following is a simplified version of the if-then-else program shown earlier using the ternary operator:

```php
<?php
  // Declare variables by assigning a value.
  $myVar = -1.234;

  // Check if the variable is true or false.
  $myVar ? print "True!" : print "False!";
?>
```

The sample code uses the ternary operator to evaluate whether or not $myVar is true. It prints true when $myVar contains a value other than zero or null, and false otherwise.

You have now reviewed conditional operations in PHP. It is important to remember that you can mix, match, and nest these structures within each other, as will become more meaningful after you cover iterative structures in the next section.

Iterative Control Structures

Iterative control structures, including do-while, for, foreach, and while loops, provide the programmer with a key tool by enabling a program to repeat a set of instructions a specified number of times or until a condition is met.

There are different structures because you can have different purposes when you want to step through data repeatedly. Sometimes you want to do it until a condition is met, as is accomplished with the for and do-while loops. On occasion you want to gate entry to an iterative structure with a condition, which is what the while loop does. In the case of a hash table or hash map, which manages a key-to-value index, PHP provides a special iterative structure—the foreach loop.

In the following section, you will examine the purpose and use of the do-while, for, foreach, and while loops. Since the next chapter covers arrays, there will be a bit of forward referencing to support the foreach loop structure. They will be presented in alphabetical order because that puts the while loop last; it behaves differently than the others by gating entry to, not exit from, a loop.

Do-While Loop

The do-while loop does not audit conditions on entry but on exit. You will find this structure useful when you always want the logic processed at least one time before exiting the loop. The prototype for a do-while loop is

```
do
{
  statements
} while (expression);
```

The DoWhile.php program illustrates the basic structure of a do-while loop:

-- **This is found in DoWhile.php on the enclosed CD.**

```php
<?php
  // Declare a variable.
  $myVar = 0;

  // Start a loop until a condition is met.
  do
  {
    // Print and increment $myVar.
    print "\$myVar [".$myVar++."]<br />\n";
  } while ($myVar < 5);
?>
```

The do-while loop allows all to enter, increments to five, and then lets the program continue to the next task. The program will generate the following output to your web page:

```
$myVar [0]
$myVar [1]
$myVar [2]
$myVar [3]
$myVar [4]
```

The do-while loop runs once or as many times as necessary until the condition in the while statement is met. Because the do-while loop checks the condition at the end of the loop, it is also called a post-test loop.

For Loop

The for loop does not audit conditions on entry but, like the do-while loop, on exit. You will find this structure useful when you want to put all streams of code through it and want the convenience of setting the initial value, exit evaluation, and incrementing pattern in one place. The pattern for a for loop is

```
for (expression1; expression2; expression3)
{
  statements
}
```

The first expression is read on entry into the loop. The second expression is read immediately after expression one during the first execution, and then after every complete execution cycle. The third expression is read at the end of each loop after the second expression evaluation.

You set a control variable in the first expression of a `for` loop, like $i, and assign it an initial value. It is also possible to leave the first expression empty and define the control variable before starting the `for` loop. The second expression contains a control statement, which governs when the exit condition is met. As with the first expression, you can leave the second expression empty, provided you have a control structure to exit the loop in the statement block of the loop. The third expression typically contains the `for` loop incrementing variable and the step value for each increment through the loop. You can exclude the third expression, but then you need to provide an incrementing operation inside the statement block of the loop.

The `For1.php` program shows the basic structure of a `for` loop:

-- **This is found in For1.php on the enclosed CD.**

```php
<?php
  // Declare a variable.
  $myVar = 0;

  // Start a loop until a condition is met.
  for ($i = $myVar; $i < 5; $i++)
  {
    // Print $myVar.
    print "\$i [".$i."]<br />\n";
  }
?>
```

The `for` loop allows all to enter, increments to five, and then lets the program continue to the next task. The program will generate the following output to your web page:

```
$i [0]
$i [1]
$i [2]
$i [3]
$i [4]
```

A modified approach to using the `for` loop as described previously is to leave expression two empty but embed the exit condition in the loop statement. This approach is shown in the following program:

-- **This is found in For2.php on the enclosed CD.**
```php
<?php
  // Declare a variable.
  $myVar = 0;

  // Start a loop until a condition is met.
  for ($i = $myVar; ; $i++)
  {
    // Print $myVar if $i is less than 5.
    if ($i < 5) // This is the exit condition.
```

```
      print "\$i [".$i."]<br />\n";
    else
      break;
  }
?>
```

By excluding the second expression from the `for` loop syntax, the exit gate is closed and you have an infinite loop. Placing a conditional statement inside the loop statement block enables you to exit the loop. There must be an internal exit statement when the second expression is left out of the `for` loop implementation. Otherwise, you will have an infinite loop.

When you remove the third expression from the `for` loop, the control variable is no longer incremented and the exit condition goes unmet. This can also be fixed in your statement block by adding a postincrement unary operator to the control variable. The following can be substituted in the `For2.php` program when you remove the third expression from the `for` loop implementation, as follows:

```
if ($i++ < 5)
```

The program produces the same results as the previous example. The `for` loop is widely used because once you master it, it is familiar and easy.

Foreach Loop

The `foreach` loop is a useful tool to navigate hash indexes or maps, which are also known as associative arrays. Associative arrays are name and value pairs stored in a structure. The names may be numeric or alphanumeric and therefore mimic the behavior of hash maps. Predefined variables also work by using name and value pairs.

While arrays are covered in the next chapter, the basic pattern of an associative array is

```
$variable = array(["key one" => "value one" , "key two" => "value two", ...])
```

The associative array syntax pattern may be new to you and deserves some description. The first string is the key, and the positional name operator, =>, points to the value of the pair. Square brackets are used to show that any pair elements are optional because you can assign an empty array to a variable. You define an associative array without any element pairs by using the following syntax:

```
$hashmap = array();
```

The following assignment declares a two-element associative array stored in the `$hashmap` target assignment variable:

```
$hashmap = array("One" => "First", "Two" => "Second");
```

You will use the `$hashmap` associative array in the `ForEach1.php` program. First, you need to see the `foreach` loop pattern, which enables you to read through the contents of any associative array:

```
foreach ($array_name as $name => $value)
{
  statements
}
```

The Foreach1.php program applies the foreach pattern and uses the $hashmap array defined previously. It prints the array key, which is also the internal name, and value pairs:

-- **This is found in Foreach1.php on the enclosed CD.**

```php
<?php
  // Declare an array variable.
  $hashmap = array("One" => "First", "Two" => "Second");

  // Start a loop until a condition is met.
  foreach ($hashmap as $hashName => $hashValue)
  {
    // Print $hashmap name and value pairs.
    print "[".$hashName."] [".$hashValue."]<br />\n";
  }
?>
```

The ForEach1.php program enables you to see the key and value pairs of an associative array. The program also renders the following results to a web page:

```
[One] [First]
[Two] [Second]
```

Recalling the predefined variables from Chapter 4, the next example will demonstrate how to use the foreach loop to read their contents. This behavior is like several operations performed by the phpInfo() function introduced in Chapter 2. The following Foreach2.php example will print the contents of the $_SERVER predefined variable into an HTML table:

-- **This is found in Foreach2.php on the enclosed CD.**

```php
<?php
  // Begin an HTML table.
  print "<table border=1>";

  // Start a loop until a condition is met.
  foreach ($_SERVER as $hashName => $hashValue)
  {
    // Print $hashmap name and value pairs in table cells.
    print "<tr>";
    print "<td>".$hashName."</td>";
    print "<td>".$hashValue."</td><tr>\n";
  }

  // Close an HTML table.
  print "</table>";
?>
```

The Foreach2.php program uses a foreach loop to read the contents of the $_SERVER predefined variable. The foreach loop takes an array variable, which contains a key and value pair. After the array variable, the arguments require using the keyword as, followed by a target variable to hold the key, a positional name operator (=>), and a target variable to hold the value. The key and value pairs are printed as $hashName and $hashValue variables into an HTML table.

When you do not care about the index value, you can dispense with the key and positional name operator (=>). The following syntax prints the values of an array and ignores the index values:

```php
<?php
  // Declare an array variable.
  $list = array("One" => "First", "Two" => "Second");

  // Read through the array values.
  foreach ($list as $element)
    print "[".$element."]<br />";
?>
```

You will see this syntax in Chapter 11 when reading lines from a file and Chapter 13 when reading rows from an Oracle database. This syntax is the more commonly used when index values are ignored.

You have now covered the `foreach` loop structure, which you will use frequently while writing PHP programs. Next, you will cover the `while` loop that gates entry and exit.

While Loop

The `while` loop enables you to gate whether or not your program enters the loop to begin with. The evaluation criterion at the top or loop entrance of the `while` loop accomplishes the preentry check and also prevents exit until the criterion is no longer met. The `while` loop has the following pattern:

```
while (expression)
{
  statements
}
```

The following `While.php` program demonstrates the use of a `while` loop:

-- **This is found in While.php on the enclosed CD**.

```php
<?php
  // Declare a variable.
  $myVar = 5;

  // Start a while loop with condition to be met.
  while ($myVar > 0)
  {
    // Print and decrement $myVar.
    print "\$myVar [".$myVar--."]<br>\n";
  }
?>
```

The `while` loop checks the condition on entry to the loop, which is also called a pretest loop. The loop runs once or as many times as necessary until the condition in the `while` statement is met.

The program generates the following output:

```
$myVar [5]
$myVar [4]
$myVar [3]
$myVar [2]
$myVar [1]
```

You have covered all of the PHP iterative structures. This background should provide you with a good foundation for writing PHP programs. At this point, it would be nice to look at a program that uses conditional and iteration structures to solve problems and explore the fall-through behavior when the break statement is excluded from a switch statement.

This program can be extended to print all the verses of the *Twelve Days of Christmas,* but at present it prints only the first three verses. This was done to demonstrate the concept and conserve space in the book. The following 12Days.php program contains the example code:

-- This is found in 12Days.php on the enclosed CD.

```php
<?php
  // Print the song title.
  print "<u>The Twelve Days of Christmas</u><p>";

  // Start a loop until a condition is met.
  for ($i = 0;$i < 3;$i++)
  {
    // Prints the beginning of a verse.
    print "On the ";

    // Demonstrate a case series using a break to exit switch statement.
    switch ($i)
    {
      case 0:
        print "first ";
        break;
      case 1:
        print "second ";
        break;
      case 2:
        print "third ";
        break;
    }

    // Print common lines in the verses.
    print "day of Christmas<br />";
    print "my true love sent to me:<br />";

    // Demonstrate an inverted case series and fall through.
    switch ($i)
    {
      case 2:
        print "Three French Hens<br />";
```

```
      case 1:
        print "Two Turtle Doves and<br />";
      case 0:
        print "A Partridge in a Pear Tree<p>";
    }
  }
?>
```

The 12Days.php program uses a for loop to manage the iterative behavior of two switch statements. The first switch statement executes only one case, while the second uses fall-through to run a series of cases. Fall-through begins with the first case that matches and continues until a break statement is encountered. In this example, it continues to the end.

The 12Days.php program generates the following output for the first three days of Christmas:

```
The Twelve Days of Christmas
On the first day of Christmas
my true love sent to me:
A Partridge in a Pear Tree
On the second day of Christmas
my true love sent to me:
Two Turtle Doves and
A Partridge in a Pear Tree
On the third day of Christmas
my true love sent to me:
Three French Hens
Two Turtle Doves and
A Partridge in a Pear Tree
```

This concludes the coverage of iterative structures. You will find them very useful in the next chapter when you learn about using arrays in PHP.

Summary

You have learned the basics of writing PHP programs in this and the preceding chapter. The sections "Conditional Structures" and "Iterative Control Structures" have demonstrated how to use the basic semantics of the language. These skills will support your exploring any part of the book, but tackling Chapters 6–9 in order will round out your basic PHP programming knowledge.

PART

II

PHP Programming

CHAPTER
6

Arrays

his chapter examines how you define, declare, assign, compare, and process arrays. It introduces the general concept of arrays before discussing the specifics of how PHP arrays work. The chapter covers the following array topics:

- Defining arrays
- Managing arrays
- Sorting arrays
- Merging and partitioning arrays

Arrays are programming structures that hold lists of like things. These lists are often indexed by a series of sequential numbers that start with zero or one and increase one value at a time. Using sequential numeric index values ensures that the index value can be used to traverse a complete list by incrementing or decrementing the index by 1 each iteration of a loop. Also, the lack of gaps in the array index leads to labeling the index values as densely populated structures. Arrays indexed by sequential numeric values are also known as numeric arrays in many programming languages.

Numeric arrays typically have a fixed size and data type when they are defined in a program. The size establishes how many like items can be put in an array, and the data type establishes what kind of variables can be stored in an array. When you define a numerical array, you allocate space for future use and can assign values immediately. Either approach provides you with a list that is indexed from zero to the size minus 1, or from 1 to the size. The values of the list are sometimes empty or null if you are only allocating space for future use. If an array is defined and assigned values at the same time, then the array elements generally contain data.

Some programming languages always assign default values or placeholder values based on the data type used to define numeric arrays, like Java. This type of default behavior means that when you define an array, it is a numerically indexed list of known default values and not a list of empty elements. Alternatively, you can have a numerically indexed list of empty elements. In both cases, you will note that the index values are created at the point you define the array and they number all possible or actual values that can be contained in the array.

A key principle of numeric arrays is that you can't remove an index and value from the middle of an array but you can assign a null or empty element to any indexed member. If you want to remove an indexed element from an array, you must typically copy the contents you want to keep from one array to another while reindexing them in the new array.

Another type of array structure is a *hash,* which contains a name and value pair for each element in an array. A hash can contain a numeric or unique string as the name or key, which acts as an index to the hash elements. The hash name points to a value, which typically can be any supported data type in a programming language. Unlike numeric arrays, hash arrays can contain both like and unlike elements. This means that the data types can differ in a hash array and traversing the content of a hash array may require a different programming technique.

It is possible to use numeric index names in a hash array, but they aren't necessarily sequential. Likewise, hash arrays aren't designed to traverse elements in the list by incrementing or decrementing index values. Numerically indexed hash arrays may have gaps in their indexing number sequence because the numbers are treated as unique names, not numbers. The presence of possible sequence gaps in numeric index names makes hash arrays *sparsely populated* structures. Hash arrays behave like linked lists in C or C++. Hash arrays have another corollary in Java collections; and like those collections, they require that you build an enumerator to traverse the collection.

Associative arrays are structures that can contain one to many of the supported data types in a programming language. They are specialized variables that contain a hash of names and values. The variable name for an associative array is an identifier or namespace for a list of address names and values. Associative arrays have no fixed size at definition and may grow or shrink dynamically in size. Elements can be added or removed at the beginning or end of an associative array, which will be discussed in the section "Managing Arrays" later in the chapter. Elements can also be removed from arrays by using the unset() function, which will be discussed in the next section, "Defining Arrays."

The behavior of PHP arrays can give the impression that they are numeric or associative arrays but *PHP arrays are always associative arrays.* Associative arrays can cause problems when you navigate through them by incrementing or decrementing their index one step at a time through a loop. If the index value is not sequential, this approach will raise a nonfatal error in your PHP environment (which is a notice, not an error); and *it can cause your program logic to fail.* You will examine how this type of error can occur in the next section. Programming techniques to work around sparsely populated numeric index gaps are presented in the section "Managing Arrays."

In the following sections, you will learn how to define, manage, sort, merge, and partition arrays in PHP. The examples will focus on primitive data types.

Defining Arrays

Arrays in PHP may be defined by two types of patterns: defining and assigning one element at a time; or declaring, which includes a definition and initial assignment of one to many elements. Both approaches are possible because PHP arrays are associative arrays and therefore not defined by a fixed-size allocation of elements. You will learn how to use both approaches in this section.

Before you explore arrays, there is another predefined PHP function that you should learn, the print_r() function. The print_r() function does two things: it prints the content of PHP arrays as name and value pairs; and it returns a Boolean true value as the default behavior. When the optional second argument is set to true, it prints nothing but returns the formatted name and value pairs. You can then assign the return value to a variable as an implicitly cast string data type.

The print_r() function has the following pattern:

```
boolean print_r(mixed var [, boolean mode ])
```

NOTE
Beginning with PHP 5, print_r() will disclose private and protected properties of PHP objects.

The following program demonstrates how to define an empty array and then add elements one at a time to it:

-- This is found in Array1.php on the enclosed CD.

```php
<?php
  // Declare string variables.
  $a = "Dr.";
  $b = "Mr.";
```

```
$c = "Mrs.";
$d = "Ms.";

// Define an array with zero members.
$salutation = array();

// Assign elements using an explicit numeric index name.
$salutation[0] = $a;
$salutation[1] = $b;
$salutation[2] = $c;
// Assign element using an implicit numeric index name.
$salutation[] = $d;

// Print array contents.
print_r($salutation);
?>
```

The Array1.php program illustrates how to declare an empty $salutation array variable and assign it values by using explicit numeric indexes. Then, it renders the following to a web page using the print_r() function:

```
Array ( [0] => Dr. [1] => Mr. [2] => Mrs. [3] => Ms. )
```

The preceding example program also demonstrated implicit numeric indexes by *using a set of empty square brackets to assign the last element.* This is possible because the PHP interpreter automatically uses the next sequential integer as the index key for the fourth element in the array. When index names or key values are not specified during element assignment, the default keys are sequential numbers. This happens whether or not assignments are one element at a time or as a group.

TIP
Adding elements to arrays by using an empty set of square brackets is effective because you will not need to maintain a counter variable for the numeric index key, which can be tedious to type.

The actual web page source will differ from the rendered page. The following is the formatted source generated by the print_r() function:

```
Array
(
    [0] => Dr.
    [1] => Mr.
    [2] => Mrs.
    [3] => Ms.
)
```

The second behavior of the print_r() function enables transferring the generated contents to a variable. This is done by overriding the default value of the optional formal parameter and setting it to true.

The first example program created individual primitive variables and then assigned them one at a time to the array. You will generally not do that because it is more convenient to build arrays in single-line statements. The simplest pattern for building an array relies on implicit key definition and is

```
array(value [, value])
```

The following program demonstrates a single-line declaration of an array and the assignment of the print_r() function output to a variable:

-- **This is found in Array2.php on the enclosed CD.**

```php
<?php
  // Declare an array variable.
  $salutation = array("Dr.","Mr.","Mrs.","Ms.");

  // Use a conditional expression to declare an array with print_r().
  if (!$output = print_r($salutation,true))
    print "The assignment failed.";

  // Concatenate string before and after the print_r() value.
  print "[".$output."].";
?>
```

The Array2.php program declares an array by using implicit numeric key assignment. Numeric keys are the default names for associative array elements when they are not explicitly provided. The conditional expression declares the $output variable by assigning it the contents returned by the print_r() function. You will find the expression is true unless the $salutation variable is a primitive data type variable containing a null value. If the $salutation variable were a no-element array, it would print the following to a web page:

```
[Array ( ) ].
```

The white space after the closing parenthesis is not a typo in the text. The output of the print_r() function will always have a trailing white space, which is actually a source formatting line return or \n. You may get rid of the extraneous white space by using rtrim($statement) or chop(print_r($statement,true)) statements. The chop() function is a familiar Perl function that is an alias in PHP for rtrim().

The Array2.php program renders the following output stream:

```
[Array ( [0] => Dr. [1] => Mr. [2] => Mrs. [3] => Ms. ) ].
```

The print_r() function provides a convenient utility to do quick array formatting. If you want to reformat the output some other way, you could use a for loop to generate similar output. The following program demonstrates the use of the for loop to produce the same output as the rtrim(print_r($salutation,true)) statement minus the \n formatting character:

-- **This is found in Array3.php on the enclosed CD.**

```php
<?php
  // Declare an array variable.
  $salutation = array("Dr.","Mr.","Mrs.","Ms.");
```

```
// Declare a starting string variable.
$output = "Array ( ";

// Read and add array keys and values to a string.
for ($i = 0; $i < count($salutation); $i++)
  $output .= " [".$i."] => ".$salutation[$i];

// Append closing parenthesis.
$output .= " )";

// Print the formatted contents.
print "[".$output."].";
?>
```

The `Array3.php` program uses an `$output` variable to hold the contents of an array by initializing the beginning of the string, adding the elements one at a time, and then appending a closing parenthesis. The program generates the same output stream shown previously by using the `print_r()` function.

While the `for` loop structure works naturally with densely populated numeric arrays, it can encounter problems in sparsely populated arrays, like associative arrays. *The problems occur because element keys in an array may become nonsequential numbers, whereas a `for` loop expects sequential numbers* that you can increment or decrement by 1 each time they iterate through the loop.

Using the `Array3.php` program, you can remove element two by using the `unset()` function immediately after you have declared the array. Then, the `for` loop structure will fail to read the complete contents of the array because the index key values are nonsequential. Therefore, the last element is never read. This type of programming error will raise a run-time notice, provided the `display_errors` directive is enabled in the `php.ini` file. Otherwise, it will exit the loop when the sequence gap is encountered without raising a fatal error. This type of error can result in myriad problems, but a common issue is failing to render properly the contents of a list of values or rows of an HTML table.

As mentioned, you can use the `unset()` function by inserting the following line immediately beneath the declaration of the `$salutation` variable to remove a key and value pair from an array:

```
// Remove a key and value pair from an array.
unset($salutation[2]);
```

An `Array3e.php` sample program is provided on the enclosed CD for your convenience. If you run the program with the `unset()` statement, you will see the following output rendered in your web page and potentially a notice if you have enabled the `display_errors` directive in the `php.ini` file:

```
[Array ( [0] => Dr. [1] => Mr. [2] => )].
```

The rendered output demonstrates that you have lost everything beyond the missing sequential index name. While this is easy to see in a small program, it can be hard to find in larger programming units, especially when the `display_errors` directive is disabled.

TIP

When it is possible that a value may be removed from a sequential list, you should rely on the `foreach` *loop structure to avoid this type of logic problem in your code. Alternatively, you should use the* `array_values()` *function to resequence a numeric array index set, which is covered later in the chapter.*

The `foreach` loop was added to PHP 4 providing an enumeration technique like that available in other programming languages. The next few examples will explore how to use `foreach` loops to enumerate through arrays.

The following `Array4.php` program demonstrates the use of the `foreach` loop to read a nonsequentially indexed numeric array:

-- This is found in Array4.php on the enclosed CD.

```php
<?php
  // Declare variable.
  $salutation = array("Dr.","Mr.","Mrs.","Ms.");

  // Remove a key and value pair from an array.
  unset($salutation[2]);

  // Declare a starting string variable.
  $output = "Array ( ";

  // Read and add array keys and values to a string.
  foreach ($salutation as $hashName => $hashValue)
      $output .= " [".$hashName."] => ".$hashValue;

  // Append trailing closed parenthesis.
  $output .= " )";

  // Print the formatted contents.
  print "[".$output."].";
?>
```

The `Array4.php` program reads through the nonsequential index values without a problem because it is managing the array as a name and value pair or hash. In the `foreach` loop, the `$salutation` array is mapped to a hash name that points to a hash value. The `foreach` loop reads and appends the array elements in order of their storage in the array. This is how you read a linked list in C/C++ or enumerate through a collection in Java. Therefore, the `foreach` loop is the natural solution to navigate sparsely populated indexes, which can occur after unsetting a name and value pair in an index sequence.

In the prior examples, the keys have been numbers. The `Array4.php` program illustrates an associative array using unique strings as the index names or keys. The same `$salutation` array is reused in this program but built by a different syntax. Whether you use numbers or unique strings as an index key, associative arrays in PHP have the following explicit key and value definition pattern:

array(key => value [, key => value])

The key is the index and the value is the data. The => symbol is a pointer that points from the key to the value. The pointer (=>) symbol is optional when building arrays using sequential numbered keys but required when using unique names as keys.

When you do not need to process or manage the index names of arrays, you can use the alternate foreach syntax. It enables you to access only the element values, not the index keys. You can test this by replacing the foreach loop in Array4.php with the following construct:

```
// Read and add array keys and values to a string.
foreach ($salutation as $hashValue)
    $output .= $hashValue;
```

The Array5.php program demonstrates using unique string index names:

-- This is found in Array5.php on the enclosed CD.

```php
<?php
  // Declare a unique string index array variable.
  $salutation = array("Bilbo"=>"A hobbit who slew a dragon."
                      ,"Frodo"=>"A hobbit that destroyed the one-ring.");

  // Declare string to print an HTML table.
  $output = "<table border=0>";

  // Read and add array keys and values to a string.
  foreach ($salutation as $hashName => $hashValue)
  {
    // Append the element name and value.
    $output .= "<tr>";
    $output .= "<td>[".$hashName."]</td>";
    $output .= "<td>[".$hashValue."]</td>";
    $output .= "</tr>";
  }

  // Close the HTML table.
  $output .= "</table>";

  // Print the formatted stringc.
  print $output;
?>
```

The Array5.php program enumerates through the array by reading the unique string names. The program uses embedded HTML tags to render the data in an HTML table. The Array5.php program renders the following HTML table:

[Bilbo]   [A hobbit who slew a dragon.]

[Frodo]   [A hobbit that destroyed the one-ring.]

The previous examples have demonstrated single-dimension arrays. PHP supports multidimensional arrays by nesting arrays as values within arrays. The ability to nest arrays allows you to build hash trees, which look like single-node hierarchies or inverted trees. The top node of the hash tree is the variable namespace, and the first list of elements is the second level in the hierarchy.

Visualizing an inverted tree is as easy as building an organization chart with the variable name at the top of the organization. Then, you use hash names as position descriptions and hash values as individual names. Assuming that the position descriptions are workers one to five, you can simply substitute a number from 0 to 4 (using zero-based numbering). Figure 6-1 illustrates an inverted tree diagram of a single-dimensional array.

The inverted tree diagram demonstrates a simple list or a single-dimensional numeric array of names. When you gain more information about the workers in the organization, you can add their first (fname), middle (mname), and last (lname) names, which you would store in a nested array. The nested array is stored as the second dimension of a multidimensional array. The second-dimension array replaces the value that contained only their first names with a programming structure. Figure 6-2 illustrates an inverted tree of a multidimensional array.

The multidimensional array displayed in Figure 6-2 is a specialized form known as a *symmetrical* multidimensional array. Symmetrical arrays share an equal depth for all nested arrays, whereas asymmetrical arrays have varying depths for nested arrays. While the single-dimensional array can be mapped to a list, the multidimensional array can be mapped to a table in two-dimensional (2D) space. The 2D figure in Figure 6-3 depicts a symmetrical multidimensional array.

The 2D view works much like what you would see in a spreadsheet, with the first dimension labeling the rows and the second dimension labeling the columns. When you nest a third dimension, you would visually see a series of stacked tables, where the third dimension resembles the Z-axis of three-dimensional (3D) space. Figure 6-4 illustrates a multidimensional array.

Beyond 3D space, the visual modeling breaks down unless we use node tree descriptions. Node tree drawings get very complex beyond a couple of levels, and language descriptions such as node and set structures seem appropriate only for mathematicians.

Nesting appears to have no officially stated physical limit, but testing shows that you can easily accommodate one hundred multidimensional arrays. This is probably sufficient for most web development applications.

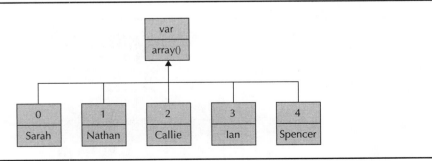

FIGURE 6-1. *An inverted tree diagram of a single-dimensional array*

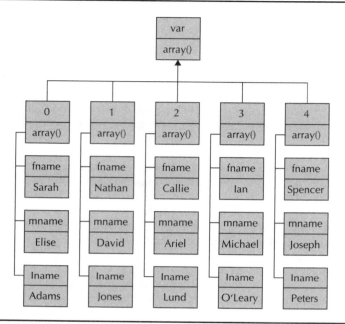

FIGURE 6-2. *An inverted tree diagram of a multidimensional array*

The following program demonstrates a pair of nested arrays in an array structure, using unique strings as the index values:

`-- This is found in Array6.php on the enclosed CD.`

```php
<?php
  // Declare variable.
```

var	fname	mname	lname
0	Sarah	Elise	Adams
1	Nathan	David	Jones
2	Callie	Ariel	Lund
3	Ian	Michael	O'Leary
4	Spencer	Joseph	Peters

FIGURE 6-3. *A 2D view of a multidimensional array*

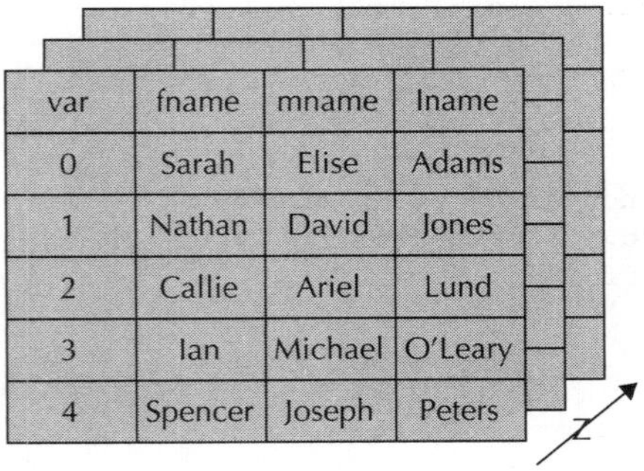

FIGURE 6-4. *A 3D view of a multidimensional array*

```
$salutation = array
            ("Bilbo"=>array
                    ("Hobbit"=>"Who slew a dragon for dwarves."
                    ,"Fellowship"=>"Left the ring for Frodo."
                    ,"Return of the King"=>"Left middle earth.")
            ,"Frodo"=>array
                    ("Fellowship"=>"Who inherited the ring."
                    ,"Return of the King"=>"Who destroyed the ring.")
            );

// Declare variable externally to the loop.
$output = "<table border=0 cellspacing=0>";

// Read and add array keys and values to a string.
foreach ($salutation as $hashName => $hashValue)
{
  // Append the element name.
  $output .= "<tr>";
  $output .= "<td valign=top>[".$hashName."]</td>";

  // Check if element value is a nested array.
  if (is_array($hashValue))
  {
    // Open an HTML table cell and nested table.
    $output .= "<td valign=top><table border=0 cellspacing=0>";

    // Read and add array keys and values to a string.
    foreach ($hashValue as $nestedName => $nestedValue)
    {
      // Append the nested element name and value.
      $output .= "<tr>";
      $output .= "<td valign=top>[".$nestedName."]</td>";
      $output .= "<td valign=top>[".$nestedValue."]</td>";
      $output .= "</tr>";
    }
```

```
      // Close nested HTML table and cell.
      $output .= "</table></td>";
    }
    else
    {
      // Append the non-array value element.
      $output .= "<td>[".$hashValue."]</td>";
      $output .= "</tr>";
    }
  }

  // Close HTML table.
  $output .= "</table>";

  // Print the formatted contents.
  print $output;
?>
```

The `Array6.php` program declares a multidimensional array of two dimensions. The two keys, Bilbo and Frodo, point to nested arrays. The nested arrays contain keys that are books from J.R.R. Tolkien's *The Hobbit* and *Lord of the Rings* trilogy. These nested keys point to values that describe actions in the books. The `is_array($salutation)` function checks whether values are arrays and then uses a nested `foreach` loop to navigate them. The program renders the following HTML table in a web page:

[Bilbo]	[Hobbit]	[Who slew a dragon for dwarves.]
	[Fellowship]	[Left the ring for Frodo.]
	[Return of the King]	[Left middle earth.]
[Frodo]	[Fellowship]	[Who inherited the ring.]
	[Return of the King]	[Who destroyed the ring.]

This section has presented the differences between numeric and associative arrays. You have learned that PHP arrays are always associative arrays regardless of index key and how to define and access them. Arrays offer a powerful tool that you will learn to exploit in subsequent chapters, as when you manage result sets returned from database tables. The next section will demonstrate how you can manage data elements in your associative arrays.

Managing Arrays

PHP arrays have a number of predefined functions that enable you to manage arrays. These include ways to test, count, traverse, and add or remove elements from an array. This section will demonstrate some of these techniques by examining the following:

- Identification functions, such as `count()` and `is_array()`
- Seeding and padding arrays with `range()` and `array_pad()` functions
- Queue management functions, such as `array_push()`, `array_pop()`, `array_shift()`, and `array_unshift()`

- Search functions, such as `array_key_exists()`, `array_keys()`, `array_search()`, `array_values()`, and `in_array()`

- Traversing functions, such as `current()`, `each()`, `end()`, `key()`, `next()`, `prev()`, and `reset()`

Identification Functions: count() and is_array()

You have already seen the `count()` and `is_array()` functions in the previous `Array6.php` programs. The `count()` function has the following pattern:

```
int count(mixed variable [, int mode ])
```

The `is_array()` function has the following pattern:

```
boolean is_array(mixed var)
```

The `count()` function enables you to count the number of array elements, but it works two ways, depending on the value of the optional `mode` variable. The default behavior of the `count()` function is demonstrated in the following program:

-- **This is found in Count1.php on the enclosed CD**.

```php
<?php
  // Declare variable.
  $salutation = array("Dr.","Mr.","Mrs.",array("Ms.","Miss."));

  // Print the return of the count() function.
  print "count(\$salutation) returns [".count($salutation)."].<br>";
?>
```

The `Count1.php` program demonstrates that the default behavior of the `count()` function adds only the number of primitive data types and arrays. *The default behavior of the count() function ignores nested array elements.* The `Count1.php` program will render the following:

```
count($salutation) returns [4].
```

As discussed in the preceding analysis of the program, the default behavior of the `count()` function treats a nested array as one element; however, the `print_r()` function returns the list of all elements, including those in nested arrays. The `print_r()` function works recursively.

Prior to PHP 4.2, the `count()` function had only one behavior, which is its current default behavior. The optional `mode` parameter was added to the `count()` function in PHP 4.2 and provides the `count()` function with the capability to count recursively.

The optional `mode` parameter's default value is `COUNT_NORMAL` or an integer of zero, but any number other than one, including a null, will also deliver the default behavior. The `count()` function enables you to get an accurate count of all base elements by using an optional `mode` value of `COUNT_RECURSIVE` or an integer of 1. Before this change, you had to write your own recursive function using the `is_array()` function to get a count of all elements in a multidimensional array. Using an integer value can save typing, but the constant `COUNT_RECURSIVE` adds clarity to how you are using the `count()` function and is the recommended approach.

The following `Count2.php` program demonstrates how you use the `count()` function recursively:

-- This is found in Count2.php on the enclosed CD.

```php
<?php
  // Declare variable.
  $salutation = array("Dr.","Mr.","Mrs.",array("Ms.","Miss."));

  // Print the return of the count() function.
  print "count(\$salutation,COUNT_RECURSIVE) returns ";
  print "[".count($salutation,COUNT_RECURSIVE)."].<br>";
?>
```

The `Count2.php` program renders the following output:

```
count($salutation,COUNT_RECURSIVE) returns [6].
```

The `count()` function's recursive ability enables it to find an accurate total of base elements in arrays. In the next section, you will explore how to use the `range()` and `array_pad()` functions.

Seeding and Padding Arrays

You have created and filled all of the arrays manually to this point. The `range()` function enables you to create and fill an array of numbers or characters based on a beginning value and an ending value. It assumes an incrementing value of 1, but you may provide another step value in the optional third formal parameter. The pattern for the `range()` function is:

```
array range(mixed low, mixed high [, int step])
```

The `range()` function returns an array, which may be numerically indexed with a list of numbers or characters. The following program demonstrates building an array of uppercase English alphabet characters and printing them to an HTML table:

-- This is found in Range1.php on the enclosed CD.

```php
<?php
  // Declare an array of uppercase alphabetic characters.
  $alphabet = range("A","Z");

  // Print opening HTML table tag.
  print "<table border=1>";

  // Read and add array keys and values to the page.
  foreach ($alphabet as $vName => $vValue)
    print "<tr><td>[".$vName."]</td><td>[".$vValue."]</td></tr>";

  // Print closing HTML table tag.
  print "</table>"
?>
```

The Range1.php program uses the range() function with a lower limit of A and an upper limit of Z to build an array of characters and renders an HTML table of numeric keys 0 to 26 and values of A to Z.

You may use the Range2.php program to duplicate the previous logic with a table composed of numbers. The only difference is that the lower and upper arguments for the range() function are numbers, not characters, as shown in the following program:

-- This is found in Range2.php on the enclosed CD.

```php
<?php
  // Declare an array of uppercase alphabetic characters.
  $alphabet = range("1","100");

  // Print opening HTML table tag.
  print "<table border=1>";

  // Loop through the array print name and value pairs.
  foreach ($alphabet as $vName => $vValue)
    print "<tr><td>[".$vName."]</td><td>[".$vValue."]</td></tr>";

  // Print closing HTML table tag.
  print "</table>"
?>
```

The Range2.php program renders an HTML table of numeric keys 0–99 and values of 1–100. The only difference between the keys and the values is that implicit keys use a zero-based number and the array uses one-based numbering.

Another useful function to extend the size of an array is the array_pad() function, which has the following pattern:

array array_pad(array *var*, int *size*, mixed *value*)

This function enables you to grow the allocated physical size of an array. The array_pad() function takes three mandatory formal arguments. The first is the target array, the second is the number of elements to be added, and the third is the value to be put in the newly added array elements. Using a null value as the third argument enables you to add null elements to an array.

You have now learned how to build integer and character arrays with the range() function and how the array_pad() function lets you grow your array size. The next section looks at how you can use predefined functions to turn your arrays into queues.

Queue Management Functions

Arrays are sometimes managed as first-in-first-out (FIFO), first-in-last-out (FILO), last-in-first-out (LIFO), and last-in-last-out (LILO) queues. There are four predefined commands to support queues. Table 6-1 provides a set of definitions that is followed by example programs demonstrating the predefined queue management functions.

Function	Description and Pattern
array_pop()	The function removes and returns the last element from a target array, which shortens the array by 1. If the formal parameter var is not an array data type, then the function returns a null value. The function has the following pattern: `mixed array_pop(array var)`

array_push()	The function adds one or more elements at the end of a target array and returns 1 for success. It has the following pattern:
	
	`int array_push(array var, mixed var`
	`   [, mixed ...])`

array_shift()	The function removes and returns the first element from a target array, which shortens the array by 1. If the formal parameter var is not an array data type, then the function returns a null value. The function has the following pattern: `mixed array_shift(array var)`

array_unshift()	The function adds an element to the front of a target array and returns 1 for success. It has the following pattern:
	
	`int array_unshift(array var, mixed var`
	`   [, mixed ...])`

TABLE 6-1. *Predefined Array Queue Management Functions*

The array_push() and array_shift() functions enable you to add one or more elements to an array in a single command, the former adding to the end of the array and the latter adding to the beginning of the array. All densely populated indexes are automatically managed by these functions.

The next PushPop.php program illustrates adding and removing a variable at the end of an array:

-- This is found in PushPop.php on the enclosed CD.

```php
<?php
  // Declare array variable.
  $salutation = array("Dr.","Mr.","Mrs.","Ms.");

  // Print the base contents.
  print "[".(print_r($salutation,true))."].<p>";

  // Push or add an element to the end of an array.
  if (array_push($salutation,"Lord"))
    print "[".(print_r($salutation,true))."].<p>";

  // Pop or remove an element from the end of an array.
  if (array_pop($salutation))
    print "[".(print_r($salutation,true))."].<p>";
?>
```

The PushPop.php program uses the array_push() function to add an element to the end of an array and the array_pop() function to remove an element from it. It generates the following output showing that Lord was momentarily an array element:

```
[Array ( [0] => Dr. [1] => Mr. [2] => Mrs. [3] => Ms. ) ].
[Array ( [0] => Dr. [1] => Mr. [2] => Mrs. [3] => Ms. [4] => Lord ) ].
[Array ( [0] => Dr. [1] => Mr. [2] => Mrs. [3] => Ms. ) ].
```

As discussed, you push on to or pop out of the end of an array with the array_push() and array_pop() functions. The opposite action is shifting into or out of an array, where you unshift with the array_unshift() function to add one or more elements at the front of an array and you shift with the array_shift() function to remove the first element. These predefined functions ensure that keys are treated as densely populated indexes and are automatically updated by the functions.

The Shifting.php program demonstrates how to put a value in and remove a value from the beginning of an array:

-- **This is found in Shifting.php on the enclosed CD.**

```php
<?php
  // Declare array variable.
  $salutation = array("Dr.","Mr.","Mrs.","Ms.");

  // Print the base contents.
  print "[".(print_r($salutation,true))."].<p>";

  // Unshift or add an element to the front of an array.
  if (array_unshift($salutation,"Lord"))
    print "[".(print_r($salutation,true))."].<p>";

  // Shift or remove an element from the front of an array.
  if (array_shift($salutation))
    print "[".(print_r($salutation,true))."].<p>";
?>
```

The Shifting.php program generates the following output:

```
[Array ( [0] => Dr. [1] => Mr. [2] => Mrs. [3] => Ms. ) ].
[Array ( [0] => Lord [1] => Dr. [2] => Mr. [3] => Mrs. [4] => Ms. ) ].
[Array ( [0] => Dr. [1] => Mr. [2] => Mrs. [3] => Ms. ) ].
```

Queues are interesting concepts in computer science or information systems. They allow one or more items to be placed in the queue at any moment and sometimes accept multiple arrivals into the queue from separate operations before any can be removed from the queue.

When you implement a FIFO queue, it requires you to pick starting and ending places, which are typically the beginning and ending elements of an array in PHP. This means you unshift into the array at the beginning and then pop out of the array at the end to implement a FIFO queue. This behavior is like getting in a queue (or line) and waiting your turn on a first-come, first-serve basis. A LILO queue would invert the process by pushing on to the array and shifting off it. Alternatively, you can implement a FILO queue by unshifting into an array and shifting out of an array; and a LIFO queue by pushing on to an array and popping out of it.

TIP
When implementing queues, make sure you're consistent on which direction does what or you will get incorrect results.

You have now learned how to manage queues in PHP arrays by using the `array_push()`, `array_pop()`, `array_shift()`, and `array_unshift()` functions. In the next section, you examine how to search and locate specific elements in an associative array.

Searching Functions

There are five predefined functions that enable searching PHP arrays for a specific key or value. Two of the functions verify whether a key or value is found in an array. Another two functions return an array of matching keys or values. One returns the value for a specified key. Table 6-2 describes the five predefined searching functions you should grow acquainted with before you work through demonstration programs later in the section.

Since you are now familiar with the search functions, the section will focus on demonstrating them. The following `ArrayKeys1.php` program demonstrates how the `array_keys()` function works when no optional search key is provided:

-- **This is found in ArrayKeys1.php on the enclosed CD.**

```php
<?php
  // Declare an array variable.
  $salutation = array("Dr.","Mr.","Mrs.","Ms.");

  // Print the formatted contents.
  print "[".(print_r($salutation,true))."].<p>";

  // Return the keys into an array.
  $result = array_keys($salutation);

  // Print the formatted contents.
  print "[".(print_r($result,true))."].";
?>
```

The `ArrayKeys1.php` program renders the following output:

```
[Array ( [0] => Dr. [1] => Mr. [2] => Mrs. [3] => Ms. ) ].
[Array ( [0] => 0 [1] => 1 [2] => 2 [3] => 3 ) ].
```

The `ArrayKeys1.php` program uses `array_keys($salutation)` to take the index keys of the `$salutation` array and put them into a new array with a fresh implicitly generated set of numeric keys. The new keys point to the old index keys, which are now values. This is not very useful when the keys in an array are integers but becomes valuable when you are working on identifying the unique string key values.

Function	Description and Pattern
array_keys()	The function takes two formal parameters: the first is a mandatory formal parameter of an array, and the second is an optional formal parameter of a search value. If an optional value is not provided, the function returns an array of all index keys. When an optional value is provided, it returns an array of index keys that point to those elements in the array that match the search value. It has the following pattern: `array array_keys(array var [, mixed search [, Boolean strict]])`
array_key_exists()	The function takes two mandatory formal parameters: the first is a key, and the second is the array to search. When the search key finds an index key match, the function returns a true; otherwise, it returns a Boolean false. It has the following pattern: `boolean array_key_exists(mixed key, array search)`
array_search()	The function takes three formal parameters: the first is a mandatory search value, the second is a mandatory array to search, and the third is a Boolean value that enforces type matching between the search value and the array element value. If the search value finds a match in the array values, the function returns the index value for the element; otherwise, it returns a Boolean false. When the optional third parameter is provided as true, the function will verify that the match is literal and type specific. It has the following pattern: `mixed array_search(mixed var, array var [, boolean strict])`
array_values()	The function takes one mandatory formal parameter that is the target array. The function returns all values in the target array with sequential numeric index keys. This provides a natural tool to repair any numerically indexed associative arrays that have lost an internal element and no longer have a densely populated set of index keys. It has the following pattern: `array array_values(array var)`
in_array()	The function takes three formal parameters: the first is a mandatory search value, the second is a mandatory array to search, and the third is a Boolean value that enforces type matching between the search value and the array element value. When the search value finds a match in the array, the function returns a Boolean true value; otherwise, it returns a Boolean false. When the optional third parameter is provided as true, the function will verify that the match is literal and type specific. It has the following pattern: `boolean in_array(mixed var, array var [, boolean strict])`

TABLE 6-2. *Predefined Array Searching Functions*

The `ArrayKeys2.php` program demonstrates how the `array_keys()` function works when the optional search key is provided:

-- **This is found in ArrayKeys2.php on the enclosed CD.**

```php
<?php
  // Declare an array variable.
  $salutation = array("Dr.","Mr.","Mrs.","Ms.");

  // Print the formatted contents.
  print "[".(print_r($salutation,true))."].<p>";

  // Return the keys into an array.
  $result = array_keys($salutation,"Mr.");

  // Print the formatted contents.
  print "[".(print_r($result,true))."].";
?>
```

The `ArrayKeys2.php` program searches for index keys that point to element values that match "Mr.", which will only be item 2 in the `$salutation` array. The `array_keys()` function returns the key that points to the matching value and displays the following output:

```
[Array ( [0] => Dr. [1] => Mr. [2] => Mrs. [3] => Ms. ) ].
[Array ( [0] => 1 ) ].
```

Submitting a key value to the `array_keys()` function lets you determine whether keys are duplicated in an array. Another way to find duplicate values is to use the `array_count_values()` function, which returns a list of keys with a value that is the number of times the key is found in an array. It has the following pattern:

```
array array_count_values(array var)
```

You can also use the `array_unique()` function to eliminate duplicate values. This is a great tool for eliminating duplicate data from a badly designed database table. You will see it demonstrated in the "Slicing Arrays" section later in this chapter. It has the following pattern:

```
array array_unique(array var)
```

Sometimes you want to check whether a key exists in an array. You use the `array_key_exists()` function to determine this. The following program demonstrates the `array_key_exists()` function:

-- **This is found in ArrayKeyExists.php on the enclosed CD.**

```php
<?php
  // Declare an array variable.
  $salutation = array("Dr.","Mr.","Mrs.","Ms.");

  // Print the formatted contents.
  print "[".(print_r($salutation,true))."].<p>";
```

```
  // Declare index search key.
  $search = 3;

  // Verify the key and then return the value.
  if (array_key_exists($search,$salutation))
    print "[".$salutation[$search]."].";
?>
```

The `ArrayKeyExists.php` program uses the `array_key_exists()` function to check whether a specific key is in the `$salutation` array before printing it as output like the following:

```
[Array ( [0] => Dr. [1] => Mr. [2] => Mrs. [3] => Ms. ) ].
[Ms.].
```

The `array_search()` function lets you search an array's list of values. It has two forms. One form finds a match that may or may not be the same data type; and the other finds a match that verifies like data types. The latter comparison is considered strictly equal, which means by value and data type.

The following program demonstrates the `array_search()` function without checking if the two are strictly equal:

-- This is found in ArraySearch1.php on the enclosed CD.

```
<?php
  // Declare an array variable.
  $salutation = array("Dr.","Mr.","Mrs.","Ms.");

  // Print the formatted contents.
  print "[".(print_r($salutation,true))."].<p>";

  // Print the value pointed to by the index key.
  print "[".$salutation[array_search("Dr.",$salutation)]."]";
?>
```

The `ArraySearch1.php` program will render the following output by using a search key of "Dr.", which points to the string literal "Dr." as noted:

```
[Array ( [0] => Dr. [1] => Mr. [2] => Mrs. [3] => Ms. ) ].
[Dr.].
```

You may elect to retest this concept by enforcing strict equality, which verifies a data and type match by substituting the following line:

```
  // Print the value pointed to by the index key.
  print "[".$salutation[array_search("Dr.",$salutation,true)]."]";
```

You will find this solution in `ArraySearch2.php` on the enclosed CD. It will not change the results because the values and data types match. When you set the third optional parameter to true, it overrides the default false value.

The `array_values()` function is a powerful tool that addresses a problem that you encountered earlier in the chapter when you examined issues with sparsely populated index keys. As presented in the `Array3e.php` program, an `unset()` function removes one of the elements in an array, which creates a sequence gap in the key list. Nonsequential key lists are called sparsely populated indexes. As seen, the `for` loop fails when it encounters a nonsequential index key value in the numeric index and stops working through the loop.

You can fix this problem by using the `array_values()` function before traversing an array with a `for` loop. This is demonstrated in the following program:

-- This is found in ArrayValues.php on the enclosed CD.

```php
<?php
  // Declare variable.
  $salutation = array("Dr.","Mr.","Mrs.","Ms.");

  // Declare the variable externally to an if statement.
  $output = "Array ( ";

  // Remove an element from an array.
  unset($salutation[2]);

  // Reset index keys from sparse to dense.
  $salutation = array_values($salutation);

  // Read and add array keys and values to a string.
  for ($i = 0;$i < count($salutation);$i++)
    $output .= " [".$i."] => ".$salutation[$i];

  // Append closing parenthesis.
  $output .= ")";

  // Print the formatted contents.
  print "[".$output."].";
?>
```

The `ArrayValues.php` program uses the `array_values()` function to copy the contents of an existing numerically indexed associative array to a new array that contains a densely populated index. This ensures that the `$salutation` array can be traversed successfully by a `for` or `while` loop. The program also renders the following output, which illustrates that the third element in the original array has been removed and the index values have been resequenced as 0 to 2:

`[Array ( [0] => Dr. [1] => Mr. [2] => Ms.)]`

The last predefined searching function you will cover is the `in_array()` function, which enables you to check if a value is found in an array list. When combined with conditional logic and the `array_search()` function, the `in_array()` function enables you to check whether a value is found in an array before attempting to process the element in the array.

The following program demonstrates the in_array() function:

```php
<?php
  // Declare an array variable.
  $salutation = array("Dr.","Mr.","Mrs.","Ms.");

  // Print the formatted contents.
  print "[".(print_r($salutation,true))."]<p>";

  // Set search string.
  $search = "Dr.";

  // Check for valid value before getting key value.
  if (in_array($search,$salutation,true))
    print "[".$salutation[array_search($search,$salutation,true)]."]";
  else
    print "[Not found.]";
?>
```

The InArray.php program uses the in_array() function to search array elements for a strictly equal string of "Dr." and then processes the element.
The program renders the following output to the web page:

You have covered the predefined searching functions. The next section covers functions that enable you to effectively traverse arrays without iteration structures, like for, while, and foreach loops.

Traversing Functions

The foreach loop provides a convenient means for traversing an array from start to finish, but sometimes you need to walk the key and value pairs differently. Seven functions provide fine-grained control of your array navigation, providing you with an alternative to loops. Concrete examples of how to use these are provided after you consider the basic definitions of the predefined traversing functions shown in Table 6-3.

The next example demonstrates using four of these predefined traversing functions to walk forward through an array within a for loop:

```php
<?php
  // Declare an array variable.
  $salutation = array("Dr.","Mr.","Mrs.","Ms.");

  // Print the formatted contents.
  print "[".(print_r($salutation,true))."]<p>";
```

Function	Description and Pattern
current()	The function takes one formal parameter, which is a target array. The current() function returns the value of the current element. It has the following pattern: mixed current(array *var*)
each()	The function takes one formal parameter, which is a target array, and returns an array of four values: the index value of 0 and *key* will point to the target array's current key value; and the index value of 1 and *value* will contain the value pointed to by the key value. It has the following pattern: array each(array *var*)
end()	The function moves the pointer to the last element of the array and returns the value of the last element. It has the following pattern: mixed end(array *var*)
key()	The function takes one formal parameter, which is a target array. The key() function returns the key of the current element. It has the following pattern: mixed key(array *var*)
next()	The function takes one formal parameter, which is a target array, and returns the next element in the array by moving the pointer forward. It has the following pattern: mixed next(array *var*)
prev()	The function takes one formal parameter, which is a target array, and returns the previous element in the array by moving the pointer backward. It has the following pattern: mixed prev(array *var*)
reset()	The function moves the pointer to the first element of the array and returns the value of the first element. It has the following pattern: mixed reset(array *var*)

TABLE 6-3.   *Predefined Array Traversing Functions*

```
// Set the array pointer to the initial element.
reset($salutation);

// Run once for the total of elements in the array.
for ($i = 0;$i < count($salutation);$i++)
{
  print "[".key($salutation)."] [".current($salutation)."]<br>";
  next($salutation);
}
?>
```

The `Traverse1.php` program uses the `reset()` function to set the pointer to the first element in the array before printing *the value returned by the* `current ()` *function* and using *the* `next ()` *function to move the pointer forward one element* in the array. The program displays the array contents using the `print_r()` function before using the `key()` and `current()` functions to list them:

```
[Array ( [0] => Dr. [1] => Mr. [2] => Mrs. [3] => Ms. ) ]

[0] [Dr.]
[1] [Mr.]
[2] [Mrs.]
[3] [Ms.]
```

Traversing the array backward, the next example shows how to use the `prev()` function using the same logic while stepping backward through an array within a `for` loop:

-- This is found in Traverse2.php on the enclosed CD.

```php
<?php
  // Declare an array variable.
  $salutation = array("Dr.","Mr.","Mrs.","Ms.");

  // Print the formatted contents.
  print "[".(print_r($salutation,true))."]<p>";

  // Set the array pointer to the initial element.
  end($salutation);

  // Run once for the total of elements in the array.
  for ($i = 0;$i < count($salutation);$i++)
  {
    print "[".key($salutation)."] [".current($salutation)."]<br>";
    prev($salutation);
  }
?>
```

The `Traverse2.php` program uses *the* `prev ()` *function to move the pointer backward one element* in the array. It displays similar results to that of `Traverse1.php`, only walking the element list backward, as is illustrated by the decrementing keys:

```
[Array ( [0] => Dr. [1] => Mr. [2] => Mrs. [3] => Ms. ) ]
[3] [Ms.]
[2] [Mrs.]
[1] [Mr.]
[0] [Dr.]
```

The last example demonstrates that the traversal can be backward while the loop moves forward from zero to the size of the array. You have now covered the basics of managing array elements. In the next section you will learn how to sort arrays.

Sorting Arrays

Arrays are lists, and you will sort them differently, depending on the end-user requirements. PHP provides a library of predefined functions to sort arrays, as shown in Table 6-4. You will review the function definitions before examining each in depth.

Function	Description and Pattern
arsort()	The function takes two formal parameters: the first is an array, and the second is a sorting flag. It sorts in reverse or descending order, preserving the native keys of the original array, and has this pattern: `void arsort(array var [, int sort_flag])`
asort()	The function takes two formal parameters: the first is an array, and the second is a sorting flag. It sorts in ascending order, preserving the native keys of the original array, and has this pattern: `void asort(array var [, int sort_flag])`
array_multisort()	The function takes a list of formal parameters that can include an array, a sort order flag, and sort type flag, followed by other array values. There can only be one actual parameter for the order or type flag value. Subsequent values will not raise an error but will not be recognized or processed in PHP 5.0 and 5.1. The possible sort order flags are SORT_ASC and SORT_DESC, and the possible sort type flags are SORT_REGULAR, SORT_NUMERIC, and SORT_STRING. Unique string keys are preserved, but numeric keys are reorganized by this function. It has the following pattern: `boolean array_multisort(array var1 [, mixed order [, mixed type [, array var2 ]] ... ])`
krsort()	The function takes two formal parameters: the first is an array, and the second is a sorting flag. It sorts in reverse or descending order by the keys while preserving the native keys of the original array; it has this pattern: `integer krsort(array var [, int sort_flag])`
ksort()	The function takes two formal parameters: the first is an array, and the second is a sorting flag. It sorts in ascending order by the keys while preserving the native keys of the original array; it has this pattern: `integer ksort(array var [, int sort_flag])`
natsort()	The function takes one formal parameter, which is an array. It sorts in ascending order, treating values as human-perceived strings. This is equivalent to the sort() function's operation when using an optional sort flag of SORT_STRING. This function does preserve keys and has this pattern: `void natsort(array var)`

TABLE 6-4. *Predefined Sorting Functions*

Function	Description and Pattern
`natcasesort()`	The function takes one formal parameter, which is an array. It sorts in ascending order by the values and uses rules like those in the `natsort()` function. The function does preserve keys during sorting and differs from the `natsort()` in ignoring case during sort operations. It has the following pattern: `void natcasesort(array `*`var`*`)`
`rsort()`	The function takes two formal parameters: the first is an array, and the second is a sorting flag. It sorts in descending or reverse order and reassigns native keys to new sequenced numeric key lists. It has this pattern: `void rsort(array `*`var`*` [, int `*`sort_flag`*`])`
`sort()`	The function takes two formal parameters: the first is an array, and the second is a sorting flag. It sorts in ascending order but reassigns the native keys to new sequenced numeric key lists. It has this pattern: `void sort(array `*`var`*` [, int `*`sort_flag`*`])`
`uksort()`	The function takes two formal parameters: the first is an array, and the second is a callback function. It sorts based on the rules provided in the callback function and preserves the original keys during sort operations. It has this pattern: `void uksort(array `*`var`*`, array `*`callback_function`*`)`
`usort()`	The function takes two formal parameters: the first is an array, and the second is a callback function. It sorts according to the rules provided in the callback function and resets the key to the value map. It has this pattern: `void usort(array `*`var`*`, array `*`callback_function`*`)`

TABLE 6-4. *Predefined Sorting Functions* (continued)

While the predefined sorting functions were presented in alphabetic order, you will examine them in the following sections:

- The `sort()` and `rsort()` functions
- The `asort()` and `arsort()` functions
- The `ksort()` and `krsort()` functions
- The `natsort()` and `natcasesort()` functions
- The `array_multisort()` function
- The `usort()` and `uksort()` functions

The functions have been grouped to cover ascending and descending patterns of like sorting functions. Understanding the basic sort operations makes comparing and contrasting them easier. You should cover these in the presented order because they build on each other.

The sort() and rsort() Functions

The sort() function examines the values in an array and sorts them in ascending order. You have the option of providing a sorting flag, which may be any of the following:

- SORT_NUMERIC—uses a numeric sort pattern that works with integers and floats.
- SORT_REGULAR—uses the ASCII value for the characters that works equally well for integers, floats, and strings.
- SORT_STRING—uses rules that relate to human perceptions of complex relationships in strings, like lists of filenames that include version numbers. The sort flag enables a more naturally human ordering of string and number combinations. The behavior of SORT_STRING is the default behavior of the natsort() function.

The Sort1.php program demonstrates a sort() operation. You will see that the sort() function acts directly on the array by converting its original keys to new keys. If the keys for an array are nonsequential or sparsely populated at the time it is sorted, they will be sequential and densely populated after the sort.

The following Sort1.php changes the familiar $salutation array by shifting the values into alphabetical order to demonstrate sort operations:

-- This is found in Sort1.php on the enclosed CD.

```php
<?php
  // Declare an array variable.
  $salutation = array("Mr.","Ms.","Mrs.","Dr.");

  // Print original ordering.
  print "[".print_r($salutation,true)."].<br>";

  // Sort the array members.
  sort($salutation);

  // Print sorted ordering.
  print "[".print_r($salutation,true)."].<br>";
?>
```

The Sort1.php program will produce the following output with the first line before and second after the sort operation:

```
[Array ( [0] => Mr. [1] => Ms. [2] => Mrs. [3] => Dr. ) ].
[Array ( [0] => Dr. [1] => Mr. [2] => Mrs. [3] => Ms. ) ].
```

The output stream demonstrates that the sort($salutation) reorders the values and builds a new set of sequential keys. *If the keys are unique strings, the sort() function replaces them with new sequential numeric keys.* The rsort() function reverses the sequencing of values and performs the same type of sort operation. You may replace the highlighted line in Sort1.php with the following statement to test it or run Sort2.php provided in the source code on the enclosed CD:

```php
  // Reverse sort the array members.
  rsort($salutation);
```

The Sort2.php program will produce the following output with the original order on the first line and the reverse sort operation on the next:

```
[Array ( [0] => Mr. [1] => Ms. [2] => Mrs. [3] => Dr. ) ].
[Array ( [0] => Ms. [1] => Mrs. [2] => Mr. [3] => Dr. ) ].
```

You learned that keys change when you use the sort() and rsort() functions to sort arrays. This is not true for other predefined sorting functions, which you will see later in the chapter. You will discover that there are a couple of options for preserving the key-to-value mapping of the original array. This can be important if you want to resort the array using the original keys after the first sort operation.

The asort() and arsort() Functions

The asort() function lets you sort arrays in ascending order but preserves the native keys, which means the key-to-value mapping remains unchanged by the sort operation. The Asort1.php program demonstrates key preservation in the following program:

-- This is found in Asort1.php on the enclosed CD.

```php
<?php
  // Declare an array variable.
  $salutation = array("Mr.","Ms.","Mrs.","Dr.");

  // Print original ordering.
  print "[".print_r($salutation,true)."].<br>";

  // Sort the array members.
  asort($salutation);

  // Print sorted ordering.
  print "[".print_r($salutation,true)."].<br>";
?>
```

You can see the *preservation of keys* by the asort($salutation) function in the following output generated by the Asort1.php program:

```
[Array ( [0] => Mr. [1] => Ms. [2] => Mrs. [3] => Dr. ) ].
[Array ( [3] => Dr. [0] => Mr. [2] => Mrs. [1] => Ms. ) ].
```

You may replace the highlighted line in Asort1.php with the following to test a descending or reverse-order sort or run Asort2.php to do the sort operation, which is provided in the online source code:

```php
  // Reverse sort the array members.
  arsort($salutation);
```

The Asort2.php program will produce the following reverse-value sort that preserves the original keys:

```
[Array ( [1] => Ms. [2] => Mrs. [0] => Mr. [3] => Dr. ) ].
```

The asort() and arsort() functions provide a vehicle for sorting and preserving the original key-to-value mapping. The preservation of the keys provides the ability to resort to the original order by using the ksort() and krsort() functions, which you will cover next.

The ksort() and krsort() Functions

The ksort() function examines the keys in an array and sorts them in ascending order. The ksort() function does not alter the original keys but preserves them for subsequent sorting operations.

The following Ksort1.php program uses an asort() function before employing a ksort() function to undo the sorting operation:

-- This is found in Ksort1.php on the enclosed CD.

```php
<?php
  // Declare an array variable.
  $salutation = array("Mr.","Ms.","Mrs.","Dr.");

  // Print original ordering.
  print "[".print_r($salutation,true)."].<br>";

  // Sort the array members.
  asort($salutation);

  // Print sorted ordering.
  print "[".print_r($salutation,true)."].<br>";

  // Sort the array members.
  ksort($salutation);

  // Print restored ordering.
  print "[".print_r($salutation,true)."].<br>";
?>
```

The Ksort1.php program produces the three lines of output. The first is the base ordering of the array, the second is the sorted order, and the third is the resorting to the original ordering of values, as shown in the following output:

```
[Array ( [0] => Mr. [1] => Ms. [2] => Mrs. [3] => Dr. ) ].
[Array ( [3] => Dr. [0] => Mr. [2] => Mrs. [1] => Ms. ) ].
[Array ( [0] => Mr. [1] => Ms. [2] => Mrs. [3] => Dr. ) ].
```

As done in the previous examples, you can switch the ksort($salutation) by using krsort($salutation) to perform a reverse-sort operation on the preserved keys. It also preserves keys during the sort operation. The Ksort2.php program, on the enclosed CD, produces the same first and second lines as Ksort1.php, but line three is a *reverse-key sort* as shown in the following output:

[Array ([0] => Mr. [1] => Ms. [2] => Mrs. [3] => Dr.)].
[Array ([3] => Dr. [0] => Mr. [2] => Mrs. [1] => Ms.)].
[Array ([3] => Dr. [2] => Mrs. [1] => Ms. [0] => Mr.)].

You have learned how to use keys as criteria in sorting arrays. The next section will address how natural language sorts work in PHP.

The natsort() and natcasesort() Functions

The natsort() function sorts values exactly like the asort() function when the optional SORT_STRING flag is provided. The SORT_STRING flag is the default sort type for the natsort() function. The natsort() function also reorganizes the keys, which changes the key-to-value map as the asort() function does.

The Natsort.php program demonstrates the natsort() function:

-- **This is found in Natsort.php on the enclosed CD.**

```php
<?php
  // Declare an array variable.
  $salutation = array("Image2.tif","Image1.tif","Image10.tif");

  // Print original ordering.
  print "[".print_r($salutation,true)."].<br>";

  // Sort the array members.
  natsort($salutation);

  // Print sorted ordering.
  print "[".print_r($salutation,true)."].<br>";
?>
```

The Natsort.php program generates the following output:

[Array ([0] => Image2.tif [1] => Image1.tif [2] => Image10.tif)].
[Array ([1] => **Image1.tif** [0] => **Image2.tif** [2] => **Image10.tif**)].

An ordinary sort operation of the filenames would have placed Image10.tif ahead of Image2.tif, because the ASCII value of 1 comes before 2. This is typically not the desired ordering of these types of filenames. The natsort() function performs case-sensitive sort operations and should not be used when case criteria are uncertain.

The natcasesort() function performs like the natsort() function but sorts strings case insensitively. Case-sensitive sorting puts uppercase alphabetical characters before lowercase characters because their ASCII values are lower. If the Image10.tif filename were IMage10.tif, the natsort() function would sort the array as follows:

[Array ([2] => IMage10.tif [1] => Image1.tif [0] => Image2.tif)].

Sorting mixed-case filenames is a challenge when the mixed case is unintentional. The natcasesort() function enables you to manage this behavior by promoting all alphabetical characters to uppercase for sorting while preserving their mixed-case values. The following Natcasesort.php program demonstrates the case-insensitive sort of mixed-case filenames:

-- **This is found in Natcasesort.php on the enclosed CD.**

```php
<?php
  // Declare an array variable.
  $salutation = array("Image2.tif","Image1.tif","IMage10.tif");

  // Print original ordering.
  print "[".print_r($salutation,true)."].<br>";

  // Sort the array members.
  natcasesort($salutation);

  // Print sorted ordering.
  print "[".print_r($salutation,true)."].<br>";
?>
```

The Natcasesort.php program produces two lines: the first is the original array order, and the second is the sorted order. The following output sorts the filename IMage10.tif without regard to the mixed case in the filename:

```
[Array ( [0] => Image2.tif [1] => Image1.tif [2] => IMage10.tif ) ].
[Array ( [1] => Image1.tif [0] => Image2.tif [2] => IMage10.tif ) ].
```

You should note that both the natsort() and natcasesort() functions preserve keys like the asort() and arsort() functions. The advantage of using natsort() over asort() is questionable when you understand their similarities. You should determine which of the two offers the clearest expression of functionality and use it consistently.

The array_multisort() Function

The array_multisort() function enables you to sort multiple arrays *provided you want to use the same sort order and type flags and they are equal sizes.* Unequal-sized arrays will raise a nonfatal warning message that the arrays are inconsistently sized. If the display_errors directive is disabled in the php.ini file, the warning error will not display and the sort will work correctly. If you want different sort orders or type behaviors, you should consider sorting the individual arrays separately by using the asort() and arsort() functions.

The following MultiSort.php program demonstrates the sorting of multiple arrays:

-- **This is found in MultiSort.php on the enclosed CD.**

```php
<?php
  // Declare array variables.
  $salutation1 = array("Mr.","Mrs.","Dr.");
  $salutation2 = array("Monsieur","Madame","Docteur");

  // Print original ordering.
  print "[English][".print_r($salutation1,true)."].<br>";
  print "[French][".print_r($salutation2,true)."].<br>";
```

```
// Sort the array members.
array_multisort($salutation1,SORT_DESC,$salutation2);

// Print sorted ordering.
print "[English][".print_r($salutation1,true)."].<br>";
print "[French][".print_r($salutation2,true)."].<br>";
?>
```

The `MultiSort.php` program produces the following output for the presorted arrays:

```
[English][Array ( [0] => Mr. [1] => Mrs. [2] => Dr. ) ].
[French][Array ( [0] => Monsieur [1] => Madame [2] => Docteur ) ].
```

Then, it prints their sorted contents as follows:

```
[English][Array ( [0] => Mrs. [1] => Mr. [2] => Dr. ) ].
[French][Array ( [0] => Madame [1] => Monsieur [2] => Docteur ) ].
```

The `array_multisort()` function treats the array arguments as parallel arrays. This is an old and awkward technique once used to work around programming languages that lacked multidimensional array structures. You may find it easier to write separate callback functions that you can use as customized sort operations in the `usort()` and `uksort()` functions, which are covered in the next section.

The usort() and uksort() Functions

The `usort()` and `uksort()` functions offer you a means to define customized sort operations. This is done by defining your own callback function. While functions are covered in Chapter 7, this forward reference is necessary to demonstrate the `usort()` or `uksort()` function. The two functions work differently. The `usort()` function does not preserve key values, while the `uksort()` function does. Also, `uksort()` can raise nonfatal undefined offset messages when the callback function uses functions like `explode()`, something that doesn't happen with `usort()`.

NOTE
If you disable the `display_errors` directive in the `php.ini` file, you can avoid these errors except in your testing environment.

The implemented callback function must take two formal parameters and return a negative integer, a zero, or a positive integer. A negative integer is returned when the first actual parameter is less than the second parameter, a zero is returned when the parameters are equal, and a positive integer is returned when the first parameter is greater than the second parameter.

The `Usort.php` program uses a custom sort to compare the default dates returned by Oracle, which has a default format mask of a two-digit day, a three-character string abbreviation for month, and a two-digit year, separated by dashes. The comparison function `calendarSort($a, $b)` sorts an array of dates by exploding the three components into separate variables. It then converts the three-character month into a numeric value. *The converted numbers representing year, month, and day are then compared to sort the values of the submitted array.*

TIP
You should note that you may also use split() *or* preg_split()
*to accomplish this task, but they incur the overhead of loading the
regular expression parser. For simple sorts that don't need regular
expression resolution, you should use the* explode() *function.*

The following Usort.php program demonstrates a custom sort algorithm:

-- This is found in Usort.php on the enclosed CD.

```php
<?php
  // Define a comparison function.
  function calendarSort($a, $b)
  {
    // Build key to value map for calendar months.
    $month = array("JAN","FEB","MAR","APR","MAY","JUN"
                   ,"JUL","AUG","SEP","OCT","NOV","DEC");

    // Check if equal.
    if ($a == $b) return 0;

    // Divide Oracle default date string into component values.
    list($day1,$month1,$year1) = explode("-",$a);
    list($day2,$month2,$year2) = explode("-",$b);

    // Create numeric dates in a YYM[M]D[D] format mask.
    $a = $year1.array_search($month1,$month).$day1;
    $b = $year2.array_search($month2,$month).$day2;

    // Check if one is greater than the other.
    return ($a > $b) ? 1 : -1;
  }

  // Declare an array variable.
  $salutation = array("10-JAN-06","14-JUL-06","01-MAY-06");

  // Print original ordering.
  print "[".print_r($salutation,true)."].<br>";

  // Perform a custom sort operation.
  usort($salutation,'calendarSort');

  // Print sorted ordering.
  print "[".print_r($salutation,true)."].<br>";
?>
```

The Usort.php program produces one line that displays the original order and another that displays the sorted order with newly indexed keys as shown in the following:

[Array ([0] => 1-0-JAN-06 [1] => 14-JUL-06 [2] => 01-MAY-06)].
[Array ([0] => 10-JAN-06 [1] => 01-MAY-06 [2] => 14-JUL-06)].

The callback function argument of the usort() function can be delimited by single or double quotes. There is no fixed rule, but you will find it more frequently using single quotes than the double quotes.

You have completed the array sorting section and covered the mechanics of defining, managing, and sorting arrays. The next section will extend your knowledge by showing you how to merge and partition arrays.

Merging and Partitioning Arrays

Once you have learned how to define, manage, and sort arrays, understanding how to merge and partition arrays is important because they enable you to slice and dice arrays to meet changing business needs. Merging arrays joins two or more arrays into a single array. Partitioning carves data from arrays. As in prior sections, first you will review the predefined functions that support merging and partitioning, and then you will explore some key examples applying the more frequently used functions. Table 6-5 captures the merging and partitioning predefined functions in alphabetic order.

Function	Description and Pattern

array_chunk()	The function takes two formal parameters. The first parameter is an array, and the second is a grouping size. The optional parameter enables you to preserve key values from the original array into the return value when set to true. The default value for the optional parameter is false, which means the standard functionality is to not preserve the original keys. The function has the following pattern:
	
	`array array_chunk(array var, int size`
	`  [, boolean preserve_keys ])`

array_combine()	The function takes two formal parameters. The first parameter is an array of keys, and the second is an array of values. They are managed as parallel arrays and must be equal in *size* to be successfully combined. The function has the following pattern: `array array_combine(array keys, array values)`

array_diff()	The function takes two or more formal parameters. All parameters are arrays. It first creates a master array of all arrays except the first parameter array and then subtracts the first array from the grouped array based on a comparison of *values*. It returns the values found in the first array that were not in the grouped array, which means it acts like a minus set operator in a database or set mathematics. It also preserves the original key values in the returned array, which means the keys are not used during the comparison operation. It has the following pattern:
	
	`array array_diff(array var1, array var2`
	`  [, array var3 ... ])`

TABLE 6-5. *Predefined Merging and Partitioning Functions*

Function	Description and Pattern

`array_diff_key()`	The function takes two or more formal parameters. All parameters are arrays. It first creates a master array of all arrays except the first parameter array and then subtracts the first array from the grouped array based on a comparison of *keys*. It returns the keys found in the first array that were not in the grouped array, which means it acts like `array_diff()` functions for keys, not values. It also preserves the original key values of the returned array. It has the following pattern:
	
	`array array_diff_key(array var1`
	`, array var2 [, array var3 ... ])`

`array_diff_uassoc()`	The function takes two or more formal parameters and was introduced into the language in PHP 5. All parameters except the last one are arrays. The last parameter is a callback function like those found in the `usort()` and `uksort()` functions. It works by first creating a grouped array of all arrays except the first parameter array. Then, it applies the callback function to compare differences between the *keys and values* of the first and grouped arrays. It returns the keys and values found in the first array that were not found in the grouped array based on the logic used by the callback function. It has the following pattern:
	
	`array array_diff_uassoc(array var1`
	`, array var2 [, array var3 ... ]`
	`, array callback_value_compare)`

`array_diff_ukey()`	The function takes two or more formal parameters and was introduced into the language in PHP 5. All parameters except the last one are arrays. The last parameter is a callback function like those found in the `usort()` and `uksort()` functions. It works by first creating a grouped array of all arrays except the first parameter array. Then, it applies the callback function to compare differences between the *keys* of the first and grouped arrays. It returns the keys and values found in the first array that were not found in the grouped array based on the logic used by the callback function. It has the following pattern:
	
	`array array_diff(array var1, array var2`
	`[, array var3 ... ]`
	`, array callback_key_compare)`

`array_filter()`	The function takes two formal parameters. The first is an array, and the second is a callback function. The function examines the *values* of the array by passing them to the callback function. If the callback function returns a true value, the value is returned in the array; otherwise, it is filtered out. It has the following pattern:
	
	`array array_filter(array var`
	`, array callback_function)`

`array_flip()`	The function takes one formal parameter, which is an array. The function transforms the array by switching the *keys* and the *values*. It has the following pattern: `array array_flip(array var)`

TABLE 6-5. *Predefined Merging and Partitioning Functions* (continued)

Function	Description and Pattern

`array_intersect()`	The function takes two or more formal parameters. All parameters are arrays. The function compares arrays to find *values* that are in all arrays. It returns an array with preserved unique string keys and values or new numeric keys and values. It has the following pattern:
	
	`array array_intersect(array var1`
	`, array var2 [, array var3 ... ])`

`array_intersect_assoc()`	The function takes two or more formal parameters. All parameters are arrays. The function compares arrays to find *keys and values* that are in all arrays. (By comparison, the `array_intersect()` function checks only values.) It returns an array with preserved keys and values. It has the following pattern:
	
	`array array_intersect_assoc(array var1`
	`, array var2 [, array var3 ... ])`

`array_intersect_key()`	The function takes two or more formal parameters. All parameters are arrays. The function compares arrays to find *keys* that are in all arrays. It returns an array with preserved keys and values of the matches between the arrays. It has the following pattern:
	
	`array array_intersect_key(array var1`
	`, array var2 [, array var3 ... ])`

`array_intersect_uassoc()`	The function takes two or more formal parameters and was introduced into the language in PHP 5. All parameters except the callback function are arrays. The function compares arrays to find elements that are in all arrays. The comparison is done by a user-defined callback function that matches same *keys and values.* The callback parameter works like those found in the `usort()` and `uksort()` functions. It returns the keys and values found in all arrays that match the criteria of the comparison callback function. It has the following pattern:
	
	`array array_intersect_uassoc(array var1`
	`, array var2 [, array var3 ... ]`
	`, array callback_value_compare)`

`array_intersect_ukey()`	The function takes two or more formal parameters and was introduced into the language in PHP 5. All parameters except the callback function are arrays. The function compares arrays to find elements that are in all arrays. The comparison is done by a user-defined callback function that matches same *keys.* The callback parameter works like those found in the `usort()` and `uksort()` functions. It returns the keys and values found in all arrays that match the criteria of the comparison callback function. It has the following pattern:
	
	`array array_intersect_ukey(array var1`
	`, array var2 [, array var3 ... ]`
	`, array callback_value_compare)`

`array_merge()`	The function takes two or more formal parameters. All parameters are arrays. It creates a master array of all arrays and returns an array with preserved keys and values. Key and value combinations are returned to the result array as many times as they are found. It has the following pattern:
	
	`array array_merge(array var1`
	`, array var2 [, array var3 ... ])`

TABLE 6-5. *Predefined Merging and Partitioning Functions* (continued)

Function	Description and Pattern

`array_merge_recursive()`	The function takes two or more formal parameters. All parameters are arrays. It creates a master array of all arrays and returns an array with preserved keys and values with one exception. Key and value pairs found more than once yield keys that point to nested arrays, which will contain multiple copies of the value, indexed by numeric keys. It has the following pattern:
	
	`array array_merge_recursive(array var1`
	`, array var2 [, array var3 ... ])`

`array_slice()`	The function requires at least two mandatory formal parameters. The first mandatory parameter is an array, and the second is an offset value. The offset value is where data begins being carved from the array. When the offset value is zero or a positive number, carving begins from that point to the end unless an optional length parameter limits the number of elements. When the offset number is negative, the carving starts by using the offset number to count right and then removes all elements to the end of the array unless a length value limits the number of spliced elements. PHP 5.0.2 added a new optional parameter to enable you to preserve numeric keys, which is disabled by default (e.g., set to false). If you override the preserve key value and set it to true, then existing numeric keys will be preserved. Unique string keys are also preserved by default. It has the following pattern:
	
	`array array_merge(array var`
	`, int offset [, int length [`
	`, boolean preserve_key_flag ]])`

`array_splice()`	The function requires at least two mandatory formal parameters. The first mandatory parameter is an array, and the second is an offset value. The offset value is where data begins being carved from the array. When the offset value is zero or a positive number, the carving begins from that point to the end unless a third optional length parameter limits the number of elements. When the offset number is negative, the carving starts by using the offset number to count from the right. It carves all elements from that point to the end of the array unless a length value limits the number of spliced elements. The second optional parameter is an integer, string, or array; and it will be appended to the array after the splice. The spliced part of the array is then assigned to a target variable. The original key values of the optional array parameter are not preserved when spliced into the target array, and unique strings are replaced by numeric index keys. It has the following pattern:
	
	`array array_splice(array var`
	`, int offset [, int length [, array var ]])`

`array_udiff()`	The function takes two or more formal parameters. All parameters are arrays except the last one, which is a callback function. It works by first creating a master array of all arrays except the first array. Then, it subtracts the first from the grouped array based on a callback function that compares *values*. It returns the values found in the first array that were not in the grouped array. It also preserves the original key values in the returned array, which means the keys are not used during the comparison operation. It has the following pattern:
	
	`array array_udiff(array var1`
	`, array var2 [, array var3 ... ]`
	`, array callback_value_compare)`

TABLE 6-5.   *Predefined Merging and Partitioning Functions* (continued)

Function	Description and Pattern

`array_udiff_assoc()`	The function takes two or more formal parameters. All parameters are arrays except the last one, which is a callback function. It works by first creating a master array of all arrays except the first array. Then, it subtracts the first from the grouped array based on a callback function that compares *keys and values.* This function is new in PHP 5 and behaves differently than `array_diff()` and `array_udiff()` functions in that it compares both keys and values. The function returns the values found in the first array that were not in the grouped array. It also preserves the original key values in the returned array, which means the keys are not used during the comparison operation. It has the following pattern:
	
	`array array_udiff_assoc(array var1`
	`, array var2 [, array var3 ... ]`
	`, array callback_value_compare)`

`array_udiff_uassoc()`	The function takes two or more formal parameters. All parameters are arrays except the last one, which is a callback function. It works by first creating a master array of all arrays except the first array. Then, it subtracts the first array from the grouped array based on a callback function to compare *keys and values.* This function is new in PHP 5 and behaves differently than the `array_diff()` and `array_udiff()` functions in that it compares both keys and values. Unlike the `array_diff_assoc()` function, it does not use an internally defined function to compare key values but a user-defined function. The function returns the values found in the first array that were not in the grouped array. It also preserves the original key values in the returned array, which means the keys are not used during the comparison operation. It has the following pattern:
	
	`array array_udiff_uassoc(array var1`
	`, array var2 [, array var3 ... ]`
	`, array callback_value_compare`
	`, array callback_key_compare)`

`array_uintersect()`	The function takes two or more formal parameters. All parameters except the callback function are arrays. The function compares arrays to find elements that are in all arrays. The comparison is done by a user-defined callback function that matches same *values.* It returns an array with preserved keys and values. It has the following pattern:
	
	`array array_uintersect(array var1`
	`, array var2 [, array var3 ... ]`
	`, array callback_value_compare)`

`array_uintersect_assoc()`	The function takes two or more formal parameters. All parameters except the callback function are arrays. The function compares arrays to find elements that are in all arrays. The comparison is done by a user-defined callback function that matches same *keys and values.* This function is new in PHP 5 and acts differently than the original `array_uintersect()` function in that it compares both keys and values. It returns an array with preserved keys and values. It has the following pattern:
	
	`array array_uintersect_assoc(array var1`
	`, array var2 [, array var3 ... ]`
	`, array callback_value_compare)`

TABLE 6-5.   *Predefined Merging and Partitioning Functions* (continued)

Function	Description and Pattern

`array_uintersect_uassoc()`	The function takes two or more formal parameters. All parameters except the callback function are arrays. The function compares arrays to find elements that are in all arrays. The comparison is done by a user-defined callback function that matches same *keys and values*. The function is new in PHP 5 and acts differently than the original `array_uintersect()` function in that it compares both keys and values. Unlike the `array_intersect_assoc()` function, it does not use an internally defined function to compare key values but a user-defined function. It returns an array with preserved keys and values. It has the following pattern:
	
	`array array_uintersect_assoc(array var1`
	`, array var2 [, array var3 ... ]`
	`, array callback_value_compare`
	`, array callback_key_compare)`

`array_unique()`	The function takes a single formal array parameter and returns a new array that has only one copy of key and value pairs. The function compares arrays elements that are in each array by using a callback function that eliminates duplicate *keys and values*. It has the following pattern: `array array_unique(array var)`

TABLE 6-5. *Predefined Merging and Partitioning Functions* (continued)

Now that you are acquainted with the list of predefined merging and partitioning function definitions, you will explore examples of the predefined functions in this section. The section focuses on the following activities:

- Combining arrays
- Merging arrays
- Slicing arrays
- Splicing arrays
- Finding the intersection of arrays
- Discovering the difference between arrays

The selected list of activities will enable you to see how to work with multiple arrays to combine, flip, merge, and slice and dice them into useful information views. Much of the activity demonstrated can also be done by the database server using SQL but is often written by web application programmers into external libraries.

Combining Arrays

As a rule, you combine two arrays together when one is a list of unique string keys and the other a list of values. The *two arrays must be the same size* for the `array_combine()` function to work. The following program demonstrates how to combine the arrays:

-- **This is found in Combine.php on the enclosed CD.**

```php
<?php
  // Declare array variables.
  $countryCode = array("dk","fi","is","no","se");
  $countryName = array("Denmark","Finland","Iceland","Norway","Sweden");

  // Print structured ordering of source arrays.
  print "[Keys][".print_r($countryCode,true)."].<br>";
  print "[Values][".print_r($countryName,true)."].<br><hr>";

  // Combine the arrays as a key and name pair.
  $countryList = array_combine($countryCode,$countryName);

  // Print restructured ordering of key and value pair array.
  foreach($countryList as $code => $name)
    print "[".$code."][".$name."].<br>";
?>
```

The $countryCode array contains a list of unique strings for five Scandinavian countries, and the $countryName array contains the English names for the countries. If you want to use the $countryCode array abbreviations as keys for the names in the $countryName array, the two arrays must be combined. *They can be combined using the* array_combine() *function by passing the array of keys as the first argument and values as the second argument.* The combined array as output from the program follows:

```
[dk][Denmark]
[fi][Finland]
[is][Iceland]
[no][Norway]
[se][Sweden]
```

The combined $countryList array is a hash composed of names and values. It provides navigational advantages if you need to pass the code back to the server as name and value pair arguments to a new page source request. Hash names can provide a meaningful relation to some data sources where unrelated numeric indexes fail to add any value.

Merging Arrays

Merging multiple arrays into a single array is a powerful feature. The array_merge() and array_merge_recursive() functions provide you with the ability to merge arrays. The key difference between these involves how they manage duplicate key and value pairs. The array_merge() function applies the concept of a set union, accepting duplicate key and value pairs; it preserves the duplicate keys by placing them in a nested numerically indexed array.

The following Merge.php program illustrates the advantages of using the ordinary merge to get uniquely indexed values by leveraging the predefined array functions:

-- **This is found in Merge.php on the enclosed CD.**

```php
<?php
  // Declare two array variables.
```

```
$one = array("Denmark","Finland","Iceland","Germany","Sweden");
$two = array("Finland","Ireland","Iceland","Denmark","United Kingdom");

// Sort the array members as unique.
$uniqueMerge = array_unique(array_merge($one,$two));

// Read and print spliced array keys and values to the page.
foreach($uniqueMerge as $code => $name)
  print "[".$code."][".print_r($name,true)."].<br>";

// Print a line break to the page.
print "<hr>";

// Sort merged array members as unique and reorder keys.
$uniqueOrderedMerge = array_values(array_unique(array_merge($one,$two)));

// Read and print spliced array keys and values to the page.
foreach($uniqueOrderedMerge as $code => $name)
  print "[".$code."][".print_r($name,true)."].<br>";
?>
```

The Merge.php program performs two merge operations on the same set of arrays. The first one merges $one and $two arrays and passes the result to the array_unique() function, which eliminates the duplicate key and value pairs. The second merge passes the result of the array_unique() function to the array_values() function, which reorders the keys to be sequentially indexed.

Applying only the array_unique() function to the merged results eliminates duplicate elements but leaves sequence gaps. If you look at the preceding Merge.php source, you will notice that index key values 1–4 come from the $one array and 6 and 9 come from the $two array. These keys are determined by the order that a unique value is found in the arrays passed to the merge() function. Arrays are evaluated from left to right. The results are shown in the following render output:

```
[0] [Denmark]
[1] [Finland]
[2] [Iceland]
[3] [Germany]
[4] [Sweden]
[6] [Ireland]
[9] [United Kingdom]
```

The sequence gaps are resolved by passing the array_unique() function return into the array_values() function, which sequentially reorders the keys of the new array. The new output generated from that operation is shown here:

```
[0] [Denmark]
[1] [Finland]
[2] [Iceland]
[3] [Germany]
[4] [Sweden]
[5] [Ireland]
[6] [United Kingdom]
```

You get the same results from the `array_merge_recursive()` function provided the base arrays are numerically indexed. When an array uses unique string indexes, the result of `array_unique(array_merge($one,$two))` will be different. However, the results of the latter `array_values()` will be the same because the function does not preserve keys, while the others do.

TIP
Unless the keys have some special merit to your application, use the combination of `array_merge()`, `array_unique()`, and `array_values()` to merge arrays.

Slicing Arrays

When you slice from an array, you remove a copy of one or more elements but leave the original keys and values intact. The `array_slice()` function enables you to carve out a chunk of an array into a new array. The array chunk is composed of one to many contiguous elements. You can carve the elements from the beginning, middle, or end of an array. When you require noncontiguous chunks, you will slice two times.

The following `Slice.php` program *slices two noncontiguous chunks from an array* and returns them into one return array:

-- This is found in Slice.php on the enclosed CD.

```php
<?php
  // Declare an array variable.
  $scandinavia = array("Denmark","Finland","Iceland","Ireland"
                       ,"Norway","Sweden","United Kingdom");

  // Read and print array keys and values to the page.
  foreach($scandinavia as $code => $name)
    print "[".$code."] [".print_r($name,true)."].<br>";

  // Print a line.
  print "<hr>";

  // Sort the array members.
  $sliced = array_values(
              array_unique(
                array_merge(
                  array_slice(
                    $scandinavia,array_search("Finland",$scandinavia),1)
                  ,array_slice(
                    $scandinavia,array_search("Norway",$scandinavia),2))));

  // Read and print spliced array keys and values to the page.
  foreach($sliced as $code => $name)
    print "[".$code."] [".print_r($name,true)."].<br>";
?>
```

This technique of slicing two noncontiguous chunks uses two separate `array_slice()` function calls as parameters to the `array_merge()` function. While it is unnecessary in the example because there are no duplicates, enclosing the return value of the `array_merge()` function in the `array_unique()` and `array_values()` functions respectively is a good habit.

Real programming solutions can slice data sets and create unexpected duplicates. You eliminate the unexpected duplicates by using the `array_unique()` function, which can create sequence gaps and cause abnormal `for` loop exits. The `array_values()` function then reindexes the keys and prevents abnormal `for` loop exits.

Slicing from the end of an array behaves differently than slicing from the beginning or middle. The sliced copies from the array are written to the function return value in reverse order, which means the last element is indexed first, the next to last element second, and so forth. You will use the `asort()` function to sort it in ascending order or `arsort()` to sort it in descending order as covered earlier in the chapter.

Splicing Arrays

Splicing arrays is a bit more than slicing them because you splice to remove from and/or add content to an array. As covered earlier in the chapter, the `array_splice()` function acts like the `array_slice()` function. The differences are that the `array_splice()` function removes original elements instead of copying them and can add new values to spliced arrays. The optional parameter is a primitive data type or array that is added to the original array.

The `array_splice()` function also returns an array of spliced values. The following `Splice.php` program demonstrates how you remove from and add elements to a target array:

-- **This is found in Splice.php on the enclosed CD.**

```php
<?php
  // Declare an array variable.
  $scandinavia = array("dk"=>"Denmark","is"=>"Iceland"
                        ,"no"=>"Norway","se"=>"Sweden");

  // Read and print array keys and values to the page.
  foreach($scandinavia as $code => $name)
    print "[".$code."] [".print_r($name,true)."]<br>";

  // Print a line.
  print "<hr>";

  // Splice out of one array to another.
  $spliced = array_splice(
              $scandinavia,array_search("Denmark",$scandinavia),1
              ,array("fi"=>"Finland"));

  // Read and print spliced array keys and values to the page.
  foreach($spliced as $code => $name)
    print "[Old] [".$code."] [".print_r($name,true)."]<br>";

  // Print a line.
  print "<hr>";

  // Read and print array keys and values to the page.
  foreach($scandinavia as $code => $name)
    print "[New] [".$code."] [".print_r($name,true)."]<br>";
?>
```

The `Splice.php` program searches and removes "Denmark" while adding "Norway" to the array. The output from the new array created by the `array_splice()` function is as follows:

```
[Out] [dk] [Denmark]
```

Examining the old array, you find that it still contains four elements. This is because one element was added to the old array when the other was removed. The following are the ordered contents of the old array after the splice:

```
[New] [0] [Finland]
[New] [is] [Iceland]
[New] [no] [Norway]
[New] [se] [Sweden]
```

While the newly added array key and value pair had a unique string key, the spliced key is numeric. This happens because the `array_splice()` function does not preserve the original keys from the appending source array. You should also note that elements are spliced into an array at the front of the array. This behavior is like the `array_unshift()` function, which also increments the older numeric keys as necessary.

You can *append one array to another by using the* `array_splice()` *function provided you use a zero for the offset and length parameters.* You can put the following statement in the `Splice.php` program immediately below the `array_splice()` function call. The following will enable you to use the splicing function as a grafting tool:

```
// Append one array to another suppressing return value.
if (!array_splice($scandinavia,0,0,array("Germany"))) null;
```

You can also use the `array_splice()` function as a conditional expression to remove unwanted values from arrays. When the `array_splice()` function carves out one or more values, it returns a true as a conditional expression. Treating the operation as a conditional expression allows you to delete values from anywhere in an array.

Finding the Intersection of Arrays

The intersection of arrays enables you to determine if values are present in multiple arrays. The `array_intersect()` function lets you compare a set of arrays to find values that are in all of them. The following `Intersect.php` program demonstrates finding *value only* intersection values:

```
-- This is found in Intersect.php on the enclosed CD.
```

```php
<?php
  // Declare three arrays.
  $one = array("Denmark","Finland","Iceland","Germany","Sweden");
  $two = array("Finland","Ireland","Iceland","Denmark","United Kingdom");
  $three = array("Denmark","Germany","Ireland","Iceland");

  // Sort the array members.
  $intersect = array_intersect($one,$two,$three);

  // Read and print spliced array keys and values to the page.
  foreach($intersect as $code => $name)
    print "[".$code."] [".print_r($name,true)."]<br>";
?>
```

The `Intersect.php` program produces the following:

```
[0] [Denmark]
[2] [Iceland]
```

Viewing the program output, you can see there are nonsequential keys for the intersection values. They exist because the `array_intersect()` function compares the first array against the second array and builds a temporary list of matches. Then, it uses the list of matches to compare against the next array, until all array parameters are processed. *After each comparison, values may be eliminated from the temporary list, which is why there are index gaps.* It is important to note that the program preserves unique string keys but does not preserve numeric keys.

You can also use the `array_intersect_assoc()` function to compare both keys and values. This function is a better choice when the keys are unique strings because it compares them independently of their positional location in arrays. You should not use this function when keys are numeric because it compares them by checking their relative positions and values. They only match when they are sequenced alike.

Discovering the Difference Between Arrays

The `array_diff()` function enables you to subtract elements in one set from another. This behavior mirrors the minus operator in sets. The `Diff.php` program merges two arrays and then subtracts one of the arrays from the other, as follows:

`-- This is found in Diff.php on the enclosed CD.`

```php
<?php
  // Declare array variables.
  $americanLeague = array("Boston","N.Y. Yankees");
  $nationalLeague = array("Dodgers","Giants");

  // Declare an empty array.
  $majorLeague = array();

  // Print structured ordering.
  print "[American]<br>[".print_r($americanLeague,true)."].<br>";
  print "[National]<br>[".print_r($nationalLeague,true)."].<br><hr>";

  // Merge array members.
  $majorLeague = array_merge($americanLeague,$nationalLeague);

  // Print restructured ordering.
  print "[Major League]<br>[".print_r($majorLeague,true)."].<br><hr>";

  // Take the difference of two arrays.
  $americanLeague = array_diff($majorLeague,$nationalLeague);
  print "[Major League - American League]<br>";
  print "[".print_r($americanLeague,true)."].<br>";
?>
```

You have completed the section on merging and partitioning arrays. The section has covered the features of predefined merging and partitioning array functions and provided example programs demonstrating concepts. The user-defined sort operation functions have not been covered, because they were qualified in the section "Sorting Arrays."

Summary

You have learned how to define, manage, sort, merge, and partition arrays. These skills will enable you to develop powerful dynamic web pages in conjunction with database queries. The next chapter will demonstrate how to define and use functions.

CHAPTER
7

Functions

his chapter examines how you define and use functions. It introduces the general concept of functions before discussing the specifics of how PHP functions work; it covers the following topics:

- Defining functions
- Understanding variable scope in functions
- Managing function parameters
    - Parameters by value or reference
    - Parameter default values
    - Variable-length parameter lists
- Using functions to return values
- Managing dynamic function calls
- Using recursive functions

All programs contain instructions to perform tasks. When sets of tasks are frequently used to perform an activity, they are grouped into units, which are known as functions or methods in most programming languages. PHP calls these units *functions*.

Functions should perform well-defined tasks. They should also hide the complexity of their tasks behind a prototype. A prototype includes a function name, a list of parameters, and a return data type. The prototype should let you see how the function can be used in your programs.

Function names should be short, declarative descriptions about what tasks they perform. The list of parameters, also known as a *signature,* is typically enclosed in parentheses and should use descriptive variable names that signal their purpose when possible. The parameters in a function signature are considered formal at definition and actual at run time. In strongly typed languages, the parameters impose positional and data type restrictions. Weakly typed languages, like C or PHP, typically impose only positional restrictions. In some programming languages, formal parameters can also designate whether run-time values are passed by value or by reference. The return type is a valid data type in the programming language or a void, which means nothing is returned by the function.

Having reviewed the general concept of functions, you will see how to define functions in PHP in the next section. PHP functions are the product of a loosely typed programming language. This lineage offers you some advantages and challenges that will be discussed throughout the balance of the chapter. While the six sections are written independently, they are positioned to support each other and should be read in sequence.

Defining Functions

PHP functions are defined by a prototype that includes a function name, a list of parameters, and a return data type. The basic prototype of a PHP function that takes no parameters and returns no values is

```
void function function_name();
```

Function names in PHP must start with an alphabetical character or an underscore and consist of only alphabetical characters, numbers, or underscores. Also, *function names are global in scope and case insensitive,* which means functions can only exist once in a page and its set of included PHP libraries.

The nature of global-scope functions differs from the convention in other popular programming languages. Whether a function is defined in a page, inside another function, or in its included libraries, it is available anywhere in the PHP program. This means you cannot define local functions inside functions with the same expectations of behavior. User-defined functions also cannot have the same name as any PHP built-in function.

PHP is a mixed-case language, which means *functions are case insensitive* while virtually everything else is not. This can be confusing at times if you forget the rule. Case-insensitive functions enable you to enter their names in lower-, mixed-, or uppercase at different times in the same program. They will always refer to a single global-scope prototype, and the convention is to consistently use the same case as the function prototype. The convention exists because it makes reading and remembering function names easier.

TIP
You should avoid using function names more than once because they can conflict or be confused by programmers.

Along with these behaviors, *functions do not support overloading.* Overloading is the practice of having multiple function signatures that are accessed according to the position and type of actual parameters that are passed to a function at run time. PHP does not support overloading because it provides variable-length parameter lists. The concept of variable-length parameter lists is covered later in the chapter, in the section "Managing Function Parameters."

You will now define a function named my_function() that takes no parameters and returns nothing. It implements the following prototype:

```
void function my_function();
```

The following Function1.php program will print to the web page the string "Hello PHP World!"

-- **This is found in Function1.php on the enclosed CD.**

```php
<?php
  // Call the user-defined function.
  print_string();

  // Define a no-parameter function that returns nothing.
  function print_string()
  {
    print "Hello PHP World!";
  }
?>
```

You can see that the keyword void in the prototype is not actually used in the program. The function keyword begins the definition, which is followed by the function name, a formal parameter list in parentheses, and a set of statements enclosed in curly braces. This function has no formal parameters and is also known as a no-argument function.

Function calls are made by using a function name followed by parentheses enclosing no parameter, one parameter, or a list of parameters separated by commas. When function calls are used as expressions in condition statements, they are not followed by a semicolon because they act in the scope of an `if` statement and are enclosed in parentheses. Functions are followed by a semicolon when they are statements. Parameters can be any type of PHP variable or numeric or string literal values. Parameters are by default copies of the value or variable used when calling the function.

You define a function that takes a single formal parameter of a string with the following prototype:

```
void function my_function(string argument);
```

While you should try to have more meaningful names for prototype variables, you can use something generic, like *argument* here. You should note that formal parameters are preceded by a $ symbol when defining function signatures.

The following `Function2.php` program demonstrates passing a string literal as the only actual parameter to the `print_string()` function:

-- This is found in Function2.php on the enclosed CD.

```php
<?php
  // Call the user-defined function.
  print_string("Hello PHP World!");

  // Define a parameter function that returns nothing.
  function print_string($argument)
  {
    print $argument;
  }
?>
```

The call to the `print_string()` function sends a string literal that will be printed to the rendered web page. As you see, *there is no type specified in the definition of function parameters.* This is by design because formal parameters are validated only by position, not data type. You will explore more on this topic in the section "Managing Function Parameters" later in the chapter.

In some programming languages, function definitions must precede function calls. This type of behavior, called *forward referencing,* is determined by how the program is parsed. Many parsers perform a single read from top to bottom, which requires a function to be defined or forward-referenced before it can be called. The PHP parser reads each delimited tag component block to load a page and then any included files to build a complete program. This is done because parts of the programs can be located between discrete tags in the same page.

After reading the PHP code segments, function definitions are first read into memory, which defines them in the page. After reading functions into memory, the rest of the page is processed. This process avoids fatal undefined function run-time errors. This works well except when a function is nested in another function, because *nested functions are not defined in the global memory space until the enclosing function is called.* This creates the possibility that a program may require forward referencing to run correctly. Large programs sharing a dependency on nested functions can be hard to debug and fix. Therefore, you should *avoid writing function **definitions** within functions.*

PHP recognizes the value of having anonymous, or lambda-style, functions because they allow you to modularize coding components without adding them to the global memory space. You define an anonymous function by using the following pattern:

```
string create_function (string args, string code)
```

The first string contains a list of formal parameters to the function, and the second contains the code for the anonymous program. You declare a variable by assigning it the predefined create_function() return value. Then, *you can treat the variable as a function and pass actual parameters to the variable in appended parentheses.*

The following DynamicFunction1.php program demonstrates this concept:

-- This is found in DynamicFunction1.php on the enclosed CD.

```php
<?php
  // Define a set of variables.
  $a = 2;
  $b = 2;
  $c = 4;

  // Call the global function.
  nested($a,$c);

  // Call the anonymous function by its variable name.
  if (isset($add))
    print "[".$add($a,$b)."]";
  else
    print "[\$add is not defined.]";

  // Define a global function.
  function nested($a,$b)
  {
    // Define an anonymous function.
    $add = create_function('$a,$b','return $a + $b;');

    // Call the anonymous function by its variable name.
    if (isset($add))
      print "[".$add($a,$b)."]<br>";
  }
?>
```

The program will add the contents of variables $a and $c by passing them as actual parameters to the nested() function. The results produced are shown in the following output:

```
[6]
[$add is not defined.]
```

Anonymous functions defined within the scope of functions are truly local in scope because they exist only in the scope of the function. When you define anonymous functions at the PHP script level, the functions' scope is equal to that of the variable. You will need to use the `unset()` function to remove the variable if you want the anonymous function destroyed after execution.

You have learned how to define functions and avoid nested functions because of their runtime-loading dependency. The next section will explore how variable scope impacts functions.

Understanding Variable Scope in Functions

PHP functions work differently than many other programming languages because they are globally defined. Likewise, the rules of scope may appear different than the norm, but they are not.

Functions can access only global variables and variables defined in them, which are known as *local* variables. You define global variables with the `define()` function that was discussed in Chapter 4. Global variables can be defined inside functions, which make them available only after calling the containing function. This behavior has benefits and problems. The benefit is that you can define conditional global variables at run time. The problem is that you can have more than one mechanism that returns values from a function, which is a potential control problem.

You can also define another type of global variable by using the `GLOBAL` keyword in a function. *Creating a variable with the GLOBAL keyword does not create an environment global variable like one created with the `define()` function.* The `GLOBAL` keyword creates a variable that you can access externally from the function where it is defined. The global variable's scope is equal to variables defined at the PHP scripting tag level. This means we have two types of global variables that have different scope. Labeling these behaviors is difficult but you can view the *GLOBAL keyword as defining script-level global variables, whereas the `define()` function creates environment-level global variables.* The latter can be accessed inside and outside of functions, while the former cannot be accessed in other functions unless passed as an actual parameter.

The following `Function3.php` program demonstrates the access privilege of a function to read an environment variable and set global environment- and script-level variables:

-- This is found in Function3.php on the enclosed CD.

```php
<?php
  // Declare a user-defined global variable.
  define('LOCAL',"[The global variable]");

  // Call function.
  print_string();

  // Print function declared local variable.
  print $function_local;

  // Define a function.
  function print_string()
  {
    // Define a global scoped variable.
    GLOBAL $function_local;
```

```
    // Print the local variable with a text literal.
    $function_local = LOCAL." is inside the function.";
    }
?>
```

The Function3.php program uses the define() function to build a global environment variable. The print_string() function *uses the GLOBAL keyword to build a script-level global variable.* You will notice that you must define a global variable on a separate line before assigning a value. The next line joins a global environment-level variable and a string literal. The program shows you can access an environment variable and define a script-level global variable inside a function. Then, you can access the variable outside of the function where it was defined. It prints the following output to a page:

```
[The global variable] is inside the function.
```

If you add the following additional function at the end of the Function3.php program, it will demonstrate the scope limit of script-level global variables:

```
// Define a function to fail on scope.
function script_global()
{
  print "[\$function_local] [".$function_local."]<br>";
}

// Call the failing function.
script_global();
```

Adding the preceding code to the Function3.php program will raise an undefined variable exception in the script_global() function. This happens because *the subsequent function lacks scope to access the $function_local script-level variable.*

When you define a script-level variable without using the GLOBAL keyword and try to access it in a function, the same scope error happens. This occurs because a variable is defined as external to the scope of the function. You must pass the variable as an actual parameter to access it inside a function. The following Function4.php program demonstrates this:

```
-- This is found in Function4.php on the enclosed CD.
```

```php
<?php
  // Declare a variable.
  $local_var = "Local variable";

  // Define a function that prints a string.
  function print_string()
  {
    // Print the local variable with a text literal.
    print "[".$local_var."]";
  }

  // Print string.
  print_string();
?>
```

The Function4.php program *will raise a nonfatal notice* if you have enabled the display_errors directive in the php.ini file, *or it will return empty brackets ([]) in the web page otherwise.* The program demonstrates that with or without a GLOBAL keyword, script-level variables are out of scope to the internal operation of functions, unless they are passed as actual parameters. Only global variables built by using the define() function are in scope to functions without explicitly passing them as actual parameters.

The same scope rules apply to the anonymous, or lambda-style, functions discussed earlier in the chapter. When an anonymous function is stored in a target variable that is defined as global within a function, the variable follows the same rules as ordinary script-level variables. You can see this principle demonstrated in the DynamicFunction2.php program:

-- This is found in DynamicFunction2.php on the enclosed CD.

```php
<?php
  // Define a set of variables.
  $a = 2;
  $b = 2;
  $c = 4;

  // Call the global function.
  nested($a,$c);

  // Call the anonymous function by its variable name.
  if (isset($add))

    print "[".$add($a,$b)."]";
  else
    print "[\$add is not defined.]";

  // Define a global function.
  function nested($a,$b)
  {
    // Define a script-level variable.
    GLOBAL $add;

    // Define an anonymous function for a script-level variable.
    $add = create_function('$a,$b','return $a + $b;');

    // Call the anonymous function by its variable name.
    if (isset($add))
      print "[".$add($a,$b)."]<br>";
  }
?>
```

The program defines a script-level $add variable internally in the nested() function. The variable $add is accessible as a function externally to where it is defined. You can redefine or delete the behavior of the function after its definition. The call to the anonymous function outside of the nested() function uses the script-level values of $a and $b, which sum to 4, as shown in the following output:

```
[6]
[4]
```

You have learned how variable scope impacts functions whether they contain ordinary data types or anonymous functions. The next section will explore how to manage the definition and use of parameters.

Managing Function Parameters

In this section, you will learn how to use and manage parameters to build effective functions. While functions that don't use parameters typically do very little, they can be very useful for fixed or static tasks. Parameterized functions provide dynamic code blocks that meet more complex programming tasks often required by business rules.

Parameters by Value or Reference

As discussed in the introduction to this chapter, parameters are passed by value or reference to functions. Passing a parameter by value means that you hand a copy of the variable or literal value to a function. The alternative to passing a parameter by value is to pass one by reference, which means that you provide a reference or pointer to the variable in memory. The former ensures that the original variable is unchanged by the function activity, while the latter enables the function to change the original variable value.

The FunctionByValue.php program demonstrates how passing by value leaves the actual parameter value unchanged:

-- This is found in FunctionByValue.php on the enclosed CD.

```php
<?php
  // Declare variable.
  $var = "Initial";

  // Print actual parameter value before function.
  print "Before function \$var [".$var."]<br>";

  // Call the user-defined function.
  print_string($var);

  // Print actual parameter value after function.
  print "After function \$var [".$var."]";

  // Define function that prints an input parameter as a string.
  function print_string($var)
  {
    // Print the local variable with a text literal.
    $var = "Updated";
```

```
      // Print actual parameter value.
      print "Inside function \$var [".$var."]<br>";
  }
?>
```

The program uses a single $var variable name, but the variable is actually two variables that share the same name but have different scope. The declaration of $var as a string sets the value as "Initial" for a script-level global variable. The second declaration is subtle because it occurs in the definition of the print_string ($var) function. The formal parameter $var has a local scope limited to the function and is passed by value, which is the default. The names are the same, but their scopes are different. Inside the function the local $var variable is redefined as a string literal of "Updated" and printed.

The output from the FunctionByValue.php program demonstrates that the value passed by the call to the print_string () function was a copy of a script-level global variable because the variable value before and after the function remains the same. The following output is produced:

```
Before function $var [Initial]
Inside function $var [Updated]
After function $var [Initial]
```

The benefit of passing by value is that the copy of a variable can be used to produce something of value to the program without altering the original variable. Passing by value is the default behavior in PHP because functions act like black boxes that take input and return a derived output.

It is possible that you want the function to return a new value to replace the old value of the actual parameter variable. You can do so by returning the modified value from the function. Then, you assign the function return value to the same variable passed as the actual parameter to the function. Assuming you now return a value from the print_string ($var) function, you can use the following syntax:

```
$var = print_string($var);
```

This solution works when there is only one variable entering and exiting a function. When you have two or more formal parameters and you want one or both changed, you will need to pass by reference.

The FunctionByReference.php program demonstrates how passing by reference changes the actual parameter value:

-- **This is found in FunctionByReference.php on the enclosed CD.**

```
<?php
  // Declare variable.
  $var = "Initial";

  // Print actual parameter value before function.
  print "Before function \$var [".$var."]<br>";

  // Call the user-defined function.
  print_string($var);
```

```
    // Print actual parameter value after function.
    print "After function \$var [".$var."]";

    // Define function that prints an input parameter as a string.
    function print_string(&$var)
    {
      // Print the local variable with a text literal.
      $var = "Updated";

      // Print actual parameter value.
      print "Inside function \$var [".$var."]<br>";
    }
?>
```

The key difference between `FunctionByReference.php` and the prior program is that here, the function *defines the formal parameter as a reference. This is done by placing an ampersand before the variable name.* The ampersand instructs the PHP compiler to pass a reference, not a copy, to the function.

The following output demonstrates that the original variable is altered inside the function:

```
Before function $var [Initial]
Inside function $var [Updated]
After function $var [Updated]
```

TIP
The `FunctionByReference.php` program uses $var as the formal parameter name to illustrate that one variable name can have two or more scopes. You can and should typically rename the $var formal parameter in the `print_string()` function to avoid confusion.

NOTE
Prior to PHP 5, you could pass a reference into a function, but that behavior has been deprecated. Now you define the function to process parameters by reference.

You have now learned how to pass parameters by value or by reference in PHP. Choosing when to do so is the trick. There are valid reasons to support both approaches, but you should consider carefully when you choose to pass by reference, because it is a form of coupling, which can add unnecessary complexity to your PHP programming library.

Parameter Default Values

When defining functions, you can define parameters as mandatory or optional. *Mandatory* parameters must be listed before optional parameters in the argument list. *Optional* parameters have a default value, which can be any scalar variable, literal, or null value.

The most generic prototype to demonstrate this behavior is

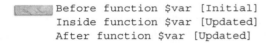
```
void function add_numbers(int a = 0, int b = 0);
```

The following `DefaultValue.php` program demonstrates default values by making both formal parameters optional and their default values zero:

-- This is found in **DefaultValue.php** on the enclosed CD.

```php
<?php
  // Call function without actual parameters.
  add_numbers();

  // Call function with two actual parameters.
  add_numbers(2,2);

  // Define a function that adds two numbers.
  function add_numbers($a = 0,$b = 0)
  {
    // Add two numbers and print the result.
    print "[(\$a + \$b)][".($a + $b)."]<br>";
  }
?>
```

The program demonstrates a call to the `add_numbers()` function without actual parameters and a call with two actual parameters. The first call will use the default zero values and results in a sum of zero, while the second call will ignore the default values and add the numbers provided in the function call. The `DefaultValue.php` program generates the following output:

```
[($a + $b)][0]
[($a + $b)][4]
```

Using default values in this example is a good fix to a simple problem. On the other hand, operational parameters pose other programming challenges. The sequential ordering dependency of optional variables requires all variables be provided from left to right. When one variable in a sequence of variables is skipped, a function can provide an incorrect result. Likewise, the absence of actual parameter run-time type identification can cause abnormal results by performing unexpected and implicit type casting operations.

Both of these problems exist because PHP uses variable-length parameter lists for function signatures. You will explore how to leverage variable-length parameter lists in the next section.

Variable-Length Parameter Lists

Variable-length parameter lists are common patterns in programming languages. The C, C++, C#, and Java programming languages all support variable-length parameter lists, but they label them differently. A *variable-length* parameter list is an array or a list of values, where the values are valid PHP data types.

When you learned earlier in the chapter how to build and implement a prototype, you had two options. One option was to use parameters, and the other was not to use them. As discussed earlier, there are two parameter options: mandatory or optional. These options make PHP function parameter lists more complex.

A function definition or prototype that uses a single mandatory parameter requires that you call the function with at least one actual parameter but does not restrict you from passing more than one. You can actually submit any number of parameters beyond the mandatory number

Function	Description and Pattern
func_get_arg()	The function takes one formal parameter, which is the index value in the variable-length parameter list. When the actual parameter is found in the range of the parameter list indexes, the function returns that argument value. If the index value is not found in the list, the function raises a warning and returns a null value. The function has the following pattern: mixed func_get_arg(int *arg_num*)
func_get_args()	The function takes no formal parameters and returns a numerically indexed array of arguments. If there are no parameters passed to the function, a null array is returned. The null array has zero elements, and attempting to access element zero will raise a nonfatal error. It has the following pattern: array func_get_args()
func_num_args()	The function takes no formal parameters and returns the number of elements in the argument list. The valid range is from 0 to the maximum number of parameters. The function has the following pattern: int func_num_args()

TABLE 7-1.   *Variable-Length Parameter List Functions*

required by a function prototype. You can define functions without any parameters and still manage a parameter list passed to the function, which means *prototypes are optional.*

After introducing some enabling functions, you will see how to manage variable-length parameter lists in PHP functions. Table 7-1 qualifies predefined functions that enable flexible parameter list management.

The *variable-length parameter list functions can **only** be used inside of a function definition and have no valid context outside of functions.* Any attempt to call these outside of the scope of a function can raise a nonfatal warning message.

The following FlexibleParameters.php program demonstrates the use of these functions:

-- **This is found in FlexibleParameters.php on the enclosed CD.**

```php
<?php
  // Call function.
  print_string("Oh yeah, baby!","There's no prototype required.");

  // Define a function that prints a string.
  function print_string()
  {
    // Check for actual parameters.
    if (func_num_args() > 0 )
```

```
      // Process list of actual parameters.
      foreach (func_get_args() as $index => $arg)
        print "Parameter List [".$index."] [".$arg."]<br>";
  }
?>
```

The program *demonstrates two actual parameters passed in the call* to the `print_string()` function, though the prototype indicates that *there are no formal parameters*. This may look quirky but it is actually a natural feature of flexible parameter passing. When you call a function, PHP checks the list of actual parameters to ensure that there are at least enough elements to match the number defined by the function prototype. Additional values are not validated because they are assumed to be optional parameters defined by the prototype or superfluous and ignored.

The `FlexibleParameters.php` program will display the following to a web page:

```
Parameter List [0] [Oh yeah, baby!]
Parameter List [1] [There's no prototype required.]
```

You have now learned how to access all actual parameters passed to user-defined functions whether defined in the prototype or not. This also completes the discussion on how you manage function parameters.

In the next section, you will examine how variable-length parameter lists and type validation functions can evaluate and process function parameters to guarantee correct return results.

Using Functions to Return Values

Up to this point, you have experimented with user-defined functions that do not return values. The traditional black-box value of functions is that inputs are processed into meaningful outputs. The outputs are return values from functions. The broadest prototype of a function that returns any data type is

```
mixed function my_function(mixed var);
```

This prototype basically says that the function has a single input of a variable that may be any data type and returns a variable of any data type. Unfortunately, many functions work accidentally this way because of careless type management of return values.

Function return types are provided by using the `return` keyword, a variable or literal value, and a semicolon. You can return any valid data type from functions. Unlike in many other programming languages, you can treat a PHP function that returns a variable like one that does not, simply ignoring the return rather than assigning it to a left operand.

The following prototype will be used to build a small calculator function:

```
float function calculate(int a = 0, int b = 0, int op = 0, array operand);
```

The function has four optional formal parameters: the first three are integers and the last is an array of operand values. The default values speak for themselves. As discussed in the preceding section, there is an immediate problem with the prototype because there is no way to enforce the ordering or provisioning of the actual parameters.

The solution to managing these optional parameters lies in effective use of the variable-length parameter list functions combined with the type identification functions. The list of type identification functions is found in Table 7-2.

Function	Description and Pattern
is_array()	The function takes one formal parameter, which can be any data type. The function returns true if the actual parameter is an array and false if it is anything else. The function has the following pattern: `bool is_array(mixed var)`
is_bool()	The function takes one formal parameter, which can be any data type. The function returns true if the actual parameter is a Boolean and false if it is anything else. The function has the following pattern: `bool is_bool(mixed var)`
is_float()	The function takes one formal parameter, which can be any data type. The function returns true if the actual parameter is a float and false if it is anything else. The is_double() and is_real() functions are aliases to the is_float() function. The function has the following pattern: `bool is_float(mixed var)`
is_int()	The function takes one formal parameter, which can be any data type. The function returns true if the actual parameter is an integer and false if it is anything else. The is_integer() and is_long() functions are aliases to the is_int() function. The function has the following pattern: `bool is_int(mixed var)`
is_null()	The function takes one formal parameter, which can be any data type. The function returns true if the actual parameter is a null and false if it is anything else. The function has the following pattern: `bool is_null(mixed var)`
is_numeric()	The function takes one formal parameter, which can be any data type. The function returns true if the actual parameter is a number or a numeric string and false if it is anything else. The function has the following pattern: `bool is_numeric(mixed var)`
is_object()	The function takes one formal parameter, which can be any data type. The function returns true if the actual parameter is an object and false if it is anything else. The function has the following pattern: `bool is_object(mixed var)`
is_scalar()	The function takes one formal parameter, which can be any data type. The function returns true if the actual parameter is a Boolean, float, integer, or string, and false if it is anything else. The function has the following pattern: `bool is_scalar(mixed var)`
is_string()	The function takes one formal parameter, which can be any data type. The function returns true if the actual parameter is a string and false if it is anything else. The function has the following pattern: `bool is_string(mixed var)`

TABLE 7-2. *Type Identification Functions*

The `Calculate.php` program demonstrates how to leverage variable-parameter lists and data type functions together to solve a problem. The program follows:

`-- This is found in Calculate.php on the enclosed CD.`

```php
<?php
  // Define a global variable.
  GLOBAL $operands;

  // Assign the global variable an array of operands.
  $operands = array("+","-","*","/");

  // Call function with each operand.
  for ($i = 0;$i < count($operands);$i++)
  {
    // Print call and return value.
    print "[(\$a = 86, \$b = 6, \$operand = ".$operands[$i].")]";
    print "[".calculate(86,(6 + $i),$i,$operands)."]<br>";
  }

  // Define a function that does binary math operations.
  function calculate($a = 0, $b = 0,$op = 0,$operands)
  {
    // Check for three actual parameters.
    if (func_num_args() == 4)
    {
      // Check and override the default value.
      if (is_numeric(func_get_arg(0)))
        $a = func_get_arg(0);
      else
        return null;

      // Check and override the default value.
      if (is_numeric(func_get_arg(1)))
        $b = func_get_arg(1);
      else
        return null;

      // Check and override the default value and choose operation.
      if ((is_numeric(func_get_arg(2)) &&
          (array_key_exists(func_get_arg(2),$operands)))
      {
        // Declare operand.
        $op = $operands[func_get_arg(2)];

        // Apply formula based on operand.
        switch (true)
```

```
      {
        case ($op == "+"):
          return (float) $a + $b;
        case ($op == "-"):
          return (float) $a - $b;
        case ($op == "*"):
          return (float) $a * $b;
        case ($op == "/"):
          return round((float) $a / $b,2);
      }
    }
    else
    {
      // Return a null argument error.
      return null;
    }
  }
  else
  {
    // Return a null argument error.
    return null;
  }
}
?>
```

The `Calculate.php` program checks if only four actual parameters are passed at run time before evaluating any arguments. If there are four actual parameters, the program validates whether the first two are numeric values and assigns the numeric values to the first two actual parameters. The program evaluates the third to see if it is a number and then uses the number to determine if a value is found in the fourth actual parameter, which is the `$operands` array. A match in the `$operands` array is assigned to the third formal parameter, which implicitly casts it to a string. *If anything doesn't meet the appropriate test, it is discarded and a null value is returned by the function.*

The return values are explicitly typecast to floats for two reasons. One is that it is possible that a real number can be returned as a division product; and the other is that all numbers should be returned as the same data type. The `case` statement selection of an operator returns the mathematical result to the calling program unit. The following output is generated by the program:

```
[($a = 86, $b = 6, $op = +)] [92]
[($a = 86, $b = 6, $op = -)] [79]
[($a = 86, $b = 6, $op = *)] [688]
[($a = 86, $b = 6, $op = /)] [9.56]
```

This technique demonstrates leveraging a variable-length parameter list and type identification functions to guarantee position and type signature behaviors. Together, variable-length parameter lists and type identification functions enable you to validate function signatures and demonstrate how to return values from functions. The last section in this chapter will explore how to build recursive functions.

Managing Dynamic Function Calls

Chapter 6 shows you how to pass a customized sort function into a predefined sorting function. The ability to do so, in your own library functions, is a powerful tool. This section will demonstrate how you pass a function name to make a dynamic function call.

The mechanism to make dynamic function calls is tied to how variables are managed in PHP. You can define a function in your page, or library, and then pass the name of the function as a string and its parameters as a list to another function. Inside the function, you append parentheses containing the actual parameter list to the variable that contains the function name. This statement makes a dynamic function call to the function represented by the string and uses a parameter list that can contain static values, variables, or an array of values.

As covered in Chapter 6, the usort() predefined function takes an array by reference and a callback function. Internally, the usort() function manages how values from the array are passed into your user-defined callback function. The function also builds a new array by replacing the old array with a sorted one.

The DynamicFunctionCall.php program demonstrates a user_sort() function that takes two parameters and has the following prototype:

 void user_sort(string *function*, array *var*)

You provide the name of the function as the first parameter and the target array as the second parameter. The array is passed by reference, which means that the array will be sorted inside the function. The DynamicFunctionCall.php program defines the user_sort() function to demonstrate dynamic function calls. *The program builds a dynamic run-time function call by concatenating a function name variable and parentheses containing the array variable.*

Three supporting functions are provided in the program. Two are classic sorting algorithms—the bubble and cocktail sorts. The third is a switch() library function that you may find very useful. The switch() function enables you to change the elements in an array to be by reference, a capability that isn't provided in the predefined array management library.

> **TIP**
> *The bubble and cocktail sort programs work only with numeric arrays and will fail if you attempt to use an associative array when the keys are unique strings as opposed to numbers.*

The following DynamicFunctionCall.php program demonstrates how you pass a function by reference to call dynamically at run time:

-- **This is found in DynamicFunctionCall.php on the enclosed CD.**

```php
<?php
  // Declare sample arrays.
  $array1 = array(7,3,2,1,6,5,4);
  $array2 = array(3,7,2,6,5,4,8);

  // Choose a bubble sort.
  user_sort('bubble_sort',$array1);
```

```php
// Choose a cocktail sort.
user_sort('cocktail_sort',$array2);

// Print the bubble sort results.
print "[".print_r($array1,true)."]<br>";

// Print the cocktail sort results.
print "[".print_r($array2,true)."]<br>";

// Performs a function by reference.
function user_sort($function,&$array)
{
  // Build function statement at runtime.
   $function($array);
}

// Performs a classic bubble sort passing array by reference.
function bubble_sort(&$array)
{
  // Read contents with one index.
  for ($i = 0;$i < count($array);$i++)
  {
    // Read contents with another index.
    for ($j = 0;$j < count($array);$j++)
    {
      // Check outer less than inner or switch by reference.
      if ($array[$i] < $array[$j])
        swap($array[$i],$array[$j]);
    }
  }
}

// Performs a classic cocktail sort passing array by reference.
function cocktail_sort(&$array)
{
  // Declare logical control variable.
  $done = false;

  // Declare boundary variables.
  $left = 0;
  $right = count($array);

  do
  {
    // Set exit criteria.
    $done = true;

    // Decrement right boundary to avoid index overrun.
    --$right;
```

```
    // Read from left to right boundary.
    for ($i = $left;$i < $right;$i++)
    {
      // Check current greater than next and switch by reference.
      if ($array[$i] > $array[$i+1])
        swap($array[$i],$array[$i+1]);
        $done = false;
    }

    // Read from right to left boundary.
    for ($i = $right;$i > $left;$i--)
    {
      // Check current less than next and switch by reference.
      if ($array[$i] < $array[$i-1])
        swap($array[$i],$array[$i-1]);
        $done = false;
    }

    // Increment left boundary.
    $left++;

  } while (!$done);
}

// Swap two variables by reference.
function swap(&$a,&$b)
{
  $c = $a;
  $a = $b;
  $b = $c;
}
?>
```

The output generated from the `DynamicFunctionCall.php` program is

```
[Array ( [0] => 1 [1] => 2 [2] => 3 [3] => 4 [4] => 5 [5] => 6 [6] => 7 ) ]
[Array ( [0] => 2 [1] => 3 [2] => 4 [3] => 5 [4] => 6 [5] => 7 [6] => 8 ) ]
```

This is a powerful tool, but there is one caveat to using it. When you call a function dynamically, the logic should ensure that all functions have the same signature. Having the same signature means that they have the same count of parameters. Alternatively, you can easily pass a single parameter, provided it is an array that contains the list of arguments. This approach leverages variable-length parameter lists covered earlier in the chapter.

Using Recursive Functions

The ability of a function to call a copy of itself is called *recursion*. Recursion is useful to solve many types of programming problems, such as parsing and node tree searches. There are two types of recursion: linear and nonlinear. In linear recursion, a function calls only one copy of itself each time. In nonlinear recursion, a function calls more than one copy of itself each time.

The only problem with recursion is that it consumes large amounts of system resources. For example, PHP *programs that perform over 200 recursive calls run the risk of collapsing the PHP stack,* which would mean a depth of 200 linear recursions. Nonlinear recursions require more memory and will probably collapse the PHP stack in half or less the depth of a linear recursion.

The following `Recursion.php` program demonstrates linear recursion by using the classic factorial problem:

-- **This is found in Recursion.php on the enclosed CD**.

```php
<?php
  // Call the recursive program.
  print "[factorial(7)] = [".factorial(7)."]<br>";

  // Define a recursive function that returns a double.
  function factorial($var)
  {
    // Check number of actual parameters.
    if (count($argv = func_get_args()) == 1);
    {
      if ($argv[0] <= 1)
        return (double) 1;
      else
        return (double) $argv[0] * factorial($argv[0] - 1);
    }
  }
?>
```

The program calls the `factorial()` function; and the `factorial()` function validates the argument list before proceeding with the calculation. If the actual parameter is not less than or equal to 1, the function calls one more copy of itself. The nested call will check the same exit condition and call itself again until it meets the exit condition of being 1 or less. The `Recursion.php` program will call itself six times before meeting the exit condition. Once the exit condition is met, it will start returning values from the deepest level to the original external call to the function.

It is unlikely that you need to use recursion to resolve mathematical problems. On the other hand, you will need to format many HTML tables. Some tables can contain one or more nested tables, and the nested tables can occur in different rows or columns. While you could write a number of programs to manage the different scenarios, writing one recursive function can make your life easier.

The following `RecursiveArray.php` program assumes a single format for each table to render a slightly modified multidimensional array from Chapter 6:

-- **This is found in RecursiveArray.php on the enclosed CD**.

```php
<?php
  // Declare an asymmetrical multidimensional array.
  $tolkien = array
              ("Bilbo"=>array
                  ("Hobbit"=>"Who slew a dragon for dwarves."
                  ,"Fellowship"=>"Left the ring for Frodo."
```

```
                    ,"Return of the King"=>array
                        ("Action 1"=>"Destroyed the one ring."
                        ,"Action 2"=>"Left middle earth."))
                 ,"Frodo"=>array
                    ("Fellowship"=>"Who inherited the ring."
                    ,"Return of the King"=>"Who destroyed the ring.")
                 ,"Gildor"=>"A high elf met on the road."
                 ,"Sam"=>array
                    ("Fellowship"=>"An eavesdropper at the window."
                    ,"Two Towers"=>"A lone companion of Frodo."
                    ,"Return of the King"=>"A ring bearer too.")
                 );


   // Print the table and nested tables.
   print nested_tables($tolkien);

   // A recursive program for rendering nested tables.
   function nested_tables($array_in)
   {
     // Declare variable with table start.
     $output = "<table border=0 cellpadding=0 cellspacing=0>";

     // Read and add array keys and values to a string.
     foreach ($array_in as $hashName => $hashValue)
     {
       // Append row tag and first column value.
       $output .= "<tr><td valign=top>[".$hashName."]</td>";

       // Check column value for nested array.
       if (is_array($hashValue))
       {
         // Call recursively a copy of itself with cell tags.
         $output .= "<td>".nested_tables($hashValue)."</td></tr>";
       }
       else
       {
         // Append non-array value with cell tags.
         $output .= "<td>[".$hashValue."]</td></tr>";
       }
     }

     // Close HTML table.
     $output .= "</table>";

     // Return the HTML table.
     return $output;
   }
?>
```

The program renders an HTML table when you submit a single-dimensional or multidimensional array; and multidimensional arrays can be asymmetrical or symmetrical. The `RecursiveArray.php` program produces the following output for the asymmetrical multidimensional array:

[Bilbo]	[Hobbit]	[Who slew a dragon for dwarves.]
	[Fellowship]	[Left the ring for Frodo.]
	[Return of the King]	[Action 1] [Destroyed the one ring.]
		[Action 2] [Left middle earth.]
[Frodo]	[Fellowship]	[Who inherited the ring.]
	[Return of the King]	[Who destroyed the ring.]
[Gildor]	[A high elf met on the road.]	
[Sam]	[Fellowship]	[An eavesdropper at the window.]
	[Two Towers]	[A lone companion of Frodo.]
	[Return of the King]	[A ring bearer too.]

The `nested_tables()` function provides a single set of code that enables you to process various scenarios of nested tables or ordinary single-dimensional tables. The recursive test is a little bit trickier to see, but it is done by the `if` statement that checks if a hash value is an array.

TIP
Where possible, you should look for recursive solutions because they can simplify your code.

NOTE
Make sure when you call recursively that you pass the hash value, not the original array variable, which would cause an infinite recursive loop that will crash your Apache server.

You have covered recursive functions and learned to be cautious of how deep your recursions may go before implementing them in your solution set. The collapse of the stack is a fatal error.

Summary
You have learned how to define, manage, and use functions. These skills will enable you to build modular code where appropriate and position you to understand object technology in the next chapter.

CHAPTER
8

Objects

his chapter examines how you define, initialize, and use objects. It lays a foundation of what objects are and how object-oriented (OO) programming works by covering the following topics:

- Defining and using objects
  - Defining and instantiating objects
  - Defining and using variables, constants, and operations
  - Getters and setters
- Defining and using inheritance and polymorphism
  - Building subclasses and overriding operations
  - Using abstract classes and interfaces
- Implementing objects
  - Cloning objects
  - Comparing objects, printing objects, and type hinting
  - Using object reflection

As discussed in the last chapter, procedural programming functions perform well-defined tasks, and they hide the details of their operation. A collection of functions can be grouped together to perform a task that requires a set of functions. Organized groups of functions are *modules*; and the process of grouping them together is *modularization.*

Modules, like functions, hide their complexity through a predefined *application programming interface (API).* Likewise, modules also mirror functions by performing operations on run-time variables. Functions do not maintain the data values of variables except in the limited scope of acting on them. The data values of variables are also known as their *operational state.* The lack of state management means that they have limits on their use and reusability.

Object-oriented (OO) programming solutions fix some of the shortcoming of functions and modules because they maintain the operational state of variables. Object types define how to store data and define API operations, also known as functions or methods. Operations are generally described as methods in OO programming languages, but they are implemented as class functions in PHP.

Exploring where OO programming started helps explain why maintaining object state is important. The idea for OO programming comes from the Simula language developed in Norway in the 1960s. The concept of an object evolved from the idea that simulated events pass through many small software factories, known as "finite-state" or "state" machines. State machines are miniature applications that simulate real-world events.

The object that moves through the series of state machines is like a software equivalent to a ball in a physical pinball machine. The software "ball" isn't really moving in response to mechanical devices but in response to state machines that simulate bumpers and other physical objects. The velocity, spin, and direction of the software ball are its internal state, which must be known and tracked to determine where it will strike and at what speed and spin. These factors determine how the next bumper, or state machine, will impact the software ball.

The possible characteristics and behaviors of the software ball are its attributes and operations. Since each ball starts with the same characteristics and behaviors, you can define a single piece of code to contain these attributes. The single piece of code you build to do this is defined as an object type, or blueprint. Each creation of a run-time unit of this code is an instantiation, or creation of an object.

Objects are also state machines. They are defined by variables that have known and unknown values; and these variables enable or constrain the operations of real-time instances. Object type instances are objects, though realistically this formalism seems lost more often than not. Object types and objects are also known as classes in many OO programming languages. This book uses *object types to describe definitions of objects and objects to describe run-time instances of object types*; and interchangeably *classes to describe definitions of objects and instances of classes to describe run-time instances of object types.*

Inside of these object types and instances of objects you have hidden data and operations. The process of hiding data storage and operations is described by two words in OO programming. The first is *encapsulation*—the process of hiding the operational details; and the second is *abstraction*— the process of using generalization to mask task complexity. The internal aspects of object types are wrapped, as a birthday present is wrapped by colorful paper. The wrappers access the hidden components through published operations, which as described earlier are often called methods and implemented in PHP as functions.

These hidden operations and data plus their wrapper operations require OO programmers to take some time to work out what should be an object and then to define the object type. This analysis and design process is called object-oriented analysis and design (OOAD). OOAD evolved from concepts in systems engineering and business process modeling. It has gone through several variations from the 1960s, including symbolic representation models like Booch and object-modeling technique (OMT). These models were merged into the Unified Modeling Language (UML) in the 1990s.

The current method for visually representing object types is generally done in UML. Object types are represented by a rectangle divided into three rectangular sections. The topmost section contains the object type name. The middle section contains the list of attributes, which are variables used in the object type. The bottom section contains the list of methods that describes the API to the object type or object. Figure 8-1 contains a sample UML diagram describing the `MyClass` object type.

OO programming has two types of API interfaces in object types. One, known as *static,* allows you to access object type variables and methods without creating an instance of a class. Static variables and methods are available like procedural libraries after the class is defined in your environment.

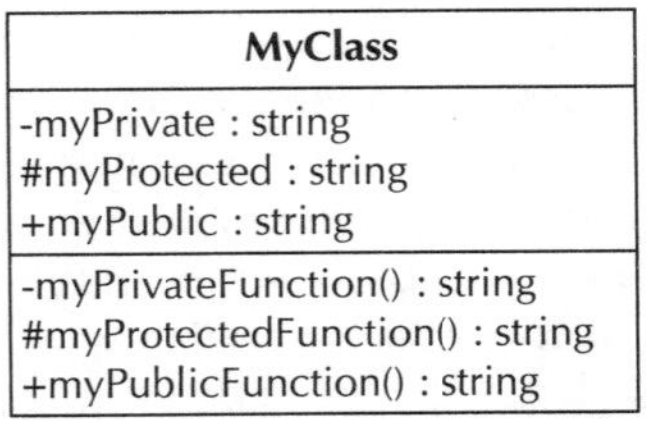

MyClass
-myPrivate : string #myProtected : string +myPublic : string
-myPrivateFunction() : string #myProtectedFunction() : string +myPublicFunction() : string

FIGURE 8-1.   *UML class diagram*

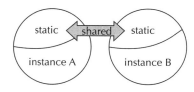

FIGURE 8-2. *Shared static area of objects*

The other type allows you to access object variables and methods of an instance of a class. They *are not static* and are only available when an instance of the class is built to manage an event.

The static area of an object type exists only once in your environment. As you create class instances, the static area becomes a shared area, as shown in Figure 8-2.

The static area of objects is generally limited to variables and functions that are common features across all class instances. Instances can exchange messages by using the static area of an object type much as operating system threads share a process control block. You will cover more about how objects share the static area later in this chapter.

You will now learn how to define and implement objects in PHP. While the sections are written independently, they are positioned to be read sequentially.

Defining and Using Objects

The same naming requirements as those used with functions apply to objects. Object names in PHP must start with an alphabetical character or underscore and consist of only alphabetical characters, numbers, or underscores. *Object names are global in scope and case insensitive,* as are functions. Prior to PHP 5, you can only have one class definition per page. *PHP 5 enables you to define multiple classes in a single program script,* avoiding all that prior nonsense with one class per file and the __autoload function, which you used to put all class files into the working environment. That being said, if you like the one-class-per-file model, you can still use it by leveraging the __autoload function.

Scope for PHP classes is global, as it is for functions, and enables you to use them anywhere in your programs. Only classes, functions, and global constants, those built by using the define() function, enjoy global environment scope.

Classes, unlike functions, cannot have return types. Class instantiation returns a copy or instance of a class. While object construction generally occurs as the source operand on the right side of an assignment operator, you can construct an object instance as an actual parameter to a function, or as a member of an array. The object instance existence is limited to the duration of the function or its membership as a component of an array variable.

You will find that objects are similar to those in many other languages but different enough to review the object operators. These are the operators that work in PHP 5. Table 8-1 provides a set of definitions that will help you read subsequent example programs in this chapter.

Having met with the general concepts, you will now work through the specifics of implementing these in PHP. You will begin by learning how to define and instantiate objects.

Operator	Description
::	The *scope resolution operator* enables you to refer to class or instance variables and functions. It is a binary operator. A class name, `parent` operator, or `self` operator must precede the scope resolution operator as its left operand. A class constant, a static variable or static function, or the `$this` operator can be the right operand. Using anything else as the right operand will raise a fatal exception. The prototype for using the scope resolution operator to reset a class variable is `ClassName::$ClassVariable = "new value";`

->	The pointer operator points to a member variable or function of an object instance. The pointer operator is a binary operator. The left operand can be `$this` or a variable holding an instance of the class, while the right operand is an instance variable or function. *The $this operator must precede the operator inside a class definition,* as the instance of an object. Outside of a class definition, the variable holding an instance of a class must precede the member variable pointer, and the class variable or function follows it. You can also *refer to a superclass by using the* `parent::$this->variable` *or* `parent::$this->function` *syntax.* The pointer operator prototype outside of a class is shown by using the instance variable as the left operand of an assignment operation:
	
	`$ClassVariableName->InstanceVariable = "new value";`
	Alternatively, the pointer operator outside of a class can point to a function, which in this case takes an actual parameter and returns nothing:
	
	`$ClassVariableName->Function("parameter");`

clone	The `clone` operator enables you to copy an instance of a class to a new instance of the same class. The `clone` operator is a binary operator. It uses variable assignment as the left operand, while the right operand must contain an instance of an object type. The prototype for cloning an object instance is: `$NewClassVariable = clone $OldClassVariable;`
instanceof	The `instanceof` operator enables you to check whether a variable is an instance of an object type. Its use mirrors that of a comparison operator, returning true when an instance is derived from an object type and false when not. The `instanceof` is a binary operator, which takes a variable holding a class instance as the left operand and the name of an object type as the right operand. It has the following prototype as a conditional expression: `if ($ClassVariable instanceof ClassName)`
new	The new operator enables you to build an instance of a class definition. The `new` operator is a binary operator. It uses variable assignment as the left operand, while the right operand must contain a constructor of an object type. The prototype for using the new operator is: `$NewClassVariable = new ClassName("parameter");`

parent	The `parent` operator refers to a superclass of an object, and *you can only use it in the class definition of a subclass or in the scope of an internal class function.* You can use it in the `__construct()` and `__destruct()` predefined functions. The parent operator uses the scope resolution operator to reference constants, static variables, or functions, and the `$this` operator, which precedes nonstatic variables and functions. The prototype for assigning values from superclass constants and static variables from within a subclass is:
	
	`$NewVariable = parent::classVariable;`
	While the prototype for calling superclass static functions from within subclasses is:
	
	`$NewVariable = parent::functionName("parameter");`
	Calling superclass instance variables and functions requires using a combination of the parent and scope resolution operators, like the following subclass function call to a superclass:
	
	`$NewVariable = parent::$this->function("parameter");`

TABLE 8-1. *Object Operators*

Operator	Description

self	The `self` operator refers to a local class of an object and *you can only use it in the definition of a class or in the scope of an internal class function.* You can use it in the `__construct()` and `__destruct()` predefined functions. The `self` operator uses the scope resolution operator to reference constants, static variables, or functions, and the `$this` operator, which precedes nonstatic variables and functions. The prototype for assigning values from class constants and static variables from within a class is:
	
	`$NewVariable = self::classVariable;`
	
	The prototype for calling class static functions from within the same classes is:
	
	`$NewVariable = self::functionName("parameter");`

$this	This operator refers to the local instance of a class, and you can only implement it in the definition of a class. The scope limits require you to use it in an internal function, which can include the `__construct()` and `__destruct()` predefined functions. The `$this` operator combined with the pointer operator enables you to access instance variables and functions. The following prototype represents assigning a value to an instance variable within a class:
	
	`$this->classVariable = "new value";`
	
	The following prototype represents calling an instance function that returns no value:
	
	`$this->classFunction("parameter");`

TABLE 8-1.   *Object Operators* (continued)

Defining and Instantiating Objects

PHP objects, like functions, have a prototype definition that includes the `class` keyword and the body of the object type in curly braces:

```
class object_name { object_body }
```

The PHP object prototype is very similar to other OO programming languages, especially the C++ syntax. All classes are publicly accessible, which is consistent with their global scope. The concept of access modifiers is new in PHP 5, and they are covered in the next section. As you may have noticed in the preceding object operator table, *there are some restrictions to when and where certain operators can be used in objects.*

Building a basic class and constructing an instance of it will enable you to see how PHP objects work. The following program defines a **BasicObject** class, declares a public class instance variable, creates an instance of the class, and prints the class variable:

```
-- This is found in BasicObject1.php on the enclosed CD.
```

```php
<?php
  // Declare a variable to hold an object instance.
  $myObject = new BasicObject();

  // Print an instance variable.
  print "[\$myObject->name] is: [".$myObject->name."]<br />";

  // Define a class that prints a message.
  class BasicObject
```

```
  {
    // Declare public instance variable.
    public $name = "BasicObject";
  }
?>
```

The PHP parser reads classes into memory immediately after placing functions into the global environment scope, as discussed in Chapter 7. The two-phase parse operation prevents class construction from failing because a class is not previously defined in the program scope.

The BasicObject class definition does one thing. It declares a public class variable, which can be accessed after constructing an instance of the object. The balance of the program constructs an instance of the BasicObject class using the new operator and references the public class instance variable.

When you build an object instance without an explicit constructor, the class typically uses the default constructor provided by the compiler. This is a no argument constructor. The BasicObject1.php program uses the default constructor to build an instance of the BasicObject class and prints the following output to a page:

[$myObject->name] is: [BasicObject]

The first class example relies on the default constructor and destructor functions provided implicitly for you by the PHP engine. Object constructors are like functions and have signatures that contain zero to many parameters in a list. The PHP default constructor, like the default constructor in Java, takes no formal parameter. *You cannot override the PHP default constructor signature without implementing an overriding constructor of your own.*

The constructor and destructor functions are class operations or methods. You can *override the default constructor by using the __construct() function*; and you can *override the default destructor by using the __destruct() function.* The __construct() function is called when you instantiate an instance of an object type with the new operator. The __destruct() function is called when you no longer hold a reference to an object instance, which may be at the time a PHP page is rendered.

The BasicObject2.php program demonstrates both the __construct() and __destruct() functions. The program defines a single parameter to build an instance of the BasicObject class and assigns an actual parameter to a publicly accessible instance variable $name. It prints a statement at construction entrance and destruction exit.

The BasicObject2.php program follows:

-- This is found in BasicObject2.php on the enclosed CD.

```
<?php
  // Declare a variable to hold an object instance.
  $myObject1 = new BasicObject("Instance of Basic Object");

  // Define a class that prints a message.
  class BasicObject
  {
    // Declare public instance variables.
    public $name = "BasicObject";

    function __construct($variable)
```

```
    {
      // Check for valid run-time parameter.
      if (isset($variable))
      {
        // Message on entrance.
        print "[Constructing Instance [".$variable."]<br />";

        // Reset class variable to instance variable.
        $this->name = $variable;
      }
    }

    function __destruct()
    {
      // Message on exit.
      print "[Destructing Instance [".$this->name."]<br />";
    }
  }
?>
```

Missing mandatory actual parameters will not cause a fatal error but will change the desired behavior of your class at run time. A missing or incorrect actual parameter can create undesired outcomes at run time. You should design classes with default variables that can be substituted when actual parameters are incomplete or incorrect.

There are two approaches to building these default class instance variables. You can define an instance variable in your class definition, or you can provide a default value for the variable in the constructor function. The code demonstrates the former, but the latter would have the following form:

```
    function __construct($variable="BasicObject")
    {
      // Message on entrance.
      print "[Constructing Instance [".$variable."]<br />";

      // Reset class variable to instance variable.
      $this->name = $variable;
    }
```

The difference between approaches is that the former requires that you verify the actual parameter is passed into the overriding constructor while the latter simply provides a default value. When you opt to provide default values as part of the signature, object construction is limited to that signature, unless you pass an array and assign an empty array by default.

Attempting to construct an object instance without providing a mandatory formal parameter to an overriding constructor can raise a warning message. *All class function formal parameters are assumed mandatory unless you provide a default value.* BasicObject2.php raises a warning message when you have enabled the display_errors directive in the php.ini file.

When you provide an overriding constructor to a PHP class, the implicit default constructor is no longer available. While other OO programming languages support the definition of overloaded constructors, PHP does not. *You can have only one overriding constructor per class.* The constraint on overloaded constructors does not present a limit because *you can use flexible parameter lists in class constructors.* You can refer to coverage of flexible parameter passing in Chapter 7.

When you don't use flexible parameter passing, you should proactively check if desired actual parameters are provided at run time. In the `BasicObject2.php` program, the `isset()` function traps whether or not it receives a run-time parameter when an object instance is built. The `BasicObject` constructor takes a parameter and replaces the default class variable `$name` contents with a run-time value.

TIP
Production environments disable the `display_errors` *directive in the* `php.ini` *file. You should ensure you check for defined run-time parameters when you have defined any in your overriding class constructor.*

The `BasicObject2.php` file uses the overriding constructor and destructor functions to render the following output to a page:

```
[Constructing Instance [Instance of Basic Object]
[Destructing Instance [Instance of Basic Object]
```

You have learned how to define and build classes in PHP and been exposed to basics components of classes. More features of object variables, constants, and operations are covered in the next sections.

Defining and Using Variables, Constants, and Operators

PHP 5 supports the use of static and nonstatic variables and operations; and it supports the use of class constants. Static variables and class constants are accessed by similar means but *you cannot reassign the value of a constant.* You can reassign the value of a static variable at run time. Class operations in PHP are class functions, which can be either static or nonstatic. Static variables and functions do not require you to create a class instance before using them. Nonstatic variables and functions do require you to create a class instance before using them.

There is only one copy of static class variables and constants in your PHP environment. These static variables and constants are accessible by your static class methods by using the scope resolution operator. When you build conditional and iterative logic in static functions, you can reference static variables or constants. You have a choice of making these function behaviors dynamic or static.

Static class functions act like ordinary functions and rely on external variables to govern their behaviors. The variables that govern behavior can be globally scoped PHP variables but are generally static class variables or constants. When two or more static class functions work together cooperatively, they often use shared static class variables. Static class variables are shared resources that can have private scope within the class.

Static class functions perform operations that are consistently executed across all instances of classes. These are collocated in classes because they are essential to class operations. While the alternative is placing them in library functions, doing so often makes little sense when you are applying OO programming concepts. Static class functions generally perform unchanging and predefined tasks, which are typically best served by using class constants.

On the other hand, you have nonstatic functions that change behaviors according to the run-time state of a class instance. The changes typically exist as a result of how you constructed or acted on class instances. You make decisions about designating a class variable or function as static or nonstatic by considering its intended use.

In addition to static, there are three access modifiers introduced in PHP 5: public, protected, and private. These are called *access modifiers* because they affect the scope of access to variables and functions. PHP 5 provides a `final` keyword that enables you to prevent overriding a class method by a subclass, and that acts as an access modifier governing inherited behaviors.

NOTE
You cannot make a variable final, as in Java, because final variables are constants in PHP.

Table 8-2 provides descriptions of the five class access modifiers.

NOTE
Prior to PHP 5 all class variables acted like public variables. It is still the expectation of some predefined functions that all class variables are public, like the `get_class_vars()` *function. Therefore, the* `get_class_vars()` *function will return only publicly accessible variables in PHP 5.*

Class instance variables differ from general variables in that you must provide a class access modifier. The class access modifier precedes the variable name whether you are defining or declaring the variable. The prototype for defining a class variable is

```
[ static ] modifier $var;
```

Access Modifier	UML Notation	Description
final		The final access modifier ensures that a class function cannot be overridden by a subclass implementation. *The final modifier can only apply to functions.*
private	–	The private access modifier hides a variable or function from direct external class access. A public class function can indirectly access private class variables and functions. Both *private class variables and functions are hidden from all subclasses of a class.*
protected	#	The protected access modifier hides a variable or function from direct external class access. A public function can indirectly access protected class variables and functions. Both *protected class variables and functions are available from subclasses of a class.*
public	+	The public access modifier, or default behavior, publishes class variables and functions.
static		The `static` keyword designates a variable or function as accessible without creating a class instance.

TABLE 8-2. *Class Access Modifiers*

Class functions are not as particular and may be included without qualifying a class access modifier. Without a class access modifier, a function is considered to have a default access modifier, which is public. The UML convention for default or friendly behavior in object-oriented analysis and design is to leave it blank. The prototype for a class function is

```
[ final ] [ static ] [ modifier ]
  function function_name( [ $var [, $var ] ] ) { function_body }
```

The following program demonstrates that you can access private, protected, and public variables from a public function. Public class functions have access to all class instance variables regardless of their access modifier. Nonstatic public class functions can also reference static variables and functions, provided they treat them as external to the class instance. You can do this by using the *ClassName*::$*VariableName* or *ClassName*::*FunctionName*() syntax inside a class function.

The BasicObject3.php program file demonstrates these nonstatic behaviors by defining a BasicObject class with overriding constructor and destructor functions and a public set_variables() function. The program create an instance of BasicObject and then calls the set_variables() function to reset the private, protected, and public class variables. The constructor displays the class type by using the reserved word __CLASS__, which can be used only inside a class definition. __CLASS__ returns the name of the object type.

The BasicObject3.php program follows:

-- This is found in BasicObject3.php on the enclosed CD.

```php
<?php
  // Declare an object instance.
  $myObject = new BasicObject();

  // Print line break.
  print "<hr />";

  // Reset the class instance variables.
  $myObject->set_variables("Reset Private"
                          ,"Reset Protected"
                          ,"Reset Public");

  // Define a class that prints a message.
  class BasicObject
  {
    // Declare class variables.
    private $myPrivate = "Privately Scoped Variable";
    protected $myProtected = "Protected Scoped Variable";
    public $myPublic = "Public Scoped Variable";

    public function __construct()
    {
      // Message on entrance.
      print "This is an [".__CLASS__."] instance.<br />";
      print "<hr />";
      print "Private Variable [".$this->myPrivate."]<br />";
```

```
    print "Protected Variable [".$this->myProtected."]<br />";
    print "Public Variable [".$this->myPublic."]<br />";
  }

  public function __destruct()
  {
    // Message on exit.
    print "Private Variable [".$this->myPrivate."]<br />";
    print "Protected Variable [".$this->myProtected."]<br />";
    print "Public Variable [".$this->myPublic."]<br />";
  }

  public function set_variables($private,$protected,$public)
  {
    $this->myPrivate = $private;
    $this->myProtected = $protected;
    $this->myPublic = $public;
  }
}
```

The overriding constructor prints the initial value of the class variables, and the overriding destructor prints their altered values. The following output is rendered by the `BasicObject3.php` program:

```
This is an [BasicObject] instance.
-------------------------------------------------------------
Private Variable [Privately Scoped Variable]
Protected Variable [Protected Scoped Variable]
Public Variable [Public Scoped Variable]
-------------------------------------------------------------
Private Variable [Reset Private]
Protected Variable [Reset Protected]
Public Variable [Reset Public]
```

The preceding program demonstrated nonstatic class variables and functions. While class instances are frequently used, sometimes you need class variables and functions that are available for all instances of an object type. You accomplish sharing class structures between class instances by defining them as static variables and functions.

Static class variables are not dependable structures to set initial object states, because they can be changed before instantiating a class instance of an object type. While you can use a private static variable like a constant, future versions of the code may introduce a setter function. The setter function can eliminate the restriction implemented by making the class variable scope private, and destabilize your application. You should implement a class constant when the program requires a known initial state value.

The `BasicObject4.php` program demonstrates defining static variables and methods by modifying the `BasicObject3.php` program. The modified program redefines the class variables as static ones. It also redefines the `set_variables()` function as a public static function. The other changes from the `BasicObject3.php` program include replacing the pointer object operator with the scope resolution operator.

The BasicObject4.php program follows:

```php
<?php
  // Reset the class instance variables.
  BasicObject::set_variables("Reset Private"
                            ,"Reset Protected"
                            ,"Reset Public");

  // Declare an object instance.
  $myObject = new BasicObject();

  // Print line break.
  print "<hr />";

  // Define a class that prints a message.
  class BasicObject
  {
    // Declare class variables.
    private static $myPrivate = "Privately Scoped Variable";
    protected static $myProtected = "Protected Scoped Variable";
    public static $myPublic = "Public Scoped Variable";

    public function __construct()
    {
      // Message on entrance.
      print "This is an [".__CLASS__."] instance.<br />";
      print "<hr />";
      print "Private Variable [".BasicObject::$myPrivate."]<br />";
      print "Protected Variable [".BasicObject::$myProtected."]<br />";
      print "Public Variable [".BasicObject::$myPublic."]<br />";
    }

    public function __destruct()
    {
      // Message on entrance.
      print "Private Variable [".BasicObject::$myPrivate."]<br />";
      print "Protected Variable [".BasicObject::$myProtected."]<br />";
      print "Public Variable [".BasicObject::$myPublic."]<br />";
    }

    public static function set_variables($private,$protected,$public)
    {
      BasicObject::$myPrivate = $private;
      BasicObject::$myProtected = $protected;
      BasicObject::$myPublic = $public;
    }
  }
?>
```

As demonstrated by the following output, the `BasicObject4.php` program demonstrates that static variables can change before class instantiation:

```
This is an [BasicObject] instance.
--------------------------------------------------------------
Private Variable [Reset Private]
Protected Variable [Reset Protected]
Public Variable [Reset Public]
--------------------------------------------------------------
Private Variable [Reset Private]
Protected Variable [Reset Protected]
Public Variable [Reset Public]
```

You use the following to declare a class constant named `A_CONSTANT` with a scalar string value:

```
const A_CONSTANT = "Scalar Value";
```

Class constants do not use access modifiers and cannot change once defined. They have class-level scope and are accessed by using the scope resolution operator. The following demonstrates how you would assign a constant `A_CONSTANT` defined in the `BasicClass` object type:

```
$var = BasicClass::A_CONSTANT;
```

The benefits of constants are twofold. First, they have a single declaration. Second, they are externally available from classes or instances of classes. While the external visibility of class constants provides programming flexibilities, it violates a principle of object-oriented programming—encapsulation. Class constants are not hidden from public access or view because they do not support access modifiers.

You can create private static variables for your constants to enforce encapsulation. The private class variables mimic the behavior of constants, by hiding them from view. However, you must avoid providing static or nonstatic functions that enable the pseudo-constants to change.

Getters and Setters

Getters and setters are common OO programming terms indicating that you get or set a class variable. In many OO programming languages, you need to write individual `getVariable()` or `setVariable($var)` functions. You can write these custom getters and setters, or you can overload the functionality with the `__get()` and `__set()` functions in PHP. Overloaded functions can only be used with nonstatic variables.

The `__get()` and `__set()` functions have the following prototypes:

```
mixed __get( $var );
void __set( $var );
```

You need to provide implementations for overloaded getter and setter functions. The following `GetAndSet.php` program demonstrates how to implement these functions:

```
-- This is found in GetAndSet.php on the enclosed CD.

<?php
  // Declare a variable to hold an object instance.
```

```
$myObject = new BasicObject();

// Print an instance variable.
print "[__get()] [".$myObject->__get("instanceName")."]<br />";

// Print the __set() call.
print "[__set()] [\"instanceName\",\"New\")]<br />";

// Reset the name instance variable.
$myObject->__set("instanceName","New");

// Print an instance variable.
print "[__get()] [".$myObject->__get("instanceName")."]<br />";

// Define a class that prints a message.
class BasicObject
{
  // Declare public instance variable.
  public $instanceName = "Old";

  // Define overloaded getter.
  public function __get($var)
  {
    return $this->$var;
  }

  // Define overloaded setter.
  public function __set($key,$value)
  {
    $this->$key = $value;
  }
}
?>
```

You pass a string into the overloaded getter, which maps to an instance variable name. The overloaded setter takes two string variables, which map to the instance variable name and value respectively. The balance of the program simply manages calling and printing the demonstration output, like the following:

```
[__get()]  [Old]
[__set()]  ["instanceName","New")]
[__get()]  [New]
```

The benefit of implementing the overloaded getter and setter functions is that you have a common interface to all nonstatic class variables. The harm of implementing these is that you must disclose the variable names. In OO programming this approach is tightly coupled and ill-advised. You should strongly consider defining your own custom getters and setters that hide your class variable names.

You have covered how to define and use class variables, constants, and operators in static and nonstatic operations. The discussion has focused on individual class definitions and behaviors. The next section will expand the discussion by examining how you extend the functionality of your classes to subclasses.

Defining and Using Inheritance and Polymorphism

Object-oriented (OO) programming languages demand a change in thinking, but sometimes you may find yourself asking why. The foregoing part of this chapter explains the mechanics of building object types as libraries. You can also build libraries by developing a collection of functions. While building libraries of object types requires more effort and design than building collections of functions, the return on your investment of time is their extensibility.

Objects are extensible because you can add to their capabilities by building subclasses. *Subclasses* inherit the behaviors of other class, which become known as *superclasses*. Subclasses can also override the behaviors of their superclass by creating functions to replace superclass functions. The idea that subclasses extend and change behaviors of their superclasses is termed *morphing*. *Polymorphing* is the process of multiple subclasses inheriting the behaviors of superclasses.

The classic example is a generalized class that defines a vehicle. You can develop specializations of the vehicle class by building car, motorcycle, truck, and van subclasses. These subclasses extend the general variables and functions provided by the vehicle class and in some cases provide overriding functions. The specialized functions manage the differences between driving a car or riding a motorcycle. When the vehicle class is subclassed, the vehicle class is promoted and called a superclass.

Objects inherit and polymorph behaviors by extending base behaviors in an organized tree called an object *hierarchy*. Object hierarchies contain libraries of object types, which are reusable programming units, or in the OO programming lexicon, reusable code artifacts.

Like the static and nonstatic class variables and functions discussed earlier, reusability has many facets. Using static variables and functions to exchange information between class instances enables you to position reusable class components. These static structures have general use across all or many class instances and support sharing function and variable states.

Subclasses are created according to two patterns: single inheritance and multiple inheritance. Single-tree OO programming languages, such as Java, support the single-inheritance model. C++ supports a multiple-inheritance model. The single-inheritance model is represented in Figure 8-3.

The semantics of Java and PHP support only the single-inheritance model, but realistically, you can use the OO principle of aggregation to overcome this limitation. Inheritance is a specialized form of aggregation, which you can implement without much effort. Ordinary aggregation requires you to define a class variable of another class, instantiate an instance of the class, and develop function wrappers that redirect action to the class instance functions. You can implement inheritance and aggregation in the same class and mimic the multiple-inheritance model.

Inheritance means that you define a class as a child of a parent class—a subclass of a class. When you create an instance of the subclass, you get an instance that has the behaviors of the parent class and subclass. If a subclass provides a function that has the same name as a parent class function, the subclass function overrides the parent class function. This means that when you call the function, it will implement the subclass function, not the parent class function.

The power of OO programming exists in extending generalized behaviors and organizing variables and functions into real-world object types. You have learned how to build and access object types and instances of objects. In the next two sections, you will learn how to extend general classes into subclasses.

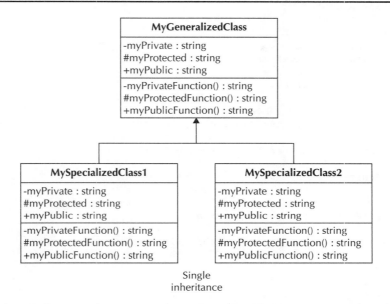

FIGURE 8-3. *Single-inheritance UML model*

Building Subclasses and Overriding Operations

In this section, you will learn how to build subclasses from classes and then how to override operations of parent classes. The next example demonstrates how you build subclasses to extend classes.

The Inheritance1.php program defines a BasicObject class and a subclass DerivedObject that extends the BasicObject class. The BasicObject class contains a protected getInstanceName() function that returns the instanceName value, while the DerivedObject does not provide a function by that name. Both overriding constructors print the __CLASS__ value and class instanceName. The subclass also calls the protected class getInstanceName() function that is inherited from the superclass only.

You should note that the protected access modifier is used for the referenced class variable and function. Class variables must be either protected or public to be available to subclasses. A subclass cannot reduce the privileges of an inherited superclass variable or method, which means protected superclass structures must be implemented as protected or public structures in the subclasses.

The Inheritance1.php program follows:

-- **This is found in Inheritance1.php on the enclosed CD.**

```php
<?php
  // Declare a variable to hold a superclass object instance.
  $myObject1 = new BasicObject("Class");

  // Declare a variable to hold a subclass object instance.
  $myObject2 = new DerivedObject("Subclass");
```

```
// Define a class.
class BasicObject
{
  // Declare instance variable.
  protected $instanceName = "";

  function __construct($instanceName)
  {
    // Message on entrance.
    print "[Constructing Instance [".__CLASS__."] [".$instanceName."]<br />";

    // Assign parameter to instance variable.
    if (isset($instanceName))
      $this->instanceName = $instanceName;
  }

  protected function getInstanceName()
  {
    return "[".__CLASS__."] [".$this->instanceName."]<br />";
  }
}

// Define a subclass.
class DerivedObject extends BasicObject
{
  // Declare instance variable.
  protected $instanceName = "";

  function __construct($instanceName)
  {
    // Message on entrance.
    print "[Constructing Instance [".__CLASS__."] [".$instanceName."]<br />";

    // Assign parameter to instance variable.
    if (isset($instanceName))
      $this->instanceName = $instanceName;

    // Call parent method as self.
    print self::getInstanceName();
  }
}
?>
```

The `Inheritance1.php` program will produce the following output:

```
[Constructing Instance [BasicObject] [Class]
[Constructing Instance [DerivedObject] [Subclass]
[BasicObject] [Subclass]
```

The call to `self::getInstanceName()` prints the parent `__CLASS__`, but the `$this` is relative to the subclass where the function was invoked. This demonstrates that the run-time `DerivedObject` instance contains a reference to the `BasicObject` variables and functions. These references are accessed by the `self` or `parent` object operators.

When a function only exists in the superclass, you can use self or parent interchangeably with the same result, but they have different processes. The self object operator examines whether there is a local class function before checking the parent class to find a function. If the immediate parent class contains the function, the self object operator will run it. When the immediate parent class doesn't contain the function, the self object operator will check for a superclass of that parent. If the function is not found in any parent superclass, the program will raise a fatal error.

The parent reference skips the local class search and immediately calls the next level superclass function. When the superclass contains the function, it will be run by the parent object operator. Like the self object operator, the parent object operator will check the immediate parent class first and then move through the hierarchy until the function is found or returns an error.

The Inheritance2.php program demonstrates how the self and parent operators work by introducing an overriding method in the DerivedObject class. It also adds a call to the parent::getInstanceName() function in the overriding constructor of the subclass.

The Inheritance2.php program follows:

-- **This is found in Inheritance2.php on the enclosed CD.**

```php
<?php
  // Declare a variable to hold a superclass object instance.
  $myObject1 = new BasicObject("Class");

  // Declare a variable to hold a subclass object instance.
  $myObject2 = new DerivedObject("Subclass");

  // Define a class.
  class BasicObject
  {
    // Declare instance variable.
    protected $instanceName = "";

    function __construct($instanceName)
    {
      // Message on entrance.
      print "[Constructing Instance [".__CLASS__."] [".$instanceName."]<br />";

      // Assign parameter to instance variable.
      if (isset($instanceName))
        $this->instanceName = $instanceName;


    }

    protected function getInstanceName()
    {
      return "Superclass [".__CLASS__."] [".$this->instanceName."]<br />";
    }
  }

  // Define a subclass.
  class DerivedObject extends BasicObject
```

```
    {
      // Declare instance variable.
      protected $instanceName = "";

      function __construct($instanceName)
      {
        // Message on entrance.
        print "[Constructing Instance [".__CLASS__."][".$instanceName."]<br />";

        // Assign parameter to instance variable.
        if (isset($instanceName))
          $this->instanceName = $instanceName;

        // Call parent method as self.
        print parent::getInstanceName();

        // Call to overriding method as self.
        print self::getInstanceName();
      }

      protected function getInstanceName()
      {
        return "Subclass [".__CLASS__."][".$this->instanceName."]<br />";

      }
    }
?>
```

The `Inheritance2.php` program will produce the following output:

```
[Constructing Instance [BasicObject][Class]
[Constructing Instance [DerivedObject][Subclass]
Superclass [BasicObject][Subclass]
Subclass [DerivedObject][Subclass]
```

The call to the `parent::getInstanceName()` function demonstrates that it was managed by the superclass because the `__CLASS__` value returned is the `BasicObject` class. What the `self::getInstanceName()` function returns is `DerivedObject`, which indicates a call to the overriding subclass function.

You can also call the superclass constructor by using the following syntax *inside the overriding subclass constructor*:

```
parent::__construct();
```

Calling the superclass constructor is equivalent to a `super` call in the Java programming language. *The `parent::__construct()` function enables you to morph the parent class behaviors in terms of how the subclass is instantiated with a parameter list.* You customize a set of instance variables and functions when you call the superclass constructor. Any shared class variable names between superclass and subclasses that are set during construction of the superclass will contain the values set in the superclass.

TIP
*You should call the parent constructor only when subclasses do not
override common static variable values or use equivalent instance
variable names.*

The section has demonstrated how to define a subclass and an overriding function. The class
getInstanceName() function produces a different result when run by a superclass versus a
subclass, demonstrating the principle of polymorphism. This type of run-time difference demonstrates
the benefit of object inheritance hierarchies in OO programming.

Using Abstract Classes and Interfaces

Abstract classes are object types that define concrete variables and functions, as well as
abstract functions. Abstract functions define a prototype that is also known as a *specification*
but no implementation details. When subclasses extend abstract classes, they must provide all
implementation details of abstract functions. You cannot instantiate abstract classes, which
have the following prototype:

```
abstract class object_name( [ var [, var ] ] ) { object_body }
```

The purpose of using abstract classes is twofold. One purpose is to build common reference
models that contain implementation details of shared variables and nonpolymorphic functions. The
other is to define reference prototypes for all required polymorphic functions. Providing prototype
functions in abstract classes ensures that subclasses will have a consistent look and feel.

The Abstract.php program demonstrates defining an abstract class that contains abstract
and concrete functions. The abstract function is called a *specification* and cannot contain a body,
which would be in curly braces. Curly braces are replaced by a semicolon when you define an
abstract function. The following prototype qualifies how you define a function specification:

```
[ modifier ] function function_name( [ $var [, $var ] ] );
```

Developing a concrete class that extends the behavior of an abstract class requires you to
provide the implementation details of abstract functions. The subclass of an abstract class can use
the parent operator to reference any concrete functions in the inherited abstract class.

The following Abstract.php program demonstrates extending an abstract class and calling
back to a concrete function of the superclass:

-- This is found in Abstract.php on the enclosed CD.

```php
<?php
  // Declare a instance of the concrete class.
  $myObject = new PageHeader();

  // Call the concrete class instance.
  $myObject->writePage("Concrete Class!");

  // Define an abstract class.
  abstract class PageWriter
```

```
   {
     // Define an abstract function specification.
     abstract function writePage($var);

     // Define a function.
     protected function getClassName()
     {
       // Return class name.
       return __CLASS__;
     }
   }

   // Define a concrete class.
   class PageHeader extends PageWriter
   {
     // Provide implementation of the abstract function.
     public function writePage($var)
     {
       // Print local class name and actual parameter.
       print "[".__CLASS__."] [".$var."]<br />";

       // Print parent class name and actual parameter.
       print "[".parent::getClassName()."] [Abstract Class!]<br />";
     }
   }
?>
```

The Abstract.php program will print the following output to a page:

```
[PageHeader] [Concrete Class!]
[PageWriter] [Abstract Class!]
```

Abstract classes are excellent solutions when you want to define a set of function specifications to be shared across subclasses while providing concrete variables and functions too. When all you want to do is provide a series of function specifications, you should use interfaces.

Interfaces provide another, more general, structure. They do not provide any concrete variables or functions but may provide class constants. Interfaces define collections of prototype functions that a series of objects must implement. For example, you may define an interface that governs how you want objects built to support the database access layer or file input and output.

Interfaces have the following prototype:

```
interface interface_name { interface_specification }
```

Interfaces are the most generalized definition in OO programming. Abstract or concrete classes can implement interfaces. During design you will see common functions that may have varying implementations based on class and subclass implementations. You should consider defining the common functions as interfaces and then implement the interfaces in classes, which will provide you with a standard approach to functions across like classes.

The getClassName() function introduced in the Abstract.php program is qualified in a ClassInformation interface. Interfaces have the widest possible use, and as a rule, all function specifications in interfaces are publicly accessible. The access modifier for the getClassName()

function implementation has changed from protected to public. Also, the abstract class now implements the ClassInformation interface, which requires that the abstract PageWriter class implement a concrete getClassName() function.

TIP
You must define interfaces and classes that implement interfaces or are derived from classes that implement interfaces at the beginning of a page. If you attempt to construct them ahead of the interface and classes, you will raise a fatal exception, which appears to be a parsing quirk.

The following Interface.php program demonstrates how you can implement an interface:

-- This is found in Interface.php on the enclosed CD.

```php
<?php
  // Define an interface.
  interface ClassInformation
  {
    // Define interface function.
    public function getClassName();
  }

  // Define an abstract class.
  abstract class PageWriter implements ClassInformation
  {
    // Define an abstract function specification.
    abstract function writePage($var);

    // Define a function.
    public function getClassName()
    {
      // Return class name.
      return __CLASS__;
    }
  }

  // Define a concrete class.
  class PageHeader extends PageWriter
  {
    // Provide implementation of the abstract function.
    public function writePage($var)
    {
      // Print local class name and actual parameter.
      print "[".__CLASS__."] [".$var."]<br />";

      // Print parent class name and actual parameter.
      print "[".parent::getClassName()."] [Abstract Class!]<br />";
    }
  }
```

```
// Declare a instance of the concrete class.
$myObject = new PageHeader();

// Call the concrete class instance.
$myObject->writePage("Concrete Class!");
?>
```

The `Interface.php` program generates the same output as the `Abstract.php` program. These two programs demonstrate the syntax and actions required to define and implement interfaces and abstract classes.

Implementing Objects

Having learned the syntax of defining, using, and extending object types, in this section, you will examine utilities to leverage OO programming. Utilities enable you to manage objects in the procedural programming structures. Table 8-3 qualifies the PHP predefined functions that enable you to evaluate and obtain information about object types and object instances.

The `get_declared_classes()` and `get_declared_interfaces()` functions are useful views into your installed environment. They enable you to discover what interfaces and classes are available to you. You can use object reflection to discover their properties, as discussed in the section "Using Object Reflection" later in this chapter.

Beyond knowing the syntax to define objects, you will need to understand how to copy, compare, and inspect them. The next three sections explore how you can do these things.

Function Name	Description

`class_exists()`	The function checks if a class is defined in the current environment scope. It returns a Boolean true if the object type is defined or false when not. You have an optional second parameter that has a default true value, which means that it attempts to run the `__autoload()` function when the class doesn't exist in the environment. You can set the optional parameter to false when you want to disable the `__autoload()` function call. It has this pattern:
	
	`bool class_exists(`
	`  string class_name`
	`  [, bool autoload])`

`get_class()`	The function returns the object type of an object instance. It has two behaviors—one inside an object and the other outside. When you use the `get_class()` function in an object instance, you do not provide an actual parameter because it assumes that you're referring to the current object instance. An external call to the `get_class()` function requires that you provide an object as a formal parameter. If you provide an actual parameter that is not an object, it will return a null string, which is interpreted as a Boolean false. It has the following pattern:
	
	`string get_class(`
	`  [ object obj_name])`

TABLE 8-3. *Object Management Predefined Functions*

Function Name	Description

`get_class_methods()`	The function returns an array of class functions that are publicly accessible. As of PHP 5.1, this function ignores functions with private or protected access modifiers. If there are no publicly accessible class functions, it will return an empty array. The actual parameter can be a string that maps to a valid class definition or a variable containing an instance of a class definition. It has the following pattern:
	
	`array get_class_methods(`
	`  mixed obj_name)`

`get_class_vars()`	The function returns an array of class variables that are publicly accessible. As of PHP 5.1, this function ignores functions with private or protected access modifiers. If there are no publicly accessible class variables, it will return an empty array. The actual parameter can be a string that maps to a valid class definition or a variable containing an instance of a class definition. It has the following pattern:
	
	`array get_class_vars(`
	`  string class_name)`

`get_declared_classes()`	The function returns an array of declared classes in the environment. The declared classes are relevant to the libraries that you've loaded through directives in your `php.ini` file. Appendix D demonstrates how you can use this predefined function and lists the typical classes in a PHP 5.1 environment. It has the following pattern: `array get_declared_classes()`
`get_declared_interfaces()`	The function returns an array of declared interfaces in the environment. The declared interfaces are relevant to the libraries that you've loaded through directives in your `php.ini` file. Appendix D demonstrates how you can use this predefined function and lists the typical interfaces in a PHP 5.1 environment. It has the following pattern: `array get_declared_interfaces()`

`get_object_vars()`	The function returns an array of object instance variables that are publicly accessible. As of PHP 5.1, this function ignores object instance variables with private or protected access modifiers. If there are no publicly accessible object instance variables, it will return an empty array. The actual parameter must be a variable that holds an instance of an object. It has the following pattern:
	
	`array get_object_vars(`
	`  object obj_name)`

`get_parent_class()`	The function returns the parent class of an instance of a subclass. It has the following pattern:
	
	`string get_parent_class(`
	`  object obj_name)`

TABLE 8-3. *Object Management Predefined Functions* (continued)

Function Name	Description
`interface_exists()`	The function checks if an interface is defined in the current environment scope. It returns a Boolean true if the interface is defined or false when not. You have an optional second parameter that has a default true value, which means that it attempts to run the `__autoload()` function when the interface doesn't exist in the environment. You can set the optional parameter to false when you want to disable the `__autoload()` function call. It has this pattern: ```boolean interface_exists(\n string name\n [, boolean autoload])```
`is_a()`	The function checks if an object instance is an implementation of an object type. When the object instance is an implementation of the object type, the function returns a true value. When it is not, the function returns a false value. It has the following pattern: ```boolean is_a(\n object obj_name\n , string object_name)```
`is_subclass_of()`	The function checks if an object instance is an implementation of a subclass of an object type. When the object instance is an implementation of a subclass of an object type, the function returns a true value. When it is not, the function returns a false value. It has the following pattern: ```boolean is_subclass_of(\n object obj_name\n , string subclass_name)```
`method_exists()`	The function checks if a function has been implemented in an object instance. When the object contains an implemented function, the function returns a true value. When it is not, the function returns a false value. It has the following pattern: ```boolean method_exists(\n object obj_name\n , string function_name)```
`property_exists()`	The function returns a true value if a class property is found, provided that it is publicly accessible. When there is not a matching property, it will return a false value. It has the following pattern: ```array property_exists(\n object obj_name\n , string property_name)```

TABLE 8-3. *Object Management Predefined Functions* (continued)

Cloning Objects

You don't have to use an assignment operator to copy the contents of one object to another. Just as you use the `new` object operator to construct an instance of an object type, you use the `clone` object operator to create a copy of an object instance.

The ability to make a copy of an object instance after you have created and acted upon it is a very essential part of OO programming. The general prototype to clone an object instance is

```
$new_object = clone $old_object;
```

When you clone an instance of an object, the default or overriding object constructor is not read. The object uses the default or overriding clone operation, which is a function like all operations in PHP. The prototype for an overriding clone function is:

```
public function __clone() { function_body }
```

The overriding __clone() function is a no-argument function. Any formal parameter in the __clone() function signature will generate a fatal exception. When you have a mechanism for keeping track of the number of active instances of an object type, you should ensure that it is implemented in both your overriding constructor and your clone functions.

The Cloning.php program demonstrates how to implement an overriding __clone() function. Both the overriding constructor and clone functions implement logic to track the number of object instances.

The Cloning.php program follows:

-- This is found in Cloning.php on the enclosed CD.

```php
<?php
  // Declare a variable to hold an object instance.
  $myAddress1 = new Address("Ian","McLaughlin"
                            ,"1111 Broadway","Oakland","CA","94601");

  // Print instance contents.
  print $myAddress1->get_address();

  // Insert paragraph return.
  print "<p>";

  // Clone a copy of an object.
  $myAddress2 = clone $myAddress1;

  // Update first name.
  $myAddress2->set_first_name("Elise");

  // Print instance contents.
  print $myAddress2->get_address();

  // Define a class that prints a message.
  class Address
  {
    // Declare instance counter.
    public static $instances = 0;

    // Declare instance number.
    private $instance;
```

```php
   // Define instance variables.
   private $first_name = "";
   private $last_name = "";
   private $street_address = "";
   private $city = "";
   private $state = "";
   private $zip = "";

   // Define overriding constructor.
   public function __construct($first_name,$last_name
                                ,$street_address
                                ,$city,$state,$zip)
   {
     // Set the instance counter and number instance.
     $this->instance = ++self::$instances;

     // Instantiate the class properties.
     $this->first_name = $first_name;
     $this->last_name = $last_name;
     $this->street_address = $street_address;
     $this->city = $city;
     $this->state = $state;
     $this->zip = $zip;
   }

   // Define an overriding clone function.
   public function __clone()
   {
     // Set the instance counter and number instance.
     $this->instance = ++self::$instances;
   }

   // Define address getter.
   public function get_address()
   {
     // Declare and append values to return variable.
     $out  = $this->first_name." ".$this->last_name."<br />";
     $out .= $this->street_address."<br />";
     $out .= $this->city.", ".$this->state."  ".$this->zip."<br />";

     // Return address string.
     return $out;
   }

   // Define first name setter.
   public function set_first_name($first_name)
   {
     // Assign first name.
     $this->first_name = $first_name;
   }
 }
?>
```

The `Cloning.php` program defines an `Address` object type and creates an instance of the object type with a first name of Ian. Then, the program clones the instance and calls an instance function to change the first name to Elise; printing the following output to a web page:

```
Ian McLaughlin
1111 Broadway
Oakland, CA 94601
Elise McLaughlin
1111 Broadway
Oakland, CA 94601
```

The logic for managing the number of instance objects uses a static variable that is shared across all instances. Once the static variable is incremented, the new value is assigned to a local instance variable. The approach illustrates the earlier discussion in this chapter supporting the utility and scope of static variables.

Comparing Objects, Printing Objects, and Type Hinting

The comparison operators covered in Chapter 4 do not work when comparing objects. Object comparison requires you to write an instance operation for each object type. The object comparison function checks whether an external object instance is equal to its own instance. You compare instances by verifying all internal instance variable values against those of an external instance.

The Java programming language provides a recommended comparison operation name— `equals()`. You should consider labeling your comparison function as an `equals()` function. Choosing the `equals()` function name has the benefits of simplicity and common practice. You should implement a comparison function in each of your concrete classes to support object comparison operations.

You write OO programming comparison functions by using a single formal parameter, which is an instance of the same object type. As you have seen in Chapter 7, enforcing type is generally not supported in PHP. *Type verification is supported **only** in the context of object types.* You enforce object type validation by using type hinting. Type hinting is done by defining the object type before the parameter value in function prototype signatures.

If PHP didn't support type hinting, you would need to take any type as an actual parameter and then validate the parameter internally within the function. While a bit more work, that is not complex because you can use the `instanceof` object operator. Assuming that you add an `equals()` comparison function to the `Address` object type without using type hinting, you compare the actual parameter variable, as shown in the following code snippet:

```php
// Define an instance comparison function.
public function equals($obj)
{
  if (($obj instanceof $this) &&
       ($this->first_name == $obj->first_name) &&
       ($this->last_name == $obj->last_name) &&
        ($this->street_address == $obj->street_address) &&
         ($this->city == $obj->city) &&
          ($this->state == $obj->state) &&
           ($this->zip == $obj->zip))
```

```
        // They are equal.
        return true;

    else

        // They are unequal.
        return false;
    }
```

The `instanceof` object comparison accomplishes the same thing as type hinting because it ensures that the actual parameter must be an instance of the same object type. After confirming the object type, the compound `if` statement evaluates all private variables to determine if they are equal to the external object instance private variables. Scope availability is ignored in this case, and one object instance can see the object instance hidden variables.

You should take note that *the `$this` object operator can be used inside the function but not as the object type in the function prototype signature.* When using type hinting, you must provide the explicit name of the object type.

Another useful tool is the `__toString()` function. When you implement a `__toString()` function, you define how to translate your object into a string. This functionality lets you print the class instance contents. It is recommended that you define the `__toString()` function for each class definition.

Building on the cloning example, you can put the `Address` object type into an included file, like the `Address.inc` file. The benefit of using an `.inc` file type is that the Apache server will never render it outside of your environment unless you enable it to reset the directive explicitly. After creating the `Address.inc` include file, you can add both the `equals()` and `__toString()` functions. The `equals()` function enables you to compare any instance against an external instance. The `__toString()` function lets you convert an object to a string, which can then be parsed with the library of predefined string manipulation functions.

TIP
Always use `.inc` files for libraries and components that you don't want to share and `.php` and `.phps` types otherwise.

The following `Address.inc` program demonstrates a separate library file containing the definition for the `Address` object type. It uses type hinting for the object comparison function:

`-- This is found in Address.inc on the enclosed CD.`

```php
<?php
  // Define a class.
  class Address
  {
    // Declare instance counter.
    public static $instances = 0;

    // Declare instance number.
    private $instance;
```

```php
// Define instance variables.
private $first_name = "";
private $last_name = "";
private $street_address = "";
private $city = "";
private $state = "";
private $zip = "";

// Define overriding constructor.
public function __construct($first_name,$last_name
                           ,$street_address
                           ,$city,$state,$zip)
{
  // Set the instance counter and number instance.
  $this->instance = ++self::$instances;

  // Instantiate the class properties.
  $this->first_name = $first_name;
  $this->last_name = $last_name;
  $this->street_address = $street_address;
  $this->city = $city;
  $this->state = $state;
  $this->zip = $zip;
}

// Define overriding clone.
public function __clone()
{
  // Set the instance counter and number instance.
  $this->instance = ++self::$instances;
}

// Define how to convert the object to a string.
public function __toString()
{
  // Declare and append values to return variable.
  $out  = $this->first_name." ".$this->last_name.", ";
  $out .= $this->street_address.", ";
  $out .= $this->city.", ".$this->state."  ".$this->zip;

  // Return address string.
  return $out;
}

// Define address getter.
public function get_address()
{
  // Declare and append values to return variable.
  $out  = $this->first_name." ".$this->last_name."<br />";
  $out .= $this->street_address."<br />";
  $out .= $this->city.", ".$this->state."  ".$this->zip."<br />";
```

```
      // Return address string.
      return $out;
    }

    // Define first name setter.
    public function set_first_name($first_name)
    {
      // Assign first name.
      $this->first_name = $first_name;
    }

    // Define a type hinting instance comparison function.
    public function equals(Address $obj)
    {
      // Assign first name.
      if (($this->first_name == $obj->first_name) &&
          ($this->last_name == $obj->last_name) &&
           ($this->street_address == $obj->street_address) &&
            ($this->city == $obj->city) &&
             ($this->state == $obj->state) &&
              ($this->zip == $obj->zip))

        // They are equal.
        return true;

      else

        // They are unequal.
        return false;
    }
  }
?>
```

Using type hinting is clearly the best implementation decision if you are building reusable components. (Note, however, that *type hinting forces a fatal error when some object type other than the desired one is the actual function parameter.*) The other benefit of type hinting is that the `instanceof` object operator is more appropriate for managing subclasses at run time than for vetting actual parameter types.

The `Comparing.php` program leverages the `Address.inc` file by extending the example in the `Cloning.php` program. It compares two different instances of the `Address` object type. The program now uses the `include_once()` predefined function from Chapter 4 to include the `Address.inc` file in the run-time environment.

The following `Comparing.php` program demonstrates object comparison:

-- **This is found in Comparing.php on the enclosed CD.**

```php
<?php
  // Include a library class.
  include_once("Address.inc");
```

```
// Declare a variable to hold an object instance.
$myAddress1 = new Address("Joseph","McLaughlin"
                         ,"1111 Broadway","Oakland","CA","94601");

// Print instance contents.
print $myAddress1->get_address();

// Insert paragraph return.
print "<p />";

// Clone a copy of an object.
$myAddress2 = clone $myAddress1;

// Update first name.
$myAddress2->set_first_name("Ariel");

// Print instance contents.
print $myAddress2->get_address();

// Print a visual line break.
print "<hr />";

// Print whether they are equal.
print "[\$myAddress1] and [\$myAddress2] are ";
print "[".compare($myAddress1,$myAddress2)."].";

// Print a visual line break.
print "<hr />";

// Convert the object to a string.
print $myAddress1->__toString();

// Substitute a string for true or false.
function compare(&$obj1,&$obj2)
{
  // Compare the objects.
  if ($obj1->equals($obj2))

    return "equal";
  else
    return "not equal";
}
?>
```

The Comparing.php program includes an Address object type from a library class file. It creates an instance of the Address object type with a first name of Joseph. Then, the program clones the instance and calls an instance function to change the first name to Ariel. The program has a local compare() function that translates the boolean return value of the equals() function into an equal or not equal string. The __toString() function prints the object into a string.

The `Comparing.php` program prints the following output to a web page:

```
Joseph McLaughlin
1111 Broadway
Oakland, CA 94601
Ariel McLaughlin
1111 Broadway
Oakland, CA 94601
----------------------------------------------------------
[$myAddress1] and [$myAddress2] are [not equal].
----------------------------------------------------------
Joseph McLaughlin, 1111 Broadway, Oakland, CA 94601
```

This section has demonstrated how you compare objects and use type hinting; it has also revisited the concept of included files. You should be careful to choose the approach to using comparison functions that works in your environment. The recommended approach is to use type hinting in the function prototype signature.

Using Object Reflection

Another feature introduced in PHP 5 is object reflection. *Reflection* is the ability to discover the structure of PHP objects in your environment. It is like a magic mirror that lets you see the published attributes and operations of interfaces and object types. As qualified earlier in the chapter and illustrated in Appendix D, you have a number of predefined interfaces, object types, and extensions loaded in your environment. While knowing the interface and class names is useful, the class name alone does not enable you to access and use predefined interfaces and objects.

PHP 5 introduces several reflection classes to access these structures. They are summarized in Table 8-4.

Reflection provides visibility into the structures of object types and enables you to see what is available inside object types. Reflection enables you to discover the constants, static variables and functions, and instance functions of classes. You can use the static `export()` function with any of the reflection classes. The `export()` function enables you to discover otherwise hidden definitions and functions.

You will use the `ReflectionClass` to explore unknown class definitions. The static `export()` function has the following prototype:

```
ReflectionClass::export('class_name');
```

This static function prints the output of a class definition to a web page. The output appears to be a string that wraps across several lines. Unfortunately, the output from the `export()` function does not support conversion to a string or parsing of the output stream. You can convert the reflected contents to a string by creating an instance of the `ReflectionClass` and using the `__toString()` function.

There are some tricks and techniques to parsing this string because of reserved characters and hidden formatting tabs and carriage returns. The `Reflection.php` program demonstrates *the*

Class Name	Description
ReflectionClass	The class enables you to reflect into defined classes in your environment. You can discover the list of classes by using the `get_declared_classes()` function discussed earlier in this chapter. It supports the following static method to access the contents of defined classes: `ReflectClass::export('class_name');`
ReflectionExtension	The class enables you to reflect into defined extensions in your environment. You can discover the list of extensions by using the `get_loaded_extensions()` function. It supports the following static method to access the contents of defined extensions: `ReflectExtension::export('extension_name');`
ReflectionFunction	The class enables you to reflect into defined functions in your environment. It supports the following static method to access the contents of defined functions: `ReflectFunction::export('function_name');`
ReflectionObject	The class enables you to reflect into defined objects in your environment. It supports the following static method to access the contents of defined objects: `ReflectObject::export('object_name');`
ReflectionMethod	The class enables you to reflect into defined methods in your environment. It supports the following static method to access the contents of defined methods: `ReflectMethod::export('method_name');`
ReflectionParameter	The class enables you to reflect into defined parameters in your environment. It supports the following static method to access the contents of defined parameters: `ReflectParameter::export('parameter_name');`
ReflectionProperty	The class enables you to reflect into defined properties in your environment. It supports the following static method to access the contents of defined properties: `ReflectProperty::export('property_name');`

TABLE 8-4. *Predefined Reflection Classes*

reflect() function that enables you to format the object type definition into a human friendly format. The `reflect()` function does some preconditioning of the string before parsing and formatting it.

The `Reflection.php` program follows:

-- **This is found in Reflection.php on the enclosed CD.**

```php
<?php
  // Discover the OCI-Collection Object.
  print "<hr />".reflect_class('OCI-Collection')."<hr />";

  // Define an object reflector function.
  function reflect_class($object_name)
  {
    // Declare a global constant.
    define('INDENT',"  ");

    // Declare a reflection class base on input string.
    $class = new ReflectionClass($object_name);
    $class_str = $class->__toString();

    // Set control variables for do-while loop.
    $minus = true;
    $start = 0;

    // Strip dashes, which are reserved characters in preg_replace().
    do
    {
      if (strpos($class_str,'-',$start))
      {
        $class_str = substr_replace($class_str,""
                                ,strpos($class_str,'-',$start),1);
        $start = strpos($class_str,'-',$start);
      }
      else
      {
        $minus = false;
      }
    } while ($minus);

    // Replace HTML characters with HTML macros.
    $class_str = htmlspecialchars($class_str);

    // Put the words and symbols into an array.
    $raw = explode(' ',$class_str);

    // Define an array for words and symbols.
    $words = array();

    // Eliminate non-rendered formatting.
    for ($i = 0;$i < count($raw);$i++)
    {
      if (strlen($raw[$i]) > 0)
      {
        $temp = "";
```

```
      // Capture a word character stream for rendered characters.
      for ($j = 0;$j < strlen($raw[$i]);$j++)
        if ((ord(substr($raw[$i],$j,1)) != 10) && // Tab           :\t
            (ord(substr($raw[$i],$j,1)) != 12) && // Line feed      :\n
            (ord(substr($raw[$i],$j,1)) != 15))   // Carriage return:\r
          $temp .= substr($raw[$i],$j,1);

      // Assign new word.
      $words[] = $temp;
    }
}

// Declare return string.
$desc = "";

// Declare indentation offset variable.
$offset = 0;

// Parse the array of words.
for ($i = 0;$i < count($words);$i++)
{
  switch(true)
  {
    // Append first word of word set to line.
    case ($i == 0):

      $desc .= $words[$i];
      break;

    // Treat terminal element as piggy-backed curly braces.
    case ((count($words) - 1) == $i):

      $desc .= substr($words[$i],0,1)."<br />\n".indent_str(--$offset);
      $desc .= substr($words[$i],-1,1)."<br />\n";
      break;

    // Prior not open and current close curly brace.
    case (($words[$i-1] != "{") && ($words[$i] == "}")):

      // Shave off the one indent set.
      $desc = substr($desc,0,strlen($desc) - strlen(INDENT));
      $desc .= $words[$i]."<br />\n".indent_str(--$offset);
      break;

    // Prior open and current close curly brace.
    case (($words[$i-1] == "{") && ($words[$i] == "}")):

      $desc .= $words[$i]."<br />\n".indent_str($offset);
      break;

    // Current open and next close curly brace.
    case (($words[$i] == "{") && ($words[$i+1] == "}")):
```

```php
      $desc .= " ".$words[$i];
      break;

    // Current open and next not close curly brace.
    case (($words[$i] == "{") && ($words[$i+1] != "}")):

      $desc .= " ".$words[$i]."<br />\n".indent_str(++$offset);
      break;

    // Current close square bracket and next Parameter or Property.
    case (($words[$i] == "]") && (substr($words[$i+1],0,1) == "P")):

      $desc .= " ".$words[$i]."<br />\n".indent_str($offset);
      break;

    // Current close square bracket and next closed curly brace.
    case (($words[$i] == "]") && ($words[$i+1] == "}")):

      $desc .= " ".$words[$i]."<br />\n".indent_str($offset);
      break;

    // Middle words.
    default:
      $desc .= " ".$words[$i];
      break;
    }
  }

  // Return reflected class.
  return $desc;
}

// Define indentation builder.
function indent_str($offset)
{
  $spacer = "";
  for ($j = 0;$j < $offset;$j++)
    $spacer .= INDENT;

  return $spacer;
}
?>
```

The Reflection.php program introduces some techniques for working around string parsing limitations. For example, a do-while loop is used to overcome the limitations of the preg_replace() predefined function, which disallows parsing a dash because it is a reserved character in regular expression evaluation. The htmlspecialchars() function is used to convert less-than and greater-than symbols to HTML macros, < and >, respectively. Finally, a loop removes nonrendered formatting remnants that did not get cleaned up by the explode() function, which used a white space as its delimiter.

You can check Appendix B for details on the string handling functions that parse and manipulate strings. *Removing formatting characters that do not render in HTML is done by using the ord() function, which identifies their ASCII values.* The *population of the $words array is done with auto-indexing using the empty square brackets ([]),* as was covered in Chapter 6.

The preceding `Reflection.php` program generates a mirrored view into the definition of the Oracle library OCI-Collection class:

```
Class [ <internal:oci8> class OCICollection ] {
    Constants [0] {}
    Static properties [0] {}
    Static methods [0] {}
    Properties [0] {}
    Methods [8] {
      Method [ <internal> public method append ] {}
      Method [ <internal> public method getelem ] {}
      Method [ <internal> public method assignelem ] {}
      Method [ <internal> public method assign ] {}
      Method [ <internal> public method size ] {}
      Method [ <internal> public method max ] {}
      Method [ <internal> public method trim ] {}
      Method [ <internal> public method free ] {}
    }
}
```

The `reflect()` function in the `Reflection.php` program should enable you to discover what features are provided in the predefined interfaces and classes. This function should also serve as an example that you can leverage to format other types of reflection classes.

This section has provided you with a toolset to explore your environment. You should be able to discover details about code components that you can use in your programs.

Summary

You have learned the basics of defining and using PHP objects in this chapter. You have learned how to implement them and some key techniques in managing objects in your environment.

CHAPTER
9

Error Management and Exception Handling

his chapter examines error management and exception handling. Error management qualifies how you configure and manage errors in your PHP environment. Errors can be compile-time or run-time failures. Run-time errors are not run-time exceptions but behave differently, requiring proactive management in your programming code. Prior to PHP 5, run-time errors were often simply suppressed by the error control operator.

Beginning with PHP 5, you manage known run-time errors by both suppressing and rethrowing them as exceptions. Exceptions are also new to PHP 5. Run-time events raise exceptions, which don't happen during the parsing phase like compile-time errors. Exception handling qualifies how you manage run-time failures in your programs.

How you manage errors and run-time exceptions can impact the perception of your web site because unhandled exceptions erode customer confidence. When you plan how you'll handle errors and exceptions, you minimize unplanned or unexpected events in your web applications. The chapter will cover the following topics:

- Error management
    - Configuring error management
    - Managing errors
- Exception handling
    - Using `try-catch` blocks
    - Understanding the `Exception` class
    - Applying exception management

The process of developing programs is fraught with errors because there isn't a perfect typist in the world. If there were one, there wouldn't be a need for the BACKSPACE or DELETE keys. The simplest errors are syntax errors, which include missing semicolons, variable designators, the $ symbol, or incorrect operator use. These types of errors are generally found during unit test.

Harder errors to work through are sometimes found in unit test but are more often not found until integration or acceptance testing. These types of errors are run-time errors, which come in many varieties. They can be loosely grouped into two categories: logical and dependency errors.

The classic logic errors are: (a) using *and* where *or* is needed to evaluate a compound logical expression or vice versa; (b) using an assignment operator where a comparison operator is needed; (c) using a variable without checking its type on entry to a function or construction of an object instance; and (d) using implicit typecasting, which can accidentally result in a loss of data variable precision, like losing the cents on monetary transactions. These types of problems are hard to find but easy to fix.

The dependency errors are likewise well understood and typically involve resources like files and sockets. Dependency errors include: (a) attempting to read or write a file that isn't there or has the wrong ownership permissions; (b) attempting to open a socket that fails to reply; and (c) attempting to access a variable, function, or class that is unavailable because it isn't defined or doesn't have the proper scope. These are typically integration and release issues, which are found more frequently as the size of your application grows. Integration and release issues are often not easy to find and can sometimes be hard to fix because they involve version control conflicts or issues.

Agile Software Development and Extreme Programming

Agile Software Development is a conceptual framework for effective software engineering, qualified by four principles:

- Individuals and interactions over processes and tools
- Working software over comprehensive documentation
- Customer collaboration over contract negotiation
- Responding to change over following a plan

These maxims have led some to label Agile Software Development as hacking or cowboy coding when it is far from that. It is a system engineering approach that recognizes that the best laid plans of mice and men are imperfect, and advocates that programmers take independent initiative to create solutions to problems as they are encountered.

The simplified approaches put forth by the Agile method are also known as Extreme Programming because the method advocates pushing beyond stagnant and nonproductive processes to get software written. Those who believe defining and adhering to process leads to successful software development have maligned the Agile method and Extreme Programming as haphazard and cavalier. However, those who adhere to the Agile method and Extreme Programming mantra are not haphazard or cavalier because they really advocate more testing, thinking, and attention to detail.

The best way to avoid these errors is to invest time in your analysis and design by building well-qualified test cases before writing code. Some programmers think that test cases are not part of Extreme Programming as advocated by the Agile Software Development method. These developers also believe that building test cases will slow down the development process, but in fact test cases often speed it up.

TIP
You should consider building test cases to shorten your development time and minimize the cost of supporting your applications.

This chapter covers the configuration of your PHP error management before covering exception management. The sections are written to be read sequentially. When you have no control over your development environment, there is a temptation to skip the next section, "Error Management," but you should at least glance through it. You may find something that you want changed in your environment and the basis for requesting the change from your system administrator.

The next section qualifies how you configure and manage errors in your PHP environment. It can help identify ways that you can use your environment to eliminate potential errors in unit test and integration testing.

Error Management

Error management is defined by directives in the php.ini file. These directives are read and set when the environment starts. When you want to make changes to the current default environment behaviors, you must start and stop the PHP engine. When running PHP with Apache or Microsoft IIS, this means you must restart the HTTP server to make the changes.

You will examine how to configure error management in the php.ini file, and then how to use the information provided by the raised errors. Both sections should help you understand more about the environment and provide ideas to enable you to use error management to help you write good error and exception handling code.

Configuring Error Management

The settings for error management are found in the php.ini file. The recommended settings change between production and development environments. Table 9-1 shows the possible error level settings that you can use.

The error levels can be combined as bits, using the bitwise operators discussed in Chapter 4. This means you can mix and match behaviors according to your needs. You can choose all

Constant Name	Value	Definition
E_ALL	2047	All errors and warnings excluding deprecation notices and forward compatibility suggestions.
E_COMPILE_ERROR	64	Fatal compile-time errors.
E_COMPILE_WARNING	128	Warnings at compile time.
E_CORE_ERROR	16	Fatal errors that happen when starting PHP.
E_CORE_WARNING	32	Warnings that happen when starting PHP.
E_ERROR	1	Fatal run-time errors.
E_NOTICE	8	Run-time notices, which can result from intentional choices. An example of an intentional choice is failing to initialize variables because you're willing to accept their default value—a null string.
E_PARSE	4	Compile-time parse errors.
E_STRICT	2048	All run-time errors, deprecation warnings, and future interoperability suggestions.
E_USER_ERROR	256	User-generated error message.
E_USER_NOTICE	1024	User-generated notice message.
E_USER_WARNING	512	User-generated warning message.
E_WARNING	2	All run-time warnings, which are nonfatal errors.

TABLE 9-1. *Error-Level Directives*

Directive Name	Default	Definition
display_errors	Off	This displays all errors to web pages when enabled. It is strongly recommended that you turn this feature off for production web sites.
display_startup_errors	Off	This displays any PHP environment startup errors. This parameter is disabled by default and should be enabled only when debugging library inclusions.
log_errors	On	This logs error messages consistent with the error management level set in the php.ini file.
log_errors_max_len	1024	This sets the line length for logging errors to file. When you set this to zero, the log file line length is unlimited.
ignore_repeated_errors	Off	This logs the same error for a given file and line number.
ignore_repeated_source	Off	This logs different errors from different files for the same source.

TABLE 9-2.   *Error Display and Log Directives*

errors, excluding notices, as follows with the *and* bitwise operator, which is a & symbol, and the bitwise *negation* operator, which is a ~ symbol:

```
E_ALL & ~E_NOTICE
```

Beyond setting the error level, you can enable or disable displaying, logging, and tracking errors. Table 9-2 contains the php.ini directives to set these.

It is recommended that you adopt a set of error management values for your development and production servers. This requires a careful evaluation of what you want to achieve in each environment.

Development environments should be verbose unless you have an IDE tool to help you troubleshoot your code. It is recommended that you enable the E_ALL or E_STRICT and display_errors directives in the development environment. They display all fatal and nonfatal errors to your web pages during unit testing. The nonfatal errors, or warning messages, identify when you take shortcuts in your programs. It is never a good idea to rely on shortcuts, because they can cause unexpected errors, which can be time-consuming to debug. When you have E_ALL or E_STRICT set, you will be reminded to avoid shortcuts because they will raise warning messages.

Production environments should hide errors from customers and testers. It is recommended that you minimize the number of errors raised by enabling the E_ERROR directive and disabling the display_errors directive. You should also make sure that you manage any run-time exceptions in your code and suppress their unhandled display to your customers. Likewise, you should enable the `log_errors` directive to keep track of any raised errors, or build your own log file and write both stage and production environment errors to it.

You can dynamically change the error management level for a given program by using the `error_reporting()` function, which can take one or more of the bit values shown in Table 9-1 as an actual parameter. It has the following prototype:

```
int error_reporting([int level])
```

When no argument is provided to the `error_reporting()` function, the return value is the current error level. The previous error level is returned when an actual parameter is provided to the `error_reporting()` function. The possible valid values for the `error_reporting()` function are listed in Table 9-1. When you use two or more error-level constants, you will use the result of a logical bitwise expression.

The `OverrideErrorLevel.php` program *demonstrates dynamic error level setting by using the error_reporting() function.* The program also expects you to enable the `display_errors` directive in your `php.ini` file when you want to see the warning message displayed in the web page.

The `OverrideErrorLevel.php` program follows:

-- This is found in OverrideErrorLevel.php on the enclosed CD.

```php
<?php
  // Override the error level.
  if (error_reporting(E_ALL))
    $myVar;

  // Print the assigned value.
  print "[".$myVar."]";
?>
```

The `OverrideErrorLevel.php` program renders an undefined variable notice to the web page, which is a type of warning message. This notice occurs when values and types are not assigned to variables explicitly. Internally, an unassigned variable in PHP contains a null value without a data type. The missing data type raises the exception.

Managing Errors

Managing errors outside of the default behaviors provided in the language enables you to take control of error handling. This section will explore how you can dynamically manage run-time error handling in your environment.

A lazy way to suppress errors is provided by the *error control operator,* which is the @ symbol. The error control operator works with expressions. As discussed in Chapter 4, expressions are things that have or return values. You cannot use the error control operator with conditional expressions, loop structures, or functions.

When the error control operator prepends an expression, it will suppress any raised exception. Extending the `OverrideErrorLevel.php` program from the preceding section, an error control operator is prepended to the $myVar variable, where it previously raised a warning message.

The following `ErrorControlOperator.php` program demonstrates the change:

-- This is found in ErrorControlOperator.php on the enclosed CD.

```php
<?php
```

```php
  // Override the error level.
  if (error_reporting(E_ALL))
    $myVar;

  // Print the assigned value.
  print "[".@$myVar."]";
?>
```

Running the `ErrorControlOperator.php` program no longer raises a notice message because it is suppressed by the error control operator. While this is convenient to suppress errors, it does nothing to improve the code. In the case of an uninitialized variable, you can avoid the run-time notice by explicitly assigning a null string to the `$myVar` variable before the `if` statement.

TIP

You should declare, not define, variables. This means you should assign a value when you use a variable the first time. In weakly typed languages, like PHP, this ensures that they are assigned a type and will not raise a warning message during compile-time parsing.

A set of predefined functions enable you to define, set, and restore error handlers, debug activities, and trigger errors. Table 9-3 summarizes these functions.

You implement error management by building a library of user-defined error handlers. The error handlers can then be set and unset during the run-time execution of your application programs. It is recommended that you place your error handlers in an include file that cannot be directly accessed by your Apache or IIS server. Include files have an extension type of `.inc` and are typically not defined in your `httpd.conf` file `AddType` directives.

The `UserErrorHandler.inc` file contains only a single example of a user-defined error handling function. It uses a switch statement to evaluate the error type before selecting a message to render. There are many opportunities for custom error handling when you build an application.

The following `UserErrorHandler.inc` file defines a custom error handler:

-- This is found in **UserErrorHandler.inc** on the enclosed CD.

```php
<?php
  // Override the error level.
  function user_error_handler($e_number,$e_string,$e_file,$e_line)
  {
    switch ($e_number)
    {
      case E_USER_ERROR:
        print "This is the User Defined Error [".$e_string."]";
        break;
      case E_USER_WARNING:
        print "This is the User Defined Warning [".$e_string."]";
        break;
      case E_USER_NOTICE:
        print "This is the User Defined Notice [".$e_string."]";
        break;
    }
  }
?>
```

Function Name	Function Description
`debug_backtrace()`	The `debug_backtrace()` function creates an error message trace, which includes the file, line, function, class, type, and arguments involved in the triggering event. You can access the contents of the array with either the `print_r()` or `var_dump()` function. It has the following prototype: `array debug_backtrace()`
`debug_print_backtrace()`	The `debug_print_backtrace()` function prints an error message trace, which includes the file, line, function, class, type, and arguments involved in the triggering event. It has the following prototype: `void debug_print_backtrace()`

`error_log()`	The `error_log()` function lets you send a message to a web server's log, TCP port, or physical file. The function has one mandatory parameter, which is a string. Three optional parameters define where the error log is directed. The `error_log()` function returns true if it successfully writes an error log message and false if not. It has the following prototype:
	
	`boolean error_log(`
	`  string message`
	`[,int message_type`
	`[,string destination`
	`[,string extra_headers]]])`
	
	The optional `message_type` parameter has four valid values:
	
	■ 0 – Indicates that the error will be logged to the default file set by the `error_log` directive in the `php.ini` file.
	
	■ 1 – Indicates the error will be sent by e-mail to the address provided in the destination parameter.
	
	■ 2 – Is no longer very meaningful and only supported in PHP 3, which enables sending the message to another listening socket.
	
	■ 3 – Indicates that the message will be appended to the error log.
	
	The last optional parameter is used when the error message is sent by e-mail, and contains copies sent and blind copies sent.

`restore_error_handler()`	The `restore_error_handler()` function restores the prior error handler, which can be a user-defined or system handler. The function always returns true. It has the following prototype: `boolean restore_error_handler()`

TABLE 9-3. *Error Debug, Handler, and Trigger Functions*

Function Name	Function Description

set_error_handler()	The set_error_handler() function creates a user-defined error handler, which overrides the standard PHP error handler. The php.ini file and dynamic error reporting settings will be ignored, but you can query these settings with the error_reporting() function. Only three user-defined constants in Table 9-1 can be used in user-defined error handler functions. It has the following prototype:
	
	`mixed set_error_handler(`
	`  callback error_handler()`
	`[,int error_types])`
	
	The callback error_handler() function can have any valid function name and implements the generic handler() function definition, which is represented by the following prototype:
	
	`handler (`
	`    int errno`
	`  ,string errstr`
	`[,string errfile`
	`[,int errline`
	`[,array errcontext]]])`
	
	The valid values of the errno are the E_USER_ERROR, E_USER_NOTICE, and E_USER_WARNING constants. The errstr message is a user-defined string. The other three are optional parameters. The errfile returns the file that raises the error, the errline returns the line number at which an error is raised, and the array errcontext contains the active symbol set at the point of the error. The active symbol set contains all variables and values in the active execution scope at the point of the error.

trigger_error()	The trigger_error() function triggers a built-in or user-defined error handler. It has two formal parameters: the first is a string error message, and the second is an integer error type. When the value of the error type is found, the function returns true; if it is not found, the function returns false. The following is the function prototype:
	
	`boolean trigger_error(`
	`  string error_msg`
	`, int error_type)`

user_error()	The user_error() function is an alias for the trigger_error() function and triggers a built-in or user-defined error handler. It has the same two formal parameters as the trigger_error() function. The following is the function prototype:
	
	`boolean user_error(`
	`  string error_msg`
	`, int error_type)`

TABLE 9-3. *Error Debug, Handler, and Trigger Functions* (continued)

The custom error handler returns a message before the thrown error message string that is contained inside the square brackets. *Each case and error message indicates whether the error number was a user-defined fatal error, warning, or notice.* You should make sure that you manage all three cases even when you think it unlikely that one or more may be used, because business requirements always change. Your application design improves by adding user-defined error handlers that consistently manage fatal, warning, or notice errors.

In a real application, you implement code to write error log messages to physical files, e-mail messages, or database tables in each of these cases. The sample custom error handler prints messages to illustrate that you take a different action for each type of error.

The UserErrorTrigger.php program demonstrates the necessary steps to call your user-defined exception handler. This code would normally be in your application programs where you anticipate the need to raise a run-time error.

The following UserErrorTrigger.php program demonstrates setting and triggering an error message:

-- This is found in UserErrorTrigger.php on the enclosed CD.

```php
<?php
  // Include a library class.
  include_once("UserErrorHandler.inc");

  // Set override error level and capture old level.
  $base = error_reporting(E_USER_ERROR | E_USER_WARNING | E_USER_NOTICE);

  // Set the user error handler.
  set_error_handler("user_error_handler");

  // Define a variable.
  $myVar;

  // Raise a user-defined notice error when variable is not set.
  if (!isset($myVar))
    trigger_error("Variable is not set!",E_USER_NOTICE);

  // Restore the generic or prior error handler.
  restore_error_handler();

  // Reset the error reporting level.
  error_reporting($base);

  // Print current error reporting level.
  print "[".error_reporting()."]<br>";
?>
```

The UserErrorTrigger.php program grabs a copy of your include file, resets the error reporting to a user-defined level, sets the error handler to your user-defined error handler, and triggers a user-defined notice error when the variable is not defined. It also restores the prior error handler and resets the error management level. The reset is done by capturing the base level as the $base variable value when setting the custom error level. The $base variable is used to reset the error management level via a call to the error_reporting() function.

This section has shown you how to configure error handling and manage errors. Now you are ready to take up the Exception class introduced in PHP 5 in the next section.

Exception Handling

Exception handling deals with managing run-time errors. The process is very similar to run-time error management as covered in the preceding section. Run-time error management was the only exception handling process available prior to PHP 5.

PHP 5 exception handling was introduced by adopting into the language a set of tools familiar to C++ and Java programmers. These tools include an Exception class, try and catch blocks, and a throw operator. You will review these features of the language in the next four sections.

Using Try-Catch Blocks

The try block encloses code that can encounter an error. For every try block, there must be at least one catch block, but there can be more than one catch block. The benefit of having more than one catch block is to manage different ways of exception handling for different user-defined subclasses of the default Exception class. You can also use multiple catch blocks when the try block throws both user-defined and standard exceptions.

TIP
You must catch your subclass exceptions first because both user-defined and standard exceptions are successfully caught by using the Exception class type hint.

The try block has two principal prototypes. The simplest encloses only one statement that will automatically throw an exception, and the other requires you to manually throw an exception. The generic prototype is the former, as follows:

```
try
{
    statement;
}
```

When the statement doesn't implicitly throw an exception on failure, you will need to throw one manually. This is a bit more involved because in PHP there are two run-time error management systems that can work against each other. When a statement raises an error and not an exception, you should use the following prototype:

```
try
{
    if (@!statement)
        throw new Exception(string error_msg,int error_code);
}
```

You'll notice that the statement becomes an expression within a conditional statement. Also, that the *error control* and *logical negation* operators precede the expression. *Together these act to suppress run-time errors when the statement fails.* Then, you throw a user-defined Exception.

The catch block prototype is straightforward and has only one version. You define a catch block by providing a single formal parameter that uses type hinting. Type hinting works only with object variables and was covered in Chapter 7. The catch block takes a type hint for the Exception class or any subclass of the Exception class, provided that it is defined within the active variable scope of the program. The following is the catch block prototype:

```
catch (Exception $e)
{
   statement;
}
```

The try and catch blocks are elements of a single structure and cannot exist independently. The following TryCatch.php program demonstrates raising a run-time error that is then rethrown as an exception. It implements the try and catch block structure:

```
-- This is found in TryCatch.php on the enclosed CD.

<?php
  // Declare a nonexistent filename.
  $file = "User.inc";

  // Raise an error on a nonexistent resource and rethrow an exception.
  try
  {
    if (@!include_once($file))
      throw new Exception("The $file is not found.",1);
  }
  catch (Exception $e)
  {
    // Convert exception into an array.
    $error_detail = array();
    $error_detail["getCode()"] = $e->getCode();
    $error_detail["getMessage()"] = $e->getMessage();
    $error_detail["getFile()"] = $e->getFile();
    $error_detail["getLine()"] = $e->getLine();
    $error_detail["getTrace()"] = $e->getTrace();

    // Print rendered table.
    print render_table($error_detail);
  }

  // A recursive program for rendering nested tables.
  function render_table($error_array)
  {
    // Declare variable with table start.
    $output = "<table border=0 cellpadding=0 cellspacing=0>";

    // Read and add array keys and values to a string.
    foreach ($error_array as $hashName => $hashValue)
    {
      // Append row tag and first column value.
      $output .= "<tr><td valign=top>[".$hashName."]</td>";
```

```
      // Check column value for nested array.
      if ((is_array($hashValue)) && (count($hashValue) > 0))
      {
        // Call recursively a copy of itself with cell tags.
        $output .= "<td>".render_table($hashValue)."</td></tr>";
      }
      else
      {
        // Append nonarray value or white space for a zero-element array.
        if (!is_array($hashValue))
          $output .= "<td>[".$hashValue."]</td></tr>";
        else
          $output .= "<td>[ ]</td></tr>";
      }
    }

    // Close HTML table.
    $output .= "</table>";

    // Return the HTML table.
    return $output;
  }
?>
```

The `TryCatch.php` program uses the `include_once()` function to trigger a run-time error that must be suppressed before converting it into an exception. As discussed when defining the `try` block prototype, the *error control* and *logical negation* operators precede the expression to suppress a run-time error. You convert run-time errors to exceptions by capturing the statements in conditional expressions.

Within the `catch` block, the program converts the exception to an array. The `Exception` class's instance functions capture information about the error, which is then assigned to associative array elements. The array is passed to a variant of the recursive HTML table rendering function shown in Chapter 7. There is a subtle change between this version of the `render_table()` function and the one introduced in the earlier chapter. This one tests for a hash value containing a zero-element array. The `render_table()` function appends a zero-element array as a square-bracketed white space when it finds a zero-element array. This fixes a shortcoming of the prior example and is necessary to manage a no-argument stack trace array element.

The `TryCatch.php` program renders the following error message to a web page:

[getCode()]	[1]
[getMessage()]	[The UserErrorHandler2.inc is not found.]
[getFile()]	[/var/www/html/TryCatch.php]
[getLine()]	[24]
[getTrace()]	[ ]

The result of the `getCode()` and `getMessage()` functions returns the thrown error code and message values. The `Exception` class captures the filename and line number when an exception is thrown. This is a bit misleading because the error is thrown on line 23, not line 24, but it is the best we can do when an error, not an exception, is thrown on a file resource availability error.

When you throw a user-defined exception into a *standard* Exception class from a system-generated error, you do not capture the standard stack trace information. This behavior limits available diagnostic information by disallowing you to access the value of the debug_ backtrace() function. You can work around this limitation by creating a subclass of the Exception class to capture the stack trace information and use the debug_backtrace() function.

This section has provided the basic syntax for building a try-catch block using the standard Exception class. The next section will explore how you use the Exception class and extend its behavior through subclasses.

Understanding the Exception Class

Understanding what functions are available in the Exception class will help you understand how to use them. Table 9-4 presents and summarizes the available functions in the Exception class.

You extend the Exception class to provide unique subclasses when you need to implement more than one catch block for raised exceptions or to capture thrown errors and exceptions from a single try block. You can also add functions to your subclasses and override the behavior of the __construct() and __toString() functions. All other class functions of the Exception object type are final, which means they cannot be overridden.

You can replace the hard-coded call to the *OCI-Collection* class in the Reflection.php program by using a predefined $_GET variable from Table 4-10, which is found in Chapter 4. The change enables you to submit an ordinary URL with a single parameter to display any class definition. The following line of code is the recommend change to make that program into a dynamic object reflection tool:

```
print reflect_class($_GET['CLASS']);
```

Once you have made the change to the program, you can use the following URL to render the Exception class definition:

```
http://dev.techtinker.com/Reflection.php?CLASS=Exception
```

The following object definition will be rendered for the Exception class:

```
Class [ <internal> class Exception ] {
    Constants [0] {}
    Static properties [0] {}
    Static methods [0] {}
    Properties [6] {
      Property [ <default> protected $message ]
      Property [ <default> private $string ]
      Property [ <default> protected $code ]
      Property [ <default> protected $file ]
      Property [ <default> protected $line ]
      Property [ <default> private $trace ]
    }
```

Function Name	Function Description
getMessage()	The getMessage() function returns the value of the actual parameter passed to the Exception class constructor function. It cannot be overridden because it is defined as final. It has the following prototype: `final string getMessage()`
getCode()	The getCode() function returns the value of the actual parameter passed to the Exception class constructor function. It cannot be overridden because it is defined as final. It has the following prototype: `final int getCode()`
getFile()	The getFile() function returns the absolute path and filename of the program that threw the exception, which is equivalent to the magic __ FILE__ constant. It cannot be overridden because it is defined as final. It has the following prototype: `final string getFile()`
getLine()	The getLine() function returns the line number where the exception is thrown, which is equivalent to the magic __LINE__ constant. When a run-time error is suppressed and an exception is then thrown, the line value is actually one greater than where the error occurs. It cannot be overridden because it is defined as final. It has the following prototype: `final string getLine()`
getTrace()	The getTrace() function returns the stack trace of the thrown exception and returns it as an associative array. It cannot be overridden because it is defined as final. It has the following prototype: `final array getTrace()` The getTrace() function returns the magic constants __FUNCTION__, __LINE__, __FILE__, and __CLASS__, as well as the type and a list of arguments. The pointer operator, "->", is returned when triggered by a function or object instance, and the scope resolution operator, "::", is returned when triggered by a static function.
getTraceAsString()	The getTraceAsString() function returns the stack trace of the thrown exception and returns it as a string. It cannot be overridden because it is defined as final. It has the following prototype: `final string getTraceAsString()`
__toString()	The __toString() function returns a combination string of the exception message thrown, the magic __FILE__ constant, and a stack trace for system-generated errors. The stack trace is unavailable for subclasses of the Exception class, unless you provide it by overriding the function. It isn't defined as final and has the following prototype: `string __toString()`

TABLE 9-4. *The Exception Class Functions*

```
Methods [9] {
  Method [ <internal> final private method __clone ] {}
  Method [ <internal, ctor> public method __construct ] {
    Parameters [2] {
      Parameter #0 [ <required> $message ]
      Parameter #1 [ <required> $code ]
    }
  }
  Method [ <internal> final public method getMessage ] {}
  Method [ <internal> final public method getCode ] {}
  Method [ <internal> final public method getFile ] {}
  Method [ <internal> final public method getLine ] {}
  Method [ <internal> final public method getTrace ] {}
  Method [ <internal> final public method getTraceAsString ] {}
  Method [ <internal> public method __toString ] {}
  }
}
```

The process of extending the Exception class is the same as that for creating other subclasses as presented in Chapter 8. While you can override the __toString() function, generally the information provided is not superior to what you can get from the predefined functions. The default __toString() function returns a concatenation of the error message, filename, line, and stack trace.

When you opt to override the __toString() function, you should consider whether or not to override the class constructor function. You can change the default constructor signature by overriding the __construct() function. Your overriding constructor should use at least the default $message and $code formal parameters in its construction signature. Also, you should initialize the *protected superclass instance* $message and $code variables in the overriding constructor.

The following MyException.inc program demonstrates an overriding Exception subclass:

-- **This is found in MyException.inc on the enclosed CD.**

```php
<?php
  // Define a subclass of Exception.
  class MyException extends Exception
  {
    // Define a backtrace class instance variable.
    protected $backtrace = "";

    // Define overriding constructor.
    public function __construct($e_msg,$e_code,$e_override)
    {
      if (is_string($e_msg))
        $this->message = $e_msg;

      if (is_int($e_code))
        $this->code = $e_code;
```

Uniform Resource Locator

A Uniform Resource Locator (URL) has a service, a port, a machine name, a domain name, a directory path, and a filename at a minimum. Dynamic web pages append one or more name and value pair parameters to the URL. The actual parameter pairs begin after a question mark and are separated by ampersand symbols. The name and value are separated by an equal sign, which is like the PHP assignment operator:

```
http://<machine>.<domain>:<port>/<path>/<file>?<name>=<value>
```

This approach to passing information in a URL is known as the GET method. The names and values are sent in clear text across the network. The URL contains both the parameter name and the value, which are typically logged where they can be read by other users. This method is an inherent security risk that can disclose information to unintended parties and enable man-in-the-middle attacks to your web site. Except in the scope of internal testing, you should always use the POST method. The POST method sends the name and value pair as an encrypted string.

```php
    if (is_string($e_override))
      $this->override = $e_override;

    // Get the error stack.
    $this->backtrace = debug_backtrace();
  }

  // Add a function to return the trace information.
  public function getBackTrace()
  {
    return $this->backtrace;
  }

  // Define how to convert the object to a string.
  public function __toString()
  {
    return $this->override;
  }
}
?>
```

The MyException class overrides the __construct() and __toString() functions and adds a new getBackTrace() function. The getBackTrace() function enables you to retrieve stack trace information for a thrown error. *This is done in a three-step process: (a) creating a local $backtrace instance variable; (b) assigning the debug_backtrace() function return value to the $backtrace instance variable; and (c) providing a function to access the stack trace information.* This three-step process is necessary because the $trace variable has a private class access modifier, which disallows a subclass to access or override its value.

The next section will demonstrate the use of the `MyException` subclass. You should catch your subclasses when they are thrown. This is done by providing a `catch` block that uses your `Exception` subclass as a type hint object for the formal parameter. *A fatal error will be raised when you attempt to handle a standard exception by using a subclass type hint.*

You can send an object subclass as an actual parameter to a superclass type hint, but cannot send an object superclass to a subclass type hint. As qualified in Chapter 7, subclasses are (a) derived from superclasses and contain at least all of the superclass variables and functions; and (b) known as a type of the superclass. This means that a subclass meets the expectation of a type hint of the superclass. Superclasses are not types of their subclasses and fail to meet a type hint of a subclass.

The following `TryCatchBySubclass.php` program demonstrates attempting to catch a standard thrown `Exception` by using the `MyException` type hint:

 -- This is found in TryCatchBySubclass.php on the enclosed CD.

```php
<?php
  // Declare an Exception subclass filename.
  $override = "MyException.inc";

  // Declare a nonexistent filename.
  $file = "User.inc";

  // Raise an error on a nonexistent resource and rethrow an exception.
  try
  {
    if (@!include_once($override))
      throw new MyException("include_once($file) not found.",1,"Override");

    if (@!include_once($file))
      throw new Exception("include_once($file) not found.",1);
  }
  catch (MyException $e) {}
?>
```

The `TryCatchBySubclass.php` program raises a fatal error because you cannot stuff a square peg into a round hole. At least, this is true when the diameter of the hole is equal to or less than the *diagonal* width of the square. Likewise, superclasses are never recognized as types of their derived subclasses because subclasses are assumed to contain more than the parent. Subclasses typically contain specialization, which means additional variables and methods that are unknown to the superclass. This is a basic tenet of OO programming and polymorphic behavior.

NOTE
Always place `catch` blocks with user-defined subclasses of the `Exception` class before a generic `Exception` catch block, and never forget to include a generic `Exception` catch block to avoid fatal run-time errors.

Applying Exception Management

Resource failures trigger exceptions and you manage them by coding `catch` blocks to handle them. The `TryCatchOverride.php` program relies on the fact that a resource failure occurs when you attempt to open a file that is missing or has restricted permissions. The program's `catch` block contains code to document the failure in a log file and mask the failure to your end user.

As qualified earlier, the `include_once()` function raises a run-time warning error when the file is missing or unavailable. You can suppress and redirect run-time errors to exceptions. The exception can then be caught in a `catch` block that uses a type hint for either the subclass or the superclass.

The following `TryCatchOverride.php` program demonstrates a user-defined subclass:

-- This is found in TryCatchOverride.php on the enclosed CD.

```php
<?php
  // Declare an Exception subclass filename.
  $override = "MyException.inc";

  // Declare a nonexistent filename.
  $file = "User.inc";

  // Raise an error on a nonexistent resource and rethrow an exception.
  try
  {
    if (@!include_once($override))
      throw new MyException("include_once($file) not found.",1,"Override");

    if (@!include_once($file))
      throw new MyException("include_once($file) not found.",1,"Override");
  }
  catch (MyException $e)
  {
    // Convert exception into an array.
    $error_detail = array();
    $error_detail["getCode()"] = $e->getCode();
    $error_detail["getMessage()"] = $e->getMessage();
    $error_detail["getFile()"] = $e->getFile();
    $error_detail["getLine()"] = $e->getLine();
    $error_detail["getTrace()"] = $e->getTrace();
    $error_detail["getBackTrace()"] = $e->getBackTrace();
    $error_detail["__toString()"] = $e->__toString();

    // Print rendered table.
    print render_table($error_detail);
  }
  catch (Exception $e)
  {
    // Convert exception into an array.
```

```php
    $error_detail = array();
    $error_detail["getCode()"] = $e->getCode();
    $error_detail["getMessage()"] = $e->getMessage();
    $error_detail["getFile()"] = $e->getFile();
    $error_detail["getLine()"] = $e->getLine();

    // Print rendered table.
    print render_table($error_detail);
  }

  // A recursive program for rendering nested tables.
  function render_table($error_array)
  {
    // Declare variable with table start.
    $output = "<table border=0 cellpadding=0 cellspacing=0>";

    // Read and add array keys and values to a string.
    foreach ($error_array as $hashName => $hashValue)
    {
      // Append row tag and first column value.
      $output .= "<tr><td valign=top>[".$hashName."]</td>";

      // Check column value for nested array.
      if ((is_array($hashValue)) && (count($hashValue) > 0))
      {
        // Call recursively a copy of itself with cell tags.
        $output .= "<td>".render_table($hashValue)."</td></tr>";
      }
      else
      {
        // Append nonarray value or white space for a zero element array.
        if (!is_array($hashValue))
          $output .= "<td>[".$hashValue."]</td></tr>";
        else
          $output .= "<td>[ ]</td></tr>";
      }
    }

    // Close HTML table.
    $output .= "</table>";

    // Return the HTML table.
    return $output;
  }
?>
```

The `TryCatchOverride.php` program uses a three-argument overriding constructor and adds the `getBackTrace()` function to capture stack trace information. Also, there are two `catch` blocks even though only the first will be run. The second `catch` block serves to illustrate two things.

You need to sequence `catch` blocks so that the subclass type hints precede the `Exception` superclass, and you need to provide a standard exception handler. Using both your user-defined and standard handlers ensures that your code will continue to run successfully whether predefined functions raise run-time errors or exceptions.

The `TryCatchOverride.php` program also uses the familiar recursive `render_table()` function, which formats stack trace information, as follows:

```
[getCode()]            [1]
[getMessage()]         [include_once(UserErrorHandler2.inc) not found.]
[getFile()]            [/var/www/html/TryCatchOverride.php]
[getLine()]            [29]
[getTrace()]           [ ]
[getBackTrace()]       [0] [file]      [/var/www/html/TryCatchOverride.php]
                           [line]      [29]
                           [function]  [__construct]
                           [class]     [MyException]
                           [object]    [Object id #1]
                           [type]      [->]
                           [args]      [0] [include_once(User.inc) not found.]
                                       [1] [1]
                                       [2] [Override]
[__toString()]         [Override]
```

The default `getTrace()` function returns nothing, but the added `getBackTrace()` function returns the run-time error stack trace. As shown in the output, only the `catch` block that contains the `getBackTrace()` function has caught the user-defined exception.

This section has shown you how to implement a user-defined subclass of the `Exception` class. This example should enable you to build robust error and exception handling into your programs.

Summary

You have learned the basics of defining error management for your environment and run-time error and exception handling for your programs. This chapter has illustrated the two approaches to run-time error management and how to blend them into one effective tool.

CHAPTER
10
File I/O

his chapter deals with the ins and outs of accessing files on your application server, which are known as inputs and outputs or I/O. Anytime a program interacts with the operating system, it performs an I/O operation. These operations involve moving data from a program variable in memory to: (a) another local program; (b) another remote program; (c) a shared memory segment; or (d) the file system. Local and remote programs that share memory segments and file systems are also known as resources, as are files.

This chapter examines the ins and outs of using system resources in the following sequence:

- Understanding files and file systems
  - File information functions
  - File location functions
  - File management functions
  - File status functions
  - File system functions
- Reading and writing files
  - Reading files
  - Writing files
  - Uploading files

Chapter 4 introduces PHP variable types as scalar and compound. You've worked extensively in the preceding chapters with the `bool`, `int`, `float`, and `string` scalar variables and the special null type. Chapter 7 covers the special function data type, and Chapter 8 demonstrates how to use PHP objects. The remaining data type is the resource type. PHP resources are things that are external to your PHP program, like files, sockets, and database connections. You also have the ability to run operating system commands in subshells from your programs and develop cross-platform scripting solutions in PHP.

Sockets support distributed applications and external calls to another computer. The availability of socket communication is qualified by the functions that support it. Only those functions that have an optional socket parameter in their prototype signature support socket communication.

The PHP resource features are powerful tools that are routinely deployed in applications. You should understand that *there are significant security risks when you enable file and system input/ output (I/O) functions.* You enable or disable these functions in your PHP configuration file.

After considering the application business requirements, some companies restrict risky PHP functions to prevent hackers from mounting potentially successful intrusions. The `disable_functions` directive in the `php.ini` file lets you disable PHP functions. You put the functions you want disabled into a comma-delimited list as the value argument of the directive.

Screening attacks at the front end of your application is the safest course of action and preferred over disabling selected PHP functions. You can prevent most application intrusion attacks by simply parsing all incoming parameters. Parsing these parameters filters end-user inputs into your application and lets you block or monitor suspicious data inputs. When you fail to filter incoming parameters, you expose your site and data to insertion attacks and potential data corruption, loss, or manipulation.

TIP
You should always *parse incoming parameters from URLs, whether or not they're coming from the HTTP GET or POST method. This is the most thorough way to prevent insertion attacks on your web site.*

PHP Security Briefing

The Open Web Application Security Project (OWASP) is a foundation established to fight the causes of insecure applications. You can find more about the foundation, current risks, and approaches to risk mitigation at the www.owasp.org web site.

Like David Letterman's top ten, OWASP has developed a top ten list of web application security problems. Whether you count up or down, *the greatest vulnerability of web applications is failing to validate input parameters.* Naturally, failing to validate input parameters opens your web application to insertion attacks.

The worst possible opening in PHP is created by both failing to validate incoming parameters and enabling PHP I/O functions, like the eval() function. The eval() function enables dynamic evaluation and execution of statements. It takes a string as an argument and runs the string in a subshell using the result as part of the program. It is a very useful development tool in building algorithmic programs.

You should never use the $_GET() or $_REQUEST predefined variables to read parameters, because they're less secure than the $_POST variable. The Attack.php program demonstrates the vulnerability created by unfiltered parameters and the eval() function. This works in PHP 5 but will fail due to a parsing error in earlier releases.

The Attack.php program uses the $_GET() function for presentation and testing simplicity.

```
-- This is found in Attack.php on the enclosed CD.
<?php
  // Assign an unfiltered parameter.
  $any_var = $_GET['p_name'];

  // Open a hole.
  eval($any_var);
?>
```

Calling the Attack.php with the following URL will read and return the contents of the target file from a Linux system, You can substitute type for cat as the operating system command argument in the system() function call when working on a server running Microsoft Windows XP:

```
http://dev.techtinker.com/Attack.php?p_name=system("cat Attack.php");
```

The Attack.php file will not be rendered in the web page because of the embedded HTML tags, but you can see the program code by viewing the page source. This type of behavior is not an intended result of placing your code on the application server tier. It is an aberration made possible by an exploitive application insertion attack.

(continued)

You can substitute any valid operating system command as the parameter value to the `system()` function. The semicolon in the actual parameter ensures that it will execute when evaluated. The execution will be with the rights and privileges of the Apache or IIS server when run. This opens your system data to writes, which can be directed to your `/tmp` directory in Linux and your `C:\TEMP` directory in Microsoft Windows XP.

You can fix this vulnerability by disabling resource functions or parsing parameters. Disabling the `eval()` in the `php.ini` file eliminates the exposure but limits the flexibility of your development environment. Parsing incoming parameters for keywords and semicolons is a better solution because it closes the security hole without limiting your development options. *You can close **this** security hole by parsing and removing semicolons from incoming parameters.*

Contrary to popular urban programmer myth, the `eval()` command is not bad juju. Its vulnerability is caused by dynamic function call behavior, which is covered in Chapter 7. Application security requires taking precautions in application development. While disabling the `eval()` function appears to close a risk, it does not eliminate unseen risks. Only parsing all incoming parameters to audit for risks provides effective security filters.

This chapter explores the file and system resource functions and their usage. Chapter 13 discusses and demonstrates database connection resources. The sections in this chapter should be read in sequence. The chapter covers how you set file permissions to read, write, and execute files. Then, the chapter demonstrates how you can read and write files. The chapter concludes by showing how you can call the operating system or external programs and how you can use the run-time command-line interpreter to build platform-independent PHP scripting tools.

Understanding Files and File Systems

Various operating systems have different approaches to file organization and management. The basics of operating systems define whether or not commands are case sensitive or insensitive and govern user privileges. Likewise, the basics of file systems define how files are organized, who can act on them, and what actions can be performed on them.

How you think of organizing files into directories or folders depends on your perspective. The base directory for Linux is called a *mount point* and for Microsoft Windows is called a *logical drive*. All directories and files are assigned a number in the operating system `inode` table, which tracks files as they are created, modified, and deleted.

File systems are further qualified by two characteristics, file ownership and permission. The superuser `root` in Linux has comprehensive system and file access and ownership. Beneath the superuser there are less privileged users or the rest of the users. All users can own files and grant read, write, or execute privileges to groups and other users. This means that files can have different privileges for the owner, the group, and other users.

In Microsoft Windows, all administrators are superusers. This means you can have many superusers. Also, *Microsoft Windows supports only two file permission types: read/write and read-only.* Regardless of whether a file is read/write or read-only, all files are executable on Microsoft Windows. There is also no concept of owner, group, and user permissions. Permissions are more or less the same for the owner and other users.

File permissions are changed in Linux via the chmod command; Microsoft Windows uses the attrib command. The chmod() command can use r, w, and x characters or three octal numbers to set file permissions, which are integers from 0 to 7. There are no permissions to the file when permission value is set to 0. Table 10-1 maps these two command alternatives.

The PHP chmod() function supports both approaches for all platforms. The ported libraries adjust for the differences between Linux and Microsoft Windows. You should note that the chmod() function does not support the shared concurrently, or sticky, bit; or the POSIX-compliant system file bit. Both of these specialized values can be set by making an external operating system chmod() call in the Linux operating system with the –t and –s option flags. As noted, Microsoft Windows supports only two file privilege sets, which can be found by using a PHP function or the attrib command.

NOTE
The Portable Operating System Interface (POSIX) is a widely adopted standard by the Linux and Unix operating systems. The POSIX library is typically enabled by default but can be disabled using the configuration tool, with the –disable-posix syntax.

PHP provides several predefined functions that enable you to discover information about files and file systems. The following subsection will explore some of these file and file system functions:

- File information functions, such as the fileowner(), filegroup(), fileperms(), filesize(), and stat() functions

- File location functions, such as the dirname(), mkdir(), realpath(), and rmdir() functions

- File management functions, such as the chgrp(), chmod(), chown(), copy(), delete(), move_uploaded_file(), and touch() functions

- File status functions, such as the is_dir(), is_executable(), is_file(), is_link(), and is_readable() functions

- File system functions, such as the disk_free_space() and disk_total_space() functions

Permission	Characters	Octal Value
Execute only	x	1
Write only	w	2
Write and execute only	wx	3
Read only	r	4
Read and execute only	rx	5
Read and write only	rw	6
Read, write, and execute	rwx	7

TABLE 10-1.   *Character-to-Octal File Permission Map*

File Information Functions

Information functions enable you to discover file ownership, privilege, and statistics. The information you gather using these functions enables you to work with files more efficiently. For example, when you discover that a file is very large, you know that you should read that file through a buffer.

Several of the functions behave differently on Microsoft Windows XP than they do on Linux or Unix systems. All testing for this segment was done using Linux because of the functional limitations of the other file system. A synopsis of POSIX-compliant library functions is found in Appendix E. You should note that they only work on POSIX-compliant Linux and Unix operating systems.

Table 10-2 summarizes the file information functions. After the table you will examine programs demonstrating some of these functions.

The file information functions can be divided into three types. One type enables you to secure information about the access, change, and modification times of files. Another type lets you determine the permissions of files or environment umask value. The umask value is the inverse of the group and user permissions for any system and determines the default file creation properties. The last set of functions provides a set of tools to collect statistics on files. The statistics functions enable you to capture specific operations or gather a complete set of file statistics.

The fileatime(), filectime(), and filemtime() functions all work alike, returning an integer value that identifies when the file was last accessed, changed, or modified, respectively. The Linux operating system stores the changed and modified time stamp as one value in the inode table and the accessed time stamp as another. The Microsoft Windows operating system stores a distinct value for each in its file system map, which is like an inode table. The IdentifyFiles .php program later in this section will demonstrate the stored contents of these time stamps. The date() function enables you to convert the integer value to a meaningful date and time stamp.

The following FileDate.php program demonstrates how you can use the access, change, or modification file functions:

-- This is found in FileDate.php on the enclosed CD.

```php
<?php
  // Read the parameter from the URL.
  $file = $_GET["p_name"];

  // Declare variable to system date and avoid a notice error.
  $info = date('d-M-Y h:i:s');

  // Verify file exists and assign local time in a European date mask.
  if (file_exists($file))
    $info = date('d-M-Y h:i:s',fileatime($file));

  // Print file statistics.
  print $info;
?>
```

The FileDate.php program formats the scalar integer to a human-friendly string using the date() function. The date() function is covered in Appendix F. The program uses the $_GET["p_name"] for simplicity in presentation, but as mentioned previously, the $_GET predefined variable is an

Function	Description and Pattern
clearstatcache()	The clearstatcache() function clears cached values generated by the stat(), lstat(), or related functions. It has the following pattern: void clearstatcache()
file_exists()	The file_exists() function finds whether a file exists. It returns true when it finds a filename and false when it fails to find the file or encounters an error. The filename is a fully qualified path and filename. It has the following pattern: bool file_exists(string *file_name*)
fileatime()	The fileatime() function finds the last access time of a file or returns false when encountering an error. The return value is an operating system time stamp or null. The filename parameter is a fully qualified path and filename. You should note that the function results are cached until you remove them by running the clearstatcache() function. It has the following pattern: int fileatime(string *file_name*)
filectime()	The filectime() function finds the last change time of a file or returns false when encountering an error. The return value is an operating system time stamp or null. The filename parameter is a fully qualified path and filename. You should note that the function results are cached until you remove them by running the clearstatcache() function. In Linux, you will find that filectime() and filemtime() are synonymous, but they have different values in the Microsoft Windows operating system. The filectime() function has the following pattern: int filectime(string *file_name*)
filegroup()	The filegroup() function finds the group ID number of a file or returns false when encountering an error. The filename is a fully qualified path and filename. The return value is the group ID value from the /etc/group file. You should note that the function results are cached until you remove them by running the clearstatcache() function. It has the following pattern: int filegroup(string *file_name*)
fileinode()	The fileinode() function finds the inode of a file or returns false when encountering an error. The return value is the inode number of the file. The filename is a fully qualified path and filename. You should note that the function results are cached until you remove them by running the clearstatcache() function. It has the following pattern: int fileinode(string *file_name*)
filemtime()	The filemtime() function finds the last modified time of a file or returns false when encountering an error. The return value is an operating system time stamp or null. The filename is a fully qualified path and filename. You should note that the function results are cached until you remove them by running the clearstatcache() function. In Linux, you will find that filectime() and filemtime() are synonymous, but they have different values in the Microsoft Windows operating system. The filemtime() function has the following pattern: int filemtime(string *file_name*)
fileowner()	The fileowner() function finds the owner ID number of a file or returns false when encountering an error. The filename is a fully qualified path and filename. The return value is the ID assigned by the operating system to a given user. These values are found in the /etc/passwd file on Linux. You should note that the function results are cached until you remove them by running the clearstatcache() function. It has the following pattern: int fileowner(string *file_name*)

TABLE 10-2. *File Information Functions*

Function	Description and Pattern
fileperms()	The fileperms() function finds the file permissions of a file or returns false when an error is encountered. The filename is a fully qualified path and filename. The return value is an integer that must be converted to an octal number set. You can explicitly convert the integer by using the sprintf() function covered in Chapter 3. You should note that the function results are cached until you remove them by running the clearstatcache() function. It has the following pattern: int fileperms(string *file_name*)
filesize()	The filesize() function finds the physical size of a file or returns false when encountering an error. This function can also raise an error, which you should suppress and throw as an exception in PHP 5, as discussed in Chapter 9. This function will likely return an unexpected result when the file is larger than 2GB and 4GB because PHP uses a 32-bit integer to calculate the file size. You can use the following sprintf() function call to convert the number: sprintf("%u",*filesize($file*)). The filename is a fully qualified path and filename. You should note that the function results are cached until you remove them by running the clearstatcache() function. It has the following pattern: int filesize(string *file_name*)
fstat()	The fstat() function gets an array of information about a file or returns false when encountering an error. This function does not work on remote files, like those on an NFS mount or a storage area network (SAN). The function takes a single parameter, which is a file handle or pointer. It has the following pattern: array fstat(file *file_pointer*)
filetype()	The filetype() function finds the file type of a file or returns false when encountering an error. The possible return values of this function are: fifo, char, dir, block, link, file, and unknown. The filename is a fully qualified path and filename. This function can also raise an error, which you should suppress and throw as an exception in PHP 5, as discussed in Chapter 9. You should note that the function results are cached until you remove them by running the clearstatcache() function. It has the following pattern: string filetype(string *file_name*)
linkinfo()	The linkinfo() function verifies whether a link points to a valid file. It is not implemented in Microsoft Windows ports of PHP. The function returns a positive integer when validating the link and zero when the link is invalid. It has the following pattern: int linkinfo(string *path*)
lstat()	The lstat() function is a mirror to the stat() function. It gets an array of information about a file when successful, and raises a run-time error on failure. You should use the error control operator to suppress run-time errors and throw an exception in PHP 5, as discussed in Chapter 9. It has the following pattern: array lstat(string *file_name*)
stat()	The stat() function gets an array of information about a file when successful or raises a run-time error on failure. You should use the error control operator to suppress run-time errors and throw an exception in PHP 5, as discussed in Chapter 9. This function has been in the language since PHP 3 and returns all values twice in the array. It uses a set of numeric indexes for one set of values to be backward compatible. The other set of values uses string names as index values. It has the following pattern: array stat(string *file_name*)
umask()	The umask() function gets the current umask value or sets a temporary overriding umask value. When you call the function without a parameter, the umask() function returns the current umask value. You override the current umask value by calling the function with an actual parameter, which returns the new value. The integer returned by the function represents an octal number. You can use the following sprintf() function call to convert the number: sprintf("%u",*filesize($file*)). It has the following pattern: int umask([int *mask*])

TABLE 10-2. *File Information Functions* (continued)

insecure way to pass parameters in clear text because you are appending them to the end of an URL. It prints the following to a web page:

```
03-May-2006 10:06:18
```

File permissions work differently between Linux servers and Microsoft Windows servers as qualified earlier in the chapter. File permissions are more important on Linux systems because they determine multiuser read, write, and execute privileges. The integer returned by the fileperms() function is an octal number and must be converted from a scalar number into an octal representation by using the sprintf() function.

The following FilePermissions.php program demonstrates how to read file and umask values:

```
-- This is found in FilePermissions.php on the enclosed CD.
```

```php
<?php
  // Read the parameter from the URL.
  $file = $_GET["p_name"];

  // Format the Octal number.
  print "File [$file] permission [".
        substr(sprintf('%o',fileperms($file)),-4)."]<br>";

  // Print the system umask value.
  print "The system umask is [".
        substr(sprintf('%o',umask()),-2)."]";
?>
```

The FilePermissions.php program will print file permissions on a Linux or Microsoft Windows system. Permissions will differ between the file owner and other levels—both the group and the user. The umask value will be returned as the inverse of the file permissions on a Linux system.

The Windows system does not use the umask value to set default file privileges and return a zero or false value. Likewise, Microsoft Windows has only two types of file privileges: read and execute and read, write, and execute. Windows does not support groups. The program converts integer returns from the fileperms() and umask() functions into octal numbers by using the sprintf() function.

The FilePermissions.php program produces different output by server operating system, as shown here:

Linux

```
File [RedRabbit.html] permission [0644]
The system umask is [22]
```

Windows

```
File [RedRabbit.html] permission [0666]
The system umask is [0]
```

The last set of file information functions lets you identify a single statistic or set of statistics for a file. Some of these also behave differently between the Microsoft Windows and Linux operating systems. Linux supports the POSIX standards and likewise the POSIX libraries for PHP. The POSIX library provides utilities that let you convert owner and user ID values to meaningful names on Linux systems.

The following `FileOwner.php` program reads a single statistic about a file, which is the ownership ID value. The program then converts it to a meaningful user name when run on a POSIX-compliant operating system with the POSIX extension loaded in the environment:

 -- **This is found in FileOwner.php on the enclosed CD.**

```php
<?php
  // Read the parameter from the URL.
  $file = $_GET["p_name"];

  //Check POSIX operating system and converts the file owner number to name.
  if ((!ereg("Win32",$_SERVER["SERVER_SOFTWARE"])) &&
      (array_search("posix",get_loaded_extensions())))
  {
    $user = posix_getpwuid(fileowner($file));
    print $user["name"];
  }
  else
    print fileowner($file);
?>
```

The `ereg()` function is used to govern the behavior of the program to suit the operating system of the application server. When the operating system is a POSIX-compliant Linux system, the `$_SERVER["SERVER_SOFTWARE"]` element does not contain a Win32 string. The `ereg()` function is a regular expression search utility. The `posix_getpwuid()` function returns an associative array of values about a file owner or group.

The `get_loaded_extensions()` function verifies that the POSIX library is installed to avoid raising a fatal error. The `get_loaded_extensions()` function is demonstrated in Appendix D.

The name index points to the user or group name tied to a user or group ID. It renders the group ID on a Windows system and group name on a Linux system.

NOTE
The `/etc/passwd` and `/etc/group` files contain the user and group names accessed by the POSIX functions respectively. This is considered a security vulnerability by some, who disable the library.

The remaining file information single statistical functions work the same way as the `fileowner()` function. The `lstat()` and `stat()` functions let you get a set of statistics about a file. You will probably use one of these more often than the single-element functions because they enable building library functions.

The following `IdentifyFiles.php` program demonstrates capturing a set of statistics about a file. You should notice that the preceding date mask and POSIX library techniques are used in the `IdentifyFiles.php` program.

-- This is found in IdentifyFiles.php on the enclosed CD.

```php
<?php
  // Read the parameter from the URL.
  $file = $_GET["p_name"];

  // Verify the file exists.
  if (file_exists($file))
  {
    // Assign statistics to a local variable.
    $info = stat($file);

    // Declare variable with table start.
    $out = "<table border=0 cellpadding=0 cellspacing=0>";

    // Read the statistics on the file.
    foreach ($info as $name => $value)
    {
      // Eliminate numerically index row set.
      if (!ereg("[0-9]",$name))
      {
        // Append row tags and column values.
        $out .= "<tr><td valign=top>[".$name."]</td>";

        // Leverage fall through and simplify logic.
        switch (true)
        {
          case ($name == "atime"):
          case ($name == "mtime"):
          case ($name == "ctime"):
            // Convert the integer value to a meaningful date.
            $out .= "<td>[".date('d-M-Y h:i:s',$value)."]</td></td>";
            break;
          case ($name == "gid"):
          case ($name == "uid"):
            // Check for non-POSIX compliant server.
            if ((!ereg("Win32",$_SERVER["SERVER_SOFTWARE"])) &&
                (array_search("posix",get_loaded_extensions())))
            {
              // POSIX library converts the number.
              $user_name = posix_getpwuid($value);
              $out .= "<td>[".$user_name['name']."]</td></tr>";
            }
            else
              $out .= "<td>[".$value."]</td></tr>";
            break;
          default:
            $out .= "<td>[".$value."]</td></tr>";
        }
      }
    }
```

```
      // Close HTML table.
      $out .= "</table>";

      // Print file statistics.
      print $out;
    }
?>
```

The `stat()` function has been in PHP since version 3. In version 3, it returned values into a numerically indexed array. For backward compatibility it now returns two sets of statistics. One is numerically indexed, and the other is an associative array. The first `ereg()` function is used with a regular expression to filter out the numeric indexes. The second `ereg()` function call prevents executing the `posix_getpwuid()` function on Microsoft Windows servers or Linux servers where the POSIX library is not installed. Failing to screen for the platform will raise a run-time error.

The `IdentifyFiles.php` program produces the following output from a Linux System:

Microsoft Windows XP		**Linux Red Hat Enterprise 3.0**	
[dev]	[2]	[dev]	[5635]
[ino]	[0]	[ino]	[227144]
[mode]	[33206]	[mode]	[33188]
[nlink]	[1]	[nlink]	[1]
[uid]	[0]	[uid]	[mclaughlinm]
[gid]	[0]	[gid]	[oracle]
[rdev]	[2]	[rdev]	[-1]
[size]	[1861]	[size]	[1831]
[atime]	[03-May-2006 10:06:18]	[atime]	[04-May-2006 04:07:49]
[mtime]	[24-Apr-2006 02:02:54]	[mtime]	[03-May-2006 09:43:52]
[ctime]	[30-Apr-2006 08:00:34]	[ctime]	[03-May-2006 09:43:52]
[blksize]	[-1]	[blksize]	[-1]
[blocks]	[-1]	[blocks]	[-1]

Neither the Linux nor the Microsoft Windows file systems provide block size or count. You will also notice that `inode`, `uid`, and `gid` values are not available on Microsoft Windows, but they are found on Linux. The `posix_getpwuid()` function enables you to view the user and default group name for the file. The formatted dates are helpful toward human uptake of the information, but the underlying scalar variables are more useful for sorting or comparing files to find the older or newer ones.

File Location Functions

There are ten file location functions. They are typically useful when uploading or downloading files to your web applications, and building PHP programs to perform shell operations. PHP shell scripts operate by using the command-line interpreter, which is covered in the "Command-Line

PHP Scripting" sidebar later in this chapter. Table 10-3 summarizes the file location functions before you examine how to use them in programs.

The `RealPath.php` program demonstrates how you can expand details from a relative filename. The `$_GET["p_name"]` lets you assign a filename. Filenames are either absolute,

Function	Description and Pattern

basename()	The `basename()` function captures the filename minus the directory path and file extension. The function has the following pattern:
	
	``
	string basename(
	  string path
	  [,string extension])
	``

closedir()	The `closedir()` function closes a directory handle, which like a file handle is an open resource. It has one mandatory parameter, which is *an open directory handle*. When the function fails, it throws a run-time warning error. This function can also raise an error, which you should suppress and throw as an exception in PHP 5, as discussed in Chapter 9. It has the following pattern: ``` void closedir(resource directory_handle) ```
dirname()	The `dirname()` function returns a directory name. It has one mandatory parameter, which should contain a fully qualified path and filename. The `dirname()` function returns the current path of the running program minus the filename and extension. It has the following pattern: ``` string dirname(string file_name) ```
getcwd()	The `getcwd()` function returns the fully qualified directory for the current working directory of the running program file. It has the following pattern: ``` string getcwd() ```

glob()	The `glob()` function performs wildcard searches based on partial filenames. It has two formal parameters, one mandatory and the other optional. The required parameter is a search pattern. The second parameter is an optional flag from the enclosed table. The valid flag values for the optional parameter follow:
	
	■ GLOB_MARK Adds a slash to returned items.
	
	■ GLOB_NOSORT Returns files in order retrieved.
	
	■ GLOB_NOCHECK Returns a search pattern when no matches are found.
	
	■ GLOB_NOESCAPE Suppresses backquoting of metacharacters.
	
	■ GLOB_BRACE Expands {a,b,c} to 'a', 'b', or 'c'.
	
	■ GLOB_ONLYDIR Returns directory entries that match the search criteria.
	
	■ GLOB_ERR Stops when encountering a non-readable directory.
	
	The `glob()` function returns an array of filename matches, which are fully qualified absolute references. The return values match the search criteria. Upon encountering an error, the function returns false. It has the following pattern:
	
	``
	array glob(
	  string pattern
	  [,int flag])
	``

TABLE 10-3. *File Location Functions*

Function	Description and Pattern

opendir()	The opendir() function returns a directory handle. It has two parameters—one is mandatory, and the other is optional. The mandatory parameter is a string that designates the directory path. The optional second parameter is a resource, like a stream from a socket. When the function fails, it returns a false or null string value. It has the following pattern:
	
	`resource opendir(`
	`  string path`
	`  [,resource context)`

pathinfo()	The pathinfo() function returns an array that includes the directory name, base filename, and extension or any one of the three as a string. It has two parameters—one is mandatory, and the other is optional. The mandatory parameter is a filename, which can be a qualified relative or absolute path and filename. The optional second parameter designates a parameter value—PATHINFO_EXTENSION, PATHINFO_BASENAME, or PATHINFO_DIRNAME. When the function fails, it returns a false or null string value. It has the following pattern:
	
	`mixed pathinfo(`
	`  string file_name`
	`  [,int parameter_option)`

readdir()	The readdir() function is used to read a directory handle, which is like a file resource. The required parameter is *an open resource handler*. When the function fails, it returns a false or null string value. It has the following pattern: `string readdir(resource directory_handle)`
rewinddir()	The rewinddir() function resets the directory handle to the directory starting point. The required parameter is *an open resource handler*. When the rewinddir() function is successful, the function returns a string, which maps to a valid file system directory. When it fails, the function returns a false or null string value. It has the following pattern: `void rewinddir(resource directory_handle)`
realpath()	The realpath() function is used to build canonical paths from relative path references. When the function fails, it returns a false or null string value. It has the following pattern: `string realpath(string path)`

scandir()	The scandir() function reads the file system to capture, sort, and assign directory files to an array. The required parameter is a string containing a valid directory path. The second optional parameter is a sorting order flag, which is zero by default for ascending alphabetical order. When the second parameter is set to 1, the files are sorted in descending order. The optional third parameter is a resource, like a stream from a socket. When the function fails, it returns a false or null string value. It has the following pattern:
	
	`array scandir(`
	`  string path`
	`  [,int sort_order`
	`  [,resource context]])`

TABLE 10-3. *File Location Functions* (continued)

which means canonical, or relative. When you provide a relative filename, the location is relative to the program file processing it. Alternatively, an absolute filename includes a fully qualified path beginning from a Linux mount point or Microsoft Windows logical drive.

A filename that has no relative or absolute directory path is assumed to be found in the current working directory, which is the same directory as the program file that calls the file. The `RealPath.php` program is best suited to discovery of the absolute path of a file location, as follows:

-- This is found in RealPath.php on the enclosed CD.

```php
<?php
  // Read the parameter from the URL.
  $file = $_GET["p_name"];

  // Expand the relative path to an absolute path.
  $file_name = realpath($file);

  // Parse the directory minus the file.
  $directory = dirname($file_name);

  // Print the absolute filename and directory path.
  print $file_name."<br>".$dir;
?>
```

When you submit the following URL to the `RealPath.php` program, it evaluates the relative path to a fully qualified filename:

```
http://dev.techtinker.com/RealPath.php?p_name=RedRabbit.html
```

It then strips the file to find the fully qualified `$directory` and generates the following web page output from a Linux server:

```
/var/www/html/RedRabbit.html
/var/www/html
```

You take a different approach when you receive filenames that include fully qualified filenames as an actual parameter to your program because they include the absolute directory and filename. In this scenario, you may want to find the physical filename exclusive of the directory path. You can do this using the following statement:

```
$file = basename($file_name);
```

An easier approach to securing the present working directory (or to `csh` the current working directory) is to use the `getcwd()` function. The `getcwd()` function returns the fully qualified directory path to the current file. It works on both Linux and Microsoft Windows and can simplify cross-platform development.

The `opendir()`, `readdir()`, `rewinddir()`, `closedir()`, and `scandir()` functions are demonstrated in the next section. The combination of file location and management functions better illustrates how file location functions work in real programs by using relative and absolute file references. They are useful for web application program and critical for PHP scripting.

File Management Functions

File management functions let you manipulate files without reading them into and writing them out of memory. File management functions let you change file permissions; copy and delete files, updating their last accessed, modified, and changed attributes; and upload files. These functions are critical tools when you want to manipulate files without changing their contents.

Table 10-4 summarizes the file management functions. The `chgrp()`, `chmod()`, and `chown()` functions are not implemented on Microsoft Windows. After reviewing the basic functions in the table, you will examine how to use them in sample programs. Many of these have limited utility in web applications when run with the `apache` user's privileges. File management functions are most useful when you are running them in scripts that enjoy superuser privileges.

Function	Description and Pattern
`chgrp()`	The `chgrp()` function changes the group provided your user is a member of the group or has a privilege level to set a new group. *The group must exist in the /etc/group file, and you can use the gid or group name as the second actual parameter.* The function returns true when successful and false when you encounter an error. It has the following pattern: `bool chgrp(string file_name, mixed group)`
`chdir()`	The `chdir()` function changes the present working directory. The function takes a single parameter of a string, which needs to be a valid qualified path. It has the following pattern: `bool chdir(string directory)`
`chmod()`	The `chmod()` function changes the read, write, and execute privileges of a file or set of files. The integer value for the permission must be a four-digit number with a zero in position one and an octal number from the list of values found in Table 10-1. The function returns true when you successfully change file permissions and false when you encounter an error. It has the following pattern: `bool chmod(string file_name, int permissions)`
`chown()`	The `chown()` function changes the file owner. The user of the program must have permissions to make this change. *The user must exist in the /etc/passwd file, and you can use the uid or user name as the second actual parameter.* The function returns true when you successfully change file ownership and false when you encounter an error. It has the following pattern: `bool chown(string file_name, mixed user)`
`chroot()`	The `chroot()` function lets you change the present process root directory, which is the relative point for file and directory access. When you use this function within a web application, the Apache or IIS server must have read and execute privileges to the target directory. The function takes a single parameter of a string. The function returns true when you successfully change the process root directory and false when you encounter an error changing the directory. It has the following pattern: `bool chdir(string directory)`
`closedir()`	The `closedir()` function closes a directory handle. It takes one mandatory parameter, which is a resource handle for an open directory. The function returns no value. It has the following pattern: `void closedir( resource directory_handle)`

TABLE 10-4. *File Management Functions*

Function	Description and Pattern
copy()	The copy() function copies files. It requires two fully qualified filenames, which include the absolute or relative path and filename. The function returns true when successfully copying a file, and false when the copy action encounters an error. It has the following pattern: `bool copy(string source,, string dest)`

mkdir()	The mkdir() function creates a directory on the local file system or across a socket to an external resource. It has four parameters. The single mandatory parameter designates the relative directory path where the directory will be created. The optional parameters are: (a) a file mode, (b) a recursive flag, and (c) a resource context. The new directory has read, write, and execute permissions by default when the file mode is unspecified. It returns true when creating the directory and false on failure. It has the following pattern:
	
	`bool mkdir(`
	`  string path_directory`
	`  [, int mode`
	`  [, bool recursive`
	`  [, resource context]]])`

rmdir()	The rmdir() function removes a directory on the local file system or across a socket to an external resource. It has two parameters. The mandatory parameter designates the relative directory path where the directory will be removed. The optional parameter is a resource context, like a socket. It returns true when creating the directory and false on failure. It has the following pattern:
	
	`bool rmdir(`
	`  string path_directory`
	`  [, resource context])`

touch()	The touch() function updates an existing file access, change, or modification time and creates a new file of zero bytes when one does not exist. The first parameter is the filename, which may be a fully qualified or absolute path and filename. The second optional parameter modifies the access, change, and modification times when the third option parameter is not provided. The third optional parameter modifies the access time only. When neither of the optional parameters is provided, they are updated by the current system time value. The function returns true when successfully updating or creating a file; and false when the attempt encounters an error. Errors occur when the file ownership or permissions restrict the change. It has the following pattern:
	
	`bool touch(`
	`  string file_name`
	`  [,int time [,int atime]])`

unlink()	The unlink() function removes files from the local file system. It requires a fully qualified filename, which includes the absolute or relative path and filename. The optional resource parameter can access a valid stream of data, which can be a resource built using PHP sockets. The program returns true when successfully deleting the file and false when the program encounters an error removing the file. It has the following pattern:
	
	`bool unlink(`
	`  string file_name`
	`  [,resource context)`

TABLE 10-4.   *File Management Functions* (continued)

The file management utilities have some distinct limitations in web applications because they run under the ownership of the `apache` user. As a rule, the `apache` user is disabled after configuring Apache, and the Apache server is started as a background process on the application-tier server. This is critical to ensure a more secure operating environment for your web applications.

The `chown()` and `chgrp()` functions *have virtually no use in your web applications because the* `apache` *user does not have adequate permissions to overwrite files owned by other users.* The `chown()` and `chgrp()` commands are typically reserved to scripts run by the superuser or root account.

The file management limitations are removed when you run PHP programs as operating system scripts. Then, the PHP scripts run with the permissions of the user that started the program. A PHP script run by the root user can use the `chown()` and `chgrp()` functions.

Command-Line PHP Scripting

You can use the run-time PHP interpreter from the command line. When you run programs from the command line, a special set of parameters are added to the `$_SERVER` array. These values are identified by the `$_SERVER["argc"]` and `$_SERVER["argv"]`. The `argc` element contains an integer value that contains the list of arguments passed to the PHP interpreter, which includes the program name as argument zero. The `argv` element contains an array of string values.

These values are not available when the program is started by a web browser. There is a special requirement when you build a script that can be run by both the command line and the browser. You must use the error control operator to suppress a run-time error when checking for either the argc or argv elements in the `$_SERVER` array because one will be raised when calling the script from a browser.

The following `CommandLine.php` program demonstrates parameter evaluation for both command-line- and browser-originated script execution:

```
-- This is found in CommandLine.php on the enclosed CD.

<?php
  // Run script as command-line script.
  if (@$_SERVER["argv"])
    if ($_SERVER["argc"] > 1)
      for ($i = 1;$i < $_SERVER["argc"];$i++)
        print "Command-line [".($i - 1)."]\t[".$_SERVER["argv"][$i]."]\n";
    else
      print "Command-line arguments are not provided.\n";

  // Run script as URL with GET method that has arguments.
  else if (count($_GET))
    foreach ($_GET as $name => $value)
      print "\$_GET[\"$name\"] = [$value]<br>";
```

(continued)

```
  // Run script as URL with POST method that has arguments.
  else if (count($_POST))
    foreach ($_POST as $name => $value)
      print "\$_POST[\"$name\"][$value]<br>";

  // Run script as URL without arguments.
  else
    print "Browser URL arguments are not provided.<br>";
?>
```

The CommandLine.php program will print any actual parameters passed to the program or a no argument message. The style for printing the message differs between the command line and the browser. You dispense with HTML tags when running from the command line but use HTML tags when using the browser as the execution tool.

Realistically, you want to make sure there are no external HTML tags to the PHP program when the script should run in both environments. If there are external HTML tags and text in the file, they will be rendered as part of standard output from the PHP interpreter because they're managed as part of standard output for the program.

You run programs at the command line by using the php executable, a filename that contains PHP programming code, and a list of arguments. When you want to treat two words separated by a white space as single parameter, you enclose them in double quotes. The following demonstrates calling the CommandLine.php program with one argument that consists of two words separated by a white space:

```
php CommandLine.php "Hello World"
```

There is no practical limit to the number of arguments that you pass to these programs. Command-line PHP scripts can replace shell scripts written in various shell scripting languages or Perl.

The ChangePermission.php program demonstrates using the touch() and chmod() functions in a PHP script run as a web page. Seeing how the data changes requires using two file information functions from Table 10-2, fileperms() and clearstatcache(). Together these let you check the file permissions, clear the information cache, and recheck file permissions.

The fileperms() function discovers the file permissions but sets the value into a cache, which suppresses updates. *Unless you clear the cache, any subsequent call to the fileperms() function will return the original value, which may be incorrect.* Using the clearstatcache() function, you can reuse the fileperms() function in a program to get changes in file permissions.

TIP

When you want to change permissions on files in a Linux system, the user running the PHP program must have execute permissions on the directory. Without those permissions, you will encounter a run-time error.

The following `ChangePermission.php` program demonstrates creating an empty file and changing its default permissions:

-- **This is found in ChangePermission.php on the enclosed CD.**

```php
<?php
  // Read the parameter from the URL.
  $file = $_GET["p_name"];

  // Check for file before creating it.
  if (!file_exists($file))
    touch($file);

  // Print initial permissions.
  print "Permissions: [".get_permissions($file)."]<br>";

  try
  {
    // Set to all for owner, read and execute for others.
    if (@!chmod($file,0755))
      throw new Exception("Change to ".realpath($file)." disallowed.",1);
  }
  catch (Exception $e)
  {
    print $e->getMessage()."<br />";
  }

  // Print changed permissions.
  print "Permissions: [".get_permissions($file)."]<br>";

  // Get file permissions.
  function get_permissions($file)
  {
    // Declare file permission variable.
    $perms = substr(sprintf('%o',fileperms($file)),-4);

    // Clear the program file statistics.
    clearstatcache();

    // Return current file parameters.
    return $perms;
  }
?>
```

The `ChangePermission.php` program is called by using the following URL:

http://dev.techtinker.com/ChangePermission.php?p_name=Test.html

There is no magic to the choice of `Test.html` as a filename, and you can substitute whatever file you prefer in the URL. The `ChangePermission.php` program will check if the file already exists in the same relative directory before creating a zero-character file. You typically create the file with the owner having read, write, and execute permissions, and the group and users having read-only permission. The program then prints the file permissions before attempting to change file permissions. The owner permissions are set to read, write, and execute, and both the group and user permissions are changed to read and execute.

NOTE
The file permissions will be read, write, and execute for all users on a Windows server. Windows does not differentiate between owner, group, and user privileges.

If the file does not exist prior to running the ChangePermission.php program, the program renders the following results for a Linux server in a web page:

```
Permissions: [0644]
Permissions: [0755]
```

If you test the ChangePermission.php program on a Microsoft Windows application server, you will see only read and write permissions because all programs are executable by default. Windows will display octal 0666 for both permission statements in the ChangePermission.php program.

The calls to fileperms() and clearstatcache() functions are inside a function to make sure that *each call that sets the cache is immediately cleared.* As noted earlier in the chapter, failing to clear the cache can return obsolete values.

NOTE
The ChangePermission.php uses a try-catch block and requires PHP 5 to avoid throwing a run-time parsing error.

The MoveFile.php program blends the opendir(), readdir(), rewinddir(), and closedir() functions from the prior section with the touch(), copy(), and unlink() functions from this section. The program shows you how to create, copy, and delete files and mimics moving a file in the local operating system. Unlike earlier programs in the chapter, MoveFile.php does not take a parameter in the URL.

The following MoveFile.php program uses a function to read and rewind the directory resource because it is traversed three times by calling the user-defined find_files() function:

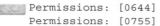 **-- This is found in MoveFile.php on the enclosed CD.**

```php
<?php
  // Declare file variables.
  $file1 = "NewFile1.txt";
  $file2 = "NewFile2.txt";

  // Declare array of files.
  $list = array($file1,$file2);

  // Check for file before creating it.
  if (!file_exists($file1))
    touch($file1);
```

```php
// Secure a directory handle.
$dhandle = opendir(getcwd());

// Print matching files from directory.
print "<hr />".find_files($list,$dhandle);

// Copy first file to second file.
copy($file1,$file2);

// Print matching files from directory.
print "<hr />".find_files($list,$dhandle);

// Delete first file from directory.
unlink($file1);

// Print matching files from directory.
print "<hr />".find_files($list,$dhandle)."<hr />";

// Close directory handle.
@closedir($dhandle);

// Find a list of files in a directory passed by reference.
function find_files($set,&$dhandle)
{
  // Declare a return string.
  $list = "";

  // Read through the list of files.
  while (($file = readdir($dhandle)) !== false)
  {
    // Check if they're members of the search array.
    if (in_array($file,$set))
      $list .= $file."<br />";
  }

  // Rewind the directory handle so that it can be reused.
  rewinddir($dhandle);

  // Return the formatted string.
  return $list;
}
?>
```

The program checks if a file exists before creating one with the touch command and then opens a directory handle for the present working directory. Then, the program calls the find_files() function, which (a) reads directory contents looking for matches against an array of values, (b) rewinds the directory handle, and (c) returns any matches. The program copies the files, recalls the find_files() function, deletes the first file with the unlink() function, and closes the directory handle.

Assuming that you do not have `NewFile1.txt` and `NewFile2.txt` in your testing directory, you should see the following output to a web page:

```
NewFile1.txt

-----------------------------------------------------------
NewFile1.txt
NewFile2.txt

-----------------------------------------------------------
NewFile2.txt
```

This demonstrates that the first file is created by the `touch` command, the first file is copied to the second, and the first file is deleted after having created the original file. Line breaks delimit the three phases of the program.

You can eliminate managing the file handles by using the `scandir()` function. It replaces the `opendir()`, `readdir()`, `rewinddir()`, and `closedir()` functions and simplifies your programming solution. The following `ScanFile.php` program illustrates the simplified approach by modifying the user-defined `find_files()` function:

-- This is found in ScanFile.php on the enclosed CD.

```php
<?php
  // Declare file variables.
  $file1 = "NewFile1.txt";
  $file2 = "NewFile2.txt";

  // Declare array of files.
  $list = array($file1,$file2);

  // Check for file before creating it.
  if (!file_exists($file1))
    touch($file1);

  // Print matching files from directory.
  print "<hr />".find_files($list);

  // Copy first file to second file.
  copy($file1,$file2);

  // Print matching files from directory.
  print "<hr />".find_files($list);

  // Delete first file from directory.
  unlink($file1);

  // Print matching files from directory.
  print "<hr />".find_files($list)."<hr />";

  // Find a list of files in a directory passed by reference.
  function find_files($set)
```

```
  {
    // Declare a return string.
    $list = "";

    // Declare an array with the directory files.
    $dir = scandir(getcwd());

    // Read through the list of files.
    for ($i = 0;$i < count($dir);$i++)
    {
      // Check if they're members of the search array.
      if (in_array($dir[$i],$set))
        $list .= $dir[$i]."<br />";
    }
      // Return the formatted string.
      return $list;
  }
?>
```

The scandir() function fits nicely inside the user-defined find_files() function and populates a local array of strings each time the function is called. This simplifies the PHP code by eliminating the need to build and pass a reference to a directory handle, and then into the function where it is rewound. Also, the more complex while-loop syntax required by the readdir() function is replaced by a simpler for-loop syntax.

You can further simplify the user-defined find_files() function by replacing the scandir() function with the glob() function. The glob() function only returns those files that match the criteria. This change eliminates the conditional check inside the function, as shown in the following Glob.php program:

-- **This is found in Glob.php on the enclosed CD.**

```
  // Find a list of files in a directory passed by reference.
  function find_files($search_string)
  {
    // Declare a return string.
    $list = "";

    // Declare an array with the wildcard matching files.
    $dir = glob($search_string);

    // Read through the list of files.
    for ($i = 0;$i < count($dir);$i++)
      $list .= $dir[$i]."<br />";

      // Return the formatted string.
      return $list;
  }
```

You can find the complete code on the enclosed CD in the Glob.php file. The balance of the Glob.php program code is a mirror to that found in the ScanFile.php program presented earlier in the chapter. The glob() function eliminates the need to do a comparison of values and limits the number of elements that the for loop iterates through. There are times when one will work better than the other, but you now have three approaches to traversing directory contents and managing files.

This section has demonstrated how you can combine the file location and management functions to write effective programs. While you have used the file_exists() function, the next section covers other file status functions.

File Status Functions

There are a series of file status functions that let you verify when a resource is a directory, file, or link. Likewise, you can check when files are executable, uploaded, readable, and writable. They differ from the information functions in that they only return a Boolean true or false value.

These file status functions are useful when you want to verify a specific fact about a resource before attempting another action, as by using the is_dir() function before calling the glob() function. File status functions enable you to check before doing something, which avoids subsequent error handling operations. Table 10-5 summarizes the file status functions.

Function	Description and Pattern
is_dir()	The is_dir() function checks whether a resource is a directory. The function returns true when the directory path exists and returns false when it is not a directory. It has the following pattern: bool is_dir(string *file_name*)
is_executable()	The is_executable() function checks whether a resource exists and has execution permissions. The function returns true when the filename exists and the file has the execute privilege on Linux. The function does not work on Microsoft Windows because all files are executable and no formal execute privilege exists in the file system. When the file is not there or does not have an execute privilege, the function returns false. The function has the following pattern: bool is_executable(string *file_name*)
is_file()	The is_file() function checks whether a resource is a file. The function returns true when the filename resolves to an ordinary file and false when it does not. It has the following pattern: bool is_file(string *file_name*)
is_link()	The is_link() function checks whether a resource is a link on Linux. The function returns true when the filename resolves to a link and false when it does not. It has the following pattern: bool is_link(string *file_name*)

TABLE 10-5. *File Status Functions*

Function	Description and Pattern
is_readable()	The is_readable() function checks whether a resource exists and has read permission. The function returns true when the filename exists and the file has the read privilege on Linux and Microsoft Windows. When the file is not there or does not have the read privilege, the function returns false. It has the following pattern: bool is_readable(string *file_name*)
is_uploaded_file()	The is_uploaded_file() function checks whether a resource is a file uploaded through a POST operation to the server. When the file is uploaded via a POST operation, the function returns true. Otherwise, the function returns false. It has the following pattern: bool is_uploaded_file(string *file_name*)
is_writable()	The is_writable() function checks whether a resource exists and has write permission. The function returns true when the filename exists and the file has the write privilege on Linux and Microsoft Windows. When the file is not there or does not have the write privilege, the function returns false. It has the following pattern: bool is_writable(string *file_name*)
is_writeable()	The is_writeable() function is an alias for the is_writable() function, which checks whether a resource exists and has write permission. The function has the following pattern: bool is_writeable(string *file_name*)

TABLE 10-5. *File Status Functions* (continued)

Status functions store their results in the file statistics cache. When some statistic changes on the operating system, you need to clear the cache before reacquiring its status. You do this by calling the clearstatcache() function. Failure to clear the cache before a subsequent call can return misleading information and cause your program to perform unexpectedly or fail.

The following Status.php program shows how to use several of these status functions:

-- **This is found in Status.php on the enclosed CD.**

```php
<?php
  // Build the canonical filename.
  $file = realpath($_GET["p_name"]);

  // Print the canonical filename.
  print "The file is: [".$file."]<br>";
```

```
    // Checks whether a string maps to a directory.
    if (is_dir($file))
      print "It's a directory.<br />";
    else
      print "It's not a directory.<br />";

    // Checks whether a string maps to a file.
    if (is_file($file))
      print "It's a file.<br />";
    else
      print "It's not a file.<br />";

    // Checks whether a string maps to an executable file.
    if (is_executable($file))
      print "It's executable.<br />";
    else
      print "It's not executable.<br />";

    // Checks whether a string maps to a readable file.
    if (is_readable($file))
      print "It's readable.<br />";
    else
      print "It's not readable.<br />";

      // Checks whether a string maps to a writable file.
    if (is_writable($file))
      print "It's writable.<br />";
    else
      print "It's not writable.<br />";
?>
```

The `realpath()` function lets you run this program against any directory, not just the default process directory. In this example, however, the `realpath()` function resolves the default process directory. The `Status.php` program will return the following output to a web page on the different server platforms:

Linux

```
The file is: [/var/www/html/RedRabbit.html]
It's not a directory.
It's a file.
It's not executable.
It's readable.
It's not writable.
```

Windows

```
The file is: [C:\Apache\RedRabbit.html]
It's not a directory.
It's a file.
It's not executable.
It's readable.
It's writable.
```

Function	Description and Pattern
`disk_free_space()`	The `disk_free_space()` function finds the amount of free space on a Linux mount point or a Microsoft Windows logical partition. It takes a single parameter of a directory string, which can be the `getcwd()` function, which works across platforms. The function is limited to local file systems and will not work on remote file systems. It has the following pattern: `float disk_free_space(string directory)`
`disk_total_space()`	The `disk_total_space()` function finds the amount of free space on a Linux mount point or a Microsoft Windows logical partition. It takes a single parameter of a directory string, which can be a nested call to the `getcwd()` function, which works across platforms. The function is limited to local file systems and will not work on remote file systems. It has the following pattern: `float disk_total_space(string directory)`
`diskfreespace()`	The `diskfreespace()` function is an alias for the `disk_free_space()` function. It has the same signature or pattern: `float disk_free_space(string directory)`

TABLE 10-6. *File System Functions*

The `Status.php` program demonstrates how to verify the status of physical directories or files. You should note that the `is_executable()` function does not work on Microsoft Windows because that is not a valid file system property.

File System Functions

Finding the amount of free space on a disk is critical when you are uploading files through a web application. PHP provides two functions and one alias to probe the available and total disk space. Table 10-6 summarizes the file system functions.

The `DiskSystem.php` program calculates and formats the output of both the available free space and the total disk space for a Linux mount point or Microsoft Windows logical drive. The program uses the `getcwd()` function discussed in the file location section, which makes the script platform neutral. Platform-neutral scripts run equally well across different operating systems, such as Linux or Microsoft Windows.

The following `DiskSystem.php` program also demonstrates some formatting techniques that mirror standard methods for calculating disk space:

```
-- This is found in DiskSystem.php on the enclosed CD.

<?php
  // Get the mount point free disk space.
  $free = number_format(disk_free_space(getcwd())/1073741824,2);

  // Get the mount point total disk space.
  $available = number_format(disk_total_space(getcwd())/1073741824,2);
```

```
// Get percentage free space.
$percentage = substr(($free/$available*100),0,4);

// Build an associative array to print in HTML table.
$display = array();
$display['Free Disk Space'] = substr($free,0,4)." GB";
$display['Available Disk Space'] = substr($available,0,4)." GB";
$display['Percentage Free Disk Space'] = $percentage."%";

// Open HTML table.
print "<table border=0 cellpadding=0 cellspacing=0>";

// Read and add array keys and values to a string.
foreach ($display as $name => $value)
{
   // Prepend row tag and first column value.
   print "<tr><td valign=top>[".$name."]</td>";

   // Append row tag and second column value.
   print "<td>[".$value."]</td></tr>";
}

// Close HTML table.
   print "</table>";
?>
```

The `DiskSystem.php` program generates the following output to a web page:

[Free Disk Space]	[43.9 GB]
[Available Disk Space]	[55.8 GB]
[Percentage Free Disk Space]	[78.7%]

The `number_format()` function is used to put in commas for thousands and a decimal point where appropriate. The actual bytes are divided by 1024 cubed, and a `substr()` function is used to truncate anything less than a tenth of a gigabyte from the displayed value.

This section has introduced you to the core functions that enable you to navigate and evaluate the application server operating system. The next section will demonstrate how you use these and other functions to read and write files.

Reading and Writing Files

This section integrates file management and system concepts while demonstrating how to read and write files from your PHP programs. Reading and writing files is an integral part of web application design in dynamic pages. While reading and writing data files has migrated in many instances to reading data from and writing data to databases, there are still many opportunities to read and write files.

Files contain many things, which can vary from simple text to collections of highly organized data structures. In the mix of varieties, you can have simple comma- or tab-delimited files. The data in these files are typically scalar values, like numbers and strings. They are also known as flat files. The flat-file label is not derived from their lack of character but from their traditional two-dimensional (2D) structure. The first dimension is the row, and the second dimension is the number of data elements delimited in each row.

This type of structure is often called a record and field structure or spreadsheet format. When the delimiter is a comma, the format is also known as comma-separated values (CSV), and the corresponding rule holds for tab-separated values (TSV). The only difference between these two formats is the delimiter. These file structures let you easily move data into and out of spreadsheets or databases. These files are frequently processed by your programs line-by-line when reading or writing them.

NOTE
Text files that are CSV are defined by one of the following MIME types: text/csv, application/csv, or text/x-csv as defined in RFC 4180. Tab-delimited files generally use the same MIME types but sometimes use text/tsv, application/tsv, or text/x-tsv.

On the more complex end of files, you have files that include data structures. Data structures are built to preserve compound as opposed to scalar data. As discussed in Chapter 4, compound data contains arrays and objects. Traditional structures preserve a position and data type signature, but as PHP is a dynamically typed language, only position matters in PHP structures. This behavior enables associative arrays to describe structures. Compound data structures add a third dimension to 2D files; an example is a spreadsheet software workbook that contains worksheets.

Delimited 2D and 3D files are useful tools when preserving complex related data, such as file application source, version, or organization information. These files contain sets of data that are valuable only when preserved in their structural context. How you read 2D and 3D files or files containing structures is typically done by reading lines as records and comma- or tab-delimited values as fields.

When data is stored in native structures the mechanisms vary widely because compound data structures require customized delimiters and parsing algorithms to both read and write their contents. You typically read and write these types of delimited files element by element by using a metadata file that explains how the compound data is organized. These metadata files are less frequent since Extended Markup Language (XML) has been adopted widely. XML provides the metadata to read and write these files through user-defined tags.

Table 10-7 summarizes the available functions to read and write files. There is no difference between resource pointers and handles. Resource handles are variables that let you keep open connections to external files. After Table 10-7, there will be examples demonstrating a selection of these functions to read and write files.

The reading and writing examples are divided into two subsections, "Reading Files" and "Writing Files." As discussed in Table 10-7, there are more ways to read files than there are to write them. You will cover how to read files before considering how to write data to files. As you work through the examples, you will find similar approaches to both activities. You can read and write files as whole units, lines, or characters.

The last subsection demonstrates how to upload files from client web browsers to your server. This section should empower you to make effective choices in PHP application and program design and, probably, to decide which file I/O approaches to use in your applications.

Function	Description and Pattern
fclose()	The fclose() function closes an open file pointer. It requires a file handle as its one parameter. It returns true when successful and false when it fails. The function has the following pattern: bool fclose(resource *file_handle*)
feof()	The feof() function checks to determine when you've reached the end of an open file pointer, which can also be a socket. It requires a file handle as its one parameter. It returns true when successful and false when it fails or the socket connection is interrupted. The function has the following pattern: bool feof(resource *file_handle*)
fflush()	The fflush() function forces a buffer write to a file or resource, which is referenced by the file handle. It requires a file handle as its one parameter. It returns true when successful and false when it fails or the socket connection is interrupted. The function has the following pattern: bool fflush(resource *file_handle*)
fgetc()	The fgetc() function reads a single character from a file into a PHP string variable. It returns false or a null string when it reads the end-of-file (eof) marker. It requires a file handle as its one parameter. The function has the following pattern: string fgetc(resource *file_handle*)

fgetcsv()	The fgetcsv() function reads a line of text as an array of comma-separated values. While the default delimiter is a comma, you can also substitute other single characters as the delimiter, such as a tab. The fgetcsv() function has one mandatory and three optional parameters. The mandatory parameter is a file handle. The optional parameters are respectively: a length parameter greater than the longest line in the file, a one-character string delimiter (by default a comma), and a one-character field enclosure (by default a double quote). The character field enclosure lets you embed a delimiting character in a field. The function returns an array of strings when successful and false when reading the end-of-file (eof) marker or when encountering an error. The function has the following pattern:
	
	array fgetcsv(resource *file_handle*
	  [,int *length*
	  [,string *delimiter*
	  [,string *enclosure*]]])

TABLE 10-7. *File Read Functions*

Function	Description and Pattern

fgets()	The fgets() function reads a line of text as a string. The fgets() function has one mandatory parameter and one optional parameter. The mandatory parameter is a file handle. The optional parameter is the line length. When the lines of text are greater than 8KB, you should set the line length and read portions of the file through a buffer. This will increase the efficiency of your file reads. The function returns a string when successful and false when reading the end-of-file (eof) marker or when encountering an error. The function has the following pattern:
	
	`string fgets(resource file_handle`
	`  [,int length])`

fgetss()	The fgetss() function reads a line of text as a string while removing HTML tags. The fgetss() function has one mandatory and two optional parameters. The mandatory parameter is a file handle. The optional parameters are the line length and allowable HTML tags. The function returns a string when successful and false when encountering an error. The function has the following pattern:
	
	`string fgetss(resource file_handle`
	`  [,int length`
	`  [,string allowed_tags]])`

file()	The file() function reads a file or portion of a file into a string. The file() function has one mandatory and two optional parameters in PHP 5. The mandatory parameter is a filename, which can be a qualified relative or absolute path and filename. The first optional parameter by default is set to false. You set it to true when you want to search the include_path directive from the php.ini file. The second optional parameter is a resource context, like a socket to a remote URL. The function returns a string when successful and false when encountering an error. The function has the following pattern:
	
	`array file(resource file_handle`
	`  [,bool use_include_path`
	`  [,resource context]])`

file_get_contents()	The file_get_contents() function reads a file or portion of a file into a string. The file_get_contents() function has one mandatory and four optional parameters in PHP 5. The mandatory parameter is a file handle. The first optional parameter by default is false. You set it to true when you want to search the include_path directive from the php.ini file. The second optional parameter is a resource context, like a socket to a remote URL. The third optional parameter sets the offset or beginning character to read the file. The fourth optional parameter added in PHP 5.1 sets a maximum length on the string read. The function

TABLE 10-7. *File Read Functions* (continued)

Function	Description and Pattern
	returns a string when successful and false when encountering an error. The function has the following pattern: ```\nstring file_get_contents(\n resource file_handle\n [,bool use_include_path\n [,resource context\n [,int offset\n [,int maxlen]]]])\n```
file_put_contents()	The file_put_contents() function puts a string or array into a file or socket. The file_put_contents() function has two mandatory and two optional parameters. The first mandatory parameter is a fully qualified path and filename. The second mandatory parameter is a string or array variable. The first optional parameter is a flag value, which can be one of the following: FILE_APPEND, LOCK_EX, and FILE_USE_INCLUDE_PATH. The second optional parameter is a resource context, such as a socket to a remote URL. The function returns the number of bytes written to the file or resource when successful and returns false when encountering an error. The function has the following pattern: ```\nint file_put_contents(string file_name\n [,mixed data\n [,int flag\n [,resource context]]])\n```
flock()	The flock() function locks a file resource while working with it. It has two mandatory and one optional parameters. The first mandatory parameter is an open file handle, and the second is one of four defined locking operations. The first optional parameter is set to true when the process should acquire a blocking lock on the file. The flock() function does not work on remote file systems, such as NFS-mounted file systems. The problem is that it cannot guarantee a blocking lock on a remote file system. The four operation constants arrived in PHP 4:

- LOCH_SH = 1   A reader sets a shared lock, which lets other readers access the file.

- LOCH_EX = 2   A writer sets an exclusive lock, which prevents other writers from accessing the file.

- LOCH_UN = 3   A reader or writer unsets a shared or exclusive lock.

- LOCH_NB = 4   A reader or writer can disable the blocking behavior by using this behavior.

The flock() function returns true when successful and false when unsuccessful or encountering an error. It has the following pattern:

```
bool flock(resource file_handle
  , int operation
  [, int &would_block])
```

TABLE 10-7. *File Read Functions* (continued)

Function	Description and Pattern
fopen()	The fopen() function opens a resource, like a file. You can then read or write to the file. The fopen() function has two mandatory and two optional parameters. The first mandatory parameter is a qualified path and filename. The second mandatory parameter is a mode value. The mode value has the following possible values:

- Mode [r] Opens for reading only, while placing the file pointer at the beginning of the file.

- Mode [r+] Opens for reading and writing, while placing the file pointer at the beginning of the file.

- Mode [w] Opens a new file for writing only when one does not already exist, or opens an existing file for writing only. It deletes the previous content by truncating the file to zero length. In both cases, the file pointer is placed at the beginning of the file.

- Mode [w+] Opens a new file for reading and writing when one does not already exist, or opens an existing file for reading and writing. It deletes any previous content by truncating the file to zero length. In both cases, the file pointer is placed at the beginning of the file.

- Mode [a] Opens a new file for writing only when one does not already exist, or opens an existing file for writing only. In both cases, the file pointer is placed at the end of the file.

- Mode [a+] Opens a new file for reading and writing when one does not already exist, or opens an existing file for reading and writing only. In both cases, the file pointer is placed at the end of the file.

- Mode [x] Opens a new file for writing only when one does not already exist, or raises an exception if one does exist. The file pointer is placed at the beginning of the file. This only works for local files.

- Mode [x+] Opens a new file for reading and writing only when one does not already exist, or raises an exception if one does exist. The file pointer is placed at the beginning of the file. This only works for local files.

The first optional parameter by default is false; set it to true when you want to search the include_path directive from the php.ini file. The second optional parameter is a resource context, like a socket to a remote URL. The function has the following pattern:

```
resource fopen(resource file_handle
  [,string mode
  [,bool use_include_path
  [,resource context]]])
```

TABLE 10-7. *File Read Functions* (continued)

Function	Description and Pattern
fpassthru()	The fpassthru() function reads a file and passes it through to standard out. *Standard out is the web page when you call fpassthru() from a web page and the console when you call it from a command-line script.* The function reads from the current position of the file pointer until arriving at the end-of-file (eof) marker. It returns the number of characters read from the file. The function has the following pattern: int fpassthru(resource *file_handle*)
fputcsv()	The fputcsv() function writes a line of text as comma-separated values. You can also substitute other single characters as the delimiter instead of a comma. The fputcsv() function has one mandatory and three optional parameters. The mandatory parameter is a file handle. The optional parameters are, respectively: an array of values, a one-character string delimiter that has a comma as a default value, and a one-character field enclosure that has a double quote character as a default value. The function returns true when successful and false when encountering an error while writing the file. The function has the following pattern: int fputcsv(resource *file_handle* [,array *data* [,string *delimiter* [,string *enclosure*]]])
fputs()	The fputs() function is an alias for the fwrite() function and writes a line of text to a file. The function has two mandatory parameters and one optional parameter. The mandatory parameters are a file handle and a string. The optional parameter is a length value that sets the line size written to a file. The function returns the number of characters written to the file or the maximum set by the length value. The function returns false when encountering an error. The function has the following pattern: int fputs(resource *file_handle* ,string *data* [,int *length*]]])
fread()	The fread() function is a binary-safe file reading utility. It has two mandatory parameters. The mandatory parameters are a file handle and a maximum number of characters to read. The function returns a string containing the characters read, which can be the whole file or the maximum number of characters. It implicitly moves the file pointer to the next sequential position following the previously read data set. The function returns false when encountering an error. The function has the following pattern: string fread(resource *file_handle* ,int *length*)
fscanf()	The fscanf() function reads a line of text from a file. It moves the file pointer position implicitly to the next line. The fscanf() function has two mandatory parameters and one optional parameter. The mandatory parameters are a file handle and a string format. When only the mandatory

TABLE 10-7. *File Read Functions* (continued)

Function	Description and Pattern

	parameters are passed, the function will return an array of values. You can submit a list of optional values that will be read. The function has the following pattern:
	
	```mixed fscanf(resource file_handle```
	  ```,string format```
	  ```[,mixed var1```
	  ```[,mixed var2]])```

`fseek()`	The `fseek()` function sets the position of the file pointer in an opened file. The `fseek()` function has two mandatory parameters and one optional parameter. The mandatory parameters are a file handle and an offset value. The optional parameter sets the way the position handle is moved or advanced in the file handle.
	
	■ `SEEK_SET` Sets the file pointer position to the offset value from the beginning of the file. This is the default value when the third parameter is not included.
	
	■ `SEEK_CUR` Sets the file pointer position to the sum of the current position plus the offset value.
	
	■ `SEEK_END` Sets the file pointer position to the end-of-file (eof) marker plus the offset, which should generally be a negative number. This enables you to move the position a specified distance backward from the eof value. It is possible to set the value beyond the eof marker and not raise an error.
	
	The `fseek()` function returns a zero on success and a negative 1 when it fails. Successful positioning is then read as false and failure read as true. The function has the following pattern:
	
	```int fseek(resource file_handle```
	  ```,int offset```
	  ```[,int whence])```

`ftell()`	The `ftell()` function finds the current position of the file pointer in an open file or resource. The `ftell()` function has one mandatory parameter, which is an open file handle. When successful, the function returns the file pointer position; upon encountering an error, it returns false. The function has the following pattern: ```int ftell(resource file_handle)```

`ftruncate()`	The `ftruncate()` function lets you truncate a file to a specified length. The `ftruncate()` function has two mandatory parameters. One is an open file handle, and the other is the desired file size. The function will remove everything beyond the value specified as the second parameter. It returns a true on success and false when encountering an error. The function has the following pattern:
	
	```int ftruncate(resource file_handle```
	  ```,int size)```

TABLE 10-7. *File Read Functions* (continued)

Function	Description and Pattern

fwrite()	The fwrite() function writes a line of text to a file. The function has two mandatory parameters and one optional parameter. The mandatory parameters are a file handle and a string. The optional parameter is a length value that sets the line size written to a file. The function returns the number of characters written to the file or the maximum set by the length value. The function returns false when encountering an error. The function has the following pattern:
	
	`int fwrite(resource file_handle`
	`  ,string data`
	`  [,int length]]])`

move_uploaded_file()	The move_uploaded_file() function moves a file that has been uploaded by PHP to a new location. It requires two fully qualified path and filenames. It returns true when successful and false when encountering an error. It has the following pattern:
	
	`bool move_uploaded_file(string source`
	`      ,string dest)`

readfile()	The readfile() function lets you read a file and pass it through to standard out. Standard out is the web page when you call readfile() from a web page and the console when you call it from a command-line script. The readfile() function has one mandatory and two optional parameters. The mandatory parameter is an open file handle. The first optional parameter enables you to search the include_path directive set in the php.ini file. The second optional parameter enables you read a resource context, such as a socket to a remote URL. The function reads from the current position of the file pointer until the end-of-file (eof) marker. It returns the number of characters read from the file when successful and false when encountering an error. The function has the following pattern:
	
	`int readfile(string file_name`
	`  [,bool use_include_path`
	`  [,resource context]])`

rename()	The rename() function renames a file or directory. The rename() function has two mandatory parameters. One is for the existing directory or filename and the other for the new filename. The optional third parameter enables you read a resource context, such as a socket to a remote URL. The function returns true when successful and false when encountering an error. The function has the following pattern:
	
	`bool rename(string old_name`
	`  ,string new_name`
	`  [,resource context])`

rewind()	The rewind() function rewinds the file pointer to the beginning position of a file. It takes one mandatory parameter, which is an open file handle. The function returns true when successful and false when encountering an error. The function has the following pattern: `bool rewind(resource file_handle)`

TABLE 10-7. *File Read Functions* (continued)

Reading Files

PHP programs can read any files that are available to their program owner with read, read/write, or read/write/execute permissions. You will need to know what type of file you are opening to read it correctly. A common convention for identifying files before reading them is to check their file types. File types are generally indicated by a suffix known as an *extension* following the rightmost period in the filename.

File extensions typically follow a common convention, which is that they are three characters in length. HTML web pages often violate that rule by having four-character file extensions. The development guidelines of your organization will set whether or not these are three-character (.htm) or four-character (.html) extensions.

As a rule, you will know the file types in your application and organization. This section will use plain text, comma-separated value (CSV), and HTML files to demonstrate how to read files. These file types typically have .txt, .csv, and .htm extensions respectively.

You can read files character-by-character, chunk-by-chunk, line-by-line, as comma-separated values (CSV), or as a whole unit. The examples in this section will demonstrate how to use each of these approaches to read local files.

Character-by-Character File Reads

Character-by-character file reads are done when you need to parse a file for some specific detail or to create a buffered string to transmit data across a socket. The use for character-by-character reads can be infrequent in web applications.

The following GetFileByCharacters.php program reads the local php.ini file character by character into a string and then prints the string to the web page:

-- **This is found in GetFileByCharacters.php on the enclosed CD.**

```php
<?php
  // Set directory and backquote directory delimiters.
  $directory = "C:\\php\\";

  // Set the filename.
  $fname = "php.ini";

  // Declare an array to hold character buffers.
  $contents = "";

  // Check for a valid read-only file handle.
  if ($fp = fopen($directory.$fname,'r'))
  {
    // Read to end-of-file by character.
    while (!feof($fp))
      $contents .= fgetc($fp);

    // Close the open file handle.
    fclose($fp);
  }

  // Print the string containing the file characters.
  print $contents;
?>
```

The GetFileByCharacters.php program uses the fopen() function to return a file handle for a fully qualified filename. A fully qualified filename includes an absolute or relative directory path and a valid filename. The directory path is physically set in this example file for a Microsoft Windows application server. You should substitute the following line for declaration of the $directory variable for a Linux system:

```
$directory = "/etc/";
```

The program uses a while loop to open the file in read-only mode and make sure that the file handle has not reached the end-of-file marker as the gating condition. The check is made at each iteration through the loop before using the fgetc() function to read the next character of data.

The fgetc() functions reads one character from the file handle current position. When the last character is read, the current file handle position reaches the end-of-file marker and the loop exit condition is met. The program closes the file resource after reading the file and before working with the file contents.

Chunk-by-Chunk File Reads

Chunk-by-chunk file reads are typically more efficient in PHP, especially when line lengths exceed 8KB. When you know that the line length can exceed this limit, it is more efficient to read the file in chunks. The rule of thumb relates to the 8KB size of typical data blocks. You can read single blocks more efficiently than multiple blocks. Since many file systems store data in 8KB blocks, this is the general guideline.

The following GetFileByChunks.php program demonstrates reading the plain text php.ini file by 100-character chunks into an array:

-- **This is found in GetFileByChunks.php on the enclosed CD.**

```php
<?php
  // Set directory and backquote directory delimiters.
  $directory = "C:\\php\\";

  // Set the filename.
  $fname = "php.ini";

  // Declare an array to hold character buffers.
  $contents = array();

  // Check for a valid read-only file handle.
  if ($fp = fopen($directory.$fname,'r'))
  {
    // Read to end-of-file by chunks of 100 characters.
    while (!feof($fp))
      $contents[] = fgets($fp, 100)."<br />";

    // Close the open file handle.
    fclose($fp);
  }

  // Read and print the file by buffer chunks.
  foreach ($contents as $key => $value)
    print $value;
?>
```

The GetFileByChunks.php program uses the fopen() function to return a file handle for a fully qualified filename. A fully qualified filename includes an absolute or relative directory path and filename. A while loop checks to make sure that the file handle has not reached the end-of-file marker before using the fgets() function to read the next chunk of data. You can also use the fgetss() function when you want to strip designated HTML and XML tags.

The fgets() function reads from the file handle current position the number of characters specified by the second optional parameter, which is 100 characters in this case. Absent a second parameter, fgets() reads lines of text. When the length of the chunk from the current file handle position to the end-of-file marker is less than the optional length parameter, the function reads the last chunk as the shorter segment. The program closes the file resource after reading the file and before working with the file contents, which are printed to a web page.

Line-by-Line File Reads

Line-by-line file reads are exactly like chunk-by-chunk reads because the default for the fgets() function is to read files by lines. You should note that the line delimiter differs between Linux and Windows, as you can see when plain text files are transferred from Windows to Linux systems in binary file transfer mode.

The following GetFileByLines.php program virtually mirrors the logic of the GetFileByChunks.php program. It differs in that it excludes the optional second parameter to the fgets() function. It reads the plain text php.ini file by lines instead of chunks into an array and prints it to the web page:

-- **This is found in GetFileByLines.php on the enclosed CD.**

```php
<?php
  // Set directory and backquote directory delimiters.
  $directory = "C:\\php\\";

  // Set the filename.
  $fname = "php.ini";

  // Declare an array to hold character buffers.
  $contents = array();

  // Check for a valid read-only file handle.
  if ($fp = fopen($directory.$fname,'r'))
  {
    // Read to end-of-file by line.
    while (!feof($fp))
      $contents[] = fgets($fp)."<br />";

    // Close the open file handle.
    fclose($fp);
  }

  // Read and print the file by buffer chunks.
  foreach ($contents as $key => $value)
    print $value;
?>
```

There is only one difference between the GetFileByLines.php and the GetFileByChunks .php programs, which is the lack of a chunk setting in the former. Line-by-line reads are frequently used when you want to render a text file in an HTML web page and improve readability by appending a <br /> tag to each line. You can also use the fgetss() function when you want to strip designated HTML tags when reading files line by line.

The fgets() function requires you to manually code a while loop to get the output into an array, but the file() function will put the file into an array in one step. The file() function is covered in the section "Whole File Reads" later in this chapter.

Comma-Separated Value File Reads

Comma-separated value (CSV) and tab-separated value (TSV) files are used frequently. Commas and tabs are the typical delimiters used to separate values, which are also known as fields in CSV and TSV files. CSV and TSV files are the natural ways to import and export data from a spreadsheet program such as Microsoft Excel. CSV and TSV files are generally two-dimensional array structures as discussed in Chapter 6, which means they represent only scalar data from a single worksheet. The first array dimension is the number of rows, and the second array dimension is the number of columns.

You will find that CSV files come in two varieties. One is symmetrical, which means each row contains the same number of columns. The other is asymmetrical, which means that rows can contain different numbers of columns. Asymmetrical columns are rare because they're tedious to use. When you manage asymmetrical CSV files, you will require some type of metadata to decode the irregular structure in terms of index names. Alternatively, you can pass through an fgetcsv() function–generated array twice. The first pass through the array sets the maximum number of columns in any row. The second pass will read the contents into a structure, padding missing columns with null values. This extra processing overhead to decode data generally means that comma-delimited null values are provided when generating the file.

TIP
You really need a very good reason to bother with asymmetrical arrays in 2D flat files that use scalar values. A rule of thumb is that the first two dimensions should always be padded with nulls when creating CSV files. When compound values are in the flat file, only their 3D element should support asymmetry through a defined associative array or object type.

The following GetFileByCSV.php program demonstrates the use of a symmetrical array of statistics for the twelve calendar months of the year:

-- **This is found in GetFileByCSV.php on the enclosed CD.**

```php
<?php
  // Set the filename.
  $fname = realpath("csvfile.csv");

  // Declare an array to hold CSV values.
  $contents = array();
```

```php
// Check for a valid read-only file handle.
if ($fp = fopen($fname,'r'))
{
  // Read to end-of-file by CSV.
  while (!feof($fp))
    $contents[] = fgetcsv($fp,1000,",");

  // Close the open file handle.
  fclose($fp);
}

// Read and parse CSV file.
print render_csv_to_table($contents);

// Define function to render CSV file in HTML table.
function render_csv_to_table($csv_array)
{
  // Declare variable with table start.
  $out = "<table border=0 cellpadding=0 cellspacing=0>";

  // Loop through the rows.
  foreach ($csv_array as $key => $value)
  {
    // Prepend the open table row tag.
    $out .= "<tr>";

    // Loop through the columns and add HTML cell tags.
    foreach ($value as $skey => $svalue)
      $out .= "<td>".$svalue."</td>";

    // Append the close table row tag.
    $out .= "</tr>";
  }

  // Close HTML table.
  $out .= "</table>";

  // Return formatted CSV array.
  return $out;
}
?>
```

The GetFileByCSV.php program uses the fopen() function to return a file handle for a fully qualified filename. It uses a while loop to check that the file handle has not reached the end-of-file marker. Then, it uses the fgetcsv() function to read the next delimited value set from the file. The program assumes no line is greater than 1000 characters and uses a comma as the field delimiter.

The fgetcsv() function reads values from the file handle between (a) the beginning of a line and the first delimiter, (b) any two delimiters or commas, and (c) the last delimiter or comma and the end-of-line character. The program closes the file resource after reading the file and before working with the file contents.

Compartmentalizing your code into read and write processing modules ensures that you don't forget to release resources. This becomes even more important when the reads are against a database through a cursor, as will be shown in Chapter 13.

The GetFileByCSV.php also includes a formatting function. The formatting function translates the CSV values into an HTML table, which is rendered into a web page.

Whole File Reads

On numerous occasions, you will read small text files or streams into your application. You can read these as whole files or partial files. The file() function enables you to map a file or partial file to a string array. After converting the file to a string array, you can manage or manipulate the data in the array.

The following GetFile.php program shows you how to use the file() function to read a complete file into a string array:

-- **This is found in GetFile.php on the enclosed CD.**

```php
<?php
  // Set the filename.
  $fname = realpath("RedRabbit.htm");

  // Read the file into an array.
  $contents = file($fname);

  // Render the file text to the web page.
  foreach ($contents as $name => $value)
    print $value;
?>
```

Many programmers prefer the file() function to the fgets() function because of its greater ease of use. That is especially true when you want to read the data into a string array. However, the fgetss() function provides the ability to filter out selected HTML tags, making it superior to the file() function in certain situations.

The GetFile.php program renders the following excerpt from *Red Rabbit* by Tom Clancy:

Okay, how to fool them? *Foley asked himself. Give the other guy something he expected to see, and he'd see it, whether it was really there or not. They wanted the Soviets to believe that the Rabbit and his family had ... not skipped town, but had ... died?*

Dead people, so Captain Kidd had supposedly said, tell no tales. And neither did the wrong dead people.

Another alternative to using the fgets() and file() functions is the file_get_contents() function, which reads the file directly into a string variable. When reading a file into a string is the desired outcome, the file_get_contents() function is easier to use than the fgets() and file() functions.

You can also read a file directly to standard out, which is your web page or console, without storing it in an intermediate variable, by using either the readfile() and fpassthru() function. This is a useful technique when you have some fixed disclaimer that you want to append or a text-based document you want to display to a web page. These two functions work identically.

The following `FilePassThru.php` program shows how you can use the `fpassthru()` function to direct a file to standard out:

-- This is found in FilePassThru.php on the enclosed CD.

```php
<?php
  // Enable script to run at command line.
  if (@$_SERVER["argv"])
    for ($i = 1;$i < $_SERVER["argc"];$i++)
      print "Argument [".($i - 1)."]\t[".$_SERVER["argv"][$i]."]\n";

  // Declare a filename when no parameters are provided.
  if (count($_GET) == 0)
    $fn= "RedRabbit.htm";

  // Declare a read-only file pointer to a file in the local directory.
  $fp = fopen($fn,"r");

  // Read the file contents into standard out.
  fpassthru($fp);

  // Close the open file handle.
  fclose($fp);
?>
```

The `FilePassThru.php` program demonstrates how to manage parameters from the command line and a URL a bit differently than the example in the earlier sidebar "Command-Line PHP Scripting." While the `fpassthru()` function redirects the file to standard out, it is dependent on a file handle being opened and closed. You should consider using these functions when the file is already formatted for presentation because they are simple and powerful tools.

This concludes the sections examining how you read files. In the next section you will examine how to write files.

Writing Files

PHP programs can write files to directories when they have permission from the file system. Writing files differs from reading files in PHP. There is no function to write characters per se, but the `fwrite()` function is binary safe and writes strings to files. The `fwrite()` function has an alias, `fputs()`. Alternatively, you can write arrays of strings by using the `file_put_contents()` function or as comma-separated value (CSV) files with the `fputcsv()` function.

Unlike the options available for reading files, you are limited to writing files as strings, CSV strings, or arrays of strings. Since strings can vary from a single character to a set of characters, you really have the same power as provided by the predefined reading functions.

This section examines how you use the `fwrite()`, `file_put_contents()`, and `fputcsv()` functions. It is divided into two sections: "Writing Strings" and "Writing CSV Strings." The `fwrite()` function example actually writes an array of strings by wrapping its native behavior in a user-defined function. This aligns the examples with the file reading examples used earlier in the chapter.

Writing Strings

This section demonstrates how to use the `fwrite()` and `file_put_contents()` functions to write strings and arrays of strings. The `fputs()` function is not presented because it is only an alias for the `fwrite()` function.

The following `WriteFileAsString.php` program demonstrates writing an array of strings by writing one string at a time:

-- This is found in **WriteFileAsString.php** on the enclosed CD.

```php
<?php
  // Declare a filename.
  $file = $_GET["p_name"];

  // Determine file path delimiter.
  if (ereg("Win32",$_SERVER["SERVER_SOFTWARE"]))
    $slash = "\\";
  else
    $slash = "/";

  // Declare a fully qualified filename.
  $fname = getcwd().$slash.$file;

  // Define an array of strings from Red Rabbit by Tom Clancy.
  $data = array();
  $data[] = "<p><i>Okay, how to fool them?</i> Foley asked himself. ";
  $data[] = "Give the other guy something he expected to see, and he'd ";
  $data[] = "see it, whether it was really there or not. They wanted ";
  $data[] = "the Soviets to believe that the Rabbit and his family had ";
  $data[] = "... not skipped town, but had ... died?</p>";

  // When the file exists, delete it.
  if (is_file($fname))
    unlink($fname);

  // Call the function to write an array to a file.
  write_string($fname,$data);

  // Read the whole file into standard out.
  readfile($fname);

  // Define function to write a CSV file.
  function write_string($file,$string)
  {
    // Declare a read-only file resource.
    if ($fp = fopen($file,'a'))
    {
      // Read the two-dimensional array and write or append to a file.
      for ($i = 0;$i < count($string);$i++)
        if (!fwrite($fp,$string[$i]))
```

```
      // Close the open file handle.
      fclose($fp);
    }
  }
?>
```

The `WriteFileAsString().php` program takes one external parameter, the target filename. The delimiter in Linux is a forward slash, and in Microsoft Windows it is a backward slash. A check against the server software enables you to dynamically provide the appropriate slash delimiter.

You can use the following URL for a Linux or Microsoft Windows system:

`http://dev.techtinker.com/WriteFileAsString.php?p_name=newfile.txt`

The filename will not overwrite another file by the same name in the target directory, because the file is opened in append mode. However, any existing file is deleted by the `unlink()` function before the code attempts to write the file to disk, avoiding multiple copies of the string being written to the file.

The `fopen()` function creates a file when none exists and places the file handle at the end of the file before writing. This appends to an existing file when one exists. The `for` loop in the `write_string()` function reads all elements of the string array, and the `fwrite()` function writes them one string at a time to the end of the file.

The alternative to using the `fopen()`, `fwrite()` and `fclose()` functions is to call the `file_put_contents()` function, which effectively does all that the other three do individually. When you want to append to an existing file, however, the `file_put_contents()` function does not work. You must use the `fwrite()` function when you want to append to an existing file.

The following `WriteFileAsArray.php` program copies the contents of an array into a file with a single call to the `file_put_contents()` function:

`-- This is found in WriteFileAsArray.php on the enclosed CD.`

```php
<?php
  // Declare a filename.
  $file = $_GET["p_name"];

  // Determine file path delimiter.
  if (ereg("(Win32)",$_SERVER["SERVER_SOFTWARE"]))
    $slash = "\\";
  else
    $slash = "/";

  // Declare a fully qualified filename.
  $fname = getcwd().$slash.$file;

  // Define an array of strings from Red Rabbit by Tom Clancy.
  $data = array();
  $data[] = "<p><i>Okay, how to fool them?</i> Foley asked himself. ";
  $data[] = "Give the other guy something he expected to see, and he'd ";
  $data[] = "see it, whether it was really there or not. They wanted ";
  $data[] = "the Soviets to believe that the Rabbit and his family had ";
  $data[] = "... not skipped town, but had ... died?</p>";
```

```php
    // Call the function to write an array to a file.
    write_string_array($fname,$data);

    // Read the whole file into standard out.
    readfile($fname);

    // Define function to write a CSV file.
    function write_string_array($file,$array)
    {
      // Read the two-dimensional array and write to a file.
      file_put_contents($file,$array);
    }
?>
```

The `WriteFileAsArray.php` program uses a `single file_put_contents()` function call to delete, open, write to, and close a file. When writing new files, it is clearly a bit easier to use than the other collection of functions. You can use the following URL for a Linux system:

```
http://dev.techtinker.com/WriteFileAsArray.php?p_name=newfile.txt
```

These examples let you write strings to new files or append strings to old files. The next section will demonstrate how to write comma-separated value files.

Writing CSV Strings

Writing comma-separated value (CSV) and tab-separated value (TSV) files is useful when you are extracting information from databases for import into spreadsheets. You generate a two-dimensional array from the database, which is more or less the result from any query of scalar values, such as dates, numbers, or strings. Then, you can use the sample program function to build a CSV file.

The `WriteFileAsCSV.php` program takes two external parameters. The first parameter is a target filename, and the second is a directory delimiter. The delimiter in Linux is a forward slash; in Microsoft Windows it is a backward slash. The filename will overwrite any matching filename in that directory. You can use the following URL for a Linux system:

```
http://dev.techtinker.com/WriteFileAsCSV.php?p_name=newfile.txt
```

This program adds an additional validation check against an incorrect actual parameter, which strips any enclosing quotes from it. When parameters are submitted via URL, they should never have delimiting quotes. You can filter these by using the `ereq_replace()` function to strip them, as is shown in the `WriteFileAsCSV.php` program file.

The following `WriteFileAsCSV.php` program builds a two-dimensional array and then passes it to the `write_csv_from_array()` function, which writes the CSV file:

-- This is found in WriteFileAsCSV.php on the enclosed CD.

```php
<?php
  // Declare a filename.
  $file = $_GET["p_name"];

  // Strip any double quotes included on the URL.
  $file = ereg_replace('"',null,$file);
```

```php
  // Determine file path delimiter.
  if (ereg("(Win32)",$_SERVER["SERVER_SOFTWARE"]))
    $slash = "\\";
  else
    $slash = "/";

  // Declare a fully qualified filename.
  $fname = getcwd().$slash.$file;

  // Declare a two-dimension data set.
  $data = array(array("","","","Cumulative","Cumulative")
              ,array("Month","Frequency","Percent","Frequency","Percent")
              ,array("-------------","-------------","-------------"
                    ,"-------------","-------------")
              ,array("January"  ,"66" ,"3.12","1262","59.7")
              ,array("February" ,"106","5.01","1368","64.71")
              ,array("March"    ,"63" ,"2.98","1431","67.69")
              ,array("April"    ,"60" ,"2.84","1491","70.53")
              ,array("May"      ,"97" ,"4.59","1588","75.12")
              ,array("June"     ,"79" ,"3.74","1667","78.86")
              ,array("July"     ,"86" ,"4.07","1753","82.92")
              ,array("August"   ,"125","5.91","1878","88.84")
              ,array("September","52" ,"2.46","1930","91.3")
              ,array("October"  ,"61" ,"2.89","1991","94.18")
              ,array("November" ,"69" ,"3.26","2060","97.45")
              ,array("December" ,"54" ,"2.55","2114","100"));

  // When the file exists, delete it.
  if (is_file($fname))
    unlink($fname);

  // Call the function to write a CSV file.
  write_csv_from_array($fname,$data);

  // Define function to write a CSV file.
  function write_csv_from_array($file,$data_array)
  {
    // Declare a read-only file resource.
    if ($fp = fopen($file,'w'))
    {
      // Read the two-dimensional array and write it to a CSV file.
      for ($i = 0;$i < count($data_array);$i++)
        if (!fputcsv($fp,$data_array[$i],","))

      // Close the open file handle.
      fclose($fp);
    }
  }
?>
```

The `WriteFileAsCSV.php` program has a reusable `write_csv_from_array()` function that opens a file in write-only mode and writes an array to a CSV file. It uses a `for` loop to read through nested arrays, which are like rows from a database query. The program assumes that the nested arrays contain only scalar values, such as date, numbers, and strings. The `fputcsv()` file explodes the array into values using the string delimiter provided as the third actual parameter. It then writes the exploded values as a comma-separated line to the target file.

You can change the delimiter to a tab by inserting a "\t" instead of the comma as the third parameter. Alternatively, you can provide the tab using the `chr()` function and the ASCII value for a tab, which is 9. There is a `WriteFileAsTSV.php` program file on the enclosed CD.

Uploading Files

PHP supports managing file uploads with the `move_uploaded_file()` function on the server. HTML supports the means to upload files in web browsers. You can develop file uploads by using the HTML `FORM` and two `INPUT` tags.

The `FORM` tag will designate an action that points to a URL-qualified server-side program. The first `INPUT` tag is designated as a file type within the scope of the `FORM` tags. When an `INPUT` tag is set as a file type, a Browse button is automatically rendered to the right of the input field. Clicking the Browse button launches the operating system file chooser, which enables you to select a local file to upload to the server.

The second `INPUT` tag is designated as a submit type, which is also within the scope of the `FORM` tags. The Submit button fires the action qualified by the action attribute of the `FORM` tag. The Submit button makes a call to the URL-qualified server-side program. Dependent on the implementation details of the web browser, you can use the `POST` or `PUT` method but not the `GET` method.

The following `UploadForm.html` file demonstrates using the `POST` method:

-- This is found in **UploadForm.html** on the enclosed CD.

```
<form id="uploadForm"
      action=http://dev.techtinker.com/UploadFile.php
      enctype="multipart/form-data"
      method="post">
  <table border=0 cellpadding=0 cellspacing=0>
    <tr>
      <td width=100>Select File</td>
        <td>
         <input id="uploadFileName"
                   name="userfile"
                   type="file">
      </td>
    </tr>
    <tr>
      <td width=100>Click Button to</td>
      <td><input type="submit" value="Upload File"></td>
    </tr>
  </table>
</form>
```

FIGURE 10-1 *Visual UploadForm.html image*

This renders the image in Figure 10-1. As discussed, when you click the Browse button the browser launches the operating system file chooser. After selecting a file, the text box will display the fully qualified or canonical path and filename. You click the Upload File button to submit the HTML form contents to the server. Submitting the form sends the file to the designated URL-qualified server-side program provided you have updated the action attribute URL.

The FORM tag includes three critical attributes: action, enctype, and method. As mentioned, the action tag contains a qualified URL and a server-side program that will process the uploaded file. The enctype attribute designates the file encoding type and qualifies that the HTML submission contains the regular array of form values. The method designates whether it is a POST or PUT method. It is recommended that you use the POST method, not the PUT method.

The INPUT tag designated as a file type has two key attributes: name and type. The type attribute renders the Browse button and enables you to read the file system. The name attribute designates the associative array index value for the selected file in the $_FILES array variable.

The following UploadFile.php program lets you process the file upload, move from a temporary file location, read the file, and render it in the web page:

-- **This is found in UploadFile.php on the enclosed CD.**

```php
<?php
  // Declare and format $_FILES array elements into HTML table.
  $out = "<table border=0 cellpadding=0 cellspacing=0>";
  foreach ($_FILES['userfile'] as $name => $value)
    $out .= "<tr><td>[$name]</td><td>[$value]</td></tr>";
  $out .= "</table>";

  // Display array elements to web page.
  print $out;

  // Declare a variable for file contents.
  $contents = "";

  // Define the upload filename for Windows or Linux.
  if (ereg("Win32",$_SERVER["SERVER_SOFTWARE"]))
    $uploadFile = getcwd()."\\temp\\".$_FILES['userfile']['name'];
```

```
  else
    $uploadFile = getcwd()."/temp/".$_FILES['userfile']['name'];

  // Check for and move uploaded file.
  if (is_uploaded_file($_FILES['userfile']['tmp_name']))
    move_uploaded_file($_FILES['userfile']['tmp_name'],$uploadFile);

  // Open a file handle and suppress an error for a missing file.
  if ($fp = @fopen($uploadFile,"r"))
  {
    // Read until the end-of-file marker.
    while (!feof($fp))
      $contents .= fgetc($fp);

    // Close an open file handle.
    fclose($fp);
  }

  // Display moved file in web page.
  print $contents;
?>
```

The first thing done by the UploadFile.php program is to render the contents of the $_FILES['userfile'] array variable, as noted here:

[name]	[RedRabbit.htm]
[type]	[text/html]
[tmp_name]	[/tmp/phpgBYU3T]
[error]	[0]
[size]	[1860]

You receive five values in the $_FILES['userfile'] array variable. They are the name of the file, the mime type of the file, the temporary name of the file, an error code, and a size. When the error code is anything other than a zero, the file upload has failed. The temporary location for the upload is set in the upload_tmp_dir directive in the php.ini file. When you have not set an override value using that directive, you will send temporary files to the /tmp directory on Linux and the C:\TEMP folder on Microsoft Windows.

 NOTE
The $_FILES array variable can receive multiple files in a single upload, which would require your using a foreach loop to process the values. You can make this type of code more generic and suited to a library function by using the foreach loop to discover the INPUT tag names when one or more files can be uploaded.

The UploadFile.php program moves the temporary file from the temporary directory to a target directory. The program assumes that you have a temp directory as a subdirectory to the directory where program file is located. If you don't have a temp directory, you should add one before testing the program.

The program uses the `ereg()` function to build the temporary directory appropriately for the server operating system. The `is_uploaded_file()` function verifies that it is an uploaded file, and the `move_uploaded_file()` function moves the file from the temporary location to a permanent location. When the uploaded file is not moved after uploading it, the file is automatically deleted from the temporary directory when the PHP program ends. The balance of the program reads the file from the permanent location and displays it in a web page.

Summary

In this chapter, you have learned the basics of File I/O and how to use the core functions to navigate and manage your local file system. You have learned how to use file information, including location, management, status, and file system functions, and how to read and write binary, text, and CSV/TSV files. You have also learned how to upload files to the server from your web pages.

PART
III

PHP Application
Development

CHAPTER
11

Basic HTTP
Authentication and Forms

his chapter examines the reply and response model for web applications and shows you how to secure your web applications using basic HTTP authentication. It also demonstrates how you build and manage user interactions through server-side PHP web forms.

The chapter is divided into the following three sections:

- Defining the Remote Procedure Call paradigm
- Using basic authentication
- Developing authenticating forms

Building web applications enables you to share information, but ultimately you want to control and manage who uses your forms. You control access to your web application by requiring valid credentials from users. Credentials are typically a username or identifier, also known as an ID. You develop roles and responsibilities for your user community when determining how you will manage their credentials.

Roles and responsibilities enable you to assign users to groups. Groups enjoy privileges to access and use some forms while they prevent the user from accessing others. This process ensures that you can let business customers view, select, and order products while preventing them from checking other customer account information. Securing your applications is a necessary step to building serviceable web business solutions.

The organization of who you authorize to do what is known as building an *Access Control List (ACL)*. ACL structures can be located in physical files or database tables. ACL structures typically contain all essential user information and access privileges required by a business application.

This chapter discusses various web application security issues along with generic approaches that show you how to secure your web applications. It will demonstrate how to build and manage an ACL file.

The IT industry has a vibrant and ongoing discussion about how you should secure your web applications. The debate centers around two issues. One issue is whether you should use basic HTTP authentication or cookies and session management to validate users. The other issue concerns which encryption algorithm you should use to protect sensitive data, like passwords. PHP supports MD5 and SHA1 encryption, which are fairly effective solutions short of deploying digital signatures.

Digest HTTP authentication will present another alternative to basic HTTP authentication, but at present it is not worth exploring because its implementation is incomplete. *The IT industry agrees that you should use the HTTPS protocol when you implement basic HTTP authentication for web applications.*

This chapter discusses and demonstrates basic HTTP authentication in PHP web application forms. The first section in this chapter discusses how web applications work by submitting interactive Remote Procedure Calls (RPCs) to a server. The second section demonstrates basic HTTP authentication. The third section explores how to implement web applications using the basic HTTP authentication model.

It is suggested that you cover Chapter 11 and 12 sequentially because a number of foundation concepts appear in this chapter. If you feel confident in your understanding of generic web application issues, you can go straight to Chapter 12 to learn how to implement application security using cookies and sessions.

Defining the Remote Procedure Call Paradigm

Remote Procedure Calls (RPCs) enable a program on one computer to call another program running on a remote computer. RPCs are supported in many frameworks, like Microsoft's DCOM or Object Management Group's CORBA definitions. They are also known as Remote Method Invocations (RMIs) in the Java programming environment.

All of these models require server-side programs listening for incoming requests. The server-side program supporting PHP web applications is an HTTP listener. Also known as the HTTPD service or HTTP daemon, it is a background process. HTTP daemons listen for incoming Uniform Resource Locators (URLs), like the Apache and IIS web application servers. When they receive a URL, they check their configuration files for instructions on how to redirect the request to local server processes.

NOTE

URLs are gradually being replaced by Uniform Resource Identifiers (URIs). A URI uniquely identifies an item in a list, like an inode table that lists physical files. URLs are URIs that contain the information and data to act on a copy of the item.

Web browsers have become the common interface to information and web page servers. Web page servers are built on the foundation of the RPC model. The first implementation of the RPC model for web applications was the Common Gateway Interface (CGI). The CGI model was the first to support mapping web pages requests to local server-side processes. CGI works by taking a URL and tokenizing it into a list of environment variables. Then, the CGI program spawns a local server-side process and passes the list of environment variables as run-time parameters to the process.

This model is specific to directory resources that are relative to the HTTP daemon. It did not scale well because each request created a new copy of the CGI control program before launching the remote process. The more efficient replacements are the Apache modules, like `mod_perl`, `mod_php`, and `mod_plsql`. Apache modules are run-time environments that spawn when the web server is launched and run as multitasking background subprograms.

In modern web applications, the Apache or IIS application server is the remote program that actively listens for and processes incoming URLs. The server's configuration files contain the required information to find, start, and hand off RPC model transactions to modules, like PHP. Modules then manage the RPC request and response model.

Each successful URL call refreshes the contents of the browser. This model requires each RPC to send, process, and receive a response. Successful responses are formatted in HTML and rewrite the contents of the browser window. This is the traditional model used to build PHP web applications. A new variation to this approach uses embedded network calls to refresh portions of web pages.

The key piece of information required to understand and use basic HTTP authentication is that each HTTP request means a complete rewrite of the web page contents. The next section will use this model to illustrate basic HTTP authentication.

Dynamic Web Page Scripting

Another pattern in web application development modifies the concepts of traditional RPC models. It is known as Asynchronous JavaScript and XML (AJAX) or Representation State Transfer (REST) architecture. The former is the commercial label assigned in 2004, and the latter is an academic description coined in 2000. They are two names for the same idea. The idea is that you should not have to replace the entire rendered web page when changing only part of the content.

More or less, this is the evolution of traditional RPC web pages to quasi-client/server computing web forms. This approach has been around for a couple of years and is relatively stable but requires adjustments to accommodate different browsers.

It is physically done by using the XMLHttpRequest object in JavaScript in most browsers or by using the ActiveXObject("Msxml2.XMLHTTP") object in Microsoft Internet Explorer. This allows you to use client-side scripting to build and send a URL to collect data, which then updates or refreshes web pages components. You can also do similar asynchronous calls by using zero-sized frames.

Using Basic Authentication

Basic HTTP authentication was released as part of the HTTP 1.0 specification and continues much as it was originally deployed. It works on the premise that a user must establish his or her browser's credentials in a realm. Browser sessions can have many concurrent realm credentials at any time, provided they authenticate against different sources.

The basic authentication prompt is nonconfigurable and a by-product of the web browser that you are using. When you want to configure the login screen's look and feel, you must implement cookies and sessions, which are covered in Chapter 12. Figure 11-1 illustrates the Microsoft Internet Explorer authentication prompt. The network realm www.techtinker.com in the authentication prompt is set by the `BasicLoginRealm.php` program covered later in the chapter.

FIGURE 11-1. *A basic HTTP authentication prompt*

You receive the authentication prompt when you launch your client browser and send a request from the browser to a remote server that is configured to support basic HTTP authentication. The server replies by sending an authentication header back to the browser. When the browser receives the authentication request, it raises the native login prompt. The user provides a valid name and password and is granted access to the system, provided the username and password match values in the server ACL.

An invalid username or password will trigger the client's receiving another authentication request. After three attempts, the basic browser authentication prompt will disappear, but the user can click the Refresh button on the browser to force another three attempts. This behavior exposes your site to hacking because the login process can repeat indefinitely. *You should consider shutting down user accounts when three unsuccessful access attempts are recorded.*

When the end user fails to validate credentials or clicks the Cancel button on the authentication dialog box, the server-side program should not render the normal contents of the target web page. Rendering the page irrespective of valid credentials discloses information about your site to an unauthorized user or potential hacker. You can prevent inadvertent disclosure by redirecting the user to an error management page or rendering alternative invalid credential content to the browser.

Basic HTTP authentication is configurable from the Apache or IIS server, or you can implement it internally in your PHP program applications. Where you implement basic authentication does not remove its key security vulnerability. *Both username and password are sent in clear text and can be captured by somebody using a network monitoring tool, like a network sniffer. Therefore, you should implement basic authentication across HTTPS in any production environment because then the URL is encrypted.*

This section demonstrates how to implement basic authentication in your web applications. The `BasicLoginRealm.php` file has the username and password values embedded in the file. You can use this approach when servers only publish nonsensitive information on an internal network and you want all users to use the same username and password.

The following `BasicLoginRealm.php` file demonstrates password validation against string constants embedded in the script:

-- This is found in BasicLoginRealm.php on the enclosed CD.

```php
<?php
  // Verify the credentials for the realm or force authentication.
  if ((@$_SERVER['PHP_AUTH_USER'] != 'username') ||
      (@$_SERVER['PHP_AUTH_PW'] != 'password'))
  {
    header('WWW-Authenticate: Basic Realm="it.techtinker.com"');
    header('HTTP/1.0 401 Unauthorized');
    print 'Please enter a valid user and password.';
    exit;
  }
  else
  {
    // Render the username and password sent.
    print '<div id=centered>';
    print '<table border="1" bordercolor="silver" cellspacing="0">';
    print '<tr>';
    print '<td><b></b> </td>';
    print '<td align="center" width="100"><b>Clear Text</b></td>';
```

```
    print '</tr>';
    print '<tr>';
    print '<td align="right" width="150"><b>PHP_AUTH_USER</b></td>';
    print '<td align="center">';
    print $_SERVER['PHP_AUTH_USER'];
    print '</td>';
    print '</tr>';
    print '<tr>';
    print '<td align="right" width="150"><b>PHP_AUTH_PW</b></td>';
    print '<td align="center">';
    print $_SERVER['PHP_AUTH_PW'];
    print '</td>';
    print '</tr>';
    print '</table>';
    print '</div>';
  }
?>
```

The `BasicLoginRealm.php` file executes the PHP script component before rendering anything to the outgoing web page stream. It uses the error control operator to suppress run-time errors that can happen when the username and password names are not sent in the request but found in the `$_SERVER` array. This occurs when the user clicks the Cancel key from the basic authentication prompt or fails to enter a username or password in any of three attempts.

NOTE
When you are using the IIS server, you will need to use the `explode(":", base64_decode(substr($_SERVER["HTTP_AUTHORIZATION"], 6)))` *syntax to capture the username and password information.*

The valid credentials are username: username, and password: password. When the username and password match the contents the web page, the `else` block is rendered to the browser; otherwise, an error message is rendered to the web page.

The following demonstrates the rendered page when the matching username and password are sent across the HTTP network, as follows:

Variable Name	Clear Text
PHP_AUTH_USER	username
PHP_AUTH_PW	password

Once a client browser authenticates to the server, all instances of the client browser have full access to the server machine in that realm. Changing realms once connected is not possible.

While embedding the username and password is a viable solution in some cases, it is not typically a good solution for web applications. Web applications should require uniquely individual credentials. ACL files map usernames to passwords and can contain as little as those two variables. You can implement this type of ACL by using the predefined .htaccess file in the Apache environment, or you can build your own.

Implementing your own ACL generally makes sense because you control the features, the location, and the naming convention for the file. Customized password files have undocumented locations and structures, which make it more difficult for potential hackers to break into your web application. Moreover, while the Apache implementation architecture is well understood and easy to implement, it is a known target for potential hackers.

When you choose to implement a custom ACL file, you should consider encrypting passwords with at least the md5() function before writing them to the file. This enables you to store only encrypted passwords in your ACL. If the file is compromised, the passwords will need to be decrypted to their natural language equivalents. The window of time that it takes a hacker to reverse-engineer the passwords may give you enough time to shut down your system and secure it with new ACL values.

The BasicFileLoginRealm.php program demonstrates how to use an ACL file to validate individual passwords against their encrypted values. It depends on finding a simplepassword.txt file in the same relative directory. The file must contain only one line of text, which mimics the traditional structure of a CSV file by substituting a colon as a delimiter. You can use the simplepassword.txt file found on the enclosed CD or create one with the following line:

```
username:5f4dcc3b5aa765d61d8327deb882cf99
```

The following BasicFileLoginRealm.php program shows how to verify basic HTTP authentication entries against a server-side ACL file:

-- This is found in BasicFileLoginRealm.php on the enclosed CD.

```php
<?php
  // Set initial state for invalid credentials.
  $valid_user = false;

  // Check for HTTP basic authentication variables.
  if ((isset($_SERVER['PHP_AUTH_USER'])) &&
      (isset($_SERVER['PHP_AUTH_PW'])))
  {
    // Read the file into an array of strings.
    $passwords = file("simplepassword.txt");

    // Read through the value list.
    foreach ($passwords as $credentials)
    {
      // Break the delimited lines into scalar variables.
      list($userid,$password) = explode(":",$credentials);

      // Find a match and exit.
      if (($_SERVER['PHP_AUTH_USER'] == $userid) &&
          (md5($_SERVER['PHP_AUTH_PW']) == trim($password)))
      {
        // Reset invalid credential state variable.
        $valid_user = true;
          break;
      }
    }
  }
```

```php
  // When credentials are invalid, prompt for them.
  if (!$valid_user)
  {
    // Send headers to force basic HTTP authentication.
    header('WWW-Authenticate: Basic Realm="www.techtinker.com"');
    header('HTTP/1.0 401 Unauthorized');

    // Print failed validation message.
    print "<html><body><font size=+2>";
    print "The site has logged your [".$_SERVER['REMOTE_ADDR']."] IP ";
    print "address, please enter a valid user and password.";
    print "</font></body></html>";
    exit;
  }
  else
  {
    // Render the username and password sent.
    print '<div id=centered>';
    print '<table border="1" bordercolor="silver" cellspacing="0">';
    print '<tr>';
    print '<td><b></b> </td>';
    print '<td align="center" width="100"><b>Clear Text</b></td>';
    print '</tr>';
    print '<tr>';
    print '<td align="right" width="150"><b>PHP_AUTH_USER</b></td>';
    print '<td align="center">';
    print $_SERVER['PHP_AUTH_USER'];
    print '</td>';
    print '</tr>';
    print '<tr align="center">';
    print '<td align="right" width="150"><b>PHP_AUTH_PW</b></td>';
    print '<td>';
    print $_SERVER['PHP_AUTH_PW'];
    print '</td>';
    print '</tr>';
    print '</table>';
    print '</div>';
  }
?>
```

Using the same general logic of validating the $_SERVER index values for username and password, the BasicFileLoginRealm.php program validates the provided results against a server-side ACL file. The error control operators are replaced by calls to the is_set() function. The program sets a $valid_user variable as a guard value. Then, the program uses a file() function to read the file contents into an array of strings, and a foreach loop to process each element in the array. The list() function is the target for the array of strings generated by the explode() function, which uses a colon as the line delimiter. Before comparing the credentials, the unencrypted password is encrypted and the read value trimmed of the line return character. When a match is found for the credential, the guard value is disabled and the desired page contents are rendered in a web page.

When no valid credentials are found, the error contents render the browser network IP address to the browser. While this won't intimidate a true hacker, the error message may discourage script kiddies. Script kiddies are amateur hackers who run programs designed to hack into your system. Script kiddies typically lack in-depth skills to independently attack your system but may have malicious or criminal intent. Crackers are hackers who have the skill and know-how to hack into your system without scripts and generally have malicious or criminal intent motivating them to attack your system.

When valid credentials are found, the successfully matched credentials will be rendered. The contents are the same as the prior example, as noted:

Variable Name	Clear Text
PHP_AUTH_USER	username
PHP_AUTH_PW	password

These examples have demonstrated how you can protect your web site with basic HTTP authentication. One example demonstrates embedding a username and password, while the other shows how to implement a server-side ACL file. ACL files enable you to provide credentials by users. This is a good mechanism, provided you do two things.

First, you must configure your web application server to process forms in HTTPS mode. This guarantees that you will send encrypted usernames and passwords, not clear text values, across the network. Second, you must ensure that all your web forms validate your HTML realm before providing access to any forms. This means you will most likely deploy your validation code module in a library function that is included once in all forms. You can review the include_ once() function in Chapter 3.

Developing Authenticating Forms

Forms are really not a PHP function per se. They are an HTML structure that enables you to submit user inputs to a remote server. You can have one or several forms in any rendered page. When you have more than one form on a page, you will have to choose how to process information. The standard RPC model is to submit one form at a time, but you can use AJAX methods to asynchronously submit and refresh components one at a time. This approach enables you to process multiple forms asynchronously by capturing a single user event and mapping it to multiple URL submissions.

The examples in this chapter adhere to the simpler RPC model because the point is to illustrate how web application forms interact to manage data. The example program will initially use two program files. The first is the BasicFileLogin.php program, which is your point of entry into the application. The second is the BasicFileWrite.php program, which recursively calls itself after every user-triggered transaction. Both of these forms enable you to add new credentials to the simplepassword.txt file.

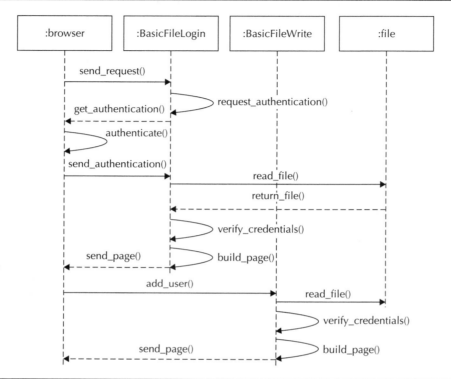

FIGURE 11-2. *UML web application sequence diagram*

Figure 11-2 contains the basic application design in a Unified Modeling Language (UML) sequence diagram. Sequence diagrams qualify object instances or module instances like barbeque skewers. The name of the module or object instance is qualified in a box that labels the skewer, and messages between skewers are represented by solid lines, while responses are shown using dotted lines.

The diagram shows the browser sending a URL to the BasicFileLogin.php program, which requests the browser provide a username and password for basic HTTP authentication. After securing the username and password, the browser sends the credentials back to the URL for verification. The BasicFileLogin.php then reads the file into an array of strings, verifies credentials, and builds a content page. The content page enables the authorized user to add new credentials to the ACL file and is returned to the browser as an HTML form.

The rendered HTML form has a target action attribute, which points to the BasicFileWrite .php program. When the user clicks the Add User button in the page rendered by the BasicFileLogin.php program, a set of credentials are sent to the server. The server validates the realm credentials before processing the submitted values. Processing then follows the previous process with one exception: The BasicFileWrite.php program renders a copy of itself. When the Add User button is clicked in the new form, it repeats the steps by recursively calling a copy of itself.

The following `BasicFileLogin.php` program is the initial starting point for this web application:

-- This is found in BasicFileLogin.php on the enclosed CD.

```php
<?php
  // Set initial state for invalid credentials.
  $valid_user = false;

  // Check for HTTP basic authentication variables.
  if ((isset($_SERVER['PHP_AUTH_USER'])) &&
     (isset($_SERVER['PHP_AUTH_PW'])))
  {
    // Read the file into an array of strings.
    $passwords = file("simplepassword.txt");

    // Read through the value list.
    foreach ($passwords as $credentials)
    {
      // Break the delimited lines into scalar variables.
      list($userid,$password) = explode(":",$credentials);

      // Find a match and exit.
      if (($_SERVER['PHP_AUTH_USER'] == $userid) &&
         (md5($_SERVER['PHP_AUTH_PW']) == trim($password)))
      {
        // Reset invalid credential state variable.
        $valid_user = true;
          break;
      }
    }
  }

  // When credentials are invalid, prompt for them.
  if (!$valid_user)
  {
    // Send headers to force basic HTTP authentication.
    header('WWW-Authenticate: Basic Realm="www.techtinker.com"');
    header('HTTP/1.0 401 Unauthorized');

    // Print failed validation message.
    print "<html><body><font size=+2>";
    print "The site has logged your [".$_SERVER['REMOTE_ADDR']."] IP ";
    print "address, please enter a valid user and password.";
    print "</font></body></html>";
    exit;
  }
  else
    // Print successful validation message.
    enter_credentials("BasicFileWrite.php");
```

```php
// Return a dynamic entry form.
function enter_credentials($form_target)
{
  $out  = '<div id=centered>';
  $out .= '<form method="post" action="'.$form_target.'">';
  $out .= '<table border="4" bordercolor="silver" cellspacing="0">';
  $out .= '<tr><td align="center" width="400">';
  $out .= '<font size=+3>New User</font>';
  $out .= '</td></tr>';
  $out .= '<tr><td>';
  $out .= '<table border="0" cellpadding="5" cellspacing="0">';
  $out .= '<tr>';
  $out .= '<td align="right" width="200">User ID:</td>';
  $out .= '<td width="200"><input name="userid" type="text"></td>';
  $out .= '</tr>';
  $out .= '<tr>';
  $out .= '<td align="right" width="200">User Password:</td>';
  $out .= '<td width="200"><input name="passwd" type="password"></td>';
  $out .= '</tr>';
  $out .= '</table>';
  $out .= '</td></tr>';
  $out .= '<tr><td align="center" colspan="2" width="400">';
  $out .= '<input name="submit" type="submit" value="Add User">';
  $out .= '</td></tr>';
  $out .= '</table>';
  $out .= '</form>';
  $out .= '</div>';

  // Render the form in a web page.
  print $out;
}
?>
```

The page rendered by the `BasicFileLogin.php` program appears in Figure 11-3. The program does the same validation as shown in the earlier example of ACL file validation. The difference between the two programs is that this one generates an interactive HTML form that can call another PHP program. The callable `BasicFileWrite.php` program is the target of the action property in the form tag using an HTTP post method. The input fields for the form are designated as a text type for the username and `password` for the password. A `password` input type replaces the typed characters with dots to prevent somebody looking over your shoulder at confidential information. The HTML button type submit, when clicked, will trigger the HTML form to send input values to the server.

The `BasicFileWrite.php` program structure is similar but more complex, managing more transaction components than the original `BasicFileLogin.php` form. The `BasicFileWrite.php` program performs all the same steps as those done by the `BasicFileLogin.php` program, plus it writes new users to an ACL file and validates username and password values. The submitted username and password are compared against the designated criteria for length and alphanumeric structure. The program also provides a status update of the last attempt to add a new user.

FIGURE 11-3. *The* `BasicFileLogin.php` *rendered page* .

The following `BasicFileWrite.php` program demonstrates how to verify, append, and audit form entry:

-- **This is found in BasicFileWrite.php on the enclosed CD.**

```php
<?php
  // Check basic authentication.
  $valid_user = verify_authentication();

  // When credentials are invalid, prompt for them.
  if (!$valid_user)
  {
    // Send headers to force basic HTTP authentication.
    header('WWW-Authenticate: Basic Realm="www.techtinker.com"');
    header('HTTP/1.0 401 Unauthorized');

    // Print failed validation message.
    print "<html><body><font size=+2>";
    print "The site has logged your [".$_SERVER['REMOTE_ADDR']."] IP ";
    print "address, please enter a valid user and password.";
    print "</font></body></html>";
    exit;
  }
  else
  {
    // Assign inputs to variables.
    $userid = $_POST['userid'];
    $passwd = $_POST['passwd'];

    // Set error default.
    $e_code = 0;
```

```php
  // Verify username and password.
  switch(true)
  {
    // Does username already exist?
    case (verified_user($userid)):
      $e_code = 1;
      break;
    // Does username start with an alphabetic character?
    case (!ereg("([a-zA-Z]+[a-zA-Z0-9]{0,1})",substr($userid,0,1))):
      $e_code = 2;
      break;
    // Is username 6-10 alphanumeric characters lead by a letter?
    case (!ereg("([a-zA-Z]+[a-zA-Z0-9]{5,10})",$userid)):
      $e_code = 3;
      break;
    // Is password 6-10 alphanumeric characters lead by a letter?
    case (!ereg("([a-zA-Z0-9]{5,10})",$passwd)):
      $e_code = 4;
      break;
  }

  // Enter only when user doesn't exist.
  if ($e_code == 0)
  {
    // Join user and encrypted password into a colon-delimited string.
    $data = implode(":",array($userid,md5($passwd)));

    // Call the function to append a line to a file.
    write_string("simplepassword.txt",$data);
  }

  // Display next user form.
  form_display($e_code,$userid);
}

// Define a Basic Authentication function.
function verify_authentication()
{
  // Check for HTTP basic authentication variables.
  if ((isset($_SERVER['PHP_AUTH_USER'])) &&
      (isset($_SERVER['PHP_AUTH_PW'])))
  {
    // Read the file into an array of strings.
    $passwords = file("simplepassword.txt");

    // Read through the value list.
    foreach ($passwords as $credentials)
    {
      // Break the delimited lines into scalar variables.
      list($username,$password) = explode(":",$credentials);
```

```
      // Find a match and exit.
      if (($_SERVER['PHP_AUTH_USER'] == $username) &&
          (md5($_SERVER['PHP_AUTH_PW']) == trim($password)))
        return true;
    }
  }
}

// Make sure user is there.
function verified_user($userid)
{
  // Read the file into an array of strings.
  $passwords = file("simplepassword.txt");

  // Read through the value list.
  foreach ($passwords as $credentials)
  {
    // Break the delimited lines into scalar variables.
    list($username,$password) = explode(":",$credentials);

    // Return there is a user.
    if ($userid == $username)
      return true;
  }

  // Return there is no existing user.
  return false;
}

// Define function to write a colon-delimited file.
function write_string($file,$string)
{
  // Declare a read-only file resource.
  if ($fp = fopen($file,'a+'))
  {
    // Read the two-dimensional array and write or append to a file.
    fwrite($fp,"\n".$string);

    // Close the open file handle.
    fclose($fp);
  }
}

// Build entry form.
function form_display($code,$userid)
{
  // Designate message by error code.
  switch ($code)
```

```php
  {
    case 0:
      $message = "You have added user [$userid] successfully.";
      break;
    case 1:
      $message = "User [$userid] is already in use.";
      break;
    case 2:
      $message = "User [$userid] must start with a character.";
      break;
    case 3:
      $message = "User [$userid] must be between 6 and 10 characters.";
      break;
    case 4:
      $message = "The password must be between 6 and 10 characters.";
  }

  // Build dynamic form.
  $out  = '<div id=centered>';
  $out .= '<form method="post" action="BasicFileWrite.php">';
  $out .= '<table border="4" bordercolor="silver" cellspacing="0">';
  $out .= '<tr><td align="center" width="400">';
  $out .= '<font size=+3>New User</font>';
  $out .= '</td></tr>';
  $out .= '<tr><td align="center" bgcolor="white" width="400">';
  $out .= '<font color=blue>'.$message.'</font>';
  $out .= '</td></tr>';
  $out .= '<tr><td>';
  $out .= '<table border="0" cellpadding="5" cellspacing="0">';
  $out .= '<tr>';
  $out .= '<td align="right" width="200">User ID:</td>';
  $out .= '<td width="200"><input name="userid" type="text"></td>';
  $out .= '</tr>';
  $out .= '<tr>';
  $out .= '<td align="right" width="200">User Password:</td>';
  $out .= '<td width="200"><input name="passwd" type="password"></td>';
  $out .= '</tr>';
  $out .= '</table>';
  $out .= '</td></tr>';
  $out .= '<tr><td align="center" colspan="2" width="400">';
  $out .= '<input name="submit" type="submit" value="Add User">';
  $out .= '</td></tr>';
  $out .= '</table>';
  $out .= '</form>';
  $out .= '</div>';

  // Render the form in a web page.
  print $out;
  }
?>
```

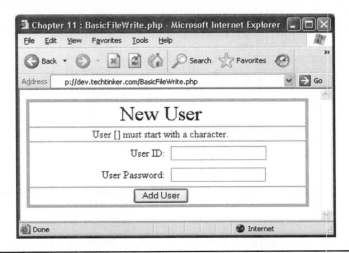

FIGURE 11-4. *The* `BasicFileWrite.php` *rendered page*

The `BasicFileWrite.php` program uses a case statement and regular expression syntax to ensure that all usernames are at least six characters in length and begin with a letter. The program also moves generic logic to do credential validation into the `verify_authentication()` function. Another `verified_user()` function checks whether a username already exists in the ACL file. You use this function to make sure a duplicate user isn't created.

The new `write_string()` function uses the `implode()` function to build a colon-delimited string before appending the string to the ACL file. The `form_display()` function in `BasicFileWrite.php` program replaces the `enter_credentials()` function in the `BasicFileLogin.php` file. While the functions render slightly different forms and have different formal parameters, you should note that they are very similar in purpose and scope. Figure 11-4 shows that they are visually near-clones of one another. The status message in blue is the one noticeable difference between the two user interfaces.

To this point you have seen how to develop and implement standard RPC application forms that use basic HTTP authentication. The initial login form enables you to add new users to a system. This method makes PHP programs independent units that post subsequent requests to another program or to copies of themselves. Many web applications start and end with this design pattern.

You can achieve a better web form design by identifying components along the lines of the model-view-controller (MVC) design pattern. The MVC pattern can be implemented by separating the view-controller components from the model. You place the view-controller components in web forms and the model components in libraries. Model components go into the libraries because they are common infrastructure items that are frequently used by many forms. Examples of model components are the file read and write functions from the earlier `BasicFileLogin.php` and `BasicFileWrite.php` programs.

UML activity diagrams help you figure out which components and program logic belong in the model or view-controller program units. Figure 11-5 demonstrates the basic activity diagram for web forms. The first action state validates that the browser has sent and authenticated credentials. The decision tree represents the revalidation of current credentials. When the credentials fail validation,

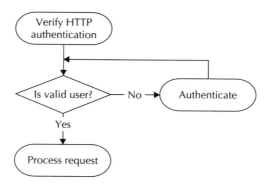

FIGURE 11-5. *UML activity diagram*

the program transfers control to an authentication state, which returns results to be validated. Valid credentials enable the form to continue to process the request action state and render the web page.

All of the action states contain components that can be relocated from individual web pages to libraries. Libraries become single shared copies of program units, typically lists of functions. The library functions are easier to maintain because there are single copies of them. When a change needs to be made, you can change the behavior of a function in one place. The downside of centralizing functions is that they must become robust enough to meet various application demands. This requires you to write algorithmic functions that can support many different uses.

The `BasicFileLogin.php` rendered page differs slightly from the `BasicFileWrite.php` page. The latter contains an additional message component that confirms a user has been added to the directory or an error message describing why the user was not created. You can create a reusable and algorithmic function that will render both pages in a library. This type of library is a view-controller component because it deals with how the page is rendered. Other view-controller components deal with the rendering and utility of widgets that control form interactivity.

The `BasicForms.inc` file contains view-controller library components necessary to move our earlier discrete examples into a collective MVC pattern. You should add other form rendering components to this file as you grow the application.

You should remember that the .inc extension is used for included library files, as discussed in Chapter 3. Likewise, you should configure the web server to not directly serve files with this extension to protect disclosing their functionality. The program code follows:

-- **This is found in BasicForms.inc on the enclosed CD.**

```php
<?php

    /* Library functions.
    ||  ------------------------------------------------------------
    ||   Function Name          Return Type   Parameters
    ||  -------------------------   -----------   ----------------------
    ||   addUserForm()           string        array      $args
    */
```

```
// Build dynamic data entry form.
function addUserForm($args)
{
  // Define local variables.
  $code;
  $form;
  $userid;

  // Parse form parameters.
  foreach ($args as $name => $value)
  {
    switch (true)
    {
      case ($name == "form"):
        $form = $value;
        break;
      case ($name == "code"):
        $code = $value;
        break;
      case ($name == "userid"):
        $userid = $value;
        break;
    }
  }

  // Initialize return variable.
  $out  = '<div id=centered>';

  // Set and append next form target file.
  $out .= '<form method="post" action="'.$form.'">';

  // Append balance of form header.
  $out .= '<table border="4"
                  bgcolor="beige"
                  bordercolor="silver"
                  cellspacing="0">';
  $out .= '<tr><td align="center" width="400">';
  $out .= '<font size=+3>New User</font>';
  $out .= '</td></tr>';

  // Verify if optional message.
  if ((isset($code)) && (is_int($code)))
  {
    $out .= '<tr><td align="center" bgcolor="white" width="400">';
    $out .= '<font color=blue>'.get_message($code,$userid).'</font>';
    $out .= '</td></tr>';
  }
```

```php
      // Append standard data entry components.
      $out .= '<tr><td>';
      $out .= '<table border="0" cellpadding="5" cellspacing="0">';
      $out .= '<tr>';
      $out .= '<td align="right" width="200">User ID:</td>';
      $out .= '<td width="200"><input name="userid" type="text"></td>';
      $out .= '</tr>';
      $out .= '<tr>';
      $out .= '<td align="right">User Password:</td>';
      $out .= '<td><input name="passwd" type="password"></td>';
      $out .= '</tr>';
      $out .= '<tr>';
      $out .= '</table>';
      $out .= '</td></tr>';
      $out .= '<tr><td align="center" colspan="2">';
      $out .= '<table border="0" cellpadding="5" cellspacing="0">';
      $out .= '<tr>';
      $out .= '<td align="center" valign="center">';
      $out .= '<input name="submit" type="submit" value="Add User">';
      $out .= '</td>';
      $out .= '</tr>';
      $out .= '</table>';
      $out .= '</td></tr>';
      $out .= '</table>';
      $out .= '</form>';
      $out .= '</div>';

      // Return the form for rendering in a web page.
      print $out;
  }
?>
```

The addUserForm() function leverages variable parameter list argument passing, which is covered in Chapter 7. This technique enables you to treat all function arguments as optional and not position specific. The implementation requires you to pass an associative array using unique string indexes. The arguments are parsed and assigned to local variables in a switch statement.

The user entered or error message HTML table row is now treated as an optional rendering component. One of the arguments to the addUserForm() function is evaluated in the function to determine if it is a required form element. Managing rendering permutations like this makes developing reusable code components easier, provided you know what you want them do to before coding them.

The model components of the application are in the BasicAuthentication.inc file. As you will see when reviewing the actual form programs later in the chapter, this library includes virtually all of the programming logic to support basic HTTP authentication and the view-controller component. The following code includes an index of functions at the top of the file that makes it easier to find what functions you have available in a library:

```php
<?php
  /* Library functions.
   || ----------------------------------------------------------------
   ||  Function Name              Return Type  Parameters
   || --------------------------  -----------  ----------------------
   ||  authenticate()             void
   ||  get_message()              string       int       $code
   ||                                          string    $userid
   ||  write_string()             void         resource  $file
   ||                                          string    $string
   ||  verify_authentication()    bool
   ||  verify_user()              bool         string    $userid
   ||  verify_valid_credentials() int          string    $userid
   ||                                          string    $passwd
   */

  // Force basic HTTP authentication.
  function authenticate()
  {
    // Send headers to force basic HTTP authentication.
    header('WWW-Authenticate: Basic Realm="www.techtinker.com"');
    header('HTTP/1.0 401 Unauthorized');

    // Print failed validation message.
    print "<html><body><font size=+2>";
    print "The site has logged your [".$_SERVER['REMOTE_ADDR']."] IP ";
    print "address, please enter a valid user and password.";
    print "</font></body></html>";
  }

  // Build entry form.
  function get_message($code,$userid)
  {
    // Designate message by error code.
    switch ($code)
    {
      case 0:
        return "You have added user [$userid] successfully.";
      case 1:
        return "User [$userid] is already in use.";
      case 2:
        return "User [$userid] must start with a character.";
      case 3:
        return "User [$userid] must be between 6 and 10 characters.";
      case 4:
        return "The password must be between 6 and 10 characters.";
    }
  }
```

```php
// Define a Basic Authentication function.
function verify_authentication()
{
  // Check for HTTP basic authentication variables.
  if ((isset($_SERVER['PHP_AUTH_USER'])) &&
      (isset($_SERVER['PHP_AUTH_PW'])))
  {
    // Read the file into an array of strings.
    $passwords = file("simplepassword.txt");

    // Read through the value list.
    foreach ($passwords as $credentials)
    {
      // Break the delimited lines into scalar variables.
      list($username,$password) = explode(":",$credentials);

      // Find a match and return valid credentials.
      if (($_SERVER['PHP_AUTH_USER'] == $username) &&
          (md5($_SERVER['PHP_AUTH_PW']) == trim($password)))
        return true;
    }
  }

  // Return invalid credentials.
  return false;
}

// Check for existing user.
function verify_user($userid)
{
  // Read the file into an array of strings.
  $passwords = file("simplepassword.txt");

  // Read through the value list.
  foreach ($passwords as $credentials)
  {
    // Break the delimited lines into scalar variables.
    list($username,$password) = explode(":",$credentials);

    // Return there is a user.
    if ($userid == $username)
      return true;
  }

  // Return there is no existing user.
  return false;
}
```

```php
// Check username and password meet rules.
function verify_valid_credentials($userid,$passwd)
{
  switch(true)
  {
    // Ensure username doesn't already exist.
    case (verify_user($userid)):
      return 1;

    // Verify username starts with an alphabetic character.
    case (!ereg("([a-zA-Z]+[a-zA-Z0-9]{0,1})",substr($userid,0,1))):
      return 2;

    // Verify username is 6-10 alphanumeric characters.
    case (!ereg("([a-zA-Z]+[a-zA-Z0-9]{5,10})",$userid)):
      return 3;

    // Verify password is 6-10 alphanumeric characters.
    case (!ereg("([a-zA-Z0-9]{5,10})",$passwd)):
      return 4;

    // Acknowledge everything is fine.
    default:
    return 0;
  }
}

  // Define function to write a colon-delimited file.
function write_string($file,$string)
{
  // Declare a write file resource.
  if ($fp = fopen($file,'a+'))
  {
    // Read the two-dimensional array and write or append to a file.
    fwrite($fp,"\n".$string);

    // Close the open file handle.
    fclose($fp);
  }
}
?>
```

The functions in this library serve as the backbone of functionality for the add user application. Several of these functions are useful throughout a larger application because they support basic HTTP authentication. Consolidating these into a library frees form developers to focus on the user interface components and not security infrastructure. A complete set of libraries to handle the model component of your application is known as a *framework*.

The `SignOn.php` program contains fewer than ten lines of code, since it can now leverage both the model and view-controller libraries. This simplification make the base code a much better starting point for a real-world application. The code follows:

-- **This is found in SignOn.php on the enclosed CD.**

```php
<?php
  // Include form library.
  @include_once("BasicAuthentication.inc");
  @include_once("BasicForms.inc");

  // Check valid credentials.
  $valid_user = verify_authentication();

  //Prompt for credentials when they're missing.
  if (!$valid_user)
  {
    authenticate();
  }
  else
  {
    // Assign inputs to variables.
    $userid = isset($_POST['userid']);
    $passwd = isset($_POST['passwd']);

    // Display next user form.
    addUserForm(array("form"=>"AddUser.php","userid"=>$userid));
  }
?>
```

The `SignOn.php` form is simple to read and understand, provided you accept the interface of the framework for the model and view-controller components. The call to the `addUserForm()` function passes an associative array to support the flexible parameter lists model in the view-controller function.

The `AddUser.php` form is likewise simple but a bit longer. The program contains the decision tree from the activity diagram in Figure 11-5, as follows:

-- **This is found in AddUser.php on the enclosed CD.**

```php
<?php
  // Include form library.
  @include_once("BasicAuthentication.inc");
  @include_once("BasicForms.inc");

  // Check valid credentials.
  $valid_user = verify_authentication();

  //Prompt for credentials when they're missing.
  if (!$valid_user)
```

```
{
  authenticate();
}
else
{
  // Assign inputs to variables.
  $userid = $_POST['userid'];
  $passwd = $_POST['passwd'];

  // Set error default and write new credentials.
  if (($code = verify_valid_credentials($userid,$passwd)) == 0)
  {
    // Join user and encrypted password into a colon-delimited string.
    $data = implode(":",array($userid,md5($passwd)));

    // Call the function to append a line to a file.
    write_string("simplepassword.txt",$data);
  }

  // Display next user form.
  addUserForm(array("code"=>$code
                 ,"form"=>"AddUser.php"
                 ,"userid"=>$userid));
}
?>
```

A subtle trick is used in the conditional statement verifying that the username and password meet the required application guidelines. Inside the `if`-statement comparison, there is a declaration of the `$code` variable. This eliminates a physical declaration line to assign the `verify_valid_credentials()` function results. It is a bit tricky to read at first but an efficient way to declare and compare a variable. The `implode()` function builds a complete entry to append to the ACL file.

TIP
You will want to create a function wrapping this when you start editing the components of existing users.

You have reviewed the concepts of the RPC model and how to implement the model in PHP web applications. The sections have demonstrated how to take two pages and build model and view-controller libraries to support a better reuse model.

Summary

The chapter has shown you how to implement the reply and response model for web applications. You covered how the reply and response model is the RPC model and is a more efficient version of CGI programming using Apache modules. The chapter has demonstrated basic HTTP authentication and demonstrated it through the use of a small application. The idea of self-contained web pages was demonstrated alongside the MVC pattern. The MVC pattern was demonstrated with both model and view-controller libraries.

CHAPTER
12

Cookies and Sessions

his chapter discusses how cookies and sessions support the reply and response model used by web applications. It demonstrates how to create and modify both cookies and sessions. Cookies are client-side information files. Cookies contain data supporting transactions across stateless HTTP network communication. Sessions are data entities and are stored as files or records in a database on the server. Sessions contain information you typically do not want to exchange between client and server, like user names and passwords.

The chapter is divided into three sections:

■ Defining and using cookies

■ Defining and using sessions

■ Applying cookies and sessions

Cookies and sessions work together to share data and build reliable transaction processing models and web applications. They work so well at maintaining transaction data that web applications using them are replacing console and client/server applications. As a team, they effectively maintain bookmarks in transactions.

Cookies maintain the identity of a remote client browser in relation to a server-side application. They are typically loaded on the client machine after the first contact with the server-side application server. Many web applications send cookies only after the client authenticates by entering a user name and password.

After authenticating the remote user, the server establishes a session and populates session data in a memory segment, physical file, or database. The server sends a cookie back to the authenticated browser that contains the session identifier. This process is effectively like the first component of a secret handshake. All subsequent communication between the client and server depends on the validity of the first handshake, which sends only a session identifier.

More than one cookie can be sent by an application, and more than one thing can be sent inside a given cookie. When the next client request is sent to the server, it also transmits the cookie as part of the URL header. The application looks for the information in the cookies to determine what it should do next. This is an effective and well-understood model, but cookies can contain confidential information. They also can disclose information when intercepted by an unauthorized third party.

Combining server-side sessions as data repositories and cookies that store only a session identifier prevents writing confidential information to client-side cookies. The confidential information can potentially contain user names and passwords, or account numbers. It is preferable that this type of information never leave the server, but sometimes writing it to web pages is unavoidable for confirmation purposes.

Privacy Illusion

Sun Microsystems founder Scott McNealy said, "You have zero privacy anyway—get over it." While he's right, not all users realize that browsing the web surrenders some of their privacy. URL rewriting inside HTML hidden inputs is probably the most elegant way of hiding the reality from the end user and average script kiddy.

Apache Setup Alert

This chapter assumes that you have enabled your `output_buffering` directive in your `php.ini` file. You enable it by setting it on or providing a physical size limit, like 4096. Zend Core for Oracle will disable this setting. When the `output_buffering` directive is disabled, all the header requests must occur before any HTML tags. These scripts will fail unless you enable the directive or modify the code.

Web browsers enable users to disallow cookies, which makes building web application transactions more difficult. The client needs a cookie to identify itself to the server and provide instructions on how it should interact with the server. When browsers disable cookies, you can use URL rewriting. URL rewriting changes the rendered web forms by including the session identifier as part of the action value for target URLs. URL rewriting sends the session identifier as part of the URL, but unfortunately, it is sent in clear text.

This can present problems when a user copies URLs and e-mails them or instant-messages them to other users. When other users copy the provided URL into a browser, they assume the original user's preauthorized standing by sending the session identifier as part of the URL. This means that the second or third user may have access to what should be confidential information because the original user didn't understand the random character sequence appended in the URL.

Sending the session identifier as part of the URL transmits it in clear text, which makes it more vulnerable to a man-in-the-middle attack. This is a risk that you should seriously consider before implementing traditional URL rewriting.

Another approach to URL rewriting embeds the session identifier as a hidden input value. This approach sends the session identifier as an encrypted POST variable to the server when the HTML form is submitted. The problem is that the session identifier is now part of the source for the rendered HTML page. URL rewriting through hidden input values is less noticeable to hackers than URL-embedded session identifiers.

Cookies or rewriting disclose the session identifier to potential hackers. The question is: How do you protect the data from a hacker who has purloined the session identifier? Two common solutions are to require reauthorization before key transaction points in your application or to surreptitiously validate the source IP before displaying the next form. The latter check does not guarantee that the user is not a hacker that is spoofing the source IP address. It does provide a way to eliminate many amateurs.

You do control your application login process when you use cookies and sessions as opposed to basic HTTP authentication. The first section shows you how to create, send, and read cookies and how to manage cookies. The second section demonstrates how to create sessions and use cookies to maintain transaction state. The third section demonstrates a small application using cookies and sessions.

Defining and Using Cookies

You can define cookies independently of sessions or in conjunction with sessions. Cookies and sessions are typically implemented as a set when managing transactions in web applications. You use cookies by themselves when building web pages that do not authenticate users visiting your site. When you define cookies without sessions, the cookies contain all the information to support your transactions.

Cookies for nonauthenticated users are convenient because you don't know if they'll revisit your site. Consuming server-side resources for these users is potentially a waste of server resources. While placing the information on the client machine exposes the behaviors of those users to anyone who accesses the cookie, it is a clean and easy process for you to code. You should avoid storing information in cookies when implementing transaction-based web applications because they can expose too much information to prying eyes.

In this section, you will learn how to define and use cookies as small client-side information files. The cookies can contain a lot of information, but you'll have to serialize the information into strings. You should avoid the PHP `serialize()` function because of its security vulnerabilities and use the `implode()` function when writing serialized strings. It is recommended that you build a couple of library modules for serializing and de-serializing the information in cookies. This will save you tremendous time in accessing and formatting the contents of the cookies in your applications and avoid the proliferation of multiple cookie formats. You can look at examples for ideas on serializing and de-serializing strings in Appendix B.

Cookies are set and then available with the next transmission of an HTTP request to the server. Cookies can be short-lived or long-lived. When you want a cookie to go away, you set the expiration time to a negative number. That means the cookie has outlived its usefulness and it will not be transmitted back to the server with the next HTTP request message.

There are two PHP functions that enable you to build cookies. They are described in Table 12-1. You will most likely only use the `setcookie()` function to encode cookies because the `setrawcookie()` uses the older encoding style, which is generally no longer valuable.

PHP makes setting your first cookie very simple. The `JustACookie.php` program demonstrates how to set a cookie and read the cookie contents. The first time you send the request to the form, you will see there is no available cookie read by the server. This is because the request for `JustACookie.php` sent an HTTP response header to the browser with the cookie information. You will see the cookie when you reload the page because the reload will send the cookie in the URL to the application server.

The following `JustACookie.php` demonstrates setting a cookie:

-- This is found in JustACookie.php on the enclosed CD.

```php
<?php
  // Check if a cookie is set and read its contents.
  if (isset($_COOKIE['MyCookie']))
    print "MyCookie is set to: [".$_COOKIE['MyCookie']."]<br>";
  else
  {
    // Print the cookie is not set.
    print "MyCookie is not set.";

    // Set the cookie for a two-minute life span.
    setcookie("MyCookie", 'A simple string value', time() + 120, '/');
  }

  // Read all available cookies sent in the URL.
  if (isset($_COOKIE))
    foreach ($_COOKIE as $name => $value)
      print "Cookie Name [$name]; cookie value [$value]<br>";
?>
```

Function	Description and Pattern
setcookie()	The setcookie() function defines a cookie that will be sent as a URL-encoded string with the HTTP headers. URL encoding substitutes a % followed by two hexadecimal numbers for all nonalphanumeric characters other than the underscore, and a + symbol for white spaces. The URL-encoded form is the same as the application/x-www-form-urlencoded MIME type. The setcookie() function has one mandatory and five optional parameters. The mandatory parameter takes a string that is the cookie name. The first optional parameter takes a string that contains the information associated with the cookie. The second optional parameter takes an int that determines the number of seconds until the cookie expires or becomes obsolete. The third optional parameter takes a string and defines the search path for the server domain. It will search all paths when set to a "/" value but only search a restricted path when set to a specific value. The fourth optional parameter takes a string and sets the domain for the cookie. The fifth optional parameter takes a bool and represents a flag that determines whether the cookie should be sent only over a secure network. You should use a 0 for false and 1 for true because a bool false will attempt to delete the cookie. The setcookie() function has the following pattern:

```
bool setcookie(string name
  [,string value
  [,int expire
  [,string path
  [,string domain
  [,bool secure ]]]]])
```

Function	Description and Pattern
setrawcookie()	The setrawcookie() function defines a cookie that will be sent as a non–URL encoded string with the HTTP headers. The older form for URL encoding, it substitutes a % followed by two hexadecimal numbers for all nonalphanumeric characters other than the underscore, and *no* + symbol for white spaces. The setrawcookie() function has one mandatory and five optional parameters. The mandatory parameter takes a string that is the cookie name. The first optional parameter takes a string that contains the information associated with the cookie. The second optional parameter takes an int that determines the number of seconds until the cookie expires or becomes obsolete. The third optional parameter takes a string and defines the search path for the server domain. It will search all paths when set to a "/" value but only search a restricted path when set to a specific value. The fourth optional parameter takes a string and sets the domain for the cookie. The fifth optional parameter takes a bool and represents a flag that determines whether the cookie should be sent only over a secure network. You should use a 0 for false and 1 for true because a bool false will attempt to delete the cookie. The setrawcookie() function has the following pattern:

```
bool setrawcookie(string name
  [,string value
  [,int expire
  [,string path
  [,string domain
  [,bool secure ]]]]])
```

TABLE 12-1. *PHP Cookie Functions*

The JustACookie.php program checks to determine if a cookie is set in the URL, which is available in the $_COOKIE predefined variable covered in Chapter 4. When the cookie is not set, the program sets the cookie with a two-minute life span. After reading or setting the cookie, the program reads all name and value pairs from the $_COOKIE predefined variable.

As mentioned, the first call to the `JustACookie.php` program will not find a cookie on the client machine but will place the cookie on the client machine. You will see the following in the web browser:

```
MyCookie is not set.
```

At this point, you can find and manually read the cookie in the `C:\Documents and Settings\Account Name\Cookies` folder for Microsoft Internet Explorer. This is the standard location when a session is unused for that browser. You should find similar content to the following, but the numbers will differ:

```
MyCookie
A+simple+string+value
dev.techtinker.com/
1536
103896320
29788830
55476320
29788830
*
```

NOTE
If you open the cookie in Notepad, it will not be formatted correctly.
WordPad will render the cookie file correctly.

When you reload the page within two minutes of your initial page load, you will see that the single cookie has been returned in the URL and processed by the PHP script. After the cookie expires, you will see nothing when refreshing the web page. The web page renders the following:

```
MyCookie is set to: [A simple string value]
Cookie Name [MyCookie]; cookie value [A simple string value]
```

The `JustCookies.php` program demonstrates how to remove a cookie by setting the life span to a negative number. The program will initially say there are no cookies, then return both cookies, and finally return the only cookie not expired.

The following `JustCookies.php` program demonstrates how to set and expire cookies:

```
-- This is found in JustCookies.php on the enclosed CD.
```

```php
<?php
  // Check if a cookie is set and read its contents.
  if ((isset($_COOKIE['MyCookie1'])) && (isset($_COOKIE['MyCookie2'])))
  {
    print "MyCookie1 is set to: [".$_COOKIE['MyCookie1']."]<br>";
    print "MyCookie2 is set to: [".$_COOKIE['MyCookie2']."]<br>";
  }
  else
  {
    // Print the cookie is not set.
    print "MyCookie1, MyCookie2, or both are not set.<br>";
```

```
    // Set the cookies for a two-minute life span.
    setcookie("MyCookie1", 'A simple string value 1', time() + 120, '/');
    setcookie("MyCookie2", 'A simple string value 2', time() + 120, '/');
}

// Print header.
print "<hr>";
print "Print all returned cookies:<br><hr>";

// Read all available cookies sent in the URL.
if (isset($_COOKIE))
  foreach ($_COOKIE as $name => $value)
    print "Cookie Name [$name]; cookie value [$value]<br>";

// Expire the cookie by setting a negative life span.
if (isset($_COOKIE['MyCookie2']))
  setcookie("MyCookie2", 'A simple string value 2', time() - 1, '/');

// Print header.
print "<hr>";
print "Print all returned cookies after expiring [MyCookie2]:<br><hr>";


// Read all available cookies sent in the URL.
if (isset($_COOKIE))
  foreach ($_COOKIE as $name => $value)
    print "Cookie Name [$name]; cookie value [$value]<br>";
?>
```

The JustCookies.php program makes a second call to the setcookie() function for the MyCookie2 cookie and sets the life span to a negative timestamp. The first time you enter the URL, you will receive the following message in the browser:

```
MyCookie1, MyCookie2, or both are not set.
-----------------------------------------------------------------------
Print all returned cookies:
-----------------------------------------------------------------------
Print all returned cookies after expiring [MyCookie2]:
```

The refresh URL will then return both cookies to the web page while sending a header back to the client to expire MyCookie2. You will see the following in the web page:

```
MyCookie1 is set to: [A simple string value 1]
MyCookie2 is set to: [A simple string value 2]
-----------------------------------------------------------------------
Print all returned cookies:
Cookie Name [MyCookie1]; cookie value [A simple string value 1]
Cookie Name [MyCookie2]; cookie value [A simple string value 2]
-----------------------------------------------------------------------
Print all returned cookies after expiring [MyCookie2]:
Cookie Name [MyCookie1]; cookie value [A simple string value 1]
Cookie Name [MyCookie2]; cookie value [A simple string value 2]
```

A subsequent URL refresh will only return the unexpired cookie from the client, as follows:

```
MyCookie1, MyCookie2, or both are not set.
--------------------------------------------------------------------
Print all returned cookies:
Cookie Name [MyCookie1]; cookie value [A simple string value 1]
--------------------------------------------------------------------
Print all returned cookies after expiring [MyCookie2]:
Cookie Name [MyCookie1]; cookie value [A simple string value 1]
```

This section has demonstrated how you set and expire a cookie. It has also demonstrated that when you set a cookie, it becomes available only on the next call to the URL, provided that call is made before the life span time-out value expires.

Defining and Using Sessions

You can define cookies when using sessions or simply let the session manage cookies. When you start a PHP session, the session implicitly creates a session identifier cookie, provided the browser is configured to accept cookies. You should consider collecting that information using JavaScript embedded in your nonauthenticated login form. You can send that browser setting as a hidden input when the user clicks the HTML input widget and transmits his or her login information. When cookies are supported, you can use them, and when they're blocked, you can implement URL rewriting.

The principal discussion in this section assumes the browser accepts cookies. The section "Applying Cookies and Sessions" later in the chapter covers how to implement URL rewriting when cookies are blocked.

Before working with sessions, you need to ensure that your PHP directives are configured correctly. They are in the `php.ini` file and typically set to the recommended values. You should check the `php.ini` file to make sure they haven't been changed. Table 12-2 summarizes the key PHP directives that support sessions. There are several others, but generally these will enable your system to support sessions.

Directive	Default	Description
session.auto_start	0	The session.auto_start directive defines whether sessions are automatically started for all served PHP files. As a rule, this should be disabled by setting it to the default value of 0.
session.cache_expire	180	The session.cache_expire directive defines the time limit before deleting the server-side cache. The default value is 180 minutes. This directive is ignored when you have configured the session.cache_limiter directive. Interestingly enough, both are enabled by default in the php.ini file. PHP therefore simply ignores the session.cache_expire value by default. You can remark it or ignore it.

TABLE 12-2. *PHP Session Directives*

Directive	Default	Description
session.cache_limiter	nocache	The session.cache_limiter directive defines whether session pages are cached. When set, this directive overrides any setting in the session.cache_expire directive. It has one of the following possible values:
		■ **none** Disables sending any cache control headers with pages containing active sessions.
		■ **nocache** Sends all requests to the server first before serving cached pages, which is the default.
		■ **private** Reserves cached pages to the original page requestor.
		■ **private_no_expire** Reserves cached pages to the original page requestor but is more generically compatible with browsers.
		■ **public** Makes all documents cached whether they require authentication or not, which is something you should avoid.
session.cookie_domain	none	The session.cookie_domain directive defines the domain for your cookies. It is prudent to set this directive to avoid other domains' reading your cookies.
session.cookie_lifetime	0	The session.cookie_lifetime directive sets the duration of the session cookie. The default is zero, which means that the cookie persists until the browser is closed. When you want a different behavior, you should set the duration value to the number of desired seconds.
session.cookie_path	/	The session.cookie_path directive defines the path where session cookies are stored. As a general rule, you should not change the default value.
session.name	PHPSESSID	The session.name directive defines the session cookie name.
session.save_handler	file	The session.save_handler directive defines where you store the session information. The default is to store it in files. You may also store it in memory (mem) or in a database (user). When you opt for storing session information in the database, you must write your own session handler. Given the weaknesses in PHP file I/O, the best solution is to store the information in the database and write your own session handler.
session.save_path	/tmp	The session.save_path directive defines where to put the session information on the server. The Linux default directory is /tmp, and Windows default folder is C:\WINDOWS\Temp.
session.use_cookies	1	The session.use_cookies directive defines whether to place cookies on the client machines. Setting this directive to 1 enables writing cookies, and setting it to 0 enables URL rewriting.

TABLE 12-2. *PHP Session Directives* (continued)

Assuming you have set the session directives correctly and restarted your Apache or ISS HTTP server, you are prepared to develop PHP forms that use sessions. There are additional directives that are less frequently used. Some of those provide advantages when you move your system into production.

Some of the directive values can be overridden by calling session setting functions in your PHP scripts. The overriding values have a limited duration to the scripts' execution cycle. Table 12-3 lists summaries of the available session functions.

Function	Description and Pattern
session_cache_expire()	The session_cache_expire() function returns the current session.cache_expire directive value, which is read in minutes. It takes one optional parameter, which is an overriding value for the session.cache_expire directive. Without an actual parameter, the function returns the current environment value for the directive. The function has the following pattern: int session_cache_expire([int *new_cache*])
session_cache_limiter()	The session_cache_limiter() function returns the current session.cache_limiter directive value, which is read in minutes. It takes one optional parameter, which is an overriding value for the session.cache_limiter directive. Without an actual parameter, the function returns the current environment value for the directive. The acceptable values are: none, nocache, private, private_no_expire, and public. Table 12-2 contains the meanings of the possible parameters. The function has the following pattern: string session_cache_limiter([string *new_limiter*])
session_commit()	The session_commit() function is an alias for the session_write_close() function. It writes session data and stores the session data. The function has the following pattern: void session_commit()
session_decode()	The session_decode() function takes a session string and writes it to the server-side session file. It returns true when successful and false when it fails. The parameter must be a valid session string, like that returned from the session_encode() function. The function has the following pattern: int session_decode(string *session_data*)
session_encode()	The session_encode() function returns the current session information in a string. It has no parameters. The function has the following pattern: string session_encode()
session_get_cookie_params()	The session_get_cookie_params() function returns the current session cookie information for the lifetime, path, domain, and secure variables. The function has the following pattern: array session_get_cookie_params()
session_id()	The session_id() function returns the session identifier for the existing session, or it enables changing the session identify by providing the new one as an actual parameter. The function acts as a getter or setter function for the session identifier. It takes one optional parameter, which is a session identifier. The function has the following pattern: string session_id([string *sessid*])

TABLE 12-3. *PHP Session Management Functions*

Function	Description and Pattern

session_is_registered()	The session_is_registered() function returns true when the actual parameter is the session cookie name. It returns false when the actual parameter is not the current session cookie name. The default session cookie name is PHPSESSID, and there's little reason to change it. The function takes one mandatory parameter that is a session cookie name as a string. The function has the following pattern:
	
	`bool session_is_registered(`
	`  string session_name)`

session_module_name()	The session_module_name() function returns the current session module name when there is no optional parameter provided. When the optional parameter is provided, the function resets the session module name and returns the new session module name. The function has the following pattern:
	
	`string session_module_name(`
	`  [string module_name])`

session_name()	The session_name() function returns the current session name when there is no optional parameter provided. When the optional parameter is provided, the function resets the session name and returns it from the function. The function has the following pattern:
	
	`string session_name(`
	`  [string name])`

session_regenerate_id()	The session_regenerate_id() function returns the current session identifier when there is no optional parameter provided. When an optional parameter is provided, the function will reset the session identifier. It returns true when successful and false when not. The function has the following pattern:
	
	`bool session_regenerate_id(`
	`  [bool reset])`

session_register()	The session_register() function is deprecated and assignments of new values to the session cookie should be directly made through the $_SESSION predefined variable.

session_save_path()	The session_save_path() function returns the current save path. When an optional parameter is provided, the function will reset the current session save path and return the new value. Omitting the optional parameter will return the current save path. The function has the following pattern:
	
	`string session_save_path(`
	`  [string path])`

session_set_cookie_params()	The session_set_cookie_params() function returns nothing but resets the current session cookie information for the lifetime, path, domain, and secure variables. The function has the following pattern:
	
	`void session_set_cookie_params(`
	`  [ int lifetime`
	`  [,string path`
	`  [,string domain`
	`  [,bool secure]]]])`

session_set_save_handler()	The session_set_save_handler() function returns a bool true when successful and false when unsuccessful. This defines the session handler when the session.save_handler directive is set to user. All five callback functions must be implemented to access a user-defined session save handler. The function has the following pattern:
	
	`bool session_set_save_handler(`
	`  [ callback open`
	`  [,callback close`
	`  [,callback read`
	`  [,callback write`
	`  [,callback gc]]]]])`

TABLE 12-3. *PHP Session Management Functions* (continued)

Function	Description and Pattern
session_start()	The session_start() function returns a bool true when the function successfully starts or resumes a session sent in the URL. It returns a bool false when the function unsuccessfully starts or resumes a session. The function has no formal parameters. The function has the following pattern: `bool session_start()`

session_unregister()	The session_unregister() function returns a bool true when the function successfully removes a variable from the $_SESSION predefined variable. It returns a bool false when the function unsuccessfully attempts to remove a variable from the $_SESSION variable. The function has one mandatory formal parameter, which is a string that maps to a name in the $_SESSION array. The function has the following pattern:
	
	`bool session_unregister(`
	`  string name)`

session_unset()	The session_unset() function returns a bool true when the function successfully removes all session variables from the $_SESSION predefined variable. It returns a bool false when the function unsuccessfully attempts to remove all variables from the $_SESSION variable. The function takes no formal parameter. The function has the following pattern: `void session_unset()`
session_write_close()	The session_write_close() function ends the current session and writes it to file. The function has the following pattern: `void session_write_close()`

TABLE 12-3.   *PHP Session Management Functions* (continued)

Session functions provide a good set of features and automation for managing sessions in files. There is marginal scalability to using files as session repositories. Putting session information into databases is a more scalable solution. Unfortunately, there is no shipped tool for managing session information in a database.

PHP does provide the session_set_save_handler() function as a wrapper to user-defined functions that manage user-defined file or database session management mechanisms. You use the session_set_save_handler() function when you implement a custom handler, and you set the session.save_handler directive to user, as is covered in Table 12-2.

This section demonstrates how to build session-enabled web pages, having summarized the PHP session functions in Table 12-3. The programs demonstrate some of the more commonly used session functions.

The SessionCookie.php program shows how to start a session. As mentioned earlier in this section, PHP automatically creates and sends cookies with the header to the client. Like ordinary cookies, they are unavailable the first time you access the web page because you can't send them with the URL until they are set on the client machine. When you reload the web page, the cookies will be available.

The SessionCookie.php program follows:

-- This is found in SessionCookie.php on the enclosed CD.

```php
<?php
  // Start a session and assign session identifier to variable.
  if (session_start())
    $session_id = session_id();
```

```
// Print description.
print "Initial Server-side State:<br />";

// Read existence of session or return not set message.
if (isset($session_id))
  print "Session Data: ['Server-side File'][".$session_id."]<br>";
else
  print "Session Data: ['Server-side File'][Not Currently Set]<br>";

// Print description.
print "<hr />";
print "Initial Client-side Cookie State:<br />";

// Read session cookie or return not set message.
if (isset($_COOKIE['PHPSESSID']))
  print "Session Cookie: ['PHPSESSID'][".$_COOKIE['PHPSESSID']."]<br>";
else
  print "Session Cookie: ['PHPSESSID'][Not Currently Set]<br>";
?>
```

The SessionCookie.php program starts the session by calling the session_start()
function. A $session_id variable is assigned the session identifier by calling the session_
id() function. This activity depends on actions having been registered on the server during the
execution of the PHP script. The session_start() function creates a session and writes an
empty file in the save directory. The filename is built by using a preface of sess_ and the session
identifier.

The initial call to the SessionCookie.php web page will render the following:

```
Initial Server-side State:
Session Data: ['Server-side File'][3uffi2h9rvmt22gl0b58k1hqn5]
------------------------------------------------------------
Initial Client-side Cookie State:
Session Cookie: ['PHPSESSID'][Not Currently Set]
```

The value of $_COOKIE['PHPSESSID'] will contain the session identifier and equal the return
of the session_id() function, provided the name index is set as the value of the session
.name directive in your php.ini file. If you changed the default session name, you can get the
correct value by calling the session_name() function.

The content of the session cookie becomes obsolete when you call the session_
regenerate_id() function because it changes the current session identifier. After regenerating
the session identifier, the value will differ from the client-side cookie value. This is an opportune
time to prompt and authenticate user credentials.

A reload of the SessionCookie.php will send the client-side cookie to the server and
render the following web page:

```
Initial Server-side State:
Session Data: ['Server-side File'][3uffi2h9rvmt22gl0b58k1hqn5]
------------------------------------------------------------
Initial Client-side Cookie State:
Session Cookie: ['PHPSESSID'][3uffi2h9rvmt22gl0b58k1hqn5]
```

The `SessionCookie.php` program demonstrates how to set and synchronize the server session and client cookies. In the example, the session file is empty. You put data into the file by assigning values to the `$_SESSION` predefined variable. The reading and writing of files from the session file is managed by the default session save handler, which reads from and writes to a serialized string in the session file. This is the default behavior when the `session.save_handler` directive is set to file.

When you set the `session.save_handler` value to mem or user, you must provide a user-defined function to manage the read and write process to the session repository. The user-defined `session_set_save_handler()` function must be placed in scope when running scripts that save the session information to memory or database resources. You will need to call an `include_once()` function to place the library function in each session-enabled script.

The `SessionFileWrite.php` demonstrates writing to and reading from the session file. It assigns values directly to the `$_SESSION` variable and reads them back from the array variable, as follows:

-- **This is found in SessionFileWrite.php on the enclosed CD.**

```php
<?php
  // Start a session and assign session identifier to variable.
  if (session_start())
    $session_id = session_id();

  // Print description.
  print "Server-side State:<br />";
  print "<hr />";

  // Read existence of the session or return not set message.
  if (isset($session_id))
  {
    // Write to the server-side session through the predefined variable.
    $_SESSION['username'] = "username";
    $_SESSION['password'] = "password";
  }

  // Read contents of server-side session file.
  foreach ($_SESSION as $name => $value)
    print "[$name][$value]<br />";
?>
```

The `SessionFileWrite.php` file sets the username and password in the session file. It is stored in the following serialized string:

```
username|s:8:"username";password|s:8:"password";
```

When `SessionFileWrite.php` reads the data from the session file, it filters it through the `$_SESSION` variable and renders the following:

```
Server-side State:
-----------------------------------------------------------------------
[username] [username]
[password] [password]
```

This section has reviewed the session directives required in the php.ini file and covered the available session functions. It has also shown how to start, use, and monitor session files. In the next section you will apply these techniques in a small application.

Applying Cookies and Sessions

This section demonstrates how you use cookies and sessions in a small login and user administration application. The web application is similar to the one in Chapter 11 but differs in how you authenticate users. Two forms are used in this application. One is a nonauthenticated SignOn.php file, and the other is an authenticated AddUser.php file.

The SignOn.php file is your preauthentication entry portal to the application. It is also your redirection target page when users fail to authenticate on other web pages. The SignOn.php form provides a generic login screen. The session will only start when the user attempts to authenticate. When the user clicks the Submit button, SignOn.php calls the AddUser.php form, which authenticates the user.

The SignOn.php code follows:

-- **This is found in SignOn.php on the enclosed CD.**

```php
<?php
  // Display login user form.
  signOnForm();

  // Build dynamic data entry form.
  function signOnForm()
  {
    // Initialize return variable.
    $out  = '<div id=centered>';

    // Set and append next form target file.
    $out .= '<form method="post" action="AddUser.php">';

    // Append balance of form header.
    $out .= '<table border="4"
                    bgcolor="beige"
                    bordercolor="silver"
                    cellspacing="0">';
    $out .= '<tr><td align="center" width="400">';
    $out .= '<font size=+3>User Login</font>';
    $out .= '</td></tr>';
    $out .= '<tr><td>';
    $out .= '<table border="0" cellpadding="5" cellspacing="0">';
    $out .= '<tr>';
    $out .= '<td align="right" width="200">User ID:</td>';
    $out .= '<td width="200"><input name="userid" type="text"></td>';
    $out .= '</tr>';
    $out .= '<tr>';
    $out .= '<td align="right">User Password:</td>';
    $out .= '<td><input name="passwd" type="password"></td>';
    $out .= '</tr>';
```

```
    $out .= '<tr>';
    $out .= '</table>';
    $out .= '</td></tr>';
    $out .= '<tr><td align="center" colspan="2">';
    $out .= '<table border="0" cellpadding="5" cellspacing="0">';
    $out .= '<tr>';
    $out .= '<td align="center" valign="center">';
    $out .= '<input name="submit" type="submit" value="Login">';
    $out .= '</td>';
    $out .= '</tr>';
    $out .= '</table>';
    $out .= '</td></tr>';
    $out .= '</table>';
    $out .= '</form>';
    $out .= '</div>';

    // Return the form for rendering in a web page.
    print $out;
  }
?>
```

There are three key lines in the `SignOn.php` file. One key line is where the HTML form tag designates an action. The value of the action property in the HTML form tag is the target page. It uses the same relative directory as the `SignOn.php` page. A second key line is where it sets the type for the password input field. This ensures that the characters entered into the password are not visible to somebody looking over your shoulder. The last key line is where the input type is set to submit. This is typically a button or link that sends the input values of the HTML from the currently rendered page to the target page.

The `SignOn.php` program renders the form in Figure 12-1 to the browser.

FIGURE 12-1. *SignOn.php form*

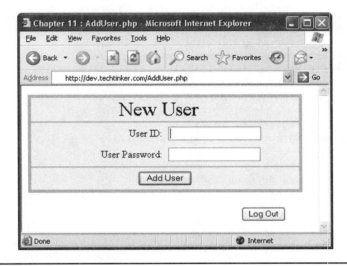

FIGURE 12-2. *Add New User form*

The AddUser.php program validates against a simplepassword.txt file like the example used in Chapter 11. While it writes data to the session file, it also writes pairs of data to its own session file. This mechanism duplicates managing data that is already managed by the session functions. It illustrates how to implement your own model for maintaining state and purging it when the user logs out.

The defined user and password in the simplepassword.txt file are the literals: username and password. The authentication file simplepassword.txt contains the following line with an encrypted password:

```
username:5f4dcc3b5aa765d61d8327deb882cf99
```

The form lets you to write new users and passwords to the simplepassword.txt file. Figure 12-2 shows the rendered AddUser.php form, which includes a Log Out button.

You should examine the file after creating one or two users of your own. It also illustrates how to log out of a web application and force reauthentication. After creating your own user, you should log out as username and log back in as your new user.

The AddUser.php program follows:

-- This is found in AddUser.php on the enclosed CD.

```php
<?php
  // Start session.
  session_start();
  $_SESSION['sessionid'] = session_id();

  // Verify if new session call.
  if ((!isset($_SESSION['userid'])) || (isset($_POST['userid'])))
```

```php
  {
    // Suppress errors and delete application-maintained file.
    @unlink($_SESSION['sessionid']);

    // Regenerate when a new user is logging in.
    if (isset($_SESSION['userid']))
      if (($_SESSION['userid'] != $_POST['userid']) ||
          ($_SESSION['passwd'] != $_POST['passwd']))
      {
        session_regenerate_id();
        $_SESSION['sessionid'] = session_id();
      }

    // Verify login account and password.
    if (verify_authentication())
    {
      // Write verified login information to a session file.
      write_session_pairs($_SESSION['sessionid']
                         ,array("userid",$_POST['userid']));
      write_session_pairs($_SESSION['sessionid']
                         ,array("passwd",$_POST['passwd']));

      // Read the current session data from the file.
      read_session_pairs($_SESSION['sessionid']);

      // Display the form.
      addUserForm(array("form"=>"AddUser.php"));
    }
    else
    {
      // Destroy the session and force reauthentication.
      session_destroy();

      // Redirect to the login form.
      signOnForm();
    }
  }
  else // Process current session new user form action.
  {
    // Read the current session data from the file.
    read_session_pairs($_SESSION['sessionid']);

    // Assign inputs to variables.
    $userid = $_POST['newuserid'];
    $passwd = $_POST['newpasswd'];

    // Set message and write new credentials.
    if (($code = verify_valid_credentials($userid,$passwd)) == 0)
    {
      // Join user and encrypted password into a colon-delimited string.
      $data = implode(":",array($userid,md5($passwd)));
```

```php
    // Call the function to append a line to a file.
    write_string("simplepassword.txt",$data);
  }

  // Display next user form.
  addUserForm(array("code"=>$code
                   ,"form"=>"AddUser.php"
                   ,"userid"=>$userid));
}

// Build user message string.
function get_message($code,$userid)
{
  // Designate message by error code.
  switch ($code)
  {
    case 0:
      return "You have added user [$userid] successfully.";
    case 1:
      return "User [$userid] is already in use.";
    case 2:
      return "User [$userid] must start with a character.";
    case 3:
      return "User [$userid] must be between 6 and 10 characters.";
    case 4:
      return "The password must be between 6 and 10 characters.";
  }
}

// Define function to read and assign $_SESSION variables.
function read_session_pairs($session)
{
  // Declare a read file resource.
  if ($fp = @fopen($session,'r'))
  {
    // Read the file into an array of strings.
    $file = file($session);

    // Write session data to environment.
    foreach ($file as $pairs)
    {
      list($name,$value) = explode(":",$pairs);
      $_SESSION[$name] = trim($value);
    }

    // Close the open file handle.
    fclose($fp);
  }
}
```

```php
// Define function to read and update server-side session file.
function update_session_pair($session,$name_in,$value_in)
{
  // Read file contents to an array of strings.
  $contents = file($session);

  // Delete the base file.
  if (unlink($session))
  {
    // Read contents.
    foreach ($contents as $pairs)
    {
      // Parse contents to variables.
      list($name,$value) = explode(":",$pairs);

      // Check for matching index value and trim line returns.
      if ($name == $name_in)
        $value = trim($value_in);
      else
        $value = trim($value);

      // Append lines to a new file.
      write_session_pairs($session,array($name,$value));
    }
  }
}

// Define a Basic Authentication function.
function verify_authentication()
{
  // Check for session variables.
  if ((isset($_SESSION['userid'])) && (isset($_SESSION['passwd'])))
    $session_valid = true;
  else
    $session_valid = false;

  // Check for input variables.
  if ((isset($_POST['userid'])) && (isset($_POST['passwd'])))
    $post_valid = true;
  else
    $post_valid = false;

  // Check that it's worth the time to validate.
  if (($session_valid) || ($post_valid))
  {
    // Read the file into an array of strings.
    $passwords = @file("simplepassword.txt");

    // Verify array contains data.
    if (isset($passwords))
```

```php
    {
      // Read through the value list.
      foreach ($passwords as $credentials)
      {
        // Break the delimited lines into scalar variables.
        list($username,$password) = explode(":",$credentials);

        // Find a match and return valid credentials or invalid ones.
        if (($session_valid) && ($_SESSION['userid'] == $username) &&
            ($_SESSION['passwd'] == $password))
          return true;
        else if (($post_valid) && ($_POST['userid'] == $username) &&
                (md5($_POST['passwd']) == trim($password)))
          return true;
      }
    }
    // Return a negative validation.
    return false;
  }

  // Return invalid credentials.
  return false;
}

// Check for existing user.
function verify_user($userid)
{
  // Read the file into an array of strings.
  $passwords = @file("simplepassword.txt");

  // Verify array contains data.
  if (isset($passwords))
  {
    // Read through the value list.
    foreach ($passwords as $credentials)
    {
      // Break the delimited lines into scalar variables.
      list($username,$password) = explode(":",$credentials);

      // Return there is a user.
      if ($userid == $username)
        return true;
    }
  }

  // Return there is no existing user.
  return false;
}

// Check user name and password meet rules.
function verify_valid_credentials($userid,$passwd)
```

```php
  {
    switch(true)
    {
      // Does user name already exist?
      case (verify_user($userid)):
        return 1;

      // Does user name start with an alphabetic character?
      case (!ereg("([a-zA-Z]+[a-zA-Z0-9]{0,1})",substr($userid,0,1))):
        return 2;

      // Does user name start with a letter for a 6-10 character string?
      case (!ereg("([a-zA-Z]+[a-zA-Z0-9]{5,10})",$userid)):
        return 3;

      // Does password start contain a 6-10 character string?
      case (!ereg("([a-zA-Z0-9]{5,10})",$passwd)):
        return 4;

      // Acknowledge everything is fine.
      default:
        return 0;
    }
  }

// Define function to write a server-side session file.
function write_session_pairs($file,$pairs)
{
  // Break array into colon-delimited string.
  $string = implode(":",$pairs);

  // Set control variable.
  $newfile = !is_file($file);

  // Declare a write file resource.
  if ($fp = fopen($file,'a+'))
  {
    // Append a line return after the first line.
    if ($newfile)
      fwrite($fp,$string);
    else
      fwrite($fp,"\n".$string);

    // Close the open file handle.
    fclose($fp);
  }
}

// Define function to write a colon-delimited file.
function write_string($file,$string)
```

```
{
  // Declare a write file resource.
  if ($fp = fopen($file,'a+'))
  {
    // Read the two-dimensional array and write or append to a file.
    fwrite($fp,"\n".$string);

    // Close the open file handle.
    fclose($fp);

  }
}

// Build dynamic data entry form.
function addUserForm($args)
{
  // Define local variables.
  $code;
  $form;
  $userid;

  // Parse form parameters.
  foreach ($args as $name => $value)
  {
    switch (true)
    {
      case ($name == "form"):
        $form = $value;
        break;
      case ($name == "code"):
        $code = $value;
        break;
      case ($name == "userid"):
        $userid = $value;
        break;
    }
  }

  // Initialize return variable.
  $out  = '<div id=centered>';

  // Set and append next form target file.
  $out .= '<form method="post" action="'.$form.'">';

  // Append balance of form header.
  $out .= '<table border="4"
                  bgcolor="beige"
                  bordercolor="silver"
                  cellspacing="0">';
  $out .= '<tr><td align="center" width="400">';
```

```
  $out .= '<font size=+3>New User</font>';
  $out .= '</td></tr>';

  // Verify if optional message.
  if ((isset($code)) && (is_int($code)))
  {
    $out .= '<tr><td align="center" bgcolor="white" width="400">';
    $out .= '<font color=blue>'.get_message($code,$userid).'</font>';
    $out .= '</td></tr>';
  }

  // Append standard data entry components.
  $out .= '<tr><td>';
  $out .= '<table border="0" cellpadding="5" cellspacing="0">';
  $out .= '<tr>';
  $out .= '<td align="right" width="200">User ID:</td>';
  $out .= '<td width="200">';
  $out .= '<input name="newuserid" type="text">';
  $out .= '</td>';
  $out .= '</tr>';
  $out .= '<tr>';
  $out .= '<td align="right">User Password:</td>';
  $out .= '<td><input name="newpasswd" type="password"></td>';
  $out .= '</tr>';
  $out .= '<tr>';
  $out .= '</table>';
  $out .= '</td></tr>';
  $out .= '<tr><td align="center" colspan="2">';
  $out .= '<table border="0" cellpadding="5" cellspacing="0">';
  $out .= '<tr>';
  $out .= '<td align="center" valign="center">';
  $out .= '<input name="submit" type="submit" value="Add User">';
  $out .= '</td>';
  $out .= '</tr>';
  $out .= '</table>';
  $out .= '</td></tr>';
  $out .= '</table>';
  $out .= '</form>';
  $out .= '<form method="post" action="SignOn.php">';
  $out .= '<table border="0" cellpadding="5" cellspacing="0">';
  $out .= '<tr>';
  $out .= '<td align="right" valign="center" width="400">';
  $out .= '<input name="submit" type="submit" value="Log Out">';
  $out .= '</td>';
  $out .= '</tr>';
  $out .= '</table>';
  $out .= '</div>';

  // Return the form for rendering in a web page.
  print $out;
}
```

```
  // Build dynamic data entry form.
  function signOnForm()
  {
    // Initialize return variable.
    $out  = '<div id=centered>';

    // Set and append next form target file.
    $out .= '<form method="post" action="AddUser.php">';

    // Append balance of form header.
    $out .= '<table border="4"
                    bgcolor="beige"
                    bordercolor="silver"
                    cellspacing="0">';
    $out .= '<tr><td align="center" width="400">';
    $out .= '<font size=+3>User Login</font>';
    $out .= '</td></tr>';
    $out .= '<tr><td>';
    $out .= '<table border="0" cellpadding="5" cellspacing="0">';
    $out .= '<tr>';
    $out .= '<td align="right" width="200">User ID:</td>';
    $out .= '<td width="200"><input name="userid" type="text"></td>';

    $out .= '</tr>';
    $out .= '<tr>';
    $out .= '<td align="right">User Password:</td>';
    $out .= '<td><input name="passwd" type="password"></td>';
    $out .= '</tr>';
    $out .= '<tr>';
    $out .= '</table>';
    $out .= '</td></tr>';
    $out .= '<tr><td align="center" colspan="2">';
    $out .= '<table border="0" cellpadding="5" cellspacing="0">';
    $out .= '<tr>';
    $out .= '<td align="center" valign="center">';
    $out .= '<input name="submit" type="submit" value="Login">';
    $out .= '</td>';
    $out .= '</tr>';
    $out .= '</table>';
    $out .= '</td></tr>';
    $out .= '</table>';
    $out .= '</form>';
    $out .= '</div>';

    // Return the form for rendering in a web page.
    print $out;
  }
?>
```

The AddUser.php form validates new users signing on and retains information for returning users who were previously the last person logged in. The client browser does not need to be shut down to change login sessions. It also deletes the user-defined file where information is stored. The password encryption md5() function is the same as that found in Chapter 11. You should really use sha1() to encrypt passwords because it provides a better algorithm.

The readSessionPairs() function is really not required, because the assignments to the $_SESSION variable have already been made. It is provided to illustrate how to read that type of file.

Enabling URL rewriting is an option when you encounter web browsers that have disabled cookies. Another alternative to URL rewriting is to include the session identifier as a hidden input parameter in an HTML form submission. The AddUser.php program can be modified to support this approach by using the following initial validation to start a session:

```
// Avoid a cookie send masquerade it as a URL component.
if (isset($_POST['sessionid']))
{
  // Start, set session ID, and read session variables.
  session_start();
  $_SESSION['sessionid'] = session_id($_POST['sessionid']);
  read_session_pairs($_SESSION['sessionid']);
}
else
{
  // Start and set session ID.
  session_start();
  $_SESSION['sessionid'] = session_id();
}
```

There needs to be a hidden input value in the form submission for the sessionid value. You can add the following line in the addUserForm() function to enable this modified type of URL rewriting:

```
$out .= '<input name="sessionid" type="hidden"
              value="'.$_SESSION['sessionid'].'">';
```

The initial logic examines the incoming form signal to determine whether or not you are relying on a cookie and session mechanism or modified URL rewriting. This approach works even when cookies are maintained by the browser.

As discussed in Chapter 11, you can move much of this code into library functions. Also, you should consider writing custom session handlers to mask the complexity required to maintain your own code. It is recommended that you define a separate script-level array variable to contain your name and value pairs externally from the $_SESSION variable, if you opt to build your own session file management utility.

This section has demonstrated a complete web application example that uses cookies and sessions to manage user authentication. It has also demonstrated how you can maintain your own session files and made a recommendation that they be separated from defined environment variables.

Summary

The chapter has shown you how to implement cookies and sessions. It has demonstrated how you authenticate using them. The chapter has explained that you have a URL rewriting option when users have disabled cookies in their browsers.

PART
IV

PHP and Oracle
Express Development

CHAPTER
13

Oracle SQL Queries
and Transactions

his chapter discusses how to connect to the Oracle Database 10*g* XE instance to both query and transact against schema objects, such as tables, views, and stored procedures. While Structured Query Language (SQL) provides the standard interface to Oracle databases, Oracle also provides the Procedural Language/ Structured Query Language (PL/SQL) interface. You will cover SQL approaches in this chapter working with both scalar variables. PL/SQL approaches working with scalar, scalar collections, and SQL reference cursors are in Chapter 14.

Chapter 2 demonstrated how to install the Oracle Database 10*g* XE product and configure and verify a connection. You must have the Apache, Oracle, and PHP product stack configured to work through the examples in this chapter. All database examples were developed and tested against PHP 5.1.4 but should work from PHP 5.1.2 forward.

Prior to PHP 5.1.2, you need to use a different set of Oracle libraries and have a diminished set of functionality. If you are migrating from an earlier version of PHP, the older function names map as alias assignments to the new function names. You should begin migrating function call names as soon as you move forward to the new release and library. It is highly recommended that you consider moving to PHP 5.1.2 or newer to take advantage of the new Oracle Call Interface 8 (OCI8) libraries.

You can review the SQL and PL/SQL primers, if you are new to the Oracle family of database products. They are Appendixes H and I respectively. Also, the complete foundation code for Chapters 13, 14, and 15 is available in Appendix J for your review.

The chapter is divided into three sections:

- Connecting to Oracle using the OCI8 libraries
- Using the OCI8 Function Library
- Querying and transacting by using SQL statements

The sections are written to be read sequentially. The section "Connecting to Oracle Using the OCI8 Libraries" discusses the three alternative connections, which have different behaviors and functionalities. The section "Using the OCI8 Function Library" reviews a summary of OCI8 functions and demonstrates the basic mechanics of processing SELECT, INSERT, UPDATE, and DELETE statements from your PHP web applications. While the section "Using the OCI8 Function Library" only demonstrates how to INSERT or UPDATE single rows, you can transact against a series of tables and set transaction controls. A single SQL statement can enable you to INSERT and UPDATE multiple rows by using dynamic SQL statements. The section "Querying and Transacting by Using SQL Statements" introduces you to *bind* variables. *Bind* variables let you to map scalar and scalar collection variables to SQL statements.

At present the OCI8 libraries are limited to only a subset of the data types provided by the Oracle Database 10*g* XE product. The development team does plan to add the ability to read and write instantiated PL/SQL objects directly from and to PHP web applications. They did not have a *firm commitment* date on when those features would be added at the time of writing. You should check http://otn.oracle.com for updates.

If you encounter problems running the programs, you have multiple places to troubleshoot once you've added Oracle Database 10*g* XE to the product stack. Appendix G provides an Oracle database primer that explains the tnsping utility, which lets you test whether the Oracle listener is up and running. The same appendix shows you how to verify whether the database is up and running, and provides you with instructions on how to connect and run queries against the database.

There are five SQL programs that you use to work through the concepts in this chapter. The first `create_user.sql` script is found in Appendix G. You should run it as the `SYSTEM` user to create the `PHP` user/schema account in your Oracle Database 10*g* XE instance. The other scripts found in Appendix J assume that you've already run the `create_user.sql` script. If you want to use a different user/schema name than `PHP`, you'll need to check and modify scripts as required.

How to Install the Oracle Instant Client

The OCI8 libraries can be installed on a local Linux or Microsoft Windows machine. You will need to take these steps if you are developing and testing your PHP programs on a different machine than the server that runs only Apache and PHP.

Installing on Linux

There are two RPM files that you download from the http://otn.oracle.com web site. They are found in the `oracle-client-10103.tar.bz2` file, which is a `tar`-format file. You should navigate to the download area and download the Oracle Database 10*g* Release 1 (10.1.0.3) Client. Place the file in the directory where you want to install the software and run the following command:

```
tar -xvjf oracle-client-10103.tar.bz2
```

Exploding the `tar` file, you will see these two files in the directory:

```
oracle-instantclient-basic-10.1.0.3-1.i386.rpm
oracle-instantclient-devel-10.1.0.3-1.i386.rpm
```

The `basic` file contains the Oracle Call Interface 8 (OCI8) libraries that will be installed in the `/usr/lib/oracle/10.1.0.3/client/lib` directory. The `devel` file contains header files and installs in the `/usr/include/oracle/10.1.0.3/client` directory. You can install these manually or use the installation script found in the install directory, as shown:

```
./runmefirst.sh
```

You can reconfigure PHP with the following option:

```
./configure \
--with-oci8-instantclient,/usr/lib/oracle/10.1.0.3/client/lib \
--prefix=$HOME/php –with-apxs=$HOME/apache/bin/apxs \
--enable-sigchild –with-config-file-path=$HOME/apache/conf
```

You rebuild PHP with the make command, set `LD_LIBRARY_PATH` to the `/usr/lib/oracle/10.1.0.3/client/lib` directory, and restart Apache. Use the Apache log files to troubleshoot misplaced or mistyped configuration steps.

For reference, you also need to set the `TNS_ADMIN` environment variable to point to the location of your `tnsnames.ora` file when using only the Oracle Instant Client. More information about Oracle networking is found in Appendix G. You can find additional operating system platform library configurations in the *Oracle Database Client Quick Installation Guide.*

(continued)

Installing on Microsoft Windows

There are three shared library files that you download from the http://otn.oracle.com web site. You should navigate to the download area and download the Oracle Database 10*g* Release 1 (10.1.0.3) Client. The download file will be in a Zip format. Place the Zip file in the directory where you want to install the software and unzip the file. You will find the following shared library files:

```
oraociei10.dll
orannzsbb10.dll
oci.dll
```

You can place these files in a directory of your choice, but using the *C:\instantclient10_1* directory name is the Oracle convention. After creating the directory, you need to add the new folder to your environment `%PATH%` variable. You should make sure it is ahead of anything else in the `%PATH%` environment variable.

If you are using a `tnsnames.ora` file, you can place it in the same directory and set the `%TNS_ADMIN%` environment variable to point to that directory. The default National Language Standard (NLS) is inherited from your operating system. If you want to override that default, you will need to set the `%NLS_LANG%` environment variable. You can find more platform information in Steve Bobrowski's *Hands-on Oracle Database 10g Express Edition for Windows* (McGraw-Hill/Osborne, 2006) or the *Oracle Database Express Edition 2 Day DBA* manual.

After installing the instant client, you should restart your Apache service. The service will generate an event log when something is mistyped in the environment or misplaced during the installation. You should use the Apache event log to troubleshoot your installation.

TIP
An OCI8 parsing limitation disallows the use of the SQL wildcard operator, which is a percent symbol, %. You need to substitute the `REGEXP_LIKE()` *function anywhere you would normally use the SQL LIKE operator. This requires using an Oracle Database 10gR2 instance.* `REGEXP_LIKE()` *is not guaranteed to work on earlier releases.*

The `create_signon_triggers.sql`, `create_store.sql`, and `seed_store.sql` scripts are required for this chapter. They are available for your review in Appendix J. You will use these scripts as described next and in their respective sections:

■ The `create_signon_triggers.sql` script supports the section "Connecting to Oracle Using the OCI8 Libraries" on connecting to an Oracle database through the OCI8 libraries.

■ The `create_store.sql` and `seed_stored.sql` scripts build and populate database tables that support the sections "Using the OCI8 Function Library" and "Querying and Transacting by Using SQL Statements" of this chapter.

This chapter requires that your server have a local Oracle 10gR2 database or Oracle Client installation. For multitiered architectures, the minimum requirement is an Oracle Client installation on the Apache and PHP server. This provides you with the necessary libraries to effect an RPC to the machine where the Oracle database and listener reside.

The next section reviews how you confirm a connection and describes the three types of possible connections that you can make to an Oracle database.

Connecting to Oracle Using the OCI8 Libraries

The Oracle Call Interface 8 (OCI8) libraries provide three connection types to the Oracle database:

■ **Standard connections**   Build an RPC connection that is good for the duration of a script's execution unless explicitly closed by the script. All calls to the database in these scripts use the same connection unless they open a unique connection by calling the `oci_new_connect()` function. Standard connections place overhead on the server to marshal and allocate resources that are dismissed when released by the script or after the script terminates. There is no preserved state between HTTP requests to the server for standard connections.

■ **Unique connections**   Build a unique RPC connection that is good for the duration of a script's execution unless explicitly closed by the script. Unique connections allow a single script to have more than one open connection to the Oracle database, which works provided you are using them to perform autonomous transactions. Autonomous transactions run simultaneously rather than sequentially, and are independent of each other's outcomes. Unique connections also place overhead on the server to marshal and allocate resources that are dismissed when released by the script or after the script terminates. There is no preserved state between HTTP requests to the server with unique connections.

■ **Persistent connections**   Build an RPC connection that is good for the duration of a script's execution unless explicitly closed by the script. All calls to the database by these scripts use the same connection unless they open a unique connection by calling the `oci_new_connect()` function. Persistent connections place overhead on the server to marshal and allocate resources that are not immediately dismissed after the script terminates. There is a preserved state between HTTP requests to the server for persistent connections. Persistent connections are closed after a period of inactivity between requests and require active DBA management to ensure that critical resources are not locked without useful purpose.

There are several OCI8 configuration options that can be set in the `php.ini` file as configuration directives. They govern how your connections work within the PHP environment. When they are not explicitly defined in the `php.ini` file, your system uses the default values. You should review and verify whether the default values work in your environment. Table 13-1 reviews the configuration directives.

Careful examination of behaviors in a test system should be monitored before you change any of the default OCI8 directives in your `php.ini` file. You can release persistent connection resources by using Apache or Oracle to terminate the connections. If you want to delegate the termination of open and unused resources to Apache, you should examine the `MaxRequestsPerChild`, `MaxSpareServers`, and `KeepAlive` directives. Oracle facilitates terminating idle connections by using the `IDLE_TIMEOUT`, which is typically set in Oracle account profiles.

Name	Default	Definition
oci8.priviliged_connect	0	This option enables you to make privileged connections under both SYSOPER and SYSDBA roles. By default these are disabled; you enable them by setting the directive to 1.
oci8.max_persistent	–1	This option enables you set the maximum number of persistent connections per process. By default there is no limit. You set a limit by using a positive integer value or 0 to disable persistent connections.
oci8.persistent_timeout	–1	This option sets the maximum time, measured in seconds, that an idle persistent connection will remain alive. The default sets persistent connections open indefinitely.
oci8.ping_interval	60	This option governs the interval between active pings of persistent connections. Disabling it does speed processing of persistent connections but simultaneously stops detection of network communication checks, which can lead to errors later in script execution. Setting it to 0 reduces the interval to every time you make an HTTP request to the persistent connection.
oci8.statement_cache_size	20	This sets the number of SQL statements that will be cached, and it is equivalent to pinning SQL statements in the SGA. You disable statement caching by setting it to 0.
oci8.default_prefetch	10	This sets the default number of rows that are prefetched after SQL statement execution. Raising the number can get performance response improvements for those scripts that return a large number of rows. It is more effective to leave this parameter at the default and call where required the oci_set_prefetch() function in your programs that will return large data sets.
oci8.old_oci_close_semantics	0	This sets a backward compatible–only feature and disables the oci_close() function from doing anything. Oracle *recommends* that you remove the oci_close() statements before enabling this parameter with a -1.

TABLE 13-1. *OCI8 Directives for the* php.ini *File*

TIP
None of these changes will have an effect when they exceed the Apache KeepAlive directive 15-second default value. You need to reset the KeepAlive to a higher value.

Whatever choice you make in managing connections, you should conduct thorough testing before implementing it in production. Testing can save embarrassing results when your web application is serving actual customers.

TIP
You should alter the cache for the SYS.AUDSES$ sequence when you will have hundreds of connections per second. You can set it initially to 10,000 and then monitor the load to determine if that is adequate. The SYS.AUDSES$ sequence is called as part of the marshaling resources for each connection.

There are only four OCI8 library functions that govern opening and closing connections. There is also the `oci_error()` function that returns error messages when you fail to connect to the database. These five functions are summarized in Table 13-2 before working through example programs. The italicized function names are the deprecated forms for the old OCI version that now *serve as aliases* to the new functions.

Having reviewed the summaries of connections, the following example programs demonstrate connection behaviors. As mentioned earlier in this chapter, you should now run the `create_signon_triggers.sql` in your environment, which requires you to have already run the `create_user.sql` script. If you want to know what these scripts do, you can review them in Appendix J.

The `OracleStandardConnection.php` program will attempt to connect to your database. It prints success to the web page when it connects, and *it prints the array of errors generated by the `oci_error()` function when encountering a connecting error,* as shown next:

`-- This is found in OracleStandardConnection.php on the enclosed CD.`

```php
<?php
  // Attempt to connect with user schema and password, then TNS alias.
  if ($c = @oci_connect("php","php","xe"))
  {
    // Print successful message to web page.
    echo "Successfully connected to Oracle.<br>";

    // Disconnect from the database.
    oci_close($c);
  }
  else
  {
    // Assign the OCI error and format double and single quotes.
    $errorMessage = oci_error();

    // Open HTML table.
    print '<table border="1" cellpadding="0" cellspacing="0">';
```

```
      // Write array elements.
      foreach ($errorMessage as $name => $value)
        print '<tr><td>'.$name.'</td><td>'.$value.'</td></tr>';

      // Close HTML table.
      print '</table>';
    }
?>
```

Function	Description
oci_close() *ocilogoff()*	The oci_close() function explicitly closes an open OCI8 connection while the script that opened the connection is running. It is the new behavior of the OCI8 library beginning with PHP 5.1.2. It has one mandatory parameter, which is a resource connection. It returns a Boolean true value when successful and false otherwise. *You do not need to explicitly include the oci_close() function, because it is implicitly called when your script ends execution.* It has the following pattern: bool oci_close(resource *connection*)
oci_error() *ocierror()*	The oci_error() function returns an array of values. It has one optional parameter, which is a resource like a connection or statement. When no parameter is provided, the error returned is for the connection. The return value array contains code, message, offset, and sqltext values. The code value maps to the raised Oracle error code. The message value maps to the raised Oracle error code message. The offset value is a line number where the error occurred. The sqltext value is the SQL statement that contains the error. The function has the following pattern: array oci_error([resource *source*])
oci_connect() *ocilogin()*	The oci_connect() function returns a connection resource when successful and a Boolean false otherwise. It has five parameters: username, password, database_name, character_set, and session_mode. The first two are mandatory, and the next three are optional. As a general rule, you will more than likely use the first three parameters when opening a database connection. The database_name parameter typically maps to the network alias you have defined in a tnsnames.ora file, but you can manually assign it in the PHP script. The character_set is inherited from your operating system unless you override it by providing a run-time value when opening the connection. The default session_mode value is OCI_DEFAULT, which excludes privileged connections. You will also need to enable the oci.privileged_connect

TABLE 13-2. *OCI8 Connection and Disconnection Functions*

Function	Description

	directive in your `php.ini` file by setting it to `1`. The overriding privileged connections session modes are `OCI_SYSOPER` and `OCI_SYSDBA`. The function has the following pattern:
	
	`oci_connect(string username`
	`, string password`
	`[,string database_name`
	`[,string character_set`
	`[,string session_mode]]])`

`oci_new_connect()`
ocinlogin()
	The `oci_new_connect()` function returns a connection resource when successful and a Boolean `false` otherwise. When you have called `oci_connect()` earlier in the script, you open another discrete connection by using the `oci_new_connect()` function. *Incomplete, not committed, transactions in one connection will be unreadable in the other connection because they are discrete sessions in the database.* The `oci_new_connect()` function has the same five parameters as the `oci_connect()` function: username, password, database_name, character_set, and session_mode. The `oci_new_connect()` function parameters work the same as those described for the `oci_connect()` function. The function has the following pattern:
	
	`oci_new_connect(string username`
	`, string password`
	`[,string database_name`
	`[,string character_set`
	`[,string session_mode]]])`

`oci_pconnect()`
ociplogin()
	The `oci_pconnect()` function returns a connection resource when successful and a Boolean `false` otherwise. Calling the `oci_pconnect()` function a second time within the time-out interval will reconnect to the same session and have access to any session-level changes made earlier. However, any incomplete SQL transactions are rolled back when scripts disconnect. The `oci_pconnect()` function has the same five parameters as the `oci_connect()` function: username, password, database_name, character_set, and session_mode. The `oci_pconnect()` function parameters work the same as those described for the `oci_connect()` function. The function has the following pattern:
	
	`oci_pconnect(string username`
	`, string password`
	`[,string database_name`
	`[,string character_set`
	`[,string session_mode]]])`

TABLE 13-2. *OCI8 Connection and Disconnection Functions* (continued)

The call to the oci_connect() function provides the *username, password,* and tnsnames.ora file network alias. You need to edit this and subsequent scripts if you are using a different *username, password,* or network alias. When the program connects to the Oracle database successfully, you will see the following message displayed in the web page:

Successfully connected to Oracle.

You can also verify that the program is connected to the database by querying the CONNECTION_LOG table. You should connect through SQL*Plus or the Oracle Database 10*g* XE web interface and run the get_connection_results.sql script to query the login and logout trigger results from the CONNECTION_LOG table:

```
-- This is found in get_connection_results.sql on the enclosed CD.

SELECT    event_id
,         event_user_name
,         event_type
,         TO_CHAR(event_date,'DD-MON-YYYY HH24:MI:SS') time
FROM      system.connection_log;
```

The dates will obviously differ, and the EVENT_ID may change, depending on your activity against the database. You will see more or less the following as a result of the SQL statement:

```
EVENT_ID EVENT_USER_NAME       EVENT_TYPE      TIME
-------- --------------------- --------------- --------------------
       3 PHP                   CONNECT         29-JUN-2006 15:30:15
       4 PHP                   DISCONNECT      29-JUN-2006 15:30:15
```

The OracleStandardConnection.php script demonstrates that the program can connect and disconnect from the Oracle database, as captured by the system event triggers in the CONNECTION_LOG table. You can see what happens when the script fails to connect by shutting down your Oracle XE listener, as qualified by Appendix G.

After shutting down the listener, you will see the following when you refresh the web page in the browser:

code	12541
message	ORA-12541: TNS:no listener
offset	0
sqltext	

The ORA-12541 error indicates that the Oracle listener is unavailable. There is a zero in the offset because the thrown exception did not happen during program execution; and a null value in the sqltext value because no SQL statement was executed. As a general rule, many applications only display the message value, but some applications store the *message* and offending *SQL statement* in error-logging tables along with the PHP program name.

The OracleNewConnection.php program demonstrates that you can have two connections in the scope of one PHP script. The oci_connect() function makes the initial connection, and the oci_new_connect() function makes the subsequent connection. *Both of these connections would close at the script termination, but they are explicitly closed by using the* oci_close() *function.* The code for this program follows:

-- **This is found in OracleNewConnection.php on the enclosed CD.**

```php
<?php
  // Attempt to connect with user schema and password, then TNS alias.
  if ($c1 = oci_connect("php","php","xe"))
  {
    // Print successful message to web page.
    echo "Successfully connected to Oracle.<br>";

    // Sleep for 5 seconds.
    if (sleep(5));

    if ($c2 = oci_new_connect("php","php","xe"))
    {
      // Print successful message to web page.
      echo "Successfully connected a new connection to Oracle.<br>";

      // Disconnect from the database.
      oci_close($c2);
    }
    else
    {
      // Assign the OCI error and format double and single quotes.
      $errorMessage = oci_error();
      print $errorMessage['message'];
    }

    // Sleep for 5 seconds.
    if (sleep(5));

    // Disconnect from the database.
    oci_close($c1);
  }
  else
  {
    // Assign the OCI error and format double and single quotes.
    $errorMessage = oci_error();
    print $errorMessage['message'];
  }
?>
```

The OracleNewConnection.php generates the following message when successful:

```
Successfully connected to Oracle.
Successfully connected a new connection to Oracle.
```

The script uses the `sleep()` function to create processing delays between connections. The delays enable you to see the connection time difference in seconds using the `get_connection_results.sql` script. As mentioned before, the `EVENT_ID` and `TIME` will differ for your results from those shown:

```
EVENT_ID EVENT_USER_NAME      EVENT_TYPE     TIME
---------- -------------------- -------------- --------------------
        5 PHP                  CONNECT        29-JUN-2006 19:45:14
        6 PHP                  CONNECT        29-JUN-2006 19:45:20
        7 PHP                  DISCONNECT     29-JUN-2006 19:45:20
        8 PHP                  DISCONNECT     29-JUN-2006 19:45:26
```

Having explored opening a connection and opening simultaneous connections, you will now examine how to open persistent connections. As discussed, a persistent connection is opened and remains open until another connection is made or a time-out releases resources. This enables any session-level status and changes to be preserved between PHP script execution cycles and resources to be conserved in opening and closing connections.

Some additional SQL and PL/SQL is required to enable the demonstration of persistent connections and their ability to preserve session-level variable context. If you are not familiar with SQL and PL/SQL, you should consider reviewing Appendixes H and I, respectively. This section also forward-references some features described in subsequent sections of this chapter and Chapter 14—*bind* variables and PL/SQL.

Oracle provides the `DBMS_APPLICATION_INFO` package for writing to and from the `CLIENT_INFO` column in the `V$SESSION` user view. The `SET_CLIENT_INFO` enables you to set a value in the column that is valid for the duration of the session. Sessions exist from the point you connect until you disconnect from the Oracle database. Unless you set a value by calling the `SET_CLIENT_INFO` procedure, the column contains a null value. Once you set the `CLIENT_INFO` column, you can read it with the `READ_CLIENT_INFO` procedure from the same package.

The `create_session_structures.sql` script builds the `SESSION_LOG` table and the `SESSION_MANAGER` package. Database packages are like code libraries that contain lists of functions. PL/SQL supports two types of subroutines: functions and procedures. Functions return a value, can be called in a SQL statement, and can be used as the right operand to an assignment operation; they use a *pass-by-copy* mode of operation. Procedures do not return a value in the classic sense of a function or method and can use a *pass-by-reference* model for parameters. The *pass-by-reference* model is similar to the PHP model discussed in Chapter 7, where you define a parameter in a function signature by reference using the ampersand, like `&$variable`. Procedures differ from PHP functions using *pass-by-reference* in that they cannot be used as the right operands of assignment operators.

The `create_session_structures.sql` script creates a table and a sequence; the latter is used for autonumbering in Oracle:

```
-- These are found in create_session_structures.sql on the enclosed CD.

CREATE TABLE session_log
( session_id          NUMBER
, session_activity    VARCHAR2(3)
, session_name        VARCHAR2(64)
, session_date        DATE);

CREATE SEQUENCE session_log_s1;
```

The Black Box Paradigms of Subroutines

There are three approaches to writing subroutines that are known as functions, methods, and procedures. They are

- A classic pass-by-value function uses formal parameters as input-only variables, which hold copies of values passed as actual parameters. The formal parameters are defined as variables with local scope and the function returns only one value, which can be a scalar or compound variable. The latter compound variable type is often passed as a memory reference or pointer. This is the defined behavior of PL/SQL functions and one of two function styles supported in PHP.

- A classic pass-by-reference function uses formal parameters as input or input and output variables. Input-only variables hold copies of values passed as actual parameters, while input and output variables hold a memory reference to a variable. The input-only formal parameters are defined as variables with local scope, and the input and output formal parameters are defined as local variables with external scope set by the calling program unit. These functions can return both (a) one value that can be a scalar or compound variable, and (b) the altered contents of any input and output actual parameters. It is possible to designate the prototype return type as a void, which limits this type of function to returning values only through input and output formal parameters. While a classic pass-by-reference function is acceptable in PHP, it is disallowed in PL/SQL functions.

- A classic procedure is a restricted pass-by-reference function that has a void return type. The argument made for this type of subroutine is that there should only be one entrance and exit from any function. Classic pass-by-reference functions have one entrance but two possible exits: the return function type and the formal reference parameter list. The classic procedure and its pass-by-reference model is the *only* pass-by-reference model supported by the Oracle OCI8 library.

Then, the script creates a package with two wrapper procedures to the DBMS_APPLICATION_INFO procedures. These procedures enable you to capture data to demonstrate that persistent connections work, as shown:

```
-- The package is found in create_session_structures.sql on the enclosed CD.

CREATE OR REPLACE PACKAGE session_manager IS
  PROCEDURE set_session
  (session_name IN VARCHAR2);
  PROCEDURE get_session
  (session_name IN OUT VARCHAR2);
END session_manager;
/
CREATE OR REPLACE PACKAGE BODY session_manager IS
  PROCEDURE set_session
  (session_name IN VARCHAR2) IS
```

```
     BEGIN
       -- Set the V$SESSION.CLIENT_INFO column for the session.
       dbms_application_info.set_client_info(session_name);
       -- Record and commit activity.
       INSERT INTO session_log VALUES
       ( session_log_s1.nextval,'SET', session_name, SYSDATE );
       COMMIT;
     END set_session;
     PROCEDURE get_session
     (session_name IN OUT VARCHAR2) IS
     BEGIN
       dbms_application_info.read_client_info(session_name);
       -- Conditionally record and commit read activities.
       IF session_name IS NOT NULL THEN
         -- Record and commit activity.
         INSERT INTO session_log VALUES
         ( session_log_s1.nextval,'GET', session_name, SYSDATE );
         COMMIT;
       END IF;
     END get_session;
   END session_manager;
   /
```

The OraclePersistentConnection.php program contains a number of forward-referenced features and functions. You will cover them later in this chapter. The program shares a single persistent connection to the database between two connections, which are passing *bind* variables between the PHP script and the Oracle database. *Bind* variables are like substitution variables; they are an Oracle structure that enables you to pass variables into SQL statements, PL/SQL statements, or across memory spaces. In PHP programs *bind* variables let you seamlessly pass a PHP variable to an Oracle variable and vice versa.

There is no persistent connection before you run OraclePersistentConnection.php, but it creates a persistent connection, writes to the session, and confirms this activity by entering data in the SESSION_LOG table. When you rerun the program, it will reuse the connection, read the session-level value of the CLIENT_INFO column, and record it in the SESSION_LOG table.

The OraclePersistentConnection.php program illustrates creating and reusing a persistent connection to the Oracle database. You should verify that you've set all necessary php.ini and httpd.conf directives, including the KeepAlive directive in httpd.conf, before testing it. *Extending the Apache* KeepAlive *directive beyond the default 15 seconds presents potential problems for high-volume sites and can subject a site to denial-of-service attacks.*

The OraclePersistentConnection.php program follows:

-- This is found in OraclePersistentConnection.php on the enclosed CD.

```php
<?php
  // Attempt to connect with user schema and password, then TNS alias.
  if ($c = @oci_pconnect("php","php","xe"))
  {
    // Set session tracking variables.
    $session_name_in = "Session at [".date('d-M-y H:i:s')."]";
    $session_name_out = "";
```

```
  // Declare statement strings.
  $stmt1 = "BEGIN session_manager.get_session(:s_name); END;";
  $stmt2 = "BEGIN session_manager.set_session(:s_name); END;";

  // Parse statement strings.
  $s1 = oci_parse($c,$stmt1);
  $s2 = oci_parse($c,$stmt2);

  // Bind IN/OUT mode variable to $s1 and IN only mode variable to $s2.
  oci_bind_by_name($s1,":s_name",$session_name_out,64,SQLT_CHR);
  oci_bind_by_name($s2,":s_name",$session_name_in,64,SQLT_CHR);

  // Run GET_SESSION procedure.
  oci_execute($s1);

  // Read result from GET_SESSION procedure.
  if (is_null($session_name_out))
  {
    // Run SET_SESSION procedure and rerun GET_SESSION procedure.
    oci_execute($s2);

    // Print successful message.
    print "Successfully created a persistent Oracle connection.<br />";
    print "Set [$session_name_in]<br>";
  }
  else
  {
    // Print successful message.
    print "Reconnected to a persistent Oracle connection.<br />";
    print "Get [$session_name_out]<br>";
  }
}
else
{
  // Assign the OCI error and format double and single quotes.
  $errorMessage = oci_error();
}
?>
```

When you run this program, like the earlier programs, a system *logon* trigger will fire and populate the values in the CONNECTION_LOG table. This will fire every time that you run the OraclePersistentConnection.php script. This behavior is similar to what happens when you *cross-connect* from one Oracle user/schema to another in the scope of a single session. The continuity of the session is described by the persistent audit trail left in the SESSION_LOG table. You should note that *no* oci_connect() *function is used in the program because it would kill the connection and session.*

When you run OraclePersistentConnection.php the first time, it will render the following in your browser:

Successfully created a persistent Oracle connection.
Set [Session at {01-Jul-06 19:33:43}]

In subsequent executions, you will see the following:

```
Reconnected to a persistent Oracle connection.
Get [Session at {01-Jul-06 19:33:43}]
```

You can query the SESSION_LOG table by using the get_connection_logs.sql program, which uses SQL*Plus formatting, which will be ignored by the Oracle Database 10*g* XE web interface. The behavior of the SQL interfaces is qualified in Appendix G. The following query from the get_session_logs.sql script queries returns the information stored by using the DBMS_APPLICTION_INFO procedures:

```
SELECT     session_id
,          session_activity
,          session_name
,          TO_CHAR(session_date,'DD-MON-YYYY HH24:MI:SS') connection
FROM       session_log
```

The query displays the following data in an interactive SQL*Plus session:

```
                                        Connection
   # Act Session Name                   Date Stamp
---- --- -------------------------------- --------------------
   1 SET Session at {01-Jul-06 19:40:41}  01-JUL-2006 19:40:41
   2 GET Session at {01-Jul-06 19:40:41}  01-JUL-2006 19:40:41
   3 GET Session at {01-Jul-06 19:40:41}  01-JUL-2006 19:40:46
   4 GET Session at {01-Jul-06 19:40:41}  01-JUL-2006 19:41:12
```

The results show a SET activity for the first call, and GET activities after that. Only the SET activity signals the opening of a persistent session. All subsequent connections are reconnections by the oci_pconnect() function and are to the same live session. This behavior is demonstrated by capturing the timestamp of the first connection and subsequent reconnections.

When you have made too many persistent connections, you will be unable to shut down the database or process more transactions. You may receive an ORA-12520 error that signals the listener cannot find a handler for the request, or an ORA-12514 error that signals the listener cannot manage the service in the connect descriptor. You may also see an ORA-24323 or ORA-24324 when the service handler cannot be accessed due to resource constraints arising from too many persistent connections. The best solution to these problems is to restart your Apache process or Windows Apache service.

TIP
You may ask yourself if the persistent connections are worth the effort. The answer to that question is found when you compare the risks of persistent connections against the availability of Virtual Private Databases, AJAX, and PL/SQL stored procedures to manage transactions.

You have now examined how to connect for the duration of a script and beyond, by establishing a persistent session. You have also seen how to connect to multiple sessions using the same script. Ordinary connections will be used through the balance of this chapter, where you explore the mechanics of the OCI8 functions and how to use *bind* variables in SQL constructs.

Using the OCI8 Function Library

The OCI8 function library contains a library function to connect to, transact against, and disconnect from the Oracle database server. It also includes libraries for working with collections and Large Objects (LOBs). The preceding section demonstrated the utility of the three connection functions and one disconnection function. This section will discuss the balance of OCI8 functions, excluding the OCI-Collection and OCI-LOB methods, which are addressed in Chapters 14 and 15 respectively.

Table 13-3 contains a list of OCI8 functions that let you work with SQL and PL/SQL. These new Oracle OCI8 functions only work in a combination of Oracle Database 10*g* and PHP 5.1.2 or newer. Backward-compatible aliases are provided for those who are migrating from older releases and listed in italics beneath the new function names in Table 13-3.

This section is divided into the following five subsections:

- An OCI8 PHP library function summary
- An introduction to the database models
- An example of querying the database
- An example of transacting against the database
- An example of changing a user password

An OCI8 PHP Library Function Summary

The OCI8 functions include libraries to support static and dynamic operations for the SQL Data Definition Language (DDL), Data Manipulation Language (DML), Data Query Language (DQL), and Data Control Language (DCL). DDL statements let you *create, alter,* or *drop* objects in the database. The italicized function names in Table 13-3 are the deprecated forms for the old OCI version that now serve as aliases to the new functions. New functionality like the `oci_bind_array_by_name()` function does not have old alias names.

DML statements let you *insert, update,* and *delete* information from database objects. DQL statements let you *query* database objects. DCL statements let you manage the properties of transactions that may span multiple database objects to ensure all or none are changed as a group. You can find more coverage of these topics in Appendix H.

As mentioned, Table 13-3 includes the majority of OCI8 PHP functions but excludes the OCI-Collection and OCI-LOB methods, which are covered respectively in Chapters 14 and 15. Also, the `oci_lob_copy()` and `oci_lob_is_equal()` functions are found in Chapter 15 as Table 15-1.

An Introduction to the Database Models

Two database models support the OCI8 example programs. One is a small video store that the sample programs use to show how to control transactions against collections of tables. The other database model is a `PRESIDENT` table of world leaders that supports associative arrays, or PL/SQL tables, reference cursors, and Oracle scalar collections as demonstrated in Chapter 14. As mentioned earlier in this chapter, the Oracle SQL and PL/SQL code for the working models is discussed in Appendix J.

Function	Description

`oci_bind_array_by_name()`	The `oci_bind_array_by_name()` function binds a numerically indexed PHP array with a PL/SQL associative array, also known as a PL/SQL table before Oracle Database 10*g*. The function returns a Boolean `true` when successful and otherwise `false`. As of PHP 5.1.4, this function can only bind arrays of scalar Oracle data types, such as `VARCHAR2`, `NUMBER`, and `DATE`. Oracle development plans to add support for arrays of PL/SQL record types in a future, and as yet unspecified, release. It has six parameters; four are mandatory, and two are optional. The first and second parameters are passed by value; one is a statement resource, and the second a string name that maps to an Oracle *bind* variable in a statement parsed by the `oci_parse()` function. The third parameter is passed by reference, which means it can change during processing but *only when* the PL/SQL parameter is set to `IN/OUT` mode. The remaining arguments are passed by value. The fourth parameter is the number of items in the list; it must be 0 or a positive number. The fifth parameter is the maximum size of the scalar values in the array. *This parameter must be the physical size of a target column when the column is defined in the data dictionary catalog, or one greater than the maximum possible field size for dynamically built columns.* You build dynamic columns by concatenating results into a single string. The sixth column is a designated data type from the following list of possible values:
	
	■ `SQLT_AFC` `CHAR` data type
	■ `SQLT_AVC` `CHARZ` data type
	■ `SQLT_CHR` `VARCHAR2` data type
	■ `SQLT_FLT` `FLOAT` data type
	■ `SQLT_INT` `INTEGER` data type
	■ `SQLT_LVC` `LONG` data type
	■ `SQLT_NUM` `NUMBER` data type
	■ `SQLT_ODT` `DATE` data type
	■ `SQLT_STR` `STRING` data type
	■ `SQLT_VCS` `VARCHAR` data type
	
	The `oci_bind_array_by_name()` function has the following pattern:
	
	`bool oci_bind_array_by_name(`
	` resource `*`statement`*
	` ,string `*`bind_variable_name`*
	` ,array &`*`numeric_reference_array`*
	` ,int `*`maximum_elements`*
	` [,int `*`maximum_field_length`*
	` [,int `*`mapped_type`*`]])`

`oci_bind_by_name()` *`ocibindbyname()`*	The `oci_bind_by_name()` function binds a defined Oracle type to a PHP variable. The variable can be any scalar variable or scalar collection but cannot be used for an Oracle 10*g* associative array, also known as a PL/SQL table in

TABLE 13-3. *OCI8 Function Library for Querying and Transacting*

Function	Description

previous releases. You must use the `oci_bind_array_by_name()` function when working with PL/SQL associative arrays. A scalar collection variable can have a VARRAY or *nested* TABLE data type; these types are covered in Appendix I. The function returns a Boolean `true` when successful and otherwise `false`. It has five parameters; three are mandatory, and two are optional. The first and second parameters are passed by value; one is a statement resource, and the second a string name that maps to an Oracle *bind* variable in a statement parsed by the `oci_parse()` function. The third parameter is passed by reference, which means it can change during processing but *only when* the PL/SQL parameter is set to IN/OUT mode. The remaining arguments are passed by value. The fourth parameter is the number of items in the list; it must be 0 or a positive number. The fifth parameter is the maximum size of the scalar values in the array. Setting the maximum field length to -1 tells the function to implicitly size the field at run time. The sixth column is a designated data type from the following list of possible values:

- SQLT_B_CURSOR   Use for reference cursors, whether weakly or strongly typed.
- SQLT_BIN   Use for RAW column data type.
- SQLT_BLOB   Use for BLOB data type, which maps Binary Large objects.
- SQLT_CFILE   Use for CFILE data type.
- SQLT_CHR   Use for VARCHAR data types.
- SQLT_CLOB   Use for CLOB data type, which maps Character Large objects.
- SQLT_FILE   Use for BFILE data type.
- SQLT_INT   Use for INTEGER and NUMBER data types.
- SQLT_LBI   Use for LONG RAW data types.
- SQLT_LNG   Use for LONG data types.
- SQLT_NTY   Use for user-defined data types and user-defined scalar collections that are either VARRAY or *nested* TABLE types.
- SQLT_RDD   Use for ROWID data type.

You need to allocate abstract types by calling the `oci_new_descriptor()` function before you bind them. Abstract types are LOB, ROWID, and BFILE data types. You also need to call the `oci_new_cursor()` function before you bind a reference cursor. The `oci_bind_by_name()` function has the following pattern:

```
bool oci_bind_by_name(
 resource statement
 ,string bind_variable_name
 ,array &numeric_reference_array
 [,int maximum_field_length
 [,int mapped_type]])
```

TABLE 13-3.   *OCI8 Function Library for Querying and Transacting* (continued)

Function	Description
`oci_cancel()` *ocicancel()*	The `oci_cancel()` function terminates a cursor and frees all available resources previously allocated to the cursor. The function returns a Boolean `true` when successful and otherwise `false`. It has one mandatory parameter, which is a resource statement. The `oci_cancel()` function has the following pattern: `bool oci_cancel(resource statement)`
`oci_commit()` *ocicommit()*	The `oci_commit()` function issues a transaction control language `COMMIT` command to the current session, which makes any changes to the data permanent. The function returns a Boolean `true` when successful and otherwise `false`. It has one mandatory parameter, which is a resource statement. The `oci_commit()` function has the following pattern: `bool oci_commit(resource connection)`

`oci_define_by_name()`
ocidefinebyname()
	The `oci_define_by_name()` function defines a PHP variable and maps it to a column name returned by a query statement. You call `oci_define_by_name()` before you execute the `oci_execute()` function, or there is no assignment to the local PHP variable. The function returns a Boolean `true` when successful and otherwise `false`. It has four parameters; three are mandatory, and one is optional. The first and second parameters are passed by value; one is a statement resource, and the second is a string name in *uppercase that maps to an Oracle column name* variable. The third is the new PHP variable that will contain the result from the query. The fourth is a data type, which uses the same types as those described in the summary of the `oci_bind_by_name()` function. The function has the following pattern:
	`bool oci_define_by_name(`
	`  resource statement`
	`  ,string column_name`
	`  ,mixed &variable`
	`  [,int type])`

`oci_execute()`
ociexecute()
	The `oci_execute()` function executes a previously parsed SQL or PL/SQL statement. The function returns a Boolean `true` when successful and otherwise `false`. It has two parameters; one is mandatory, and the other is optional. The mandatory parameter is a resource statement, which is generated as the result of an `oci_parse()` function of a SQL or PL/SQL statement. The second, optional, parameter is a mode variable that governs the behavior of the executed statement. The default mode value is the `OCI_COMMIT_ON_SUCCESS` constant; it results in an automatic commit of the executed SQL statement. The available override mode variable is `OCI_DEFAULT`; using it disables an automatic commit on successful execution of the SQL statement. It has the following pattern:
	`bool oci_execute(`
	`  resource statement`
	`  [,int mode])`

`oci_fetch()` *ocifetch()*	The `oci_fetch()` function fetches the next row from the executed cursor. The function returns a Boolean `true` when successful and otherwise `false`. It has one mandatory parameter, a resource statement. It has the following pattern: `bool oci_fetch(resource statement)`

TABLE 13-3. *OCI8 Function Library for Querying and Transacting (continued)*

Function	Description

oci_fetch_all()
ocifetchstatement()
	The oci_fetch_all() function fetches all rows from the executed cursor into a single array variable. The function returns an int value for the number of rows returned and false on failure. It has five parameters; two are mandatory, and three are optional. The first mandatory parameter is a resource statement, and the second is a target PHP array variable. The third parameter (the first optional one) is the number of rows to skip before reading rows into the array; it has a default value of 0. The fourth parameter (the second optional one) is the maximum number of rows to read; it has a default of -1, which means all rows. The fifth parameter governs the way the array is written from the query. You can use one or the other of each of the following format flags joined by a bitwise operator, or single pipe, to set the output pattern:
	
	■ OCI_FETCHSTATEMENT_BY_ROW or OCI_FETCHSTATEMENT_BY_COLUMN, and
	
	■ OCI_ASSOC or OCI_NUM
	
	The OCI_FETCHSTATEMENT_BY_COLUMN and OCI_ASSOC combination is the default value when no actual parameters are provided. Also, the OCI_ASSOC has one meaningful use when records are sorted by row: *the nested indexes are column names*. The function has the following pattern:
	`int oci_fetch_all(resource statement`
	`,array $output_array`
	`[,int skip_rows`
	`[,int max_rows`
	`[,int format_flag]]])`

oci_fetch_array() *ocifetchinto()*	The oci_fetch_array() function fetches the next row from the executed cursor. The function returns a row of data as an array when successful and false when encountering an error. It has two parameters. The first is a mandatory parameter and takes a resource statement, and the second is an optional mode variable that determines formatting of the array structure. The possible mode values are ■ OCI_BOTH Returns the row as an array with both *numeric* and *column name* indexes for each column value. *This is the default index type mode value.* ■ OCI_ASSOC Returns the row as an array with *column name* index values for each column value, which is exactly like the return from the oci_fetch_assoc() function. ■ OCI_NUM Returns the row as an array with *numeric* index values for each column value, which is exactly like the return from the oci_fetch_row() function. ■ OCI_RETURN_NULLS Returns the row as an array with *default or user-designated* index values for each column value, which is exactly like the return from the oci_fetch_assoc() function. *This is the default null behavior mode, and you should note that the converted null values are PHP null data types.*

TABLE 13-3. *OCI8 Function Library for Querying and Transacting* (continued)

Function	Description

	■ OCI_RETURN_LOBS Returns columns that have a LOB data type with a LOB descriptor as the index, which means an index value of LOB_FIELD. *This is enabled by default.*
	
	The function has the following pattern:
	`array oci_fetch_array(`
	` resource statement`
	`[,int mode])`

`oci_fetch_assoc()`	The `oci_fetch_assoc()` function fetches the next row from the executed cursor. The function returns a row of data as an array when successful and `false` when encountering an error. It has one parameter, which is a resource statement. The returned array uses the *column name from the database* as the index value. In all other behaviors, this function works exactly like the `oci_fetch_array()` function using the OCI_ASSOC mode. It has the following pattern:
	`array oci_fetch_assoc(`
	` resource statement)`

`oci_fetch_object()`	The `oci_fetch_object()` function fetches the next row from the executed cursor. The function returns an internal object that *only contains* instance attributes for each column of data. The instance variable names are *column names* from the SQL query. It returns `false` when encountering an error. It has one parameter, which is a resource statement. You will need to use the `oci_num_fields()` and `oci_field_name()` functions to access the instance attributes formally, but the generated object is also navigable as an associative array. The `oci_fetch_object` function has the following pattern:
	`object oci_fetch_object(`
	` resource statement)`

`oci_fetch_row()`	The `oci_fetch_row()` function fetches the next row from the executed cursor. The function returns a row of data as an array when successful and `false` when encountering an error. It has one parameter, which is a resource statement. The returned array uses a *numeric* index value. In all other behaviors, this function works exactly like the `oci_fetch_array()` function using the OCI_NUM mode. It has the following pattern:
	`array oci_fetch_row(`
	` resource statement)`

`oci_field_is_null()`
ocicolumnisnull()
	The `oci_field_is_null()` function checks for a *null* fetched field and returns a Boolean `true` when the value is null and `false` otherwise. It takes two mandatory parameters. The first one is a resource statement, and the second is a field to be evaluated. It has the following pattern:
	`bool oci_field_is_null(`
	` resource statement`
	`,mixed field)`

`oci_field_name()` *ocicolumnname()*	The `oci_field_name()` function returns the name of a field from a fetched row. It returns a `string` when successful and a `false` when encountering an error. It has two mandatory parameters; one is a statement resource, and the other is an `int`

TABLE 13-3.   *OCI8 Function Library for Querying and Transacting* (continued)

Function	Description

	representing the position of the field in the fetched row. Fields are numbered 1 to 999 in the Oracle Database 10*g* family of products. The function has the following pattern:
	`string oci_field_name(`
	  `resource statement`
	  `,int field_position)`

oci_field_precision()
 ocicolumnprecision()
	The `oci_field_precision()` function returns the size of an Oracle NUMBER data type. It returns the size of the number, with the possible values of 0 or a positive integer. A 0 precision value is a number with nothing to the right of the decimal place, but a positive value indicates the number has a value to the right of the decimal point. The function has two mandatory parameters; one is a statement resource, and the other is an `int` representing the position of the field in the fetched row. Fields are numbered 1 to 999 in the Oracle Database 10*g* family of products. The function has the following pattern:
	`int oci_field_precision(`
	  `resource statement`
	  `,int field_position)`

oci_field_scale()
 oci_columnscale()
	The `oci_field_scale()` function returns the size of numbers to the right of the decimal point. It returns the number of placeholders to the right of the decimal point, with the possible values of 0, a positive integer, or -127. When you return the -127 value, it indicates a FLOAT data type. The function has two mandatory parameters; one is a statement resource, and the other is an `int` representing the position of the field in the fetched row. Fields are numbered 1 to 999 in the Oracle Database 10*g* family of products. The function has the following pattern:
	`int oci_field_scale(`
	  `resource statement`
	  `,int field_position)`

oci_field_size()
 ocicolumnsize()
	The `oci_field_size()` function returns the size of Oracle variable-length strings, like the VARCHAR2 data type. It returns the size in bytes of the field. The function has two mandatory parameters; one is a statement resource. The other is an `int` representing the position of the field or the field name in the fetched row. Fields are numbered 1 to 999 in the Oracle Database 10*g* family of products. The function has the following pattern:
	`int oci_field_size(`
	  `resource statement`
	  `,mixed field_name_or_position)`

oci_field_type()
 ocicolumntype()
	The `oci_field_type()` function returns the data type of a fetched field. It returns the data type for the data field, which enables the data value to be treated as a number or date as opposed to a string. You can find the *list of possible values in Table H-2*. The function has two mandatory parameters; one is a statement resource, and the other is an `int` representing the position of the field in the fetched row. Fields are numbered 1 to 999 in the Oracle Database 10*g* family of products. The function has the following pattern:
	`mixed oci_field_type(`
	  `resource statement`
	  `,mixed field_position)`

TABLE 13-3. *OCI8 Function Library for Querying and Transacting* (continued)

Function	Description

`oci_field_type_raw()`
ocicolumntyperaw()
	The `oci_field_type_raw()` function returns the Oracle internal number of a data type from a fetched field. Oracle internally numbers data types as part of the data catalog, which is part of the Oracle metadata. You can find the *list of possible values in Table H-2.* The function has two mandatory parameters; one is a statement resource, and the other is an `int` representing the position of the field in the fetched row. Fields are numbered 1 to 999 in the Oracle Database 10g family of products. The function has the following pattern:
	`mixed oci_field_type_raw(`
	` resource statement`
	` ,mixed field_position)`

`oci_free_statement()`
ocifreecursor()
	The `oci_free_statement()` function releases all available resources previously allocated to a statement or cursor. The function returns a Boolean `true` when successful and otherwise `false`. It has one mandatory parameter, which is a resource statement. The `oci_free_statement()` function has the following pattern:
	`bool oci_free_statement(`
	` resource statement)`

`oci_internal_debug()` *ociinternaldebug()*	The `oci_internal_debug()` function enables internal Oracle debugging. The function returns nothing because it enables tracing on the Oracle database. It has one mandatory parameter, which is an `int`. You use 0 to disable and anything else to enable. The function has the following pattern: `void oci_internal_debug(int onoff)`

`oci_new_collection()`
ocinewcollection()
	The `oci_new_collection()` function creates a PHP OCI-Collection object that maps to an Oracle Collection variable. It returns an OCI-Collection on success and `false` otherwise. Table 14-1 covers the Oracle OCI-Collections library. At writing against PHP 5.1.4, these types are limited to collections of scalar variables. *Oracle may extend the collection behavior to structures and instantiated PL/SQL objects but **has made no commitment** as to when they will introduce that behavior.* The function has three parameters; two are mandatory, and one is optional. The first parameter is a resource connection, and the second is the data type name from the user/schema used to build the connection. The optional third parameter lets you specify another owning schema for the collection data type. The function has the following pattern:
	`OCI-Collection oci_new_collection(`
	` resource connection`
	` ,string collection_type_name`
	` [,string schema])`

`oci_new_cursor()`
ocinewcursor()
	The `oci_new_cursor()` function creates a system cursor resource when successful and `false` otherwise. The function has one parameter, a resource connection. The function has the following pattern:
	`resource oci_new_cursor(`
	` resource connection)`

`oci_new_descriptor()` *ocinewdescriptor()*	The `oci_new_descriptor()` function creates a PHP OCI-Lob object that maps to an Oracle LOB variable. It returns an OCI-Lob on success and `false` otherwise. Table 14-1 covers the Oracle OCI-Lob library. The function has

TABLE 13-3. *OCI8 Function Library for Querying and Transacting* (continued)

Function	Description
	two parameters; one is mandatory, and one is optional. The first parameter is a resource connection, and the second is the LOB type. LOB data types are treated as abstract types along with Oracle ROWID and FILE types. The following are the possible types:
	■ OCI_D_FILE Sets the descriptor to manage binary or character files, respectively BFILE and CFILE data types.
	■ OCI_D_LOB Sets the descriptor to manage binary or character large objects, respectively BLOB and CLOB data types.
	■ OCI_D_ROWID Sets the descriptor to manage Oracle ROWID values, which map the physical storage to file system blocks.

	The function has the following pattern:
	`OCI-Lob oci_new_descriptor(`
	` resource connection`
	` ,int lob_type)`

`oci_num_fields()` *ocinumcols()*	The `oci_num_fields()` function lets you count the number of fields fetched. The function returns an `int` on success and a `false` when encountering an error. The function returns the number of affected columns in a row. It becomes available for your use after calling the `oci_execute()` function when the resource *statement* is an INSERT, UPDATE, or DELETE. When querying the database using a SELECT statement, the function works differently—it becomes available after calling the `oci_fetch()` function and then returns the number of rows fetched. The value changes as rows are fetched, and it mirrors the behavior of the %ROWCOUNT cursor attribute in the PL/SQL language. (Note: You can check Appendix I for more information on the %ROWCOUNT cursor attribute or *Oracle Database 10g PL/SQL Programming* by Scott Urman et al. [McGraw-Hill/Osborne, 2004].) It has one mandatory parameter, which is a resource statement returned by the `oci_parse()` function call. The function has the following pattern: `int oci_num_fields(resource statement)`
`oci_num_rows()` *ocirowcount()*	The `oci_num_rows()` function lets you count the number of rows touched by a SQL statement. The function returns an `int` on success and a `false` when encountering an error. You can use it when querying or transacting against the database with an insert, update, or delete statement, or with a PL/SQL program call. It can only run after the `oci_fetch()` function with a select statement and will return the number placed in the buffer; it increments as values are fetched. It returns 1 when used after `oci_execute()` calling a PL/SQL stored procedure. It has one mandatory parameter, which is a resource statement returned by the `oci_parse()` function call. The function has the following pattern: `int oci_num_rows(resource statement)`
`oci_parse()` *ociparse()*	The `oci_parse()` function puts a statement into the Oracle SGA, which then prepares the SQL statement to run in the database. It returns a statement identifier when successful and `false` when encountering an error. It makes no attempt to

TABLE 13-3.   *OCI8 Function Library for Querying and Transacting* (continued)

Function	Description

	actually parse the SQL statement and validate its syntax; that is done when you call oci_execute(). The function has two mandatory parameters; one is a resource connection, and the other is a string representing a SQL statement. The function has the following pattern:
	
	`resource oci_parse(`
	` resource connection`
	` ,string sql_statement)`

oci_password_change()	The oci_password_change() function lets you change a user password. There are two ways to use this function. One use returns a Boolean value, and the other, a resource connection. When returning a Boolean value, it returns a true on success and false when encountering an error. The function has four mandatory parameters. The first is a resource connection or a network alias defined in your tnsnames.ora file. When the first parameter is a connection, the function returns a Boolean value. The function returns a resource when the first parameter is a connection resource. The second parameter is a username, the third, a current password, and the fourth, a new password. The function has the following patterns:
	
	`bool oci_password_change(`
	` resource connection`
	` ,string user_name`
	` ,string old_password`
	` ,string new_password)`
	
	`resource oci_password_change(`
	` resource database`
	` ,string user_name`
	` ,string old_password`
	` ,string new_password)`

oci_result()
ociresult()
	The oci_result() function returns a field value from a fetched row. It returns the field value as a string data type for everything except abstract data types, like FILE, LOB, and ROWID. It returns a false when encountering an error. The function has two mandatory parameters; one is a resource connection, and the other is an int or string representing the field position or column name from the SQL query. The function has the following pattern:
	
	`mixed oci_result(`
	` resource connection`
	` ,mixed field_reference)`

oci_rollback()
ocirollback()
	The oci_rollback() function rolls back all uncommitted transactions in the scope of a database connection. It returns a Boolean true when the value is null and false otherwise. The function has one mandatory parameter, which is a resource connection. The function has the following pattern:
	
	`bool oci_rollback(`
	` resource connection)`

TABLE 13-3. *OCI8 Function Library for Querying and Transacting* (continued)

Function	Description

`oci_server_version()` `ociserverversion()`	The `oci_server_version()` function returns the database server product version information. It returns a `string` containing the version number or a Boolean `false` otherwise. The function has one mandatory parameter, which is a resource connection. The function has the following pattern:
	`string oci_server_version(`
	`  resource connection)`

`oci_set_prefetch()` `ocisetprefetch()`	The `oci_set_prefetch()` function resets the prefetch number of rows returned from an executed query, overriding the `oci8.default_prefetch` directive in the `php.ini` file. The function returns a Boolean `true` when successful and otherwise `false`. The function has two parameters, one mandatory and the other optional. The first, mandatory, parameter is a resource connection, and the second, optional, parameter is the number of rows to prefetch when executing the query. The default for fetched rows is 1. The function has the following pattern:
	`bool oci_set_prefetch(`
	`  resource connection`
	`  [, int fetched_rows])`

`oci_statement_type()` `ocistatementtype()`	The `oci_statement_type()` function returns the type of resource statement, like SELECT, UPDATE, DELETE, INSERT, CREATE, DROP, ALTER, BEGIN, DECLARE, and UNKNOWN. It has one mandatory parameter, which is a resource statement. The function has the following pattern:
	`string oci_statement_type(`
	`  resource statement)`

TABLE 13-3.   *OCI8 Function Library for Querying and Transacting* (continued)

Figure 13-1 is an adorned UML static class diagram for the database model of the video store application. UML static class diagrams depict what are known as *entity relationship drawings (ERDs)* in other modeling techniques, like information engineering. Classes are tables without methods of operation.

Classes, or tables, are connected by relationship lines. Each relationship contains two relations defined by an adorning verb phrase and symbols of cardinality: 0, 1, and *. Cardinality has two components: the left value is the minimum cardinality and the right value is the maximum cardinality. The minimum cardinality means the fewest possible rows, and the maximum cardinality means the most possible rows in a relationship. One relation is read from a class on the left, or top, to another class on the right, or bottom, and the other relation read vice versa. You read a relationship from one class to another by substituting the starting class as the subject, the adorning phrase as the verb, and ending class as the direct object of a sentence. You read the shorthand of a relation as *a CONTACT has one or more ADDRESS,* and the longhand of the complementary, or opposite, relation as *a row of the ADDRESS table belongs to one and only one row of the CONTACT table.*

When a relationship reads that the direct object of the sentence, class, has zero, one to a limit, or many rows, the subject of the sentence holds a list of primary keys and the direct object of the sentence holds a column of foreign keys. Foreign keys are values found in the list of primary keys. The video store example uses the convention of labeling primary key columns as

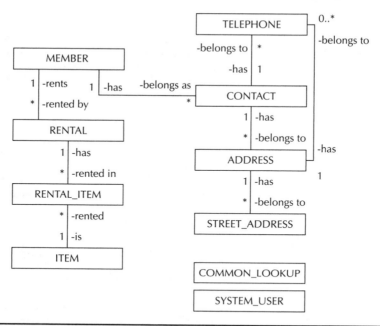

FIGURE 13-1. *Video store model*

the table name with a _ID suffix. Foreign key column names are generally but not exclusively the same name as the primary key column. Exceptions are the CREATED_BY and LAST_UPDATED_BY column names, which are *foreign key* columns to the SYSTEM_USER_ID column in the SYSTEM_USER table. The creation and update columns are part of every table in the model and support what is sometimes called the *"who audit"* or *"who done it"* columns. These columns track the user that created, or last updated, any row in any table in the model.

The balance of this subsection demonstrates how to: (a) *query, insert, update,* and *delete* rows in the video store model by individual scripts; (b) *change a user's password*; and (c) *manage an all-or-nothing transaction* using DCL functions: the oci_commit() and oci_rollback() functions.

An Example of Querying the Database

The SelectItemRecords.php program demonstrates a query from two tables in the database. It uses an ordinary connection and then parses, executes, and fetches return rows from an ANSI SQL:2003 inner join statement between two tables, as follows in the script:

```
-- This is found in SelectItemRecords.php on the enclosed CD.

<?php
  // Connect to the database.
  if ($c = @oci_connect("php","php","xe"))
```

```
{
  // Parse a query to a resource statement.
  $s = oci_parse($c,"SELECT    i.item_id id
                    ,         i.item_barcode as barcode
                    ,         c.common_lookup_type as type
                    ,         i.item_title as title
                    ,         i.item_rating as rating
                    ,         i.item_release_date release_date
                    FROM      item i inner join common_lookup c
                    ON        i.item_type = c.common_lookup_id
                    WHERE     c.common_lookup_type = 'XBOX'
                    ORDER BY i.item_title");

  // Execute query without an implicit commit.
  oci_execute($s,OCI_DEFAULT);

  // Open the HTML table.
  print '<table border="1" cellspacing="0" cellpadding="3">';

  // Read fetched headers.
  print '<tr>';
  for ($i = 1;$i <= oci_num_fields($s);$i++)
    print '<td class="e">'.oci_field_name($s,$i).'</td>';
  print '</tr>';

  // Read fetched data.
  while (oci_fetch($s))
  {
    // Print open and close HTML row tags and columns data.
    print '<tr>';
    for ($i = 1;$i <= oci_num_fields($s);$i++)
      print '<td class="v">'.oci_result($s,$i).'</td>';
    print '</tr>';
  }

  // Close the HTML table.
  print '</table>';

  // Disconnect from database.
  oci_close($c);
}
else
{
  // Assign the OCI error and format double and single quotes.
  $errorMessage = oci_error();
  print htmlentities($errorMessage['message'])."<br />";
}
?>
```

The program uses an `oci_parse()` function to place a SQL statement into a resource statement. Then it calls the `oci_execute()` function with the overriding `OCI_DEFAULT` to avoid the overhead of OCI_COMMIT_ON_SUCCESS because commits are only useful when *inserting, updating,* or *deleting* data. After the SQL SELECT statement is executed, the column name labels are available before fetching any rows. The program uses the oci_num_fields() and oci_field_name() functions to get and print the headers to an HTML table. The oci_fetch() function is called within a while statement, which executes until fetching all rows. Inside the while loop, the oci_num_fields() and oci_result() functions get and print column values for each row. This behavior uses the while loop to read data rows and the for loop to read data columns.

An Example of Transacting Against the Database

The InsertItemRecord.php program demonstrates how to *insert* a row into the video store ITEM table. It mimics the techniques of the SelectItemRecords.php program and suppresses the oci_execute() function default mode OCI_COMMIT_ON_SUCCESS to demonstrate the utility of the oci_commit() function and the isolation property of one session from another. Isolation between sessions means that partial results in one session are not seen by another session of the same user or other users with privileges to the table(s). The oci_commit() function makes partial results final when the oci_execute() function uses the OCI_DEFAULT mode.

The InsertItemRecord.php program demonstrates the principle of isolation between concurrent sessions, as qualified:

```
-- This is found in InsertItemRecord.php on the enclosed CD.

<?php
  // Connect to the database.
  if ($c = @oci_connect("php","php","xe"))
  {
    // Parse a insert to a resource statement.
    $s = oci_parse($c,"INSERT INTO item VALUES
                      ( item_s1.nextval
                      ,'9736-06125-4'
                      ,(SELECT    common_lookup_id
                        FROM      common_lookup
                        WHERE     common_lookup_type = 'DVD_WIDE_SCREEN')
                      ,'The Adventures of Indiana Jones'
                      ,''
                      ,'PG-13','21-OCT-03'
                      , 3, SYSDATE, 3, SYSDATE)");

    // Execute query without an implicit commit.
    oci_execute($s,OCI_DEFAULT);

    // Query before commit, commit insert, print line break, and requery.
    query();
    oci_commit($c);
    print "Inserted [".oci_num_rows($s)."] row(s) committed.<br />";
    query();

    // Disconnect from database.
    oci_close($c);
  }
  else
```

```php
{
  // Assign the OCI error and format double and single quotes.
  $errorMessage = oci_error();
  print htmlentities($errorMessage['message'])."<br />";
}

// Query results in another connection.
function query()
{
  // Open a new connection.
  if ($nc = @oci_new_connect("php","php","xe"))
  {
    // Parse a query to a resource statement.
    $q = oci_parse($nc,"SELECT    item_id
                        ,         item_title
                        ,         item_release_date
                        FROM      item
                        WHERE     REGEXP_LIKE(item_title,'Indiana')");

    // Query for committed records.
    oci_execute($q);

    // Assign results.
    render_query($q);

    // Close new connection.
    oci_close($nc);
  }
  else
  {
    // Assign the OCI error and format double and single quotes.
    $errorMessage = oci_error();
    print htmlentities($errorMessage['message'])."<br />";
  }
}

// Render query results.
function render_query($rs)
{
  // Declare control variable.
  $no_row_fetched = true;

  // Open the HTML table.
  print '<table border="1" cellspacing="0" cellpadding="3">';

  // Read fetched data.
  while (oci_fetch($rs))
  {
    // Only print header once.
    if ($no_row_fetched)
```

```
        {
          // Read fetched headers.
          print '<tr>';
          for ($i = 1;$i <= oci_num_fields($rs);$i++)
            print '<td class="e">'.oci_field_name($rs,$i).'</td>';
          print '</tr>';

          // Disable header printing.
          $no_row_fetched = false;
        }

        // Print open and close HTML row tags and columns data.
        print '<tr>';
        for ($i = 1;$i <= oci_num_fields($rs);$i++)
          print '<td class="v">'.oci_result($rs,$i).'</td>';
        print '</tr>';
      }

      // Close the HTML table.
      print '</table>';
    }
?>
```

The INSERT statement *inserts* a row into the ITEM table at the moment the oci_execute() function completes successfully. As mentioned, using the OCI_DEFAULT mode suppresses an automatic commit, but the oci_execute() function *does insert one row, as reported by the oci_num_rows() function.* When the user-defined query() function is called the first time, it opens a new connection and finds no *insert* into the ITEM table because it has not been committed in the other session. After committing the insertion by calling the oci_commit() function, *a fresh query finds the inserted row.*

You will see the following output rendered in your browser by the program:

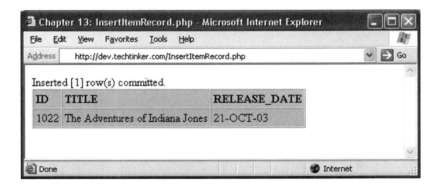

When you consistently override the default mode of the oci_execute() function for a series of INSERT statements, they can be committed as a group. However, it is critical that *you must call the oci_commit() function before closing your connection or exiting your script; otherwise, all your transactions will be rolled back.* This is the preferred transaction model for database applications. The alternative approach treats each oci_execute() call as an autonomous transaction, which makes it possible for one or more to succeed and one or more to fail in a group of related transactions. With this type of behavior, you place at risk the integrity of your data model.

Take for example how you insert an individual with an address and phone number into the video store model using autonomous transactions. When only the inserts into the INDIVIDUAL and STREET_ADDRESS tables fail and those into the ADDRESS and TELEPHONE tables succeed, you would have useless rows in the ADDRESS and TELEPHONE tables. These rows are called *orphans*. They become garbage data in your database. Autonomous transactions also raise a question about how you report to your end user the success or failure of transactions. Autonomous transactions leave you unable to report whether the transaction succeeded or failed, only that some succeeded while others failed.

Adopting an all-or-nothing transaction approach, the traditional transaction model has distinct advantages in web applications. When one or more inserts fail, those that succeed are rolled back as if they were never made. This enables you to report that the transaction failed, or enables your program to reattempt any *inserts, updates,* or *deletes* before reporting success or failure to your end user. You should be careful to make sure the choice meets your business need when choosing between normal and autonomous transaction models.

TIP
The query in the program uses the REGEXP_LIKE() function because you cannot use the Oracle SQL wildcard operator, %, in an OCI-managed statement. This means you cannot use the LIKE operator in SQL statements.

NOTE
You should note that you can have line or carriage returns in a SQL statement, but you cannot do the same thing when executing a PL/SQL statement. The difference in behavior between SQL and PL/SQL statements results from how their respective parsers work in the Oracle Server.

The method for UPDATE and DELETE statements mirrors the example demonstrated by the INSERT statement in the InsertItemRecord.php program. In the next section, the example program demonstrates how to change a user/schema password.

An Example of Changing a User Password

As covered in Table 13-3, there are two patterns for changing a user/schema password. One requires a connection, and the other simply connects and changes the password.

The ChangePassword.php program demonstrates connecting and changing the password. This pattern is the more likely scenario when using Oracle Virtual Private Databases or shared schemas with Oracle-validated usernames and passwords. The Oracle Virtual Private Database lets you share a schema among a group of users, which simplifies your server-side application development.

NOTE
Oracle Virtual Private Databases are new to Oracle Database 10g Release 2, which includes Oracle Database 10g Express Edition.

The password changing logic is in the user-defined `change_password()` function, and you can submit the username, old password, and new password via the GET method in a URL. Hopefully, you can copy it "as is" without warranty wherever you find a need for it. The `ChangePassword.php` program follows:

-- **This is found in ChangePassword.php on the enclosed CD.**

```php
<?php
  // Declare input variables.
  (isset($_GET['uname'])) ? $u_name = $_GET['uname']
                          : $u_name = "plsql";
  (isset($_GET['opasswd'])) ? $o_passwd = $_GET['opasswd']
                            : $o_passwd = "plsql";
  (isset($_GET['npasswd'])) ? $n_passwd = $_GET['npasswd']
                            : $n_passwd = "oracle";

  // Change password.
  change_password($u_name,$o_passwd,$n_passwd);

  function change_password($u_name,$o_passwd,$n_passwd)
  {
    // Connect to database and change password.
    if ($nc = @oci_new_connect($u_name,$o_passwd,"xe"))
    {
      // Change the user password.
      if (oci_password_change($nc,$u_name,$o_passwd,$n_passwd))
        print get_params($u_name,$o_passwd,$n_passwd);
      else
        print "Password Unchanged.<br>";

      // Close connection.
      oci_close($nc);
    }
    else
    {
      // Assign the OCI error and format double and single quotes.
      $errorMessage = oci_error();
      print htmlentities($errorMessage['message'])."<br />";
    }
  }

  // Return an HTML table of user, old password, and new password.
  function get_params($u_name,$o_passwd,$n_passwd)
  {
    $out  = '<table border="1" cellpadding="0" cellspacing="0">';
    $out .= '<tr><td class="e" width="125">User/Schema</td>';
    $out .= '<td class="v" width="125">'.$u_name.'</td></tr>';
    $out .= '<tr><td class="e">Old Password</td>';
    $out .= '<td class="v">'.$o_passwd.'</td></tr>';
    $out .= '<tr><td class="e">New Password</td>';
```

```
    $out .= '<td class="v">'.$n_passwd.'</td></tr>';
    $out .= '</table>';

    // Return connect elements.
    return $out;
  }
?>
```

The program can use a URL without parameters, or you can provide parameters if you have changed the default values. The three assumed values are qualified in the ternary operators used to validate the inputs. They are a username of PHP, an old password of PHP, and a new password of Oracle. It uses a new connection to make the password change and disconnects using the `oci_close()` function.

Substituting the hostname *(hn)* and domain name *(dn),* you can use the following URL to change your password:

`http://<hn>.<dn>/ChangePassword.php?uname=PHP&opasswd=PHP&npasswd=ORACLE`

It will render a page with the version of the database, and an HTML table containing the user/ schema name plus the old and new passwords. You can change them back by reversing the old and new passwords and reposting the URL through your browser refresh.

These examples use static SQL statements, which are nice and tidy example programs. The next section demonstrates how you use dynamic SQL statements by exploiting Oracle *bind* variables.

Querying and Transacting Using SQL Statements

The use of static SQL statements has practical limitations. It is impossible to know what your end users will *select, insert, update,* and *delete* in your web applications. You need the ability to collect inputs and dynamically search and insert data into your application. You need some type of substitution variable method to have this flexibility.

Oracle *bind* variables act like substitution variables. They are Oracle structures that let you pass scalar variables into and out of SQL statements and PL/SQL statements in your PHP programs. *Bind* variables also let you move data across memory spaces. In PHP programs *bind* variables let you seamlessly pass a PHP variable to Oracle and vice versa.

This section shows you how to exploit *bind* variables and explores alternatives in selecting, inserting, updating, and deleting data from the database. Oracle bind variables are identified as string literals preceded by a colon—*:bind_variable.* They are included in the `oci_bind_by_name()` and `oci_bind_by_array_name()` functions, as well as in resource *statements.*

While static SQL statement have three phases, *parse, execute,* and *fetch,* dynamic SQL statements have potentially five phases, *parse, bind, define, execute,* and *fetch.* Reference cursor or collection *bind* variables require a *define* phase. You provide *input only* or *pass-by-value* variables to SQL resource *statements. Pass-by-reference* operations require PL/SQL stored procedures, which are covered in Chapter 14.

The query programs demonstrate how to use a `SELECT` statement to return, row by row, all rows to an array by assignment and reference, and all rows into an object. Separate programs demonstrate the four qualified query processes.

The `BindFetchSQL.php` program demonstrates a `SELECT` statement returning a result set row by row, as shown:

-- **This is found in BindFetchSQL.php on the enclosed CD.**

```php
<?php
  // Return successful attempt to connect to the database.
  if ($c = @oci_connect("php","php","xe"))
  {
    // Declare input variables.
    (isset($_GET['lname'])) ? $lname = $_GET['lname']
                            : $lname = "[a-zA-Z]";

    // Declare array mapping column to display names.
    $q_title = array("FULL_NAME"=>"Full Name"
                    ,"TITLE"=>"Title"
                    ,"CHECK_OUT_DATE"=>"Check Out"
                    ,"RETURN_DATE"=>"Return");

    // Parse a query to a resource statement.
    $s = oci_parse($c,"SELECT   cr.full_name
                      ,        cr.title
                      ,        cr.check_out_date
                      ,        cr.return_date
                      FROM     current_rental cr
                      WHERE    REGEXP_LIKE(cr.full_name,:lname)");

    // Bind a variable into the resource statement.
    oci_bind_by_name($s,":lname",$lname,-1,SQLT_CHR);

    // Execute the parsed query without a commit.
    oci_execute($s,OCI_DEFAULT);

    // Print the table header using calls to the query metadata.
    print '<table border="1" cellspacing="0" cellpadding="3">';

    // Print open and close HTML row tags and column field names.
    print '<tr>';
    for ($i = 1;$i <= oci_num_fields($s);$i++)
      print '<td class="e">'.$q_title[oci_field_name($s,$i)].'</td>';
    print "</tr>";

    // Read and print statement row return.
    while (oci_fetch($s))
    {
      // Print open and close HTML row tags and columns data.
      print '<tr>';
      for ($i = 1;$i <= oci_num_fields($s);$i++)
        print '<td class="v">'.oci_result($s,$i).'</td>';
      print '</tr>';
    }
```

```
    // Print a close HTML table tag.
    print '</table>';

    // Disconnect from database.
    oci_close($c);
  }
  else
  {
    // Assign the OCI error and format double and single quotes.
    $errorMessage = oci_error();
    print htmlentities($errorMessage['message'])."<br />";
  }
?>
```

The `BindFetchSQL.php` program adds some programming techniques to how you manage the result set. The input validation operation uses a regular expression identifier for any combination of lowercase and uppercase letters when the URL does not contain an `lname` parameter. The regular expression default value uses the Oracle SQL `REGEXP_LIKE()` function embedded in the resource statement. Also, the `$q_title` array is used to map alias assignments that include white space to the column names. While it is possible in SQL*Plus to enclose aliases with white space in double quotes, you cannot do the same in PHP resource statements and this is a work-around.

Inside the resource statement, there is a bind variable, `:lname`. The same bind variable is passed as a string literal as the second argument in the `oci_bind_by_name()` function—`":lname "`. The `oci_bind_by_name()` function maps the third argument, a PHP variable, to the *bind* variable. The other parameters to the `oci_bind_by_name()` function designate the size and type. The `-1` instructs the OCI8 library to implicitly derive the type, and `SQLT_CHR` maps to a variable-length string or `VARCHAR2` Oracle SQL type. (Note: Oracle SQL data types are covered in Appendix H.) Without a parameter in the URL, the web page should render the following output:

Full Name	Title	Check Out	Return
Brian Winn	RoboCop	27-JUN-06	02-JUL-06
Brian Winn	The Hunt for Red October	27-JUN-06	02-JUL-06
Doreen Vizquel	Camelot	27-JUN-06	02-JUL-06
Doreen Vizquel	I Remember Mama	27-JUN-06	02-JUL-06
Oscar Vizquel	Star Wars I	27-JUN-06	02-JUL-06
Oscar Vizquel	Star Wars II	27-JUN-06	02-JUL-06
Oscar Vizquel	Star Wars III	27-JUN-06	02-JUL-06
Ian M Sweeney	Cars	27-JUN-06	02-JUL-06
Meaghan Sweeney	Hook	27-JUN-06	02-JUL-06

Row-by-row fetching is easy to understand and work with, plus it is more or less consistent from one database to another. The `oci_fetch_all()` function returns all potential rows as a group into an array. By default the `oci_fetch_all()` function returns each set of column values as rows, indexed by column names. The individual rows are numerically indexed column values. The numeric index is equivalent to the row numbering, except that it is a *0-based* instead of *1-based* numbering schema.

When you override the default mode, you can set the first column as either a number or a column name index by using OCI_NUM or OCI_ASSOC, respectively. Nested arrays within each row are indexed by numbers in three of four sorting operations. You can return an array that mimics the two-dimensional structure returned by the SQL cursor using the combination of OCI_FETCHSTATEMENT_BY_ROW and OCI_NUM.

The `BindFetchAll.php` program lets you see the various combinations from the `oci_fetch_all()` function:

-- **This is found in BindFetchAll.php on the enclosed CD.**

```php
<?php
  // Return successful attempt to connect to the database.
  if ($c = @oci_connect("php", "php", "xe"))
  {
    // Declare input variables.
    (isset($_GET['limit']))   ? $limit = (int) $_GET['limit']
                              : $limit = 5;
    (isset($_GET['param']))   ? $flag = (int) $_GET['param']
                              : $flag = 0;

    // Parse a query through the connection to a statement.
    $s = oci_parse($c,"SELECT cr.full_name
                       ,       cr.title
                       FROM    current_rental cr
                       ,       SELECT    cr.account_number
                               FROM      current_rental cr
                               GROUP BY cr.account_number
                               HAVING    COUNT(account_number) >= :limit) lim
                       WHERE   cr.account_number = lim.account_number");

    // Bind the array variable to the statement resource.
    oci_bind_by_name($s,":limit",$limit);

    // Execute the parsed query without a commit.
    oci_execute($s,OCI_DEFAULT);

    // Declare variables to control HTML header formatting.
    $dimensions = array("Column","Row");
    $dimension1 = "";
```

```
$dimension2 = "";
$index = 0;

// Print open HTML table tag.
print '<table border="1" cellspacing="0" cellpadding="3">';

// Dynamically alter array organization flags.
switch($flag)
{
  case 0:
    // Primary index is column name, secondary index is row number.
    oci_fetch_all($s,$array_out,0,-1
                 ,OCI_FETCHSTATEMENT_BY_COLUMN|OCI_ASSOC);
    break;
  case 1:
    // Primary index is column number, secondary index is row number.
    oci_fetch_all($s,$array_out,0,-1
                 ,OCI_FETCHSTATEMENT_BY_COLUMN|OCI_NUM);
    break;
  case 2:
    // Primary index is row number, secondary index is column name.
    oci_fetch_all($s,$array_out,0,-1
                 ,OCI_FETCHSTATEMENT_BY_ROW|OCI_ASSOC);
    break;
  case 3:
    // Primary index is row number, secondary index is column number.
    oci_fetch_all($s,$array_out,0,-1
                 ,OCI_FETCHSTATEMENT_BY_ROW|OCI_NUM);
    break;
  default:
    // Primary index is column name, secondary index is row number.
    oci_fetch_all($s,$array_out,0,-1);
    break;
}

// Print 1st dimension header.
print '<tr>';
print '<td class="e">'.$dimension1.'<br />Index</td>';

// Set initial index, string or zero.
foreach ($array_out as $name => $value)
{
  if (!is_numeric($name)) $index = $name;
  break;
}

// Print nested array headers.
for ($i = 0;$i < count($array_out[$index]);$i++)
```

```
    {
      print '<td class="e">'.$dimension2.'<br />Index</td>';
      print '<td class="e">'.$dimension2.'<br />Value</td>';
    }

    // Close HTML header row.
    print '</tr>';

    // Read through the first dimension of the record set.
    foreach ($array_out as $name => $value)
    {
      print '<tr>';
      print '<td class="e">'.$name.'</td>';

      // Read through the second dimension of the record set.
      foreach ($value as $subname => $subvalue)
      {
        print '<td class="e">'.$subname.'</td>';
        print '<td class="v">'.$subvalue.'</td>';
      }
      print '</tr>';
    }

    // Print the close HTML table tag.
    print '</table>';

    // Disconnect from database.
    oci_close($c);
  }
  else
  {
    // Assign the OCI error and format double and single quotes.
    $errorMessage = oci_error();
    print htmlentities($errorMessage['message'])."<br />";
  }
?>
```

The `BindFetchAll.php` program takes an optional parameter in the URL named `param`. Using the `param` variable in the URL lets you test various possibilities with the `oci_fetch_all()` function. The local `$flag` variable set by the `param` variable is managed in a `switch` statement. You should note that the default case produces the same result as using the `OCI_FETCHSTATEMENT_BY_COLUMN` and `OCI_ASSOC` flags.

Substituting the hostname *(hn)* and domain name *(dn)*, you can use the following URL to change your password:

```
http://<hn>.<dn>/BindFetchArraySQL.php?param=2
```

It will render a page with an array similar in organization to what you get when fetching one row at a time, except you fetch them as a set. The page is rendered as shown in the following illustration:

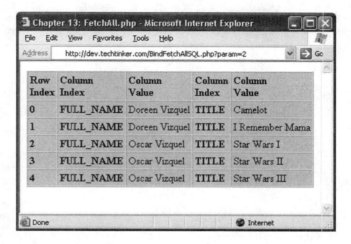

The `oci_fetch_array()` function provides a tool to pivot the output of a single row of data. You can use the function to return a row in an array indexed by *numbers, column names,* or *both*. The general behavior of the `oci_fetch_array()` function does not return null values or Oracle Large Objects (LOBs). You can override the default behavior toward nulls and LOBs by using a single pipe, |, to combine the OCI_ASSOC, OCI_BOTH, or OCI_NUM, and OCI_RETURN_NULLS and OCI_RETURN_LOBS. An example program using `oci_fetch_array()` that lets you explore the output sets of the function is found on the enclosed CD in the BindFetchArraySQL.php program.

The `oci_fetch_object()` function mirrors the behavior of the `oci_fetch()` function with an interesting twist. It returns the entire contents of the return row set from the query and assigns the return set to a PHP object. Actually, it's an OCI8 internal object that reflection shows has zero static variables, constants, or functions. The object is navigable like a standard associative array or as an object when you know the instance variable names.

NOTE
Instantiated PL/SQL objects are available in Oracle 9iR2 forward. The `oci_fetch_object()` may be extended to manage these at some future date but at present only works with rows returned from queries.

The BindFetchObjectSQL.php program demonstrates how you navigate the first row as an object:

```php
-- This is found in BindFetchObjectSQL.php on the enclosed CD.

<?php
  // Return successful attempt to connect to the database.
  if ($c = @oci_connect("php", "php", "xe"))
  {
    // Declare input variables.
    (isset($_GET['limit']))   ? $limit = (int) $_GET['limit']
                              : $limit = 5;
```

```php
      // Parse a query to a resource statement.
      $s = oci_parse($c,"SELECT    cr.full_name
                             ,        cr.title
                             ,        cr.product
                             ,        cr.check_out_date
                             ,        cr.return_date
                        FROM        current_rental cr
                             ,        (SELECT    cr.account_number
                                        FROM      current_rental cr
                                        GROUP BY cr.account_number
                                        HAVING    COUNT(account_number) >= :limit) l
                        WHERE       cr.account_number = l.account_number");

      // Bind a variable into the resource statement.
      oci_bind_by_name($s,":limit",$limit);

      // Execute the parsed query without a commit.
      oci_execute($s,OCI_DEFAULT);

      // Print open HTML table tag.
      print '<table border="1" cellspacing="0" cellpadding="3">';

      // Read and print statement row return.
      $object_out = oci_fetch_object($s);

      // Read through the first dimension of the record set.
      for ($i = 1;$i <= oci_num_fields($s);$i++)
      {
        $name = oci_field_name($s,$i);
        print '<tr>';
        print '<td class="v">'.$name.'</td>';
        if (oci_field_is_null($s,$i))
          print '<td class="v"> </td>';
        else
          print '<td class="v">'.$object_out->$name.'</td>';
        print '</tr>';
      }

      // Print the close HTML table tag.
      print '</table>';

      // Disconnect from database.
      oci_close($c);
  }
  else
  {
    // Assign the OCI error and format double and single quotes.
    $errorMessage = oci_error();
    print htmlentities($errorMessage['message'])."<br />";
  }
?>
```

The program uses the `oci_fetch_object()` function to load the first row of the SQL statement into an object. Then, the program uses the dynamic combination of `oci_num_fields()` and `oci_name_fields()` functions to secure the instance variable names. Instance variable names are the same as the column names returned from a SQL statement. Using syntax covered in Chapter 8, you reference object instance variables with the *pointer operator* syntax, as shown:

```
$object_out->$name
```

The `oci_fetch_object()` function offers no real utility other than a different access method. The utility will be frequently used when a future version of OCI supports instantiable PL/SQL objects. Copying an instantiable PL/SQL object into your PHP program as a native object lets you place your database server code directly into your PHP programs at run time.

As mentioned earlier in this chapter, you use Oracle *bind* variables in INSERT, UPDATE, and DELETE statements. The mechanism is very similar to how you work with SELECT statements. The `InsertTransaction.php` demonstrates how *bind* variables work, inserting a new member row into the MEMBER table of the video store model, as shown:

```
-- This is found in InsertTransaction.php on the enclosed CD.

<?php
  // Return successful attempt to connect to the database.
  if ($c = @oci_connect("php","php","xe"))
  {
    // Declare an array in lieu of $_POST for entry.
    $account_number = "B303-73740";
    $credit_card_no = "5555-5555-5555-5555";
    $credit_card_type = "DISCOVER_CARD";

    // Parse an insert into a resource statement.
    $s = oci_parse($c,"INSERT INTO member VALUES
                      ( member_s1.nextval
                      , :account_no
                      , :credit_card_no
                      ,(SELECT   common_lookup_id
                        FROM     common_lookup
                        WHERE    common_lookup_context = 'MEMBER'
                        AND      common_lookup_type = :credit_card_type)
                      , 3, SYSDATE, 3, SYSDATE )");

    // Bind a variable into the resource statement.
    oci_bind_by_name($s,":account_no",$account_number,-1,SQLT_CHR);
    oci_bind_by_name($s,":credit_card_no",$credit_card_no,-1,SQLT_CHR);
    oci_bind_by_name($s,":credit_card_type",$credit_card_type,-1,SQLT_CHR);

    // Execute the parsed query without a commit.
    oci_execute($s,OCI_DEFAULT);

    // Commit transaction.
    oci_commit($c);
```

```
    // Disconnect from database.
    oci_close($c);
}
else
{
    // Assign the OCI error and format double and single quotes.
    $errorMessage = oci_error();
    print htmlentities($errorMessage['message'])."<br />";
}
?>
```

You should note that you can *bind* variables anywhere in SQL statements. The INSERT statement uses three bind variables, two as direct *pass-by-value* substitutions and one in the WHERE predicate of the VALUES clause subquery. As discussed in the earlier section "Connecting to Oracle Using the OCI8 Libraries," it is *critical* to call the oci_commit() function when you override the default mode of the oci_execute() function. If you remove the oci_commit() function call from this program, nothing is inserted into the MEMBER table.

The performance of fetching one row at a time is easily surpassed by other methods that fetch the entire contents at one pass. You will examine those approaches using Oracle PL/SQL stored procedures in Chapter 14.

Summary

The chapter has shown you how to connect to the Oracle Database 10*g* XE database, query the database, and transact against the database. You have explored techniques using static and dynamic calls to SQL statements. The discussion has presented alternative approaches to accessing, querying, and transacting against the database.

CHAPTER
14

Oracle PL/SQL
Transactions

his chapter continues the discussion of how to connect to and use the Oracle Database 10*g* XE instance started in Chapter 13. The chapter focuses on how to use and leverage Oracle Procedural Language/Structured Query Language (PL/SQL) to develop web applications. PL/SQL is completely integrated with the SQL*Plus environment and has been a major part of the Oracle database since Oracle 7. The PL/SQL programming language lets you build server-side procedural programs.

The semantics for connecting and managing transactions are the same as those presented in Chapter 13. In this chapter, you learn how to use Oracle *bind* variables to *pass-by-value* and *pass-by-reference* between your PHP programs and PL/SQL stored procedures. While the focus is how you put variable values into and out of PL/SQL procedures, understanding the basics of PL/SQL is helpful to learning this information. You can review the SQL or PL/SQL primers, if you are new to the Oracle family of database products, which are found in Appendixes H and I respectively.

This chapter is divided into four sections:

- Explaining PL/SQL stored procedures

- Using reference cursors and PL/SQL stored procedures

- Using scalar associative arrays and PL/SQL stored procedures

- Using scalar collections and PL/SQL stored procedures

There are four SQL programs that you need to work through the examples in this chapter. If you have not created your PHP user/schema, you will need to run the create_user.sql script that is found in Appendix G. You run it as the SYSTEM user to create the PHP user/schema account in your Oracle Database 10*g* XE instance. The other database setup scripts are found in Appendix J; they assume that you've already run the create_user.sql script. If you want to use a different user/schema name than PHP, you'll need to check and change any scripts affected by the change.

The create_signon_triggers.sql, create_store.sql, and seed_store.sql scripts are required for Chapter 13 and should be loaded at this time. If they are not loaded, you will need to load them to work with these example programs. You will also need to run the create_world_leaders.sql script, which builds and populates a PRESIDENT table. The PRESIDENT table illustrates *pass-by-value* and *pass-by-reference* operations with Oracle reference cursors, associative arrays, and collections. All of these scripts are available for your review in Appendix J.

Explaining PL/SQL Stored Procedures

PL/SQL stored procedures are program units that reside inside the database in text form. You use SQL Data Definition Language (DDL) to create stored procedures. The creation process compiles the code by running it through a PL/SQL parser to check for syntax errors and validate the existence of dependent database objects, like tables, views, packages, procedures, and functions. Stored procedures come in two varieties, stand-alone procedures and procedures inside of packages.

Stand-alone procedures are self-contained programs, having both a definition and an implementation. As described in Appendix I, PL/SQL is a strongly typed language. Procedure definitions qualify the formal parameter list by both position and data type. As with flexible parameter passing in PHP functions, discussed in Chapter 7, you have the ability in PL/SQL to use named notation to override the positional limit of the procedure signature. You also have the ability to assign default values to formal parameters when defining your stored procedures and functions.

Unlike PHP functions, PL/SQL procedures cannot be right operands and cannot return a variable by assignment. PL/SQL procedures **only** support *pass-by-value* and *pass-by-reference* modes through the formal parameter list. Formal parameters in Oracle stored procedures use the IN mode to support *pass-by-value* and the IN OUT mode to support *pass-by-reference.* As discussed in Chapter 13, you will use *bind* variables to pass variables between programming environments.

PL/SQL also supports user-defined functions. Stand-alone functions only support a *pass-by-value* mode of operation, and all formal parameters must be defined as IN mode variables. PL/SQL functions can be right operands and return a variable by assignment, but you can only handle the return value of PL/SQL functions by using them as SQL expressions. SQL expressions use SELECT clause functions. The functions accept actual parameters and return a *scalar variable value,* but they cannot return non-scalar variables, such as reference cursors, arrays, and large objects. You should use procedures to move data to and from the database server through *bind* variables because they support both scalar and non-scalar variables the same way.

Stand-alone functions and procedures do not let you implement overloaded procedures because procedure names are unique namespaces in the context of the user/schema. Overloaded functions and procedures have the same procedure name but different formal parameter lists. Formal parameter lists are overloaded when the number, order, or data type of parameters changes between the function or procedure signatures. Signatures are the formal parameter lists of procedures, and they are the formal parameters and return data types of functions. You define a collection of overloaded procedures in PL/SQL by placing them in a database package.

PL/SQL database packages have separate definitions and implementations. The definition is a package specification. The package specification defines the names and parameter lists of procedures and the names, parameter lists, and return types of functions. The implementation is a package body, and it defines locally accessible functions and procedures while providing the implementation of procedures and functions defined by a package specification. Parameters for package functions and procedures work exactly like their stand-alone versions. Formal function parameters *only* support the IN mode, or *pass-by-value* model; while formal procedure parameters support both the IN and IN OUT modes, or *pass-by-value* and *pass-by-reference* models.

This chapter uses overloaded procedures in the WORLD_LEADERS package to demonstrate how to use reference cursors, associative arrays, and collections. Each section covers their respective PL/SQL procedure, inclusive of signatures, parameter modes, and implementation details. The PL/SQL procedures demonstrate intermediate PL/SQL programming techniques. If you require more information on the PL/SQL language, you should check *Oracle Database 10g PL/SQL Programming* by Scott Urman et al. (McGraw-Hill/Osborne, 2004) or Oracle's *PL/SQL User's Guide and Reference 10g Release 2* for more information.

Using Reference Cursors and PL/SQL Stored Procedures

PL/SQL required a look-alike data type for the result set from a SELECT statement to move return sets from one program to another. Oracle developed the system reference cursor data type to meet this need. Reference cursors act as pointers to result sets in query work areas. You use them when you want to query data in one program and process it in another, especially when the two programs are in different programming languages. You have the option of implementing a reference cursor in two ways: one is *strongly typed* and the other, *weakly typed.*

A *strongly typed* reference cursor is explicitly defined by assigning a %ROWTYPE attribute to the cursor. The %ROWTYPE attribute maps the structure from a catalog table or view in the database to the reference cursor. A reference cursor is also known as a compound data type. You use *strongly typed* reference cursors when you need to control the structure of *input* parameters to stored procedures or functions. You define a *strongly typed* reference cursor inside a PL/SQL package specification by using the following syntax:

```
TYPE president_type_cursor IS REF CURSOR RETURN president%ROWTYPE;
```

Weakly typed reference cursors are dynamically defined at run time. They are more flexible generally and can be reused by multiple structures. You also define weakly typed reference cursors in PL/SQL package specifications. The following is the definition used in the WORLD_LEADERS package:

```
TYPE president_type_cursor IS REF CURSOR;
```

The create_world_leaders.sql script defines a *weakly typed* reference cursor, as covered in Appendix J. You can change it from a weakly typed to strongly typed reference cursor if you prefer the additional structure, but you will need to change the SELECT statement inside the GET_PRESIDENT procedure. A strongly typed reference cursor requires you to mirror a catalog table or view definition. Generally, weakly typed reference cursors offer more flexibility when the result set does not mirror a table or view definition.

TIP
You should use weakly typed reference cursors when the underlying SELECT statement returns fewer columns than the complete table or view. Also, changing underlying coding components is simpler when using a weakly typed reference cursor. The inability to partition weakly typed reference cursors seldom outweighs these simplified coding considerations.

This chapter uses several overloaded procedures that share the same procedure name, GET_PRESIDENTS. Three of the overloaded procedure signatures only differ in the data types of the last four variables, whereas the reference cursor only uses one parameter to capture the four parameter values in the others. Reference cursors are ideal for developing flexible solutions that involve arrays of structures, or compound variables, as opposed to single-dimensional arrays of scalar variables.

The following excerpted GET_PRESIDENTS procedure uses three scalar input variables and one reference cursor output variable:

```
-- This is found in create_world_leaders.sql on the enclosed CD.

  -- Implement a procedure body to return a reference cursor.
  PROCEDURE get_presidents
  ( term_start_in    IN      NUMBER
  , term_end_in      IN      NUMBER
  , country_in       IN      VARCHAR2
  , presidents       IN OUT PRESIDENT_TYPE_CURSOR ) AS
```

```
BEGIN
   -- Collect data for the reference cursor.
   OPEN presidents FOR
      SELECT    president_id "#"
      ,         first_name||' '||middle_name||' '||last_name "Preisdent"
      ,         term_start||' '||term_end "Tenure"
      ,         party "Party"
      FROM      president
      WHERE     country = country_in
      AND       term_start BETWEEN term_start_in AND term_end_in
      OR        term_end BETWEEN term_start_in AND term_end_in;
END get_presidents;
```

Input variables are passed by value, while output variables are passed by reference, as is designated by their respective IN and IN OUT mode qualifiers. The scalar input variable names mirror the column names in the PRESIDENT table plus an _in suffix. You use the suffix to distinguish the formal parameter names from valid column names in the SELECT statement. Substitution variables in SELECT statements must differ from valid column names; otherwise, the SQL parser will ignore all substitution variable names that match valid column names, using the column name values instead.

TIP
Oracle reference cursors must be explicitly called and cannot be referenced in implicit cursor management tools, such as a PL/SQL for loop.

The PRESIDENTS variable is a weakly typed reference cursor defined in the WORLD_ LEADERS package specification. This means the reference cursor structure is set at run time. You use the OPEN *reference_cursor_name* FOR syntax followed by a SELECT statement to open a reference cursor. This explicitly opens a SQL cursor and assigns the query work area pointer to the run-time instance of the GET_PRESIDENTS procedure, which is then returned to the calling program.

NOTE
All rows are selected and placed in a query work area in the SGA when you explicitly open a cursor. The pointer to that query work area is a reference cursor, which is returned to the calling program, as is done in the ReferenceCursor.php script.

As mentioned in Chapter 13, SQL statements in SQL*Plus have *parse, execute,* and *fetch* phases. External programs using the OCI8 interface have at least those and possibly have *parse, define, bind, execute,* and *fetch* phases. The *bind* phase lets you *pass-by-value* variables into the Oracle server, while the combination of *define* and *bind* phases let you retrieve them when you *pass-by-reference.*

Working with SQL statements in Chapter 13 did not provide an opportunity to demonstrate *pass-by-reference* behaviors because the SELECT statements return scalar values. PL/SQL procedures let us demonstrate this powerful OCI8 feature because it supports *pass-by-reference* variables.

The `ReferenceCursor.php` program demonstrates how you use the `oci_new_cursor()` and `oci_bind_by_name()` functions to define an Oracle reference cursor; they bind input and output variables respectively. The program also demonstrates that you must use `oci_execute()` twice when dealing with a PL/SQL procedure that contains one reference cursor. The first call executes the statement, and the second call transfers the query work area pointer to a local variable. When you have more than one reference cursor as an `IN OUT` mode variable, you make incremental calls to the `oci_execute()` function for each reference cursor. Each call transfers a different query work area pointer to your PHP program.

The `ReferenceCursor.php` program takes three URL parameters, `begin`, `end`, and `country`. You limit the number of rows returned by providing values to the starting and ending term parameters—`begin` and `end` respectively. Absent those parameters, the program returns all former and current presidents of the U.S.A., as found in this code:

-- **This is found in ReferenceCursor.php on the enclosed CD.**

```php
<?php
  // Return successful attempt to connect to the database.
  if ($c = @oci_connect("php","php","xe"))
  {
    // Declare input variables.
    (isset($_GET['begin']))    ? $t_start = (int) $_GET['begin']
                               : $t_start = 1787;
    (isset($_GET['end']))      ? $t_end = (int) $_GET['end']
                               : $t_end = (int) date("Y",time());
    (isset($_GET['country'])) ? $country = $_GET['country']
                               : $country = "USA";

    // Declare a PL/SQL execution command.
    $stmt = "BEGIN
               world_leaders.get_presidents(:term_start
                                            ,:term_end
                                            ,:country
                                            ,:return_cursor);
             END;";

    // Strip special characters to avoid ORA-06550 and PLS-00103 errors.
    $stmt = strip_special_characters($stmt);

    // Parse a query through the connection.
    $s = oci_parse($c,$stmt);

    // Declare a return cursor for the connection.
    $rc = oci_new_cursor($c);

    // Bind PHP variables to the OCI input or in mode variables.
    oci_bind_by_name($s,':term_start',$t_start);
    oci_bind_by_name($s,':term_end',$t_end);
    oci_bind_by_name($s,':c',$country);

    // Bind PHP variable to the OCI output or in/out mode variable.
    oci_bind_by_name($s,':return_cursor',$rc,-1,OCI_B_CURSOR);
```

```
    // Execute the PL/SQL statement.
    oci_execute($s);

    // Access the returned cursor.
    oci_execute($rc);

    // Print the table header with known labels.
    print '<table border="1" cellpadding="3" cellspacing="0">';

    // Set dynamic labels control variable true.
    $label = true;

    // Read the contents of the reference cursor.
    while($row = oci_fetch_assoc($rc))
    {
      // Declare header and data variables.
      $header = "";
      $data = "";

      // Read the reference cursor into a table.
      foreach ($row as $name => $column)
      {
        // Capture labels for the first row.
        if ($label)
        {
          $header .= '<td class="e">'.$name.'</td>';
          $data .= '<td class="v">'.$column.'</td>';
        }
        else
          $data .= '<td class=v>'.$column.'</td>';
      }

      // Print the header row once.
      if ($label)
      {
        print '<tr>'.$header.'</tr>';
        $label = !$label;
      }

      // Print the data rows.
      print '<tr>'.$data.'</tr>';
    }

    // Print the HTML table close.
    print '</table>';

    // Disconnect from database.
    oci_close($c);
  }
  else
  {
    // Assign the OCI error and format double and single quotes.
    $errorMessage = oci_error();
    print htmlentities($errorMessage['message'])."<br />";
  }
```

```
// Strip special characters, like carriage returns or line feeds and tabs.
function strip_special_characters($str)
{
  $out = "";
  for ($i = 0;$i < strlen($str);$i++)
    if ((ord($str[$i]) != 9) && (ord($str[$i]) != 10) &&
        (ord($str[$i]) != 13))
      $out .= $str[$i];
  return $out;
}
?>
```

This program uses the `oci_new_cursor()` function to build a local reference cursor, against which you bind a *pass-by-reference* variable using the `oci_bind_by_name()` function. You also use the `oci_bind_by_name()` function to bind three input variables as *pass-by-value* variables. The optional fourth and fifth parameters in the `oci_bind_by_name()` function are unnecessary when passing the string and numeric literal values. These optional parameters are implicitly managed as VARCHAR2 data types. Oracle SQL implicitly downcasts a VARCHAR2 containing a number to a NUMBER data type because there is no loss of precision.

Reference cursors require the fifth parameter in the `oci_bind_by_name()` function to designate the proper Oracle data type, so you must also provide the fourth parameter too. Using a -1 for the maximum-length fourth parameter is the simplest way to ensure that changes in the cursor do not require that you modify the *max_field_length* parameter for each call to the `oci_bind_by_name()` function. The fifth parameter should be OCI_B_CURSOR as described in Table 13-3.

You fetch a row from the query work area using the `oci_fetch_assoc()` function. The returned array will have columns as rows and *column names* as indexes. You can read the indexes and data from the first row and then read only the data for the rest, as is done in the foregoing program.

The `strip_special_characters()` *function is provided because you cannot have any control characters in the PL/SQL string when you parse it.* This function strips tabs, line feeds, and carriage returns. The Oracle PL/SQL parser is different from the SQL parser and more particular. You can leave control characters in your SQL statements without adverse impact.

TIP
You will receive PLS-00103 *and* ORA-06550 *errors when your submitted PL/SQL statement includes a line feed or carriage return. The error message will say that it encountered a "" when expecting some other PL/SQL construct.*

Substituting the hostname *(hn)* and domain name *(dn)*, you can use the following URL to find presidents of the U.S.A. from 1849 to 1875:

```
http://<hn>.<dn>/ReferenceCursor.php?begin=1849&end=1875
```

The URL will return the four columns from the reference cursor. You will get output like that shown in Figure 14-1.

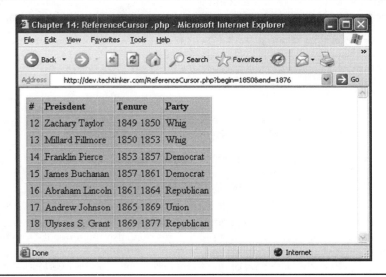

FIGURE 14-1. *ReferenceCursor.php web page*

This section has demonstrated how to use PL/SQL procedures and reference cursors to pass data structures using pass-by-reference variables. The next sections will demonstrate how you access associative arrays and collections.

Using Associative Arrays and PL/SQL Stored Procedures

Associative arrays in the Oracle Database 10*g* family of products were previously known as PL/SQL tables. PL/SQL tables were introduced in Oracle 7 as dynamic lists of scalar variables in 1993. Three years later in Oracle 7.3, PL/SQL tables were capable of managing arrays of structures, like reference cursors. PL/SQL tables were renamed with the Oracle 10*g* release because they now support both numeric and unique string indexes.

Associative arrays have many customized uses in PL/SQL, like managing bulk inserts and queries. Bulk operations improve the efficiency of the Oracle database server. They are also simpler to use than reference cursors for many programmers when they want to move data from one PL/SQL program to another. OCI8 now makes it possible to *pass-by-reference* associative arrays, but at the time of writing this book OCI8 only supports scalar value associative arrays. Scalar value associative arrays are single-dimensional arrays of scalar data types.

This limitation does not prevent working with sets of PL/SQL tables as structures. You do this by managing each column of a structure separately, and the set of collection columns as a set of parallel arrays. This is tedious to code for the moment, but Oracle has promised to support associative arrays using record structures *sometime* in the future.

Associative arrays are used in PL/SQL programs by defining them in the declaration section, which for a package is the specification. You must ensure that the array element size is at least as great as the longest possible element in the array. The following associative array type definitions are defined in the WORLD_LEADERS package specification to support the example programs:

-- **This is found in create_world_leaders.sql on the enclosed CD.**

```
-- Define an associative array (PL/SQL Table) of numbers.
TYPE president_id_table IS TABLE OF NUMBER
  INDEX BY BINARY_INTEGER;

-- Define three associative arrays (PL/SQL Table) of VARCHAR2 by size.
TYPE president_name_table IS TABLE OF VARCHAR2(60 CHAR)
  INDEX BY BINARY_INTEGER;
TYPE tenure_table IS TABLE OF VARCHAR2(9 CHAR)
  INDEX BY BINARY_INTEGER;
TYPE party_table IS TABLE OF VARCHAR2(24 CHAR)
  INDEX BY BINARY_INTEGER;
```

These statements enable package procedures to use these user-defined types as data types for formal parameters. Other packages and procedures may also reference these types by prefacing them with the package name and a period, known as attribute chaining in Oracle jargon. Each of these types is used as the data type of one formal parameter for the overloaded GET_PRESIDENTS procedure as shown:

-- **This is found in create_world_leaders.sql on the enclosed CD.**

```
-- Implement a procedure body to return parallel associative arrays.
PROCEDURE get_presidents
( term_start_in      IN      NUMBER
, term_end_in        IN      NUMBER
, country_in         IN      VARCHAR2
, president_ids      IN OUT  PRESIDENT_ID_TABLE
, president_names    IN OUT  PRESIDENT_NAME_TABLE
, tenures            IN OUT  TENURE_TABLE
, parties            IN OUT  PARTY_TABLE) AS

BEGIN

  -- Define a Bulk Collect into parallel associative arrays.
  SELECT    president_id pres_number
  ,         first_name||' '||middle_name||' '||last_name pres_name
  ,         term_start||'-'||term_end tenure
  ,         party
  BULK COLLECT
  INTO      president_ids
  ,         president_names
  ,         tenures
  ,         parties
  FROM      president
  WHERE     country = country_in
  AND       term_start BETWEEN term_start_in AND term_end_in
  OR        term_end BETWEEN term_start_in AND term_end_in;

END get_presidents;
```

This overloaded GET_PRESIDENTS procedure uses the same three scalar input variables, which are passed by value. It uses four *pass-by-reference* scalar associative array types instead of a single *pass-by-reference* cursor variable. The highlighted data types for the IN OUT mode variables are defined in the WORLD_LEADERS specification.

Unlike the explicit cursor structure to open a reference cursor, the SELECT statement uses a BULK COLLECT operation. BULK COLLECT operations build implicit cursors and read all return values INTO the target variables: president_ids, president_names, tenures, and parties. The target variables are associative arrays that are densely populated and indexed by numbers starting at 1. When the SELECT statement returns null column values, they are added to the respective array and indexed. All arrays will have the same number of elements, and indexes in one array identify the same row in another array. Using this approach, you create four parallel associative arrays. You can work these as compound structures by using the mirrored index values in a single iterative structure.

The AssociativeArray.php program demonstrates how to call a PL/SQL procedure that uses *pass-by-reference* associative arrays. It demonstrates how to *parse, bind, execute,* and *fetch* the associative arrays. Unlike when using Oracle reference cursors, you do not need to define associative arrays because they map to PHP associative arrays. Another advantage of using associative arrays over OCI-Collection objects is that you use the same method for accessing elements as you do in native PHP arrays.

AssociativeArray.php also uses the strip_special_characters() function to eliminate tabs, line feeds, and carriage returns, and the same ternary parameter validation found in the ReferenceCursor.php program, as follows:

```php
-- This is found in AssociativeArray.php on the enclosed CD.

<?php
  // Return successful attempt to connect to the database.
  if ($c = @oci_connect("php","php","xe"))
  {
    // Declare input variables.
    (isset($_GET['begin']))   ? $t_start = (int) $_GET['begin']
                              : $t_start = 1787;
    (isset($_GET['end']))     ? $t_end = (int) $_GET['end']
                              : $t_end = (int) date("Y",time());
    (isset($_GET['country'])) ? $country = $_GET['country']
                              : $country = "USA";

    // Declare a PL/SQL execution command.
    $stmt = "BEGIN
              world_leaders.get_presidents(:term_start
                                          ,:term_end
                                          ,:country
                                          ,:p_id
                                          ,:p_name
                                          ,:p_tenure
                                          ,:p_party);
            END;";
```

```php
// Strip special characters to avoid ORA-06550 and PLS-00103 errors.
$stmt = strip_special_characters($stmt);

// Parse a query through the connection.
$s = oci_parse($c,$stmt);

$r_president_id = "";
$r_president_name = "";
$r_tenure = "";
$r_party = "";

// Bind PHP variables to the OCI input or in mode variables.
oci_bind_by_name($s,':term_start',$t_start);
oci_bind_by_name($s,':term_end',$t_end);
oci_bind_by_name($s,':country',$country);

// Bind PHP variables to the OCI output or in/out mode variables.
oci_bind_array_by_name($s,':p_id',$r_president_id,100,38,SQLT_INT);
oci_bind_array_by_name($s,':p_name',$r_president_name,100,10,SQLT_STR);
oci_bind_array_by_name($s,':p_tenure',$r_tenure,100,10,SQLT_STR);
oci_bind_array_by_name($s,':p_party',$r_party,100,24,SQLT_STR);

// Execute the PL/SQL statement.
if (oci_execute($s))
{
  // Declare variable and open HTML table.
  $out = '<table border="1" cellpadding="3" cellspacing="0">';
  $out .= '<tr>';
  $out .= '<td class="e">#</td>';
  $out .= '<td class="e">President Name</td>';
  $out .= '<td class="e">Tenure</td>';
  $out .= '<td class="e">Party</td>';
  $out .= '</tr>';

  // Read parallel collections.
  for ($i = 0;$i < count($r_president_id);$i++)
  {
    $out .= '<tr>';
    $out .= '<td class="v">'.$r_president_id[$i].'</td>';
    $out .= '<td class="v">'.$r_president_name[$i].'</td>';
    $out .= '<td class="v">'.$r_tenure[$i].'</td>';
    $out .= '<td class="v">'.$r_party[$i].'</td>';
    $out .= '</tr>';
  }

  // Close HTML table.
  $out .= '</table>';
}
```

```
    // Render table.
    print $out;

    // Disconnect from database.
    oci_close($c);
  }
  else
  {
    // Assign the OCI error and format double and single quotes.
    $errorMessage = oci_error();
    print htmlentities($errorMessage['message'])."<br />";
  }

  // Strip special characters, like carriage returns or line feeds and tabs.
  function strip_special_characters($str)
  {
    $out = "";
    for ($i = 0;$i < strlen($str);$i++)
      if ((ord($str[$i]) != 9) && (ord($str[$i]) != 10) &&
          (ord($str[$i]) != 13))
        $out .= $str[$i];
    return $out;
  }
?>
```

The `AssociativeArray.php` program uses the `oci_bind_array_by_name()` function, which differs from other bind management operations. You bind Oracle associative arrays directly to PHP associative arrays. Since the PHP variables have no elements when they are sent to the Oracle server, you must specify a maximum size when binding the Oracle and PHP variables in the `oci_bind_array_by_name()` function. The program uses 100 as a maximum number of elements in the associative array. All other specialized Oracle types require the *define* phase to match variable types for both *pass-by-value* and *pass-by-reference* operations.

Access to the return results is simple because the arrays have the same size and index values. You use a for loop and the `count()` function on any returned column variable, and you simply reference the array values using standard array element syntax. You should note that the Oracle VARCHAR2 types map to the SQLT_STR type, and that the Oracle NUMBER types map to the SQLT_NUM type. *(Note: This is to work around an OCI8 bug at the time of writing.)* Unfortunately, you must increase the physical size of dynamically built types by 1 more than the longest returned value, or using the SQLT_STR type will raise an ORA-06512 error saying that the host bind array is too small. At some future date, you should be able to map the Oracle VARCHAR2 and NUMBER types to SQLT_CHR and SQLT_NUM respectively.

NOTE
Only the curious need bother with this tidbit. The bug described here was discovered while testing the referenced example program and occurs because the code presumes a null-terminated, not blank-padded, variable-length string. The issues with noncataloged columns, or columns built dynamically by concatenation, and with NUMBER types were under investigation at the time of writing.

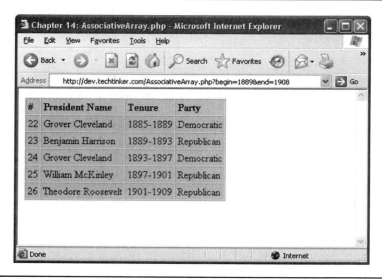

FIGURE 14-2. *AssociativeArray.php web page*

Substituting the hostname *(hn)* and domain name *(dn)*, you can use the following URL to find presidents of the U.S.A. from 1889 to 1908:

```
http://<hn>.<dn>/AssociativeArray.php?begin=1889&end=1908
```

Other than a change in which presidents are displayed, you will get the same four columns as returned by the reference cursor example. Figure 14-2 contains the rendered output.

This section has demonstrated how to use PL/SQL associative arrays as *pass-by-reference* data types, and how to map PL/SQL and PHP associative arrays. The next sections will demonstrate how you access collections.

Using Collections and PL/SQL Stored Procedures

PL/SQL associative arrays are the oldest form of collections in the Oracle database. They are limited to use in PL/SQL programs and as *pass-by-value* and *pass-by-reference* data types in the OCI8 libraries. Associative array data types cannot be used as column data types when defining column data types in tables.

Oracle added two new collections in Oracle 8*i*: the VARRAY and NESTED TABLE collection types. These collection types enable you to build scalar arrays as user-defined SQL data types. Oracle collections are defined by using Data Definition Language (DDL) to create user-defined types. As they are SQL data types, you can use these collections as data types when defining columns in database tables, as formal parameters in PL/SQL procedures and functions, and as PL/SQL function returns.

VARRAY collections are created with a fixed *maximum* number of elements, and of the two types, they are more like traditional programming arrays. NESTED TABLE collections are not created with a fixed maximum number of elements and are closer to lists in traditional programming languages.

As a rule, you will probably use NESTED TABLE collections more often than VARRAY collections for a number of reasons. Two key reasons to use NESTED TABLE data types are: (1) you cannot read a VARRAY directly in a SQL statement without using the SQL CAST() function to cast the VARRAY to a NESTED TABLE; and (2) you must define a maximum number of elements when defining the VARRAY collection type.

You must provide *parse, define, bind, execute,* and *fetch* phases to use VARRAY and NESTED TABLE collections in your PHP programs. You define an OCI-Collection object by using the oci_new_collection() function. Using the Reflection.php program presented in Chapter 8, you can generate the following object definition:

```
Class [ <internal:oci8> class OCICollection ] {
    Constants [0] {}
    Static properties [0] {}
    Static methods [0] {}
    Properties [0] {}
    Methods [8] {
      Method [ <internal> public method append ] {}
      Method [ <internal> public method getelem ] {}
      Method [ <internal> public method assignelem ] {}
      Method [ <internal> public method assign ] {}
      Method [ <internal> public method size ] {}
      Method [ <internal> public method max ] {}
      Method [ <internal> public method trim ] {}
      Method [ <internal> public method free ] {}
    }
  }
```

Table 14-1 provides a summary of the methods for the OCI-Collection class. You can access the contents of collections only by using these published methods. Some parts of the OCI-Collection class are rendered incorrectly through reflection. The class name is also returned in the older form that is now an alias, and the getElem() and assignElem() functions are represented in lowercase. You can use lowercase method names interchangeably, too, but this can change. *It is recommended that you use the published mixed-case method names.*

Method	Description
append()	The append() method adds an element at the end of an instance of the OCI-Collection object type. The method takes one formal input parameter that can be any scalar Oracle SQL data type. *The index values in an OCI-Collection are zero-based index values when they are built manually and one-based indexes when they are built and returned by the Oracle database.* The method returns true when successful and false otherwise. The method has the following pattern: bool append(mixed *value*)
assign()	The assign() method assigns an OCI-Collection instance to another OCI-Collection instance. The method takes one formal input parameter that can only be an OCI-Collection instance. The assign() method returns true when successful and false otherwise.

TABLE 14-1. *OCI-Collection Methods*

Method	Description
	The assign() method will replace any data in the left operand, or assignment target, with the contents of the right operand. The value may be a null, single-item, or multiple-item collection. The method has the following pattern: `bool assign(OCI-Collection class_instance)`
assignElem()	The assignElem() method adds an element to replace an existing element anywhere in an OCI-Collection. The method takes two formal input parameters. The first parameter is an integer in the range of existing index values. You raise an ORA-22165 error when attempting to assign an index value outside the existing range of values. It returns true when successful and false otherwise. The method has the following pattern: `bool assignElem(int index, mixed value)`
free()	The free() method releases all resources assigned to an instance of the OCI-Collection class. This does not unset the OCI-Collection object variable, but it disconnects the variable from the Oracle server collection type. After calling the free() method, you must recall oci_new_collection() to access it as an OCI-Collection instance. It returns true when successful and false otherwise. The method has the following pattern: `bool free()`
getElem()	The getElem() method returns an element from an instance of an OCI-Collection. The method takes an integer between 1 and the return value of the size() when populated by the Oracle database because those indexes are *1-based*. When you build OCI-Collection instances manually, the maximum index value is the size() function return minus 1 because the indexes are *0-based* numbers. The function returns: (a) a scalar variable when a result is found, (b) a null when a null is found, and (c) a 0 when the index value is not found in the list of indexes. The method has the following pattern: `mixed getElem(mixed value)`
max()	The max() method returns the maximum number of elements that can be contained in an OCI-Collection instance. The method has no formal parameter, and it returns: (a) a positive integer 1 or higher when the referenced Oracle data type is a VARRAY; (b) a 0 when the referenced Oracle data type is a NESTED TABLE; and (c) false when an error occurs. The method has the following pattern: `int max()`
size()	The size() method returns the number of actual elements contained in an OCI-Collection instance. The method has no formal parameter and returns the number of actual elements when successful and false otherwise. The method has the following pattern: `int size()`
trim()	The trim() method removes a specified number of elements from the end of an OCI-Collection instance. The method has one formal parameter, which is an integer signifying how many elements to remove from the collection. It returns true when successful and false otherwise. The method has the following pattern: `bool trim(int value)`

TABLE 14-1.   *OCI-Collection Methods* (continued)

The getElem() and size() functions are used in the CollectionVarray.php and CollectionNestedTable.php programs. The AppendAssign.php program uses the append(), assign(), assignElem(), and getElem() functions after defining a local collection using the oci_new_collection() function.

The `AppendAssign.php` program works without referencing any data from the Oracle database but *depends on the existence of a collection type.* The program requires a connection to a user/schema that contains the `PRESIDENT_NAME_NTABLE` nested table collection. This connection enables the `oci_bind_by_name()` function to construct an `OCI-Collection` instance. The `PRESIDENT_NAME_NTABLE` is a nested table of the scalar `VARCHAR2` data type, where each string is limited to a length of 60 Unicode characters.

The program demonstrates that you can create collections inside your PHP programs, which you *can send* to the server to support bulk `INSERT` statements. You create collections by using the `oci_new_collection()` function. `AppendAssign.php` creates an array of the first 16 American presidents, excluding the thirteenth president. The missing president is added as the value of the `$unlucky_number` variable. The program then creates two collections by using the `oci_bind_by_name()` function to demonstrates `OCI-Collection` methods, as shown:

-- This is found in AppendAssign.php on the enclosed CD.

```php
<?php
  // Return successful attempt to connect to the database.
  if ($c = @oci_connect("php","php","xe"))
  {
    // Declare array.
    $president_array = array("George Washington","John Adams"
                            ,"Thomas Jefferson","James Madison"
                            ,"James Monroe","John Quincy Adams"
                            ,"Andrew Jackson","Martin Van Buren"
                            ,"William Henry Harrison","John Tyler"
                            ,"James Polk","Zachary Taylor"
                            ,"","Franklin Pierce"
                            ,"James Buchanan","Abraham Lincoln");

    // Declare a variable containing the missing president.
    $unlucky_number = "Millard Fillmore";

    // Define NESTED TABLE OCI-Collection types.
    $president_master = oci_new_collection($c,'PRESIDENT_NAME_NTABLE');
    $president_copy = oci_new_collection($c,'PRESIDENT_NAME_NTABLE');

    // Read the array contents and add them to OCI-Collection.
    for ($i = 0;$i < count($president_array);$i++)
      if ($president_master->append($president_array[$i]));

    // Assign the original master to a copy.
    $president_copy->assign($president_master);

    // Declare variable, open HTML table and write headers.
    $out  = '<table border="1" cellpadding="3" cellspacing="0">';
    $out .= '<tr>';
    $out .= '<td align="center" colspan="2" class="e">Master</td>';
    $out .= '<td align="center" colspan="2" class="e">Copy</td>';
    $out .= '</tr>';
    $out .= '<tr>';
    $out .= '<td class="e">#</td>';
```

```php
    $out .= '<td class="e">President Name</td>';
    $out .= '<td class="e">#</td>';
    $out .= '<td class="e">President Name</td>';
    $out .= '</tr>';

    // Read collections.
    for ($j = 0;$j < $president_master->size();$j++)
    {
      // Open row and 1 to index.
      $out .= '<tr>';
      $out .= '<td class="v">'.($j + 1).'</td>';

      // Check for missing president in OCI-Collection master.
      if (!is_null($value = $president_master->getElem($j)))
        $out .= '<td class="v">'.$value.'</td>';
      else
      {
        $president_master->assignElem($j,$unlucky_number);
        $out .= '<td class="v">';
        $out .= $president_master->getElem($j);
        $out .= '</td>';
      }

      // Add 1 to index.
      $out .= '<td class="v">'.($j + 1).'</td>';

      // Check for missing president in OCI-Collection copy.
      if (!is_null($value = $president_copy->getElem($j)))
        $out .= '<td class="v">'.$value.'</td>';
      else
        $out .= '<td class="v"> </td>';

      // Close row.
      $out .= '</tr>';
    }

    // Close HTML table.
    $out .= '</table>';

    // Print the HTML table.
    print $out;

    // Disconnect from database.
    oci_close($c);
  }
  else
  {
    // Assign the OCI error and format double and single quotes.
    $errorMessage = oci_error();
    print htmlentities($errorMessage['message'])."<br />";
  }
?>
```

The program then uses the size of the $president_array variable to loop iteratively through the array and call the collection append() method to add members to the collection. The append() method allocates space to the collection and indexes elements before assigning the actual parameter passed to the method as a new collection item. The assign() method copies the contents of the $president_master collection to the $president_copy collection. The getElem() method returns an element from the collection, and the assignElem() method replaces an *existing* element with a new value.

TIP
There is no mechanism to remove an element from the middle of a collection, and the assignElem() method cannot add new elements because it cannot add space to the collection.

The index values are different between OCI-Collection instances generated by calls to PL/SQL stored procedures and those that are built manually. Oracle constructs all collections with a *1-based* index, but using the append() method in a PHP program builds collections with a *0-based* index. While you should note the difference from a handling perspective, it does not present a problem. OCI8 alters the *0-based* index to a *1-based* index implicitly when you use the oci_bind_by_name() function. This implicit reindexing works bidirectionally.

Using NESTED TABLE Data Types

As mentioned, Oracle collections are defined by using Data Definition Language (DDL) to create user-defined types. The following types are created to support the NESTED TABLE collections in the overloaded GET_PRESIDENTS procedure:

```
-- This is found in create_world_leaders.sql on the enclosed CD.

-- Define a NESTED TABLE of NUMBER data types.
CREATE OR REPLACE TYPE president_id_ntable
  AS TABLE OF NUMBER;
/

-- Define three NESTED TABLE of VARCHAR2 data types of varying size.
CREATE OR REPLACE TYPE president_name_ntable
  AS TABLE OF VARCHAR2(60 CHAR);
/
CREATE OR REPLACE TYPE tenure_ntable
  AS TABLE OF VARCHAR2(9 CHAR);
/
CREATE OR REPLACE TYPE party_ntable
  AS TABLE OF VARCHAR2(24 CHAR);
/
```

As mentioned, Oracle collections are SQL data types. They can be used in defining columns in tables, parameters in PL/SQL procedures and functions, and function return types. These SQL data types are specific to the user/schema where they are created.

These types are created as tables, and tables have no maximum row limit and NESTED TABLES likewise have no maximum element limit. You use each collection data type for only one formal parameter in the overloaded GET_PRESIDENTS procedure as noted:

-- This is found in create_world_leaders.sql on the enclosed CD.

```
-- Implement a procedure body to return parallel nested tables.
PROCEDURE get_presidents
( term_start_in    IN     NUMBER
, term_end_in      IN     NUMBER
, country_in       IN     VARCHAR2
, president_ids    IN OUT PRESIDENT_ID_NTABLE
, president_names  IN OUT PRESIDENT_NAME_NTABLE
, tenures          IN OUT TENURE_NTABLE
, parties          IN OUT PARTY_NTABLE) AS
BEGIN

  SELECT   president_id pres_number
  ,        first_name||' '||middle_name||' '||last_name pres_name
  ,        term_start||'-'||term_end tenure
  ,        party
  BULK COLLECT
  INTO     president_ids
  ,        president_names
  ,        tenures
  ,        parties
  FROM     president
  WHERE    country = country_in
  AND      term_start BETWEEN term_start_in AND term_end_in
  OR       term_end BETWEEN term_start_in AND term_end_in;

END get_presidents;
```

The CollectionNestedTable.php program demonstrates how you use NESTED TABLE collections to retrieve parallel scalar arrays of information. The program uses the same type of BULK COLLECT operation described for associative arrays. BULK COLLECT operations build implicit cursors and read all return values INTO the target variables. The target variables are NESTED TABLE collections, which are densely populated arrays indexed by numbers starting at 1. When the SELECT statement returns null column values, they are also added to the respective array and indexed. All collections will have the same number of elements, and indexes in one collection identify the same row in another collection. Using this approach, you create four parallel NESTED TABLE structures. You can work these as compound structures by using the mirrored index values in a single iterative structure.

CollectionNestedTable.php also uses the strip_special_characters() function to eliminate tabs, line feeds, and carriage returns, and the same ternary parameter validation found the previous examples, as follows:

-- This is found in CollectionNestedTable.php on the enclosed CD.

```php
<?php
  // Return successful attempt to connect to the database.
  if ($c = @oci_connect("php","php","xe"))
```

```php
{
  // Declare input variables.
  (isset($_GET['begin']))   ? $t_start = (int) $_GET['begin']
                            : $t_start = 1787;
  (isset($_GET['end']))     ? $t_end = (int) $_GET['end']
                            : $t_end = (int) date("Y",time());
  (isset($_GET['country'])) ? $country = $_GET['country']
                            : $country = "USA";

  // Declare a PL/SQL execution command.
  $stmt = "BEGIN
            world_leaders.get_presidents(:t_start
                                        ,:t_end
                                        ,:country
                                        ,:r_president_id
                                        ,:r_president_name
                                        ,:r_tenure
                                        ,:r_party);

           END;";

  // Strip special characters to avoid ORA-06550 and PLS-00103 errors.
  $stmt = strip_special_characters($stmt);

  // Parse a query through the connection.
  $s = oci_parse($c,$stmt);

  // Define variables based on the Oracle VARRAY Collection type.
  $r_president_id = oci_new_collection($c,'PRESIDENT_ID_NTABLE');
  $r_president_name = oci_new_collection($c,'PRESIDENT_NAME_NTABLE');
  $r_tenure = oci_new_collection($c,'TENURE_NTABLE');
  $r_party = oci_new_collection($c,'PARTY_NTABLE');

  // Bind PHP variables to the OCI types.
  oci_bind_by_name($s,':t_start',$t_start);
  oci_bind_by_name($s,':t_end',$t_end);
  oci_bind_by_name($s,':country',$country);
  oci_bind_by_name($s,':r_president_id',$r_president_id,-1,SQLT_NTY);
  oci_bind_by_name($s,':r_president_name',$r_president_name,-1,SQLT_NTY);
  oci_bind_by_name($s,':r_tenure',$r_tenure,-1,SQLT_NTY);
  oci_bind_by_name($s,':r_party',$r_party,-1,SQLT_NTY);

  // Execute the PL/SQL statement.
  if (oci_execute($s))
  {
    // Declare variable and open HTML table.
    $out = '<table border="1" cellpadding="3" cellspacing="0">';
    $out .= '<tr>';
    $out .= '<td class="e">#</td>';
    $out .= '<td class="e">President Name</td>';
    $out .= '<td class="e">Tenure</td>';
    $out .= '<td class="e">Party</td>';
    $out .= '</tr>';
```

```
      // Read parallel collections.
      for ($i = 0;$i < $r_president_id->size();$i++)
      {
        $out .= '<tr>';
        $out .= '<td class="v">'.$r_president_id->getelem($i).'</td>';
        $out .= '<td class="v">'.$r_president_name->getElem($i).'</td>';
        $out .= '<td class="v">'.$r_tenure->getElem($i).'</td>';
        $out .= '<td class="v">'.$r_party->getElem($i).'</td>';
        $out .= '</tr>';
      }

      // Close HTML table.
      $out .= '</table>';
    }

    // Print the HTML table.
    print $out;

    // Disconnect from database.
    oci_close($c);
  }
  else
  {
    // Assign the OCI error and format double and single quotes.
    $errorMessage = oci_error();
    print htmlentities($errorMessage['message'])."<br />";
  }

  // Strip special characters, like carriage or line returns and tabs.
  function strip_special_characters($str)
  {
    $out = "";
    for ($i = 0;$i < strlen($str);$i++)
      if ((ord($str[$i]) != 9) && (ord($str[$i]) != 10) &&
          (ord($str[$i]) != 13))
        $out .= $str[$i];
    return $out;
  }
?>
```

The `CollectionNestedTable.php` program uses the `oci_new_collection()` function to define four collections. The collections are bound to the resource statement by using the `oci_bind_by_name()` function, which is the same function you use to bind scalar variables. You should note that using a `-1` value as the maximum element count lets you dynamically return as many elements as necessary, which is different than how the VARRAY data type works. Arrays typically require you to qualify a maximum physical size for the number of elements in the array.

You can use the `oci_bind_by_name()` for collections and scalar variables because collections and scalar variables are SQL data types, not PL/SQL structures. After executing the resource statement, you access the returned collection elements by using the OCI-Collection `getElem()` method for the collection instance.

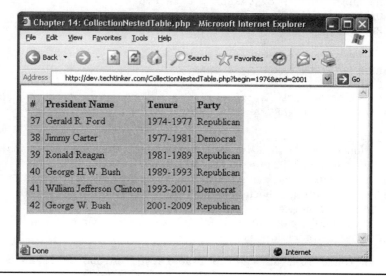

FIGURE 14-3. *CollectionNestedTable.php web page*

Substituting the hostname *(hn)* and domain name *(dn),* you can use the following URL to find presidents of the U.S.A. from 1976 to 2001:

```
http://<hn>.<dn>/NestedTable.php?begin=1976&end=2001
```

Other than a change in which presidents are displayed, you will get the same four columns as returned by the previous examples. Figure 14-3 contains the rendered output.

The CollectionNestedTable.php script has demonstrated how to retrieve an unlimited list into a defined OCI-Collection instance and access the elements. The program also demonstrates that you can work with structures if you treat them as parallel array groups.

Using VARRAY Data Types

VARRAY data types differ from NESTED TABLE data types in that you must know the maximum number of elements before using the variable type. Limiting yourself to a specific number of rows is a departure from general practices using database tables or the NESTED TABLE data type. However, there are occasions when you want to guarantee the number of rows returned, and VARRAY data types enable you to do that.

The following types are created to support the VARRAY collections in the overloaded GET_PRESIDENTS procedure:

```
-- This is found in create_world_leaders.sql on the enclosed CD.

-- Define a VARRAY of NUMBER data types.
CREATE OR REPLACE TYPE president_id_varray
  AS VARRAY(100) OF NUMBER;
/
```

```
-- Define three VARRAY of VARCHAR2 data types of varying size.
CREATE OR REPLACE TYPE president_name_varray
  AS VARRAY(100) OF VARCHAR2(60 CHAR);
/
CREATE OR REPLACE TYPE tenure_varray
  AS VARRAY(100) OF VARCHAR2(9 CHAR);
/
CREATE OR REPLACE TYPE party_varray
  AS VARRAY(100) OF VARCHAR2(24 CHAR);
/
```

As mentioned, Oracle VARRAYs are SQL data types. They can be used in defining columns in tables, parameters in PL/SQL procedures and functions, and function return types. These SQL data types are specific to the user/schema where they are created. The VARRAY collection differs from the NESTED TABLE collection in that you set a maximum element size. The maximum size is set to 100 in the examples.

You use each collection data type for only one formal parameter in the overloaded GET_PRESIDENTS procedure as noted:

-- **This is found in create_world_leaders.sql on the enclosed CD.**

```
-- Implement a procedure body to return parallel nested tables.
PROCEDURE get_presidents
( term_start_in    IN      NUMBER
, term_end_in      IN      NUMBER
, country_in       IN      VARCHAR2
, president_ids    IN OUT PRESIDENT_ID_VARRAY
, president_names  IN OUT PRESIDENT_NAME_VARRAY
, tenures          IN OUT TENURE_VARRAY
, parties          IN OUT PARTY_VARRAY) AS
BEGIN

  SELECT    president_id pres_number
  ,         first_name||' '||middle_name||' '||last_name pres_name
  ,         term_start||'-'||term_end tenure
  ,         party
  BULK COLLECT
  INTO      president_ids
  ,         president_names
  ,         tenures
  ,         parties
  FROM      president
  WHERE     country = country_in
  AND       term_start BETWEEN term_start_in AND term_end_in
  OR        term_end BETWEEN term_start_in AND term_end_in;

END get_presidents;
```

The CollectionVarray.php program demonstrates how you use VARRAY collections to retrieve parallel scalar arrays of information. The program uses the same type of BULK COLLECT operation described for associative arrays and NESTED TABLE collections. BULK COLLECT operations build implicit cursors and read all return values INTO the target variables. The target variables are VARRAY collections, which are densely populated arrays indexed by numbers starting at 1 and limited by the size value set during the DDL creation operation.

When the SELECT statement returns null column values, they are also added to the respective array and indexed. All collections will have the same number of elements and indexes in one collection that they have in all other collections. Using this approach, you create four parallel VARRAY structures. You can work these as compound structures by using the mirrored index values in a single iterative structure.

Only the oci_bind_by_name() function call changes between CollectionNestedTable .php and CollectionVarray.php. The fourth actual parameter must be equal to the maximum number of elements allowed in the VARRAY collection. *As mentioned earlier, these VARRAY types can have only 100 elements.*

These four lines differ between the two programs:

-- **This is found in CollectionVarray.php on the enclosed CD.**

```
oci_bind_by_name($s,':r_president_id',$r_president_id,100,SQLT_NTY);
oci_bind_by_name($s,':r_president_name',$r_president_name,100,SQLT_NTY);
oci_bind_by_name($s,':r_tenure',$r_tenure,100,SQLT_NTY);
oci_bind_by_name($s,':r_party',$r_party,100,SQLT_NTY);
```

There is no fixed rule for when you should use a VARRAY instead of a NESTED TABLE or vice versa in your PHP programs. Typically the casting limitation of VARRAY data types covered earlier in this chapter applies only to server-side stored procedures. It is a matter of programmer preference which collection data type you choose, but please remember a VARRAY locks you into a maximum value, whereas a NESTED TABLE does not.

Summary

The chapter has shown you how to use PL/SQL stored procedures in conjunction with your PHP programs. You have explored techniques in working with scalar, system reference cursor, and collection data types. The discussion has presented alternative approaches to accessing, querying, and transacting against the database using PL/SQL.

CHAPTER
15

Oracle Large
Object Transactions

his chapter examines how you can use Oracle Large Object (LOB) data types in your PHP web applications. There are two principal variations of LOB data type. They are *character* or *raw* file streams stored in the database, and *externally stored files*. You can store up to 4GB in LOB data types.

Character or *raw* file streams store in the database as one of three SQL data types: CLOB, NCLOB, and BLOB. CLOB and NCLOB data types store respectively *character* and *national Unicode character* LOB data, while BLOB stores raw binary data. The BLOB type can store raw structured or unstructured binary streams. Only the *descriptor* that points to the internal location of the LOB is physically stored *in-line* as the column value in a table.

LOB files stored externally from the database are known as binary files and are represented by the CFILE and BFILE data types. They can be anything from HTML web pages to image files. Only the locator that points to where the physical file is located is stored *in-line* as the column value in a table. The physical file system directory is defined as a DIRECTORY object in the database, and privileges are granted to individual user/schema accounts to read from that directory.

This chapter covers the following topics:

- Defining the OCI8 LOB functions and OCI-Lob object
- Using BLOB, CLOB, and NCLOB data types
- Using CFILE and BFILE data types

NOTE
The scripts in this chapter depend on your using Zend Core for Oracle and will not work with the generic PHP 5.1.4 libraries as of the time of writing.

The Oracle database stores LOB data types *out-of-line,* which means they are not part of the physical row structure of a table. The *in-line* LOB value is a *descriptor* or *locator,* which points to where you find the *out-of-line* data. This works like a foreign key to an internal database location for BLOB, CLOB, and NCLOB data types and is labeled typically as a *descriptor.* You can use *descriptors* to read and write large raw and text files.

The *in-line* CFILE and BFILE values, on the other hand, are known as *locators,* and they act like Unix symbolic links to external file system locations. You can *only read* externally referenced files by using the *locator.*

The addition of full regular expression matching in Oracle Database 10*g* Express Edition (or 10*g* Release 2 of the database) provides new searching mechanisms for character streams in CLOB, NCLOB, and BLOB data types. BFILE structures are effective tools for storing images, movies, and Portable Document Format (PDF) files.

Like Chapters 13 and 14, this chapter assumes you have a working understanding of the Oracle database environment, SQL, and PL/SQL. Primers are provided for these topics in Appendixes G, H, and I, respectively. You can also refer to the *Oracle Database Express Edition 2 Day Developer Guide 10*g *Release 2,* or for more specifics on LOB data types check the *Oracle Database Application Developer's Guide—Large Objects 10*g *Release 2.*

The *descriptor* is the *in-line* pointer to BLOB, CLOB, and NCLOB data types, and the *locator* is the *in-line* pointer to CFILE and BFILE data types. They are both really locators, although some documentation states otherwise, and using *descriptor* and *locator* helps people disambiguate their uses. These unofficial names for pointers are adopted in this chapter.

The SQL and PL/SQL base setup for Chapters 13 and 14 is augmented with additional Oracle database configuration steps to support LOB data types. You can review the foundation setup scripts in Appendix J, but the LOB configuration steps are covered in this chapter. You should read these sections sequentially, but at a minimum you should review the section "Defining the OCI8 LOB Functions and OCI-Lob Object" before working through the other two sections.

Defining the OCI8 LOB Functions and OCI-Lob Object

LOB and BFILE data types are highly specialized types in the Oracle database. Oracle uses the DBMS_LOB stored package to read and write to LOB data types when working inside a session and transaction scope. The constants, functions, and procedures of the DBMS_LOB package service requests from the OCI-Lob object provided in the OCI8 function library.

Chapters 13 and 14 cover most of the OCI8 library, with connection functions located in Table 13-2, operational functions in Table 13-3, and the OCI-Collection methods in Table 14-1. Two LOB-specific operational functions were left out of the prior coverage, and one merits repeating, the oci_new_descriptor() function. The three operational OCI8 library functions are summarized in Table 15-1.

Function	Description
oci_lob_copy()	The oci_lob_copy() function copies a large object, or part of a large object, to a new large object. It has three parameters; the first two are mandatory and the third is optional. The first parameter is a source object, and the second is a target object. The function copies the source object to the target object by using a *pass-by-value* model. It returns true when successful and false when it fails. The optional third parameter designates the maximum length of data to be copied from the source to the target large object. The function has the following pattern: oci_lob_copy(OCI-Lob *source_object* ,OCI-Lob *target_object* [,int *length*])
oci_lob_is_equal()	The oci_lob_is_equal() function compares a large object, or part of a large object, to another large object. It has two required parameters. Both parameters are objects for comparison. The function returns true when successful and false on any failure. You need two active *descriptors* to use this function. It has the following pattern: oci_lob_is_equal(OCI-Lob *object_1* ,OCI-Lob *object_2*)

TABLE 15-1. *OCI8 Function Library for Oracle Large Object (LOB) Data Types*

Function	Description

`oci_new_descriptor()`	The `oci_new_descriptor()` function creates a local PHP OCI-Lob object that maps to an Oracle LOB variable. It returns an OCI-Lob type variable on success and `false` when encountering an error. The function has two parameters; one is mandatory and the other is optional. The first parameter is a resource connection, and the second is an Oracle data resource type, which is conveniently `OCI_D_LOB` by default. (Note: LOB data types are treated as abstract types along with Oracle ROWID and FILE types.) The function supports the following resource types:
	
	`OCI_D_FILE` Sets the descriptor to manage binary or character files, respectively BFILE and CFILE data types.
	
	`OCI_D_LOB` Sets the descriptor to manage binary or character large objects, respectively BLOB and CLOB data types.
	
	`OCI_D_ROWID` Sets the descriptor to manage Oracle ROWID values, which map the physical storage to file system blocks.
	
	The function has the following pattern:
	
	`OCI-Lob oci_new_descriptor(`
	` resource connection`
	` [, int type])`

TABLE 15-1. *OCI8 Function Library for Oracle Large Object (LOB) Data Types* (continued)

The OCI8 `oci_lob_copy()` and `oci_lob_is_equal()` functions require you to acquire and hold a reference to the *descriptor* or *locator*. This means you *must override* the default OCI_COMMIT_ON_SUCCESS mode and use OCI_DEFAULT mode when using the `oci_execute()` function in conjunction with these two functions.

There are also limitations governing how you use *descriptors* and *locators* in SQL queries and transactions compared to anonymous and named block PL/SQL programs. The differences have to do with how they maintain references to *descriptors* or *locators* in the scope defined by the DBMS_LOB package. The DBMS_LOB package defines scope by imposing a single transaction rule, which limits both *descriptors* and *locators* to a scope that begins and ends in a single transaction.

You start a transaction against the database with an INSERT, UPDATE, or DELETE statement, or by using a SELECT statement with a FOR UPDATE or RETURNING *column_value* INTO *variable_name* clause. You end a transaction by using the COMMIT statement to make permanent any change to the data. The `oci_execute()` function starts and ends a transaction by default when executing a statement, which acts as an autonomous transaction. Autonomous transactions open and close a *descriptor* or *locator* reference before you can use the reference. Avoiding the default implicit COMMIT statement lets you use the `oci_execute()` function to interact sequentially with the database.

Oracle LOB data types are accessible through the OCI-Lob object. You must do three things to access and/or manipulate the contents of a LOB. They are: (a) you define a local descriptor variable by using the `oci_new_descriptor()` function; (b) you map the *descriptor* variable to a *bind* variable; and (c) you bind the local variable to the SQL or PL/SQL statement's *bind* variable. Then, you can use the local *descriptor* or *locator* variable name as a pointer to the instance of the OCI-Lob object and use the supplied methods summarized in Table 15-2.

Method	Description
append()	The append() method adds data to BLOB, CLOB, and NCLOB data types because CFILE and BFILE data types are *read-only*. It has one formal parameter, which is a source LOB that will be appended to the current instance of OCI-Lob. The append() method requires that buffering is disabled in the current connection. When buffering has been previously enabled during the transaction scope, you must call the setBuffering() and flush() methods before calling the append() method. The append() method returns true when successful and false when it encounters an error. It has the following pattern: bool append(OCI-Lob *from_lob*)
close()	The close() method releases resources allocated to write a temporary OCI-Lob instance. It has no formal parameter. The close() method should only be called by an object instance that previously called the writeTemporary() method. It returns true when successful and false when it encounters an error. It has the following pattern: bool close()
eof()	The eof() method tests whether it has reached the end of a LOB. It has no formal parameter and returns true when successful and false when encountering an error or a position that is not the end of the LOB. It has the following pattern: bool eof()
erase()	The erase() method lets you delete all or a portion of a BLOB, CLOB, or NCLOB data type because CFILE and BFILE data types are *read-only*. It has two optional parameters; one is an offset (starting point) and the other is the length to erase. The default value for the starting point is 1, and the default length is the size of the referenced LOB. The method returns the number of characters erased when successful and false on encountering an error. It has the following pattern: int erase([int *offset* [,int *length*]])
export()	The export() method writes a BLOB, CLOB, and NCLOB data type value to a physical file. It has three formal parameters; one is required and two are optional. The required parameter is a fully qualified filename. The first optional parameter is a starting point (or offset), and the other is the length of the LOB to export. The default value for the starting point is 1, and the default length is the size of the referenced LOB. The method returns true when successful and false on encountering an error. It has the following pattern: bool export(string *file_name* [,int *offset* [,int *length*]])
flush()	The flush() method purges an open buffer to the database server and opens a fresh buffer. It has one optional parameter that lets you free resources when you set OCI_LOB_BUFFER_FREE as its flag value. The method returns true when successful and false on encountering an error or when buffering is disabled. It is recommended that you *only* call the flush() method *after returning a true value from the getBuffering() method*. It has the following pattern: bool flush([int *flag*])
free()	The free() method releases resources previously allocated to a local PHP variable by calling the oci_new_descriptor() function. More or less, the free() method acts like the unset() function for a local *descriptor* variable. It returns true when successful and false on failure or when it encounters an error. It has the following pattern: bool free()
getBuffering()	The getBuffering() method checks to see if buffering is enabled for an instance of the OCI-Lob object. It returns true when buffering is enabled, and false when it is not enabled or it encounters an error. It has the following pattern: bool getBuffering()
import()	The import() method reads a physical file into a BLOB, CLOB, and NCLOB data type value. It has one formal parameter, which is a fully qualified filename. It returns true when successful and false when it encounters an error. It has the following pattern: bool import(string *file_name*)

TABLE 15-2. *OCI-Lob Methods*

Method	Description
load()	The load() method returns the entire contents of any LOB provided that it is smaller than the value specified in the memory_limit directive of the php.ini file. The default value is 8 MB. It has no formal parameter and returns a string when successful and false on encountering an error. It is recommended that you use the size() and read() method combination, and *not* the load() method. The load() method can exceed memory limitations and cause your application to fail. It has the following pattern: string load()
read()	The read() method writes a BLOB, CLOB, or NCLOB data type value to a string data type. It has one formal parameter, which is the length to read from the current position of the LOB pointer. Unless you have altered the default pointer by calling the seek() method, the default starting position is 1. It returns a string when successful and false on encountering any failure. It has the following pattern: string read(int *length*)
rewind()	The rewind() method moves the resource pointer to the beginning of the LOB. It has no formal parameter and returns true when successful and false on encountering any failure. It has the following pattern: bool rewind()
save()	The save() method *replaces* any contents of a large object or appends content to a large object. It has two formal parameters; one is mandatory and the other is optional. The required parameter is a string that is written into the BLOB, CLOB, or NCLOB data type. The optional value is an offset from the beginning of the LOB, which is 1 by default. The save() method returns true when successful and false when it encounters an error. It has the following pattern: bool save(string *data* [,int *offset*])
saveFile()	The saveFile() method is an *alias* to the import() method and reads a physical file into a BLOB, CLOB, or NCLOB data type value. It has one formal parameter, which is a fully qualified filename. It returns true when successful and false when encountering an error. It has the following pattern: bool saveFile(string *file_name*)
seek()	The seek() method moves the resource pointer to a position in the LOB. It has two formal parameters; one is mandatory and the other is an optional behavior flag. The required parameter is the number of characters to move. The optional flag sets the starting point and the forward or backward direction of movement. OCI_SEEK_SET Uses 1 as the starting point and increments the offset value forward from the start. OCI_SEEK_CUR Uses the current resource pointer location and increments the offset value forward from the start. OCI_SEEK_END Uses the end of the LOB as a starting point and decrements the offset value backward from the end. It returns true when successful and false on encountering an error. It has the following pattern: bool seek(int *offset* [,int *whence*])
setBuffering()	The setBuffering() method enables or disables buffering for an instance of the OCI-Lob object. It returns true when successful and false when encountering an error. It has the following pattern: bool setBuffering()
size()	The size() method finds the size of a LOB value in an instance of the OCI-Lob object. It returns the Integer size when successful and false when encountering an error. It has the following pattern: bool size()

TABLE 15-2. *OCI-Lob Methods* (continued)

Method	Description
tell()	The tell() method finds the location of the resource pointer in the LOB. It has no formal parameter and returns the int value of the pointer location in an LOB when successful or false when it encounters an error. It has the following pattern: int tell()
truncate()	The truncate() method *trims* an LOB completely or down to a specified value. The optional parameter designates where to start trimming. This function acts like the PHP rtrim() function covered in Appendix B. It returns true when successful and false on encountering an error. It has the following pattern: bool truncate([int *length*])
write()	The write() method *writes* new content into a large object. It has two formal parameters; one is mandatory and the other is optional. The required parameter is a string that is written into the BLOB, CLOB, or NCLOB data type. The optional parameter is the string length. The write() method returns the number of bytes written when successful and false otherwise. It has the following pattern: int write(string *data* [,int *length*])
writeTemporary()	The writeTemporary() method *creates* a new LOB variable and *writes* new content into it. It has two formal parameters; one is mandatory and the other is optional. The required parameter is a string that is written into the BLOB, CLOB, or NCLOB data type. The optional parameter is a flag type that sets the LOB as a BLOB or CLOB data type. The default type for the optional parameter is a CLOB data type. The following are the possible type values: OCI_TEMP_BLOB Writes a BLOB data type. OCI_TEMP_CLOB Writes a CLOB data type. The write() method returns true when successful and false otherwise. It has the following pattern: bool writeTemporary(string *data* [,int *type*])
writeToFile()	The writeToFile() method is an *alias* to the export() method, and writes a BLOB, CLOB, and NCLOB data type value to a physical file. It has three formal parameters, one is required and two are optional. The required parameter is a fully qualified file name. The optional parameters are a starting point (or offset) and the other is the length of the LOB to export. The default value for the starting point is 1, and the default length is the size of the referenced LOB. The method returns true when successful and false on encountering an error. It has the following pattern: bool writeToFile(string *file_name* [,int *offset* [,int *length*]])

TABLE 15-2.   *OCI-Lob Methods* (continued)

The subsequent sections use sample programs to demonstrate several of these OCI-Lob methods. Like object instances discussed in Chapter 8, the methods act on the contents of the OCI-Lob instances. Instances are identified by local variables that are bound by the oci_bind_by_name() function to *descriptor* or *locator* values. The contents are open resources that can be stored in other PHP variables bound to other BLOB, CLOB, and NCLOB column values in the database.

TIP
There is no way to instantiate a local OCI-Lob object instance, and you can only map them to descriptor or locator values in the database by calling the oci_execute() function.

NOTE
All OCI-Lob methods raise an error when the descriptor or locator values are invalid.

The section has covered the OCI8 LOB functions and OCI-Lob object. It has also reviewed the OCI-Lob methods. The next two sections examine how to use OCI-Lob instances in SQL and PL/SQL.

Using BLOB, CLOB, and NCLOB Data Types

This section uses CLOB values to demonstrate how to access and change LOB data types. The approaches to working with the CLOB data types map to BLOB and NCLOB data types because all three types work the same way. This section is divided into two parts:

- How to read CLOB columns
- How to update CLOB columns

Adding CLOB and BFILE columns to the PRESIDENT table extends the example from Chapters 13 and 14. You add the LOB columns by using the following statements:

```
-- This is found in alter_world_leaders.sql on the enclosed CD.

-- Add a CLOB column to the PRESIDENT table.
ALTER TABLE PRESIDENT ADD (biography CLOB);

-- Add a BFILE column to the PRESIDENT table.
ALTER TABLE PRESIDENT ADD (photograph BFILE);
```

After you run these statements or the alter_world_leaders.sql script (the latter is the preferred direction), you should describe the PRESIDENT table:

```
SQL> DESC[RIBE] president
```

The description should return the following PRESIDENT table definition:

```
Name                               Null?     Type
--------------------------------- --------- -----------------
PRESIDENT_ID                      NOT NULL  NUMBER
LAST_NAME                                   VARCHAR2(20 CHAR)
FIRST_NAME                                  VARCHAR2(20 CHAR)
MIDDLE_NAME                                 VARCHAR2(20 CHAR)
TERM_START                                  NUMBER
TERM_END                                    NUMBER
COUNTRY                                     VARCHAR2(3 CHAR)
PARTY                                       VARCHAR2(24 CHAR)
BIOGRAPHY                                   CLOB
PHOTOGRAPH                                  BINARY FILE LOB
```

Provided you find a PRESIDENT table, you should also find the BIOGRAPHY column as a CLOB data type, and the PHOTOGRAPH column as a BINARY FILE LOB data type, which is a BFILE data type. If you don't have the PRESIDENT table, you can run the create_world_leaders.sql script to create the table, as described in Chapter 13. The `alter_world_leaders.sql` script modifies the table and adds `CLOB` and `BFILE` columns. You should run the `alter_world_leaders.sql` script now, if you haven't already, because the examples depend on objects created and data inserted by it in your schema.

The two DML subsections use HTML forms to query and upload text files to the server. It draws on concepts introduced earlier in the book, like the upload example in Chapter 10. The text and images files on the enclosed CD support examples in this chapter, and you should save them to your hard disk.

The first subsection demonstrates how to read `CLOB` columns. The same techniques are then used to support the DML examples in the next section. You should consider reading these sequentially because the second subsection references material from the first one.

How to Read CLOB Columns

This section demonstrates how to populate sample data using PL/SQL, and then how to query and return it into a web page using PHP. You use the same approach for all LOB types, but when you read `BLOB` and `BFILE` variables this way, the information is not too useful.

All new column values are automatically null values when you add new columns to tables that contain existing rows. `BLOB`, `CLOB`, and `NCLOB` data types have three possible states, *null, empty,* and *populated.* You change a `CLOB` column value from a null to an empty value by updating the column value with an `EMPTY_CLOB()` function call. Moving it from an empty to a populated value requires you to use the `APPEND()`, `WRITE()`, or `WRITEAPPEND()` procedure found in the `DBMS_LOB` package.

The three possible states for `CLOB` descriptors requires conditional state testing. The sample programs contain valid logic to support testing for these possible state values. You can find more details about reading from and writing to LOB columns, and the null, empty, and populated states of `CLOB` variables, in the section "Using the DBMS_LOB Package" of Appendix I.

After adding the `CLOB` column to the `PRESIDENT` table, by running the `alter_world_leaders.sql` script, you can write to a `CLOB` column by calling the `ADD_BIOGRAPHY` procedure. The `BIOGRAPHY` column is placed in your schema by the same script. The program inserts a set of thumbnail biographical lines with three dots for et cetera for George Washington. An anonymous block PL/SQL program updates the `BIOGRAPHY` column, which is defined as a `CLOB` data type. This anonymous block program ran when you executed the `alter_world_leaders.sql` script earlier to add the `CLOB` and `BFILE` column types to the `PRESIDENT` table.

```
-- This is found in alter_world_leaders.sql on the enclosed CD.

DECLARE
   -- Define a local nested table collection.
   TYPE presidential_biography IS TABLE OF VARCHAR2(600);

   -- Define and initialize a NESTED TABLE.
   biography_in      BIOGRAPHY_TABLE := biography_table();
   biography_out     CLOB;
BEGIN
   -- Enable space.
   biography_in.EXTEND(10);
```

```
-- Add biography.
biography_in(1)   := 'On April 30, 1789, George Washington, ...<p />';
biography_in(2)   := 'Born in 1732 into a Virginia planter ...<p />';
biography_in(3)   := 'He pursued two intertwined interests: ...<p />';
biography_in(4)   := 'From 1759 to the outbreak of the American ...<p />';
biography_in(5)   := 'When the Second Continental Congress ...<p />';
biography_in(6)   := 'He realized early that the best strategy ...<p />';
biography_in(7)   := 'Washington longed to retire to his ...<p />';
biography_in(8)   := 'He did not infringe upon the policy making ...<p />';
biography_in(9)   := 'To his disappointment, two parties were ...<p />';
biography_in(10)  := 'Washington enjoyed less than three years ...<p />';

-- Add biography for one president.
add_biography(1,biography_in);
END;
/
```

The anonymous block program creates a NESTED TABLE data type manually, allocates space for ten rows, and calls the ADD_BIOGRAPHY stored procedure to write the NESTED TABLE contents into a CLOB column value. It demonstrates the concept of moving arrays of scalar variables into and out of CLOB variables.

The data inserted in the BIOGRAPHY column provides data for querying the CLOB column using PHP. The two subsections demonstrate how to query using SQL SELECT statements and PL/SQL stored procedures respectively.

Reading CLOB Columns Using SQL SELECT Statements

Five fetch operations support querying CLOB columns. They are the oci_fetch(), oci_fetch_array(), oci_fetch_assoc(), oci_fetch_object(), and oci_fetch_row() functions. This section demonstrates how to use each of these with a SQL SELECT statement to query CLOB columns in PHP programs.

The QueryLobSQL.php program demonstrates the easiest way to access a CLOB *descriptor,* by using the oci_fetch() function. The other fetching functions are demonstrated after the following QueryLobSQL.php program:

-- **This is found in QueryLobSQL.php on the enclosed CD.**

```php
<?php
  // Return successful attempt to connect to the database.
  if ($c = @oci_connect("php","php","xe"))
  {
    // Declare input variables.
    (isset($_GET['id'])) ? $id = (int) $_GET['id'] : $id = 1;
    (isset($_GET['name'])) ? $name = $_GET['name'] : $name = "Washington";

    // Declare a SQL SELECT statement returning a CLOB.
    $stmt = "SELECT    biography
             FROM      president
             WHERE     president_id = :id";

    // Parse a query through the connection.
    $s = oci_parse($c,$stmt);
```

```php
      // Bind PHP to OCI variable(s).
      oci_bind_by_name($s,':id',$id);

      // Execute the PL/SQL statement.
      if (oci_execute($s))
      {
        // Return a LOB descriptor, and access it with OCI methods.
        while (oci_fetch($s))
        {
          for ($i = 1;$i <= oci_num_fields($s);$i++)
            if (is_object(oci_result($s,$i)))
            {
              if ($size = oci_result($s,$i)->size())
                $data = oci_result($s,$i)->read($size);
              else
                $data = " ";
            }
            else
            {
              if (oci_field_is_null($s,$i))
                $data = " ";
              else
                $data = oci_result($s,$i);
            }
        } // End of the while(oci_fetch($s)) loop.

        // Format HTML table to display biography.
        $out = '<table border="1" cellpadding="3" cellspacing="0">';
        $out .= '<tr>';
        $out .= '<td align="center" class="e">Biography of '.$name.'</td>';
        $out .= '</tr>';
        $out .= '<tr>';
        $out .= '<td class="v">'.$data.'</td>';
        $out .= '</tr>';
        $out .= '</table>';
      }

      // Print the HTML table.
      print $out;

      // Disconnect from database.
      oci_close($c);
    }
    else
    {
      // Assign the OCI error and format double and single quotes.
      $errorMessage = oci_error();
      print htmlentities($errorMessage['message'])."<br />";
    }
?>
```

Using the `oci_fetch()` function in a `while` loop is clearly the most consistent and easiest approach for queries returning scalar and LOB column types from SQL statements and reference cursors. The algorithm provided loops through rows and then the columns while checking for objects and null values that require special handling. The logic shown in the program manages all possibilities because `CLOB` variables can be *null, empty,* and *populated* `CLOB` column values.

TIP
Don't attempt to skip the two-step process of sizing and reading by using the single-step `OCI-Lob->load()` method because you can run out of memory with truly large objects.

You can run this program by providing the following URL:

```
http://hostname.domain/QueryLobSQL.php?id=1&name=Washington
```

It is possible to dispense with the parameters because they're managed by ternary validation operators at the top of the script. The parameter validation statements assume by default that you are looking for the U.S. president who as a boy chopped down a cherry tree—George Washington. The results from the script are an excerpt from www.whitehouse.gov/history/presidents/, as are the rest of the biography and photographs used in this chapter.
The results of the preceding URL are shown in Figure 15-1.

NOTE
This is a much improved situation from the three states you must manage in the SQL*Plus environment, as covered in Appendix I.

There are several other approaches that have what may be considered less intuitive syntax. The first alternative uses the `oci_fetch_assoc()` function, which has the following syntax:

```
$array = oci_fetch_assoc($s);
$size = $array['BIOGRAPHY']->size();
$data = $array['BIOGRAPHY']->read($size);
```

The `oci_fetch_assoc()` function returns the *descriptor* as a value in an array indexed by column names. This is a moderately flexible way to return a `CLOB` value along with other column values. A close corollary to using the `oci_fetch_assoc()` function is the `oci_fetch_row()` function. The only difference between the two is that you use a numeric index value in lieu of the column name, like this:

```
$array = oci_fetch_row($s);
$size = $array[0]->size();
$data = $array[0]->read($size);
```

You should note the `oci_fetch_row()` function returns a *0-based* numeric index rather than a *1-based* numeric index, which is the general rule when working with database result sets.
The `oci_fetch_all()` function is handy because it automatically returns the `CLOB` as an array of strings. Specifically, it fetches an array indexed by column names, where *a CLOB variable is returned as a nested array of strings.* The index value for the array of strings is always a zero. You use the following syntax to access the return value from an `oci_fetch_all()` function:

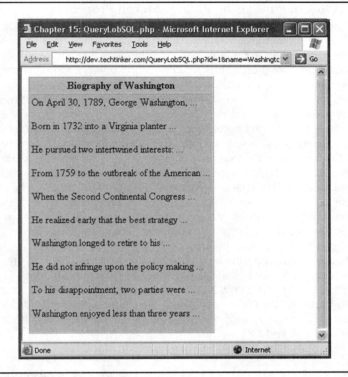

FIGURE 15-1. *Output from* `QueryLobSQL.php`

```
oci_fetch_all($s,$array);
$data = $array['BIOGRAPHY'][0];
```

The `oci_fetch_all()` function does not returns a `CLOB` descriptor. This behavior differs from the other fetching mechanisms and means you can't update the contents of the `CLOB` column value.

Another candidate for replacing the `oci_fetch()` function's simplicity is the `oci_fetch_object()` function, but it requires a bit more care and attention than you may find desirable. The `oci_fetch_object()` function returns the `CLOB` descriptor inside a `stdClass` object. You must know and explicitly use the column name as a method of the `stdClass` instance to gain access to the descriptor. Then, you can use the `size()` and `read()` methods to access the `CLOB` value, as shown:

```
$array = oci_fetch_object($s);
$size = $array->BIOGRAPHY->size();
$data = $array->BIOGRAPHY->read($size);
```

This section has demonstrated how to query and return LOB columns using a SQL `SELECT` statement. The next section demonstrates how to use a stored procedure to query a LOB column.

Reading CLOB Columns Using PL/SQL Stored Procedures

This section examines how you can query the CLOB columns using PL/SQL stored procedures. Traditional PL/SQL programming approaches must yield to the division of labor created by the OCI8 libraries. External programming language solutions, like PHP web applications, are distributed computing solutions. The OCI connection opens an RPC communication channel between the external program and the Oracle database server.

You begin an RPC transaction state when you call the oci_execute() function and pass it a PL/SQL statement that calls a stored procedure. *Unless you override the oci_execute() function's default OCI_COMMIT_ON_SUCCESS mode by substituting the OCI_DEFAULT mode, you terminate the transaction state immediately after calling the stored procedure.* When you override the default mode, a stored procedure can query the database with a SELECT statement that includes a FOR UPDATE clause. The procedure can then return the *descriptor* through a pass-by-reference parameter in the signature of the stored procedure. The returned descriptor becomes your OCI-Lob object instance. Through it, you have a direct channel to the database CLOB column value until an oci_commit() function is called to terminate the transaction. Transaction scope lives from the oci_execute() function call to the oci_commit() function call, unless there is a connection failure.

The first part of demonstrating how you use stored procedures is to create one. The alter_world_leaders.sql script creates a BIOGRAPHY package that contains three procedures. They are the READ_BIOGRAPHY, UPDATE_BIOGRAPHY, and VIEW_BIOGRAPHY procedures. The READ_BIOGRAPHY procedure supports this section, while the UPDATE_BIOGRAPHY supports the section "How to Update CLOB Columns," and the VIEW_BIOGRAPHY supports the section "Using CFILE and BFILE Data Types."

The relevant part of the BIOGRAPHY package body for this section is

```
-- This is found in alter_world_leaders.sql on the enclosed CD.

CREATE OR REPLACE PACKAGE BODY biography IS
  -- Read biography based on primary key value.
  PROCEDURE read_biography
  ( president_id_in IN     NUMBER
  , descriptor      IN OUT CLOB ) IS
  BEGIN
    -- A FOR UPDATE makes this a DML transaction.
    SELECT    biography INTO descriptor
    FROM      president
    WHERE     president_id = president_id_in
    FOR UPDATE;
  END read_biography;

  -- Update biography based on primary key value.
  PROCEDURE update_biography
  ( president_id_in IN     NUMBER
  , descriptor      IN OUT CLOB ) IS
  BEGIN
    ... shown later ...

  END update_biography;
```

```
-- Read biography based on primary key value.
PROCEDURE view_photograph
( president_id_in IN      NUMBER
, alias           IN OUT VARCHAR2
, file_name       IN OUT VARCHAR2 ) IS
BEGIN
  ... shown later ...
END view_photograph;
END biography;
/
```

The READ_BIOGRAPHY procedure takes two parameters. The first parameter maps to the primary key PRESIDENT_ID column of the PRESIDENT table, and it is passed by value.

A Nuance of Run-Time PL/SQL Parameters

There is an important detail about parameters in PL/SQL stored procedures that you need to understand. They are dynamic and have no size. Their size is inherited from the actual parameter sent to a stored procedure at run time. This can cause problems when formal parameters are VARCHAR2 *pass-by-reference* variables, entering as null values and exiting as meaningful values.

You solve this problem by sizing actual parameter inside anonymous block PL/SQL programs before they call the procedures. This sets their size before they enter the procedures and limits their return size. Likewise, you need to size SQLT_CHR type parameters in your PHP program before sending them to stored procedures, which differs from allowing their size to be implicitly derived by the oci_bind_by_name() function.

A quick example can illustrate this principle by calling the FILEGETNAME procedure in the DBMS_LOB package from a PHP program. It would use a PL/SQL statement like

```
$stmt = "BEGIN dbms_lob.filegetname(:descriptor,:alias,:f_name); END;";.
```

Since a descriptor is statically sized, you are only required to pre-size the :alias and :f_name *bind* variables as follows:

```
oci_bind_by_name($s,':descriptor',$descriptor,-1,SQLT_CLOB);
oci_bind_by_name($s,':alias',$alias,255,SQLT_CHR);
oci_bind_by_name($s,':f_name',$f_name,255,SQLT_CHR);
```

This oci_bind_by_name() function syntax using a -1 as maximum field length works for the :descriptor *bind* variable because the variable has a physical size on entry and is a *pass-by-value* actual parameter. The maximum field length is set to 255 for the :alias and :f_name *bind* variables because they're null values on entry and populated on exit, which makes them *pass-by-reference* actual parameters.

The potential problem arises when the exit value is greater than the predefined entry size. In this case, both are guaranteed to be no larger than 255 characters.

The second parameter maps to the BIOGRAPHY column of the PRESIDENT table, which is the CLOB column in the table, and the parameter is passed by reference. You get an outbound parameter value of a CLOB *descriptor* when calling the READ_BIOGRAPHY procedure.

The QueryLobPLSQL.php program demonstrates that you need to use all five phases of a statement to work with CLOB column values through PL/SQL. The five phases are: *parse, bind, define, execute,* and *fetch,* as described in Chapter 13.

You define a CLOB *descriptor* by using both the oci_new_descriptor() and oci_define_by_name() functions. The CLOB *descriptor* must be defined before you attempt to map the local and *bind* variables with the oci_bind_by_name() function, as shown in the program:

-- **This is found in QueryLobPLSQL.php on the enclosed CD.**

```php
<?php
  // Return successful attempt to connect to the database.
  if ($c = @oci_connect("php","php","xe"))
  {
    // Declare input variables.
    (isset($_GET['id'])) ? $id = (int) $_GET['id'] : $id = 1;
    (isset($_GET['name'])) ? $name = $_GET['name'] : $name = "Washington";

    // Declare a PL/SQL execution command.
    $stmt = "BEGIN
               biography.read_biography(:id,:biography);
             END;";

    // Strip special characters to avoid ORA-06550 and PLS-00103 errors.
    $stmt = strip_special_characters($stmt);

    // Parse a query through the connection.
    $s = oci_parse($c,$stmt);

    // Define a descriptor for a CLOB.
    $rlob = oci_new_descriptor($c,OCI_D_LOB);

    // Define a variable name to map to CLOB descriptor.
    oci_define_by_name($s,':biography',$rlob,SQLT_CLOB);

    // Bind PHP variables to the OCI types.
    oci_bind_by_name($s,':id',$id,-1,SQLT_INT);
    oci_bind_by_name($s,':biography',$rlob,-1,SQLT_CLOB);

    // Execute the PL/SQL statement.
    if (oci_execute($s,OCI_DEFAULT))
    {
      // Returns zero when CLOB is null or empty value.
      if ($size = @$rlob->size())
        $data = $rlob->read($size);
      else
        $data = " ";

      // End the transaction scope.
      oci_commit($c);
```

```
      // Format HTML table to display biography.
      $out = '<table border="1" cellpadding="3" cellspacing="0">';
      $out .= '<tr>';
      $out .= '<td align="center" class="e">Biography of '.$name.'</td>';
      $out .= '</tr>';
      $out .= '<tr>';
      $out .= '<td class="v">'.$data.'</td>';
      $out .= '</tr>';
      $out .= '</table>';
      $out .= '</table>';
    }

    // Print the HTML table.
    print $out;

    // Disconnect from database.
    oci_close($c);
  }
  else
  {
    // Assign the OCI error and format double and single quotes.
    $errorMessage = oci_error();
    print htmlentities($errorMessage['message'])."<br />";
  }

  // Strip special characters, like carriage or line returns and tabs.
  function strip_special_characters($str)
  {
    $out = "";
    for ($i = 0;$i < strlen($str);$i++)
      if ((ord($str[$i]) != 9) && (ord($str[$i]) != 10) &&
          (ord($str[$i]) != 13))
        $out .= $str[$i];

    // Return pre-parsed SQL statement.
    return $out;
  }
?>
```

The program uses an if statement to manage the three possible states of the CLOB descriptor, which are null, empty, and populated. The combination of the assignment, the error suppression operator, and the OCI-Lob->size() method as an expression in the if statement processes only populated CLOB variables as true. This occurs because

- Null CLOB value run-time errors are suppressed, and the suppressed call returns a false or zero value through the assignment to the $size variable.

- Empty CLOB values return a zero size to the $size variable.

- Populated CLOB values return a nonzero value through assignment to the $size variable, and a nonzero value is true under implicit evaluation rules covered in Chapter 5.

The conditional expression returns a HTML macro value for a white space when the CLOB is null or empty, and returns the CLOB value when populated. After reading the CLOB column variable, the transaction context is closed by the oci_commit() function call.

All activity managing the CLOB column value occurs in the transaction context, between the call to oci_connect() function using the OCI_DEFAULT mode, and the call to the oci_commit() function. The transaction context is the same area where you would change or remove data from the CLOB column value.

This section has demonstrated how to use a PL/SQL stored procedure to query a CLOB data type. It has also discussed the transaction context working with Oracle LOB data types. The next section will demonstrate how to update CLOB columns.

How to Update CLOB Columns

Inserting, updating, and deleting the contents of CLOB column values are similar processes. They have the same transaction context issue as querying data. The transaction context is between the calls to the oci_connect() and oci_commit() functions.

The update programs use several tools and techniques developed through the book to upload a biography text file, convert the file to a biography string, and update a presidential biography in a CLOB column with the string. The OCI-Lob->save() method writes the data to the CLOB column value.

The UploadBioSQLForm.htm is your entry form and begins the web application process. You should enter the values shown in Figure 15-2. After entering the president number and name, click the Browse button to find the WashingtonGeorge.txt file. Then, click the Upload button that calls the UploadBioSQL.php file.

```
-- This is found in UploadBioSQLForm.htm on the enclosed CD.

<form id="uploadForm"
      action=http://hostname.domain/UploadBioSQL.php
      enctype="multipart/form-data"
      method="post">
```

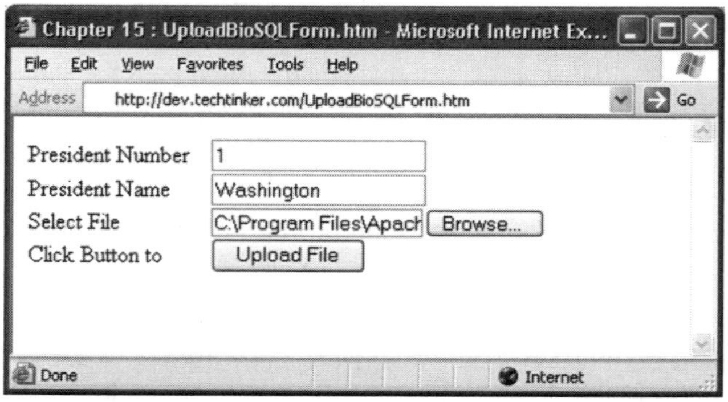

FIGURE 15-2. *UploadBioSQLForm.htm entry form*

```
<table border=0 cellpadding=0 cellspacing=0>
  <tr>
    <td width=125>President Number</td>
    <td><input id="id" name="id" type="text"></td>
  </tr>
  <tr>
    <td width=125>President Name</td>
    <td><input id="name" name="name" type="text"></td>
  </tr>
  <tr>
    <td width=125>Select File</td>
    <td><input id="uploadfilename" name="userfile" type="file"></td>
  </tr>
  <tr>
    <td width=125>Click Button to</td>
    <td><input type="submit" value="Upload File"></td>
  </tr>
</table>
</form>
```

NOTE
*You need to enter your hostname and domain into the action attribute
of the HTML FORM tag for this to work in your environment.*

After the entry form calls the UploadBioSQL.php program, it first calls the process_
uploaded_file() function. The function works the same way as the one demonstrated at the end
of Chapter 10. It gets the uploaded temporary file and moves it to the platform-dependent temporary
directory. Then, it opens the file and reads it into a string. The function returns the string assigned to
the $biography variable, which is shown in the following UploadBioSQL.php program file:

-- This is found in UploadBioSQL.php on the enclosed CD.

```php
<?php
  // Assign uploaded file contents to a string.
  $biography = process_uploaded_file();

  // Return successful attempt to connect to the database.
  if ($c = @oci_connect("php","php","xe"))
  {
    // Declare input variables.
    (isset($_POST['id'])) ? $id = (int) $_POST['id'] : $id = 1;
    (isset($_POST['name'])) ? $name = $_POST['name'] : $name = "Washington";

    // Declare a PL/SQL execution command.
    $stmt = "UPDATE    president
             SET       biography = empty_clob()
             WHERE     president_id = :id
             RETURNING biography
             INTO      :descriptor";
```

```php
  // Strip special characters to avoid ORA-06550 and PLS-00103 errors.
  $stmt = strip_special_characters($stmt);

  // Parse a query through the connection.
  $s = oci_parse($c,$stmt);

  // Define a descriptor for a CLOB.
  $rlob = oci_new_descriptor($c,OCI_D_LOB);

  // Define a variable name to map to CLOB descriptor.
  oci_define_by_name($s,':descriptor',$rlob,SQLT_CLOB);

  // Bind PHP variables to the OCI types.
  oci_bind_by_name($s,':id',$id);
  oci_bind_by_name($s,':descriptor',$rlob,-1,SQLT_CLOB);

  // Execute the PL/SQL statement.
  if (oci_execute($s,OCI_DEFAULT))
  {
    $rlob->save($biography);
    oci_commit($c);
    query_insert($id,$name);
  }

  // Disconnect from database.
  oci_close($c);
}
else
{
  // Assign the OCI error and format double and single quotes.
  $errorMessage = oci_error();
  print htmlentities($errorMessage['message'])."<br />";
}

// Query the updated record.
function query_insert($id,$name)
{
  // Return successful attempt to connect to the database.
  if ($c = @oci_new_connect("php","php","xe"))
  {
    // Declare a SQL SELECT statement returning a CLOB.
    $stmt = "SELECT    biography
             FROM      president
             WHERE     president_id = :id";

    // Parse a query through the connection.
    $s = oci_parse($c,$stmt);

    // Bind PHP variables to the OCI types.
    oci_bind_by_name($s,':id',$id);
```

```
    // Execute the PL/SQL statement.
    if (oci_execute($s))
    {
      // Return a LOB descriptor as the value.
      while (oci_fetch($s))
      {
        for ($i = 1;$i <= oci_num_fields($s);$i++)
          if (is_object(oci_result($s,$i)))
          {
            if ($size = oci_result($s,$i)->size())
              $data = oci_result($s,$i)->read($size);
            else
              $data = " ";
          }
          else
          {
            if (oci_field_is_null($s,$i))
              $data = " ";
            else
              $data = oci_result($s,$i);
          }
      } // End of the while(oci_fetch($s)) loop.

      // Format HTML table to display biography.
      $out = '<table border="1" cellpadding="3" cellspacing="0">';
      $out .= '<tr>';
      $out .= '<td align="center" class="e">Biography of '.$name.'</td>';
      $out .= '</tr>';
      $out .= '<tr>';
      $out .= '<td class="v">'.$data.'</td>';
      $out .= '</tr>';
      $out .= '</table>';
    }

    // Print the HTML table.
    print $out;

    // Disconnect from database.
    oci_close($c);
  }
  else
  {
    // Assign the OCI error and format double and single quotes.
    $errorMessage = oci_error();
    print htmlentities($errorMessage['message'])."<br />";
  }
}

// Manage file upload and return file as string.
function process_uploaded_file()
```

```
   {
     // Declare a variable for file contents.
     $contents = "";

     // Define the upload filename for Windows or Linux.
     if (ereg("Win32",$_SERVER["SERVER_SOFTWARE"]))
       $upload_file = getcwd()."\\temp\\".$_FILES['userfile']['name'];
     else
       $upload_file = getcwd()."/temp/".$_FILES['userfile']['name'];

     // Check for and move uploaded file.
     if (is_uploaded_file($_FILES['userfile']['tmp_name']))
       move_uploaded_file($_FILES['userfile']['tmp_name'],$upload_file);

     // Open a file handle and suppress an error for a missing file.
     if ($fp = @fopen($upload_file,"r"))
     {
       // Read until the end-of-file marker.
       while (!feof($fp))
         $contents .= fgetc($fp);

       // Close an open file handle.
       fclose($fp);
     }

     // Return file content as string.
     return $contents;
   }

   // Strip special characters, like carriage or line returns and tabs.
   function strip_special_characters($str)
   {
     $out = "";
     for ($i = 0;$i < strlen($str);$i++)
       if ((ord($str[$i]) != 9) && (ord($str[$i]) != 10) &&
           (ord($str[$i]) != 13))
         $out .= $str[$i];

     // Return pre-parsed SQL statement.
     return $out;
   }
?>
```

The $biography variable is assigned the contents of the uploaded file when the program calls the local process_uploaded_file() function. Then, the program calls the $rlob->save($biography) method to update the BIOGRAPHY column with the uploaded biography excerpt from the www.whitehouse.gov/history/presidents/ web site. Then, it closes the transaction context opened by the UPDATE statement by calling the oci_commit() function. After closing the transaction state, the program calls the local query_insert() function to display the uploaded biography. The new biography displayed in Figure 15-3 is more complete

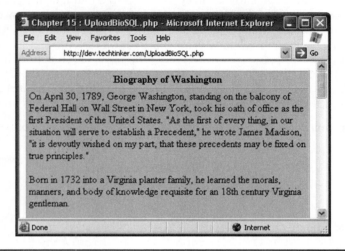

FIGURE 15-3. *UploadBioSQL.php result page*

than the thumbnail sketch loaded in the earlier section "Reading CLOB Columns using SQL SELECT Statements."

Changing the process to use a stored PL/SQL procedure is fairly simple. You replace the SQL UPDATE statement with a call to a PL/SQL stored procedure. The procedure uses an UPDATE statement and a RETURNING *column_name* INTO *variable_name* clause. This is where you use the UPDATE_BIOGRAPHY procedure from the BIOGRAPHY package introduced earlier in the chapter; here it is:

```
-- This is found in alter_world_leaders.sql on the enclosed CD.

CREATE OR REPLACE PACKAGE BODY biography IS

  ...
  -- Update biography based on primary key value.
  PROCEDURE update_biography
  ( president_id_in IN       NUMBER
  , descriptor      IN OUT CLOB ) IS
  BEGIN
    -- A FOR UPDATE makes this a DML transaction.
    UPDATE    president
    SET       biography = empty_clob()
    WHERE     president_id = president_id_in
    RETURNING biography INTO descriptor;
  END update_biography;

  ...
END biography;
/
```

This places an empty CLOB into the target column before returning the column value into the outgoing descriptor variable. You must use an UPDATE statement to avoid returning a null value as your descriptor, which is an invalid OCI-Lob instance handle. A SELECT statement with a FOR UPDATE clause only works with initialized CLOB columns.

The UploadBioPLSQLForm.htm entry form provides an action that calls the UploadBioPLSQL.php program. The other difference between the UploadBioSQL.php and UploadBioPLSQL.php programs is the $stmt variable. The UploadBioPLSQL.php calls an anonymous block shell that executes a stored procedure, as noted:

 -- This is found in UploadBioPLSQL.php on the enclosed CD.

```
$stmt = "BEGIN
            biography.update_biography(:id,:biography);
         END;";
```

NOTE
The OCI8 binding process does not support an NDS statement, such as EXECUTE IMMEDIATE biography.update_biography (:id,:biography).

The execution of the UploadBioPLSQLForm.htm and UploadBioPLSQL.php programs mirrors that done using only their SQL peers. They are found on the enclosed CD for your reference.

This section has demonstrated how to upload files, convert them to strings, and put them into CLOB columns. It has also demonstrated the behavior of DML transactions using the OCI-Lob->save() method.

The next section will explore how you work with BFILE column values and images stored externally from the database. You will see a number of similarities but a few differences.

Using CFILE and BFILE Data Types

The CFILE and BFILE data types work differently than their counterpart BLOB, CLOB, and NCLOB types. The largest differences are that they're read-only LOB data types and stored externally from the database. CFILE columns typically store character files, like static HTML pages. BFILE data types typically reference binary files, like image, Portable Document Format (PDF), and compressed files.

This section will examine the process of storing, referencing, and accessing BFILE column values containing images of U.S. presidents taken from the White House web site at www.whitehouse.gov/history/presidents/. You will find Graphics Interchange Format (GIF) and Joint Photographic Experts Group (JPG) images for the first 42 presidents on the enclosed CD. The current president is excluded because at the time of writing he didn't have a similar-sized photograph on the site.

This section is organized into four parts:

- Configuring the BFILE environment
- Querying a BFILE using SQL statements
- Querying a BFILE using PL/SQL statements
- Uploading BFILE physical files

You should read these sections sequentially, but at a minimum you'll need to review the section "Configuring the BFILE Environment" to set up your environment. As in other parts of the books, discussions reference earlier sections.

Configuring the BFILE Environment

You already covered how to add the BFILE column types to tables in the section "Using BLOB, CLOB, and NCLOB Data Types." The BFILE column name you will work with in this section is PHOTOGRAPH in the PRESIDENT table. Unlike CLOB data types that can be null, empty, or populated, BFILE columns are either null or not null. However, when the locator value fails to resolve to a fully qualified filename no file can be found.

The steps to configure your environment require you to (a) create an Oracle DIRECTORY reference, (b) create an Apache virtual alias and directory, (c) update the PHOTOGRAPH column with a BFILE locator, and (d) copy the physical file into the mapped directory. After completing these steps, you can confirm the setup with a single query using the DBMS_LOB.GETLENGTH() function.

Creating a DIRECTORY Reference

BFILE data types require you to configure a DIRECTORY reference in the database that points to a physical directory where you will store the files. You can create a customized directory for these examples by running the create_bfile_directory.sql script. The script builds a DIRECTORY reference named MY_DIRECTORY, as shown:

```
CREATE DIRECTORY my_directory AS
'C:\Program Files\Apache Group\Apache2\htdocs\photo';
```

> **NOTE**
> *Linux users will need to edit the create_bfile_directory.sql*
> *script to substitute their directory name.*

After running the script, you need to create the physical directory to support the MY_DIRECTORY reference. By design, the scripts in this chapter depend on the DIRECTORY reference pointing to a physical photo subdirectory in the directory where you are testing the PHP programs. It is assumed that you are testing in the directory pointed to by the Apache DocumentRoot directive value.

You can verify if the DIRECTORY reference has been created in the database by running the following SELECT statement as the SYSTEM user:

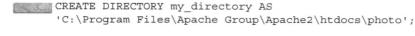
-- **This is found in create_bfile_directory.sql on the enclosed CD.**

```
SELECT    owner
,         directory_name
,         directory_path
FROM      dba_directories
WHERE     directory_name = 'MY_DIRECTORY';
```

If the query fails to find the directory, rerun the create_bfile_directory.sql script before proceeding, and make sure you create the directory with the right permissions. The output from the script should report the following on the respective platforms, assuming a default Apache 2.0.x installation.

Linux:

```
OWNER   DIRECTORY_NAME DIRECTORY_PATH
------  -------------- ---------------------------------------------------------
SYS     MY_DIRECTORY   /var/www/html/photo
```

Windows:

```
OWNER   DIRECTORY_NAME DIRECTORY_PATH
------  -------------- ---------------------------------------------------------
SYS     MY_DIRECTORY   C:\program files\apache group\apache2\htdocs\photo
```

As shown, the DIRECTORY owner is the privileged SYS user. You use a DDL GRANT statement to grant READ privilege to your PHP schema as the SYSTEM user. This lets the PHP user read from the directory. The following command grants the READ privilege to the PHP user/schema:

```
GRANT READ ON my_directory TO php;
```

Creating an Apache Virtual Alias and Directory

There is one Apache configuration step required to use this new directory in your web pages. You need to configure an alias and directory in your httpd.conf file, as follows for your respective platform.

Linux:

```
Alias /mydirectory/ "/var/www/html/photo/"

<Directory "/var/www/html/photo">
   Options None
   AllowOverride None
   Order allow,deny
   Allow from all
</Directory>
```

Windows:

```
Alias /mydirectory/ "C:/Program Files/Apache Group/Apache2/htdocs/photo/"

<Directory "C:/Program Files/Apache Group/Apache2/htdocs/photo">
   Options None
   AllowOverride None
   Order allow,deny
   Allow from all
</Directory>
```

Updating the PHOTOGRAPH Column with a BFILE Locator

You need to insert a BFILE *locator* into the PHOTOGRAPH column of the PRESIDENT table for the George Washington row. This step should already have been completed when you ran the alter_world_leaders.sql script earlier. That script contains the following UPDATE statement to set the BFILE *locator*:

-- This is found in alter_world_leaders.sql on the enclosed CD.

```
UPDATE president
SET photograph = BFILENAME('MY_DIRECTORY','Washington.gif')
WHERE president_id = 1;
```

The UPDATE statement uses the BFILENAME() function to insert a BFILE locator into the column value. The BFILENAME() function has two parameters, the first is a DIRECTORY reference and the second is a physical filename.

Copy the Physical File into the Mapped Directory

After updating the column value and copying the WashingtonGeorge.gif file into the designated directory, you can test your Oracle configuration by running the following query from the PHP schema:

```
SELECT    dbms_lob.getlength(photograph) AS bfile_size
FROM      president
WHERE     president_id = 1
```

It should return the following:

```
BFILE_SIZE
----------
     32474
```

The physical size of the external file is not stored internally in the database. The call to the GETLENGTH() function of the DBMS_LOB package uses the locator value and DIRECTORY reference to find the physical file and get its size through an operating system call.

This section has set up the BFILE environment and confirmed that it is working. The next section demonstrates how to query and display BFILE images in your PHP web applications.

Querying a BFILE Using SQL Statements

Querying a BFILE name requires calling the FILEGETNAME procedure of the DBMS_LOB package, and mapping the directory alias to a filename. This can lead some to say that you can't use SQL to navigate the BFILE locator. There are actually several alternative approaches to supplementing the default Oracle database environment. The easiest way is to write a wrapper function over the DBMS_LOB.FILEGETNAME procedure.

The GET_BFILENAME() function creates an effective wrapper to the DBMS_LOB.FILEGETNAME procedure, as

-- This is found in get_bfilename.sql on the enclosed CD.

```
CREATE OR REPLACE FUNCTION get_bfilename
( president_id_in IN     NUMBER )
RETURN VARCHAR2 IS
  -- Define a locator.
  locator              BFILE;

  -- Define alias and filename.
  dir_alias            VARCHAR2(255);
```

```
directory            VARCHAR2(255);
file_name            VARCHAR2(255);

-- Define a local exception for size violation.
directory_num EXCEPTION;
PRAGMA EXCEPTION_INIT(directory_num,-22285);
BEGIN
  -- A FOR UPDATE makes this a DML transaction.
  FOR i IN (SELECT    photograph
            FROM      president
            WHERE     president_id = president_id_in) LOOP
    locator := i.photograph;
  END LOOP;

  -- Check for available locator.
  IF locator IS NOT NULL THEN
    dbms_lob.filegetname(locator,dir_alias,file_name);
  END IF;

  -- Return filename.
  RETURN file_name;
EXCEPTION
  WHEN directory_num THEN
  RETURN NULL;
END get_bfilename;
/
```

You can test the GET_BFILENAME() function by running the following SQL statement against the DUAL pseudo-table, which will return a filename:

```
SELECT    get_bfilename(1) AS file_name
FROM      dual;
```

The script outputs

```
FILE_NAME
------------------------------------------------------------
WashingtonGeorge.gif
```

Having created and tested a wrapper function to the DBMS_LOB.GETFILENAME procedure, you can now write a simpler PHP file to render an image file. This approach is documented in the QueryPhotoSQL.php program, which is

```
-- This is found in QueryPhotoSQL.php on the enclosed CD.
```

```php
<?php
  // Return successful attempt to connect to the database.
  if ($c = @oci_connect("php","php","xe"))
  {
    // Declare input variables.
    (isset($_GET['id'])) ? $id = (int) $_GET['id'] : $id = 1;
    (isset($_GET['name'])) ? $name = $_GET['name'] : $name = "Washington";
```

```
        // Declare a PL/SQL execution command.
        $stmt = "SELECT    GET_BFILENAME(president_id) AS file_name
                 FROM      president
                 WHERE     president_id = :id";

        // Parse a query through the connection.
        $s = oci_parse($c,$stmt);

        // Bind PHP variables to the OCI types.
        oci_bind_by_name($s,':id',$id,-1,SQLT_INT);

        // Execute the PL/SQL statement.
        if (oci_execute($s))
        {
          // Return a LOB descriptor as the value.
          while (oci_fetch($s))
          {
            for ($i = 1;$i <= oci_num_fields($s);$i++)
              $file_name = oci_result($s,$i);
          } // End of the while(oci_fetch($s)) loop.

          // Format HTML table to display photograph.
          $out = '<table border="1" cellpadding="3" cellspacing="0">';
          $out .= '<tr>';
          $out .= '<td align="center" class="e">Photo of '.$name.'</td>';
          $out .= '</tr>';
          $out .= '<tr>';
          $out .= '<td align="center" class="v" valign="center">';
          if (!is_null($file_name))
            $out .= '<img src="/mydirectory/'.$file_name.'">';
          else
            $out .= 'No available photo';
          $out .= '</td>';
          $out .= '</tr>';
          $out .= '</table>';
        }

        // Print the HTML table.
        print $out;

        // Disconnect from database.
        oci_close($c);
      }
      else
      {
        // Assign the OCI error and format double and single quotes.
        $errorMessage = oci_error();
        print htmlentities($errorMessage['message'])."<br />";
      }
    ?>
```

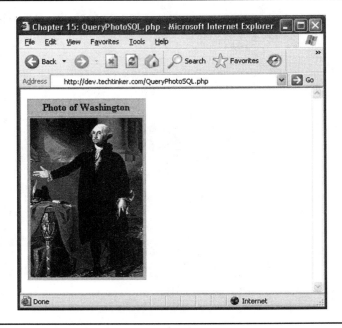

FIGURE 15-4. *QueryPhotoPLSQL.php result page*

The SQL SELECT statement calls the GET_BFILENAME function and returns the filename to a SQL statement. The DIRECTORY reference for the image is managed in the program as a relative reference to the script's current directory. This outputs the page shown in Figure 15-4.

This section has demonstrated how to query a BFILE object using a SQL SELECT statement. The processing is artificial to the generic rules governing the use of the DBMS_LOB.GETFILENAME procedure because you have wrapped the procedure in a function. Stored functions, unlike procedures, can be called in the SELECT clause of a SQL statement. You have now seen that using a wrapper like GET_BFILENAME makes using Oracle built-in packages quite easy. The next section demonstrates how to build a complete solution using PL/SQL.

Querying a BFILE Using PL/SQL Statements

It is the desire of many programmers and businesses to simplify web application development. Writing business rules into stored functions, procedures, and packages in PL/SQL helps you do that. It requires better planning and coordination, but as you've seen in the preceding section, a small wrapper simplified how the PHP program could access the image.

This section uses the VIEW_PHOTOGRAPH procedure in the BIOGRAPHY package. The VIEW_PHOTOGRAPH procedure hides some of the complexity required to access the filename, such as the GET_BFILENAME() function presented in the last section. There are many alternatives to using wrappers. One alternative is writing anonymous block PL/SQL programs into your PHP scripts. Typically, writing PL/SQL anonymous block programs in web pages is not a better choice than writing a stored function, procedure, or package.

NOTE
Anonymous block PL/SQL programs, like SQL statements, generally proliferate with slight variations that cause multiple copies to be stored in the Oracle Shared Global Area (SGA). Stored programs typically eliminate useless variations, make better use of the cache, and improve database performance.

The `VIEW_PHOTOGRAPH` procedure hides type definition, error handling, cursor execution, null validation, and a built-in procedure call. The PHP anonymous block is a single line of code because of the wrapper procedure. The implementation of the `VIEW_PHOTOGRAPH` follows:

```
-- This is found in alter_world_leaders.sql on the enclosed CD.

CREATE OR REPLACE PACKAGE BODY biography IS

  ...
  -- Read biography based on primary key value.
  PROCEDURE view_photograph
  ( president_id_in IN      NUMBER
  , alias           IN OUT VARCHAR2
  , file_name       IN OUT VARCHAR2 ) IS

    -- Define local variables.
    descriptor BFILE;
    directory_num EXCEPTION;
    PRAGMA EXCEPTION_INIT(directory_num,-22285);
  BEGIN
    -- A FOR UPDATE makes this a DML transaction.
    SELECT     photograph
    INTO       descriptor
    FROM       president
    WHERE      president_id = president_id_in
    FOR UPDATE;

    IF descriptor IS NOT NULL THEN
      dbms_lob.filegetname(descriptor,alias,file_name);
    END IF;
  EXCEPTION
    WHEN directory_num THEN
    RETURN;
  END view_photograph; END biography;
/
```

The if statement checks the descriptor to make sure it is not null before calling the `DBMS_LOB.FILEGETNAME()` function. This avoids a different type of raised exception, which is currently unhandled in the exception block. When an error occurs, the `VIEW_PHOTOGRAPH` simply returns null values for the alias and the filename to the caller.

The QueryPhotoPLSQL.php program calls the VIEW_PHOTOGRAPH procedure in the $stmt variable. The program renders an image when one is found and a text message when the filename is null. The code follows:

-- **This is found in QueryPhotoPLSQL.php on the enclosed CD.**

```php
<?php
  // Return successful attempt to connect to the database.
  if ($c = @oci_connect("php","php","xe"))
  {
    // Declare input variables.
    (isset($_GET['id'])) ? $id = (int) $_GET['id'] : $id = 1;
    (isset($_GET['name'])) ? $name = $_GET['name'] : $name = "Washington";

    // Declare a PL/SQL execution command.
    $stmt = "BEGIN biography.view_photograph(:id,:alias,:f_name); END;";

    // Parse a query through the connection.
    $s = oci_parse($c,$stmt);

    // Bind PHP variables to the OCI types.
    oci_bind_by_name($s,':id',$id,-1,SQLT_INT);

    // Set OUT mode procedure variables physical run-time size.
    // Avoids an ORA-21560: argument 2 is null, invalid, or out of range
    oci_bind_by_name($s,':alias',$alias,255,SQLT_CHR);
    oci_bind_by_name($s,':f_name',$f_name,255,SQLT_CHR);

    // Execute the PL/SQL statement.
    if (oci_execute($s,OCI_DEFAULT))
    {
      // Format HTML table to display photograph.
      $out = '<table border="1" cellpadding="3" cellspacing="0">';
      $out .= '<tr>';
      $out .= '<td align="center" class="e">Photo of '.$name.'</td>';
      $out .= '</tr>';
      $out .= '<tr>';
      $out .= '<td align="center" class="v" valign="center">';
      if (!is_null($f_name))
        $out .= '<img src="/mydirectory/'.$f_name.'">';
      else
        $out .= 'No available photo';
      $out .= '</td>';
      $out .= '</tr>';
      $out .= '</table>';
    }

    // Print the HTML table.
    print $out;
```

```
      // Disconnect from database.
      oci_close($c);
    }
    else
    {
      // Assign the OCI error and format double and single quotes.
      $errorMessage = oci_error();
      print htmlentities($errorMessage['message'])."<br />";
    }
?>
```

The call to the VIEW_PHOTOGRAPH wrapper does not eliminate the possibility of returning a failure due to invalid run-time parameter size. This is covered earlier in the chapter in the sidebar "A Nuance of Run-Time PL/SQL Parameters." This program does not rely on the implicit size for the :alias and :f_name *bind* variables. This program returns the same image as that displayed in preceding Figure 15-4.

This section has demonstrated how to use PL/SQL to access BFILE images. It has also demonstrated using a procedure wrapper around the DBMS_LOB built-in package.

Uploading BFILE Physical Files

Uploading BFILE images works very similarly to the process of uploading text biographies. However, when you upload the files, you do not copy them to a temporary directory where you read the contents and load them into the CLOB column value. The image files must be placed in your virtual directory.

The UploadPhotoSQLForm.htm contains the same code as the earlier examples used to upload CLOB biographies. Only the action attribute changes to point to the UploadPhotoSQL .php program, as qualified:

-- **This is found in UploadPhotoSQL.htm on the enclosed CD.**

```
<form id="uploadForm"
      action=http://hostname.domain/UploadPhotoSQL.php
      enctype="multipart/form-data"
      method="post">
  <table border=0 cellpadding=0 cellspacing=0>
    <tr>
      <td width=125>President Number</td>
      <td><input id="id" name="id" type="text"></td>
    </tr>
    <tr>
      <td width=125>President Name</td>
      <td><input id="name" name="name" type="text"></td>
    </tr>
    <tr>
      <td width=125>Select File</td>
      <td><input id="uploadfilename" name="userfile" type="file"></td>
    </tr>
    <tr>
```

```
        <td width=125>Click Button to</td>
        <td><input type="submit" value="Upload File"></td>
      </tr>
    </table>
  </form>
```

The form works the same way as the others, provided you updated the action attribute in the HTML FORM tag to point to your web site. You must ensure that you have the right primary key value before uploading an image file. The UploadPhotoSQL.php program puts the files in a physical photo subdirectory of the directory where you are testing the PHP programs. It is assumed that you are testing in the directory pointed to by the Apache DocumentRoot directive value.

The following is the UploadPhotoSQL.php code:

-- **This is found in UploadPhotoSQL.php on the enclosed CD.**

```php
<?php
  // Assign the photograph file name.
  $f_name = process_uploaded_file();

  // Return successful attempt to connect to the database.
  if ($c = @oci_connect("php","php","xe"))
  {
    // Declare input variables.
    (isset($_POST['id'])) ? $id = (int) $_POST['id'] : $id = 1;
    (isset($_POST['name'])) ? $name = $_POST['name'] : $name = "Washington";

    // Declare a PL/SQL execution command.
    $stmt = "UPDATE    president
             SET       photograph = BFILENAME('MY_DIRECTORY',:f_name)
             WHERE     president_id = :id";

    // Strip special characters to avoid ORA-06550 and PLS-00103 errors.
    $stmt = strip_special_characters($stmt);

    // Parse a query through the connection.
    $s = oci_parse($c,$stmt);

    // Bind PHP variables to the OCI types.
    oci_bind_by_name($s,':id',$id);
    oci_bind_by_name($s,':f_name',$f_name);

    // Execute the PL/SQL statement.
    if (oci_execute($s))
       query_insert($id,$name);

    // Disconnect from database.
    oci_close($c);
  }
  else
```

```php
{
  // Assign the OCI error and format double and single quotes.
  $errorMessage = oci_error();
  print htmlentities($errorMessage['message'])."<br />";
}

// Query results after an insert.
function query_insert($id,$name)
{
  // Return successful attempt to connect to the database.
  if ($c = @oci_new_connect("php","php","xe"))
  {
    // Declare a PL/SQL execution command.
    $stmt = "BEGIN biography.view_photograph(:id,:alias,:f_name); END;";

    // Parse a query through the connection.
    $s = oci_parse($c,$stmt);

    // Define a descriptor for a CLOB.
    //$rlob = oci_new_descriptor($c,OCI_D_FILE);

    // Bind PHP variables to the OCI types.
    oci_bind_by_name($s,':id',$id,-1,SQLT_INT);

    // Set OUT mode procedure variables physical run-time size.
    // Avoids an ORA-21560: argument 2 is null, invalid, or out of range
    oci_bind_by_name($s,':alias',$alias,255,SQLT_CHR);
    oci_bind_by_name($s,':f_name',$f_name,255,SQLT_CHR);

    // Execute the PL/SQL statement.
    if (oci_execute($s,OCI_DEFAULT))
    {
      // Format HTML table to display photograph.
      $out = '<table border="1" cellpadding="3" cellspacing="0">';
      $out .= '<tr>';
      $out .= '<td align="center" class="e">Photo of '.$name.'</td>';
      $out .= '</tr>';
      $out .= '<tr>';
      $out .= '<td align="center" class="v" valign="center">';
      if (!is_null($f_name))
        $out .= '<img src="/mydirectory/'.$f_name.'">';
      else
        $out .= 'No available photo';
      $out .= '</td>';
      $out .= '</tr>';
      $out .= '</table>';
    }

    // Print the HTML table.
    print $out;
```

```php
      // Disconnect from database.
      oci_close($c);
    }
    else
    {
      // Assign the OCI error and format double and single quotes.
      $errorMessage = oci_error();
      print htmlentities($errorMessage['message'])."<br />";
    }
  }

  // Manage file upload and return file as string.
  function process_uploaded_file()
  {
    // Declare a variable for file contents.
    $contents = "";

    // Define the upload filename for Windows or Linux.
    if (ereg("Win32",$_SERVER["SERVER_SOFTWARE"]))
      $upload_file = getcwd()."\\photo\\".$_FILES['userfile']['name'];
    else
      $upload_file = getcwd()."/photo/".$_FILES['userfile']['name'];

    // Check for and move uploaded file.
    if (is_uploaded_file($_FILES['userfile']['tmp_name']))
      move_uploaded_file($_FILES['userfile']['tmp_name'],$upload_file);

    return $filename = basename($upload_file);
  }

  // Strip special characters, like carriage or line returns and tabs.
  function strip_special_characters($str)
  {
    $out = "";
    for ($i = 0;$i < strlen($str);$i++)
      if ((ord($str[$i]) != 9) && (ord($str[$i]) != 10) &&
          (ord($str[$i]) != 13))
        $out .= $str[$i];

    // Return pre-parsed SQL statement.
    return $out;
  }
?>
```

The important detail in the UploadPhotoSQL.php program is the dynamic selection of the subdirectory based on the operating system. The details behind this functionality are covered in Chapter 10.

This section has demonstrated how to read and write BFILE column values. It has also demonstrated how to configure and verify the configuration of your test machine.

Summary

The chapter has shown you how to use Oracle LOB data types in with your PHP programs. You have worked with creating, defining, populating, and accessing LOB column values, and with configuring the Apache HTTP server to work with external binary image files. You have also explored techniques working with these data types, using both SQL and PL/SQL approaches to read and write CLOB and read BFILE column values.

PART
V

Appendixes

APPENDIX
A

HTML Tag Index

ypertext Markup Language (HTML) tags designate behaviors or format contents in your web pages. HTML tags are embedded tags. Embedded tags do not render in documents. An HTML browser treats a set of *reserved words enclosed between less-than and greater-than symbols as tags.* That is why you must use the `&gt;` and `&lt;` macros to render a greater-than or less-than symbol in a browser.

There are many more macros provided for otherwise reserved characters, such as `&amp;` for an ampersand or ` ` for a white space. Macros start by using an ampersand and end with a semicolon. Some browsers will let you enter a macro without the semicolon, but others won't. As in other environments, slight deviations from definitions can cause negative outcomes, and it is recommended that you follow the syntax definitions carefully to ensure cross-browser support.

Browsers ignore carriage returns and line feeds, `\r` and `\n`. They also ignore tabs, `\t`, and treat white space as single when you have multiple spaces. You use the ` ` macro when you want more than one white space together. This is why HTML provides the break tag, `<br />`, to let you control where line breaks should appear in your web page displays.

Browsers process embedded tags by looking for the starting and ending tags, which contain keywords. Starting tags contain only a keyword, while ending tags contain both a forward slash and a keyword. You enclose a word in starting and ending tags to render the word bolded, like the following:

```
<b>bold_word</b>
```

Some keywords historically had no closing tag, like `<br>`, `<hr>`, `<link>`, `<meta>`, and `<p>`. XHTML standards have changed that convention, and these tags now support two syntax forms, one to be backward compatible and the other to comply with XHTML standards. The XHTML standard works very much like the Extensible Markup Language (XML), which requires a closing tag in all cases. While HTML tags are case insensitive, XHTML tags are case sensitive like the XML tags, and both tags and attribute names are represented in lowercase text. XHTML attempts to fulfill all requirements in the HTML 4.01 standard.

XHTML-compliant paragraph breaks should now be represented as `<p />`, whereas they were once simply `<p>` in your documents. Table A-1 describes some basic tags used for examples in this book, but it is not a comprehensive guide to HTML or XHTML tags. You should check the HTML home page—www.w3.org/MarkUp/—for a comprehensive treatment of these tags.

Tag Name	Description
`<!--...-->`	This tag identifies a comment. Text within the comment tags is not printed in the browser. Example: `<!-- Text not displayed in browser -->`
`<a>...</a>`	This tag defines an anchor within documents. An anchor is used to link to another document or serves as a label in a document. You use the attributes to specify the purpose of an anchor tag. Attributes: ■ `href=url` Specifies a relative or absolute path to a document or a client-side scripting function. The former is captured by the HTTPD listener virtual directory, and the latter, by a document event listener.

TABLE A-1. *HTML Basic Tag Resource*

Tag Name	Description
	■ `name=text` Assigns a name locator.
	■ `tabindex=number` Specifies the tab order of the current link with a number between 0 and 32,767.
	■ `target=text` Specifies the name of the window or frame in which the document opens.
	Examples:
	■ A relative local file reference: `<a href="fname.pdf">...</a>`
	■ An absolute local file reference: `<a href="C:\data\fname.pdf">...</a>`
	■ A virtual HTTP listener reference, where *hn* is the hostname and *dn* is the domain name: `<a href="http://hn.dn/fname.htm">...</a>`
	■ A relative locator in a local file reference: `<a href="fname.pdf#anchor_name">...</a>`
	■ A named label: `<a name="anchor_name">...</a>`
	■ An e-mail link where *dn* is the domain name: `<a href="mailto:uname@dn">...</a>`
`<body>...</body>`	This tag defines the beginning and end of the document body, and the body contains all content statically rendered in a web browser. When you set the attributes of the body tag, they impact the entire rendered document. Attributes:
	■ `background=url` Specifies the fully qualified filename for an image that is used as the tiled page background.
	■ `bgcolor="#rrggbb"	"color_name"` Sets the background color for a page.
	■ `text="#rrggbb"	" color_name"` Sets the default font color for a page.
	Example: `<body>page_body</body>`
` ` or XHTML ` `	This tag breaks lines of text. To be XHTML compliant, you must use an end tag or use the alternate forward slash at the end of the tag. Example: `first_line second_line`
`<form>...</form>`	This creates a FORM body, which can include several HTML objects and typically one SUBMIT button. The form tags cannot be nested or overlapped with one another, but you can have more than one form in an HTML document.

TABLE A-1.   *HTML Basic Tag Resource* (continued)

Tag Name	Description

	`input` tags are placed inside forms and passed by their *name* attribute as parameters.
	Attributes:
	
	■ `action=`*url* Designates the target *url* acted on when an event listener triggers it.
	
	■ `id=`*text* Provides an *id* attribute that you can use in a reference by another tag or in a client-side scripting language like JavaScript.
	
	■ `method=`*get* | *post* Defines the *url* method used when the form is submitted. More on this can be found in Chapter 11. The get method submits the argument list and values as clear text, which can easily be hacked, whereas the post method polls the server and then sends the argument list separately. You should generally use the post method.
	
	■ `name=`*text* Provides a *name* attribute that you can use in a reference by another tag or in a client-side scripting language like JavaScript.
	
	Example:
	
	■ A virtual HTTP listener reference, where *hn* is the hostname and *dn* is the domain name:
	`<form action=`*http://hn.dn/php/code.php*`>`
	`... `*various_input_tags*` ...`
	`</form>`

`<hr>` or XHTML `<hr />`	This tag renders a line to the page. To be XHTML compliant, you must use an end tag or use the alternate forward slash at the end of the tag. Example: `<hr />`

`<head>...</head>`	This tag defines the header segment of a document. The header segment contains `<link>`, `<meta>`, `<script>`, `<style>`, and `<title>` tags that need to be present before rendering the document's body segment. The header segment displays no rendered content to the client browser, unless it is part of a client-side scripting definition.
	Example:
	`<head>`
	`... `*select_administrative_tags*` ...`
	`</head>`

`<html>...</html>`	This tag defines the document as an HTML-rendered document.
	Example:
	`<html>`
	`... `*all_tags_and_content*` ...`
	`</html>`

`<input>...</input>`	This tag provides widgets for entering text, selecting check boxes, radio buttons, and generic buttons. This tag should be used in preference to older format tags like `<button>` that were never cross-platform compatible.

TABLE A-1.   *HTML Basic Tag Resource* (continued)

Tag Name	Description

Description

Attributes:

- `id=text`   Provides an *id* attribute that you can use in a reference by another tag or in a client-side scripting language like JavaScript.

- `name=text`   Provides a *name* attribute that you can use in a reference by another tag or in a client-side scripting language like JavaScript.

- `onclick=action`   Specifies a relative or absolute path to a document or a client-side scripting function. The former is captured by the HTTPD listener virtual directory, and the latter, by a document event listener.

- `type=type_value`   Provides a *type* attribute that lets you designate the input as an *action button, checkbox, file, hidden, password, radio button,* or *submit* widget.

Examples:

- An action button:
  ```
  <input name="button_name" type="button"
   onclick="action" />
  ```

- A file:
  ```
  <input name="f_name" type="file" />
  ```

- A hidden element:
  ```
  <input name="enter_it" type="hidden" />
  ```

- A text field:
  ```
  <input name="hide_me" type="text" />
  ```

- A password field:
  ```
  <input name="passwd" type"password" />
  ```

- A submit button:
  ```
  <input name="submit"
   text="Submit Button"
   type="submit" />
  ```

`<link>` or XHTML `<link>...</link>`

This tag goes in the header segment of HTML documents. It often references external style sheets and client-side scripting libraries.

Attributes:

- `href=url`   Identifies a target document.

- `rel=relation`   Describes the relationship between the current source and target documents. Some common relationships are *stylesheet, next, prev, copyright, index,* and *glossary.*

- `title=text`   Provides a reference title for the target document in the tag.

TABLE A-1.   *HTML Basic Tag Resource* (continued)

Tag Name	Description

`<meta>` or XHTML `<meta>...</meta>`	This tag provides global settings to an HTML document. It should be placed within the header segment of the document at or near the beginning. It is commonly used for making documents searchable by adding keywords or specifying character sets and scripting languages.
	Attributes:
	■ `content=text` A required attribute that specifies the value of the *meta* tag. This attribute is always used in conjunction with the *name* attribute.
	■ `name=text` Specifies a name attribute for a *meta* tag.
	■ `scheme=text` Provides additional information to interpret *meta* tag data.
	Example:
	<pre>`<meta http-equiv=Content-Type`
	` content=text/html;`
	` http-equiv=Content-Script-Type`
	` text/javascript`
	` charset=iso-8859-1`
	`/>`</pre>

`<ol>...</ol>`	This tag defines an ordered list in an HTML-rendered document. It uses the `<li>` and `</li>` tags to specify elements in the list.
	Example:
	<pre>`<ol>`
	` <li>item_1</li>`
	` <li>item_(n+1)</li>`
	`</ol>`</pre>

`<script>...</script>`	This tag lets you include client-side scripting in your HTML form. You can designate different scripting languages in different scripting tags or set a single scripting language in a *meta* tag for the document.
	Example:
	<pre>`<script language=javascript`
	` type=text/javascript>`
	`. . .scripting_code. . .`
	`</script>`</pre>

`<select>...</select>`	This tag provides a drop-down widget for selecting an entry from a list. Attributes: ■ `id=text` Provides an *id* attribute that you can use in a reference by another tag or in a client-side scripting language like JavaScript. ■ `name=text` Provides a *name* attribute that you can use in a reference by another tag or in a client-side scripting language like JavaScript. ■ `onchange=action` Designates the target *url* acted on when an event listener triggers for a drop-down box.

TABLE A-1. *HTML Basic Tag Resource* (continued)

Tag Name	Description

Example:

```
<select name="name"
 onchange="action"
 size="1">
<option value="0" selected>
 default_choice
</option>
<option value=1>
 choice(n+1)
</option>
</select>
```

`<style>...</style>`

This tag defines local style values that can override those imported by using the style tag following the link tag. This tag lets you localize styles that are referenced using the *class* attribute.

Example:

```
<style>
 .tableheader { style_formatting }
</style>
```

`<table>...</table>`

This tag defines a table. Attributes placed in this tag work throughout the table subordinate components, like `<tr>` and `</tr>`, `<th>` and `</th>`, or `<td>` and `</td>` to create table rows, table header cells, and table row cells respectively.

Attributes:

- `border=value` Specifies whether the table will have lines delimiting cell values.

- `cellspacing=value` Specifies the spacing between cells.

- `cellborder=value` Specifies the width of the cell border.

Example:

```
<table>
 <tr><th>header_cell_text</th></tr>
 <tr><td>row_cell_text</td></tr>
</table>
```

`<title>...</title>`

This tag defines the document title that is rendered in the window frame of an HTML document.

Example:

```
<title>page_title</title>
```

`<ul>...</ul>`

This tag defines an unordered list in an HTML-rendered document. It uses the `<li>` and `</li>` tags to specify elements in the list.

Example:

```
<ul>
 <li>item_1</li>
 <li>item_(n+1)</li>
</ul>
```

TABLE A-1. *HTML Basic Tag Resource* (continued)

After you define the widgets in your web pages, there are a number of HTML tags that let you format your text. These are summarized in Table A-2.

This appendix has reviewed basic widget and formatting HTML tags. It has focused on tags that support the embedded HTML in the PHP sample programs.

Tag Name	Description
`<b>...</b>`	This tag bolds text. Example: `<b>important_text</b>`
`<big>...</big>`	This tag makes text bigger. Example: `<big>bigger_text</big>`
`<div>...</div>`	This tag lets you define specialized formatting that can override the defaults for the web page. The `div` and `span` tags are recommended over using the `font` tag. Example: `<div>altered_text</div>`
`<i>...</i>`	This tag italicizes text. Example: `<i>italicized_text</i>`
`<s>...</s>`	This tag strikes through text. Example: `<s>strike_through_text</s>`
`<small>...</small>`	This tag makes text small. Example: `<small>small_text</small>`
`<span>...</span>`	This tag lets you define specialized formatting that can override the defaults for the web page. The `span` and `div` tags are recommended over using the `font` tag. Example: `<span>altered_text</span>`
`<tt>...</tt>`	This tag makes text monospaced. Example: `<tt>monospaced_text</tt>`
`<u>...</u>`	This tag underlines text. Example: `<u>underlined_text</u>`

TABLE A-2. *HTML Basic Formatting Tags*

APPENDIX
B

Strings, Tools, and Techniques

his appendix lists string functions that you will use often while developing PHP programs. Not all of these are thread safe, and you should review the list before you choose how you will manipulate strings. As to the aliases, be careful which ones you use and be consistent in use. If you're going to use the `chop()` function because you like the Perl tone of it, then don't intermingle it with the PHP `rtrim()` function.

These functions let you create substrings, manipulate strings, or collect information to parse strings. The `explode()` and `implode()` functions are frequently found in example code accessing the MySQL database. Alternatives to using the `explode()` and `implode()` functions are found in Chapter 13. Table B-1 lists and describes the most common string functions, and it includes small example programs following the description and function.

The sample programs are designed for you to run from the PHP run-time interpreter (not in a web page). You can check details of how to do that in the "Command-Line PHP Scripting" sidebar found in Chapter 10. Thread-safe functions are noted in italics beneath the function name.

Function	Description
chop()	The chop() function is an *alias* for the rtrim() function. Please cross-reference the rtrim() function for complete details on how the chop() function works. The chop() function has the following prototype: `string chop(string str [, character_list])`

chr()	The chr() function returns a single character equivalent to an ASCII value. It requires one int value parameter that maps to an ASCII value, and returns a null when the actual parameter is outside the ASCII values 1 to 255. The chr() function has the following prototype:
	`string chr(int ascii_value)`
	The following sample program uses the chr() function to convert an ASCII 65 to a capital A:
	`<?php`
	`  $string = chr(65);`
	`  print "[".$string."]\n";`
	`?>`
	It produces the following standard output stream:
	`[A]`
	The following demonstrates a *null* return value:
	`<?php`
	`  if (is_null(chr(300)))`
	`    print "[null value]\n";`
	`?>`
	It produces the following standard output stream:
	`[null value]`

TABLE B-1. *Summary of String Management Functions*

Function	Description
explode()	The explode() function returns an array of numerically indexed strings. It has three parameters; the first two are mandatory and the third is optional. The first required parameter is a string separator, the second is the string to parse, and the third is an optional limit value. The limit value caps the number of elements returned in the array. The function returns false when the string separator is a null element string. PHP 5.1 introduces a negative limit value, which excludes that limit value from the end of the array of substrings. The explode() function has the following prototype:

```
array explode(string separator
  , string string
  [, int limit])
```

The following sample program uses the explode() function with a white space separator:

```php
<?php
  $str = "One Two Three";
  $list = explode(" ",$str)
  foreach($list as $name => $value)
  print "[".$name."]["".$value."]\n";
?>
```

It produces the following standard output stream:

```
[0][One]
[1][Two]
[2][Three]
```

Function	Description
implode()	The implode() function returns a string built from an array. It has two mandatory parameters. The first is a glue string, or joining string. The second is the array to convert into a string. The implode() function has the following prototype:

```
array implode(string glue
  , array element_list)
```

The following sample program uses the implode() function with a white space separator:

```php
<?php
  $list = array("One","Two","Three");
  $str = implode(" ",$list);
  print "[".$str."]\n";
?>
```

It produces the following standard output stream:

```
[One Two Three]
```

Function	Description
join()	The join() function is an *alias* for the implode() function. Please cross-reference the implode() function for complete details on how

TABLE B-1. *Summary of String Management Functions* (continued)

Function	Description
	the `join()` function works. The `join()` function has the following prototype: ``` string join(string glue [, array element_list]) ```

`ltrim()`	The `ltrim()` function lets you strip white space and line terminators from the beginning of strings unless you specify that you want to keep them. It has two parameters; one is mandatory and the other is optional. The required parameter is the starting string, which will be trimmed of leading white space and special characters before returning the modified string by the `ltrim()` function. The optional parameter is a list of allowed trailing characters that should remain in the output string, like:
	
	■ " " (ASCII *32* [*0x20*]), an ordinary space.
	
	■ "\t" (ASCII *9* [*0x09*]), a tab.
	
	■ "\n" (ASCII *10* [*0x0A*]), a newline (line feed).
	
	■ "\r" (ASCII *13* [*0x0D*]), a carriage return.
	
	■ "\0" (ASCII *0* [*0x00*]), the *NUL*-byte.
	
	■ "\x0B" (ASCII *11* [*0x0B*]), a vertical tab.
	
	The `ltrim()` function has the following prototype:
	
	``
	ltrim(string string_in [, character_list])
	``
	
	The following sample program uses the `ltrim()` function to trim leading white space from a string:
	
	``php
	<?php
	  $string = " leading whitespaces.";
	  print "[".$string."]\n";
	  $string = ltrim($string);
	  print "[".$string."]\n";
	?>
	``
	
	It produces the following standard output stream, which removes leading white spaces:
	
	``
	[leading whitespace.]
	[leading whitespace.]
	``

`number_format()`	The `number_format()` function takes a `float` data type and formats the number as a string. It has one mandatory and three optional parameters. The mandatory first parameter is the number. The optional second parameter is the number of decimal places, the third is the decimal format symbol (typically a period), and the fourth is the

TABLE B-1. *Summary of String Management Functions* (continued)

Function	Description
	thousands symbol (typically a comma). The `number_format()` function has the following prototype:

```
string number_format(float number
  [, int decimals
  [, string decimal_symbol
  [, string thousands_symbol]]])
```

The following sample program uses the `number_format()` function to format a number:

```php
<?php
 $number = 123456789.01;
 $str = number_format($number,2,".",",");
 print "[".$str."]\n";
?>
```

It produces the following standard output stream:

```
[123,456,789.01]
```

Function	Description
`ord()`	The `ord()` function returns an ASCII value for a single character. It has one required parameter, which is a one-character `string` value. The `ord()` function has the following prototype:

```
string ord(string character)
```

The following sample program uses the `ord()` function to covert an *A* to an ASCII 65 value:

```php
<?php
 $int = ord("A");
 print "[".$int."]\n";
?>
```

It produces the following standard output stream:

```
[65]
```

Function	Description
`quotemeta()`	The `quotemeta()` function places a back-quote in front of: . \ + * ? [^] ($) symbols. It takes a single string parameter and returns a back-quoted string as a result. The `quotemeta()` function has the following prototype:

```
string quotemeta(string str)
```

The following sample program uses the `quotemeta()` function to back-quote a symbol:

```php
<?php
 $str = quotemeta("a * b = c");
 print "[".$str."]\n";
?>
```

It produces the following standard output stream:

```
[a \* b = c]
```

TABLE B-1. *Summary of String Management Functions* (continued)

Function	Description
`rtrim()`	The `rtrim()` function lets you strip white space and line terminators from the end of strings unless you specify that you want to keep them. It has two parameters; one is mandatory and the other is optional. The required parameter is the starting string, which is trimmed of white space and line termination characters at the end of the string. The optional parameter is a list of allowed trailing characters:

- " " (ASCII *32* [*0x20*]), an ordinary space.
- "\t" (ASCII *9* [*0x09*]), a tab.
- "\n" (ASCII *10* [*0x0A*]), a newline (line feed).
- "\r" (ASCII *13* [*0x0D*]), a carriage return.
- "\0" (ASCII *0* [*0x00*]), the *NUL*-byte.
- "\x0B" (ASCII *11* [*0x0B*]), a vertical tab.

The `rtrim()` function has the following prototype:

```
rtrim(string string_in [, character_list])
```

The following sample program uses the `rtrim()` function to trim trailing white space from a string:

```php
<?php
  $string = "This is trailing whitespace ";
  print "[".$string."]\n";
  $string = rtrim($string);
  print "[".$string."]\n";
?>
```

It produces the following standard output stream:

```
[This is trailing whitespace ]
[This is trailing whitespace]
```

Function	Description
`strcasecmp()`	The `strcasecmp()` function returns a sorting number based on a case-insensitive comparison operation. It has two mandatory parameters, which are case-sensitive strings to compare. When the first string is greater than the second, the function returns a positive number. When the first string is less than the second, the function returns a negative number. When both strings are equal, the function returns a zero. The `strcasecmp()` function has the following prototype:

```
int strcasecmp(string str1
  , string str2)
```

The following sample program uses the `strcasecmp()` function:

```php
<?php
  $value = strcasecmp("One","one");
```

TABLE B-1. *Summary of String Management Functions* (continued)

Function	Description
| | ```php
print "[".$value."]\n";
?>
``` |
| | It returns an int value as described based on a case-insensitive comparison: |
| | ```
[0]
``` |
| strchr() | The strchr() function is an *alias* for the strstr() function. Please cross-reference the strstr() function for complete details on how the strchr() function works. The strchr() function has the following prototype: |
| | ```
int strchr(string haystack
, string needle)
``` |
| strcmp() | The strcmp() function returns a sorting number based on a case-sensitive comparison operation. It has two mandatory parameters, which are case-sensitive strings to compare. When the first string is greater than the second, the function returns a positive number. When the first string is less than the second, the function returns a negative number. When both strings are equal, the function returns a zero. The strcmp() function has the following prototype: |
| | ```
int strcmp(string str1
, string str2)
``` |
| | The following sample program uses the strcmp() function: |
| | ```php
<?php
$value = strcasecmp("One","one");
print "[".$value."]\n";
?>
``` |
| | It produces the following standard output stream on finding the first string less than the second because the ASCII values of capital characters are lower than those of lowercase characters: |
| | ```
[-1]
``` |
| strip_tags() | The strip_tags() function returns a string without any HTML or PHP tags. It has two parameters; one is mandatory and the other is optional. The first parameter is a target string, and the second parameter is a list of tags that you don't want to remove from the string. The strip_tags() function has the following prototype: |
| | ```
int strip_tags(string str
, string allowable_tags)
``` |
| | The following sample program uses the strip_tags() function: |
| | ```php
<?php
$value = strip_tags("<B>Bold</B>");
print "[".$value."]\n";
?>
``` |

TABLE B-1. *Summary of String Management Functions* (continued)

Function	Description
	It produces the following standard output stream by removing the HTML bold formatting tag: `[Bold]`

`stripos()`	The `stripos()` function returns a positional int value from a case-insensitive substring comparison. It has two mandatory parameters, which are case-insensitive strings, and one optional parameter, which is an offset position. The first parameter is the string to search, or the *haystack*. The second parameter is the substring to look for in the string, also known as the *needle*. The third parameter is a starting place to search in the string. It returns the first position where the substring starts in the haystack after the offset or `false` when it doesn't find the needle in the haystack. The default for the offset is the first position in the string. The `stripos()` function has the following prototype:
	
	`int stripos(string haystack`
	`  , string needle`
	`  [, int offset])`
	
	The following sample program uses the `stripos()` function:
	
	`<?php`
	`  $value = stripos("Abstract","ACT");`
	`  print "[".$value."]\n";`
	`?>`
	
	It returns a case-insensitive *needle* match and returns the int value position of the match, which is
	
	`[5]`

`stripslashes()`	The `stripslashes()` function removes backslashes from a string and returns the remaining string. It has one parameter, which is a target string. The `stripslashes()` function has the following prototype:
	
	`string stripslashes(string str)`
	
	The following sample program uses the `stripslashes()` function to remove a back-quote symbol:
	
	`<?php`
	`  $str = quotemeta("a \* b = c");`
	`  print "[".$str."]\n";`
	`?>`
	
	It produces the following standard output stream:
	
	`[a * b = c]`

`stristr()`	The `stristr()` function returns a substring from a case-insensitive substring comparison point to the end of the string. It has two

TABLE B-1. *Summary of String Management Functions* (continued)

Function	Description

	mandatory parameters, which are case-insensitive strings. The first parameter is the string to search, or the *haystack*. The second parameter is the substring to look for in the string, also known as the *needle*. It returns a substring from the first occurrence of the needle in the haystack. The `stristr()` function has the following prototype:
	
	``php
	string stristr(string haystack
	  , string needle)
	``
	
	The following sample program uses the `stristr()` function:
	
	``php
	<?php
	 $value = stristr("Abstract","ACT");
	 print "[".$value."]\n";
	?>
	``
	
	It returns a case-insensitive *needle* match, which is returned in lowercase, matching the searched string, not the search needle:
	
	``
	[act]
	``

`strlen()`	The `strlen()` function returns the length of a string. It has one parameter, which is a target string to analyze. It has the following prototype:
	
	``php
	int strlen(string target)
	``
	
	The following sample program uses the `strlen()` function:
	
	``php
	<?php
	 $value = strlen("String Length");
	 print "[".$value."]\n";
	?>
	``
	
	It returns the string length:
	
	``
	[13]
	``

`strpos()`	The `strpos()` function returns a positional `int` value from a case-sensitive substring comparison. It has two mandatory parameters, which are case-sensitive strings, and one optional parameter, which is an offset position. The first parameter is the string to search, or the *haystack*. The second parameter is the substring to look for in the string, also known as the *needle*. The third parameter is a starting place to search in the string. It returns the first position where the substring starts in the haystack after the offset or `false` when it doesn't find the *needle* in the *haystack*. The default for the offset is the first position in the string. The `strpos()` function has the following prototype:
	
	``php
	int strpos(string haystack
	  , string needle
	  [, int offset])
	``

TABLE B-1. *Summary of String Management Functions* (continued)

Function	Description
	The following sample program uses the `strpos()` function:

	``php
	<?php
	 $value = strpos("Abstract","ACT");
	 print "[".$value."]\n";
	?>
	``

	It returns a case-insensitive *needle* match and returns the position of the match, which is
	`[5]`
strstr()	The `strstr()` function returns a substring from a case-sensitive substring comparison point to the end of the string. It has two mandatory parameters, which are case-sensitive strings. The first parameter is the string to search, or the *haystack*. The second parameter is the substring to look for in the string, also known as the *needle*. It returns a substring from the first occurrence of the needle in the haystack. The `strstr()` function has the following prototype:
	``` string strstr(string haystack , string needle) ```
	The following sample program uses the `strstr()` function:

	``php
	<?php
	 $value = strstr("Abstract","act");
	 print "[".$value."]\n";
	?>
	``

	It returns the needle because nothing follows the needle value:
	`[act]`
strtok()	The `strtok()` function tokenizes a string into an array. This is useful when reading comma- or tab-delimited files. It has two mandatory variables; one is the target variable and the other is the token, or delimiter. It has the following prototype:
	``` string strtok(string target , string token) ```
	The following sample program uses the `strtok()` function:

	``php
	<?php
	 $string = "One,Two,Three";
	 $token = strtok($string,",");
	 while ($token !== false)
	 {
	  print "Word [$token]\n";
	  $token = strtok(",");
	 }
	?>
	``

TABLE B-1. *Summary of String Management Functions* (continued)

Function	Description
	It uses the token to create three separate words in an array, as shown:

	`Word [One]`
	`Word [Two]`
	`Word [Three]`

`strtolower()`	The `strtolower()` function converts a string to a lowercase string. It has one mandatory parameter, which is a target string. The `strtolower()` function has the following prototype:
	`string strtolower(string target)`
	The following sample program uses the `strtolower()` function:

	`<?php`
	`  $value = strtolower("Mixed Case String");`
	`  print "[".$value."]\n";`
	`?>`

	It returns a lowercase string:
	`[mixed case string]`
`strtoupper()`	The `strtoupper()` function converts a string to a lowercase string. It has one mandatory parameter, which is a target string. The `strtoupper()` function has the following prototype:
	`string strtoupper(string target)`
	The following sample program uses the `strtoupper()` function:

	`<?php`
	`  $value = strtoupper("Mixed Case String");`
	`  print "[".$value."]\n";`
	`?>`

	It returns an uppercase string:
	`[MIXED CASE STRING]`
`substr()`	The `substr()` function lets you pull a substring from a larger string when you know the starting and ending points, which you can get by using the `stripos()` function. It has three parameters; two are mandatory and the third is optional. The first parameter is the target string to search. The second parameter is where to begin the substring. The optional third parameter is the length of the substring. When the third parameter is not provided, you get everything from the starting position to the end of the string. It has the following prototype:

	`string substr(string target`
	`, int start_position`
	`[, int ending_position])`

TABLE B-1.   *Summary of String Management Functions* (continued)

Function	Description
	The following sample program uses the `substr()` function:

```php
<?php
 $str = "Grab me from here.";
 $value = substr($str,5,2);
 print "[".$value."]\n";
?>
```

It returns a two-character word:

```
[me]
```

TABLE B-1. *Summary of String Management Functions* (continued)

Summary

This section has introduced commonly used PHP string management functions. They should help you get up and running, writing your own web applications.

APPENDIX
C

PHP Environment
Constants

s discussed in Chapter 4, a long list of standard constants changes with point releases of the PHP engine. They are contributed by the PHP community, Zend Corporation, and SAPI modules. There are also variations based on the modules used in your server environment.

Finding the defined constants in your environment can be done by using the `get_defined_constants()` function, but it does not render them in a user-friendly way. Sorting the returned array is a bit tricky too because it will require a user-defined sort function.

The `GetConstants.php` program demonstrates how you can discover your environment constants and provides a user-defined sort function to alphabetize them. The program formats the output into an HTML table that uses cascading style sheet definitions. The following table is produced as output from the `GetConstants.php` program. It represents a standard Apache, PHP 5.1, and Oracle Express Edition environment.

Constant Name	Constant Value
[ASSERT_ACTIVE]	[1]
[ASSERT_BAIL]	[3]
[ASSERT_CALLBACK]	[2]
[ASSERT_QUIET_EVAL]	[5]
[ASSERT_WARNING]	[4]
[CAL_DOW_DAYNO]	[0]
[CAL_DOW_LONG]	[2]
[CAL_DOW_SHORT]	[1]
[CAL_EASTER_ALWAYS_GREGORIAN]	[2]
[CAL_EASTER_ALWAYS_JULIAN]	[3]
[CAL_EASTER_DEFAULT]	[0]
[CAL_EASTER_ROMAN]	[1]
[CAL_FRENCH]	[3]
[CAL_GREGORIAN]	[0]
[CAL_JEWISH]	[2]
[CAL_JEWISH_ADD_ALAFIM]	[4]
[CAL_JEWISH_ADD_ALAFIM_GERESH]	[2]
[CAL_JEWISH_ADD_GERESHAYIM]	[8]
[CAL_JULIAN]	[1]
[CAL_MONTH_FRENCH]	[5]
[CAL_MONTH_GREGORIAN_LONG]	[1]

Constant Name	Constant Value
[CAL_MONTH_GREGORIAN_SHORT]	[0]
[CAL_MONTH_JEWISH]	[4]
[CAL_MONTH_JULIAN_LONG]	[3]
[CAL_MONTH_JULIAN_SHORT]	[2]
[CAL_NUM_CALS]	[4]
[CASE_LOWER]	[0]
[CASE_UPPER]	[1]
[CHAR_MAX]	[127]
[CLSCTX_ALL]	[23]
[CLSCTX_INPROC_HANDLER]	[2]
[CLSCTX_INPROC_SERVER]	[1]
[CLSCTX_LOCAL_SERVER]	[4]
[CLSCTX_REMOTE_SERVER]	[16]
[CLSCTX_SERVER]	[21]
[CONNECTION_ABORTED]	[1]
[CONNECTION_NORMAL]	[0]
[CONNECTION_TIMEOUT]	[2]
[COUNT_NORMAL]	[0]
[COUNT_RECURSIVE]	[1]
[CP_ACP]	[0]
[CP_MACCP]	[2]
[CP_OEMCP]	[1]
[CP_SYMBOL]	[42]
[CP_THREAD_ACP]	[3]
[CP_UTF7]	[65000]
[CP_UTF8]	[65001]
[CREDITS_ALL]	[-1]
[CREDITS_DOCS]	[16]
[CREDITS_FULLPAGE]	[32]
[CREDITS_GENERAL]	[2]
[CREDITS_GROUP]	[1]
[CREDITS_MODULES]	[8]
[CREDITS_QA]	[64]

Constant Name	Constant Value
[CREDITS_SAPI]	[4]
[CRYPT_BLOWFISH]	[0]
[CRYPT_EXT_DES]	[0]
[CRYPT_MD5]	[1]
[CRYPT_SALT_LENGTH]	[12]
[CRYPT_STD_DES]	[1]
[DATE_ATOM]	[Y-m-d\TH:i:sO]
[DATE_COOKIE]	[D, d M Y H:i:s T]
[DATE_ISO8601]	[Y-m-d\TH:i:sO]
[DATE_RFC1036]	[l, d-M-y H:i:s T]
[DATE_RFC1123]	[D, d M Y H:i:s T]
[DATE_RFC2822]	[D, d M Y H:i:s O]
[DATE_RFC822]	[D, d M Y H:i:s T]
[DATE_RFC850]	[l, d-M-y H:i:s T]
[DATE_RSS]	[D, d M Y H:i:s T]
[DATE_W3C]	[Y-m-d\TH:i:sO]
[DEFAULT_INCLUDE_PATH]	[.;C:\php5\pear]
[DIRECTORY_SEPARATOR]	[\]
[DISP_E_BADINDEX]	[-2147352565]
[DISP_E_DIVBYZERO]	[-2147352558]
[DISP_E_OVERFLOW]	[-2147352566]
[DOMSTRING_SIZE_ERR]	[2]
[DOM_HIERARCHY_REQUEST_ERR]	[3]
[DOM_INDEX_SIZE_ERR]	[1]
[DOM_INUSE_ATTRIBUTE_ERR]	[10]
[DOM_INVALID_ACCESS_ERR]	[15]
[DOM_INVALID_CHARACTER_ERR]	[5]
[DOM_INVALID_MODIFICATION_ERR]	[13]
[DOM_INVALID_STATE_ERR]	[11]
[DOM_NAMESPACE_ERR]	[14]
[DOM_NOT_FOUND_ERR]	[8]
[DOM_NOT_SUPPORTED_ERR]	[9]
[DOM_NO_DATA_ALLOWED_ERR]	[6]

Constant Name	Constant Value
[DOM_NO_MODIFICATION_ALLOWED_ERR]	[7]
[DOM_PHP_ERR]	[0]
[DOM_SYNTAX_ERR]	[12]
[DOM_VALIDATION_ERR]	[16]
[DOM_WRONG_DOCUMENT_ERR]	[4]
[ENT_COMPAT]	[2]
[ENT_NOQUOTES]	[0]
[ENT_QUOTES]	[3]
[EXTR_IF_EXISTS]	[6]
[EXTR_OVERWRITE]	[0]
[EXTR_PREFIX_ALL]	[3]
[EXTR_PREFIX_IF_EXISTS]	[5]
[EXTR_PREFIX_INVALID]	[4]
[EXTR_PREFIX_SAME]	[2]
[EXTR_REFS]	[256]
[EXTR_SKIP]	[1]
[E_ALL]	[2047]
[E_COMPILE_ERROR]	[64]
[E_COMPILE_WARNING]	[128]
[E_CORE_ERROR]	[16]
[E_CORE_WARNING]	[32]
[E_ERROR]	[1]
[E_NOTICE]	[8]
[E_PARSE]	[4]
[E_STRICT]	[2048]
[E_USER_ERROR]	[256]
[E_USER_NOTICE]	[1024]
[E_USER_WARNING]	[512]
[E_WARNING]	[2]
[FALSE]	[]
[FILE_APPEND]	[8]
[FILE_IGNORE_NEW_LINES]	[2]
[FILE_NO_DEFAULT_CONTEXT]	[16]

Constant Name	Constant Value
[FILE_SKIP_EMPTY_LINES]	[4]
[FILE_USE_INCLUDE_PATH]	[1]
[FORCE_DEFLATE]	[2]
[FORCE_GZIP]	[1]
[FTP_ASCII]	[0]
[FTP_AUTORESUME]	[-1]
[FTP_AUTOSEEK]	[1]
[FTP_BINARY]	[1]
[FTP_FAILED]	[0]
[FTP_FINISHED]	[1]
[FTP_IMAGE]	[1]
[FTP_MOREDATA]	[2]
[FTP_TEXT]	[0]
[FTP_TIMEOUT_SEC]	[0]
[GLOB_BRACE]	[128]
[GLOB_ERR]	[4]
[GLOB_MARK]	[8]
[GLOB_NOCHECK]	[16]
[GLOB_NOESCAPE]	[4096]
[GLOB_NOSORT]	[32]
[GLOB_ONLYDIR]	[1073741824]
[HTML_ENTITIES]	[1]
[HTML_SPECIALCHARS]	[0]
[ICONV_IMPL]	["libiconv"]
[ICONV_MIME_DECODE_CONTINUE_ON_ERROR]	[2]
[ICONV_MIME_DECODE_STRICT]	[1]
[ICONV_VERSION]	[1.9]
[IMAGETYPE_BMP]	[6]
[IMAGETYPE_GIF]	[1]
[IMAGETYPE_IFF]	[14]
[IMAGETYPE_JB2]	[12]
[IMAGETYPE_JP2]	[10]
[IMAGETYPE_JPC]	[9]

Constant Name	Constant Value
[IMAGETYPE_JPEG]	[2]
[IMAGETYPE_JPEG2000]	[9]
[IMAGETYPE_JPX]	[11]
[IMAGETYPE_PNG]	[3]
[IMAGETYPE_PSD]	[5]
[IMAGETYPE_SWC]	[13]
[IMAGETYPE_SWF]	[4]
[IMAGETYPE_TIFF_II]	[7]
[IMAGETYPE_TIFF_MM]	[8]
[IMAGETYPE_WBMP]	[15]
[IMAGETYPE_XBM]	[16]
[INF]	[1.#INF]
[INFO_ALL]	[-1]
[INFO_CONFIGURATION]	[4]
[INFO_CREDITS]	[2]
[INFO_ENVIRONMENT]	[16]
[INFO_GENERAL]	[1]
[INFO_LICENSE]	[64]
[INFO_MODULES]	[8]
[INFO_VARIABLES]	[32]
[INI_ALL]	[7]
[INI_PERDIR]	[2]
[INI_SYSTEM]	[4]
[INI_USER]	[1]
[LC_ALL]	[0]
[LC_COLLATE]	[1]
[LC_CTYPE]	[2]
[LC_MONETARY]	[3]
[LC_NUMERIC]	[4]
[LC_TIME]	[5]
[LIBXML_COMPACT]	[65536]
[LIBXML_DOTTED_VERSION]	[2.6.22]
[LIBXML_DTDATTR]	[8]

Constant Name	Constant Value
[LIBXML_DTDLOAD]	[4]
[LIBXML_DTDVALID]	[16]
[LIBXML_ERR_ERROR]	[2]
[LIBXML_ERR_FATAL]	[3]
[LIBXML_ERR_NONE]	[0]
[LIBXML_ERR_WARNING]	[1]
[LIBXML_NOBLANKS]	[256]
[LIBXML_NOCDATA]	[16384]
[LIBXML_NOEMPTYTAG]	[4]
[LIBXML_NOENT]	[2]
[LIBXML_NOERROR]	[32]
[LIBXML_NONET]	[2048]
[LIBXML_NOWARNING]	[64]
[LIBXML_NOXMLDECL]	[2]
[LIBXML_NSCLEAN]	[8192]
[LIBXML_VERSION]	[20622]
[LIBXML_XINCLUDE]	[1024]
[LOCK_EX]	[2]
[LOCK_NB]	[4]
[LOCK_SH]	[1]
[LOCK_UN]	[3]
[LOG_ALERT]	[1]
[LOG_AUTH]	[32]
[LOG_AUTHPRIV]	[80]
[LOG_CONS]	[2]
[LOG_CRIT]	[1]
[LOG_CRON]	[72]
[LOG_DAEMON]	[24]
[LOG_DEBUG]	[6]
[LOG_EMERG]	[1]
[LOG_ERR]	[4]
[LOG_INFO]	[6]
[LOG_KERN]	[0]
[LOG_LPR]	[48]

Constant Name	Constant Value
[LOG_MAIL]	[16]
[LOG_NDELAY]	[8]
[LOG_NEWS]	[56]
[LOG_NOTICE]	[6]
[LOG_NOWAIT]	[16]
[LOG_ODELAY]	[4]
[LOG_PERROR]	[32]
[LOG_PID]	[1]
[LOG_SYSLOG]	[40]
[LOG_USER]	[8]
[LOG_UUCP]	[64]
[LOG_WARNING]	[5]
[MK_E_UNAVAILABLE]	[-2147221021]
[M_1_PI]	[0.31830988618379]
[M_2_PI]	[0.63661977236758]
[M_2_SQRTPI]	[1.1283791670955]
[M_E]	[2.718281828459]
[M_LN10]	[2.302585092994]
[M_LN2]	[0.69314718055995]
[M_LOG10E]	[0.43429448190325]
[M_LOG2E]	[1.442695040889]
[M_PI]	[3.1415926535898]
[M_PI_2]	[1.5707963267949]
[M_PI_4]	[0.78539816339745]
[M_SQRT1_2]	[0.70710678118655]
[M_SQRT2]	[1.4142135623731]
[NAN]	[0]
[NORM_IGNORECASE]	[1]
[NORM_IGNOREKANATYPE]	[65536]
[NORM_IGNORENONSPACE]	[2]
[NORM_IGNORESYMBOLS]	[4]
[NORM_IGNOREWIDTH]	[131072]
[NULL]	[]
[OCI_ASSOC]	[1]

Constant Name	Constant Value
[OCI_BOTH]	[3]
[OCI_B_BFILE]	[114]
[OCI_B_BIN]	[23]
[OCI_B_BLOB]	[113]
[OCI_B_CFILEE]	[115]
[OCI_B_CLOB]	[112]
[OCI_B_CURSOR]	[116]
[OCI_B_INT]	[3]
[OCI_B_NTY]	[108]
[OCI_B_NUM]	[2]
[OCI_B_ROWID]	[104]
[OCI_COMMIT_ON_SUCCESS]	[32]
[OCI_DEFAULT]	[0]
[OCI_DESCRIBE_ONLY]	[16]
[OCI_DTYPE_FILE]	[56]
[OCI_DTYPE_LOB]	[50]
[OCI_DTYPE_ROWID]	[54]
[OCI_D_FILE]	[56]
[OCI_D_LOB]	[50]
[OCI_D_ROWID]	[54]
[OCI_EXACT_FETCH]	[2]
[OCI_FETCHSTATEMENT_BY_COLUMN]	[16]
[OCI_FETCHSTATEMENT_BY_ROW]	[32]
[OCI_LOB_BUFFER_FREE]	[1]
[OCI_NUM]	[2]
[OCI_RETURN_LOBS]	[8]
[OCI_RETURN_NULLS]	[4]
[OCI_SEEK_CUR]	[1]
[OCI_SEEK_END]	[2]
[OCI_SEEK_SET]	[0]
[OCI_SYSDATE]	[SYSDATE]
[OCI_SYSDBA]	[2]
[OCI_SYSOPER]	[4]

Constant Name	Constant Value
[OCI_TEMP_BLOB]	[1]
[OCI_TEMP_CLOB]	[2]
[ODBC_BINMODE_CONVERT]	[2]
[ODBC_BINMODE_PASSTHRU]	[0]
[ODBC_BINMODE_RETURN]	[1]
[ODBC_TYPE]	[Win32]
[PATHINFO_BASENAME]	[2]
[PATHINFO_DIRNAME]	[1]
[PATHINFO_EXTENSION]	[4]
[PATH_SEPARATOR]	[;]
[PEAR_EXTENSION_DIR]	[C:\php5]
[PEAR_INSTALL_DIR]	[C:\php5\pear]
[PHP_BINDIR]	[C:\php5]
[PHP_CONFIG_FILE_PATH]	[C:\WINDOWS]
[PHP_CONFIG_FILE_SCAN_DIR]	[ ]
[PHP_DATADIR]	[C:\php5]
[PHP_EOL]	[ ]
[PHP_EXTENSION_DIR]	[C:\php5]
[PHP_INT_MAX]	[2147483647]
[PHP_INT_SIZE]	[4]
[PHP_LIBDIR]	[C:\php5]
[PHP_LOCALSTATEDIR]	[C:\php5]
[PHP_OS]	[WINNT]
[PHP_OUTPUT_HANDLER_CONT]	[2]
[PHP_OUTPUT_HANDLER_END]	[4]
[PHP_OUTPUT_HANDLER_START]	[1]
[PHP_PREFIX]	[C:\php5]
[PHP_SAPI]	[apache2handler]
[PHP_SHLIB_SUFFIX]	[dll]
[PHP_SYSCONFDIR]	[C:\php5]
[PHP_URL_FRAGMENT]	[7]
[PHP_URL_HOST]	[1]
[PHP_URL_PASS]	[4]

Constant Name	Constant Value
[PHP_URL_PATH]	[5]
[PHP_URL_PORT]	[2]
[PHP_URL_QUERY]	[6]
[PHP_URL_SCHEME]	[0]
[PHP_URL_USER]	[3]
[PHP_VERSION]	[5.1.2]
[PREG_GREP_INVERT]	[1]
[PREG_OFFSET_CAPTURE]	[256]
[PREG_PATTERN_ORDER]	[1]
[PREG_SET_ORDER]	[2]
[PREG_SPLIT_DELIM_CAPTURE]	[2]
[PREG_SPLIT_NO_EMPTY]	[1]
[PREG_SPLIT_OFFSET_CAPTURE]	[4]
[PSFS_ERR_FATAL]	[0]
[PSFS_FEED_ME]	[1]
[PSFS_FLAG_FLUSH_CLOSE]	[2]
[PSFS_FLAG_FLUSH_INC]	[1]
[PSFS_FLAG_NORMAL]	[0]
[PSFS_PASS_ON]	[2]
[SEEK_CUR]	[1]
[SEEK_END]	[2]
[SEEK_SET]	[0]
[SORT_ASC]	[4]
[SORT_DESC]	[3]
[SORT_LOCALE_STRING]	[5]
[SORT_NUMERIC]	[1]
[SORT_REGULAR]	[0]
[SORT_STRING]	[2]
[SQLT_AFC]	[96]
[SQLT_AVC]	[97]
[SQLT_BFILEE]	[114]
[SQLT_BLOB]	[113]
[SQLT_CFILEE]	[115]

Constant Name	Constant Value
[SQLT_CHR]	[1]
[SQLT_CLOB]	[112]
[SQLT_FLT]	[4]
[SQLT_INT]	[3]
[SQLT_LNG]	[8]
[SQLT_LVC]	[94]
[SQLT_NTY]	[108]
[SQLT_NUM]	[2]
[SQLT_ODT]	[156]
[SQLT_RDD]	[104]
[SQLT_RSET]	[116]
[SQLT_STR]	[5]
[SQLT_UIN]	[68]
[SQLT_VCS]	[9]
[SQL_BIGINT]	[-5]
[SQL_BINARY]	[-2]
[SQL_BIT]	[-7]
[SQL_CHAR]	[1]
[SQL_CONCURRENCY]	[7]
[SQL_CONCUR_LOCK]	[2]
[SQL_CONCUR_READ_ONLY]	[1]
[SQL_CONCUR_ROWVER]	[3]
[SQL_CONCUR_VALUES]	[4]
[SQL_CURSOR_DYNAMIC]	[2]
[SQL_CURSOR_FORWARD_ONLY]	[0]
[SQL_CURSOR_KEYSET_DRIVEN]	[1]
[SQL_CURSOR_STATIC]	[3]
[SQL_CURSOR_TYPE]	[6]
[SQL_CUR_USE_DRIVER]	[2]
[SQL_CUR_USE_IF_NEEDED]	[0]
[SQL_CUR_USE_ODBC]	[1]
[SQL_DATE]	[9]
[SQL_DECIMAL]	[3]

Constant Name	Constant Value
[SQL_DOUBLE]	[8]
[SQL_FETCH_FIRST]	[2]
[SQL_FETCH_NEXT]	[1]
[SQL_FLOAT]	[6]
[SQL_INTEGER]	[4]
[SQL_KEYSET_SIZE]	[8]
[SQL_LONGVARBINARY]	[-4]
[SQL_LONGVARCHAR]	[-1]
[SQL_NUMERIC]	[2]
[SQL_ODBC_CURSORS]	[110]
[SQL_REAL]	[7]
[SQL_SMALLINT]	[5]
[SQL_TIME]	[10]
[SQL_TIMESTAMP]	[11]
[SQL_TINYINT]	[-6]
[SQL_VARBINARY]	[-3]
[SQL_VARCHAR]	[12]
[STREAM_CLIENT_ASYNC_CONNECT]	[2]
[STREAM_CLIENT_CONNECT]	[4]
[STREAM_CLIENT_PERSISTENT]	[1]
[STREAM_CRYPTO_METHOD_SSLv23_CLIENT]	[2]
[STREAM_CRYPTO_METHOD_SSLv23_SERVER]	[6]
[STREAM_CRYPTO_METHOD_SSLv2_CLIENT]	[0]
[STREAM_CRYPTO_METHOD_SSLv2_SERVER]	[4]
[STREAM_CRYPTO_METHOD_SSLv3_CLIENT]	[1]
[STREAM_CRYPTO_METHOD_SSLv3_SERVER]	[5]
[STREAM_CRYPTO_METHOD_TLS_CLIENT]	[3]
[STREAM_CRYPTO_METHOD_TLS_SERVER]	[7]
[STREAM_ENFORCE_SAFE_MODE]	[4]
[STREAM_FILTER_ALL]	[3]
[STREAM_FILTER_READ]	[1]
[STREAM_FILTER_WRITE]	[2]
[STREAM_IGNORE_URL]	[2]

Constant Name	Constant Value
[STREAM_IPPROTO_ICMP]	[1]
[STREAM_IPPROTO_IP]	[0]
[STREAM_IPPROTO_RAW]	[255]
[STREAM_IPPROTO_TCP]	[6]
[STREAM_IPPROTO_UDP]	[17]
[STREAM_MKDIR_RECURSIVE]	[1]
[STREAM_MUST_SEEK]	[16]
[STREAM_NOTIFY_AUTH_REQUIRED]	[3]
[STREAM_NOTIFY_AUTH_RESULT]	[10]
[STREAM_NOTIFY_COMPLETED]	[8]
[STREAM_NOTIFY_CONNECT]	[2]
[STREAM_NOTIFY_FAILURE]	[9]
[STREAM_NOTIFY_FILE_SIZE_IS]	[5]
[STREAM_NOTIFY_MIME_TYPE_IS]	[4]
[STREAM_NOTIFY_PROGRESS]	[7]
[STREAM_NOTIFY_REDIRECTED]	[6]
[STREAM_NOTIFY_RESOLVE]	[1]
[STREAM_NOTIFY_SEVERITY_ERR]	[2]
[STREAM_NOTIFY_SEVERITY_INFO]	[0]
[STREAM_NOTIFY_SEVERITY_WARN]	[1]
[STREAM_OOB]	[1]
[STREAM_PEEK]	[2]
[STREAM_PF_INET]	[2]
[STREAM_PF_INET6]	[23]
[STREAM_PF_UNIX]	[1]
[STREAM_REPORT_ERRORS]	[8]
[STREAM_SERVER_BIND]	[4]
[STREAM_SERVER_LISTEN]	[8]
[STREAM_SOCK_DGRAM]	[2]
[STREAM_SOCK_RAW]	[3]
[STREAM_SOCK_RDM]	[4]
[STREAM_SOCK_SEQPACKET]	[5]
[STREAM_SOCK_STREAM]	[1]

Constant Name	Constant Value
[STREAM_URL_STAT_LINK]	[1]
[STREAM_URL_STAT_QUIET]	[2]
[STREAM_USE_PATH]	[1]
[STR_PAD_BOTH]	[2]
[STR_PAD_LEFT]	[0]
[STR_PAD_RIGHT]	[1]
[SUNFUNCS_RET_DOUBLE]	[2]
[SUNFUNCS_RET_STRING]	[1]
[SUNFUNCS_RET_TIMESTAMP]	[0]
[TRUE]	[1]
[T_ABSTRACT]	[345]
[T_AND_EQUAL]	[271]
[T_ARRAY]	[359]
[T_ARRAY_CAST]	[292]
[T_AS]	[326]
[T_BAD_CHARACTER]	[313]
[T_BOOLEAN_AND]	[279]
[T_BOOLEAN_OR]	[278]
[T_BOOL_CAST]	[290]
[T_BREAK]	[331]
[T_CASE]	[329]
[T_CATCH]	[337]
[T_CHARACTER]	[312]
[T_CLASS]	[352]
[T_CLASS_C]	[360]
[T_CLONE]	[298]
[T_CLOSE_TAG]	[369]
[T_COMMENT]	[365]
[T_CONCAT_EQUAL]	[273]
[T_CONST]	[334]
[T_CONSTANT_ENCAPSED_STRING]	[315]
[T_CONTINUE]	[332]
[T_CURLY_OPEN]	[374]

Constant Name	Constant Value
[T_DEC]	[296]
[T_DECLARE]	[324]
[T_DEFAULT]	[330]
[T_DIV_EQUAL]	[274]
[T_DNUMBER]	[306]
[T_DO]	[317]
[T_DOC_COMMENT]	[366]
[T_DOLLAR_OPEN_CURLY_BRACES]	[373]
[T_DOUBLE_ARROW]	[357]
[T_DOUBLE_CAST]	[294]
[T_DOUBLE_COLON]	[375]
[T_ECHO]	[316]
[T_ELSE]	[303]
[T_ELSEIF]	[302]
[T_EMPTY]	[350]
[T_ENCAPSED_AND_WHITESPACE]	[314]
[T_ENDDECLARE]	[325]
[T_ENDFOR]	[321]
[T_ENDFOREACH]	[323]
[T_ENDIF]	[304]
[T_ENDSWITCH]	[328]
[T_ENDWHILE]	[319]
[T_END_HEREDOC]	[372]
[T_EVAL]	[260]
[T_EXIT]	[300]
[T_EXTENDS]	[354]
[T_FILE]	[364]
[T_FINAL]	[344]
[T_FOR]	[320]
[T_FOREACH]	[322]
[T_FUNCTION]	[333]
[T_FUNC_C]	[362]
[T_GLOBAL]	[340]

Constant Name	Constant Value
[T_HALT_COMPILER]	[351]
[T_IF]	[301]
[T_IMPLEMENTS]	[355]
[T_INC]	[297]
[T_INCLUDE]	[262]
[T_INCLUDE_ONCE]	[261]
[T_INLINE_HTML]	[311]
[T_INSTANCEOF]	[288]
[T_INTERFACE]	[353]
[T_INT_CAST]	[295]
[T_ISSET]	[349]
[T_IS_EQUAL]	[283]
[T_IS_GREATER_OR_EQUAL]	[284]
[T_IS_IDENTICAL]	[281]
[T_IS_NOT_EQUAL]	[282]
[T_IS_NOT_IDENTICAL]	[280]
[T_IS_SMALLER_OR_EQUAL]	[285]
[T_LINE]	[363]
[T_LIST]	[358]
[T_LNUMBER]	[305]
[T_LOGICAL_AND]	[265]
[T_LOGICAL_OR]	[263]
[T_LOGICAL_XOR]	[264]
[T_METHOD_C]	[361]
[T_MINUS_EQUAL]	[276]
[T_MOD_EQUAL]	[272]
[T_MUL_EQUAL]	[275]
[T_NEW]	[299]
[T_NUM_STRING]	[310]
[T_OBJECT_CAST]	[291]
[T_OBJECT_OPERATOR]	[356]
[T_OPEN_TAG]	[367]
[T_OPEN_TAG_WITH_ECHO]	[368]

Constant Name	Constant Value
[T_OR_EQUAL]	[270]
[T_PAAMAYIM_NEKUDOTAYIM]	[375]
[T_PLUS_EQUAL]	[277]
[T_PRINT]	[266]
[T_PRIVATE]	[343]
[T_PROTECTED]	[342]
[T_PUBLIC]	[341]
[T_REQUIRE]	[259]
[T_REQUIRE_ONCE]	[258]
[T_RETURN]	[335]
[T_SL]	[287]
[T_SL_EQUAL]	[268]
[T_SR]	[286]
[T_SR_EQUAL]	[267]
[T_START_HEREDOC]	[371]
[T_STATIC]	[346]
[T_STRING]	[307]
[T_STRING_CAST]	[293]
[T_STRING_VARNAME]	[308]
[T_SWITCH]	[327]
[T_THROW]	[338]
[T_TRY]	[336]
[T_UNSET]	[348]
[T_UNSET_CAST]	[289]
[T_USE]	[339]
[T_VAR]	[347]
[T_VARIABLE]	[309]
[T_WHILE]	[318]
[T_WHITESPACE]	[370]
[T_XOR_EQUAL]	[269]
[UPLOAD_ERR_CANT_WRITE]	[7]
[UPLOAD_ERR_FORM_SIZE]	[2]
[UPLOAD_ERR_INI_SIZE]	[1]

Constant Name	Constant Value
[UPLOAD_ERR_NO_FILE]	[4]
[UPLOAD_ERR_NO_TMP_DIR]	[6]
[UPLOAD_ERR_OK]	[0]
[UPLOAD_ERR_PARTIAL]	[3]
[VARCMP_EQ]	[1]
[VARCMP_GT]	[2]
[VARCMP_LT]	[0]
[VARCMP_NULL]	[3]
[VT_ARRAY]	[8192]
[VT_BOOL]	[11]
[VT_BSTR]	[8]
[VT_BYREF]	[16384]
[VT_CY]	[6]
[VT_DATE]	[7]
[VT_DECIMAL]	[14]
[VT_DISPATCH]	[9]
[VT_EMPTY]	[0]
[VT_ERROR]	[10]
[VT_I1]	[16]
[VT_I2]	[2]
[VT_I4]	[3]
[VT_INT]	[22]
[VT_NULL]	[1]
[VT_R4]	[4]
[VT_R8]	[5]
[VT_UI1]	[17]
[VT_UI2]	[18]
[VT_UI4]	[19]
[VT_UINT]	[23]
[VT_UNKNOWN]	[13]
[VT_VARIANT]	[12]
[XML_ATTRIBUTE_CDATA]	[1]
[XML_ATTRIBUTE_DECL_NODE]	[16]

Constant Name	Constant Value
[XML_ATTRIBUTE_ENTITY]	[6]
[XML_ATTRIBUTE_ENUMERATION]	[9]
[XML_ATTRIBUTE_ID]	[2]
[XML_ATTRIBUTE_IDREF]	[3]
[XML_ATTRIBUTE_IDREFS]	[4]
[XML_ATTRIBUTE_NMTOKEN]	[7]
[XML_ATTRIBUTE_NMTOKENS]	[8]
[XML_ATTRIBUTE_NODE]	[2]
[XML_ATTRIBUTE_NOTATION]	[10]
[XML_CDATA_SECTION_NODE]	[4]
[XML_COMMENT_NODE]	[8]
[XML_DOCUMENT_FRAG_NODE]	[11]
[XML_DOCUMENT_NODE]	[9]
[XML_DOCUMENT_TYPE_NODE]	[10]
[XML_DTD_NODE]	[14]
[XML_ELEMENT_DECL_NODE]	[15]
[XML_ELEMENT_NODE]	[1]
[XML_ENTITY_DECL_NODE]	[17]
[XML_ENTITY_NODE]	[6]
[XML_ENTITY_REF_NODE]	[5]
[XML_ERROR_ASYNC_ENTITY]	[13]
[XML_ERROR_ATTRIBUTE_EXTERNAL_ENTITY_REF]	[16]
[XML_ERROR_BAD_CHAR_REF]	[14]
[XML_ERROR_BINARY_ENTITY_REF]	[15]
[XML_ERROR_DUPLICATE_ATTRIBUTE]	[8]
[XML_ERROR_EXTERNAL_ENTITY_HANDLING]	[21]
[XML_ERROR_INCORRECT_ENCODING]	[19]
[XML_ERROR_INVALID_TOKEN]	[4]
[XML_ERROR_JUNK_AFTER_DOC_ELEMENT]	[9]
[XML_ERROR_MISPLACED_XML_PI]	[17]
[XML_ERROR_NONE]	[0]
[XML_ERROR_NO_ELEMENTS]	[3]
[XML_ERROR_NO_MEMORY]	[1]

Constant Name	Constant Value
[XML_ERROR_PARAM_ENTITY_REF]	[10]
[XML_ERROR_PARTIAL_CHAR]	[6]
[XML_ERROR_RECURSIVE_ENTITY_REF]	[12]
[XML_ERROR_SYNTAX]	[2]
[XML_ERROR_TAG_MISMATCH]	[7]
[XML_ERROR_UNCLOSED_CDATA_SECTION]	[20]
[XML_ERROR_UNCLOSED_TOKEN]	[5]
[XML_ERROR_UNDEFINED_ENTITY]	[11]
[XML_ERROR_UNKNOWN_ENCODING]	[18]
[XML_HTML_DOCUMENT_NODE]	[13]
[XML_LOCAL_NAMESPACE]	[18]
[XML_NAMESPACE_DECL_NODE]	[18]
[XML_NOTATION_NODE]	[12]
[XML_OPTION_CASE_FOLDING]	[1]
[XML_OPTION_SKIP_TAGSTART]	[3]
[XML_OPTION_SKIP_WHITE]	[4]
[XML_OPTION_TARGET_ENCODING]	[2]
[XML_PI_NODE]	[7]
[XML_SAX_IMPL]	[libxml]
[XML_TEXT_NODE]	[3]
[ZEND_THREAD_SAFE]	[1]

APPENDIX
D

Environment Interfaces and Object Types

s discussed in the section "Using Object Reflection" in Chapter 8, several loaded extensions run in your PHP environment. The loaded extensions and PHP version determine the object interfaces and classes in your environment. The following functions are the keys to discovering what are available in your environment:

Function Name	Function Description
`get_declared_interfaces()`	This function returns an array of declared interfaces in your environment.
`get_declared_classes()`	This function returns an array of declared object types or classes in your environment.
`get_loaded_extensions()`	This function returns an array of loaded extensions in your environment.

The array returns values that do not sort well without writing an uppercase sort operation, as done in Chapter 4 to access environment constants. The `GetComponents.php` program enables you to query your environment to list loaded extensions and declared interfaces and classes. The implementation of the `GetComponents.php` program follows its formatted output list:

Declared Extensions

[apache2handler]	[iconv]	[SPL]
[bcmath]	[libxml]	[standard]
[calendar]	[oci8]	[tokenizer]
[com_dotnet]	[odbc]	[wddx]
[ctype]	[pcre]	[xml]
[date]	[Reflection]	[xmlreader]
[dom]	[session]	[xmlwriter]
[ftp]	[SimpleXML]	[zlib]

Declared Interfaces

[ArrayAccess]	[OuterIterator]	[Serializable]
[Countable]	[RecursiveIterator]	[SplObserver]
[Iterator]	[Reflector]	[SplSubject]
[IteratorAggregate]	[SeekableIterator]	[Traversable]

Declared Classes

[AppendIterator]	[DOMNamedNodeMap]	[ParentIterator]
[ArrayIterator]	[DOMNameList]	[php_user_filter]
[ArrayObject]	[DOMNameSpaceNode]	[RangeException]
[BadFunctionCallException]	[DOMNode]	[RecursiveArrayIterator]
[BadMethodCallException]	[DOMNodeList]	[RecursiveCachingIterator]
[CachingIterator]	[DOMNotation]	[RecursiveDirectoryIterator]
[com]	[DOMProcessingInstruction]	[RecursiveFilterIterator]
[COMPersistHelper]	[DOMStringExtend]	[RecursiveIteratorIterator]
[com_exception]	[DOMStringList]	[Reflection]
[com_safearray_proxy]	[DOMText]	[ReflectionClass]
[Directory]	[DOMTypeinfo]	[ReflectionException]
[DirectoryIterator]	[DOMUserDataHandler]	[ReflectionExtension]
[DomainException]	[DOMXPath]	[ReflectionFunction]
[DOMAttr]	[dotnet]	[ReflectionMethod]
[DOMCdataSection]	[EmptyIterator]	[ReflectionObject]
[DOMCharacterData]	[ErrorException]	[ReflectionParameter]
[DOMComment]	[Exception]	[ReflectionProperty]
[DOMConfiguration]	[FilterIterator]	[RuntimeException]
[DOMDocument]	[InfiniteIterator]	[SimpleXMLElement]
[DOMDocumentFragment]	[InvalidArgumentException]	[SimpleXMLIterator]
[DOMDocumentType]	[IteratorIterator]	[SplFileInfo]
[DOMDomError]	[LengthException]	[SplFileObject]
[DOMElement]	[LibXMLError]	[SplObjectStorage]
[DOMEntity]	[LimitIterator]	[SplTempFileObject]
[DOMEntityReference]	[LogicException]	[stdClass]
[DOMErrorHandler]	[NoRewindIterator]	[UnderflowException]
[DOMException]	[OCI-Collection]	[UnexpectedValueException]
[DOMImplementation]	[OCI-Lob]	[variant]
[DOMImplementationList]	[OutOfBoundsException]	[XMLReader]
[DOMImplementationSource]	[OutOfRangeException]	[XMLWriter]
[DOMLocator]	[OverflowException]	[__PHP_Incomplete_Class]

The `GetComponents.php` program uses the predefined discovery functions and two user-defined functions. One function enables writing a list into a three-column table, and the other provides an uppercase sort. The program also uses a style sheet consistent with the formatting generated by the `phpInfo()` function, as follows:

```
<style>
.e {background-color: #ccccff; font-weight: bold; color: #000000;}
.h {background-color: #9999cc; font-weight: bold; color: #000000;}
.v {background-color: #cccccc; color: #000000;}
</style>
```

The `GetComponents.php` program follows:

-- **This is found in the GetComponents.php file on the enclosed CD.**

```php
<?php
  // Declare an array of environment classes.
  $extensions = get_loaded_extensions();

  // Sort by uppercase values.
  usort($extensions,'uppercase_sort');

  // Print the table with column labels.
  print to_table($extensions,'Declared Extensions');

  // Print break between tables.
  print "<p>";

  // Declare an array of environment interfaces.
  $interfaces = get_declared_interfaces();

  // Sort by uppercase values.
  usort($interfaces,'uppercase_sort');

  // Print the table with column labels.
  print to_table($interfaces,'Declared Interfaces');

  // Print break between tables.
  print "<p>";

  // Declare an array of environment classes.
  $classes = get_declared_classes();

  // Sort by uppercase values.
  usort($classes,'uppercase_sort');

  // Print the table with column labels.
  print to_table($classes,'Declared Classes');

  // Function renders three column table.
  function to_table($array_in,$title)
```

```
{
  // Declare variable with table start.
  $output = "<table border=0 cellpadding=0 cellspacing=0>";
  $output .= "<tr>";
  $output .= "<td align=center class=h colspan=3 width=600>";
  $output .= $title;
  $output .= "</td>";
  $output .= "</tr>";

  // Check integer division by three and adjust for remainder.
  if ((count($array_in) % 3) == 0)
    $chunks = count($array_in) / 3;
  else
    $chunks = (int) (count($array_in) / 3) + 1;

  // Read and add array keys and values to a string.
  for ($i = 0;$i < $chunks;$i++)
  {
    // Append non-array value with cell tags.
    $output .= "<tr>";
    $output .= "<td class=v width=200>";
    $output .= "[".$array_in[$i]."]";
    $output .= "</td>";
    $output .= "<td class=v width=200>";
    $output .= "[".$array_in[$i+$chunks]."]";
    $output .= "</td>";

    // Check if values exceed array elements and print placeholders.
    if (($i + (2*$chunks)) < count($array_in))
    {
      $output .= "<td class=v width=200>";
      $output .= "[".$array_in[$i+(2*$chunks)]."]";
      $output .= "</td>";
    }
    else
      $output .= "<td class=v width=200> </td>";

    // Append row close.
    $output .= "</tr>";
  }

  // Close HTML table.
  $output .= "</table>";

  // Return the HTML table.
  return $output;
}
```

```
// Function to sort uppercase.
function uppercase_sort($a,$b)
{
  // Promote all keys to uppercase.
  $a = strtoupper($a);
  $b = strtoupper($b);

  // Check which one is greater.
  return ($a > $b) ? 1 : -1;
}
?>
```

The trick to balancing the columns is using the modulus operator and integer division. When there is a remainder, the result of the division is cast to an integer value plus one, which ensures that it has a balanced set of rows. Then, as elements are placed in the third column, the number of elements for a column is evaluated against the array size and overruns are padded with an HTML macro for a formatting placeholder.

The GetComponents.php file should help you determine what's in your environment. With knowledge of the available modules, you can use the reflection concepts covered in Chapter 8 to check out how you can use these modules. Also, you should note that the dl() function, previously used to load shared libraries, is deprecated in PHP 5. All modules should be loaded through the php.ini file or a configuration option on Linux.

APPENDIX
E

POSIX
File Functions

he POSIX library works on compliant versions of the Unix operating system, such as Red Hat Linux Advanced Server 3/4. It provides additional views into physical information about files, directories, and processes. It does present information that can expose what should be secure information to unauthorized users, like hackers. You should take appropriate precautions to secure data when you enable this library.

Table E-1 lists the POSIX functions, summaries of their behaviors, and prototypes for the functions. The appendix then demonstrates how you determine whether the POSIX libraries are available in your environment and how you use some of them. It is recommended that you use this library when writing PHP programs as internal scripting solutions or server administration web applications on POSIX-compliant servers.

Function Name	Function Description

`posix_access()`	The `posix_access()` function checks user file permissions. The function checks whether the files have the same permission as the script owner when safe mode is set. It has two parameters; one is mandatory and the other is optional. It has the following pattern:
	
	`bool posix_access (string file`
	`    [,int mode])`

`posix_ctermid()`	The `posix_ctermid()` function returns the pathname of the controlling terminal, which begins with the `/dev/tty` path. It has no formal parameter and the following pattern: `string posix_ctermid()`
`posix_get_last_error()`	The `posix_get_last_error()` function gets the last errno (error number) set by the last failed POSIX library function. The function returns a `bool` false when there is no reported error code. It has the following pattern: `int posix_get_last_error()`
`posix_getcwd()`	The `posix_getcwd()` function returns the absolute pathname of the current work directory. It takes no parameters and returns a `bool` false when encountering an error. It has the following pattern: `string posix_getcwd()`
`posix_getegid()`	The `posix_getegid()` function returns the primary group identifier of the owner running the program. This is typically the apache user. It has no formal parameter and the following pattern: `int posix_getegid()`

TABLE E-1. *POSIX Library Functions*

Function Name	Function Description
`posix_getgid()`	The `posix_getgid()` function returns the real group identifier of the running program owner. It has no formal parameter and has the following pattern: `int posix_getgid()`
`posix_getgrgid()`	The `posix_getgrgid()` function returns an array describing the definition of a user group. It returns a `bool` false on failure, which happens when the mandatory group identifier parameter is not found in the `/etc/group` file. Failing to find a submitted group identifier raises a run-time `e_warning` message unless suppressed. The `posix_getgrgid()` function and `posix_getgrnam()` functions return the same array of values: ■ **name** The group name from the `/etc/group` file. ■ **passwd** The marker for the group password, which is represented as a string literal *x*. ■ **members** An array of system users in the group, which is defined in the `/etc/group` file. ■ **gid** The group identifier from the `/etc/group` file. The function has the following pattern: `array posix_getgrgid(int gid)`
`posix_getgrnam()`	The `posix_getgrnam()` function returns an array describing the definition of a user group. It returns a `bool` false on failure, which happens when the mandatory group name parameter is not found in the `/etc/group` file. Failing to find a submitted group identifier raises a run-time `e_warning` message unless suppressed. The `posix_getgrnam()` function and `posix_getgrgid()` function return the same array of values: ■ **name** The group name from the `/etc/group` file. ■ **passwd** The marker for the group password, which is represented as a string literal *x*.

TABLE E-1.   *POSIX Library Functions* (continued)

Function Name	Function Description
	■ **members** An array of system users in the group, which is defined in the /etc/group file.
	■ **gid** The group identifier from the /etc/group file.
	The function has the following pattern:
	`array posix_getgrnam(string name)`
posix_geteuid()	The `posix_geteuid()` function returns the primary user identifier of the owner running the program. It has no formal parameter and has the following pattern:
	`int posix_geteuid()`
posix_getgroups()	The `posix_getgroups()` function returns an array of group identifiers for the user executing this script. It returns 0 and 48 when executed by a web page because web requests are served by the apache user. The 0 group is returned because apache is started as a background job and 48 is the apache group. As a rule, this function is more useful in server-side PHP scripting than web pages. It has no formal parameter and has the following pattern:
	`array posix_getgroups()`
posix_getlogin()	The `posix_getlogin()` function returns the login name of the owner of the program. This returns a null value when run from a web page because the apache process is run as a background process and has no reference to a login user. It returns the initial login user when the script is run by an active process or forked subshell from the command line. It has the following pattern:
	`string posix_getlogin()`
posix_getpgid()	The `posix_getpgid()` function returns the process group identifier of the program. This returns the process identifier for the background job that starts the HTTPD service when run from a web page. This process is the parent process identifier for the HTTPD listener processes and is the same value as that returned by the `posix_getppid()` function when run from a browser window. It returns the forked process identifier when called from an interactive shell execution. It takes a current process identifier as its one mandatory parameter. It is recommended that you use the `posix_getpid()` function as the actual parameter. It has the following pattern:
	`int posix_getpgid(int pid)`

TABLE E-1.   *POSIX Library Functions* (continued)

Function Name	Function Description
posix_getpgrp()	The posix_getpgrp() function returns the group process, which is also the parent process identifier of the program. This returns the process identifier for the background job that starts the HTTPD services when run from a web page and is a mirror to the posix_getppid() function. It is also the same value that the posix_getpgid() function returns when run from a browser window. It returns the forking process identifier when called from an interactive shell execution. It has no formal parameter and has the following pattern: int posix_getpgrp()
posix_getpid()	The posix_getpid() function returns the process identifier for the running script. It has no formal parameter and has the following pattern: int posix_getpid()
posix_getppid()	The posix_getppid() function returns the parent process identifier of the program. This returns the process identifier for the background job that starts the HTTPD services when run from a web page. It is also the same value that the posix_getpgid() function returns when run from a browser window. It returns the forking process identifier when called from an interactive shell execution. It has no formal parameter and has the following pattern: int posix_getppid()
posix_getpwnam()	The posix_getpwnam() function returns an array describing the definition of a user. It takes a single mandatory parameter of a user identifier. The posix_getuid() function can be used to get the current user running any script. It returns a bool false on failure, which happens when the mandatory group name parameter is not found in the /etc/password file. Failing to find a submitted user identifier raises a run-time e_warning message unless suppressed. The posix_getpwnam() and posix_getpwuid() functions return the same array of values: ■ **name** The user name from the /etc/password file. ■ **passwd** The marker for the user password, which is represented as a string literal *x*.

TABLE E-1. *POSIX Library Functions* (continued)

Function Name	Function Description
	■ **uid** The user numeric identifier from the /etc/password file.
	■ **gid** The primary group identifier for the user taken from the /etc/password file.
	■ **gecos** The GECOS was originally a definition from the Honeywell batch processing system but is now the descriptive user name and other information from the /etc/password file.
	■ **dir** The absolute directory path for the user home directory.
	■ **shell** The default shell for the user taken from the /etc/passwd file.
	The function has the following pattern:
	`array posix_getpwnam(string name)`
posix_getpwuid()	The posix_getpwuid() function returns an array describing the definition of a user running the current process. The posix_getpwuid() function has one mandatory parameter, which is a valid user name. It returns a bool false on failure, which happens when the mandatory user name parameter is not found in the /etc/password file. Failing to find a submitted user identifier raises a run-time e_warning message unless suppressed. Both the posix_getpwnam() and posix_getpwuid() functions return the same array of values:
	■ **name** The user name from the /etc/password file.
	■ **passwd** The marker for the user password, which is represented as a string literal *x*.
	■ **uid** The user numeric identifier from the /etc/password file.
	■ **gid** The primary group identifier for the user taken from the /etc/password file.
	■ **gecos** The GECOS was originally a definition from the Honeywell batch processing system but is now the descriptive user name and other information from the /etc/password file.

TABLE E-1.   *POSIX Library Functions* (continued)

Function Name	Function Description
	■ **dir** The absolute directory path for the user home directory.
	■ **shell** The default shell for the user taken from the /etc/passwd file.
	The function has the following pattern:
	`array posix_getpwuid(string name)`
posix_getrlimit()	The posix_getrlimit() function returns the system default values, as noted in this table for a Red Hat Linux Advanced Server version:
	■ soft core 0
	■ hard core Unlimited
	■ soft data Unlimited
	■ hard data Unlimited
	■ soft stack 10485760
	■ hard stack Unlimited
	■ soft totalmem Unlimited
	■ hard totalmem Unlimited
	■ soft rss Unlimited
	■ hard rss Unlimited
	■ soft maxproc 7168
	■ hard maxproc 7168
	■ soft memlock 4096
	■ hard memlock 4096
	■ soft cpu Unlimited
	■ hard cpu Unlimited
	■ soft filesize Unlimited
	■ hard filesize Unlimited
	■ soft openfiles 1024
	■ hard openfiles 1024
	It has no formal parameter and has the following pattern:
	`array posix_getrlimit()`

TABLE E-1. *POSIX Library Functions* (continued)

Function Name	Function Description
posix_getsid()	The posix_getsid() function returns the connection process identifier for a process identifier. When a user connects to a Linux server, an initial process identifier is assigned. This is visible by issuing an echo $$ command. When a user switches users by using the su (substitute user) utility, the prior command no longer resolves to the session identifier. You can use the posix_getsid() function to find out the initial entry point process identifier for any running PHP script. It takes a valid process identifier (PID) to work and returns a bool false when the PID value is invalid. The function also raises a warning when an incorrect PID is provided as the actual parameter value. It has the following pattern: int posix_getsid()
posix_getuid()	The posix_getuid() function returns the user identifier of the current running program. It has the following pattern: int posix_getuid()
posix_isatty()	The posix_isatty() function determines if the process is being executed from a current terminal. The function has one mandatory parameter and takes STDIN, STDOUT, or STDERR as a value. It returns false if the script is run from a web page and true when it is run from the command line. You should use this before attempting to run the posix_isatty() function. It has the following pattern: bool posix_isatty(int *fd*)
posix_kill()	The posix_kill() function kills a running process. It has two mandatory parameters: a valid process identifier and a signal code. The most common signal codes are: (a) 15 for kill normally or without prejudice; and (b) 9, which means kill immediately or with prejudice. When killing a process normally, the process cleans up after itself. Abnormally stopping a running process can leave resources in an incomplete state. The function returns a bool true when it successfully kills the process and false when it fails to do so. The function has the following pattern: int posix_kill(int *pid*, int *signal*)

TABLE E-1. *POSIX Library Functions* (continued)

Function Name	Function Description

`posix_mkfifo()`	The `posix_mkfifo()` function creates a special file, known as a pipe or bidirectional first-in, first-out (FIFO) pipe. The function returns a `bool` true when it successfully creates the FIFO pipe and false when it fails to do so. The functions has the following pattern:
	
	`bool posix_mkfifo(string pathname`
	`    ,int mode)`

`posix_mknod()`	The `posix_mknod()` function creates an ordinary or special file. The function has two mandatory and two optional parameters. The first required parameter is a fully qualified filename. A fully qualified path has either a relative path or absolute pathname before the physical file name. The second parameter is a file mode from the list:
	
	■ `POSIX_S_IFBLK` This mode designates the file a special block file.
	
	■ `POSIX_S_IFCHR` This mode designates the file a special character file.
	
	■ `POSIX_S_IFIFO` This mode designates the file a named FIFO pipe file.
	
	■ `POSIX_S_IFREG` This mode designates the file a normal file.
	
	■ `POSIX_S_IFSOCK` This mode designates the file a socket.
	
	The two optional parameters are required when the specified mode is either `POSIX_S_IFBLK` or `POSIX_S_IFCHR`. The major and minor parameters address the characteristics of the device kernel. The function returns a `bool` true when it successfully creates the FIFO pipe and false when it fails to do so. The function has the following pattern:
	
	`bool posix_mknod(string file_name`
	`    ,int mode`
	`    [,int major`
	`    [,int minor]])`

`posix_setegid()`	The `posix_setegid()` function sets the effective group identifier of the current program. It usually requires superuser permissions and is only suitable for command-line scripting. The function returns a `bool`

TABLE E-1. *POSIX Library Functions* (continued)

Function Name	Function Description
	true when it is successful and false when it is not. It has the following pattern: `bool posix_setegid(int `*`gid`*`)`
`posix_seteuid()`	The `posix_seteuid()` function sets the effective user identifier of the current program. It usually requires superuser permissions and is only suitable for command-line scripting. The function returns a `bool` true when it is successful and false when it is not. It has the following pattern: `bool posix_seteuid(int `*`uid`*`)`
`posix_setgid()`	The `posix_setgid()` function sets the real group identifier of the current program. It usually requires superuser permissions and is only suitable for command-line scripting. The function returns a `bool` true when it is successful and false when it is not. It has the following pattern: `bool posix_setgid(int `*`gid`*`)`

`posix_setpgid()`	The `posix_setpgid()` function sets the process group identifier of the spawned background job process. It usually requires superuser permissions and is only suitable for command-line scripting. The function returns a `bool` true when it is successful and false when it is not. It has the following pattern:
	
	`bool posix_setpgid(int `*`pid`*`,`
	`    ,int `*`gpid`*`)`

`posix_setsid()`	The `posix_setsid()` function makes the current process the session identifier. This is useful when spawning processes during job control. It requires superuser permissions and is only suitable for command-line scripting. The function returns an `int` value for the new session identifier and null when it fails. It has the following pattern: `int posix_setsid()`
`posix_setuid()`	The `posix_setuid()` function sets the real user identifier of the current program. It usually requires superuser permissions and is only suitable for command-line scripting. The function returns a `bool` true when it is successful and false when it is not. It has the following pattern: `bool posix_setuid(int `*`uid`*`)`

TABLE E-1. *POSIX Library Functions* (continued)

Function Name	**Function Description**
posix_strerror()	The posix_strerror() function casts the error to a POSIX-compliant error code. A 0 indicates that the process completed successfully. The function returns a string value that represents the error message or the literal *Success* string. It has the following pattern: bool posix_strerror(int *error_code*)
posix_time()	The posix_time() function returns relative times for the process. It returns the following array of values: ■ **ticks** The number of clock ticks since the last reboot of the system, which is equivalent to the return value from uptime at the Linux command line. ■ **utime** The time used by the current process. ■ **stime** The system time used by the current process, which is rounded down to the last completed second. ■ **cutime** The current time used by the current process and its child processes, which is rounded down to the last completed second. ■ **cstime** The current system time used by the current process and its child processes, which is rounded down to the last completed second. The posix_time() function has no formal parameter and has the following pattern: array posix_time()
posix_ttyname()	The posix_ttyname() function gets the current terminal name. The function has one mandatory parameter. The possible actual parameter values are STDIN, STDOUT, or STDERR. It returns a string value for terminal name. This can only be run from the command line. It has the following pattern: string posix_ttyname(int *fd*)
posix_uname()	The posix_uname() function gets the current information and returns an array with the following attributes: ■ **sysname** The operating system name. ■ **nodename** The hostname for the system.

TABLE E-1.   *POSIX Library Functions* (continued)

Function Name	Function Description
	■ **release** The kernel release of the operating system.
	■ **version** The kernel version information of the operating system
	■ **machine** The machine architecture of the system.
	It has no mandatory or optional parameters and has the following pattern:
	`array posix_uname()`

TABLE E-1.   *POSIX Library Functions* (continued)

You can use the `GetExtensions.php` script to determine if you have loaded the POSIX library. The mechanism for doing this is covered in Chapter 7 and Appendix D but slightly modified to target only library extensions in this chapter.

The `GetExtensions.php` script returns all extensions or one extension. When you want to verify only one extension or library, you submit a single parameter using the following type of URL:

`http://dev.techtinker.com/`**GetExtensions.php?extension=posix**

You can use the POSIX functions when the script returns the POSIX library in the rendered table. The `GetExtensions.php` script uses a simple `$_GET` because it is simply a diagnostic script, as follows:

`-- This is found in GetExtensions.php on the enclosed CD.`

```php
<?php
  // Declare an array of environment classes.
  $extensions = get_loaded_extensions();

  // Sort by uppercase values.
  usort($extensions,'uppercase_sort');

  // Print the table with column labels.
  if (isset($_GET['extension']))
    print to_table(array($_GET['extension']),'Declared Extension');
  else
    print to_table($extensions,'Declared Extensions');

  // Function renders three-column table.
  function to_table($array_in,$title)
  {
    // Declare variable with table start.
    $output = "<table border=0 cellpadding=0 cellspacing=0>";
    $output .= "<tr>";
```

```php
    $output .= "<td align=center class=h colspan=3 width=600>";
    $output .= $title;
    $output .= "</td>";
    $output .= "</tr>";

    // Check integer division by three and adjust for remainder.
    if ((count($array_in) % 3) == 0)
      $chunks = count($array_in) / 3;
    else
      $chunks = (int) (count($array_in) / 3) + 1;

    // Read and add array keys and values to a string.
    for ($i = 0;$i < $chunks;$i++)
    {
      // Append non-array value with cell tags.
      $output .= "<tr>";
      $output .= "<td class=v width=200>";
      $output .= "[".$array_in[$i]."]";
      $output .= "</td>";

      // Check if values exceed array elements and print placeholders.
      if (($i + ($chunks)) < count($array_in))
      {
        $output .= "<td class=v width=200>";
        $output .= "[".$array_in[$i+$chunks]."xx]";
        $output .= "</td>";
      }
      else
        $output .= "<td class=v width=200> </td>";

      // Check if values exceed array elements and print placeholders.
      if (($i + (2*$chunks)) < count($array_in))
      {
        $output .= "<td class=v width=200>";
        $output .= "[".$array_in[$i+(2*$chunks)]."]";
        $output .= "</td>";
      }
      else
        $output .= "<td class=v width=200> </td>";

      // Append row close.
      $output .= "</tr>";
    }

    // Close HTML table.
    $output .= "</table>";

    // Return the HTML table.
    return $output;
}
```

```
// Function to sort uppercase.
function uppercase_sort($a,$b)
{
  // Promote all keys to uppercase.
  $a = strtoupper($a);
  $b = strtoupper($b);

  // Check which one is greater.
  return ($a > $b) ? 1 : -1;
}
?>
```

After verifying that you can run the functions, the posix_getpwuid() or posix_getpwnam() function provides you with the largest set of information about the current process user. The posix_get_process_info.php program demonstrates how to use either function to collect information on the process user. You should note that they return the same data. This is demonstrated by the following program:

-- **This is found in posix_get_process_info.php on the enclosed CD.**

```
<?php
  // Print title.
  print "The result of <b>posix_getpwuid(posix_getuid()).</b><br />";

  // Secure information based on user identifier.
  foreach ($userinfo = posix_getpwuid(posix_getuid()) as $name => $value)
    print "[$name][$value]<br />";

  // Print line break.
  print "<hr />";

  // Print title.
  print "The result of <b>posix_getpwnam(<i>user_name</i>).</b><br />";

  // Use the name to display information on user identifier.
  foreach (posix_getpwnam($userinfo['name']) as $name => $value)
    print "[$name][$value]<br />";
?>
```

The posix_get_process_info.php program demonstrates that the posix_getpwuid() and posix_getpwnam() functions return the same array set. The only difference between the two programs is the argument. The former takes a user identifier, which can be supplied by calling the posix_getuid() function, while the latter requires a user name.

The posix_get_process_info.php displays details about each running process as qualified in Table E-1 and renders the following to a web page:

```
The result of posix_getpwuid(posix_getuid()).
[name][apache]
[passwd][x]
[uid][48]
```

```
[gid] [48]
[gecos] [Apache]
[dir] [/var/www]
[shell] [/sbin/nologin]
------------------------------------------------------------------------
The result of posix_getpwnam(user_name).
[name] [apache]
[passwd] [x]
[uid] [48]
[gid] [48]
[gecos] [Apache]
[dir] [/var/www]
[shell] [/sbin/nologin]
```

While the posix_getpwuid() and posix_getpwnam() functions return an information set about users, the posix_getgruid() and posix_getgrname() functions return information about groups.

The following posix_get_group_info.php program demonstrates how these functions work:

-- **This is found in posix_get_group_info.php on the enclosed CD.**

```php
<?php
  // Check if command line executed.
  if ($_SERVER['argc'] > 0)
    $script = true;
  else
    $script = false;

  // Print title.
  print "The result of <b>posix_getgrgid(posix_getuid()).</b><br />";

  // Secure information based on user identifier.
  foreach ($groupinfo = posix_getgrgid(posix_getgid()) as $name => $value)
    if ((is_array($value)) && (count($value) == 0))
      if ($script)
        print "[$name] [Array()]\n";
      else
        print "[$name] [Array()]<br />";
    else if ((is_array($value)) && (count($value) > 0))
      foreach ($value as $sname => $svalue)
        if ($script)
          print "[$name] [$sname] [$svalue]\n";
        else
          print "[$name] [$sname] [$svalue]<br />";
    else
      if ($script)
        print "[$name] [$value]\n";
      else
        print "[$name] [$value]<br />";
```

```
// Print line break.
print "<hr />";

// Print title.
print "The result of <b>posix_getgrnam(<i>group_name</i>).</b><br />";

// Use the name to display information on user identifier.
foreach (posix_getgrnam($groupinfo['name']) as $name => $value)
  if ((is_array($value)) && (count($value) == 0))
    if ($script)
      print "[$name][Array()]\n";
    else
      print "[$name][Array()]<br />";
  else if ((is_array($value)) && (count($value) > 0))
    foreach ($value as $sname => $svalue)
      if ($script)
        print "[$name][$sname][$svalue]\n";
      else
        print "[$name][$sname][$svalue]<br />";
  else
    if ($script)
      print "[$name][$value]\n";
    else
      print "[$name][$value]<br />";
?>
```

The posix_get_group_info.php displays details about a given group as qualified in Table E-1 and renders the following to a web page:

```
The result of posix_getgrgid(posix_getuid()).
[name] [apache]
[passwd] [x]
[members] [Array()]
[gid] [48]
-----------------------------------------------------------------------
The result of posix_getgrnam(group_name).
[name] [apache]
[passwd] [x]
[members] [Array()]
[gid] [48]
```

The members of the apache group are empty. This is done by design to limit access through the HTTPD listener. The script is also enabled to print formatted text differently when run from the command line where the members array is most likely not empty. Again, these scripts are available for web applications but more useful for command-line scripting in PHP.

APPENDIX
F

Date Functions

ates are typically seen as strings that represent a calendar date, but the `date` data type is a scalar number in PHP and most other programming languages. Dates are the subject of extensive international discourse and standards because systems must be able to agree on transaction dates and timestamps.

The conversion process from `date` to `string` data types and vice versa is an interesting process. Programming languages take common approaches by providing libraries that enable you to format date variables into various human-readable strings and create `date` variable types from `string` and `int` data type variables.

This appendix introduces the PHP 5 date management library functions. They are summarized in Table F-1 and then discussed and expanded by examples. You should note that it is possible to map Oracle and PHP `date` types, but it is more likely that programs render dates as strings, transmit them as strings to server-side programs, and convert strings into `date` variables before binding them to and performing SQL operations. The conversion from `string` to `date` variable types often occurs by binding a `string` variable to a dynamic SQL statement that uses a SQL `TO_DATE()` function.

Aside from reading and storing dates, `date` types are used to calculate differences between two timestamps or dates. Calculations evaluate whether a specific period of time has elapsed and enable setting a future ending date for a period of time. These are especially useful in setting and expiring cookies as discussed in Chapter 12.

Function Name	Function Description

`checkdate()`	The `checkdate()` function checks whether a date is valid in a standard calendar. The function takes three required `int` parameters. The first value is a number from 1 to 12 for a *Georgian* month in a year. The second value is a number from 1 to 31 for the day of the month. The third value is a number between 1 and 32,767 for the year. It returns true if the numbers create a valid date and false when they do not. It has the following pattern:
	
	`bool checkdate(int month,`
	` ,int day`
	` ,int mode)`

`date()`	The `date()` function returns the date as a `string` type. It has two formal parameters, and one is mandatory while the other is optional. The mandatory parameter designates the format of the returned date. When the optional parameter is provided, it specifies a timestamp that overrides the default current system or output from the `time()` function. Formatting commands can be by themselves or combined in the format parameter and are available to manage *day, week, month, year, time of day, time zone,* or *a combination of day and time,* as qualified in the following list describing formatting options: ■ `d` A two-digit value between `01` and `31` for a day in a month. ■ `D` A three-letter string representing a day in a week, like *Mon* to *Sun.* ■ `j` A one- to two-digit value between `1` and `31` for a day in a month. ■ `l` A full word for a day in a week, like *Monday* to *Sunday.* ■ `N` A one-digit number representing a day in a week where `1` means *Monday* and `7` means *Sunday.* This is ISO-8601 compliant and new in PHP 5.1.

TABLE F-1. *Date Library Functions*

Function Name	Function Description
	■ S English ordinal suffix that is only meaningful when combined as a jS formatting command, such as *1st, 2nd, 3rd*.
	■ w A one-digit number representing a day in a week, where 0 means *Sunday* and 6 means *Saturday*.
	■ z A one- to three-digit number representing a day in a Georgian year, starting with 0 and ending with 365 during leap years on the calendar.
	■ W A one- to two-digit number representing a week in a year. It defines weeks as beginning with *Monday* and ending with *Sunday*. This is ISO-8601 compliant and was introduced in PHP 4.1.
	■ F A full word for the month in a year, like *January* to *December*.
	■ m A two-digit value between 01 and 12 for a month in a year.
	■ M A three-letter string representing a month in a year, like *Jan* to *Dec*.
	■ n A one- to two-digit value between 1 and 12 for a month in a year.
	■ t A two-digit value between 28 and 31 for the number of days in a Georgian calendar month.
	■ L 1 for leap year and 0 for all others.
	■ o A four-digit value for the current year based on ISO-8601, which uses rules that can return the prior or next year for days at the beginning or end of the year. The prior year is returned when the day falls in a week where the Monday of that week is in the last year. Likewise, the next year is returned when the day falls in a week where the Sunday of that week is in the next year.
	■ Y A four-digit value for the current year based on the day falling in the Georgian calendar year.
	■ y A two-digit value for the current year based on the day falling in the Georgian calendar year. The year is presented with leading zeros.
	■ a A two-character lowercase *ante* or *post meridiem*, like *am* or *pm*.
	■ A A two-character uppercase *ante* or *post meridiem*, like *AM* or *PM*.
	■ B A three-character *Swatch* time, which was introduced in 1998 and is more or less a *decimal minute* like that introduced during the French Revolution. Swatch time does not recognize daylight saving time and is calculated by dividing a 24-hour value by 1000. Each unit is called a beat and is represented as a zero-based number from 000 to 999.
	■ g A one- to two-digit value between 1 and 12 for an hour in a day.
	■ G A one- to two-digit value between 0 and 24 for an hour in a day, which is like a modified military time.
	■ h A two-digit value between 01 and 12 for an hour in a day.
	■ H A two-digit value between 00 and 24 for an hour in a day, which is also known as military time.
	■ i A two-digit value between 00 and 59 for the minute in an hour.
	■ s A two-digit value between 00 and 59 for the second in a minute.
	■ e A string time zone identifier, which can return UTC, GMT, or a valid time zone as qualified in Table F-2. This was added in PHP 5.1.

TABLE F-1. *Date Library Functions* (continued)

Function Name	Function Description
	■ I A 1 for daylight saving time and 0 when not daylight saving time.
	■ O The difference to Greenwich (GMT) time in hours.
	■ P The difference to Greenwich (GMT) time in hours and minutes with a colon separating hours from minutes. This was added in PHP 5.1.3.
	■ T The time zone setting for the machine, such as PDT or MST.
	■ Z The time zone offset in seconds. Positive numbers are used to represent values west of UTC, and negative number represent values east.
	■ c The ISO-8601 date, represented as year, month, and day separated by hyphens, then a T and then the local time and offset from GMT also separated by a hyphen, as follows: `2006-06-20T22:24:23-06:00`
	■ r The RFC 2822 format date, represented as a three-character day of the week, date, time, and GMT offset.
	■ U The seconds since the Unix Epoch that started on 1/1/1970 GMT.
	Unrecognized formatting commands will be rendered as desired characters in the date representation. You can back-quote formatting characters when you want those characters rendered as characters in the return string. The `date()` function has the following pattern: `string date(string format [,int timestamp])`
`date_default_timezone_get()`	The `date_default_timezone_get()` function returns the current system time zone value. The function takes no parameters. The list of possible return values are found in Table F-2. The function looks for the `TZ` environment variable first, followed by the `date.timezone` value from the `php.ini` file, and then the UTC value on Linux. It finds the time zone on Microsoft Windows in the `TimeZoneInformation\StandardName` registry key found in the active `ControlSetnnn` key of the `HKEY_LOCAL_MACHINE\SYSTEM` directory. It has the following pattern: `string date_default_timezone_get()`
`date_default_timezone_set()`	The `date_default_timezone_set()` function returns a `bool` true or false value when setting the run-time time zone for a script. It has one formal parameter, which is a valid time zone. Table F-2 lists valid time zones. Beginning with PHP 5.1, this function will return a run-time notice when the actual parameter is an invalid time zone value, and a run-time error when overriding a system setting or `TZ` environment variable on a Linux system. It has the following pattern: `bool date_default_timezone_set( string timezone_value)`
`date_sunrise()`	The `date_sunrise()` function returns the time of sunrise for a given location as a `string`, `int`, or `float` type. The default format is a `string` type represented in a 24-hour military clock style with hours and minutes. It has one mandatory and five optional parameters. The mandatory parameter is a timestamp, like that for the `time()` function, that captures the current system clock value. The first optional `int` parameter is the format value, which sets the return type of the function:
	■ `SUNFUNCS_RET_STRING` string
	■ `SUNFUNCS_RET_DOUBLE` float
	■ `SUNFUNCS_RET_TIMESTAMP` int

TABLE F-1.   *Date Library Functions* (continued)

Function Name	Function Description
	The next four optional parameters are float variables representing the `latitude`, `longitude`, `zenith`, and `gmt_offset`. The `latitude` is a positive value north of the equator and negative value south of it. The `longitude` is a positive number west of Greenwich mean time and a negative number east of it. The `zenith` is always approximately 90 degrees. The `gmt_offset` is a positive number moving west away from the oncoming sun, and a negative number moving east toward the sun. It has the following pattern:

```
mixed date_sunrise(int timestamp
 [,int output_format
 [,float latitude
 [,float longitude
 [,float zenith
 [,float gmt_offset]]]]])
```

Function Name	Function Description
date_sunset()	The `date_sunset()` function returns the time of sunset for a given location as a `string`, `int`, or `float` type. The default format is a `string` type represented in a 24-hour military clock style with hours and minutes. It has one mandatory and five optional parameters. The mandatory parameter is a timestamp, like that for the `time()` function, that captures the current system clock value. The first optional `int` parameter is the format value, which sets the return type of the function:

- ■   `SUNFUNCS_RET_STRING`   String

- ■   `SUNFUNCS_RET_DOUBLE`   Float

- ■   `SUNFUNCS_RET_TIMESTAMP`   Int

The next four optional parameters are float variables representing the `latitude`, `longitude`, `zenith`, and `gmt_offset`. The `latitude` is a positive value north of the equator and negative value south of it. The `longitude` is a positive number west of Greenwich mean time and a negative number east of it. The `zenith` is always approximately 90 degrees. The `gmt_offset` is a positive number moving west away from the oncoming sun, and a negative number moving east toward the sun. It has the following pattern:

```
mixed date_sunrise(int timestamp
 [,int output_format
 [,float latitude
 [,float longitude
 [,float zenith
 [,float gmt_offset]]]]])
```

Function Name	Function Description
getdate()	The `getdate()` function returns an associative array of date information. The function has one optional parameter, which is a *timestamp* value. When no optional *timestamp* is provided, the function returns the array for the current system date or result of the `time()` function. The array contains the following elements:

- ■   `seconds`   A two-digit value between 00 and 59 for the second in a minute.

- ■   `minutes`   A two-digit value between 00 and 59 for the minute in an hour.

- ■   `hours`   A two-digit value between 00 and 23 for an hour in a day.

- ■   `mday`   A one- to two-digit value between 1 and 31 for a day in a month.

- ■   `wday`   A one-digit number representing a day in a week where *0* means *Sunday* and *6* means *Saturday*.

- ■   `mon`   A two-digit value between 01 and 12 for a month in a year.

TABLE F-1.   *Date Library Functions* (continued)

Function Name	Function Description
	■ year A four-digit value for the current year based on the day falling in the Georgian calendar year.
	■ yday A one- to three-digit number representing a day in a year, starting with 0 and ending with 365 during leap years on the Georgian calendar.
	■ weekday A full word for a day in a week, like *Monday* to *Sunday*.
	■ month A full word for the month in a year, like *January* to *December*.
	■ 0 The seconds since the Unix Epoch that started on 1/1/1970 GMT.
	■ The getdate() function has the following pattern: array getdate([int *timestamp*])
gettimeofday()	The gettimeofday() function returns an associative array of time information. The function has one optional parameter *beginning with PHP 5.1*, which is a bool variable that changes the return type of the function. When you call the gettimeofday() function without a parameter, it returns an array by assuming the return_float flag is false. On the other hand, you will return only the Unix epoch value expressed to the microsecond level of precision as a float data type when you call the function with the optional parameter set to true. The array contains the following elements: ■ sec The seconds since the Unix Epoch that started on 1/1/1970 GMT, expressed as an int data type. ■ usec The microseconds beyond the sec value since the Unix Epoch that started on 1/1/1970 GMT, expressed as an int data type. ■ minuteswest A one- to five-digit value between 0 and 86399 for the number of minutes west of GMT. ■ dsttime A one- to two-digit value qualifying the adjustment difference for Daylight Saving Time (DST). *While displayed in PHP 5.1.4 as a legacy, the DST values are deprecated in favor of time zones and can be ignored.* The gettimeofday() function has the following pattern: mixed gettimeofday([int *timestamp*])
gmdate()	The gmdate() function returns the date as a string type and functions like the date() function except it returns the GMT value, not local time. It has two formal parameters; one is mandatory while the other is optional. The mandatory parameter designates the format of the returned date. When the optional parameter is provided, it specifies a timestamp that overrides the default current system or output from the time() function. Formatting commands can be by themselves or combined in the format parameter and are available to manage *day, week, month, year, time of day, time zone,* or *a combination of day and time,* as qualified in the table describing formatting options of the date() function. Unrecognized formatting commands will be rendered as desired characters in the date representation. You can back-quote formatting characters when you want those characters rendered as characters in the return string. The gmdate() function has the following pattern: string gmdate(string *format* [,int *timestamp*])
gmmktime()	The gmmktime() function returns a GMT Unix timestamp. The timestamp corresponds to the seconds since the Unix Epoch that started on 1/1/1970 GMT. The timestamp is returned as an int data type. The gmmktime() function has seven optional arguments but ignores the seventh beginning in PHP 5.1 because DST is deprecated for time zones. The valid optional parameters are for *hour, minute, second, month, day,* and *year.*

TABLE F-1. *Date Library Functions* (continued)

Function Name	Function Description

	The gmmktime() function has the following pattern:
	
	```int gmmktime([int hour```
	 ```[,int minute```
	 ```[,int second```
	 ```[,int month```
	 ```[,int day```
	 ```[,int year```
	 ```[,int dst]]]]]]])```

gmstrftime()	The gmstrftime() function returns the date as a string type and functions like the strftime() function except that it returns the GMT value, not local time; it is available only on Linux because there is *no* equivalent C library produced by the Microsoft Corporation. It has two formal parameters; one is mandatory while the other is optional. The mandatory parameter designates the format of the returned date. When the optional parameter is provided, it specifies a timestamp that overrides the default current system or output from the time() function. Formatting commands can be by themselves or combined in the format parameter and are available to manage *day, week, month, year, time of day, time zone,* or *a combination of day and time,* as qualified in the table describing the formatting options of the strftime() function. Unrecognized formatting commands will be rendered as desired characters in the date representation. You can back-quote formatting characters when you want those characters rendered as characters in the return string. The gmstrftime() function has the following pattern:
	
	```string gmstrftime(string format```
	 ```[,int timestamp])```

idate()	The idate() function returns the format date values as an int type; unlike the date() function, it accepts only one format parameter. It has two formal parameters; one is mandatory while the other is optional. The mandatory parameter designates the format of the returned date. When the optional parameter is provided, it specifies a timestamp that overrides the default current system or output from the time() function. It uses only one formatting command. ■ B A one- to three-character *Swatch* time, which was introduced in 1998 and is more or less a *decimal minute* like that introduced during the French Revolution. Swatch time does not recognize daylight saving time and is calculated by dividing a 24-hour time value by 1000. Each unit is called a beat and is represented as a zero-based number from 0 to 999. ■ d A one- to two-digit value between 1 and 31 for a day in a month. ■ h A one- to two-digit value between 1 and 12 for an hour in a day. ■ H A one- to two-digit value between 0 and 24 for an hour in a day, which is also known as military time. ■ i A one- to two-digit value between 0 and 59 for a minute in an hour. ■ I 1 for daylight saving time and 0 when not daylight saving time. ■ L 1 for leap year and 0 for all others. ■ m A one- to two-digit value between 1 and 12 for a month in a year. ■ s A one- to two-digit value between 0 and 59 for a second in a minute. ■ t A two-digit value between 28 and 31 for the number of days in a Georgian calendar month.

TABLE F-1. *Date Library Functions* (continued)

Function Name	Function Description
	■ U The seconds since the Unix Epoch that started on 1/1/1970 GMT.
	■ w A one-digit number representing a day in a week, where 0 means *Sunday* and 6 means *Saturday*.
	■ W A one- to two-digit number representing a week in a year. It defines weeks as beginning with *Monday* and ending with *Sunday*. This is ISO 8601 compliant.
	■ y A one- to two-digit value for the current year based on the day falling in the Georgian calendar year. The year is *not* presented with leading zeros.
	■ Y A four-digit value for the current year based on the day falling in the Georgian calendar year.
	■ z A one- to three-digit number representing a day in a Georgian year, starting with 0 and ending with 365 during leap years on the calendar.
	■ Z The time zone offset in seconds. Positive numbers are used to represent values west of UTC, and negative numbers represent values east.

	The idate() function has the following pattern:
	`int idate(string format`
	`[,int timestamp])`

localtime()	The localtime() function returns an array of timestamp values, including *day, month, year, hour, minute, second, day of the week, day of the year,* and whether *daylight saving is enabled.* The function has two optional parameters. The first optional parameter is a timestamp. When a timestamp is not furnished, the function uses the result from the time() function. The second optional parameter is a bool value that determines whether the output array is numerically or string indexed. The default false value returns a numeric array of values. When you want an associative array returned, the first optional parameter must also be provided. The function has the following pattern:
	`array localtime([int timestamp`
	`[,bool is_associative]])`

microtime()	The microtime() function returns a string with the microseconds, a white space, and the Unix Epoch seconds by default. The function takes one optional bool parameter. When the optional parameter is set to true, the function returns a float type that displays seconds on the left of the decimal point and microseconds on the right. The function has the following pattern: `string microtime([bool is_float])`

mktime()	The mktime() function returns a local Unix timestamp. The timestamp corresponds to the seconds since the Unix Epoch that started on 1/1/1970 GMT. The timestamp is returned as an int data type. The mktime() function has seven optional arguments but ignores the seventh beginning in PHP 5.1 because DST is deprecated for time zones. The valid optional parameters are for *hour, minute, second, month, day,* and *year.* The function has the following pattern:
	`int mktime([int hour`
	`[,int minute`
	`[,int second`
	`[,int month`
	`[,int day`
	`[,int year`
	`[,int dst]]]]]]])`

TABLE F-1.   *Date Library Functions* (continued)

Function Name	Function Description
strftime()	The strftime() function returns the date as a string type and functions like the strptime() function except it returns the GMT value, not local time; it is available only on Linux because there is *no* equivalent C library produced by the Microsoft Corporation. It has two formal parameters; one is mandatory while the other is optional. The mandatory parameter designates the format of the returned date. When the optional parameter is provided, it specifies a timestamp that overrides the default current system or output from the time() function. Formatting commands can be by themselves or combined in the format parameter and are available to manage *day, week, month, year, time of day, time zone,* or *a combination of day and time,* as qualified in the following list describing formatting options:

- %a A three-letter string representing a day in a week, like *Mon* to *Sun.*

- %A A full word for a day in a week, like *Monday* to *Sunday.*

- %b A three-letter string representing a month in a year, like *Jan* to *Dec.*

- %B A full word for the month in a year, like *January* to *December.*

- %c The complete local timestamp-date representation, like:
  Wed 21 Jun 2006 07:32:01 PM

- %C A two-digit value representing the first century digits of a year.

- %d A one- to two-digit value between 1 and 31 for a day in a month.

- %D This is the classic U.S. representation of two-digit *month, day,* and *year* separated by forward slashes, and equivalent to %m/%d/%y. This format does not map internationally because the international convention is: *day, month,* and *year* or %d/%m/%y.

- %e A two-character representation for a day, where the 0 in the two-digit form is replaced by a white space.

- %F A four-digit year, two-digit month, and two-digit day separated by hyphens. This is the ISO-8601 date format and is equal to a %Y-%m-%d syntax.

- %g A two-digit value between 01 and 12 for a month in a year.

- %G A four-digit year value.

- %h A three-letter string representing a month in a year, like *Jan* to *Dec* and equal to %b.

- %H A two-digit value between 00 and 24 for an hour in a day, which is also known as military time.

- %I A two-digit value between 01 and 12 for an hour in a day.

- %j A one- to three-digit number representing a day in a year, starting with 1 and ending with 366 during leap years on the Georgian calendar.

- %l A two-digit value between 01 and 12 for an hour in a day.

- %m A two-digit value between 01 and 12 for a month in a year.

- %M A two-digit value between 00 and 59 for the minute in an hour.

- %n A newline character.

- %P A two-character lowercase *ante-* or *postmeridian,* like *am* or *pm.*

TABLE F-1. *Date Library Functions* (continued)

Function Name	Function Description
	■ `$p` A two-character uppercase *ante-* or *postmeridian,* like *AM* or *PM.*
	■ `%r` The time of day in an *hour, minute, second,* and meridian format, like `%I:%M%S %p.`
	■ `%R` The time of day in 24-hour notation of *hours* and *minutes,* like `%H%M.`
	■ `%s` The seconds since the Unix Epoch that started on 1/1/1970 GMT.
	■ `%S` A two-digit value between 00 and 59 for the second in a minute.
	■ `%t` A tab character, or ASCII 32.
	■ `%T` The time of day in 24-hour notation of *hours, minutes,* and *seconds,* like `%H%M%S.`
	■ `%u` A one-digit number representing a day in a week where 1 means *Monday* and 7 means *Sunday.*
	■ `%U` A one- to two-digit number representing a week in a year. It defines weeks as beginning with *Monday* and ending with *Sunday* and has a range of 1 to 53.
	■ `%V` A one- to two-digit number representing a week in a year. It defines weeks as beginning with *Monday* and ending with *Sunday.* This is ISO-8601 compliant. The first week of the year must have four days of the current year in it.
	■ `%w` A one-digit number representing a day in a week where *0* means *Sunday* and 6 means *Saturday.*
	■ `%W` A one- to two-digit number representing a week in a year. It defines weeks as beginning with *Monday* and ending with *Sunday,* has a range of 1 to 53, and starts with the first day of the year to occur on a *Monday.*
	■ `%x` The preferred local timestamp date without qualifying time.
	■ `%X` The preferred local timestamp date without qualifying date.
	■ `%y` A two-digit value for the current year based on the day falling in the Georgian calendar year. The year is presented with leading zeros.
	■ `%Y` A four-digit value for the current year based on the day falling in the Georgian calendar year.
	■ `%z` The time zone offset in seconds. Positive numbers are used to represent values west of UTC and negative numbers represent values east.
	■ `%Z` The time zone abbreviation, like MDT.
	■ `%+` The date in UTC format.
	■ `%%` The % acts like a back-quote operator inside the function to print a % value.
	Unrecognized formatting commands will be rendered as desired characters in the date representation. You can back-quote formatting characters when you want those characters rendered as characters in the return string. The `strftime()` function has the following pattern:

```
string strftime(string format
  [,int timestamp])
```

TABLE F-1. *Date Library Functions* (continued)

Function Name	Function Description

strptime()	The strptime() function returns an array of timestamp values, including *day, month, year, hour, minute, second, day of the week, day of the year*, and whether *daylight saving is enabled*; it is available only on Linux because there is *no* equivalent C library produced by the Microsoft Corporation. The function has two mandatory parameters. The first parameter is a string date and the second is a format mask. It uses the same format masks as qualified in the strftime() function. The function has the following pattern:
	`array strptime([string date`
	` ,string format])`

strtotime()	The strtotime() function converts a string date into a int timestamp. The function has two parameters. One is mandatory, and the other is optional. The mandatory parameter is the date string for conversion. The optional parameter is the current timestamp, which provides a reference for converting the string value. It has the following pattern: `int strtotime()`
time()	The time() function takes no parameter and returns an int timestamp. It has the following pattern: `int time()`

TABLE F-1. *Date Library Functions* (continued)

You have now reviewed the date function summaries. Most are cross-platform available, but the strftime() and strptime() functions are limited in general to Linux at the time of writing. The platform limitation is due to the C library shipped with the respective operating systems.

The date() function is one that you will use quite frequently. An example reviewing how the date() function works is in the Date.php program. It demonstrates formatting a date according to the default timestamp and using both the time() and mktime() functions to override the default. Using the time() function only explicitly states what the function does implicitly by default. The mktime() function call is the only truly overriding use of the date() function in the program.

The Date.php program is:

-- This is found in Date.php on the enclosed CD.

```php
<?php
  // Print default timestamp as day, month, and year.
  print "Using default [".date("d M Y")."]<br />";

  // Print current timestamp as day, month, and year.
  print "Using time() [".date("d M Y",time())."]<br />";

  // Print future timestamp as day, month, and year.
  print "Using mktime() [".date("d M Y",mktime(12,0,0,4,6,2010))."]<br />";
?>
```

The Date.php program prints

```
Using default: [22 Jun 2006]
Using time(): [22 Jun 2006]
Using mktime(): [06 Apr 2010]
```

The strtotime() is another function that you'll use quite frequently in your programs because it enables you to calculate relative dates. You are able to instruct the function to get a date several years, months, or days in the future or past. This can be very helpful when setting cookie expiration dates as discussed in Chapter 12. While some documentation may lead you to believe that date formatting is not formal, you will find that it is. Stick to basic date formats, like two-digit *day, month,* and *year* or better yet a two-digit *day,* three-character *month,* and four-digit *year.*

The Strtotime.php program demonstrates these relative and absolute conversions:

-- This is found in Strtotime.php on the enclosed CD.

```php
<?php
  // Convert relative and absolute references to dates.
  print date("d M Y",strtotime("now"))."<br>";
  print date("d M Y",strtotime("13 June 2030"))."<br>";
  print date("d M Y",strtotime("+1 day"))."<br>";
  print date("d M Y",strtotime("+1 year"))."<br>";
  print date("d M Y",strtotime("-1 year",time()))."<br>";
?>
```

The Strtotime.php program was run June 22, 2006, and generated:

```
22 Jun 2006
13 Jun 2030
23 Jun 2006
22 Jun 2007
22 Jun 2005
```

Sometimes when you need details about a timestamp, the localtime() function enables you to secure an array of details without manually parsing a timestamp. The same values are available in the Linux strptime() function. The cross-platform localtime() function is used to demonstrate the return set. It is recommended that you set the second optional parameter to true because that lets you see meaningful index values. *When both parameters are optional, you need to provide all optional parameters because they're evaluated by position,* as discussed in Chapter 7.

The Localtime.php program uses the optional flag to return an associative as opposed to a numeric array. The associative array returned by the localtime() function contains the *day, month, year, hour, minute, second, day of the week, day of the year,* and whether *daylight saving is enabled.* You can access by index name the values returned by the associative array to calculate the interval between system access.

The Localtime.php program follows:

-- This is found in Localtime.php on the enclosed CD.

```php
<?php
  // Print HTML table and column headers.
```

```
  print '<table border="1" cellpadding="3" cellspacing="0">';
  print '<tr>';
  print '<td colspan="3" align="center" class="e">';
  print 'Today ['.date("d M y").']';
  print '</td>';
  print '</tr>';
  print '<tr>';
  print '<td class="e">Name</td>';
  print '<td class="e">Value</td>';
  print '</tr>';

  // Define the local times.
  $elements = localtime(time(),true);

  // Print array contents into HTML table.
  foreach ($elements as $name => $value)
  {
    print '<tr>';
    print '<td class="v">'.$name.'</td>';
    print '<td class="v">'.$value.'</td>';
    print '</tr>';
  }

  // Print HTML table close.
  print '</table>';
?>
```

The localtime() function call provides the time() function as the first parameter, which enables setting the second parameter to true. This makes sure that the right variables are passed in the correct positional sequence. The time() function is the default value for the first optional parameter. The results of the Localtime.php program are shown in Figure F-1.

Several of the date management functions have extensive libraries of formatting options. The Format_idate.php program shows how you can capture the meaning for electronic reference. It was chosen because the list of options is not terribly unmanageable. The program follows:

-- **This is found in Format_idate.php on the enclosed CD.**

```
<?php
  // Declare an array of format characters and short definitions.
  $formats = array(array("B","Swatch Beat/Internet Time")
                  ,array("d","Day of the month")
                  ,array("h","Hour (12 hour format)")
                  ,array("H","Hour (24 hour format)")
                  ,array("i","Minutes")
                  ,array("I","1 if daylight savings enabled")
                  ,array("L","1 if leap year")
                  ,array("m","Month number")
                  ,array("s","Seconds")
                  ,array("t","Days in current month")
                  ,array("U","Seconds since Unix Epoch")
```

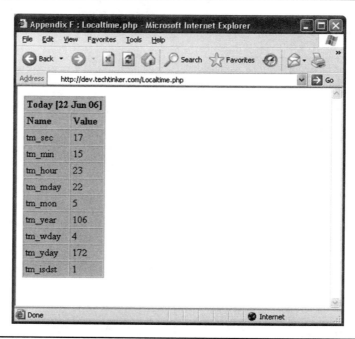

FIGURE F-1. *Localtime.php*-rendered web page

```
                ,array("w","Day of the week")
                ,array("W","ISO-8601 week number of year")
                ,array("y","Year (1 or 2 digits)")
                ,array("Y","Year (4 digits)")
                ,array("z","Day of the year")
                ,array("Z","Timezone offset in seconds"));

// Print HTML table and column headers.
print '<table border="1" cellpadding="3" cellspacing="0">';
print '<tr>';
print '<td colspan="3" align="center" class="e">';
print 'Today ['.date("d M y").']';
print '</td>';
print '</tr>';
print '<tr>';
print '<td class="e">Format</td>';
print '<td class="e">Definition</td>';
print '<td class="e">Value</td>';
print '</tr>';

// Print array contents into HTML table.
for ($i = 0;$i < count($formats);$i++)
```

```
  {
    print '<tr>';
    print '<td class="v">'.$formats[$i][0].'</td>';
    print '<td class="v">'.$formats[$i][1].'</td>';
    print '<td class="v">'.idate($formats[$i][0]).'</td>';
    print '</tr>';
  }

  // Print HTML table close.
  print '</table>';
?>
```

You can do this for the `date()` and `strftime()` functions if you want a quick shorthand reference to the formatting commands. The rendered output is shown in Figure F-2.

The last date functions left are the `date_default_timezone_get()` and `date_default_timezone_set()` functions. These are important because of the global nature of web transactions. When a user logs in to your site, you do not want to share date information relative to your location but to the user's location. You can capture it by using the JavaScript in your form, as follows:

```
<script type="text/javascript">
var now = new Date();
var time = now.gettimezoneOffset();
</script>
```

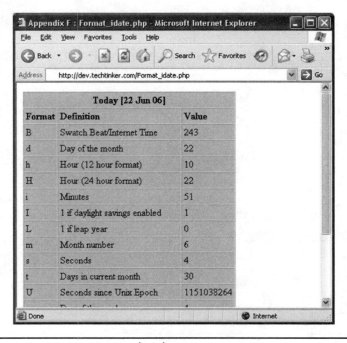

FIGURE F-2.   *Format_idate.php-rendered page*

You can then write a local JavaScript function and set it to return the `time` variable back as a parameter `tz` in the next HTTP request or via AJAX. Then, the value will be read by the next PHP program as `$_GET['tz ']` or `$_POST['tz ']`. This will enable you to calculate the proper time offset and render it in subsequent web pages. You should also write the time zone value to the local session or remote cookie too, as discussed in Chapter 12.

The `Timezone.php` program demonstrates reading the server-side time zone value:

-- This is found in Timezone.php on the enclosed CD.

```php
<?php
  // Print current time zone.
  print "Timezone is [".date_default_timezone_get()."]<br />";
?>
```

The program outputs the following:

```
Timezone is [America/Denver]
```

Table F-2 lists all valid time zones that you may encounter. You can use these to detect and set values for your display, like languages and currency values.

Africa		
Africa/Abidjan	Africa/Djibouti	Africa/Maputo
Africa/Accra	Africa/Douala	Africa/Maseru
Africa/Addis_Ababa	Africa/El_Aaiun	Africa/Mbabane
Africa/Algiers	Africa/Freetown	Africa/Mogadishu
Africa/Asmera	Africa/Gaborone	Africa/Monrovia
Africa/Bamako	Africa/Harare	Africa/Nairobi
Africa/Bangui	Africa/Johannesburg	Africa/Ndjamena
Africa/Banjul	Africa/Kampala	Africa/Niamey
Africa/Bissau	Africa/Khartoum	Africa/Nouakchott
Africa/Blantyre	Africa/Kigali	Africa/Ouagadougou
Africa/Brazzaville	Africa/Kinshasa	Africa/Porto-Novo
Africa/Bujumbura	Africa/Lagos	Africa/Sao_Tome
Africa/Cairo	Africa/Libreville	Africa/Timbuktu
Africa/Casablanca	Africa/Lome	Africa/Tripoli
Africa/Ceuta	Africa/Luanda	Africa/Tunis
Africa/Conakry	Africa/Lubumbashi	Africa/Windhoek
Africa/Dakar	Africa/Lusaka	
Africa/Dar_es_Salaam	Africa/Malabo	

TABLE F-2. *International Time Zones*

America

America/Adak	America/Chicago	America/Indiana/Vevay
America/Anchorage	America/Chihuahua	America/Indianapolis
America/Anguilla	America/Coral_Harbour	America/Inuvik
America/Antigua	America/Cordoba	America/Iqaluit
America/Araguaina	America/Costa_Rica	America/Jamaica
America/Argentina/Buenos_Aires	America/Cuiaba	America/Jujuy
America/Argentina/Catamarca	America/Curacao	America/Juneau
America/Argentina/ComodRivadavia	America/Danmarkshavn	America/Kentucky/Louisville
America/Argentina/Cordoba	America/Dawson	America/Kentucky/Monticello
America/Argentina/Jujuy	America/Dawson_Creek	America/Knox_IN
America/Argentina/La_Rioja	America/Denver	America/La_Paz
America/Argentina/Mendoza	America/Detroit	America/Lima
America/Argentina/Rio_Gallegos	America/Dominica	America/Los_Angeles
America/Argentina/San_Juan	America/Edmonton	America/Louisville
America/Argentina/Tucuman	America/Eirunepe	America/Maceio
America/Argentina/Ushuaia	America/El_Salvador	America/Managua
America/Aruba	America/Ensenada	America/Manaus
America/Asuncion	America/Fort_Wayne	America/Martinique
America/Atka	America/Fortaleza	America/Mazatlan
America/Bahia	America/Glace_Bay	America/Mendoza
America/Barbados	America/Godthab	America/Menominee
America/Belem	America/Goose_Bay	America/Merida
America/Belize	America/Grand_Turk	America/Mexico_City
America/Boa_Vista	America/Grenada	America/Miquelon
America/Bogota	America/Guadeloupe	America/Monterrey
America/Boise	America/Guatemala	America/Montevideo
America/Buenos_Aires	America/Guayaquil	America/Montreal
America/Cambridge_Bay	America/Guyana	America/Montserrat
America/Campo_Grande	America/Halifax	America/Nassau
America/Cancun	America/Havana	America/New_York
America/Caracas	America/Hermosillo	America/Nipigon
America/Catamarca	America/Indiana/Indianapolis	America/Nome
America/Cayenne	America/Indiana/Knox	America/Noronha
America/Cayman	America/Indiana/Marengo	America/North_Dakota/Center

TABLE F-2.   *International Time Zones* (continued)

America

America/Panama	America/St_Thomas	Canada/Mountain
America/Pangnirtung	America/St_Vincent	Canada/Newfoundland
America/Paramaribo	America/Swift_Current	Canada/Pacific
America/Phoenix	America/Tegucigalpa	Canada/Saskatchewan
America/Port-au-Prince	America/Thule	Canada/Yukon
America/Port_of_Spain	America/Thunder_Bay	Chile/Continental
America/Porto_Acre	America/Tijuana	Chile/EasterIsland
America/Porto_Velho	America/Toronto	Mexico/BajaNorte
America/Puerto_Rico	America/Tortola	Mexico/BajaSur
America/Rainy_River	America/Vancouver	Mexico/General
America/Rankin_Inlet	America/Virgin	US/Alaska
America/Recife	America/Whitehorse	US/Aleutian
America/Regina	America/Winnipeg	US/Arizona
America/Rio_Branco	America/Yakutat	US/Central
America/Rosario	America/Yellowknife	US/East-Indiana
America/Santiago	Brazil/Acre	US/Eastern
America/Santo_Domingo	Brazil/DeNoronha	US/Hawaii
America/Sao_Paulo	Brazil/East	US/Indiana-Starke
America/Scoresbysund	Brazil/West	US/Michigan
America/Shiprock	Canada/Atlantic	US/Mountain
America/St_Johns	Canada/Central	US/Pacific
America/St_Kitts	Canada/East-Saskatchewan	US/Pacific-New
America/St_Lucia	Canada/Eastern	US/Samoa

Antarctica

Antarctica/Casey	Antarctica/McMurdo	Antarctica/Syowa
Antarctica/Davis	Antarctica/Palmer	Antarctica/Vostok
Antarctica/DumontDUrville	Antarctica/Rothera	
Antarctica/Mawson	Antarctica/South_Pole	

Arctic

Arctic/Longyearbyen

TABLE F-2. *International Time Zones* (continued)

Asia

Asia/Aden	Asia/Jakarta	Asia/Seoul
Asia/Almaty	Asia/Jayapura	Asia/Shanghai
Asia/Amman	Asia/Jerusalem	Asia/Singapore
Asia/Anadyr	Asia/Kabul	Asia/Taipei
Asia/Aqtau	Asia/Kamchatka	Asia/Tashkent
Asia/Aqtobe	Asia/Karachi	Asia/Tbilisi
Asia/Ashgabat	Asia/Kashgar	Asia/Tehran
Asia/Ashkhabad	Asia/Katmandu	Asia/Tel_Aviv
Asia/Baghdad	Asia/Krasnoyarsk	Asia/Thimbu
Asia/Bahrain	Asia/Kuala_Lumpur	Asia/Thimphu
Asia/Baku	Asia/Kuching	Asia/Tokyo
Asia/Bangkok	Asia/Kuwait	Asia/Ujung_Pandang
Asia/Beirut	Asia/Macao	Asia/Ulaanbaatar
Asia/Bishkek	Asia/Macau	Asia/Ulan_Bator
Asia/Brunei	Asia/Magadan	Asia/Urumqi
Asia/Calcutta	Asia/Makassar	Asia/Vientiane
Asia/Choibalsan	Asia/Manila	Asia/Vladivostok
Asia/Chongqing	Asia/Muscat	Asia/Yakutsk
Asia/Chungking	Asia/Nicosia	Asia/Yekaterinburg
Asia/Colombo	Asia/Novosibirsk	Asia/Yerevan
Asia/Dacca	Asia/Omsk	Indian/Antananarivo
Asia/Damascus	Asia/Oral	Indian/Chagos
Asia/Dhaka	Asia/Phnom_Penh	Indian/Christmas
Asia/Dili	Asia/Pontianak	Indian/Cocos
Asia/Dubai	Asia/Pyongyang	Indian/Comoro
Asia/Dushanbe	Asia/Qatar	Indian/Kerguelen
Asia/Gaza	Asia/Qyzylorda	Indian/Mahe
Asia/Harbin	Asia/Rangoon	Indian/Maldives
Asia/Hong_Kong	Asia/Riyadh	Indian/Mauritius
Asia/Hovd	Asia/Saigon	Indian/Mayotte
Asia/Irkutsk	Asia/Sakhalin	Indian/Reunion
Asia/Istanbul	Asia/Samarkand	

TABLE F-2. *International Time Zones* (continued)

Atlantic

Atlantic/Azores	Atlantic/Faeroe	Atlantic/South_Georgia
Atlantic/Bermuda	Atlantic/Jan_Mayen	Atlantic/St_Helena
Atlantic/Canary	Atlantic/Madeira	Atlantic/Stanley
Atlantic/Cape_Verde	Atlantic/Reykjavik	

Australia

Australia/ACT	Australia/LHI	Australia/South
Australia/Adelaide	Australia/Lindeman	Australia/Sydney
Australia/Brisbane	Australia/Lord_Howe	Australia/Tasmania
Australia/Broken_Hill	Australia/Melbourne	Australia/Victoria
Australia/Canberra	Australia/North	Australia/West
Australia/Currie	Australia/NSW	Australia/Yancowinna
Australia/Darwin	Australia/Perth	
Australia/Hobart	Australia/Queensland	

Europe

Europe/Amsterdam	Europe/Lisbon	Europe/Sarajevo
Europe/Andorra	Europe/Ljubljana	Europe/Simferopol
Europe/Athens	Europe/London	Europe/Skopje
Europe/Belfast	Europe/Luxembourg	Europe/Sofia
Europe/Belgrade	Europe/Madrid	Europe/Stockholm
Europe/Berlin	Europe/Malta	Europe/Tallinn
Europe/Bratislava	Europe/Mariehamn	Europe/Tirane
Europe/Brussels	Europe/Minsk	Europe/Tiraspol
Europe/Bucharest	Europe/Monaco	Europe/Uzhgorod
Europe/Budapest	Europe/Moscow	Europe/Vaduz
Europe/Chisinau	Europe/Nicosia	Europe/Vatican
Europe/Copenhagen	Europe/Oslo	Europe/Vienna
Europe/Dublin	Europe/Paris	Europe/Vilnius
Europe/Gibraltar	Europe/Prague	Europe/Warsaw
Europe/Helsinki	Europe/Riga	Europe/Zagreb
Europe/Istanbul	Europe/Rome	Europe/Zaporozhye
Europe/Kaliningrad	Europe/Samara	Europe/Zurich
Europe/Kiev	Europe/San_Marino	

TABLE F-2. *International Time Zones* (continued)

Pacific

Pacific/Apia	Pacific/Johnston	Pacific/Ponape
Pacific/Auckland	Pacific/Kiritimati	Pacific/Port_Moresby
Pacific/Chatham	Pacific/Kosrae	Pacific/Rarotonga
Pacific/Easter	Pacific/Kwajalein	Pacific/Saipan
Pacific/Efate	Pacific/Majuro	Pacific/Samoa
Pacific/Enderbury	Pacific/Marquesas	Pacific/Tahiti
Pacific/Fakaofo	Pacific/Midway	Pacific/Tarawa
Pacific/Fiji	Pacific/Nauru	Pacific/Tongatapu
Pacific/Funafuti	Pacific/Niue	Pacific/Truk
Pacific/Galapagos	Pacific/Norfolk	Pacific/Wake
Pacific/Gambier	Pacific/Noumea	Pacific/Wallis
Pacific/Guadalcanal	Pacific/Pago_Pago	Pacific/Yap
Pacific/Guam	Pacific/Palau	
Pacific/Honolulu	Pacific/Pitcairn	

TABLE F-2.   *International Time Zones* (continued)

This appendix has explored the date management functions and qualified the differences between cross-platform and platform-specific functions. The summaries have covered the large number of formatting command options for the date functions. The programs in the appendix have shown brief examples of how to use the `date()`, `strtotime()`, `localtime()`, `idate()`, and `date_default_timezone_get()` functions. You have also been provided with the JavaScript to capture the client local time zone.

APPENDIX
G

Oracle Database Primer

his appendix will introduce you to the general concepts of database architecture, expose you to the Oracle Database architecture, teach you how to start and stop both the database instance and the database listener, and show you how to access SQL to build database components. These skills are critical to deploying PHP web applications using the Oracle Database 10*g* Express Edition (XE), especially if you don't have any background with the Oracle database.

The appendix covers material in the following sequence:

- Oracle Database architecture
- Starting and stopping the Oracle database
- Starting and stopping the Oracle listener
- Accessing and using SQL*Plus

There are several books that provide general introductions to the Oracle database product stack, such as Kevin Loney's *Oracle Database 10g: The Complete Reference* (McGraw-Hill/ Osborne, 2004). Also, you can find step-by-step details in Steve Bobrowski's platform-specific *Hands-on Oracle Database 10g Express Edition for Linux* or *Hands-on Oracle Database 10g Express Edition for Windows* (McGraw-Hill/Osborne, 2006).

The appendix assumes that you will read it sequentially, and each section may reference material introduced earlier. Naturally, you can zoom forward to an area of interest when you already understand the earlier material.

Oracle Database Architecture

The Oracle Database 10*g* Express Edition (XE) is a limited version of the premier Oracle Database 10*g* Enterprise Edition (EE) product. The Oracle Database 10*g* XE product contains all the standard relational database management system components that set Oracle apart in the database industry. These components enable Oracle database management systems to manage small to large data repositories consistently while data is concurrently accessed and altered by users.

You can divide the components of Oracle database management systems into two groups of services. The groups are

- *Data repositories,* also known as databases, which enable accessing any column value in one or more rows of a table or result set. Result sets are selected values of a single table or the product of joins between multiple tables (SQL joins are described in Appendix H). Tables are persistent two-dimensional structures that are organized by rows of defined structures. You create these structures when defining and creating tables in a database instance. Databases are relational databases when they include a data catalog that tracks the definitions of structures.

- *Programs,* which enable administering and accessing the data repository and provide the infrastructure to manage a data repository. The combination of a data repository and enabling programs is known as an *instance* of a database because the programs process and manage the data repository and catalog. A data catalog stores data about data, which is also known as metadata. The catalog also defines how the database management system programs will access and manage user-defined databases. The programs are background processes that manage the physical input and output to physical files and other required processing activities. Opening a relational database instance starts these background processes.

Integrating the data repository and administrative programs requires a relational programming language that (a) has a linear structure; (b) can be accessed interactively or within procedural programs; and (c) supports data definition, manipulation, and query activities. The Structured Query Language (SQL) is the relational programming language used by the Oracle database and most other relational database products.

Appendix H provides you with an introduction on how to work with Oracle SQL. Like any spoken or written language, SQL has many dialects. The Oracle Database 10*g* XE product supports two dialects of SQL. One is the Oracle-proprietary SQL syntax, and the other is the ANSI SQL: 2003. The SQL language provides users with high-level *definition, set-at-a-time, insert, update,* and *delete* operations, as well as the ability to *select* data. SQL is a high-level language because it enables you to access data without dealing with physical file access details.

Data catalogs are tables mapping data that defines other database tables, views, stored procedures, and structures. Database management systems define frameworks, which qualify what can belong in data catalogs to support database instances. They use SQL to define, access, and maintain the data catalog. Beneath the SQL interface and background processes servicing SQL commands, the database management system contains a set of library programs that manage transaction control.

The architecture of the Oracle database instance is shown in Figure G-1. The figure shows that inside a relational database instance, you have shared memory segments, active background processes, and files. The shared memory segment is known as the *shared global area (SGA)*. The SGA contains various buffered areas of memory that support access to and activities in databases. The active background processes support the database instance. The five required Oracle background processes are in fact required in every Oracle database instance; they are the *Process Monitor (PMON), System Monitor (SMON), Database Writer (DBWRn), Log Writer (LGWR),* and *Checkpoint (CKPT).* An optional background process for backup is the *Archiver (ARCn).* These six background process are found in Figure G-1. The files supporting database instances are divisible into three segments: files that contain instance variables, files that contain the physical data and data catalog, and files that contain an archive file of the data and data catalog.

The Oracle database five required instance background processes perform the following services:

- *Process Monitor (PMON)* cleans up the instance after failed processes by rolling back transactions, releasing database locks and resources, and restarting deceased processes.

- *System Monitor (SMON)* manages system recovery by opening the database, rolling forward changes from the online redo log files, and rolling back uncommitted transactions. SMON also coalesces free space and deallocates temporary segments.

- *Database Writer (DBWn)* writes data to files when checkpoints occur, dirty buffers reach their threshold or there are no free buffers, timeouts occur, Real Application Cluster (RAC) ping requests are made, tablespaces are placed in OFFLINE or READ ONLY state, tables are dropped or truncated, and tablespaces begin backup processing.

- *Log Writer (LGWR)* writes at user commits or three-second intervals; when one-third full or there is 1MB of redo instructions; and before the *Database Writer* writes.

- *Checkpoint (CKPT)* signals the *Database Writer* at checkpoints and updates the file header information for database and control files at checkpoints.

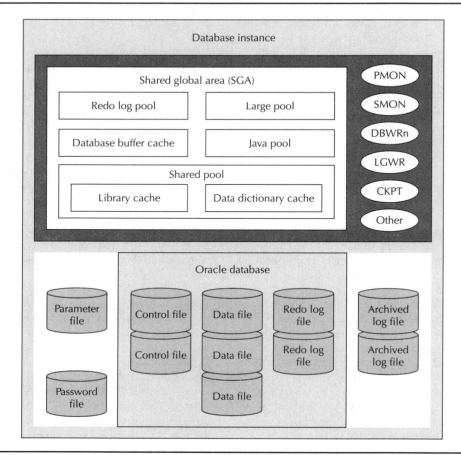

FIGURE G-1. *Oracle instance architecture diagram*

The optional *Archiver (ARCn)* process is critical to recovering databases. When an Oracle database instance is in archive mode, the *Archiver* writes to the redo log file are mirrored in the archive log files as the database switches from one redo log file to another. You should have the database in archive mode unless it is a test system and the time to rebuild it is trivial or unimportant.

The other, optional background processes for the Oracle 10g database family are the *Coordinator Job Queue (CJQ0), Dispatcher (Dnnn), RAC Lock Manager – Instance (LCKn), RAC DLM Monitor – Remote (LMDn), RAC DLM Monitor – Global Locks (LMON), RAC Global Cache Service (LMS), Parallel Query Slaves (Pnnn), Advanced Queuing (QMNn), Recoverer (RECO),* and *Shared Server (Snnn)*. Naturally, only a few of these are available in the Oracle Database 10g XE product. You have access to configuring the *Coordinator Job Queue, Dispatcher,* and *Recoverer* processes.

Understanding the *details* of how shared memory, processes, and files interact is the responsibility of the database administrator (DBA). You can find a fairly comprehensive guide to how to manage databases in the *Oracle Database 10g DBA Handbook* by Kevin Loney and Bob Bryla (McGraw-Hill/

Osborne, 2005). Immediately available to you on the enclosed CD is the *Oracle Database Express Edition 2 Day DBA* manual. You will find it on the CD as the `B25107.pdf` file.

Beyond the database instance, the Oracle database management system provides many utilities. These utilities support database backup and recovery, Oracle database file integrity verification (via the DB Verify utility – dbv), data import and export (using the `imp` and `exp` utilities), and a network protocol stack. The network protocol stack is a critical communication component that enables local and remote connections to the Oracle database by users other than the owner of the Oracle executables. The networking product stack is known as the Net8. Net8 is a complete host layer that conforms to the Open System Interconnection (OSI) Reference Model, and provides the session, presentation, and application layers. You can find more on the OSI model at http://en.wikipedia.org/wiki/OSI_model.

Oracle Net8 enables connectivity between both local and remote programs, and the database instance. Remote programs whether implemented on the same physical machine or different physical machines use an RPC communication model, like that discussed in Chapter 11. Net8 provides the packaging and de-packaging of network packets between local and remote programs to a database instance that supports RPC communications across TCP/IP.

Like the HTTPD listener model discussed in Chapter 11, Oracle has its own listener. Unlike the HTTPD listener, the Oracle listener listens for Net8-packaged transmissions on a specific port. The packaged transmissions are Oracle Net8-encoded packages. Packages are received from a network transport layer, like TCP/IP, at a designated port number, by default port 1521, where the Oracle listener hears, receives, and connects the transactions to the local database instance.

As illustrated in Figure G-2, the package arrives at the listening port where a listener thread hears it and then hands it to the OCI thread. Then, the transaction is sent through the Net8 transport layer

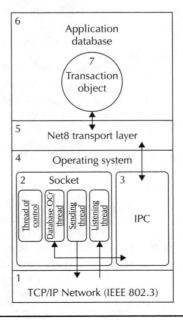

FIGURE G-2. *Oracle listener architecture*

to remove the packaging and pass the SQL command to a transactional object in a database instance, like a table, view, or stored procedure.

This process has two variations; one is called thick-client and the other is called thin-client. Thick-client communication, the old model, supports client/server computing, which worked like `telnet` or *secure shell* (`shh`) across state-aware network sockets. The thick-client communication model requires you install an Oracle client software application on the client. The Oracle client software contains the necessary programs and libraries to effect bidirectional state-aware sockets between client and server computers. The newer thin-client communication supports both state-aware and stateless transaction patterns, but it does so differently. All you need is an *Oracle Call Interface (OCI)* library that enables you to package the communication into a compatible Net8 packet. PHP uses the thin-client communication model by accessing the OCI8 library file.

Inside the database instance, user accounts are called schemas. The superuser schemas are known as `SYS` and `SYSTEM`. The `SYS` schema contains the data catalog and as a rule should never be used for routine administration. The `SYSTEM` schema has a master set of roles and privileges that enable the DBA to use it like a superuser account, and it contains administrative views to the data catalog. The `SYSTEM` schema views are typically easier to use than trying to kludge through the physical tables that contain the data catalog.

TIP
A small mistake in the data catalog can destroy your database instance and provide you with no way to recover it. Also, changing things in the `SYS` schema is not supported by your license agreement unless you are instructed to do so by Oracle to fix a specified problem.

Linux requires that you set an `$ORACLE_HOME` environment variable that maps to the physical Oracle database management home directory. Windows does not automatically create a `%ORACLE_HOME%` environment variable because it adds the fully qualified directory path to your `%PATH%` variable. You will find the environment setup script instructions in the *Oracle Database Express Edition Installation Guide* included on the enclosed CD.

The internal process that we should discuss is the HTTPD listener. It is configured inside Oracle Database 10*g* XE, but when you upgrade to the licensed product, you will need to configure the stand-alone HTTPD server or buy a supplemental license to the Oracle Application Server 10*g*. Configuration of the stand-alone HTTPD server is found in Chapter 11 of the *Expert Oracle PL/SQL* by Ron Hardman and Michael McLaughlin (McGraw-Hill/Osborne, 2005). You can find configuration instructions for the Oracle Application Server 10*g* in the *Oracle Application Server 10g Administration Handbook* by John Garmany and Donald K. Burleson (McGraw-Hill/Osborne, 2004).

NOTE
The design of Microsoft Windows compels Oracle to deploy services to start and stop the database and listener. This is done by the platform-specific utility `ORADIM`. Fortunately, the Oracle Database 10g XE installation builds these services for you. Only change them when you truly understand how to do so. A mistake working with the `ORADIM` facility can force you to refresh your operating system or manually clean up the registry.

This section has provided you with a summary of the Oracle database architecture and pointed you to some additional useful references. You can also review white papers and administration-related database architecture notes posted on http://otn.oracle.com for additional information. In the next sections, you will learn how to start and stop the database and listener, and learn how to access SQL*Plus to run SQL statements.

Starting and Stopping the Oracle Database

This section demonstrates how to start and stop the Oracle Database 10*g* XE server. The command-line utility, sqlplus, works the same for both the Linux and Microsoft Windows versions. The only difference is linked to account ownership of the database. As discussed in Chapter 10, the file system and ownership model in Microsoft Windows differs substantially from that of Linux. The differences evoke strong emotions from some people who prefer one over the other, but they simply present different opportunities and hurdles from varying perspectives.

The Oracle database management system can support multiple database instances. The ability to support multiple instances makes it necessary to assign each instance a unique System Identifier (SID). The generic database SID value is XE when installing the Oracle Database 10*g* XE server. The assignment of the SID is the same regardless of platform.

While the versions for the two operating systems are very similar, you will cover them separately. You can choose to read one or the other because both cover the same material from the perspective of the operating system. These subsections teach you how to start and shut down the database in Linux and Microsoft Windows environments.

Linux Operations

Oracle Database 10*g* XE installs as the superuser, root, on the Linux system, and is set up to start at boot. When you want to shut down or start the database after the system has booted, use the *substitute user,* su, command. The *substitute user* command lets you become another user and inherit that user's environment variables. The following command lets you change from a less privileged user to the superuser:

```
su - root
```

You will assume the mantle of root by providing the correct password to the superuser account. Then, you have two choices as to how you start or stop the database. You can use the script built during installation to *start, stop, restart, configure,* or check the *status* of the database and all attendant services by typing the following:

```
/etc/init.d/oracle-xe {start|stop|restart|configure|status}
```

Alternatively, you can use the sqlplus utility to *start, stop, restart, configure,* or check the *status* **only** of the database. You can determine whether the executable is in your current path by using the which utility, as shown:

```
which -a sqlplus
```

You can add the required directory path when the executable is not found in your current $PATH environment variable. A temporary change for the duration of your connection can be made by using

```
set PATH=/usr/lib/oracle/xe/app/oracle/product/10.2.0/server/bin:$PATH
export $PATH
```

You can then issue a `sqlplus` command to connect to the Oracle Database 10*g* XE instance as the privileged user `SYS`, using a specialized role for starting and stopping the database. The connection command is

```
sqlplus '/ as sysdba'
```

NOTE
You can connect directly to the Oracle database only when you are the owner of the Oracle database. This type of connection is a direct connection between the shell process and database, which means that the communication is not routed through Net8 and the Oracle listener does not need to be running.

After connecting to the `SQL>` prompt, you will need to provide the Oracle superuser password. Once authenticated, you will be the `SYS` user in a specialized role known as `SYSDBA`. The `SYSDBA` role exists for starting and stopping your database instance and performing other administrative tasks. You can see your current Oracle username by issuing the following SQL*Plus command:

```
SQL> show user
USER is "SYS"
```

Assuming the database is already started, you can use the following command to see the current SGA values:

```
SQL> show sga

Total System Global Area   285212672 bytes
Fixed Size                   1247544 bytes
Variable Size               71304904 bytes
Database Buffers           209715200 bytes
Redo Buffers                 2945024 bytes
```

You can *shut down* the database by choosing `abort`, `immediate`, `transactional`, or `normal`. Only the `abort` fails to secure transaction integrity, which means that database recovery is required when restarting the database. The other three *shutdown* methods do not require recovery when restarting the database. The optional arguments perform the following types of *shutdown* operations:

- *Shutdown* `normal` stops any new connections to the database and waits for all connected users to disconnect; then the Oracle instance writes completed database transactions from redo buffers to data files and marks them closed, terminates background processes, closes the database, and dismounts the database.

- *Shutdown* `transactional` stops any new connections to the database and disconnects users as soon as the current transactions complete; when all transactions complete the Oracle instance writes database and redo buffers to data files and marks them closed, terminates background processes, closes the database, and dismounts the database.

- *Shutdown* `immediate` stops all current SQL statements, rolls back all active transactions, and immediately disconnects users from the database; then the Oracle instance writes database and redo buffers to data files and marks them closed, terminates background processes, closes the database, and dismounts the database.

- *Shutdown* `abort` stops all current SQL statements and immediately shuts down without writing database and redo buffers to data files; the Oracle instance does not roll back uncommitted transactions but terminates running processes without closing physical files and the database, and it leaves the database in a mounted state requiring recovery when restarted.

The following illustrates the immediate *shutdown* of a database instance:

```
SQL> shutdown immediate
Database closed.
Database dismounted.
ORACLE instance shut down.
```

When you want to start the database, you have three options. You can start the database by using the `startup` command and either the `nomount`, `mount`, or `open` (default) option. The optional arguments perform the following types of `startup` operations:

- *Startup* `nomount` starts the instance by reading the parameter file in the `$ORACLE_HOME/dbs` directory. This file can be `spfile.ora` or `pfile.ora`. The former can't be read in a text editor but is the default parameter file option beginning with Oracle 9*i*. You can create an editable `pfile.ora` using SQL as the `SYS` user in the role of `SYSDBA` *from an open database.* This *startup* starts the background processes, allocates the SGA shared memory segment, and opens the `alertSID.log` and trace files. The SID is the name of an Oracle database instance. The value is stored in the data catalog and control files. This type of *startup* is only done when creating a new database or rebuilding control files during a backup and recovery operation.

- *Startup* `mount` does everything the `nomount` process does, and then it continues by locating, opening, and reading the control files and parameter files to determine the status of the data files and online redo log files, but no check is made to verify the existence or state of the data files. This type of *startup* is useful when you need to rename the data files, change the online redo file archiving process, or perform full database recovery.

- *Startup* `open` does everything the `mount` process does, and then it continues by locating, opening, and reading the online data files and redo log files. This is the default *startup* operation, and you use it when opening the database for user transactions.

After reconnecting to the database, if you disconnected, you can issue the `startup` command. If you provide a `nomount` or `mount` argument to the `startup` command, only those processes qualified earlier will occur. When you provide the `startup` command with no argument, the default argument `open` is applied and the database will be immediately available for user transactions. The following demonstrates a standard startup of the database instance:

```
SQL> startup
ORACLE instance started.
```

```
Total System Global Area   285212672 bytes
Fixed Size                   1247544 bytes
Variable Size               62916296 bytes
Database Buffers           218103808 bytes
Redo Buffers                 2945024 bytes
Database mounted.
Database opened.
```

Viewing how the database moves from *shutdown* to *nomount* to *mount* to *open* is helpful. The following syntax demonstrates moving the database one step at a time from a *shutdown* instance to an open database:

```
SQL> startup nomount
ORACLE instance started.

Total System Global Area   285212672 bytes
Fixed Size                   1247544 bytes
Variable Size               62916296 bytes
Database Buffers           218103808 bytes
Redo Buffers                 2945024 bytes
SQL> ALTER DATABASE MOUNT;

Database altered.

SQL> ALTER DATABASE OPEN;

Database altered.
```

The preceding output demonstrates that the Oracle instance creates the shared memory segment before opening the database, even in a `startup nomount` operation. The memory segment is created first because it is the container where you store the open instance. You can use an `ALTER` SQL statement against the database to `mount` and `open` the database instance.

This section has shown you how to shut down and restart your database instance. It has also laid a foundation for some insights into routine database administration tasks, which you can explore in the Oracle documentation provided on the enclosed media or by referencing the *Oracle Database 10*g *DBA Handbook.*

Microsoft Windows Operations

Oracle Database 10*g* XE installs as a standard program on the Microsoft Windows system. You have full access from any user account that has Administrator privileges. Oracle Database 10*g* XE also installs several services using the platform-specific `ORADIM` utility. You can find these services by opening your Control Panel and navigating to the Services icon. The navigation path changes whether you are in the Classic view or the Category view. In the Classic view, click the Administrative Tools icon and then the Services icon. In the Category view, first click the Performance and Maintenance icon, next click the Administrative Tools icon, and then the Services icon. This will bring you to the Services view displayed in Figure G-3.

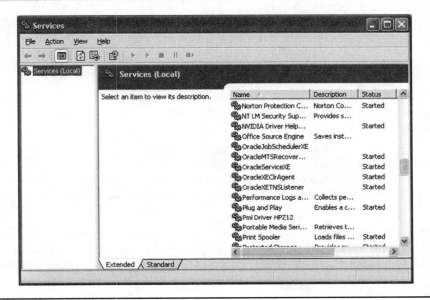

FIGURE G-3. *The Services view*

As a general rule, you are best served starting, restarting, and shutting down the services from this GUI view. However, you will need the command-line utility when you want to perform data backup and recovery activities. You can access the `sqlplus` utility from any command prompt session to manually *start, stop, restart, configure,* or check the *status* of the database. This is possible because the fully qualified directory path is placed in the generic `%PATH%` environment for all *Administrator* accounts during the product installation. Making changes in the database requires that you connect to the Oracle Database 10*g* XE instance as the privileged user `SYS`.

You'll use the SQL*Plus executable, `sqlplus`, to connect to the database. There is a specialized role for starting and stopping the database, known as `SYSDBA`. You connect using the following syntax:

```
sqlplus '/ as sysdba'
```

After you connect to the `SQL>` prompt, Oracle will prompt you for the Oracle superuser password that you set during product installation. Once authenticated, you will be the `SYS` user in a specialized role known as `SYSDBA`. The `SYSDBA` role exists for starting and stopping your database instance and performing other administrative tasks. You can see your current Oracle user name by issuing the following SQL*Plus command:

```
SQL> show user
USER is "SYS"
```

Assuming the database is already started, you use the following command to see the current SGA values:

```
SQL> show sga

Total System Global Area  285212672 bytes
Fixed Size                  1247544 bytes
Variable Size              71304904 bytes
Database Buffers          209715200 bytes
Redo Buffers                2945024 bytes
```

You can *shut down* the database by choosing `abort`, `immediate`, `transactional`, or `normal`. Only the `abort` fails to secure transaction integrity, which means that database recovery is required when restarting the database. The other three *shutdown* methods do not require recovery when restarting the database. The optional arguments perform the following types of *shutdown* operations:

- *Shutdown* `normal` stops any new connections to the database and waits for all connected users to disconnect; then the Oracle instance writes completed database transactions from redo buffers to data files and marks them closed, terminates background processes, closes the database, and dismounts the database.

- *Shutdown* `transactional` stops any new connections to the database and disconnects users as soon as the current transactions complete; when all transactions complete, the Oracle instance writes database and redo buffers to data files and marks them closed, terminates background processes, closes the database, and dismounts the database.

- *Shutdown* `immediate` stops all current SQL statements, rolls back all active transactions, and immediately disconnects users from the database; then the Oracle instance writes database and redo buffers to data files and marks them closed, terminates background processes, closes the database, and dismounts the database.

- *Shutdown* `abort` stops all current SQL statements and immediately shuts down without writing database and redo buffers to data files; the Oracle instance does not roll back uncommitted transactions but terminates running processes without closing physical files and the database, and it leaves the database in a mounted state requiring recovery when restarted.

The following illustrates the immediate *shutdown* of a database instance:

```
SQL> shutdown immediate
Database closed.
Database dismounted.
ORACLE instance shut down.
```

When you want to start the database, you have three options. You can start the database by using the `startup` command and either the `nomount`, `mount`, or `open` (default) option. The optional arguments perform the following types of `startup` operations:

- *Startup* `nomount` starts the instance by reading the parameter file in the `%ORACLE_HOME%\` `dbs` directory. This file can be `spfile.ora` or `pfile.ora`. The former can't be read in a text editor but is the default parameter file option beginning with Oracle 9*i*. You can create an editable `pfile.ora` using SQL as the `SYS` user in the role of `SYSDBA` *from* *an open database.* This *startup* starts the background processes, allocates the SGA shared memory segment, and opens the `alertSID.log` and trace files. The SID is the name of an Oracle database instance. The value is stored in the data catalog and control files. This type of *startup* is only done when creating a new database or rebuilding control files during a backup and recovery operation.

- *Startup* `mount` does everything the `nomount` process does, and then it continues by locating, opening, and reading the control files and parameter files to determine the status of the data files and online redo log files, but no check is made to verify the existence or state of the data files. This type of *startup* is useful when you need to rename the data files, change the online redo file archiving process, or perform full database recovery.

- *Startup* `open` does everything the `mount` process does, and then it continues by locating, opening, and reading the online data files and redo log files. This is the default *startup* operation and used when you want to transact against the database.

As discussed earlier, all *Administrator* user accounts have the `sqlplus` executable in their working `%PATH%` environment variable. Using the `sqlplus` command, you connect to the Oracle Database 10*g* XE instance as the privileged user `SYS` under the `SYSDBA` role. This role lets you start, stop, and perform database administration tasks on a database instance. The command is

```
sqlplus '/ as sysdba'
```

After connecting to the database, you can issue the `startup` command. If you provide a `nomount` or `mount` argument to the `startup` command, only those processes qualified will occur. When you provide the `startup` command with no argument, the default argument `open` is applied and the database will be immediately available for transactions. The following demonstrates a standard startup of the database instance:

```
SQL> startup
ORACLE instance started.

Total System Global Area   285212672 bytes
Fixed Size                   1247544 bytes
Variable Size               62916296 bytes
Database Buffers           218103808 bytes
Redo Buffers                 2945024 bytes
Database mounted.
Database opened.
```

Viewing how the database moves from *shutdown* to *nomount* to *mount* to *open* is helpful. The following syntax demonstrates moving the database one step at a time from a *shutdown* instance to an open database:

```
SQL> startup nomount
ORACLE instance started.

Total System Global Area   285212672 bytes
Fixed Size                   1247544 bytes
Variable Size               62916296 bytes
Database Buffers           218103808 bytes
Redo Buffers                 2945024 bytes
```

```
SQL> ALTER DATABASE MOUNT;

Database altered.

SQL> ALTER DATABASE OPEN;

Database altered.
```

The preceding output demonstrates that the Oracle instance creates the shared memory segment before opening the database, even in a `startup nomount` operation. The memory segment is created first because it is the container where you store the open instance. You can use an `ALTER` SQL statement against the database to `mount` and `open` the database instance.

This section has shown you how to shut down and restart your database instance. It has also laid a foundation for some insight into routine database administration tasks, which you can explore in the Oracle documentation provided on the enclosed CD or by referencing the *Oracle Database 10*g *DBA Handbook*.

Starting and Stopping the Oracle Listener

The Oracle `lsnrctl` utility lets you start the server-side Oracle listener process on a port that you set in the `listener.ora` configuration file. There are actually three files used in configuring the Oracle Net8 listener—they are the `listener.ora`, `tnsnames.ora`, and `sqlnet.ora` configuration files. The `sqlnet.ora` file is not necessary for basic operations and is not configured in the shipped version of Oracle Database 10*g* XE. You can use the `sqlnet.ora` file to set network tracing commands, which are qualified in the *Oracle Database Net Services Administrator's Guide 10*g *Release 2* and *Oracle Database Net Services Reference 10*g *Release 2* documentation. You may browse or download these from http://otn .oracle.com for supplemental information.

The network configuration files are in the `network/admin` subdirectory of the Oracle Database 10*g* XE product home directory. The following qualifies the default Oracle product home by platform:

Linux:

```
/usr/lib/oracle/xe/app/oracle/product/10.2.0/server
```

Microsoft Windows:

```
C:\oraclexe\app\oracle\product\10.2.0\server
```

The Oracle product home path is typically set as an environment variable for all user accounts. Environment variables are aliases that point to something else and exist in all operating systems. You can set an Oracle product home directory as follows by platform:

Linux:

```
export set ORACLE_HOME=/usr/lib/oracle/xe/app/oracle/product/10.2.0/server
```

Microsoft Windows:

```
set ORACLE_HOME=C:\oraclexe\app\oracle\product\10.2.0\server
```

You can then navigate to the Oracle product home by using the `$ORACLE_HOME` in Linux or `%ORACLE_HOME%` in Microsoft Windows. These settings are temporary unless you put them in a configuration file that gets sourced when you connect to your system in Linux. It is a convention for you to put these in your `.bashrc` file or have your system administrator put them in the standard .profile account in Linux. You can also configure permanent environment variables in your *System Properties* in Microsoft Windows.

You will find the instructions for setting the Oracle Database XE Client environment variables in the *Oracle Database Express Edition Installation Guide* included on the CD. The Linux installation guide is in the `B25144.pdf` file, and the Microsoft Windows installation guide is in the `B25143.pdf` file.

TIP
You can set your environment variables by going to the Control Panel, launching the System icon, choosing the Advanced tab, and clicking the Environment Variable button.

The sample `listener.ora` file is a configuration file. A `listener.ora` file exists after you install Oracle Database 10g XE. You will find that your `listener.ora` file contains the *Oracle product home directory*, your server machine *hostname,* and a *port number.* These values are critical pieces of information that enable your listener to find your Oracle installation. These data components mirror the configuration directives that enable Apache or IIS to hand off HTTP requests to appropriate services.

The only differences between the Linux and Microsoft Windows operating system versions are different path statement for the Oracle product home and the case sensitivity or insensitivity of the hostname. The *hostname* is lowercase for a Linux system and uppercase for Microsoft Windows.

```
-- This is an example of a default listener.ora file.

LISTENER =
  (DESCRIPTION_LIST =
    (DESCRIPTION =
      (ADDRESS = (PROTOCOL = IPC)(KEY = EXTPROC1))
      (ADDRESS = (PROTOCOL = TCP)(HOST = hostname)(PORT = port_number))
    )
  )

SID_LIST_LISTENER =
  (SID_LIST =
    (SID_DESC =
      (SID_NAME = PLSExtProc)
      (ORACLE_HOME = oracle_product_home_directory)
      (PROGRAM = extproc)
    )
    (SID_DESC =
      (SID_NAME = CLRExtProc)
      (ORACLE_HOME = oracle_product_home_directory)
      (PROGRAM = extproc)
    )
  )

DEFAULT_SERVICE_LISTENER = (XE)
```

The `listener.ora` file has two key addressing components. The first is the actual listener name, which by default isn't too original because it is an uppercase string, `LISTENER`. The default listener name is implicitly assumed unless you provide an overriding listener name to any `lsnrctl` command. You must explicitly provide the listener name when you use anything other than the default as your actual listener name.

The listener name is also appended to the `SID_LIST` descriptor, which registers static maps for external procedures and the Oracle Heterogeneous Server. Oracle Database 10*g* XE uses two external procedure configurations—`PLSExtProc` and `CLRExtProc`. Oracle recommends that you have discrete listeners for IPC and TCP traffic, but the standard listener configuration file will work unless you attempt to access user-defined shared libraries or DLLs and encounter an ORA-28595 error.

TIP
Using user-defined shared libraries, DLLs, and PL/SQL wrappers will require you to break up IPC and TCP listening activities into separate IPC and TCP listeners. You can find more on that topic in Chapter 11 of Oracle Database 10*g* PL/SQL Programming *by Scott Urman, Ron Hardman, and Michael McLaughlin (McGraw-Hill/Osborne, 2004).*

The `DEFAULT_SERVICE_LISTENER` is set to *XE* in the `listener.ora` file. XE also is the global name of the current database instance. The `SERVICE_NAME` parameter defaults to the global database name when one is not specified in the `spfileSID.ora` or `pfileSID.ora` file. The service name for any Oracle database is the database name concatenated to the database domain. Oracle Database 10*g* XE defines the database name as XE and assigns no database domain. You can find this information by connecting as the `SYS` user under the `SYSDBA` role, formatting the return values, and running the following query:

```
COL name FORMAT A30
COL value FORMAT A30

SELECT    name
,         value
FROM      v$parameter
WHERE     name LIKE '%name'
OR        name LIKE '%domain';
```

The query returns the following data:

```
NAME                              VALUE
------------------------------    ------------------------------
db_domain
instance_name                     xe
db_name                           XE
db_unique_name                    XE
```

Net8 is designed to support client load balancing and connect-time failover. The `SERVICE_NAME` replaces the `SID` parameter that previously enabled these features. The `tnsnames.ora` file is a mapping file that enables client requests to find the Oracle listener. The `tnsnames.ora` file contains a network alias that maps to the Oracle `SERVICE_NAME` and connection configurations to facilitate access to external procedures. The *hostname* and *port_number* enable the network alias, XE, to find the Oracle listener. Naturally, there is an assumption that your *hostname* maps through DNS resolution or the local host file to a physical Internet Protocol (IP) address.

TIP
You can add the hostname and IP address to your local host file when you do not resolve to a server through DNS. The /etc/host *file is the Linux host file, and the* C:\WINDOWS\system32\drivers\etc *file is the Microsoft Windows host file.*

A sample tnsnames.ora file is

```
-- This is an example of a default tnsnames.ora file.

XE =
  (DESCRIPTION =
    (ADDRESS = (PROTOCOL = TCP)(HOST = hostname)(PORT = port_number))
    (CONNECT_DATA =
      (SERVER = DEDICATED)
      (SERVICE_NAME = XE)
    )
  )

EXTPROC_CONNECTION_DATA =
  (DESCRIPTION =
    (ADDRESS_LIST =
      (ADDRESS = (PROTOCOL = IPC)(KEY = EXTPROC1))
    )
    (CONNECT_DATA =
      (SID = PLSExtProc)
      (PRESENTATION = RO)
    )
  )

ORACLR_CONNECTION_DATA =
  (DESCRIPTION =
    (ADDRESS_LIST =
      (ADDRESS = (PROTOCOL = IPC)(KEY = EXTPROC1))
    )
    (CONNECT_DATA =
      (SID = CLRExtProc)
      (PRESENTATION = RO)
    )
  )
```

Some strings in these configuration files are case sensitive. An example is the PROGRAM value in the listener.ora file and the KEY value in the tnsnames.ora file. These values are case sensitive and must match exactly between files or you will receive an ORA-28576 error when accessing the external procedure.

These files support the `lsnrctl` utility regardless of platform. The `lsnrctl` utility enables you to *start, stop,* and check the *status* of the listener process. As discussed when covering how to start and stop the database instance, you will need to be the `root` user in the Linux environment and an *Administrator* user in the Microsoft Windows environment.

The default installation starts the Oracle listener when the system boots, but we should check whether it is running before attempting to shut it down. You can use the following to check the status of the Oracle listener:

```
lsnrctl status
```

As discussed, the command implicitly substitutes `LISTENER` as the default second argument. You will need to explicitly provide the listener name when *starting, stopping,* or *checking status* when you have changed the default listener name. You should see the following on a Microsoft Windows system when you check the status of a running Oracle Database 10*g* XE listener and only slight differences on a Linux system:

```
LSNRCTL for 32-bit Windows: Version 10.2.0.1.0 - Beta on 17-JUN-2006

Copyright (c) 1991, 2005, Oracle.  All rights reserved.

Connecting to (DESCRIPTION=(ADDRESS=(PROTOCOL=IPC)(KEY=EXTPROC1)))
STATUS of the LISTENER
------------------------
Alias                     LISTENER
Version                   TNSLSNR for 32-bit Windows: Version 10.2.0.1.0 -
Start Date                17-JUN-2006 20:11:37
Uptime                    0 days 0 hr. 0 min. 21 sec
Trace Level               off
Security                  ON: Local OS Authentication
SNMP                      OFF
Default Service           XE
Listener Parameter File   C:\oraclexe\app\ ... \network\admin\listener.ora
Listener Log File         C:\oraclexe\app\ ... \network\log\listener.log
Listening Endpoints Summary...
  (DESCRIPTION=(ADDRESS=(PROTOCOL=ipc)(PIPENAME=\\.\pipe\EXTPROC1ipc)))
  (DESCRIPTION=(ADDRESS=(PROTOCOL=tcp)(HOST=MCLAUGHLIN-DEV)(PORT=1521)))
Services Summary...
Service "CLRExtProc" has 1 instance(s).
  Instance "CLRExtProc", status UNKNOWN, has 3 handler(s) for this service
Service "PLSExtProc" has 1 instance(s).
  Instance "PLSExtProc", status UNKNOWN, has 1 handler(s) for this service
The command completed successfully
```

You can stop the service by using

```
lsnrctl stop
```

You can restart the service by using

```
lsnrctl start
```

After stopping and starting the listener, you should check if you can make a network connection from your user account to the listener. This is very similar to the idea of a network ping operation, except you are pinging the Oracle Net8 connection layer. You use the `tnsping` utility to verify an Oracle Net8 connection, as follows:

tnsping xe

You should see the following type of return message but with a real *hostname* as opposed to the substituted `hostname` value; provided you haven't changed the default network *port number*:

```
Disconnected from Oracle Database 10g Express Edition Release 10.2.0.1.0

C:\Documents and Settings\Client>tnsping xe

TNS Ping Utility for 32-bit Windows: Version 10.2.0.1.0
Copyright (c) 1997, 2005, Oracle.  All rights reserved.

Used parameter files:
C:\oraclexe\app\oracle\product\10.2.0\server\network\admin\sqlnet.ora

Used TNSNAMES adapter to resolve the alias
Attempting to contact (DESCRIPTION = (ADDRESS = (PROTOCOL = TCP)(HOST =
hostname)(PORT = 1521)) (CONNECT_DATA = (SERVER = DEDICATED) (SERVICE_NAME =
XE)))

OK (10 msec)
```

The `tnsping` checks the `sqlnet.ora` parameter file for any instructions that it may contain. Net8 connections first check the `sqlnet.ora` file to find any network tracing instructions before proceeding with connection attempts. The Oracle Net8 tracing layers are very powerful tools and can assist you in diagnosing complex connection problems. You will find answers to configuring `sqlnet.ora` in the *Oracle Database Net Services Reference 10g Release 2.*

You can use a GUI tool to *start, stop,* and check the *status* of the Oracle listener when you are running on Microsoft Windows. You can find it by navigating to Control Panel, then if you are using a Classic view, choose Administrative Tools and then Services; but if you are using a Category view, choose Performance and Maintenance | Administrative Tools and Services. Right-click OracleXETNSListener in the list of services in the right panel and click Stop the Service.

This section has explained where the configuration files are and how they work to enable you to *start, stop,* and check the *status* on the Oracle listener. In the next section you will see how users connect using the Oracle listener.

Accessing and Using SQL*Plus Interface

The Oracle Database 10g XE product provides you with two interfaces to access, insert, update, or delete data, as well as to create, alter, and drop structures in database instances. Both interfaces enable you to interact with the database by using Structured Query Language (SQL). If you are unfamiliar with the concepts of SQL, please check Appendix H before continuing with this segment.

Oracle SQL*Plus is both an interactive environment where you can enter SQL statements and process them one by one, or where you can run scripts as batch submissions. Scripts are small SQL programs or collections of programs found in a single file.

You have two ways to use SQL with the Oracle Database 10*g* XE product. One is through the web page interface, and the other is through a command-line interface. This section will cover the command-line tool first and then the web page interface. The web page interface has restrictions when performing database administration tasks and disallows dynamic changes between sessions, but you can log out as the current user and back in as the new user.

The Oracle SQL and PL/SQL examples used in Chapters 13 and 14 require you to create an Oracle user account or schema named PHP. You can create the user in the web pages, but you cannot assign the new user a default storage clause other than the default *user* tablespace. Storage clauses enable you to designate where a user will physically store data. Tablespaces are logical structures that act as portals to one to many physical files.

The basic architecture of a user schema is disconnected from physical storage through a series of software abstractions. A user can access and store data in one or more tablespaces, and a tablespace can reference one or more files. This architecture enables a user to store more data than the physical file limits imposed by an operating system. You designate a default storage tablespace when you define a user/schema, but Oracle Database 10*g* XE plans on all users being stored in the USER tablespace.

The enclosed scripts do not attempt to override the planned intent of the product but assume you will use the default USER tablespace. If you are working in an Oracle Standard or Enterprise Edition version of the database, you should consider creating a *php* tablespace and modifying the scripts to place all data there.

You will work with the command-line interface first because doing so provides an opportunity to discuss the differences between the SQL*Plus and SQL environments. The discussion lays a foundation for the subsequent web page interface materials. You can further your understanding of Oracle SQL*Plus by referring to the *SQL*Plus User Guide and Reference Release 2,* or Oracle SQL by referring to the *Oracle Database SQL Reference 10g Release 2* found on http://otn.oracle.com.

SQL Command-Line Interface

The SQL*Plus command-line interface requires that you have an account on the server or that you install Oracle client software on your local machine. The command-line tool requires a thick-client connection to build a socket between a client and server. The interactive SQL*Plus interface is provided by the Oracle client software.

You can access the SQL*Plus application directly when you are working on the same machine as the Oracle database. If you are working on a Linux machine, you will need to put the $ORACLE_HOME/bin directory in your environment path and set several other environment variables. You will find the instructions for setting the Oracle Database XE Client environment variables in the *Oracle Database Express Edition Installation Guide* included on the CD. The Linux installation guide is in the B25144.pdf file, and the Microsoft Windows installation guide is in the B25143.pdf file.

Only Linux users will need to set the environment file. You do it by running oracle_env.csh when your account uses c or tcsh shell, or oracle_env.sh when your account uses Bash or Korn shell. They are in the following directory after a standard Oracle Database 10*g* XE installation:

```
/usr/lib/oracle/xe/app/oracle/product/10.2.0/client/bin
```

After creating your environment variable file, you source the file into your environment and copy the `create_user.sql` and `create_world_leaders.sql` files to a working directory owned by your user account. These files build your Oracle PHP user account and seed database objects that you will use in Chapters 13, 14, and 15.

Microsoft Windows users will need to open a *Command Prompt* session to access the SQL*Plus command-line tool. There is no GUI version of SQL*Plus delivered as part of the Oracle Database 10*g* XE product.

NOTE
*The GUI version of SQL*Plus is set to be deprecated in the next release of the database.*

In the directory *where you have copied the two files,* you can now connect to the SQL*Plus environment by typing the following command:

```
sqlplus system/password@xe
```

This assumes you own or have access to the Oracle superuser accounts, `SYS` and `SYSTEM`, and know the password. If you don't own the superuser account, you should contact your DBA to run the `create_user.sql` script from the `SYSTEM` account. The `@xe` is an instruction to use the network alias in your `tnsnames.ora` file to find the database. When you append a TNS alias, the connection only resolves through a running Oracle listener.

You can execute scripts from the SQL*Plus environment by prefacing them with an `@` symbol. This reads the file directly into a line-by-line execution mode. Alternatively, you can use the `GET` command to read the file into the current SQL*Plus buffer, before running it. The latter method is fine when you have only a SQL statement in the file and no SQL*Plus statements. *DO **not** use the GET command with these scripts* because they contain a mix of SQL and SQL*Plus statements.

NOTE
*SQL commands let you interact with the database, while SQL*Plus commands let you configure your SQL*Plus environment. They also enable you to format and secure feedback from the database on the success or failure of your SQL statements.*

You create the PHP user and schema with the `create_user.sql` script. The script contains SQL*Plus, SQL, and PL/SQL components. PL/SQL, which stands for Procedural Language/Structured Query Language, was created by Oracle to let users write stored procedures in the database. Appendix I reviews the basics of the PL/SQL language, or you may consider reviewing the *Oracle Database 10*g *PL/SQL Programming* book.

You have two options as to how you run the script. The first option is to connect to SQL*Plus and run the script from the command line. The second option is to run the script as an actual parameter to the `sqlplus` executable. The easiest way for new Oracle users is to connect to SQL*Plus and run the script. You connect with the command

```
sqlplus system/password@xe
```

The script will fail unless you run it as the SYSTEM user. After connecting as the SYSTEM user, you use this syntax to run the script from a local Linux directory or Microsoft Windows folder:

```
SQL> @create_user.sql
```

This script checks whether there is an existing PHP user in your database before creating one. It removes the PHP user when found. Dropping a user wipes out all objects owned by that user. This script can be rerun in case you make an error and want to wipe out your working area to start over, but remember that it wipes everything owned by the previous PHP user. The create_user.sql follows:

```
-- This is found in create_user.sql on the enclosed CD.

SET FEEDBACK ON
SET PAGESIZE 999
SET SERVEROUTPUT ON SIZE 1000000

DECLARE
  -- Define an exception.
  wrong_schema EXCEPTION;
  PRAGMA EXCEPTION_INIT(wrong_schema,-20001);

  -- Define a return variable.
  retval VARCHAR2(1 CHAR);

  /*
  || Define a cursor to identify whether the current user is either the
  || SYSTEM user or a user with the DBA role privilege.
  */
  CURSOR privs IS
    SELECT   DISTINCT null
    FROM     user_role_privs
    WHERE    username = 'SYSTEM'
    OR       granted_role = 'DBA';
BEGIN
  -- Open cursor and read through it.
  OPEN privs;
  LOOP

    -- Read a row.
    FETCH privs INTO retval;

    -- Evaluate if cursor failed.
    IF privs%NOTFOUND THEN
      -- Raise exception.
      RAISE wrong_schema;
    ELSE
      -- Evaluate whether PLSQL user exists and drop it.
      FOR i IN (SELECT null FROM dba_users WHERE username = 'PHP') LOOP
        EXECUTE IMMEDIATE 'DROP USER php CASCADE';
      END LOOP;
```

```
      -- Create user and grant privileges.
      EXECUTE IMMEDIATE 'CREATE USER php IDENTIFIED BY php';
      EXECUTE IMMEDIATE 'GRANT connect TO php';
      EXECUTE IMMEDIATE 'GRANT resource TO php';

      -- Print successful outcome.
      DBMS_OUTPUT.PUT_LINE(CHR(10)||'Created PHP user.');
    END IF;

    -- Exit the loop.
    EXIT;

  END LOOP;

  -- Close cursor.
  CLOSE privs;

EXCEPTION
  -- Handle a defined exception.
  WHEN wrong_schema THEN
    DBMS_OUTPUT.PUT_LINE('The script requires the SYSTEM user and '
      ||                 'you are using the <'||user||'> schema or '
      ||                 'the script requires a user with DBA role '
      ||                 'privileges.');

  -- Handle a generic exception.
  WHEN others THEN
    DBMS_OUTPUT.PUT_LINE(SQLERRM);
    RETURN;
END;
/

-- Define SQL*Plus formatting.
COL grantee          FORMAT A8
COL granted_role     FORMAT A30
COL grantor          FORMAT A12
COL privilege        FORMAT A12
COL owner            FORMAT A6
COL table_name       FORMAT A10

-- Query user granted roles.
SELECT   grantee
,        granted_role
FROM     dba_role_privs
WHERE    grantee = 'PHP';

-- Query resources.
SELECT   grantor
,        owner
,        table_name
```

```
,          grantee
,          privilege
FROM       dba_tab_privs
WHERE      grantee = 'PHP';

COL admin_option        FORMAT A3
COL privilege           FORMAT A30
COL username            FORMAT A10

-- Query user system privileges.
SELECT     grantee
,          privilege
,          admin_option
FROM       dba_sys_privs
WHERE      grantee = 'PHP';
```

Coming from a MySQL background, the script may look like the new stored procedures introduced in version 5. This file uses Oracle PL/SQL to manage the process of creating a user. The script then uses formatting commands to govern the output from two SQL queries, and the queries determine the permissions of the new user.

The COL [UMN] and SET commands belong to the SQL*Plus environment and are specific to Oracle. They let you configure the way output is rendered in the command-line SQL*Plus environment. You will not need to worry about these through the web page because they generate result sets in HTML tables.

You should see the following output after running the script:

```
GRANTEE   GRANTED_ROLE
--------  ------------------------------
PHP       DBA
PHP       CONNECT

2 rows selected

no rows selected

GRANTEE   PRIVILEGE                       ADM
--------  ------------------------------  ---
PHP       UNLIMITED TABLESPACE            NO

1 rows selected.
```

These are the base permissions required for the PHP user. The password is set trivially as PHP, but you can change it to whatever you like. You have two options to change a password. The first option is to type password at the SQL prompt, as shown:

```
SQL> password
Changing password for PHP
Old password:
New password:
Retype new password:
Password changed
```

The second option for changing your password is to use the ALTER SQL command to change the PHP user password. The syntax is

```
SQL> ALTER USER php IDENTIFIED BY secret_password;
```

After you connect through the Oracle Database 10*g* XE web page login page, the second query against the DBA_TAB_PRIVS table in the create_user.sql script will return a different set of granted privileges. These are granted as part of your initial login through the web applications. The new granted privileges for the PHP user are

```
GRANTOR        OWNER    TABLE_NAME  GRANTEE   PRIVILEGE
-------------  ------   ----------  --------  ------------
FLOWS_020100   SYS      DBMS_RLS    PHP       EXECUTE
FLOWS_020100   CTXSYS   CTX_DDL     PHP       EXECUTE
FLOWS_020100   CTXSYS   CTX_DOC     PHP       EXECUTE
```

While keeping your SQL*Plus session active, you should connect as the PHP user to the database instance. Log in as the PHP user using the Oracle Database 10*g* XE homepage found at http://*hostname*:8080/apex/ unless you've changed the embedded HTTPD listener port number to something other than the default 8080. On Microsoft Windows, Oracle will use a different port number if you have something running on port 8080, like Tomcat. By the way, don't forget to change the *hostname* to your correct hostname.

After logging in as the PHP user through the web form, return to the SQL*Plus session and rerun *only* the second query. You should probably copy the query out of the script so that you don't inadvertently recreate the user with fewer granted privileges by rerunning create_user.sql.

You can now disconnect from the SQL*Plus session by using the word **quit** and a return key:

```
SQL> quit
```

There is a great deal more information about the SQL*Plus environment but you will need to review it in the *SQL*Plus User Guide and Reference Release 2* manual, which is over 500 pages long. There is also a client/server GUI version of SQL*Plus that ships with the Oracle Database 10*g* Standard and Enterprise Editions, but remember the GUI SQL*Plus is deprecated in the next database release. Only the command-line version will ship in future releases.

SQL Web Application Interface

The SQL*Plus web application interface provides you with some nice query-by-example (QBE) and SQL wizards to develop your applications. These tools are nice for both novice and experienced developers. They do, however, have some keen limitations that you will encounter as you use them.

This section will demonstrate how you use the web application interface to create a user, upload SQL scripts to the server, and run your uploaded SQL scripts in your user account. The upload utility stores your scripts inside the database as character large objects (CLOBs). They become a code repository that you can edit and update. When you run scripts from your repository, you read them from the database source and dynamically execute them in a SQL*Plus session.

NOTE
*The Oracle Database 10*g *XE web application uses URL rewriting to maintain your session information, which is covered in Chapter 11.*

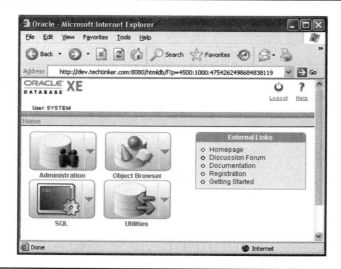

FIGURE G-4. *Oracle Database 10*g *XE home page*

Log in as the SYSTEM user at http://*hostname*:8080/apex/ but don't forget to change the *hostname* to the correct hostname. Figure G-4 illustrates what you see when you log in to the Oracle Database 10*g* XE web application.

You should click the SQL button on the home page to navigate to the SQL page. As found in Figure G-5, you will see three icons: SQL Commands, SQL Scripts, and Query Builder. These icons lead you to three development environments.

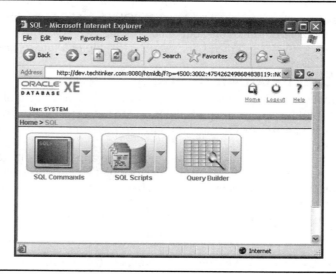

FIGURE G-5. *Oracle Database 10*g *XE SQL page*

The SQL Commands button takes you to an interactive SQL session manager. Unlike the command-line SQL*Plus session, the web interface does not support SQL*Plus formatting commands. The best you can do is click the CSV Export link to download the results to your client as a comma-delimited file. You can then open it in Microsoft Excel or open Office Calc to format the output.

The SQL Scripts button takes you to an interactive page that lets you upload SQL program to the database. Once uploaded, your scripts are stored as CLOB data types in a table. You can edit them by double-clicking the image representing the file in the web page. This will place the code in an editable object in the web page, where you can edit the script and then run it.

The Query Builder button takes you to a QBE console, where you can build queries without having to write them in SQL. This is a very helpful point-and-click tool for developing SQL queries. You can learn about SQL while using this interface because it lets you see the SQL statements before you run them. The web page also lets you save the queries to run again.

You should double-click the SQL Scripts button and upload the `create_user.sql` script to the database. The refreshed page will show a file icon with the name of the script below it. Double-click the script to load it into the Script Editor web page and click the Run button. The Run Script web page will prompt with a warning message (shown in Figure G-6) that the `create_user.sql` script contains statements that will be ignored. You can safely ignore the warning and click the Run button because those statements are SQL*Plus commands and will not alter the purpose of the script.

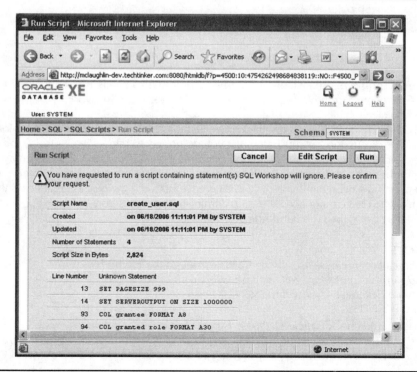

FIGURE G-6.   *Run Script warning message page*

After you click the Run button, you will be brought to the Manage Script Result web page. This page will tell you that the results have been submitted to the database. Job submission means that any diagnostic script results will not be displayed as output. This means you will need to submit the three diagnostic queries about roles, grants, and privileges in the SQL Commands web page. Using your favorite text editor, you can copy the queries into the SQL Commands web page and run them. Alternatively, you can adopt a policy of writing diagnostic results to a tracking table, which can be populated by the submitted jobs. Make sure you look up autonomous transactions and configure these table writes as autonomous when you choose this direction.

NOTE
On Linux you're probably using the vim editor, but if you're on Microsoft Windows you might want to download notepad++. It is a nice text editor and supports the HTML, JavaScript, PHP, and SQL languages very well. Unfortunately, it does not support Oracle PL/SQL at present; for that, you should try Toad by Quest Software.

There shouldn't be much load on your Oracle Database 10*g* XE instance, and the job should complete fairly quickly. You can check the job status by navigating to the SQL Scripts web page and clicking the Manage Results bullet in the grayed task box at the far right. This will display all jobs run and their respective completion time.

You can confirm the PHP user is created by running the following query in the SQL Commands web page:

```
SELECT    username
FROM      all_users
WHERE     username = 'PHP';
```

The query should return a single username column with a single row containing the string literal PHP. This means you have successfully created the PHP user for work in Chapters 13, 14, and 15 of the book.

You have learned how to use the Oracle Database 10*g* web application to upload, edit, and run scripts. The discussion has illustrated that you do not get to interactively display the results of script performance because they are submitted as remote scheduled jobs. While you may recognize that there are benefits and costs to both command-line and web application interfaces, not all differences have been highlighted. One difference between the two approaches is that privileged users like SYSTEM cannot access certain administrative views from the web application that can be accessed by using the command-line SQL*Plus session.

NOTE
You can create new uses by navigating through the Home | Administration | Manage Database Users web pages to the Create Database User web page.

You should check *Oracle Database Express Edition Application Express User's Guide* and the *Oracle Database Express Edition 2 Day Developer Guide* for more complete coverage. You will find the *User's Guide* in the B25309.pdf file and *2 Day Developer Guide* in the B25108.pdf file on the enclosed CD. Also, you may benefit from books like *Oracle Database 10g: The Complete Reference* and step-by-step details in the platform-specific *Hands-on Oracle Database 10g Express Edition for Linux* or *Hands-on Oracle Database 10g Express Edition for Windows* book.

Summary

This appendix has introduced you to the architecture of relational databases and demonstrated how you start and stop database instances on Linux and Microsoft Windows. It has also shown you how to start, stop, and check the status of an Oracle listener and access the SQL*Plus environment to interact with the database.

APPENDIX
H

SQL Primer

he *Structured Query Language (SQL)* is the mechanism for accessing information in relational databases. The SQL acronym has different pronunciations, but many use the word *sequel* because IBM originally named it the *Structured English Query Language.* The SEQUEL acronym mutated to SQL when IBM discovered the original acronym was trademarked by Hawker Siddeley.

SQL is a nonprocedural programming language designed to work with data sets in relational database management systems. SQL lets you define, modify, and remove database objects, transact against data, control the flow of transactions, and query data. The SQL language commands are often grouped by function into four groups that are also called languages: *Data Definition Language (DDL), Data Manipulation Language (DML), Data Control Language (DCL),* and *Data Query Language (DQL).*

As a SQL primer, this appendix covers these languages in the order required to build database applications. The primer will refer to examples provided in Appendix J that support Chapters 13, 14, and 15. The appendix covers

- Oracle SQL data types
- Data Definition Language (DDL)
- Data Query Language (DQL)
- Data Manipulation Language (DML)
- Data Control Language (DCL)

DCL and DQL are not universally accepted in many published references. DCL was originally called *Transaction Control Language (TCL),* and DQL was considered part of the DML language commands. While Oracle Corporation used the TCL acronym for years to describe the *Data Control Language,* even Oracle is adopting DCL to avoid confusion with the *Tool Command Language (TCL)* created at Berkeley in 1987. You will use DCL to describe transaction control commands, like SAVEPOINT, ROLLBACK, and COMMIT. DQL describes using the SELECT statement to query data without locking the rows, whereas SELECT statements that lock rows for subsequent transactions are more than a query but less than data manipulation, although they are often classified as DML statements. You will use DQL to describe all SELECT statement queries.

SQL implementations differ for many reasons. They vary in their level of compliance with different ANSI standards. For example, Oracle SQL supports two semantic join models—one is the Oracle Proprietary method and the other is ANSI SQL 2003–compliant. Table H-1 covers the SQL standards.

Oracle 10*g* is ANSI SQL:2003 compliant. The regular expressions have matured in Oracle 10*g* Release 2 over Release 1. Window functions calculate aggregates over a window of data. You can find more about the ANSI SQL:2003–compliant features of the Oracle 10*g* family of products by reading the *Oracle SQL Standard Support in Oracle Database 10g White Paper* on the http://otn.oracle.com web site.

While these topics are arranged for the beginner from start to finish, you should be able to use individual sections as independent references. A more gradual approach to Oracle SQL is found in *Oracle Database 10g SQL* by Jason Price (McGraw-Hill/Osborne, 2004). The comprehensive reference is the *Oracle Database SQL Reference 10g Release 2* manual, which has slightly over 1,200 printed pages and is available online at http://otn.oracle.com.

Name	Year	Description
SQL-86	1986	This is the first standardized version of SQL. It was ratified by ISO in 1987.
SQL-89	1989	This is a minor revision of SQL-86.
SQL-92	1992	This is a major revision of SQL-89 and also known as SQL2.
SQL:1999	1999	This is a major revision of SQL-92 that added recursive queries, regular expression handling, database triggers, nonscalar data types, and object-oriented features.
SQL:2003	2003	This is a major revision of SQL:1999 that added auto-generated columns, standardized sequences, window functions, and XML-related functions.

TABLE H-1.   *ANSI SQL Standards*

Oracle SQL Data Types

Oracle Database 10*g* Express Edition supports *character, numeric, timestamp, binary,* and *row address* data types. These are also known as SQL data types or built-in types because they can be used to define columns in tables and parameter data types in PL/SQL. Table H-2 summarizes these SQL data types and qualifies two widely used data subtypes by groups. While the list is not comprehensive of all subtypes, which can be found in the *Oracle Database SQL Reference 10*g *Release 2* manual, it should cover the most frequently used data subtypes.

Data Type	Raw Code	Description
CHAR	96	The CHAR data type stores fixed-length character data in bytes or characters. You can override the default by providing a formal *size* parameter. The BYTE or CHAR qualification is optional and will be applied from the NLS_LENGTH_SEMANTICS parameter by default. It has the following prototype: CHAR [(*size* [BYTE | CHAR])]
NCHAR	96	The NCHAR data type stores fixed-length Unicode national character data in bytes or characters. Unicode variables require two or three bytes, depending on the character set, which is an encoding schema. The AL16UTF16 character set requires two bytes, and UTF8 requires three bytes. You can override the default by providing a formal *size* parameter. It has the following prototype: NCHAR [(*size*)]
STRING	1	The STRING data type is a subtype of VARCHAR2 and stores variable length strings in bytes or characters up to 32,767 characters in length. If BYTE or CHAR is not specified, the type uses the NLS_LENGTH_SEMANTICS parameter defined for the database instance. You define a VARCHAR2 data type by providing a required *size* parameter. It has the following prototype: STRING [(*size* [BYTE | CHAR])]
VARCHAR2	1	The VARCHAR2 data type stores variable-length strings in bytes or characters up to 32,767 characters in length. If BYTE or CHAR is not specified, the type uses the NLS_LENGTH_SEMANTICS parameter defined for the database instance. You define a VARCHAR2 data type by setting its maximum *size* parameter. It has the following prototype: VARCHAR2 [(*size* [BYTE | CHAR])]

TABLE H-2.   *SQL Data Types*

Data Type	Raw Code	Description
NVARCHAR2	1	The NVARCHAR2 data type stores variable-length strings in bytes or characters up to 32,767 characters in length. The size per character is determined by the Unicode setting for the database instance. You define a NVARCHAR2 data type by setting its maximum *size* parameter. It has the following prototype: NVARCHAR2 (*size*)
CLOB	112	The CLOB data type stands for Character Large Object. It stores character strings up to 4GB in size. Variables with Unicode character sets are also supported up to the same maximum size. CLOB types are defined without any formal parameter for size. It has the following prototype: CLOB
NCLOB	112	The NCLOB data type stands for Unicode national Character Large Object. It stores character strings up to 4GB in size. Variables with Unicode character sets are also supported up to the same maximum size. NCLOB types are defined without any formal parameter for size. It has the following prototype: NCLOB
LONG	8	The LONG data type is provided for backward compatibility and will soon become unavailable because the CLOB and NCLOB data types are its future replacement types. *(NOTE: Oracle recommends you should begin migrating LONG data types, but no firm date for its deprecation has been announced.)* It contains a variable-length string up to 2GB of characters per row of data, which means you can have only one LONG data type in a table definition. You define a LONG without any formal parameter. It has the following prototype: LONG
BINARY_FLOAT	100	The BINARY_FLOAT is a 32-bit floating-point number that takes four bytes of storage. It is defined without a formal parameter. It has the following prototype: BINARY_FLOAT
BINARY_DOUBLE	101	The BINARY_DOUBLE is a 64-bit floating-point number that takes eight bytes of storage. It is defined without a formal parameter. It has the following prototype: BINARY_DOUBLE
FLOAT	2	The FLOAT is a 126-position subtype of the NUMBER data type. You can define it without a formal parameter or with a formal parameter of *size*. It has the following prototype: FLOAT [(*size*)]
NUMBER	2	The NUMBER is a 38-position numeric data type. You can declare its precision, or size, and its scale, or number of digits to the right of the decimal point. You can define it without a formal parameter, with a single *precision* parameter, or with both *precision* and *scale* parameters. It has the following prototype: NUMBER [(*precision* [, *scale*])]
DATE	12	The DATE is a seven-byte-representation timestamp representing time from 1 Jan 4712 B.C.E. to 31 Dec 9999 using a Gregorian calendar representation. The default format mask, DD-MON-RR, is set as a database parameter and found as the NLS_DATE_FORMAT parameter in the V$PARAMETER table. It has the following prototype: DATE
INTERVAL YEAR	182	The INTERVAL YEAR is a five-byte representation of year and month, and the default display is YYYY MM. You can define it with or without a formal parameter of *year*. The *year* must be a value between 0 and 9 and defaults to 2. The default limits of the year interval are –99 and 99. It has the following prototype: INTERVAL YEAR [(*year*)] TO MONTH

TABLE H-2. *SQL Data Types* (continued)

Data Type	Raw Code	Description
INTERVAL DAY	183	The INTERVAL DAY is an 11-byte representation of *days, hours, minutes,* and *seconds* in an interval. The default display is DD HH:MI:SS, or *days, hours, minutes,* and *seconds*. The *days* and fractions of *seconds* must be values between 0 and 9. The default limits the *days* and interval is between 1 and 31, and *seconds* are returned without fractions. It has the following prototype: INTERVAL YEAR [(*years*)] TO SECOND [(*seconds*)]
TIMESTAMP	180	The TIMESTAMP is a 7–11 byte representation of date and time, and it includes fractional seconds when you override the default seconds parameter. The default *seconds* parameter returns seconds without any fractional equivalent. The fractions of *seconds* must be values between 0 and 9 and have a maximum display precision of microseconds. It has the following prototype: TIMESTAMP [(*seconds*)]
TIMESTAMP WITH TIME ZONE	231	The TIMESTAMP WITH TIME ZONE is a 13-byte representation of date and time including offset from UTC; it includes fractional seconds when you override the default seconds parameter. The default *seconds* parameter returns seconds without any fractional equivalent. The fractions of *seconds* must be values between 0 and 9 and have a maximum display precision of microseconds. It has the following prototype: TIMESTAMP [(*seconds*)] WITH TIME ZONE
BLOB	113	The BLOB data type may contain any type of unstructured binary data up to a maximum size of 4GB. It has the following prototype: BLOB
BFILE	114	The BFILE data type contains a reference to a file stored externally on a file system. The file must not exceed 4GB in size. It has the following prototype: BFILE
RAW	23	The RAW data type is provided for backward compatibility and will soon become unavailable because the BLOB data type is its future replacement. *(NOTE: Oracle recommends that you begin migrating RAW data types, but no firm date for the type's deprecation has been announced.)* It can contain a variable-length raw binary stream up to two thousand bytes per row of data, which means you can only have one RAW data type in a table definition. It has the following prototype: RAW (*size*)
LONG RAW	24	The LONG RAW data type is provided for backward compatibility and will soon become unavailable because the BLOB data type is its future replacement. *(NOTE: Oracle recommends that you begin migrating LONG RAW data types, but no firm date for the type's deprecation has been announced.)* It can contain a variable length raw binary stream up to 2GB bytes. It has the following prototype: LONG RAW
ROWID	69	The ROWID data type is a ten-byte representation of a Base 64 binary data representation retrieved as the ROWID pseudo-column. The ROWID pseudo-column maps to a physical block on the file system or raw partition. It has the following prototype: ROWID
UROWID	208	The UROWID data type is a maximum of 4,000 bytes, and it is the Base 64 binary data representation of the logical row in an index-organized table. The optional parameter sets the size in bytes for the UROWID values. It has the following prototype: ROWID [(*size*)]

TABLE H-2.   *SQL Data Types* (continued)

You can also find examples using these Oracle SQL data types in the *Oracle Database Application Developer's Guide—Fundamentals* and *Oracle Database Application Developer's Guide—Large Objects.* The most frequently used data types are the BLOB, BFILE, CLOB, DATE,

FLOAT, NUMBER, STRING, TIMESTAMP, and VARCHAR2 data types. International implementations also use the TIMESTAMP WITH LOCAL TIME ZONE to regionalize Virtual Private Databases available in the Oracle Database 10*g* product family.

Data Definition Language (DDL)

The DDL commands let you *create, replace, alter, drop, rename,* and *truncate* database objects, permissions, and settings. You require a database instance before you can you *create, replace, alter, drop, rename,* and *truncate* database objects. When you installed the Oracle database, the installation script created a clone of a sample database. Alternatively, the installation program could have used the CREATE command to build a database instance. After creating the database instance, you can then use the ALTER command to change settings for the instance or for given sessions. Sessions last the duration of a connection to the database instance.

The DDL section is organized into subsections and covers

- Managing tables and constraints
- Managing views
- Managing stored programs
- Managing sequences
- Managing user-defined types

You will most frequently use DDL commands to manage tables, constraints, views, stored programs (such as functions, procedures, and packages), sequences, and user-defined types. This section works through the general form and application for these commands.

Managing Tables and Constraints

Database tables are the typically two-dimensional structures that hold the raw data that make databases useful. The first dimension defines the column names and their data types, and the second dimension defines the rows of data. Rows of data are also known as records and instances of the table structure.

Tables are the backbone of the database instance. Tables are built by using the CREATE statement. You have several options when building database tables, but the basic decision is whether you are creating a structure to hold data or copying a data structure to a newly named table.

Assuming you are building a table for the first time as a structure where you will hold information, you need to determine whether the table will have database constraints. Database constraints are rules that define how you will allow users to *insert* and *update* rows or records in the table. Five database constraints are available in an Oracle database: *check, foreign key, not null, primary key,* and *unique.* Constraints restrict DML commands as follows:

- *Check* constraints check whether a column value meets criteria before allowing a value to be inserted or updated into a column. They check whether a value is between two numbers, a value is greater than a number, or a combination of logically related compound rules is met. Also, *not null* and *unique* constraints are specialized types of *check* constraints.

■ *Foreign key* constraints check whether a column value is found in a list of values in a column designated as a *primary key* column in the same or a different table. *Foreign key* constraints are typically managed in the application programs, rather than as database constraints, because of their adverse impact on throughput.

■ *Not null* constraints check whether a column value contains a value other than null.

■ *Primary key* constraints identify a column as the *primary key* for a table and impose both a *not null* and *unique* constraint on the column. A *foreign key* can only reference a valid *primary key* column.

■ *Unique* constraints check whether a column value will be unique among all rows in a table.

Database constraints are assigned during the creation of a table or by using the ALTER command after a table is created. You can include constraints in the CREATE statement by using *in-line* or *out-of-line* constraints. While some maintain that this is a matter of preference, it is more often a matter of finding working examples. You should consider using *out-of-line* constraints because they're organized at the end of your table creation and can be grouped for increased readability. Unfortunately, only *in-line* NOT NULL constraints are visible when you describe a table. The following demonstrates creating a table using SQL:

```
-- This is found in create_store.sql on the enclosed CD.
```

```
CREATE TABLE member
( member_id                 NUMBER
, account_number            VARCHAR2(10)
, credit_card_number        VARCHAR2(19)
, credit_card_type          NUMBER
, created_by                NUMBER
, creation_date             DATE
, last_updated_by           NUMBER
, last_update_date          DATE
, CONSTRAINT pk_member_1    PRIMARY KEY(member_id)
, CONSTRAINT nn_member_1    CHECK(account_number IS NOT NULL)
, CONSTRAINT nn_member_2    CHECK(credit_card_number IS NOT NULL)
, CONSTRAINT nn_member_3    CHECK(credit_card_type IS NOT NULL)
, CONSTRAINT nn_member_4    CHECK(created_by IS NOT NULL)
, CONSTRAINT nn_member_5    CHECK(creation_date IS NOT NULL)
, CONSTRAINT nn_member_6    CHECK(last_updated_by IS NOT NULL)
, CONSTRAINT nn_member_7    CHECK(last_update_date IS NOT NULL)
, CONSTRAINT fk_member_1    FOREIGN KEY(credit_card_type)
  REFERENCES common_lookup  (common_lookup_id)
, CONSTRAINT fk_member_2    FOREIGN KEY(created_by)
  REFERENCES system_user    (system_user_id)
, CONSTRAINT fk_member_3    FOREIGN KEY(last_updated_by)
  REFERENCES system_user    (system_user_id));
```

The CREATE statement for a table cannot include the REPLACE clause because you must DROP a table before altering its definition. This limitation exists because of the linkages between database constraints and indexes that reference the table, both of which are implicitly dropped when you DROP a table. The preceding MEMBER table is created by using out-of-line constraints. The CREATE TABLE statement demonstrates *primary key, check,* and *foreign key* constraints.

You have the option of building constraints without names, but all of these constraints have meaningful names, which enable programmers to sort out errors much faster when they occur. The database assigns system-generated names when you fail to provide explicit names, and you will find that they are not very helpful to you when you're troubleshooting an application failure. You should always use meaningful constraint names.

You can create a copy of the original table by using a CREATE statement that uses a SELECT statement to implicitly derive the table structure, as follows:

```
CREATE TABLE member_clone AS SELECT * FROM member;
```

This implicit cloning of one table into another has the downside of naming all database constraints for the table using a meaningless sequence, like SYS_C0020951. However, it is convenient for building a place to store data until you can perform maintenance on the table. Using the SQL*Plus describe command,

```
SQL> describe member_clone
```

you will see a mirror to the original table, as follows:

```
Name                                      Null?    Type
----------------------------------------- -------- ------------
MEMBER_ID                                 NOT NULL NUMBER
CREDIT_CARD_NUMBER                        NOT NULL VARCHAR2(19)
CREDIT_CARD_TYPE                          NOT NULL NUMBER
CREATED_BY                                NOT NULL NUMBER
CREATION_DATE                             NOT NULL DATE
LAST_UPDATED_BY                           NOT NULL NUMBER
LAST_UPDATE_DATE                          NOT NULL DATE
```

The ALTER command provides you with the opportunity to *add, rename,* or *drop* columns while keeping the table active in the database. The ALTER command demonstrates how to *add* a column to the MEMBER table when it contains data:

```
ALTER TABLE member ADD (demo_column VARCHAR2(10));
```

You can use an *in-line* constraint when the table does not contain any data, like the following:

```
ALTER TABLE member ADD (demo_column VARCHAR2(10)
CONSTRAINT nn_member_8 NOT NULL);
```

This syntax will not work when one or more rows do not contain data in the target column. You should note that the *in-line* constraint does not identify itself as a check constraint but simply denotes the NOT NULL condition. This is typical of *in-line* constraints, whereas *out-of-line* NOT NULL constraints must be qualified as CHECK constraints. After you populate the new column in all existing rows with a value, you can add a named NOT NULL constraint by using the following ALTER command syntax:

```
ALTER TABLE member ADD CONSTRAINT nn_member_8
CHECK(demo_column IS NOT NULL);
```

You can then drop the column explicitly, which also drops the nn_member_8 NOT NULL constraint. The following ALTER command drops the column, including any values that you've added:

```
ALTER TABLE member DROP COLUMN demo_column;
```

You can also *rename* a table whether it has dependents or not. All *foreign key* constraint references are implicitly changed to point to the new table name when their respective *primary key* column exists. This happens because the ALTER command changes only a non-identifying property of a catalog table reference. Application code references in stored program units are not altered to reflect the change because they are not part of the database catalog. You can rename a table with the ALTER command, like so:

```
ALTER TABLE member RENAME TO membership;
```

Then, you can use the alternate syntax to rename it back by using

```
RENAME membership TO member;
```

The TRUNCATE command lets you remove all data from a table but keep the structure of the table. There is no rolling back the TRUNCATE command when you issue it. *Truncating a table is final!* Since we don't need the MEMBER_CLONE table created earlier, you can truncate its results with the following syntax:

```
TRUNCATE TABLE member_clone;
```

Database tables typically stand alone in the database, but when you add a foreign key constraint that references another table, that table has a dependent. You drop tables without dependents differently than tables with dependents. You can drop a table that has no dependents by using the following command syntax:

```
DROP TABLE member_clone;
```

You append the CASCADE CONSTRAINTS phrase when dropping tables with dependents, like this:

```
DROP TABLE member CASCADE CONSTRAINTS;
```

What the CASCADE CONSTRAINTS phrase does is tell the database to ignore the *foreign key* dependency. However, you will need to repopulate the table with the *primary key* data to support the *foreign key* values in the dependent tables, or they become orphan rows. You should identify orphan rows and discover why they've been orphaned, which is typically due to an error caused by an insertion or update anomaly.

The error can be harmless or harmful. Harmless errors mean that you meant to delete the rows and forgot. Harmful errors are that the parent rows were deleted in error, which means you'll need to recover the data.

NOTE
*If you dropped the MEMBER table, please rerun the database seeding
scripts described in Appendix J.*

This section has covered the basic mechanics of some DDL statements. There are other commands that you can use. Your best reference to more details about the DDL statements in the primer is the index for the `ALTER`, `CREATE`, `DROP`, `RENAME`, and `TRUNCATE` commands in the *Oracle Database SQL Reference 10g Release 2* manual.

Managing Views

Views are constructed by using `SELECT` statements to provide subsets of columns from tables, a subset of rows, a subset of columns and rows combination, or a combination of columns from two or more tables. Views are often built to display complex information in an easily queried database objects. The `SELECT` statement can contain aggregation, conversion, calculation, and various types of grouping and set operations.

An example of a conversion function is using a `TO_CHAR()` function to convert a `DATE` data type column into a `VARCHAR2` data type when you want to return a known date format mask. Aggregation functions *count, average,* and *sum* are examples using the `COUNT()`, `AVG()`, and `SUM()` functions respectively. Grouping operators reduce the number of actual rows to summary levels by paring the repeating column values into a single row in the result set. A result set is the number of rows and columns returned from a `SELECT` statement. You can also limit the number of returned rows from a `VIEW` by using a `WHERE` clause in the `SELECT` statement to narrow selected rows based on criteria evaluation.

Views are powerful structures but they have some clearly defined limits when you want to transact against them using DML statements. The `SELECT` statement for the views cannot have any of the following in order to let you *insert, update,* and *delete* records through the view:

- **Expressions**   Expressions can be conversion or aggregation functions.
- **Set operators**   These can be `UNION`, `UNION ALL`, `INTERSECT`, or `MINUS`.
- **Sorting operations**   These can be `DISTINCT`, `GROUP BY`, `HAVING`, or `ORDER BY` clauses.

Eliminating these from `SELECT` statements used in views solves most problems related to `INSERT` and `UPDATE` statements. One remaining element of a `SELECT` statement can enable insertion and update anomalies, and that problem is a `WHERE` clause narrowing returned rows by some criteria evaluation. You can eliminate the potential anomalies by appending the `WITH CHECK OPTION` phrase to the end of the view creation statement.

TIP
You can check whether a view is updatable by inspecting the list of columns in the USER_UPDATABLE_COLUMNS table when in doubt.

Views are typically built by using the `CREATE OR REPLACE` clause because you cannot alter a view without replacing it completely. The `ALTER` statement can only compile a view when it has been invalidated because a referenced catalog table or view in the `SELECT` statement has been dropped and re-created. Sometimes you need to build views before underlying tables exist. You can do that by using the `CREATE OR REPLACE FORCE` syntax, but after creating the view it will immediately become invalid because of the missing table. The benefit of using a `FORCE` option is that you can check whether the syntax for the view is fine except for the missing table.

The following SQL statement builds a `CURRENT_RENTAL` view that should only be used to query data:

```
-- This is found in seed_store.sql on the enclosed CD.

CREATE OR REPLACE VIEW current_rental AS
  SELECT    m.account_number
  ,         c.first_name
  ||        DECODE(c.middle_initial,NULL,' ',' '||c.middle_initial||' ')
  ||        c.last_name FULL_NAME
  ,         i.item_title TITLE
  ,         i.item_subtitle SUBTITLE
  ,         SUBSTR(cl.common_lookup_meaning,1,3) PRODUCT
  ,         r.check_out_date
  ,         r.return_date
  FROM      common_lookup cl
  ,         contact c
  ,         item i
  ,         member m
  ,         rental r
  ,         rental_item ri
  WHERE     r.customer_id = c.contact_id
  AND       r.rental_id = ri.rental_id
  AND       ri.item_id = i.item_id
  AND       i.item_type = cl.common_lookup_id
  AND       c.member_id = m.member_id
  ORDER BY 1,2,3;
```

This view cannot be updated because the concatenation and two functions in the SELECT statement make it ineligible for insert or update operations. However, try querying the USER_UPDATABLE_COLUMNS table with the following query:

```
SELECT    table_name
,         column_name
FROM      user_updatable_columns
WHERE     table_name = 'CURRENT_RENTAL';
```

You will see the column names appear as updatable when they're not:

```
TABLE_NAME                       COLUMN_NAME
-------------------------------  --------------
CURRENT_RENTAL                   MEMBER_ID
CURRENT_RENTAL                   FULL_NAME
CURRENT_RENTAL                   TITLE
CURRENT_RENTAL                   SUBTITLE
CURRENT_RENTAL                   PRODUCT
CURRENT_RENTAL                   CHECK_OUT_DATE
CURRENT_RENTAL                   RETURN_DATE
```

This type of output from USER_UPDATABLE_COLUMNS can be misleading, but you should notice that the column names do not match actual columns in tables. The column names are aliases from the SELECT statement that builds the CURRENT_RENTAL view. If you attempt to *insert* values, you would receive an ORA-01732 error message, and it would tell you that the data manipulation operation is not legal on this view.

The RENAME and DROP operations are the same as those for tables. You cannot use a TRUNCATE operation because views contain no data of their own. They are only reflections of tables that contain data.

Managing Stored Programs

Stored programs in Oracle are written in PL/SQL programming language or other languages with PL/SQL wrappers. You can build libraries in C/C++, C#, or Java programming languages.

You use CREATE OR REPLACE syntax to build functions, procedures, and packages. Packages contain functions, procedures, and user-defined types. The ALTER statement works the same for stored programs as it did for views: you *alter* stored programs to compile them when they've become invalid. Stored programs become invalid when referenced tables, views, or other stored programs become invalid.

NOTE
User-defined data types can be dropped, but when they are, columns referencing them are dropped from tables and stored programs become invalid.

Stored programs cannot be renamed but can be dropped from the database, and recreated under a new name. The TRUNCATE statement does not apply because they do not contain raw data components. You will cover more about stored programs in Appendix I.

Managing Sequences

Sequences are counting structures that maintain a persistent awareness of their current value. They are simple to create when you want them to start at one; increment one at a time; set no *cache, minimum,* or *maximum* value; and accept both NOCYCLE and NOORDER properties. Sequence cache values are 20 by default, but you can overwrite the cache size when creating the sequence or by altering it after creation. As done in the sample code found in Appendix J, you build the generic SEQUENCE with this command:

 `-- This is found in create_world_leaders.sql on the enclosed CD.`

```
CREATE SEQUENCE president_s1;
```

Many designs simply build these generic sequences and enable rows to be inserted by the web application interface. Some tables require specialized setup rows that are manually inserted by administrators. When you have a table requiring manual setup rows, some begin the sequence at 1001, which provides you flexibility to add more setup rows after initial implementation.

The SYSTEM_USER, RENTAL_LOOKUP, and other tables in the video store example require setup data, which is often called seeding data. The sequences for both of these tables add an initial START WITH clause that sets the starting number for the sequence values, as shown:

 `-- This is found in create_store.sql on the enclosed CD.`

```
CREATE SEQUENCE system_user_s1 START WITH 1001;
```

Sequences are typically built to support *primary key* columns in tables. *Primary key* columns impose a combination constraint on their values—they use both UNIQUE and NOT NULL constraints.

During normal Online Transaction Processing (OLTP), some insertions are rolled back because other transactional components fail. When transactions are rolled back, the captured sequence value is typically lost. This means that you may see numeric gaps in the *primary key* column sequence values.

Typically, you ignore small gaps. Larger gaps in sequence values occur during *after-hours* batch processing, where you are performing bulk inserts into tables. Failures in batch processing typically involve operation staff intervention in conjunction with programming teams to fix the failure and process the data. Part of fixing this type of failure is resetting the next sequence value. While it would be nice to simply use an ALTER statement to reset the next sequence value, you cannot reset the START WITH number using an ALTER statement. You can reset every other criterion of a sequence with the ALTER statement, but you must drop and recreate the sequence to change the START WITH value.

There are three steps in the process to successfully modify a sequence START WITH value. You modify a sequence START WITH value by: (a) querying the *primary key* that uses the *sequence* to find the highest current value; (b) dropping the existing sequence with the DROP SEQUENCE *sequence_name*; command; and (c) recreating the sequence with a *START WITH* value *one greater than the highest value in the primary key column.* Naturally, the gap doesn't hurt anything, and you can skip this step, but as a rule, it is recommended.

You can alter properties of a sequence by using the ALTER statement as illustrated by the following prototype:

```
ALTER SEQUENCE sequence_name    [INCREMENT BY increment_value]
       [MINVALUE minimum | NOMINVALUE]
       [MAXVALUE maximum | NOMAXVALUE]
       [CACHE | NOCACHE]
       [ORDER | NOORDER]
```

You use sequences by appending (with a *dot* notation) two *pseudo-columns* to the sequence name: .nextval and .currval. The .nextval pseudo-column *initializes* the sequence in a session and gets the *next value,* which is initially the START WITH value. After accessing the .nextval pseudo-column, you get the *current value* by using the .currval pseudo-column. You receive an ORA-08002 error when attempting to access the .currval pseudo-column before having called the .nextval pseudo-column in a session. The error message says that you have tried to access a sequence *not defined* in the session because .nextval *initializes* or *defines* the sequence in the session.

There are several ways to access sequences with the .nextval pseudo-column. The basic starting point is querying the pseudo-table DUAL, as shown:

```
SELECT    president_s1.nextval
FROM      dual;
```

Then, you can see the value again by querying:

```
SELECT    president_s1.currval
FROM      dual;
```

The number will be the same, provided you did not connect to another schema and/or reconnect to the SQL*Plus session. You can also use the .nextval and .currval pseudo-columns in the VALUES clause of INSERT or UPDATE statements. The next example demonstrates their use in the *inserts* of data to related tables:

 `-- This is found in seed_store.sql on the enclosed CD.`

```
INSERT INTO member VALUES
( member_s1.nextval
,'B293-71445'
,'1111-2222-3333-4444'
,(SELECT    common_lookup_id
  FROM      common_lookup
  WHERE     common_lookup_context = 'MEMBER'
  AND       common_lookup_type = 'DISCOVER_CARD')
, 2, SYSDATE, 2, SYSDATE);

INSERT INTO contact VALUES
( contact_s1.nextval
, member_s1.currval
,(SELECT    common_lookup_id
  FROM      common_lookup
  WHERE     common_lookup_context = 'CONTACT'
  AND       common_lookup_type = 'CUSTOMER')
,'Winn','Randi','', 2, SYSDATE, 2, SYSDATE);
```

The first INSERT statement accesses the member_s1.nextval sequence to insert a *primary key* value into the MEMBER table. The .nextval pseudo-column *defines* the sequence in the session and returns a number. The member_s1.currval pseudo-column in the second INSERT statement calls the *defined* sequence and returns the same number, which is used as a *foreign key* column in the CONTACT table. You guarantee *primary key* and *foreign key* value matches when you combine the .nextval and .currval pseudo-columns as demonstrated in the seed_store.sql script.

NOTE
A DQL or SELECT statement runs as a subquery inside both INSERT statements. These subqueries ensure the INSERT statement uses the right foreign key by querying on meaningful information the correct primary key from the COMMON_LOOKUP table. This type of subquery, also known as a SQL expression, returns only one column and one row. Only SQL expressions can be used inside the VALUES clause of an INSERT statement.

You can use the RENAME command to change a syntax name. Sequences have no direct dependencies at the database level but often have dependencies in stored programs and database triggers that access the sequence to mimic automatic numbering behaviors of *primary key* values.

Managing User-Defined Types

User-defined types have been available since Oracle 8 and were dramatically increased in scope by Oracle 9*i* Release 2. You have the ability to define two groups of user-defined types in the Oracle Database 10g family of products. They are collections and object types. Object types are not *currently* supported by the Oracle Call Interface (OCI8) library and therefore cannot be used in your PHP programs. Oracle collections are supported by the OCI8 library.

There are two types of OCI8-supported collections—one is a VARRAY, and the other is a NESTED TABLE. After you create these types, you can use them as column data types when defining SQL objects, such as tables and stored procedures. VARRAY collections are defined as fixed-sized arrays of scalar variables, like DATE, NUMBER, and VARCHAR2 data types. VARRAY collections are the closest Oracle programming structure to a native *array* in most programming languages. NESTED TABLE collections are defined as variable-sized *lists* of scalar variables and naturally behave like *lists* in other programming languages. Elements in both collection types are indexed by sequential positive integers starting with the number 1.

You create a VARRAY by using the following syntax:

-- This is found in create_world_leaders.sql on the enclosed CD.

```
CREATE OR REPLACE TYPE president_name_varray
  AS VARRAY(100) OF VARCHAR2(60 CHAR);
/
```

This builds a 100-element VARRAY collection of variable-length strings that are 60 characters in length. You raise an ORA-06502 when you attempt to enter an element greater than the maximum length of the scalar variable, and an ORA-22165 when you attempt to enter a list of elements greater than the boundary size of 100 elements.

There is no boundary set when you build a NESTED TABLE because they act more like *lists* than *arrays*. You use the following syntax to create a NESTED TABLE collection for a scalar variable-length string of up to 60 characters:

-- This is found in create_world_leaders.sql on the enclosed CD.

```
CREATE OR REPLACE TYPE president_name_ntable
  AS TABLE OF VARCHAR2(60 CHAR);
/
```

The ALTER, RENAME, and TRUNCATE statements cannot be used against user-defined collections. You can use the ALTER statement to *add* and *drop* member attributes from user-defined object types, and you can *alter* those object types from *instantiable* to *final* and back again.

The REPLACE command enables you to alter the definition of collection types. However, replacing and dropping user-defined types becomes complex when you have defined other objects that reference them. The problem can be demonstrated by creating a table using the president_name_ntable as a column data type:

```
CREATE TABLE president_name
( president_name_id    NUMBER
, president_names      PRESIDENT_NAME_NTABLE)
NESTED TABLE president_names STORE AS PRESIDENT_NAMES_TABLE;
```

After a table is defined referencing the user-defined SQL collection data type, attempting CREATE OR REPLACE or DROP statements raises an ORA-02303 error. The error message explains that you cannot *drop* or *replace* a type with type or table dependents. You can override this limitation by using the FORCE option for both statements but it will remove the dependents types from tables.

The trick to using user-defined collection types is to understand the hierarchy of sequencing dependencies, and work within the hierarchy. This means *drop* the lowest item that depends on a *type* up to the user-defined type, and replace the user-defined type before any objects that reference the *type* or the *type dependents*.

Data Query Language (DQL)

DQL commands are basically SELECT statements. SELECT statements let you *query* the database to find information in one or more tables, and return the query as a *result set*. A *result set* is an array structure, or more precisely in computerese, a result set is a two-dimensional array. You can find a discussion of two-dimensional arrays in Chapter 6.

NOTE
A SELECT statement with a FOR UPDATE clause is a transaction and DML statement, not a DQL query. This is a fine distinction, but critical should you encounter an ORA-22292 error while working with the DBMS_LOB package covered in Chapter 15.

The first dimension of the array is a list of values indexed by *column names* from one or more tables. The elements in the list of values are sometimes called column or field values, and to the fraternity- (or sorority-) pledged database designers, they are attributes, like matrices in linear algebra. The combination of these column values is also known as a record structure. The second dimension of the array is the row, or a numerically indexed list of record structures. So, a *result set* is a collection of data values organized by column name and row number.

NOTE
Attributes and tuples are columns and rows, respectively, in linear algebraic vocabulary and suitable to hear about in college classrooms, but really they're nothing more than columns and rows.

DQL statements can be stand-alone *queries, in-line views* (or *tables*), *subqueries,* or *correlated subqueries.* They can return *scalar* or *compound* values in the Oracle database because Oracle can store *instantiable* object types as *column* data types. Since OCI8 library *currently* can't manage *instantiable* object types, all column values here will be assumed as scalar data types.

TIP
Databases do not like zero-based numbering schemas, and queries return rows by row numbers starting with 1.

All SQL statements have the ability to join multiple tables; otherwise, database systems would be little more than complex file systems. Oracle Database 10g XE supports two join semantics. One is known as the Oracle Proprietary SQL semantic, and the other is the ANSI 2003:SQL semantic. The original join approach used by Oracle is similar to IBM SQL/DS (Structured Query Language/Data System) and simply predates ANSI standards. You will be exposed to both and then decide which you like best.

Queries

The SQL SELECT statement has several components, known variously and interchangeably as clauses, phrases, and predicates. A *clause* is the generally accepted term but the others work too, provided they convey the concept to your audience. The *basic* SELECT clauses and their descriptions are listed in Table H-3 for your convenience.

Clause	Description

SELECT	The SELECT clause contains a list of columns. Columns can also be defined by SQL expressions. Expressions are the result of *single-row* SQL functions. Oracle provides a set of *single-row* SQL functions, along with the ability for you to develop *user-defined single-row* SQL functions. Either type of *single-row* SQL function is supported in the SELECT clause. Columns and expressions are delimited by commas and support alias naming without white space and alias naming enclosed in quote marks with intervening white space. The Oracle SQL parser assumes an AS predicate when one is not provided in the SELECT clause. You precede duplicate column names with the table name or alias of the table name. The prototype of the SELECT clause is
	
	```SELECT column1 [AS alias1]```
	``` [, column2 [AS alias2]```
	``` [, column(n+1) [AS alias(n+1)]]]```

FROM	The FROM clause contains a list of tables when using Oracle Proprietary SQL, and a list of tables and join conditions between the listed tables when using ANSI SQL:2003. Tables can be tables, views, or *in-line views* (subqueries embedded in the FROM clause). Table names can have aliases composed of characters, numbers and underscores. Table name aliases are a shorthand notation for table names. The prototype for Oracle Proprietary SQL is
	
	```FROM table1 [alias1]```
	``` [, table2 [alias2]```
	``` [, (in_line_view) [alias3]```
	``` [, table(n+1) [alias(n+1)]]]```
	The prototype for ANSI SQL:2003 differs when joining on two columns that share the same name, or two columns that have different names. The SQL parser assumes an INNER JOIN when no optional join qualifier is provided. The prototype for two columns with different names is
	
	``FROM table1 [INNER
		LEFT [OUTER]	RIGHT [OUTER] |```
			``` FULL [OUTER]] JOIN table2```
			``` ON table1.column_name1 = table2.column_name2```
			The prototype for two columns with the same name is
			
			``FROM table1 [INNER
				LEFT [OUTER]	RIGHT [OUTER] |```
					``` FULL [OUTER]] JOIN table2```
					``` USING(column_name)```
					A NATURAL JOIN links tables using all matching columns found in both tables, and produces a *Cartesian product* or CROSS JOIN when both tables have mutually exclusive lists of column names. The prototype for a NATURAL JOIN is
					
					```FROM table1 NATURAL JOIN table2```
					The CROSS JOIN syntax forces a *Cartesian product* between two tables, which is a result set with row(s) of the left table matched with all the row(s) of the right table. The prototype is
					
					```FROM table1 CROSS JOIN table2```

TABLE H-3.   *SELECT Statement Clauses*

Clause	Description

WHERE	The WHERE clause contains a list of column names compared against column names or string literals. Using the equal operator, the comparison operator supports joins in the Oracle Proprietary SQL syntax. You also have inequality operators, like *less than or equal to* or *greater than or equal to,* and the IS NULL or IS NOT NULL for comparison to columns containing null values. Each qualifying comparison statement is separated by an AND or OR operator. The prototype for Oracle Proprietary SQL is
	
	`WHERE table1.columna = table2.columnb`
	`AND table1.columnb = literal_value`
	`OR table1.columnc = subquery`

HAVING	The HAVING clause eliminates groups. The prototype uses a SUM() SQL *row-level* function to group a result set: `HAVING SUM(column) > 30`
ORDER BY	The ORDER BY clause does sorting of the result set. You can use column names or numbers for the positional columns. The prototype is `ORDER BY column1 [, column2 [, column(n+1)]]`
GROUP BY	The GROUP BY clause groups ordinary columns when the query includes a row-level function in the SELECT or HAVING clause. It requires you to mirror column descriptions from the SELECT clause. The prototype is `GROUP BY column1 [, column2 [, column(n+1)]]`

RETURNING INTO	The RETURNING INTO clause lets you transfer SELECT clause variables into a bind variable. This clause is necessary when working with Oracle CLOB and NCLOB data types and OCI8. The prototype is:
	
	`RETURNING select_clause_variable`
	`INTO :bind_variable`

TABLE H-3.   *SELECT Statement Clauses* (continued)

There are two subtypes of queries. One returns only one column and row and is known as a SQL *expression.* Expressions have wide uses in other than the SELECT statement, as seen in the subsection "Managing Sequences" earlier in this appendix. The other query subtype is the general rule for queries, and what most people think of when using the word *query*—a query returns zero, one, or many rows in a result set.

The following example demonstrates a standard query from two tables using an INNER JOIN on different column names:

```
-- This is found in SelectItemRecords.php on the enclosed CD.

SELECT     i.item_id AS id
,          i.item_barcode AS barcode
,          c.common_lookup_type AS type
,          i.item_title AS title
,          i.item_rating AS rating
,          i.item_release_date AS release_date
FROM       item i INNER JOIN common_lookup c
ON         i.item_type = c.common_lookup_id
WHERE      c.common_lookup_type = 'XBOX'
ORDER BY i.item_title;
```

The query demonstrates a standard query that returns a result set of zero, one, or many rows. It uses the ANSI SQL:2003 syntax for the join between tables but really only uses features that exist in the ANSI SQL:1999 standard. The query also demonstrates both column and table aliases.

The following query demonstrates a SQL expression:

```
SELECT    COUNT(*)
FROM      ITEM
WHERE     item_type = (SELECT    common_lookup_id
                       FROM      common_lookup
                       WHERE     common_lookup_context = 'ITEM'
                       AND       common_lookup_type = 'XBOX');
```

The SQL expression determines how many XBOX items are in the video store inventory. It uses a subquery of the COMMON_LOOKUP table to find the ITEM_TYPE *foreign key* for a context of ITEM and type of XBOX. The SELECT clause contains only a SQL *row-level* function, which guarantees a single column and row in the result set.

The subquery in the foregoing example is not a *correlated subquery. Correlated subqueries* have a join to the outer query in the inner query and are prefaced by the EXISTS or NOT EXISTS operator. *In-line views* are subqueries that are found in the FROM clause. In-line views generally have an alias, and joins between them are resolved in the same way as joins between normal tables and views.

You can also reference subqueries by using equalities and nonequalities with the ALL, ANY, or SOME operators. In lieu of equalities and nonequalities, you can use IN or NOT IN for subqueries, and as noted, EXISTS or NOT EXISTS for correlated subqueries.

Data Manipulation Language (DML)

INSERT, UPDATE, and DELETE statements define the DML commands. All of these may use joins, subqueries, correlated subqueries, and in-line views. The in-line views must be contained within a subquery or correlated subquery. DML commands can insert, update, or delete one to many rows of data.

INSERT Statements

The INSERT statement acts on rows of data. Inserting data into tables can be done row by row or by groups of rows. You have two potential ways to create *insertion anomalies* when inserting data.

One type of *insertion anomaly* happens when you insert two rows with the same information. *Primary key* constraints typically reduce the likelihood that the entire rows are duplicated, but it is possible to create repeating sets that will disable some queries from tables. You can use *unique indexes* across sets of columns to prevent this type of *insertion anomaly,* as demonstrated later in the section.

Another type of *insertion anomaly* happens when you insert incorrect data. The incorrect data can be *foreign key* columns or descriptive *nonkey* columns. The foreign key error occurs when you fail to properly leverage a sequence of .nextval and .currval attributes or fail to use SQL expressions to find the foreign keys. You should refer to the sequence coverage earlier in this appendix to understand how to use .nextval and .currval for managing *primary* and *foreign keys* in transaction sets. As demonstrated in the INSERT statements found in Appendix J, it is important to match foreign keys by using SQL expressions.

INSERT statements differ from other DML statements in that they use the metadata definition of the table. The metadata is stored when a table is created, and acts like a function or method signature for the INSERT statement. It lists the formal parameters in the same order used by the CREATE TABLE statement, and the database appends columns to the list when they are added later by using the ALTER statement.

You can determine a table signature by querying the USER_TAB_COLUMNS view using the following query:

```
SELECT    column_id
,         column_name
,         data_type
,         nullable
FROM      user_tab_columns
WHERE     table_name = 'MEMBER';
```

The query returns the default signature of the MEMBER table, which was created earlier in the appendix. INSERT statements use the default signature unless you specify an overriding column list before the VALUES clause. Overriding the default signature is a common practice when inserting into tables that have many *null allowed* columns. The following are the results from the query against USER_TAB_COLUMNS for the MEMBER table:

```
COLUMN_ID COLUMN_NAME            DATA_TYPE  N
---------- -------------------- ---------- -
        1 MEMBER_ID              NUMBER     N
        2 ACCOUNT_NUMBER         VARCHAR2   Y
        3 CREDIT_CARD_NUMBER     VARCHAR2   Y
        4 CREDIT_CARD_TYPE       NUMBER     Y
        5 CREATED_BY             NUMBER     Y
        6 CREATION_DATE          DATE       Y
        7 LAST_UPDATED_BY        NUMBER     Y
        8 LAST_UPDATE_DATE       DATE       Y
```

The results from this view can be deceiving when tables are defined using *out-of-line* CHECK constraints instead of *in-line* NOT NULL constraints. Only *in-line* and *primary key* constraints will show an 'N' in the NULLABLE column. You can check the USER_CONSTRAINTS and USER_CONS_COLUMNS views to determine whether or not there is a NOT NULL check constraint.

The following inserts a row into the MEMBER table by using the default signature just described:

```
-- This is found in seed_store.sql on the enclosed CD.

INSERT INTO member VALUES
( member_s1.nextval                               -- 1   MEMBER_ID
, 'B293-71445'                                     -- 2   ACCOUNT_NUMBER
, '1111-2222-3333-4444'                            -- 3   CREDIT_CARD_NUMBER
, (SELECT   common_lookup_id                       -- 4   CREDIT_CARD_TYPE
   FROM     common_lookup
   WHERE    common_lookup_context = 'MEMBER'
   AND      common_lookup_type = 'DISCOVER_CARD')
, 2                                                -- 5   CREATED_BY
, SYSDATE                                          -- 6   CREATION_DATE
, 2                                                -- 7   LAST_UPDATED_BY
, SYSDATE);                                        -- 8   LAST_UPDATE_DATE
```

When you need to override the default signature, you add an overriding column list, as shown in the following prototype:

```
INSERT INTO table_name
( column1, column2, column(n+1))
VALUES
( column_value1, column_value2, column_value(n+1));
```

The INSERT statement uses a SQL expression to find the appropriate foreign key value for the CREDIT_CARD_TYPE column. While the SELECT statement returns a single row and column, the structure of the query does not guarantee that behavior by itself. A *unique* INDEX guarantees the business rule and that the SQL expression cannot return more than one row:

```
-- This is found in create_store.sql on the enclosed CD.

CREATE UNIQUE INDEX common_lookup_u1
  ON common_lookup(common_lookup_context,common_lookup_type);
```

You can insert multiple rows with a single INSERT statement by using a SELECT statement in place of the VALUES clause, just as you created a new table by querying an old table earlier in this appendix. When you insert from data residing somewhere else in the database, you use the following prototype:

```
INSERT INTO table_name
AS select_statement;
```

UPDATE Statements

The UPDATE statement lets you update one or more column values in one or a set of rows in a table. It supports different direct assignments to each column value by using bind variables, literal values, and subqueries. The WHERE clause in the UPDATE statement qualifies which rows are changed by the UPDATE statement. You can check the DQL section earlier in this appendix for more coverage on the WHERE clause.

NOTE
All rows in the table are updated when you run an UPDATE statement without a WHERE clause.

Update anomalies occurs much like the *insertion anomalies* that happen when you insert two rows with the same information. The only difference is that the UPDATE statement alters a second row when it shouldn't. You eliminate updating multiple rows in error by using *unique indexes* across sets of columns to prevent it, as described in the preceding subsection, "INSERT Statements.".
The UPDATE statement has the following prototype:

```
UPDATE    table_name [alias]
SET       column1 = {value | select_statement}
,         column2 = {value | select_statement}
,         column(n+1) = {value | select_statement}
WHERE     list_of_comparative_operations
[RETURNING column_name INTO :bind_variable];
```

You should note that *unlike when using the alias assignment in the SELECT clause,* you must exclude the AS clause or you raise an ORA-00971 error that says you are missing the SET clause. The RETURNING INTO clause is used to shift a column value reference for an Oracle LOB data type into a *bind* variable, as demonstrated by UploadBioSQL.php in Chapter 15. A sample UPDATE statement using a correlated subquery updates the middle initial for a single row in the CONTACT table as follows:

```
UPDATE      contact c1
SET         c1.middle_initial = 'B'
WHERE       EXISTS (SELECT   NULL
                    FROM     contact c2
                    WHERE    c1.contact_id = c2.contact_id
                    AND      c2.last_name = 'Vizquel'
                    AND      c2.first_name = 'Oscar');
```

The correlated query could have been eliminated by putting the LAST_NAME and FIRST_NAME column value comparisons in the WHERE clause. This illustrates that there are many ways to do equivalent things using SQL statements.

DELETE Statements

The DELETE statement, like the INSERT statement, works at the row level. You delete one to many rows with a DELETE statement. As when using the UPDATE statement, you generally will have a WHERE clause; otherwise, you delete all rows in the table.

Deleting data can be tricky when you have *dependent* foreign key columns in other tables. While generally most businesses do not enable foreign key referential integrity at the database level, they maintain the logic in the application interface. You should make sure the application programming logic is correct, because incorrect logic can cause *deletion anomalies.* Deletion anomalies manifest themselves in orphaned rows, join failures, and erroneous query result sets.

The prototype for a DELETE statement is

```
DELETE
FROM        table_name
WHERE       list_of_comparative_operations;
```

The following deletion statement against the video store will fail because it violates the foreign key referential integrity rules maintained by foreign key database constraints:

```
DELETE
FROM        item i
WHERE       i.item_title = 'Camelot';
```

The row in the ITEM table that contains the ITEM_TITLE value of *Camelot* cannot be deleted because there is a dependent row in the RENTAL_ITEM table. It raises an integrity constraint violation, ORA-02292, because of a foreign key dependency.

Deleting rows is clearly simple, but the downside is that all too many rows can be deleted in error. You should use care when deleting data, to delete only the right data. It is also a great time to back up the table in case you need to recover due to an error.

Statement	Description
COMMIT	The COMMIT statement makes permanent all DML changes to data up to that point in the user session. Once you commit data changes, they are *permanent* unless you perform some form of point-in-time database recovery. It has the following prototype: COMMIT
ROLLBACK	The ROLLBACK statement reverses changes to data that have not yet become permanent through being committed during a user session. The ROLLBACK makes sure all changes are undone from the most recent DML statement to the oldest one in the current user session, or since the last commit action. Alternatively, when a SAVEPOINT has been set during the user session, the ROLLBACK can undo transactions only since either that SAVEPOINT or the last commit. It has the following prototype: ROLLBACK [TO *savepoint_name*]
SAVEPOINT	The SAVEPOINT statement sets a point-in-time marker in a current user session. It enables the ROLLBACK command to only roll back all transactions after the SAVEPOINT is set. It has the following prototype: SAVEPOINT *savepoint_name*

TABLE H-4. *DCL Statements*

Data Control Language (DCL)

Data Control Language (DCL) is the ability to guarantee an all-or-nothing approach when changing data in more than one table. Table H-4 covers the key commands involved in DCL to manage transactions.

A good programming practice is to set a SAVEPOINT statement before beginning a set of DML statements to change related data. Then, if you encounter a failure in one of the DML statements, you can use the ROLLBACK statement to undo the DML statements that completed. You use the COMMIT command to make the changes permanent when all changes have been made successfully.

Summary

The appendix has reviewed the Structured Query Language (SQL) and explained how and why basic SQL statements work. The coverage should enable you to work through the Oracle Database 10*g* XE examples in the book.

APPENDIX

I

PL/SQL Primer

he *Procedure Language/Structured Query Language (PL/SQL)* was developed by Oracle in the late 1980s. Originally, PL/SQL had limited capabilities, but that changed in the early 1990s. PL/SQL provides the Oracle database with an interpreted and operating system–independent programming environment. SQL is natively integrated in the PL/SQL language, and PL/SQL programs can be called directly from the command-line SQL*Plus interface covered in Appendix G. This appendix assumes you have basic familiarity with operating in the SQL*Plus environment, and that you will read it sequentially.

The PL/SQL language is a robust tool with many options. As a PL/SQL primer, the appendix introduces

- Oracle PL/SQL block structure
- Variables, assignments, and operators
- Control structures
  - Conditional structures
  - Iterative structures
- Stored functions, procedures, and packages
- Database triggers
- Collections
- Using the DBMS_LOB package

PL/SQL is a case-insensitive programming language, like SQL. While the language is case insensitive, there are many conventions different people use to write their PL/SQL programs. Most choose combinations of uppercase, lowercase, title case, or mixed case. Among these opinions there is no standard approach to follow. The PL/SQL code in this book uses uppercase for command words and lowercase for variables, column names, and stored program calls.

After understanding the basics of PL/SQL, you can explore other references, such as *Oracle Database 10g PL/SQL Programming* by Scott Urman et al. (McGraw-Hill/Osborne, 2004) and *Expert Oracle PL/SQL* by Ron Hardman and Michael McLaughlin (McGraw-Hill/Osborne, 2005), as well as the *Oracle PL/SQL User's Guide and Reference 10g, Release 2* manual.

Oracle PL/SQL Block Structure

PL/SQL was developed by modeling the concepts of structured programming, static data typing, modularity, exception management, and parallel processing found in the Ada programming language. The Ada programming language, developed for the United States Department of Defense, was designed to support military real-time and safety-critical embedded systems, such as those in airplanes and missiles. The Ada programming language borrowed significant syntax from the Pascal programming language, including the assignment and comparison operators and the single-quote string delimiters.

Choosing the Ada programming language made sense for a number of reasons. Three reasons were that SQL adopted the Pascal operators, string delimiters, and declarative scalar data types. Pascal and Ada have declarative scalar data types. Declarative data types are also known as strong data types, which mean they do not change at run time. Strong data types were critical to tightly integrating Oracle SQL and PL/SQL data types. Matching operators and string delimiters meant simplified parsing because SQL statements are natively embedded in PL/SQL programming units.

NOTE
Primitives in the Java programming language describe scalar variables, which only hold one thing at a time.

The Oracle Call Interface (OCI) libraries have over the years enabled mapping other programming language data types to these strongly typed variables. The OCI libraries abstract the Oracle SQL and PL/SQL variable details from the interface, simplifying programmer access. The combination of using OCI to interact directly with SQL and PL/SQL has made the PL/SQL language and environment extremely extensible. OCI8 is the newest version of the library.

PL/SQL implemented modularity concepts with only slight modification from Ada. PL/SQL supports two types of programs: one is an anonymous block program, and the other is a named block program. Both types of programs have *declaration, execution,* and *exception* handling sections or blocks. The anonymous block program is basically designed to support batch scripting, while the named block program supports stored programming units.

The basic prototype for an anonymous block PL/SQL program is

```
[DECLARE]
  Declaration_statements
BEGIN
  execution_statements
[EXCEPTION]
  exception_handling_statements
END;
/
```

As shown and highlighted in the prototype, PL/SQL requires only the execution section for an anonymous block program. The execution section of PL/SQL programs starts with a `BEGIN` statement and stops at the beginning of the optional `EXCEPTION` block or the `END` statement of the program. *A semicolon ends the anonymous PL/SQL block, and the forward slash executes the block.*

TIP
This is why you see a semicolon inside a PL/SQL resource statement in PHP but not inside a SQL statement in Chapters 13, 14, and 15.

Declaration sections can contain variable definitions and declarations, user-defined PL/SQL type definitions, cursor definitions, reference cursor definitions, and local function or procedure definitions. *Execution* sections can contain variable assignments, object initializations, conditional structures, iterative structures, nested anonymous PL/SQL blocks, or calls to local or stored named PL/SQL blocks. *Exception* sections can contain error-handling phrases that can use all of the same items as the execution section.

NOTE
You declare *a variable by giving it a name and assigning it a type. You* define *a variable by giving it a name and assigning it both a type and a value.*

The `hello_world.sql` program demonstrates the minimal components of a PL/SQL program. You require a `BEGIN` statement, execution statements, and an `END` statement, plus a block terminating semicolon and forward slash execution operator. The `hello_world.sql` follows:

`-- This is found in hello_world.sql on the enclosed CD.`

```
SET SERVEROUTPUT ON SIZE 1000000
BEGIN
  dbms_output.put_line('Hello World');
END;
/
```

The program uses a SQL*Plus `SET` operation to open a buffer for output from the PL/SQL program. The `DBMS_OUTPUT.PUT_LINE()` function is like a call to standard out with one exception: the standard out console is the SQL*Plus session. This is why you must first open a buffer in SQL*Plus to print to console. The call to the standard out procedure is an execution statement and terminated by a semicolon. Procedures act like functions but have no return type and cannot be used as right operands.

All declarations, statements, and blocks are terminated by a semicolon. The declaration block contains all *declarations* and *named PL/SQL program units,* while the execution block contains *execution, if-then-else,* and *case statements,* as well as *anonymous block PL/SQL programs.* The exception block contains *error handlers* and supports all items that you can put in the execution block.

NOTE
Every PL/SQL block must contain something, at least a NULL;
statement, or it will fail run-time compilation, also known as parsing.

SQL*Plus supports the use of substitution variables in the interactive console, which are prefaced by an ampersand (`&`). Substitution variables are variable-length strings or numbers. Oracle implicitly downcasts a numeric substitution variable to a SQL `NUMBER` data type when you assign it to a variable of the same data type. Variable-length strings can contain white space because the `enter` command signals the end of the string.

The `substitution.sql` program uses a `DECLARE` block to demonstrate how you assign a substitution variable to a local variable in your program:

`-- This is found in substitution.sql on the enclosed CD.`

```
DECLARE
  my_var VARCHAR2(30) := '&input';
BEGIN
  dbms_output.put_line('Hello '|| my_var );
END;
/
```

The `DECLARE` section encloses the `&input` substitution variable in single quotes to designate the run-time value as a string literal. The assignment operator in PL/SQL is a colon plus an equal sign, `:=` (a legacy from Pascal and Ada). The difference between PL/SQL string literals and PHP string literals is that the former are always delimited by single quotes and the latter are delimited by either single or double quotes.

You run this program by calling it from an Oracle SQL*Plus section. The @ symbol in Oracle SQL*Plus loads and executes a file script. The default file extension is .sql, but you can override it with whatever you prefer. You should see the following print to your console:

```
SQL> @substitution.sql
Enter value for input: Henry Wadsworth Longfellow
old    3:    my_var VARCHAR2(30) := '&input';
new    3:    my_var VARCHAR2(30) := 'Henry Wadsworth Longfellow';
Hello Henry Wadsworth Longfellow
PL/SQL procedure successfully completed.
```

The line starting with old designates where your program planned to make the substitution, and new designates the run-time substitution. While this works in the example, you should only *make assignments in the execution block of anonymous block* programs. They should go in the *execution* block because exceptions are not caught in the *exception* block when triggered by errors in the *declaration* block.

The exception.sql program is built to demonstrate how to properly assign a substitution variable and manage a triggered exception. The physical size of the my_var variable has been reduced to a ten-character VARCHAR2 string. The smaller variable size is too small for our dead poet's name and will throw an exception when you try to put it in the variable, as done here:

```
-- This is found in exception.sql on the enclosed CD.

DECLARE
  my_var VARCHAR2(10);
BEGIN
  my_var := '&input';
  dbms_output.put_line('Hello '|| my_var );
EXCEPTION
  WHEN others THEN
    dbms_output.put_line(SQLERRM);
    RETURN;
END;
/
```

Assigning a string literal that is too large for the designated my_var variable triggers an error in the exception.sql program. The raised error is then managed by the generic exception handler, OTHERS. The exception handler prints the raised error message to the console, it returns control to the next line in the *execution* block, and the program terminates successfully, although it actually failed. This is an atypical behavior that lets you see how to use the RETURN call in an exception handler. You use the RETURN call when a nonfatal error occurs and your handler fixes or records it. The SQLERRM built-in function returns the raised error for standard Oracle errors, as described in Chapter 6 of *Oracle Database 10g PL/SQL Programming*.

The console output is

```
SQL> @exception.sql
Enter value for input: Henry Wadsworth Longfellow
old    7:    my_var := '&input';
new    7:    my_var := 'Henry Wadsworth Longfellow';
ORA-06502: PL/SQL: numeric or value error: character string buffer too small
PL/SQL procedure successfully completed.
```

As mentioned, you can have: (a) nested anonymous block programs in the *execution* section of anonymous programming units; (b) named block programs in the *declaration* section that can in turn contain nested programs of the same type; and (c) calls to stored named block programs. The outermost programming block controls the total program flow, while nested programming blocks control their subordinate programming flow. Each anonymous or named block programming unit can contain an *exception* section.

Often exception handlers manage all possible errors by using the OTHERS exception, which catches all raised errors. Sometimes exception handlers only manage specific exceptions and expect unhandled exceptions to be reported back to calling programs. When an error is triggered in the innermost execution block, it raises the error and passes it to the local exception block. The calling program is never made aware of local errors when they are managed in the *local* exception section.

Calling programs learn about errors when they are not managed by the local exception handler. The called program reports the error as a reason for its execution failure. This alerts the calling program, which can handle the exception or report the raised error back to a higher-level calling program. This is a continuous cycle of decision making from the lowest programming unit to the highest, as demonstrated in Figure I-1.

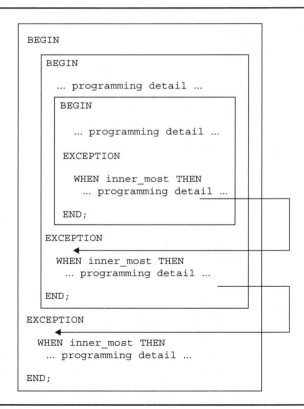

FIGURE I-1. *Error stack management*

Whether errors are thrown from called local or named PL/SQL blocks, the stack management process is the same. Errors are raised and put in a *first-in, last-out* queue, which is known as a *stack*. As raised errors are placed on the stack, they are passed to calling program units until they reach the outermost program. The outermost program reports the error stack to the end user. The end user can be a physical person, a SQL statement, or a batch processing script external to the database.

This was a very tedious process to manage in PL/SQL prior to Oracle 10*g*, when the FORMAT_ ERROR_BACKTRACE procedure was added to the DBMS_UTILITY package. This procedure now provides PL/SQL with a formal error stack management process.

You have explored the basic structure of PL/SQL block programs and error stack management. You have also forward-referenced the definition and declaration of variables, and the assignment process in PL/SQL. The block structure is foundation knowledge to support later sections in this appendix.

Variables, Assignments, and Operators

Data types in PL/SQL include all SQL data types and subtypes described in Table H-2, plus you have five PL/SQL-specific data types covered in Table I-1. There are a number of implicit casting operations performed by Oracle, and they follow the common rule of programming: *implicitly cast when there is no loss of precision.* Likewise, there are a series of functions to let you *explicitly* cast when there is risk of losing run-time precision. You should choose carefully when you *explicitly* downcast variables.

Data Type	Description

Associative Array PL/SQL Tables	The *associative array* type is a user-defined collection of scalar variables, user-defined PL/SQL record types, or user-defined object types. *Associative arrays* are one of three collection types defined by Oracle. The other two, VARRAY and NESTED TABLE, can be used to define column values in the database, as covered in Appendix H. *Associative arrays* can only be used as variable data types for PL/SQL block variables and formal parameters in the signatures of stored functions and procedures. You define an *associative array* as
	
	`TYPE my_array IS TABLE OF data_type`
	`  INDEX BY BINARY_INTEGER;`

BOOLEAN	The BOOLEAN type works like most Boolean variables but has a nasty twist for inexperienced PL/SQL programmers. The PL/SQL BOOLEAN variable can be *true, false,* or *null.* A BOOLEAN variable is *null* until you have assigned it a value. As in SQL, *null* values cannot be evaluated using traditional comparison operators. You must use the IS NULL or IS NOT NULL comparison operator to compare a BOOLEAN data type or other variable types before they're initialized with a value. You assign a case-insensitive *true* or *false* to initialize a BOOLEAN variable. A full prototype declaration is `my_var BOOLEAN [:= true	false];`

Record Type	*Record types* are user-defined compound variables. A record type is a single row of data made up of multiple columns. You can use record types to capture a row from a reference cursor, like the one used in Chapter 14. *Record types* can only be used as variable data types for PL/SQL block variables and formal parameters in the signatures of stored functions and procedures. You define an *explicit* record type by
	
	`TYPE my_variable_record IS RECORD`
	`( variable_name1 sql_data_type`
	`[, variable_name2 sql_data_type`
	`[, variable_name(n+1) sql_data_type]]);`

TABLE I-1.   *PL/SQL Data Types*

Data Type	Description
	Alternatively, you define an *implicit* record type, also known as anchoring your variable to a table, by
	`TYPE my_variable_record IS RECORD` `OF catalog_table%ROWTYPE;`
REF CURSOR	A REF CURSOR is an Oracle *reference cursor* structure that enables you to capture the entire result set of SQL SELECT statements. A REF CURSOR is user defined as either *strongly* or *weakly* typed. A strongly typed reference cursor is explicitly defined by assigning a %ROWTYPE attribute to the cursor. The %ROWTYPE attribute maps the structure from a catalog table or view in the database to a reference cursor. You can only use *strongly* typed cursors when working with row sets that match catalog objects, while *weakly* typed reference cursors support run-time row sets that are generated by a SELECT statement. The process of mapping a run-time row set to a cursor is the closest you get to run-time type identification in Oracle. You define a *strongly typed* REF CURSOR as follows:
	`TYPE my_var_cursor IS REF CURSOR` `RETURN catalog_row_type%ROWTYPE;`
	Alternatively, you define a *weakly typed* REF CURSOR as follows:
	`TYPE my_var_cursor IS REF CURSOR;`
XMLType	The XMLType data type enables you to store and reference HTML links in the database. The XMLType data type is a specialized CLOB data type that contains member functions, or methods, to support rendering HTML content. The type is rendered in mixed case for convenience and is case insensitive as are all other types. You define a XMLType as follows:
	`my_var XMLType;`

TABLE I-1. *PL/SQL Data Types* (continued)

There are several other product specific types created to support various add-on products in the Oracle Database 10*g* family of products. You can find those in the *Oracle Database PL/SQL Packages and Type Reference 10*g *Release 2* on the http://otn.oracle.com web site.

An anonymous PL/SQL block was developed to test the *weakly typed* REF CURSOR used in the WORLD_LEADER package. It demonstrates how to define a record type, a variable using a user-defined record type, and a variable using the REF CURSOR structure. The anonymous block also demonstrates how to declare variables using scalar SQL data types.

While you can define reference cursors in anonymous block programs, typically you define them in package specifications. Package specifications act as a declaration section for a package body. The following *weakly typed* reference cursor is defined in the WORLD_LEADERS package:

```
-- This is found in create_world_leaders.sql on the enclosed CD.

    -- Define a PL/SQL Reference Cursor.
    TYPE president_type_cursor IS REF CURSOR;
```

Only the *declaration* section is covered in the excerpt. You will see the *execution* block later in the chapter. The declaration section is

```
-- This is found in create_world_leaders.sql on the enclosed CD.

DECLARE
    -- Define local PL/SQL record type as target for reference cursor.
    TYPE president_record IS RECORD
    ( president_id     NUMBER
    , president        VARCHAR2(60 CHAR)
```

```
, tenure              VARCHAR2(9 CHAR)
, party               VARCHAR2(24 CHAR));

-- Define a variable of the PL/SQL record.
presidents PRESIDENT_RECORD;

-- Declare local variables.
t_start               NUMBER := '1914';
t_end                 NUMBER := '1943';
t_country             VARCHAR2(3 CHAR) := 'USA';
president_info        WORLD_LEADERS.PRESIDENT_TYPE_CURSOR;
BEGIN
 ...
END;
/
```

The user-defined `president_record` record type is called an *explicit* definition. You can also make an *implicit* definition by using a `%ROWTYPE` attribute against any catalog table or view. An explicit record type is required here because the `SELECT` statement returns a `REF_CURSOR` that *is not* equivalent to a catalog table or view. After defining the record type, a `presidents` variable is defined using the user-defined *weakly typed* `CURSOR` data type. The other three variables are defined because they have names, data types, and assigned values.

The assignment operator is not the only operator in the PL/SQL programming language. PL/SQL also supports the comparison, concatenation, logical, and mathematical operators listed in Table I-2.

Operator	Type	Description
:=	Assignment	Assigns a right operand to a left operand.
=>	Assignment	This is the named notation operator, which lets you pass a parameter by name to a stored function or procedure. It only works in an exclusively PL/SQL environment and cannot be called in the SQL*Plus environment.
=	Comparison	Compares whether two scalar variable values are equal.
<>, !=, ~=, ^=	Comparison	Compares whether two scalar variable values are not equal.
<	Comparison	Compares whether the left operand is less than the right operand.
>	Comparison	Compares whether the left operand is greater than the right operand.
<=	Comparison	Compares whether the left operand is less than or equal to the right operand.
>=	Comparison	Compares whether the left operand is greater than or equal to the right operand.
BETWEEN	Comparison	Compares whether the left operand is BETWEEN two right operands conjoined by the AND operator.
IS NULL	Comparison	Compares whether the left operand is a null value, which can happen when a variable is not initialized.

TABLE I-2. *Assignment, Comparison, Concatenation, and Arithmetic Operators*

Operator	Type	Description
IS NOT NULL	Comparison	Compares whether the left operand is *not* a null value, which is the general case when variables are initialized.
LIKE	Comparison	Compares whether a variable is like another variable. You use the underscore (_) for a single character wildcard, and the percent symbol (%) for a series of characters.
NOT	Comparison	Logical negation operations.
||	Concatenation	Concatenates one string to another.
AND	Logical	Operator conjoins two logical expressions.
OR	Logical	Operator includes two logical expressions.
+	Math	Dual-purpose operator for identity and addition.
/	Math	Operator for division of the left operand by the right operand.
**	Math	Operator for taking the exponential of the left operand to the power of the right operand.
*	Math	Operator for multiplication of the two operands.
-	Math	Operator for subtraction or negation of the right operand.

TABLE I-2. *Assignment, Comparison, Concatenation, and Arithmetic Operators* (continued)

You define CURSOR statements in the declaration section. A CURSOR statement can have formal arguments. The prototype for a local CURSOR statement is

```
CURSOR my_cursor
  [ (parameter1      VARCHAR2
  [,(parameter2      NUMBER
  [,(parameter(n+1)  DATE ]] ) ] IS
    SELECT    column1 [AS alias1]
    [,        column2 [AS alias2]
    [,        column(n+1) [AS alias(n+1)]]]
    FROM      table1     [table_alias1]
    [,        table2     [table_alias2]
    [,        table(n+1) [table_alias(n+1)]]]
    WHERE     column1 = parameter1
    [,        column2 = parameter2];
```

You can extend the SELECT statement to include any valid SQL statement syntax. CURSOR parameter types, like functions and procedures, do not specify size, relying on the run-time size of the actual parameter. All CURSOR parameters are *pass-by-value*, or IN mode–only, variables.

You have now reviewed variables, assignments, and operators. You have also been exposed to PL/SQL-specific user-defined types.

Control Structures

Control structures do one of two things: they check a logical condition to branch program execution, or they iterate over a condition until it is met or they are instructed to exit. The section "Conditional Structures" covers *if, elsif, else,* and *case* statements, and the section "Iterative Structures" covers looping with *for* and *while* structures.

Conditional Structures

Conditional statements check whether a value meets a condition before taking action. There are two types of conditional structures in PL/SQL: the IF statement and the CASE statement. The IF statement that has two subtypes: *if-then-else* and *if-then-elsif-then-else*. The *elsif* is not a typo but the correct reserved word in PL/SQL, as well as Pascal and Ada programming languages.

IF Statement

All IF statements are blocks in PL/SQL and end with the END IF phrase; and CASE statements are also blocks, ending with END CASE phrase. The following is the basic prototype for an if-then-else PL/SQL block:

```
IF [NOT] left_operand1 = right_operand1 [AND|OR
   [NOT] left_operand2 = right_operand2 [AND|OR
   [NOT] boolean_operand ]] THEN
  NULL;
END IF;
```

The Open Universe of NULL Variables

A formalism governing Boolean variables in computer science raises its ugly head like a mythological beast from time to time. The ugly head is how to tell what something is when it isn't true. Is it false or something else?

The choice involves how we define the concept for a compiler or interpreter. Computational lexicography determines whether a Boolean operates in a closed or open universe. The closed universe idea was pioneered by Einstein in his 1917 musing about a spherical universe. A spherical universe, according to his paper, was fixed in size and led to his famous cosmological constant in the *special* theory of relativity, which was later recanted when Russian mathematician Alexander Friedmann theorized the universe was constantly expanding in 1922 and this hypothesis was confirmed by the noted American astronomer Edwin Hubble in 1929.

How it came to apply to the scope and behavior of variables is unknown. Applying a closed-universe model to a Boolean variable means that if it is not true, it is false, and vice versa. By contrast, applying an open-universe model to a Boolean variable means that if is not true, it may be false or something else, and vice versa. Null variables are false by default in some programming languages that use the closed-universe model, such as PHP. In databases, Boolean variables are true, false, or null because databases use an open-universe model.

The foregoing if-then-else block prototype uses an equality comparison, but you can substitute any of the comparison operators from Table I-2 for the equal symbol. You can evaluate one or more conditions by using the AND or the OR to link statements together as compound Boolean expressions, and you can negate outcomes by using the NOT operator. Logical operators support conjoining and including operations. A conjoining operator, AND, means that *both statements must evaluate as true or false.* An include operator, OR, means that *one or the other must be true.* Include operators stop processing when one statement evaluates as true.

BOOLEAN variables are comparisons in and of themselves. Other operands can be any valid data type that works with the appropriate comparison operator, but remember that the variables must be initialized. Problems occur when you fail to initialize or handle noninitialized variables in conditional statements. For example, when you use an IF statement to evaluate a noninitialized BOOLEAN as *true,* it fails and processes the ELSE block; however, when you use an IF NOT statement to evaluate a noninitialized BOOLEAN as *false,* it also fails and processes the ELSE block. This happens because a noninitialized BOOLEAN variable isn't *true* or *false.*

The solution to this problem is to use the SQL NVL() function, which substitutes a value for any *null* value variables. The NVL() function takes two parameters: the first is a variable, and the second is a literal, which can be a numeric, string, or constant value. The two parameters must share the same data type. *You can access all the standard SQL functions natively in your PL/SQL programs.* The if_then.sql program demonstrates how you use the NVL() against a noninitialized BOOLEAN variable. The IF NOT statement would return *false* for an noninitialized BOOLEAN variable without the NVL() function, as shown:

 `-- This is found in if_then.sql on the enclosed CD.`

```
DECLARE
  -- Define a Boolean variable.
  my_var BOOLEAN;
BEGIN
  -- Use a NVL function to substitute a value for evalution.
  IF NOT NVL(my_var,false) THEN
    dbms_output.put_line('This should happen!');
  ELSE
    dbms_output.put_line('This can''t happen!');
  END IF;
END;
/
```

The if_then.sql program finds the NVL() function value to be *false,* or NOT *true,* and it prints the following message:

```
This should happen!
```

NOTE
The ELSE block contains a back-quoted string. The single quote mark is a reserved character for delimiting strings. You back-quote an apostrophe by using another apostrophe, or a single quote, inside a delimited string.

The if-then-*elsif*-then-else statement works like the if-then-else statement but lets you perform multiple conditional evaluations in the same IF statement. The following is the basic prototype for an if-then-*elsif*-then-else PL/SQL block:

```
IF     [NOT] left_operand1 > right_operand2 [AND|OR
   NULL;
ELSIF [NOT] left_operand1 = right_operand1 [AND|OR
        [NOT] left_operand2 = right_operand2 [AND|OR
        [NOT] boolean_operand ]] THEN
   NULL;
END IF;
```

CASE Statement

The other conditional statement is a CASE statement. A CASE statement works like the if-then-*elsif*-then-else process. There are two types of CASE statements; one is a *simple* CASE and the other is a *searched* CASE. A simple CASE statement takes a scalar variable as an expression and then evaluates it against a list of like scalar results. A searched CASE statement takes a BOOLEAN variable as an expression and then compares the Boolean result in the WHEN clause. When the Boolean result is true, the program runs the WHEN clause subroutine. The following is the prototype of the CASE statement:

```
CASE expression
WHEN result1 THEN
   statement1;
WHEN result2 THEN
   statement2;
WHEN result(n+1) THEN
   statement(n+1);
ELSE
   else_statement;
END CASE;
```

The case_statement.sql program demonstrates a searched CASE statement:

```
-- This is found in case_statement.sql on the enclosed CD.

BEGIN
  CASE TRUE
  WHEN (1 > 3) THEN
    dbms_output.put_line('One is greater than three.');
  WHEN (3 < 5) THEN
    dbms_output.put_line('Three is less than five.');
  WHEN (1 = 2) THEN
    dbms_output.put_line('One equals two.');
  ELSE
    dbms_output.put_line('Nothing worked.');
  END CASE;
END;
/
```

The program evaluates WHEN clause results as expressions, finding that 3 is less than 5. It then prints

```
Three is less than five.
```

This subsection has demonstrated the conditional expressions available to you in PL/SQL. It has also covered how noninitialized variables must be treated as NULL values.

Iterative Structures

The PL/SQL language supports FOR, SIMPLE, and WHILE loops. It does not support a *repeat until* loop block. Loops typically work in conjunction with cursors but can work to solve other problems, such as searching or managing Oracle collections.

FOR Loops

PL/SQL supports *numeric* and *cursor* FOR loops. The *numeric* FOR loop iterates across a defined range, while the *cursor* FOR loop iterates across rows returned by a SELECT statement cursor. FOR loops manage how they begin and end implicitly. You can override the *implicit* END LOOP phrase by using an explicit EXIT statement placed inside the FOR loop to force a premature exit.

Numeric FOR loops take two implicit actions. They automatically declare and manage their own loop index, and they create and manage their exit from the loop. A *numeric* FOR loop has the following prototype:

```
FOR i IN starting_number..ending_number LOOP
   statement;
END LOOP;
```

The *starting_number* and *ending_number* must be integers. The *loop index* is the i variable, and the loop index scope is limited to the FOR loop. When you have previously defined or declared a variable i, the numeric loop will ignore the externally scoped variable and create a new locally scoped variable.

The *cursor* FOR loop requires a locally defined CURSOR. You cannot use a *cursor* FOR loop to iterate across a reference cursor (REF CURSOR) because *reference cursors can only be traversed by using explicit loop structures, like simple and while loops.* The cursor FOR loop can also use a SELECT statement in lieu of a locally defined CURSOR; it has the following prototype:

```
FOR i IN cursor_name [(parameter1,parameter(n+1))] | (statement) LOOP
   statement;
END LOOP;
```

The *cursor_name* can have an optional parameter list, which is enclosed in parentheses. A *cursor_name* without optional parameters does not require parentheses. You are using an *explicit* cursor when you use a *cursor_name* and an *implicit* cursor when you provide a SELECT statement.

NOTE
Every SQL statement runs as an implicit cursor whether inside a PL/SQL block or not.

The *statement* must be a valid SELECT statement, but you can dynamically reference locally scoped variable names without any special syntax in all clauses except the FROM clause.

Unless you override the exit criteria, the *cursor* FOR loop will run through all rows returned by the *cursor* or *statement*.

Simple Loops

Simple loops are explicit structures. They require that you manage both loop index and exit criteria. Typically, simple loops are used in conjunction with both locally defined CURSOR statements and reference cursors (REF CURSOR). Reference cursors are typically returned by stored functions or procedures. They are returned by stored functions as the user-defined return type, whereas they are returned as *pass-by-reference* parameters in procedures. Both of these approaches are demonstrated later in this appendix.

Oracle provides six CURSOR attributes that help you manage activities in loops. They are covered in Table I-3. Four of these attributes are used for ordinary cursor operations, while two support BULK operations. Oracle provides BULK operations to let you perform DQL and DML operations against sets of rows, as opposed to the traditional row-by-row mechanics.

The FORALL statement is a hybrid loop structure that lets you *insert, update,* or *delete* a bulk set of records in a single DML statement. DQL statements use the BULK COLLECT statement to query all rows in a result set and place them into a *user-defined* associative array.

The simple loops have a variety of uses. The following is the prototype for a simple loop, using an explicit CURSOR:

```
OPEN cursor_name [(parameter1,parameter(n+1))];
LOOP
  FETCH cursor_name
  INTO   row_structure_variable | column_variable1 [,column_variable(n+1)];
    EXIT WHEN cursor_name%NOTFOUND;
    statement;
END LOOP;
CLOSE cursor_name;
```

Attribute	Description
%BULK_ROWCOUNT	The %BULK_ROWCOUNT attribute returns the number of rows modified by the FORALL statement.
%BULK_EXCEPTIONS	The %BULK_EXCEPTIONS attribute returns exceptions encountered when modifying rows with the FORALL statement.
%FOUND	The %FOUND returns *true* when the last FETCH statement returned a row and *false* otherwise.
%ISOPEN	The %ISOPEN returns *true* when the CURSOR is open and *false* when it is closed.
%NOTFOUND	The %NOTFOUND returns true when the last FETCH statement failed to return a row and false otherwise.
%ROWCOUNT	The %ROWCOUNT returns the current number of rows fetched by the FETCH statement at a moment in time.

TABLE I-3. *CURSOR Attributes*

The prototype demonstrates that you OPEN a CURSOR before starting the simple loop, and then you FETCH a row. While rows are returned, you process them, but when a FETCH fails to return a row, you exit the loop. Place the EXIT WHEN statement as the last statement in the loop when you want the behavior of a repeat until loop. Repeat until loops typically process statements in a loop at least once regardless of whether the CURSOR returns records.

The WHILE loop differs from the simple loop in that it guards entry to the loop, not the exit. It sets the entry guard as a *condition* expression. The loop is entered only when the guard condition is met. The basic syntax is

```
OPEN cursor_name [(parameter1,parameter(n+1))];
WHILE condition LOOP
  FETCH cursor_name
  INTO  row_structure_variable | column_variable1 [,column_variable(n+1)];
    EXIT WHEN cursor_name%NOTFOUND;
    statement;
END LOOP;
CLOSE cursor_name;
```

When the condition checks for an opened CURSOR, then the WHILE *condition* would be an expression like *cursor_name*%ISOPEN. There are many other possible condition values that you can use in WHILE loops.

This section has demonstrated how you can use implicit and explicit looping structures. It has also introduced you to the management of the CURSOR statement in the execution section of PL/SQL programs.

Stored Functions, Procedures, and Packages

PL/SQL stored programming units are functions, procedures, packages, and triggers. Oracle maintains a unique list of stored object names for tables, views, sequences, stored programs, and types. This list is known as a *namespace*. Stored functions, procedures, and packages provide a way to hide implementation details in a program unit. While triggers work along the same lines as functions and procedures, they serve a different purpose that is covered in the next section of this appendix. Triggers also have their own separate namespace in Oracle, which means a trigger can have the same name as a table, view, stored program, sequence, or type.

PL/SQL implements *functions* with *pass-by-value* parameters and *procedures* with *pass-by-reference* parameters, as done in the Ada programming language. A package has two parts: a specification that acts like a declaration block and a body that provide implementations of those things defined in the specification or its own local declaration block. A package specification is a container of user-defined data type, function, and procedure definitions, and a package body is an implementation library for the components defined in the package specification. Package bodies can also have locally defined user-defined data type, function, and procedure definitions. These locally defined modules can be used inside the functions and procedures of the package but are not available externally.

The PL/SQL parser is a single-pass parser. A single-pass parser requires that all variables, types, and program units be defined before they are referenced. Package specifications serve the purpose of defining package functions, procedures, and types, eliminating the process of forward-referencing required for locally defined variables and structures. This means that if you have two local procedures A and B defined in sequence, you cannot call procedure B in procedure A because B has not yet been defined. Local procedures can be forward-referenced by providing a stub like those found in package specifications.

The following demonstrates an anonymous block using forward referencing:

```
DECLARE
  -- A forward referencing stub for a local procedure.
  PROCEDURE b;

  -- A local procedure calling a forward referenced procedure.
  PROCEDURE a IS
  BEGIN
    b;
    dbms_output.put_line('This is procedure A.');
  END a;

  -- A local procedure implementation for the forward referencing stub.
  PROCEDURE b IS
  BEGIN
    dbms_output.put_line('This is procedure B.');
  END b;
BEGIN
  a;
END;
/
```

You will see the following output:

```
This is procedure B.
This is procedure A.
```

The subsections will address stored functions, procedures, and packages. You are encourgaged to cover them sequentially.

Stored Functions

Stored functions are convenient structures because you can call them directly from SQL statements or in PL/SQL programs. All stored functions in Oracle must return a value, and they can also be used as right operands with assignment operators because they return a value. You can also define local named block programs in their declaration sections, like anonymous block programs.

The prototype for a stored function is

```
CREATE [OR REPLACE] FUNCTION function_name
[(parameter1     [IN] data_type [:= null_default1]
[,parameter2     [IN] data_type [:= null_default2]
[,parameter(n+1) [IN] data_type [:= null_default(n+1)]])]
RETURN return_data_type
[AUTHID {CURRENT_USER | DEFINER}] {IS | AS}
  declaration_statements;
BEGIN
  execution_statements;
  RETURN return_data_variable;
END function_name;
/
```

You can define functions with or without formal parameters. Formal parameters in functions are *pass-by-value,* or IN mode, variables by default. You can type the IN phrase or leave it out because when you leave out the mode value, the function compilation process implicitly provides it. Formal parameters support optional default values, which serve to make formal parameters optional. Optional parameters are typically implemented at the end of a formal parameter list. You must submit null values for optional parameters when they are intermingled with required parameters.

An optional AUTHID clause, introduced in Oracle 8*i,* lets you define how a function resolves references. AUTHID sets the *execution authority model* for stored functions, procedures, and packages. The default is DEFINER, and the override is CURRENT_USER; these are known as definer's rights and invoker's rights references. You can read more about these execution authority models in the *Oracle Database 10g PL/SQL Programming* and *Expert Oracle PL/SQL* books.

The *declaration* block is between the IS and BEGIN phrases. Stored functions return a value defined by a data type. The *execution* and *exception* blocks appear exactly as they do in anonymous block programs.

You should run the create_world_leaders.sql script (covered in Chapter 13 and Appendix J) before running the next script; otherwise, it will fail because of missing objects. The get_presidents_function.sql program demonstrates a stored function that returns a user-defined reference cursor:

```
-- This is in get_presidents_function.sql on the enclosed CD.

CREATE OR REPLACE FUNCTION get_presidents_function
( term_start_in    IN      NUMBER := 1787
, term_end_in      IN      NUMBER := TO_NUMBER(TO_CHAR(SYSDATE,'YYYY'))
, country_in       IN      VARCHAR2 := 'USA')
RETURN WORLD_LEADERS.PRESIDENT_TYPE_CURSOR IS

  presidents       WORLD_LEADERS.PRESIDENT_TYPE_CURSOR;

BEGIN

  -- Collect data for the reference cursor.
  OPEN presidents FOR
    SELECT    president_id "#"
    ,         first_name||' '
    ||        DECODE(middle_name,NULL,NULL,middle_name||' ')
    ||        last_name "Preisdent"
    ,         term_start||' '||term_end "Tenure"
    ,         party "Party"
    FROM      president
    WHERE     country = country_in
    AND       term_start BETWEEN term_start_in AND term_end_in
    OR        term_end BETWEEN term_start_in AND term_end_in;

  -- Return user-defined REF CURSOR.
  RETURN presidents;

END get_presidents_function;
/
```

The GET_PRESIDENTS_FUNCTION takes three optional formal parameters, which means you can call it without providing any actual parameters. It uses all three parameters in the WHERE clause of the SELECT statement. The SELECT statement also uses a DECODE() function to avoid returning a double white space when there is no middle initial. Unlike earlier examples of the OPEN phrase, this usage is unique. It both populates a reference cursor variable and opens and fetches all rows into the reference cursor. After opening and fetching the rows, the function returns the user-defined reference cursor as a complete result set.

Functions can be used as right operands in PL/SQL assignments or called directly from SQL statements. Procedures cannot be right operands or called from SQL statements. The OCI8 libraries do not let you return a function return value to external language programs, like PHP. After running the get_presidents_function.sql program, try out the following script; it demonstrates a call without actual parameters to the function from SQL using the pseudo-table DUAL:

```
-- This is found in get_president1.sql on the enclosed CD.

SELECT    get_presidents_function
FROM      dual;
```

The SELECT statement returns all 42 United States presidents, and the output advises you that the function returned a CURSOR statement. You should note that the parentheses are *optional* when calling a function that does not require actual parameters. You can also use actual parameters, as shown in the next query, which select the first two United States presidents:

```
-- This is found in get_president1.sql on the enclosed CD.

SELECT    get_presidents_function(1787,1800)
FROM      dual;
```

You are limited to passing actual parameters by positional order in SQL statements. That means you cannot pass the second actual parameter without providing the first, et cetera. Stored functions and procedures do support *named notation* to fix this problem, but you can use it only in the context of PL/SQL programs. The limit is imposed because of how the SQL parser works with the *named notation* operator. The *named notation* operator is an assignment operator and covered in Table I-2.

The following anonymous block program demonstrates named positional notation:

```
-- This is found in get_president1.sql on the enclosed CD.

-- Define anonymous block PL/SQL program to test named notation.
DECLARE

  -- Define local PL/SQL record type as target for reference cursor.
  TYPE president_record IS RECORD
  ( president_id    NUMBER
  , president       VARCHAR2(60 CHAR)
  , tenure          VARCHAR2(9 CHAR)
  , party           VARCHAR2(24 CHAR));

  -- Define a local variable using the user-defined record type.
  president_rs      PRESIDENT_RECORD;
```

```
      -- Define a variable for the user-defined reference cursor.
      presidents       WORLD_LEADERS.PRESIDENT_TYPE_CURSOR;

BEGIN

      -- Assign the function to a matching left operand.
      presidents := get_presidents_function(term_end_in => 1820);

      -- Explicit fetches are required for reference cursors.
      LOOP
        FETCH presidents
        INTO  president_rs;
        EXIT WHEN presidents%NOTFOUND;
        dbms_output.put      ('['||president_rs.president_id||']');
        dbms_output.put      ('['||president_rs.president||']');
        dbms_output.put      ('['||president_rs.tenure||']');
        dbms_output.put_line ('['||president_rs.party||']');
      END LOOP;
END;
/
```

The anonymous block program defines a RECORD data type using the four column values returned by the GET_PRESIDENTS_FUNCTION. Then, it defines a variable with the user-defined RECORD data type, and another variable with the reference cursor defined in the WORLD_LEADERS package. Only the second formal parameter is passed as an actual parameter by *named notation* to the GET_PRESIDENTS_FUNCTION. The function return value is then assigned to the reference cursor variable, which is accessed by the FETCH statement INTO the RECORD data type variable. The field elements of the record are printed by using the RECORD data type variable and *dot notation* to the field names.

TIP
While it would be convenient to call the function directly as the target of the FETCH phrase, the parser disallows this syntax. You must assign the function result to a REF CURSOR variable before attempting to access the structure.

Functions offer a great deal of power to database development because they can be called by SQL statements and used in PL/SQL program units. Unfortunately, functions use only *pass-by-value* parameters and do not let you move data directly through OCI8 into programs written in external languages.

Procedures

Procedures cannot be right operands or called from SQL statements, but as discussed in Chapter 14, the OCI8 libraries let you move data into and out of PL/SQL stored procedures using *bind* variables by using a *pass-by-reference* model. The scope of *bind* variables is a database session. This means *bind* variables are able to exchange data between different programs running in the same session. A session begins when you connect to and ends when you disconnect from a user/schema in the database. As when working with stored functions, you can also define local named block programs in the declaration section of procedures.

The prototype for a stored *procedure* is

```
CREATE [OR REPLACE] PROCEDURE procedure_name
[(parameter1     [IN [OUT]] data_type [:= null_default1]
[,parameter2     [IN [OUT]] data_type [:= null_default2]
[,parameter(n+1) [IN [OUT]] data_type [:= null_default(n+1)]])]
[AUTHID {CURRENT_USER | DEFINER}] {IS | AS}
  declaration_statements;
BEGIN
  execution_statements;
END procedure_name;
```

You can define procedures with or without formal parameters. Formal parameters in procedures can be either *pass-by-value* or *pass-by-reference* variables in stored procedures. *Pass-by-reference* variables have both IN and OUT modes. Like functions, when you don't provide a parameter mode, the procedure creation assumes you want the mode to be a *pass-by-value*. Compiling the procedure implicitly assigns the IN mode phrase when none is provided. As in functions, formal parameters in procedures also support optional default values. The AUTHID clause and execution authority models are discussed in the preceding section, "Stored Functions." As in functions, the *declaration* block is between the IS and BEGIN phrases, while other blocks mirror the structure of anonymous block programs.

If you haven't already run it, you should run the create_world_leaders.sql script (covered in Chapter 13 and Appendix J) before running the next script; otherwise, it will fail because of missing objects. The get_presidents_procedure.sql program demonstrates a stored procedure has three *pass-by-value* parameters and four *pass-by-reference* parameters. The *pass-by-value* parameters are scalar variables, while the *pass-by-reference* parameters are PL/SQL associative arrays. Associative arrays are also known as PL/SQL tables.

Associative arrays must be locally defined or externally defined in a package specification. When you want to use them externally to your program, you should define them in a package specification. The four *pass-by-reference* parameters use associative arrays that are in defined in the WORLD_LEADER package specification that is created by the create_world_leaders .sql script.

The get_presidents_procedure.sql is

```
-- This is found in get_presidents_procedure.sql on the enclosed CD.

CREATE OR REPLACE PROCEDURE get_presidents_procedure
( term_start_in    IN      NUMBER
, term_end_in      IN      NUMBER
, country_in       IN      VARCHAR2
, president_ids    IN OUT  WORLD_LEADERS.PRESIDENT_ID_TABLE
, president_names  IN OUT  WORLD_LEADERS.PRESIDENT_NAME_TABLE
, tenures          IN OUT  WORLD_LEADERS.TENURE_TABLE
, parties          IN OUT  WORLD_LEADERS.PARTY_TABLE) IS

BEGIN

  -- Define a Bulk Collect into parallel associative arrays (PL/SQL tables)
  SELECT    president_id pres_number
  ,         first_name||' '
```

```
     ||          DECODE(middle_name,NULL,NULL,middle_name||' ')
     ||          last_name "President"
     ,           term_start||'-'||term_end tenure
     ,           party
  BULK COLLECT
  INTO        president_ids
     ,           president_names
     ,           tenures
     ,           parties
  FROM        president
  WHERE       country = country_in
  AND         term_start BETWEEN term_start_in AND term_end_in
  OR          term_end BETWEEN term_start_in AND term_end_in;

END get_presidents_procedure;
/
```

The get_presidents_procedure.sql script uses a BULK COLLECT operation to optimize query run time. The three *pass-by-value* parameters determine the number of rows selected by the query; they work like those in the GET_PRESIDENTS_FUNCTION previously demonstrated in the get_presidents_function.sql script. The *pass-by-reference* parameters are output targets, and they return query results. Combining the BULK COLLECT and INTO clauses implicitly creates a loop and populates the associative array columns with individual scalar arrays.

NOTE
External language calls through OCI8 require that you externally size IN and OUT mode variables before calling stored procedures because they don't have an implicit starting size.

The following anonymous block program demonstrates how to access stored procedures with both *pass-by-value* and *pass-by-reference* parameters:

```
-- This is found in get_president2.sql on the enclosed CD.

DECLARE

  -- Declare local variables.
  t_start           NUMBER := '1914';
  t_end             NUMBER := '1943';
  t_country         VARCHAR2(3 CHAR) := 'USA';
  president_ids     WORLD_LEADERS.PRESIDENT_ID_TABLE;
  president_names   WORLD_LEADERS.PRESIDENT_NAME_TABLE;
  tenures           WORLD_LEADERS.TENURE_TABLE;
  parties           WORLD_LEADERS.PARTY_TABLE;

BEGIN

  -- Call the overloaded procedure.
  get_presidents_procedure
```

```
( t_start
, t_end
, t_country
, president_ids
, president_names
, tenures
, parties);

  -- Read the contents of one of the arrays.
  FOR i IN 1..president_names.COUNT LOOP
    dbms_output.put      ('['||president_ids(i)||']');
    dbms_output.put      ('['||president_names(i)||']');
    dbms_output.put      ('['||tenures(i)||']');
    dbms_output.put_line('['||parties(i)||']');
  END LOOP;

END;
/
```

The anonymous block program returns a list of presidents between the specified years. The numeric FOR loop starts with 1 and ends with the highest index value of the array. All Oracle collections and cursors use *1-based* numbering. The COUNT phrase is actually a method from the Oracle Collection API and is discussed later in the appendix. Elements of Oracle collections are referenced by index values, but by contrast with many modern programming languages, PL/SQL uses ordinary parentheses, not square brackets, to hold the index values.

Packages

Packages are the backbone of stored programs in the Oracle database. They enable you to define and share user-defined types, such as Oracle collections, record types, and reference cursors. Packages also enable you to overload the signatures of stored functions and procedures. The package specification serves as a schema-level declaration section for the package, where you define user-defined data types, functions, and procedures. Elements defined in the package specification are known as *published* because they are externally available from the package.

You provide implementation details in package bodies for user-defined data types, functions, and procedures defined in the package specification. Published user-defined types, functions, and procedures are accessible to any anonymous block or named block PL/SQL program in the schema. Granting an EXECUTE privilege on the package makes them available to other schemas. You can also define local user-defined data types, functions, and procedures, but they have limited scope, which is limited to package functions and procedures.

When package bodies reference other package functions or procedures, they actually reference the definition of the function or procedure found in the other packages. This makes package specifications, like tables and views, referenced objects. Changes in package specifications invalidate dependent package specifications and bodies, while changing package bodies does not invalidate dependent functions, procedures, and packages. Package specification changes invalidate dependents because they change the definition of types, reference cursors, functions, and procedures. Package body changes do not invalidate dependents, because they alter only the hidden, or encapsulated, details of the implementation, and dependencies rely *only* on the definitions.

NOTE
Package body changes can introduce new behaviors that break application programming logic or integrity but pass compilation parsing tests. These errors can cause run-time failure or DML anomalies that you must identify through your normal data analysis process.

Oracle controls the referential integrity between stored programs by building a dependency tree and monitoring the timestamp of referenced and dependent programs. A change in the timestamp of a referenced stored function, procedure, or package invalidates dependent programs. This would require manually recompiling all dependent programs, but Oracle provides a lazy compile feature that lets invalidated programs attempt to recompile when they are called by another run-time program.

While timestamp monitoring is the default behavior, you can use an alternate, signature model. The signature model maintains the same dependency tree, but rather than compare timestamps, the database examines altered function and procedure signatures in a referenced package to find signatures changes. When the signature has changed, the database invalidates those dependent programs that reference only changed signatures. Function signatures are defined by the function name, list of formal parameters, execution authority model, and return data type. Procedure signatures are defined by everything in a function signature but the return data type.

The difference between the two ways of defining signatures is linked to the scope of the parameter lists for functions and procedures. Function parameter lists use only *pass-by-value*, using the exclusive IN mode, while using the return type to output results. Procedure parameter lists use both *pass-by-value* and *pass-by-reference*, or exclusive IN and IN OUT modes, the latter of which returns altered variables through the parameter list.

The *package* specification prototype demonstrates only one use of each, as follows:

```
CREATE [OR REPLACE] PACKAGE package_name
[AUTHID {CURRENT_USER | DEFINER}] {IS | AS}

[TYPE type_name IS {RECORD | REF CURSOR | TABLE} OF data_type [%ROWTYPE]
[(parameter 1    data_type [:= null_default1]
[,parameter2     data_type [:= null_default2]
[,parameter(n+1) data_type [:= null_default(n+1)]]])]
[INDEX BY BINARY_INTEGER];

FUNCTION function_name
[(parameter1    [IN] data_type [:= null_default1]
[,parameter2    [IN] data_type [:= null_default2]
[,parameter(n+1) [IN] data_type [:= null_default(n+1)])]
RETURN return_data_type;

PROCEDURE procedure_name
[(parameter1    [IN [OUT]] data_type [:= null_default1]
[,parameter2    [IN [OUT]] data_type [:= null_default2]
[,parameter(n+1) [IN [OUT]] data_type [:= null_default(n+1)]]])];

END package_name;
/
```

Package specifications also include a default `DEFINER` *execution model authority* that applies to the package. As discussed, user-defined types, functions, and procedures in package specifications are merely stubs that are implemented by the package body. The `WORLD_LEADERS` package in Appendix J demonstrates defining associative arrays, reference cursors, and an overloaded `GET_PRESIDENTS` procedure. The procedures demonstrate signatures using scalar, collection, and reference cursor data types as formal parameters.

The *package body* prototype demonstrates only one use of each, as follows:

```
CREATE [OR REPLACE] PACKAGE BODY package_name {IS | AS}

-- Define package body only types.
[TYPE type_name IS {RECORD | REF CURSOR | TABLE} OF data_type [%ROWTYPE]
[(parameter 1    data_type [:= null_default1]
[,parameter2    data_type [:= null_default2]
[,parameter(n+1) data_type [:= null_default(n+1)]]])]
[INDEX BY BINARY_INTEGER];

FUNCTION function_name
[(parameter1     [IN] data_type [:= null_default1]
[,parameter2     [IN] data_type [:= null_default2]
[,parameter(n+1) [IN] data_type [:= null_default(n+1)]])]
RETURN return_data_type {IS | AS}
  declaration_statements;
BEGIN
  execution_statements;
  RETURN return_data_variable;
END function_name;

PROCEDURE procedure_name
[(parameter1     [IN [OUT]] data_type [:= null_default1]
[,parameter2     [IN [OUT]] data_type [:= null_default2]
[,parameter(n+1) [IN [OUT]] data_type [:= null_default(n+1)]]])];
  declaration_statements;
BEGIN
  execution_statements;
END procedure_name;

END package_name;
/
```

Package bodies must mirror the function and procedure signatures provided in the package specifications. Since many people copy their package specification to have a starting set of signatures, you should make sure to change `PACKAGE` to `PACKAGE BODY`. That is recommended because the returned compilation error is not very helpful when you try to compile a package body as a package.

Package bodies also contain locally defined types, functions, and procedures. These structures are available only inside the package body and mimic the concept of private access levels in other modern programming languages, like C++ and Java. The `WORLD_LEADERS` package body provides an implementation example without local functions and procedures in Appendix J.

This section has explained how to define packages and referred you to the WORLD_LEADERS package and package body found in Appendix J for working examples. Packages are the backbone of stored procedures in an Oracle environment.

Database Triggers

Database *triggers* are specialized stored programs that are triggered by events in the database. They run between the time you issue a command and the time you perform the database management system action. For this reason, you cannot use SQL Data Control Language in these triggers: SAVEPOINT, ROLLBACK, or COMMIT. You can define four types of triggers in the Oracle Database 10g family of products:

- **Data Definition Language (DDL) triggers** These triggers fire when you *create, alter, rename,* or *drop* objects in a database schema. They are useful to monitor poor programming practices, such as when programs *create* and *drop* temporary tables rather than use Oracle collections effectively in memory. Temporary tables can fragment disk space and degrade database performance over time.

- **Data Manipulation Language (DML) or row-level triggers** These triggers fire when you *insert, update,* or *delete* data from a table. You can use these types of triggers to audit, check, save, and replace values before they are changed. Automatic numbering of pseudo-numeric *primary keys* is frequently done by using DML triggers.

- **Instead-of triggers** These triggers enable you to stop performance of a DML statement and redirect the DML statement. INSTEAD OF triggers are often used to manage how you write to views that disable a direct write because they're not updatable views. The INSTEAD OF triggers apply business rules and directly *insert, update,* or *delete* rows in appropriate tables related to these updatable views.

- **System or database event triggers** These triggers fire when a system activity occurs in the database, like the logon and logoff event triggers used in Chapter 13. These triggers enable you to track system events and map them to users.

You will cover all four trigger types in this section but only work with examples of the DML and system triggers that support the book. It is assumed that you will read these from start to end. While most of the material stands independently in the sections, there are some flow dependencies.

DDL Triggers

DDL triggers can fire on CREATE, ALTER, RENAME, TRUNCATE, and DROP statements and several other DDL statements. DDL triggers support both BEFORE and AFTER triggers on the same event at either the database or schema level. You often use these triggers to monitor how new release patching changes the database.

TIP
The overhead of these types of triggers should be avoided in production systems; they should only be used in test systems.

The prototype for building DDL triggers is

```
CREATE [OR REPLACE] TRIGGER trigger_name
{BEFORE | AFTER} ddl_event ON {DATABASE | SCHEMA}
[WHEN (logical_expression)]
[DECLARE]
  declaration_statements;
BEGIN
  execution_statements;
END [trigger_name];
/
```

The DDL triggers can also track the creation and modification of tables by application programs that lead to database fragmentation. They are also effective security tools when you monitor GRANT and REVOKE privilege statements.

DML Triggers

DML triggers can fire *before* or *after* insert, update, and delete events, and they can be *statement-* or *row-level* activities. *Statement-level* triggers fire and perform a statement or set of statements once no matter how many rows are affected by the DML event. *Row-level* triggers fire and perform a statement or set of statements for *each* row changed by the DML.

The prototype for building DML triggers is

```
CREATE [OR REPLACE] TRIGGER trigger_name {BEFORE | AFTER}
{INSERT | UPDATE | UPDATE OF column1 [, column2 [, column(n+1)]] | DELETE}
[FOR EACH ROW]
[WHEN (logical_expression)]
[DECLARE]
  declaration_statements;
BEGIN
  execution_statements;
END [trigger_name];
/
```

The BEFORE and AFTER clauses determine whether the trigger fires *before* or *after* the change is written to your local copy of the data. The FOR EACH ROW clause specifies that the trigger should fire for each row as opposed to once per statement, while the WHEN clause acts as a filter specifying when the trigger fires. Unlike when working with other stored program units, you must qualify a DECLARE block when you require it in your trigger.

There are two *pseudo*-records when you use the FOR EACH ROW clause in a trigger. They both refer to the columns referenced in the DML statement. The pseudo-records are compound variables represented as NEW and OLD. The variable names are NEW or OLD in the WHEN clause, and as *bind* variables they are :new and :old in the trigger body. *Bind* variables let you pass variables *by value* or *by reference* between PL/SQL blocks in the same database session.

When you use the SQL web interface to define new tables in the Oracle Database 10g Express Edition, you build row-level DML triggers to transparently *insert* pseudo-numeric *primary keys*. This type of trigger mimics automatic numbering in other products, like Microsoft Access.

Generically built triggers do not have a WHEN clause to filter when the trigger should let you *insert* a manual primary key value. This means you cannot leverage the sequence pseudo-columns

.nextval and .currval and synchronize *primary* and *foreign keys* during multiple table insertion processes. It also compromises your ability to perform BULK inserts into the table. Actually, you can still do the BULK operation, but you won't get the desired performance, because this trigger will fire for each row instead of once for the INSERT statement.

The *row-level* trigger CONNECTION_LOG_T1 demonstrates the proper way to write a pseudo-automatic numbering trigger:

```
-- This is found in create_signon_trigger.sql on the enclosed CD.

CREATE OR REPLACE TRIGGER connection_log_t1
  BEFORE INSERT ON connection_log
  FOR EACH ROW
  WHEN (new.event_id IS NULL)
BEGIN
  SELECT    connection_log_s1.nextval
  INTO      :new.event_id
  FROM      dual;
END;
/
```

The CONNECTION_LOG_T1 trigger fires only when you fail to provide a primary key value during an INSERT statement. This row-level trigger demonstrates two processing rules. One rule is that you can reference a *pseudo*-row column as an *ordinary* variable in the WHEN clause because the actual trigger fires in the same memory scope as the DML transaction. The other rule is that you must reference a *pseudo*-row column as a *bind* variable inside the actual trigger scope, where it is running in a different memory space. The *pseudo*-rows NEW and OLD are *pass-by-reference* structures, and they contain your active DML session variable values when arriving at the trigger body. The *pseudo*-row NEW and OLD variables also receive any changes made in the trigger body when they are returned to your active DML session.

All the OLD pseudo-row columns are null when you execute an INSERT statement, and the NEW pseudo-row columns are null when you run a DELETE statement. Both OLD and NEW pseudo-row columns are present during UPDATE statements, but only for those columns referenced by the SET clause.

This section has covered how to use DML triggers and examined a *row-level* trigger implementation. You should be able to use DML triggers by drawing on what you have learned in this section.

INSTEAD OF Triggers

You can use the INSTEAD OF trigger to intercept INSERT, UPDATE, and DELETE statements and replace those instructions with alternative procedural code. Nonupdatable views generally have INSTEAD OF triggers to accept the output and resolve the issues that make the view nonupdatable.

The prototype for building an INSTEAD OF trigger is

```
CREATE [OR REPLACE] TRIGGER trigger_name
INSTEAD OF {dml_statement | ddl_statement}
ON {object_name | database | schema}
FOR EACH ROW
[WHEN (logical_expression)]
```

```
[DECLARE]
  declaration_statements;
BEGIN
  execution_statements;
END [trigger_name];
/
```

INSTEAD OF triggers are powerful alternatives that resolve how you use complex and nonupdatable views. When you know how the SELECT statement works, you can write procedural code to update the data not directly accessible through nonupdatable views.

You can also use INSTEAD OF triggers for DDL statements against both database and schema. INSTEAD OF triggers provide alternatives to database administrators when they want to guarantee behaviors of DDL statements; for instance, when they want to ensure all new tables are partitioned.

System or Database Event Triggers

System triggers enable you to audit *server startup* and *shutdown, server errors,* and *user logon* and *logoff* activities. They are convenient for tracking the duration of connections by user and the uptime of the database server.

The prototype for building a database SYSTEM trigger is

```
CREATE [OR REPLACE] TRIGGER trigger_name
{BEFORE | AFTER} database_event ON {database | schema}
[DECLARE]
  declaration_statements;
BEGIN
  execution_statements;
END [trigger_name];
/
```

The example developed in Chapter 13 uses both *logon* and *logoff* triggers to monitor the duration of PHP connections. The DML statements for these triggers are in the USER_CONNECTION package. Both the CONNECTING_TRIGGER and DISCONNECTING_TRIGGER call procedures in the USER_CONNECTION package to insert *logon* and *logoff* information by user.

The CONNECTING_TRIGGER provides an example of a SYSTEM trigger, as shown:

```
-- This is found in create_signon_trigger.sql on the enclosed CD.

CREATE OR REPLACE TRIGGER connecting_trigger
  AFTER LOGON ON DATABASE
BEGIN
  user_connection.connecting(sys.login_user);
END;
/
```

The USER_CONNECTION package is also found in Appendix J for your reference. The CONNECTING procedure uses an INSERT statement to write to the CONNECTION_LOG table. SYSTEM triggers let you track basic usage by capturing *entry* and *exit* points without the overhead of enabling database auditing.

Collections

There are three types of collections in the Oracle Database 10g family of products. They are the VARRAY, NESTED TABLE, and associative array data types.

VARRAY and NESTED TABLE are both SQL and PL/SQL data types. As SQL data types, they can define user-specified column data types. Both the VARRAY and NESTED TABLE data types are structures indexed by sequential integers. Sequentially indexed structures disallow gaps in the index values and are also known as densely populated structures. While VARRAY has a fixed number of elements when defined, NESTED TABLE does not.

The associative array, previously known as a PL/SQL table, is *only* a PL/SQL data type. Associative array data types can only be referenced in a PL/SQL scope. They are typically defined in package specifications when they are to be used externally from an anonymous or named block program. Associative array data types support both numeric and string indexes. Numeric indexes for associative arrays do not need to be sequential and so are nonsequential structures. Nonsequential structures can have gaps in index sequences and are known as sparsely populated structures. Associative arrays are dynamically sized and have no fixed maximum size, like the NESTED TABLE data type.

All three have access to the Oracle Collection API but each uses a different set of methods. The recent changes to OCI8 enable it to support scalar, arrays of scalar, and reference cursor variables to external languages, like PHP. The VARRAY and NESTED TABLE data types require that you use the OCI-Collection class to access them externally from the SQL*Plus environment. OCI8 also has a new function that supports passing a PL/SQL table by reference.

The subsections cover the VARRAY, NESTED TABLE, and associative array data types, as well as the Oracle Collection API. These sections are designed to be read in order but should support an *experienced* developer poking around for targeted explanations.

VARRAY Data Type

The VARRAY data type works like a standard array in most programming languages. When you define a variable as a VARRAY data type, you must specify its maximum size. The VARRAY data type definition lets you specify whether elements are *nullable* and *not null constrained*; the default is *nullable.* By contrast with how the C# and Java programming languages treat arrays, Oracle does not immediately allocate physical space for collection elements at definition of a VARRAY data type. Part of the reason has to do with the fact that you can designate VARRAY elements as *not null constrained.* Most programming languages that allocate space when defining data types work because they store null values as the default array element values.

You use the following prototype to define SQL VARRAY data types:

```
CREATE [OR REPLACE] TYPE type_name AS {VARRAY | VARYING ARRAY}(size)
OF sql_base_data_type [NOT NULL];
```

The SQL *base data type* can be any scalar variable, like a DATE, NUMBER, or VARCHAR2 data type. Defining a SQL VARRAY data type sets its scope of use to the schema. You can extend that scope by granting privileges of use to other schemas in the database. As a rule, you should consider defining VARRAY data type variables as SQL data types to maximize their flexibility and scope.

You can also define VARRAY data types in anonymous and named block programs. You cannot access a VARRAY data type outside of where it is defined in PL/SQL, which determines its scope of use. Scope can be defined by an anonymous block, a named block, or a package.

Only defining the VARRAY data types in the package specification lets you use the data type like a restricted-use SQL data type. They are restricted from being used as column data types, which are reserved to only SQL data types.

The following type definitions of VARRAY data types are used to support the PL/SQL code in Chapter 14:

```
-- This is found in create_world_leaders.sql on the enclosed CD.

CREATE OR REPLACE TYPE president_id_varray
  AS VARRAY(100) OF NUMBER;
/
CREATE OR REPLACE TYPE president_name_varray
  AS VARRAY(100) OF VARCHAR2(60 CHAR);
/
```

Creating data types requires a semicolon to terminate the block, and a forward slash to execute the SQL DDL statement. You access a variable using a VARRAY data type as demonstrated in this example:

```
-- This is found in create_world_leaders.sql on the enclosed CD.

DECLARE
  -- Declare local variables.
  t_start            NUMBER := '1914';
  t_end              NUMBER := '1943';
  t_country          VARCHAR2(3 CHAR) := 'USA';
  president_ids      PRESIDENT_ID_VARRAY;
  president_names    PRESIDENT_NAME_VARRAY;
  tenures            TENURE_VARRAY;
  parties            PARTY_VARRAY;
BEGIN
  -- Call the overloaded procedure.
  world_leaders.get_presidents
  ( t_start, t_end, t_country
  , president_ids, president_names, tenures, parties);


  -- Read the contents of one of the arrays.
  FOR i IN 1..president_names.COUNT LOOP
    dbms_output.put_line('Testing ['||president_names(i)||']');
  END LOOP;
END;
/
```

The president_names variable is a VARRAY data type. Combining the variable name through dot notation with the COUNT method lets you use it as the maximum value in the numeric FOR loop. The COUNT method is part of the Oracle Collection API covered last in this section. Rather than the square brackets more common to other programming languages, Oracle collections use standard parentheses to reference index values.

NESTED TABLE Data Type

The NESTED TABLE data type works like *lists* in many programming languages. Unlike when using VARRAY data types, you do not define in advance how many elements can fit in a NESTED TABLE. NESTED TABLE data types are essentially unlimited size structures.

As with the VARRAY data type, defining NESTED TABLE data types does not implicitly allocate physical space for list elements. You manually allocate space by using the overloaded EXTEND method found in the Oracle Collection API. Alternatively, you can use a BULK COLLECT to populate a variable defined as a NESTED TABLE data type.

You use the following prototype to define SQL NESTED TABLE data types:

```
CREATE [OR REPLACE] TYPE type_name
AS TABLE OF sql_base_data_type [NOT NULL];
```

The SQL *base data type* can be any scalar variable, like the VARRAY covered earlier. The NESTED TABLE data type definition also lets you specify whether elements are *nullable* and *not null constrained*; the default is *nullable*. You can also define variables using NESTED TABLE data types in anonymous and named block PL/SQL programs. They have the same scope restrictions as variables defined as VARRAY data types. As an observation, you should probably define variables as NESTED TABLE data types rather than VARRAY data types because NESTED TABLE data types are easier to work with in SQL and are a better fit against table and view data.

NESTED TABLE SQL data type definitions are used to support the PL/SQL code in Chapter 14:

```
-- This is found in create_world_leaders.sql on the enclosed CD.

CREATE OR REPLACE TYPE president_id_ntable
  AS TABLE OF NUMBER;
/
CREATE OR REPLACE TYPE president_name_ntable
  AS TABLE OF VARCHAR2(60 CHAR);
/
```

As shown in the program, you access a variable using a NESTED TABLE data type as you do any Oracle collection type:

```
-- This is found in create_world_leaders.sql on the enclosed CD.

DECLARE
  -- Declare local variables.
  t_start            NUMBER := '1914';
  t_end              NUMBER := '1943';
  t_country          VARCHAR2(3 CHAR) := 'USA';
  president_ids      PRESIDENT_ID_NTABLE;
  president_names    PRESIDENT_NAME_NTABLE;
  tenures            TENURE_NTABLE;
  parties            PARTY_NTABLE;

BEGIN
  -- Call the overloaded procedure.
  world_leaders.get_presidents
```

```
( t_start, t_end, t_country
, president_ids, president_names, tenures, parties);

-- Read the contents of one of the arrays.
FOR i IN 1..president_names.COUNT LOOP
  dbms_output.put_line('Testing ['||president_names(i)||']');
END LOOP;
END;
/
```

The president_names variable is a NESTED TABLE data type, and like the VARRAY data type, it uses the COUNT method from the Oracle Collection API to find the highest index value. Standard parentheses enclose all Oracle collection indexes.

Associative Array Data Type

The associative array data type works like an associative array in JavaScript or PHP. As of the Oracle Database 10*g* family of products, it supports both numeric and string indexes. Associative arrays dynamically assign without first allocating space; in this they differ from the other two collection types. Associative arrays can also use many of the Oracle Collection API methods.

While you can build associative arrays of compound data types, like RECORD data types, you cannot export those at present through the OCI to external programs. Oracle plans to add that feature at some *future* date.

You cannot define associative arrays as SQL data types. They are exclusively PL/SQL data types. You must define them in a PACKAGE specification to use them externally from a specific anonymous or named block programming unit.

The following examples of defining PL/SQL associative array data types support the PL/SQL code in Chapter 14:

-- **This is found in create_world_leaders.sql on the enclosed CD.**

```
TYPE president_id_table IS TABLE OF NUMBER
  INDEX BY BINARY_INTEGER;
TYPE president_name_table IS TABLE OF VARCHAR2(60 CHAR)
  INDEX BY BINARY_INTEGER;
/
```

Aside from the fact that you can only create an associative array in PL/SQL, the difference between defining a NESTED TABLE and an associative array is small. You must explicitly index an associative array with a PLS_INTEGER, BINARY_INTEGER, or VARCHAR2 data type, while NESTED TABLE data types are numerically indexed.

You access a variable using an associative array data type that is numerically indexed sequentially, as you do for a NESTED TABLE. This is shown in the following anonymous block program that depends on a sequential index:

-- **This is found in create_world_leaders.sql on the enclosed CD.**

```
DECLARE
  -- Declare local variables.
  t_start          NUMBER := '1914';
  t_end            NUMBER := '1943';
```

```
     t_country               VARCHAR2(3 CHAR) := 'USA';
     president_ids           WORLD_LEADERS.PRESIDENT_ID_TABLE;
     president_names         WORLD_LEADERS.PRESIDENT_NAME_TABLE;
     tenures                 WORLD_LEADERS.TENURE_TABLE;
     parties                 WORLD_LEADERS.PARTY_TABLE;

BEGIN
  -- Call the overloaded procedure.
  world_leaders.get_presidents
  ( t_start, t_end, t_country
  , president_ids, president_names, tenures, parties);

  -- Read the contents of one of the arrays.
  FOR i IN 1..president_names.COUNT LOOP
    dbms_output.put_line('Testing ['||president_names(i)||']');
  END LOOP;
END;
/
```

Nonsequential numeric or string indexes require a different approach; they fail in a numeric FOR loop because they are sparsely populated and contain gaps. The following `reading_string_index.sql` script pulls from several components in this appendix. It demonstrates how you can navigate using an ascending string index:

```
-- This is found in reading_string_index.sql on the enclosed CD.

DECLARE
  -- Define control variables.
  current VARCHAR2(60 CHAR);
  element INTEGER;

  -- Define an associative array of numbers.
  TYPE president_table IS TABLE OF NUMBER
    INDEX BY VARCHAR2(60 CHAR);

  -- Declare an associative array variable.
  presidents PRESIDENT_TABLE;

  -- Define a dynamic cursor.
  CURSOR get_presidents
  ( term_start_in NUMBER
  , term_end_in   NUMBER
  , country_in    VARCHAR2) IS
    SELECT   president_id
    ,        last_name||', '
    ||       first_name
    ||       DECODE(middle_name,NULL,NULL,' '||middle_name) president
```

```
      FROM       president
      WHERE      country = country_in
      AND        term_start BETWEEN term_start_in AND term_end_in
      OR         term_end BETWEEN term_start_in AND term_end_in
      ORDER BY 1;
BEGIN
  -- Swap index and name.
  FOR i IN get_presidents(1787,2009,'USA') LOOP
      presidents(i.president) := TO_CHAR(i.president_id);
  END LOOP;

  -- Start with first alphabetically index column.
  FOR i IN 1..presidents.COUNT LOOP
    IF i = 1 THEN
      current := presidents.FIRST;
      element := presidents(current);
    ELSE
      IF presidents.NEXT(current) IS NOT NULL THEN
        current := presidents.NEXT(current);
        element := presidents(current);
      ELSE
        EXIT;
      END IF;
    END IF;

    -- Print current value and index.
    IF element < 10 THEN
      DBMS_OUTPUT.PUT_LINE('Old Index ['||element||']  is ['||current||']');
    ELSE
      DBMS_OUTPUT.PUT_LINE('Old Index ['||element||'] is ['||current||']');
    END IF;
  END LOOP;
END;
/
```

This demonstrates reading two columns from the PRESIDENT_TABLE and putting the value as a string index and the numeric primary key as the value. The second loop reads an associative array by using the Oracle Collection API FIRST method to get the current index value, and the returned current index identifies the current element value. On subsequent loops, the NEXT method and current index traverse the string-indexed array in ascending alphabetical order.

Collection API

Table I-4 contains a list of the Oracle Collection API methods. Several of the methods are overloaded, and the different signatures are covered in their prototypes.

Table I-4 is provided to enlarge understanding of the OCI-Collection methods discussed in Chapter 14. The OCI-Collection methods are mirrors to the Oracle Collection API methods.

Method	Description
COUNT	The COUNT method returns the number of elements with allocated space in VARRAY and NESTED TABLE data types. The COUNT method returns all elements in associative arrays. The return value of the COUNT method can be smaller than the return value of LIMIT for the VARRAY data types. It has the following prototype: `Integer COUNT`

DELETE	The DELETE method lets you delete members from the collection. It has two formal parameters; one is mandatory and the other is optional. Both parameters accept PLS_INTEGER, VARCHAR2, and LONG variable types. Only one actual parameter, *n*, is interpreted as the index value to delete from the collection. When you supply two actual parameters, the function deletes everything from the parameter *n* to *m*, inclusively. It has the following prototypes:
	
	`void DELETE(n)`
	`void DELETE(n,m)`

EXISTS	The EXISTS method checks to find an element with the supplied index in a collection. It returns true when the element is found and false otherwise. The element may contain a value or a null value. It has one mandatory parameter, which can be a PLS_INTEGER, VARCHAR2, or LONG type. It has the following prototype: `Boolean EXISTS(n)`

EXTEND	The EXTEND method allocates space for one or more new elements in a VARRAY or NESTED TABLE collection. It has two optional parameters. It adds space for one element by default without any actual parameter. A single optional parameter designates how many physical spaces should be allocated, but it is constrained by the LIMIT value for VARRAY data types. When two optional parameters are provided, the first designates how many elements should be allocated space and the second designates the index it should use to copy the value to the newly allocated space. It has the following prototypes:
	
	`void EXTEND`
	`void EXTEND(n)`
	`void EXTEND(n,i)`

FIRST	The FIRST method returns the lowest subscript value in a collection. It can return a PLS_INTEGER, VARCHAR2, or LONG type. It has the following prototype: `mixed FIRST`
LAST	The LAST method returns the highest subscript value in a collection. It can return a PLS_INTEGER, VARCHAR2, or LONG type. It has the following prototype: `mixed LAST`
LIMIT	The LIMIT method returns the highest possible subscript value in a collection. It can only return a PLS_INTEGER type and *can only be used by a VARRAY data type*. It has the following prototype: `mixed LIMIT`
NEXT(n)	The NEXT method returns the next higher subscript value in a collection when successful or a false. The return value is a PLS_INTEGER, VARCHAR2, or LONG type. It requires a valid index value as a parameter. It has the following prototype: `mixed NEXT(n)`
PRIOR(n)	The PRIOR method returns the next lower subscript value in a collection when successful or a false. The return value is a PLS_INTEGER, VARCHAR2, or LONG type. It requires a valid index value as a parameter. It has the following prototype: `mixed PRIOR(n)`

TRIM	The TRIM method removes a subscripted value from a collection. It has one optional parameter. Without an actual parameter, it removes the highest element from the array. An actual parameter is interpreted as the number of elements removed from the end of the collection. It has the following prototypes:
	
	`void TRIM`
	`void TRIM(n)`

TABLE I-4. *Oracle Collection API Method List*

You have now reviewed all three Oracle collection types. Only VARRAY and NESTED TABLE require using the OCI-Collection class when called through externally defined languages. This section has demonstrated how to navigate numeric and string-indexed collections, and reviewed the Oracle Collection API.

Using the DBMS_LOB Package

Oracle provides many built-in packages. These are often wrapped procedures. You can't see the implementation details of wrapped packages. An example of a wrapped package is the DBMS_OUTPUT package, which has been used to redirect standard out from the PL/SQL environment to the SQL*Plus console. There are many more built-in packages that you can find in the *PL/SQL Packages and Types Reference 10*g *Release 2.*

This section reviews the basics of the DBMS_LOB package and supports how you use the DBMS_LOB package in conjunction with Oracle LOB data types covered in Chapter 15. CLOB and BFILE columns are added to the PRESIDENT table to support the OCI-Lob object discussion in Chapter 15.

This section is divided into three subsections:

- "Verifying or Configuring the LOB Environment"
- "Writing and Reading a CLOB Data Type"
- "Positioning and Reading a BFILE Data Type"

The mechanism for working with read and write LOB data types differs from the process for reading BFILE data type values. While the BLOB, CLOB, and NCLOB types store a only descriptor value *in-line* for each row, the CFILE and BFILE data types store a locator value *in-line*. These are more or less the same thing because they point to the location of the data, but descriptors describe an internal database location and locators point to an external location in the file system. The DBMS_LOB package lets you access both types of LOB columns by using descriptor and locator references.

You should consider reviewing "Positioning and Reading a BFILE Data Type" to gain background knowledge about BFILE data types before reading "Writing and Reading a CLOB Data Type," but again it is left to your discretion to decide what works best for you. Also, if your environment is set up completely, you can skip directly to either "Writing and Reading a CLOB Data Type" or "Positioning and Reading a BFILE Data Type" section.

Verifying or Configuring the LOB Environment

You can describe the PRESIDENT table in SQL*Plus to check whether you have the right base object, by using

```
SQL> DESC[RIBE] president
```

This should return the following PRESIDENT table definition:

```
Name                                 Null?    Type
----------------------------------- -------- ----------------
PRESIDENT_ID                        NOT NULL NUMBER
LAST_NAME                                    VARCHAR2(20 CHAR)
FIRST_NAME                                   VARCHAR2(20 CHAR)
```

MIDDLE_NAME	VARCHAR2(20 CHAR)
TERM_START	NUMBER
TERM_END	NUMBER
COUNTRY	VARCHAR2(3 CHAR)
PARTY	VARCHAR2(24 CHAR)
BIOGRAPHY	CLOB
PHOTOGRAPH	BINARY FILE LOB

Provided you find a PRESIDENT table, you should also find the BIOGRAPHY column as a CLOB data type, and the PHOTOGRAPH column as a BINARY FILE LOB data type, which is a BFILE data type. If you don't have the PRESIDENT table, you run the create_world_leaders.sql script to create the table. You modify the table to add CLOB and BFILE columns by running the alter_world_leaders.sql script found in Chapter 15.

BLOB, CLOB and NCLOB data types are stored internally in the database and require no other validation here than checking for the correct column data type in the table. However, the section "Writing and Reading a CLOB Data Type" requires the ADD_BIOGRAPHY procedure from Chapter 15. You need to compile it into your schema if you haven't done so already.

The ADD_BIOGRAPHY stored procedure is in the alter_world_leaders.sql script, and the implementation details are in the section "Writing and Reading a CLOB Data Type" later in this appendix. You can check if it is in your environment by describing it:

```
SQL> DESCRIBE add_biography
```

This should return the following ADD_BIOGRAPHY procedure definition:

```
PROCEDURE add_biography
```

Argument Name	Type	In/Out	Default?
PRESIDENT_ID_IN	NUMBER	IN	
BIOGRAPHY	BIOGRAPHY_TABLE	IN	

CFILE and BFILE are externally stored on the file system and require that you identify their physical directory location by building an internal *directory* reference. You do this by connecting as a privileged user, like SYSTEM, and creating a DIRECTORY by running the create_bfile_directory.sql script or this statement:

```
CREATE DIRECTORY my_directory AS
'C:\Program Files\Apache Group\Apache2\htdocs\photo';
```

> **NOTE**
> *Linux users will need to edit the create_bfile_directory.sql
> script to replace their directory.*

After running the script, you need to create the MY_DIRECTORY reference. By design, other scripts depend on the DIRECTORY reference pointing to a physical photo subdirectory in the directory pointed to by the Apache DocumentRoot directive value.

You can verify if the DIRECTORY has been created in the database by running the following SELECT statement as the SYSTEM user, as is also covered in Chapter 15:

```
-- This is found in create_bfile_directory.sql on the enclosed CD.

SELECT    owner
,         directory_name
,         directory_path
FROM      dba_directories
WHERE     directory_name = 'MY_DIRECTORY';
```

If the query fails to find the directory, rerun the create_bfile_directory.sql script before proceeding. The output from the script should report the values shown next on the respective platforms, assuming a default Apache 2.0.x installation.

Linux:

```
OWNER   DIRECTORY_NAME DIRECTORY_PATH
------  -------------- -----------------------------------------------------------
SYS     MY_DIRECTORY   /var/www/html/photo
```

Windows:

```
OWNER   DIRECTORY_NAME DIRECTORY_PATH
------  -------------- -----------------------------------------------------------
SYS     MY_DIRECTORY   C:\program files\apache group\apache2\htdocs\photo
```

As shown, the DIRECTORY owner is the privileged SYS user. You use a DDL GRANT statement to grant READ privilege to your PHP schema. This lets the PHP user read from the directory. The following command grants the READ privilege to the PHP user/schema:

```
GRANT READ ON my_directory TO php;
```

The last configuration step requires that you copy the WashingtonGeorge.gif image file from the enclosed CD to the MY_DIRECTORY physical location. After completing these steps, you should have a valid environment for running the remaining examples found in this appendix.

Writing and Reading a CLOB Data Type

This section examines how you write data because you'll need the data in the table to read it. After writing the data to the table, you will examine how to read CLOB column values.

Both writing and reading CLOB data types are a bit tedious when their size actually exceeds 4,000 characters, because you can't simply map the data to a VARCHAR2 variable. Likewise, you can't insert values directly when they exceed the length of a VARCHAR2 data type. In both cases, you need to use specialized procedures from the DBMS_LOB package. Three DBMS_LOB procedures support writing to a LOB data type: the APPEND(), WRITE(), and WRITEAPPEND() procedures.

Writing a CLOB Data Type

You typically define LOB columns as *nullable* columns in tables because you often update them with values after inserting the other scalar data type columns. Alternatively, you can insert an empty_clob() function when you have a *null disallowed* column.

NOTE
An empty_clob() is not a null value; it is an initialized empty CLOB data type containing an empty object or a populated object. This is an example of something that is not necessarily true when it is found not null by a Boolean expression. It demonstrates that truth can require a compound Boolean expression to check whether a CLOB is both not null and not empty to be true.

LOB data types require a transaction context to write data to the database. You create a transaction context by using a SELECT statement that includes the FOR UPDATE clause, or by using a SELECT, INSERT, or UPDATE statement with the RETURNING *column_variable* INTO *program_variable* clause.

The ADD_BIOGRAPHY procedure lets you update a LOB column by encapsulating the logic of the transaction context and then calls to the DBMS_LOB package. It uses two mandatory formal parameters: one is a unique primary key value, and the other is a SQL collection. Collections let you write and read chunks of BLOB, CLOB, and NCLOB variables. The ADD_BIOGRAPHY procedure reads the elements of a collection and writes them into a CLOB column value, as follows:

```
-- This is found in alter_world_leaders.sql on the enclosed CD.

CREATE OR REPLACE PROCEDURE add_biography
( president_id_in IN      NUMBER
, biography       IN      BIOGRAPHY_TABLE ) IS
  -- Define a local CLOB variable.
  descriptor  CLOB;
BEGIN
  -- Update row with empty CLOB, and return value into local variable.
  SELECT    biography INTO descriptor
  FROM      president
  WHERE     president_id = president_id_in FOR UPDATE;

  -- Open the CLOB variable for bidirectional I/O.
  dbms_lob.open(descriptor,dbms_lob.lob_readwrite);

  -- Append the nested table elements to CLOB.
  FOR i IN 1..biography.COUNT LOOP
    dbms_lob.writeappend(descriptor,LENGTH(biography(i)),biography(i));
  END LOOP;

  -- Close the CLOB.
  dbms_lob.close(descriptor);

  -- Commit the change.
  COMMIT;

END add_biography;
/
```

The ADD_BIOGRAPHY procedure uses a SELECT statement with a FOR UPDATE clause to start a transaction and a COMMIT to end it. The SELECT statement also captures the LOB descriptor, which is then used by the DBMS_LOB procedures to: (a) open the CLOB column for reading and writing, (b) append a VARCHAR2 value to the end of the CLOB column value, and (c) close the CLOB column. The appended values are elements in a collection because the WRITEAPPEND procedure supports only RAW and VARCHAR2 streams. All three phases must occur within the context of a single transaction.

The following anonymous block program demonstrates populating a SQL collection and sending the collection variable as an actual parameter to the procedure:

```
-- This is found in alter_world_leaders.sql on the enclosed CD.

DECLARE
  -- Define a local nested table collection.
  TYPE presidential_biography IS TABLE OF VARCHAR2(600);

  -- Define and initialize a NESTED TABLE.
  biography_in       BIOGRAPHY_TABLE := biography_table();
  biography_out      CLOB;
BEGIN
  -- Enable space.
  biography_in.EXTEND(10);

  -- Add biography.
  biography_in(1)   := 'On April 30, 1789, George Washington, ...<p />';
  biography_in(2)   := 'Born in 1732 into a Virginia planter ...<p />';
  biography_in(3)   := 'He pursued two intertwined interests: ...<p />';
  biography_in(4)   := 'From 1759 to the outbreak of the American ...<p />';
  biography_in(5)   := 'When the Second Continental Congress ...<p />';
  biography_in(6)   := 'He realized early that the best strategy ...<p />';
  biography_in(7)   := 'Washington longed to retire to his ...<p />';
  biography_in(8)   := 'He did not infringe upon the policy making ...<p />';
  biography_in(9)   := 'To his disappointment, two parties were ...<p />';
  biography_in(10)  := 'Washington enjoyed less than three years ...<p />';

  -- Add biography for one president.
  add_biography(1,biography_in);
END;
/
```

The anonymous block program reinforces the "Collection" section discussion from earlier in the appendix. By contrast with the previous examples, this program creates a NESTED TABLE data type manually, which requires an explicit constructor call to the user-defined type. It also requires allocation of ten rows of space using the EXTEND method from the Oracle Collection API. It makes assignments of truncated strings to mimic what it would do with strings 4,000 characters long. Then, it calls the ADD_BIOGRAPHY procedure.

This script populates the BIOGRAPHY column for the row identified by a PRESIDENT_ID primary key of 1, which should map to George Washington in the PRESIDENT table. It provides you with something to test in the next section. However, you already have test data, if you're reviewing this after working through the examples in Chapter 15.

This section has demonstrated how to write data from a SQL collection to a LOB column. It has also covered the basic steps involved in a single transaction context for each LOB write operation. The next section demonstrates how to read LOB data types.

Reading a CLOB Data Type

This section demonstrates how you read and access LOB columns, and discusses the three possible data states of LOB variables. Unlike scalar variables that have one of two states, null and not null respectively, LOB variables can be null, empty, and populated. Empty and populated column values both contain a descriptor and are also not-null values. This is a classic example of when a not-null test acts like a not-false test where the result isn't necessarily true because it can be something else, as discussed in the box "The Open Universe of NULL Variables" earlier in this appendix.

When you insert a row into a table using *named value* syntax and opt to not provide a value for a nullable LOB column, the LOB column contains a null value. The same behavior occurs when you use the ALTER statement to add a LOB column to a table after rows already exist; all existing rows will contain a null LOB column value.

The following query uses a *substitution* variable for the primary key and checks the status of a BIOGRAPHY column in the PRESIDENT table:

```
SELECT    DECODE(NVL(dbms_lob.getlength(biography),-1)
          , -1,'Null'             -- Null when a negative one.
          , 0,'Empty'            -- Zero when an empty LOB.
          ,'Populated') status   -- Anything else contains data.
FROM      president
WHERE     president_id = &primary_key;
```

Whether or not you've done Chapter 15 first, the forty-first and forty-second presidents should have empty CLOB column values. Run the preceding query, and provide a value of 41 when prompted for the primary_key. You will see the following output, which says the column contains a null value:

```
STATUS
---------
Null
```

You can update a row with an EMPTY_CLOB() value to change its null state. Run the following query, and provide a value of 42 when prompted for the primary_key:

```
UPDATE    president
SET       biography = EMPTY_CLOB()
WHERE     president_id = &primary_key;
```

After running the UPDATE statement, type a COMMIT statement to make the change permanent. Then, you should run the SELECT statement run earlier but use 42 when prompted for the value of a primary_key, and you will see the following output:

```
STATUS
---------
Empty
```

The last step in testing this concept is to query the row updated in the "Writing a CLOB Data Type" section by providing a 1 for the `primary_key` value. You will see the following output:

```
STATUS
---------
Populated
```

This demonstration has shown the three states of CLOB columns. You need to anticipate that you have more than a null or not-null value when dealing with CLOB data types. You should avoid if-then-else statements simply checking for a null or not-null value because they can process empty CLOB values by mistake.

NOTE
The clob_query.sql script contains a conditional statement that excludes null and empty CLOB values.

The actual length of the BIOGRAPHY column for row 1 is 472 characters, which you can read using a normal SQL SELECT statement. This works because the SQL*Plus environment actually attempts to implicitly cast CLOB data types to VARCHAR2 data types when the return value is smaller than 4,000 characters. When the actual value is *longer* than 4,000 characters, you use a collection data type in an anonymous block PL/SQL program with the DBMS_LOB package procedures to read CLOB column values.

The clob_query.sql program demonstrates this and illustrates a few tricks and techniques for managing and parsing a CLOB variable in PL/SQL:

```sql
-- This is found in clob_query.sql on the enclosed CD.

DECLARE

  -- Define a local associative array collection.
  TYPE presidential_biography IS TABLE OF VARCHAR2(600)
    INDEX BY BINARY_INTEGER;

  -- Control Variables
  chunk           NUMBER := 80;
  clob_size       NUMBER;
  counter         NUMBER := 1;
  position        NUMBER := 1;

  -- Define a CLOB and maximum-sized variable string.
  descriptor      CLOB;
  biography_line  VARCHAR2(4000);

BEGIN
  -- A FOR UPDATE makes this a DML transaction.
  SELECT    biography
  INTO      descriptor
  FROM      president
  WHERE     president_id = &primary_key FOR UPDATE;
```

```
-- Check that descriptor is not null and not empty.
IF (descriptor IS NOT NULL) AND (dbms_lob.getlength(descriptor) > 0) THEN
  -- Set the CLOB size.
  clob_size := dbms_lob.getlength(descriptor);

  -- Only enter when current position is less than size.
  WHILE (position < clob_size) LOOP

    -- Get the position of the next HTML tag.
    chunk := dbms_lob.instr(descriptor,'<p />',position,1) - position + 5;

    -- Read the chunk including the HTML tag.
    dbms_lob.read(descriptor,chunk,position,biography_line);

    -- Format lines per return value.
    IF counter < 10 THEN
      dbms_output.put_line('[ '||counter||'] ['||biography_line||']');
    ELSE
      dbms_output.put_line('['||counter||'] ['||biography_line||']');
    END IF;

    -- Set next position and increment counter.
    position := position + chunk;
    counter := counter + 1;

  END LOOP;
 END IF;
END;
/
```

The clob_query.sql program uses a combination of a conditional expression to avoid reading an empty CLOB variable and a while loop to gate entrance to an out-of-range position variable. It also uses the DBMS_LOB.INSTR() function to calculate where to end the next chunk of data, by finding the XHTML paragraph tag. Then, it reads a line from the BIOGRAPHY column using the descriptor, a chunk size, and a starting position in the CLOB variable.

Run the clob_query.sql and provide 1 when prompted as the primary_key value. You will get the following output in the same organization as what was previously inserted by the anonymous block program in the section "Writing a CLOB Data Type":

```
[ 1] [On April 30, 1789, George Washington, ...<p />]
[ 2] [Born in 1732 into a Virginia planter ...<p />]
[ 3] [He pursued two intertwined interests: ...<p />]
[ 4] [From 1759 to the outbreak of the American ...<p />]
[ 5] [When the Second Continental Congress ...<p />]
[ 6] [He realized early that the best strategy ...<p />]
[ 7] [Washington longed to retire to his ...<p />]
[ 8] [He did not infringe upon the policy making ...<p />]
[ 9] [To his disappointment, two parties were ...<p />]
[10] [Washington enjoyed less than three years ...<p />]
```

This section has demonstrated how to read data from a SQL LOB column to a collection. It also covered the null, empty, and populated types of CLOB values.

Positioning and Reading a BFILE Data Type

This section examines how you work with BFILE columns. Unlike the CLOB type covered in the preceding section, the BFILE is a read-only LOB. As covered in the section "Verifying or Configuring the LOB Environment," a BFILE column only contains a *locator* that points to an externally stored file.

You also create a DIRECTORY object in the database, which serves as a virtual mapping to a physical directory. DIRECTORY objects are owned by the privileged SYS user/schema, and you must grant READ privilege to schemas that have BFILE columns. You can only grant that privilege as the SYS or SYSTEM user in a default Oracle environment.

A BFILE column can have either a null or not-null value. You insert a filename into a BFILE column by using the BFILENAME() function. The following UPDATE statement inserts a filename for the image of President George Washington:

```
-- This is found in alter_world_leaders.sql on the enclosed CD.

UPDATE president
SET photograph = BFILENAME('MY_DIRECTORY','Washington.gif')
WHERE president_id = 1;
```

The BFILENAME() function requires a virtual directory as its first parameter, and the virtual directory must be defined in the database as a DIRECTORY reference. The second required parameter is a physical filename. A DIRECTORY reference becomes invalid when it no longer resolves correctly to the file system. Unlike with some database objects, no report is made when virtual mapping becomes invalid. This behavior mirrors what happens when privilege grants are revoked.

TIP
You can implement DDL triggers on CREATE and DROP DIRECTORY to manage DIRECTORY objects, which support BFILE columns.

After you have updated the BFILE column with a valid DIRECTORY and filename, you need to place the file in the target location. There is no way to view the image file in SQL*Plus. Chapter 15 demonstrates how to retrieve and display the actual image in PHP.

NOTE
You do not have to place the file in the target location before inserting the physical location with the BFILENAME() function, but when you attempt to run a DBMS_LOB procedure against the file, it will fail at run time if it is missing.

BFILE data types do not impose transaction context limits like BLOB, CLOB, and NCLOB data types. This makes querying them easier because you can place the logic directly into a function that can be easily queried by SQL. The FIND_BFILENAME() function finds the file name in a BFILE locator, as follows:

```
-- This is found in find_bfilename.sql on the enclosed CD.

CREATE OR REPLACE FUNCTION find_bfilename
( president_id_in IN    NUMBER )
RETURN VARCHAR2 IS
  -- Define a locator.
  locator           BFILE;

  -- Define alias and file name.
  alias             VARCHAR2(255);
  file_name         VARCHAR2(255);

  -- Define a local exception for size violation.
  directory_num EXCEPTION;
  PRAGMA EXCEPTION_INIT(directory_num,-22285);
BEGIN
  -- A FOR UPDATE makes this a DML transaction.
  FOR i IN (SELECT photograph FROM president
            WHERE  president_id = president_id_in) LOOP
    locator := i.photograph;
  END LOOP;

  -- Check for available locator.
  IF locator IS NOT NULL THEN
    dbms_lob.filegetname(locator,alias,file_name);
  END IF;

  -- Return file name.
  RETURN file_name;

EXCEPTION
  WHEN directory_num THEN
  RETURN NULL;
END find_bfilename;
/
```

You query the result for George Washington by using the *primary key* value of 1, as follows:

```
SELECT bfilename(1) FROM dual;
```

This produces the following output:

```
FIND_BFILENAME(1)
-----------------
Washington.gif
```

Much as you created the FIND_BFILENAME function, you can also define a function to return the size of a physical image or external file. All you need to do is change the return type from a VARCHAR2 to a NUMBER and call the DBMS_LOB.GETLENGTH() function instead of the DBMS_LOB.FILEGETNAME() function.

You have now seen how to enter and retrieve a BFILE column value and size. The BFILE data type enables you to centralize image files for your web pages. The risk of implementing this type of solution is that you must synchronize files to BFILE columns with physical files and make sure links resolved through DIRECTORY references don't become obsolete.

This section has introduced the concept of *built-in packages* and demonstrated the basics of how you use the DBMS_LOB package. It has focused on writing and reading CLOB and BFILE data types, as well as on laying a foundation to support the OCI8 discussion in Chapter 15. For more extensive coverage of LOB data types, you are referred to LOB chapter in the *PL/SQL Packages and Types Reference 10g Release 2.*

Summary

The appendix has reviewed the *Procedural Language/Structured Query Language (PL/SQL)* and explained how and why basic PL/SQL statements and structures work. The coverage should enable you to work through the Oracle Database 10g XE examples in the book.

APPENDIX
J

Database Setup Scripts

his appendix contains the database environment scripts from the enclosed CD. They are too long to print conveniently in Chapters 13, 14, and 15 but do provide written patterns that may be useful to readers. This appendix assumes you will answer basic questions about the Oracle database languages in the SQL and PL/SQL primers, respectively Appendixes H and I.

Database environment scripts are presented in this sequence:

- Create system login and logout structures—`create_signon_trigger.sql`
- Create media store structures—`create_store.sql`
- Seed media store data—`seed_store.sql`
- Create and seed PL/SQL example—`create_world_leaders.sql`

These scripts introduce many concepts of SQL and PL/SQL programming in an Oracle environment. You should take note of these implementations because they're designed to provide a basis of code for your Oracle environment. You may consider augmenting these descriptions with *Oracle SQL by Example* by Alice Rischert (Prentice Hall, 2004) or *Oracle Database 10g PL/SQL Programming* by Scott Urman, Ron Hardman, and Michael McLaughlin (McGraw-Hill/Osborne, 2004).

Create System Login and Logout Structures

The `create_signon_trigger.sql` must run in the SYSTEM account to build triggers with access to all user logins and logouts. This script is rerunnable by searching and deleting preexisting objects in the database. It then builds a connection_log table and row-level trigger to automatically populate the surrogate primary key, the package with a procedure for connecting and disconnecting, and two system-level triggers to capture login and logout events.

The `create_signon_trigger.sql` program follows:

-- This is found in create_signon_trigger.sql on the enclosed CD.

```
DECLARE

  -- Define an exception.
  wrong_schema EXCEPTION;
  PRAGMA EXCEPTION_INIT(wrong_schema,-20001);

  -- Define a return variable.
  retval VARCHAR2(1 CHAR);

  /*
  || Define a cursor to identify whether the current user is either the
  || SYSTEM user or a user with the DBA role privilege.
  */
  CURSOR privs IS
    SELECT   DISTINCT null
    FROM     user_role_privs
```

```
    WHERE     username = 'SYSTEM'
    OR        granted_role = 'DBA';

BEGIN

  -- Open cursor and conditionally drop table in correct schema.
  OPEN privs;
  LOOP
    FETCH privs INTO retval;
    IF privs%NOTFOUND THEN
      RAISE wrong_schema;
    ELSE
      FOR i IN (SELECT null
                FROM   user_tables
                WHERE  table_name = 'CONNECTION_LOG') LOOP
        EXECUTE IMMEDIATE 'DROP TABLE connection_log CASCADE CONSTRAINTS';
      END LOOP;
      FOR i IN (SELECT null
                FROM   user_sequences
                WHERE  sequence_name = 'CONNECTION_LOG_S1') LOOP

        EXECUTE IMMEDIATE 'DROP SEQUENCE connection_log_s1';

      END LOOP;
    END IF;
    EXIT;
  END LOOP;
  CLOSE privs;

EXCEPTION

  -- Handle a defined exception.
  WHEN wrong_schema THEN
    DBMS_OUTPUT.PUT_LINE('The script requires the SYSTEM user and '
      ||                 'you are using the <'||user||'> schema or '
      ||                 'the script requires a user with DBA role '
      ||                 'privileges.');

  -- Handle a generic exception.
  WHEN others THEN
    DBMS_OUTPUT.PUT_LINE(SQLERRM);
    RETURN;

END;
/
```

```
-- Create connection audit log table.
CREATE TABLE connection_log
( event_id            NUMBER(10)
, event_user_name     VARCHAR2(30) CONSTRAINT log_event_nn1 NOT NULL
, event_type          VARCHAR2(14) CONSTRAINT log_event_nn2 NOT NULL
, event_date          DATE         CONSTRAINT log_event_nn3 NOT NULL
, CONSTRAINT connection_log_p1    PRIMARY KEY (event_id));

CREATE SEQUENCE connection_log_s1;

-- Create a trigger to automate the primary (surrogate) key generation.
CREATE OR REPLACE TRIGGER connection_log_t1
  BEFORE INSERT ON connection_log
  FOR EACH ROW
  WHEN (new.event_id IS NULL)
BEGIN
  SELECT    connection_log_s1.nextval
  INTO      :new.event_id
  FROM      dual;
END;

/


-- Grant access rights to PHP user.
GRANT SELECT ON connection_log TO PHP;

-- Define a package with connecting and disconnecting procedures.
CREATE OR REPLACE PACKAGE user_connection AS
  PROCEDURE Connecting
  (user_name        IN VARCHAR2);
  PROCEDURE Disconnecting
  (user_name        IN VARCHAR2);
  END user_connection;
/

-- Define a package body with procedure implementation details.
CREATE OR REPLACE PACKAGE BODY user_connection AS

  PROCEDURE connecting
  (user_name        IN VARCHAR2) IS
  BEGIN
    INSERT INTO connection_log
    (event_user_name, event_type, event_date)
    VALUES
    (user_name,'CONNECT',SYSDATE);
  END connecting;
```

```
  PROCEDURE disconnecting
  (user_name        IN VARCHAR2) IS
  BEGIN
    INSERT INTO connection_log
    (event_user_name, event_type, event_date)
    VALUES
    (user_name,'DISCONNECT',SYSDATE);
  END disconnecting;

END user_connection;
/

-- Define system login trigger.
CREATE OR REPLACE TRIGGER connecting_trigger
  AFTER LOGON ON DATABASE
BEGIN
  user_connection.connecting(sys.login_user);
END;
/

-- Define system logout trigger.
CREATE OR REPLACE TRIGGER disconnecting_trigger
  BEFORE LOGOFF ON DATABASE
BEGIN
  user_connection.disconnecting(sys.login_user);
END;
/
```

Create Media Store Structures

The create_store.sql script builds a set of tables and views to run a video store. It also creates SYSTEM_USER and COMMON_LOOKUP tables to introduce some application design components to the model. The script seeds data in the infrastructure tables. These seeded values enable the seed_store.sql script to use subqueries in the insert statements to capture foreign key values from the table that holds the lists of primary keys.

Building the environment enables you to query and transact against multiple tables in Chapter 13 example programs; enables you to examine transaction patterns; and illustrates the purpose of persistent connections. This model also highlights the benefits of building stored procedures on the server to reduce the complexity of transaction management in your web application pages.

The create_store.sql program is rerunnable, but don't forget that when you rerun it, you must then seed the transactional data by running the seed_store.sql program. Also, the create_store.sql program uses out-of-line constraints exclusively in building the tables, as follows:

-- **This is found in create_store.sql on the enclosed CD.**

```
-- Conditionally drop objects.
BEGIN
  FOR i IN (SELECT null
            FROM   user_tables
```

```
                      WHERE  table_name = 'SYSTEM_USER') LOOP
        EXECUTE IMMEDIATE 'DROP TABLE system_user CASCADE CONSTRAINTS';
      END LOOP;
      FOR i IN (SELECT null
                 FROM   user_sequences
                 WHERE  sequence_name = 'SYSTEM_USER_S1') LOOP
        EXECUTE IMMEDIATE 'DROP SEQUENCE system_user_s1';
      END LOOP;
    END;
    /


    -- ----------------------------------------------------------------
    -- Create SYSTEM_USER table and sequence and seed data.
    -- ----------------------------------------------------------------

    CREATE TABLE system_user
    ( system_user_id           NUMBER
    , system_user_name         VARCHAR2(20)
    , system_user_group_id     NUMBER
    , system_user_type         NUMBER
    , last_name                VARCHAR2(20)
    , first_name               VARCHAR2(20)
    , middle_initial           VARCHAR2(1)
    , created_by               NUMBER
    , creation_date            DATE
    , last_updated_by          NUMBER
    , last_update_date         DATE
    , CONSTRAINT pk_system_user_1 PRIMARY KEY(system_user_id)
    , CONSTRAINT nn_system_user_1 CHECK(system_user_name IS NOT NULL)
    , CONSTRAINT nn_system_user_2 CHECK(system_user_group_id IS NOT NULL)
    , CONSTRAINT nn_system_user_3 CHECK(system_user_type IS NOT NULL)
    , CONSTRAINT nn_system_user_4 CHECK(created_by IS NOT NULL)
    , CONSTRAINT nn_system_user_5 CHECK(creation_date IS NOT NULL)
    , CONSTRAINT nn_system_user_6 CHECK(last_updated_by IS NOT NULL)
    , CONSTRAINT nn_system_user_7 CHECK(last_update_date IS NOT NULL));

    CREATE SEQUENCE system_user_s1 START WITH 1001;

    INSERT INTO system_user
    ( system_user_id
    , system_user_name
    , system_user_group_id
    , system_user_type
    , created_by
    , creation_date
    , last_updated_by
    , last_update_date)
    VALUES ( 1,'SYSADMIN', 1, 1, 1, SYSDATE, 1, SYSDATE);

    ALTER TABLE system_user ADD CONSTRAINT fk_system_user_1
```

```
FOREIGN KEY(created_by) REFERENCES system_user(system_user_id);

ALTER TABLE system_user ADD CONSTRAINT fk_system_user_2
FOREIGN KEY(last_updated_by) REFERENCES system_user(system_user_id);

-- Conditionally drop objects.
BEGIN
  FOR i IN (SELECT null
            FROM   user_tables
            WHERE  table_name = 'COMMON_LOOKUP') LOOP
    EXECUTE IMMEDIATE 'DROP TABLE common_lookup CASCADE CONSTRAINTS';
  END LOOP;
  FOR i IN (SELECT null
            FROM   user_sequences
            WHERE  sequence_name = 'COMMON_LOOKUP_S1') LOOP
    EXECUTE IMMEDIATE 'DROP SEQUENCE common_lookup_s1';
  END LOOP;
END;
/


-- ------------------------------------------------------------------
-- Create COMMON_LOOKUP table and sequence and seed data.
-- ------------------------------------------------------------------

CREATE TABLE common_lookup
( common_lookup_id            NUMBER
, common_lookup_context       VARCHAR2(30)
, common_lookup_type          VARCHAR2(30)
, common_lookup_meaning       VARCHAR2(30)
, created_by                  NUMBER
, creation_date               DATE
, last_updated_by             NUMBER
, last_update_date            DATE
, CONSTRAINT pk_c_lookup_1     PRIMARY KEY(common_lookup_id)
, CONSTRAINT nn_c_lookup_1     CHECK(common_lookup_context IS NOT NULL)
, CONSTRAINT nn_c_lookup_2     CHECK(common_lookup_type IS NOT NULL)
, CONSTRAINT nn_c_lookup_3     CHECK(common_lookup_meaning IS NOT NULL)
, CONSTRAINT nn_c_lookup_4     CHECK(created_by IS NOT NULL)
, CONSTRAINT nn_c_lookup_5     CHECK(creation_date IS NOT NULL)
, CONSTRAINT nn_c_lookup_6     CHECK(last_updated_by IS NOT NULL)
, CONSTRAINT nn_c_lookup_7     CHECK(last_update_date IS NOT NULL)
, CONSTRAINT fk_c_lookup_1     FOREIGN KEY(created_by)
  REFERENCES system_user      (system_user_id)
, CONSTRAINT fk_c_lookup_2     FOREIGN KEY(last_updated_by)
  REFERENCES system_user      (system_user_id));

CREATE INDEX common_lookup_n1
  ON common_lookup(common_lookup_context);
CREATE UNIQUE INDEX common_lookup_u2
  ON common_lookup(common_lookup_context,common_lookup_type);
```

```
CREATE SEQUENCE common_lookup_s1 START WITH 1001;

INSERT INTO common_lookup VALUES
( 1,'SYSTEM_USER','SYSTEM_ADMIN','System Administrator'
, 1, SYSDATE, 1, SYSDATE);

INSERT INTO common_lookup VALUES
( common_lookup_s1.nextval,'SYSTEM_USER','DBA','Database Administrator'
, 1, SYSDATE, 1, SYSDATE);

INSERT INTO common_lookup VALUES
( common_lookup_s1.nextval,'CONTACT','EMPLOYEE','Employee'
, 1, SYSDATE, 1, SYSDATE);

INSERT INTO common_lookup VALUES
( common_lookup_s1.nextval,'CONTACT','CUSTOMER','Customer'
, 1, SYSDATE, 1, SYSDATE);

INSERT INTO common_lookup VALUES
( common_lookup_s1.nextval,'MEMBER','INDIVIDUAL','Individual Membership'
, 1, SYSDATE, 1, SYSDATE);

INSERT INTO common_lookup VALUES
( common_lookup_s1.nextval,'MEMBER','GROUP','Group Membership'
, 1, SYSDATE, 1, SYSDATE);

INSERT INTO common_lookup VALUES
( common_lookup_s1.nextval,'MEMBER','DISCOVER_CARD','Discover Card'
, 1, SYSDATE, 1, SYSDATE);

INSERT INTO common_lookup VALUES
( common_lookup_s1.nextval,'MEMBER','MASTER_CARD','Master Card'
, 1, SYSDATE, 1, SYSDATE);

INSERT INTO common_lookup VALUES
( common_lookup_s1.nextval,'MEMBER','VISA_CARD','VISA Card'
, 1, SYSDATE, 1, SYSDATE);

INSERT INTO common_lookup VALUES
( common_lookup_s1.nextval,'MULTIPLE','HOME','Home'
, 1, SYSDATE, 1, SYSDATE);

INSERT INTO common_lookup VALUES
( common_lookup_s1.nextval,'MULTIPLE','WORK','Work'
, 1, SYSDATE, 1, SYSDATE);

INSERT INTO common_lookup VALUES
( common_lookup_s1.nextval,'ITEM','DVD_FULL_SCREEN','DVD: Full Screen'
, 1, SYSDATE, 1, SYSDATE);
```

```
INSERT INTO common_lookup VALUES
( common_lookup_s1.nextval,'ITEM','DVD_WIDE_SCREEN','DVD: Wide Screen'
, 1, SYSDATE, 1, SYSDATE);

INSERT INTO common_lookup VALUES
( common_lookup_s1.nextval,'ITEM','NINTENDO_GAMECUBE','Nintendo GameCube'
, 1, SYSDATE, 1, SYSDATE);

INSERT INTO common_lookup VALUES
( common_lookup_s1.nextval,'ITEM','PLAYSTATION2','PlayStation2'
, 1, SYSDATE, 1, SYSDATE);

INSERT INTO common_lookup VALUES
( common_lookup_s1.nextval,'ITEM','XBOX','XBOX'
, 1, SYSDATE, 1, SYSDATE);

INSERT INTO common_lookup VALUES
( common_lookup_s1.nextval,'ITEM','VHS_SINGLE_TAPE','VHS: Single Tape'
, 1, SYSDATE, 1, SYSDATE);

INSERT INTO common_lookup VALUES
( common_lookup_s1.nextval,'ITEM','VHS_DOUBLE_TAPE','VHS: Double Tape'
, 1, SYSDATE, 1, SYSDATE);
ALTER TABLE system_user ADD CONSTRAINT fk_system_user_3
 FOREIGN KEY(system_user_type) REFERENCES common_lookup(common_lookup_id);

-- Conditionally drop objects.
BEGIN
  FOR i IN (SELECT null
            FROM   user_tables
            WHERE  table_name = 'MEMBER') LOOP
    EXECUTE IMMEDIATE 'DROP TABLE member CASCADE CONSTRAINTS';
  END LOOP;
  FOR i IN (SELECT null
            FROM   user_sequences
            WHERE  sequence_name = 'MEMBER_S1') LOOP
    EXECUTE IMMEDIATE 'DROP SEQUENCE member_s1';
  END LOOP;
END;
/

-- -------------------------------------------------------------------
-- Create MEMBER table and sequence and seed data.
-- -------------------------------------------------------------------

CREATE TABLE member
( member_id                 NUMBER
, account_number            VARCHAR2(10)
, credit_card_number        VARCHAR2(19)
, credit_card_type          NUMBER
```

```
,  created_by                  NUMBER
,  creation_date               DATE
,  last_updated_by             NUMBER
,  last_update_date            DATE
,  CONSTRAINT pk_member_1      PRIMARY KEY(member_id)
,  CONSTRAINT nn_member_1      CHECK(account_number IS NOT NULL)
,  CONSTRAINT nn_member_2      CHECK(credit_card_number IS NOT NULL)
,  CONSTRAINT nn_member_3      CHECK(credit_card_type IS NOT NULL)
,  CONSTRAINT nn_member_4      CHECK(created_by IS NOT NULL)
,  CONSTRAINT nn_member_5      CHECK(creation_date IS NOT NULL)
,  CONSTRAINT nn_member_6      CHECK(last_updated_by IS NOT NULL)
,  CONSTRAINT nn_member_7      CHECK(last_update_date IS NOT NULL)
,  CONSTRAINT fk_member_1      FOREIGN KEY(credit_card_type)
   REFERENCES common_lookup    (common_lookup_id)
,  CONSTRAINT fk_member_2      FOREIGN KEY(created_by)
   REFERENCES system_user      (system_user_id)
,  CONSTRAINT fk_member_3      FOREIGN KEY(last_updated_by)
   REFERENCES system_user      (system_user_id));

CREATE INDEX member_n1 ON member(credit_card_type);
CREATE SEQUENCE member_s1 START WITH 1001;

-- Conditionally drop objects.
BEGIN
  FOR i IN (SELECT null
            FROM   user_tables
            WHERE  table_name = 'CONTACT') LOOP
    EXECUTE IMMEDIATE 'DROP TABLE contact CASCADE CONSTRAINTS';
  END LOOP;
  FOR i IN (SELECT null
            FROM   user_sequences
            WHERE  sequence_name = 'CONTACT_S1') LOOP
    EXECUTE IMMEDIATE 'DROP SEQUENCE contact_s1';
  END LOOP;
END;
/


-- ----------------------------------------------------------------
-- Create CONTACT table and sequence and seed data.
-- ----------------------------------------------------------------

CREATE TABLE contact
( contact_id                   NUMBER
, member_id                    NUMBER
, contact_type                 NUMBER
, last_name                    VARCHAR2(20)
, first_name                   VARCHAR2(20)
, middle_initial               VARCHAR2(1)
, created_by                   NUMBER
, creation_date                DATE
```

```
, last_updated_by              NUMBER
, last_update_date             DATE
, CONSTRAINT pk_contact_1      PRIMARY KEY(contact_id)
, CONSTRAINT nn_contact_1      CHECK(contact_type IS NOT NULL)
, CONSTRAINT nn_contact_2      CHECK(last_name IS NOT NULL)
, CONSTRAINT nn_contact_3      CHECK(first_name IS NOT NULL)
, CONSTRAINT nn_contact_4      CHECK(created_by IS NOT NULL)
, CONSTRAINT nn_contact_5      CHECK(creation_date IS NOT NULL)
, CONSTRAINT nn_contact_6      CHECK(last_updated_by IS NOT NULL)
, CONSTRAINT nn_contact_7      CHECK(last_update_date IS NOT NULL)
, CONSTRAINT fk_contact_1      FOREIGN KEY(member_id)
  REFERENCES member            (member_id)
, CONSTRAINT fk_contact_2      FOREIGN KEY(contact_type)
  REFERENCES common_lookup     (common_lookup_id)
, CONSTRAINT fk_contact_3      FOREIGN KEY(created_by)
  REFERENCES system_user       (system_user_id)
, CONSTRAINT fk_contact_4      FOREIGN KEY(last_updated_by)
  REFERENCES system_user       (system_user_id));

CREATE INDEX contact_n1 ON contact(member_id);
CREATE INDEX contact_n2 ON contact(contact_type);
CREATE SEQUENCE contact_s1 START WITH 1001;

-- Conditionally drop objects.
BEGIN
  FOR i IN (SELECT null
            FROM   user_tables
            WHERE  table_name = 'ADDRESS') LOOP
    EXECUTE IMMEDIATE 'DROP TABLE address CASCADE CONSTRAINTS';
  END LOOP;
  FOR i IN (SELECT null
            FROM   user_sequences
            WHERE  sequence_name = 'ADDRESS_S1') LOOP
    EXECUTE IMMEDIATE 'DROP SEQUENCE address_s1';
  END LOOP;
END;
/


-- ------------------------------------------------------------------
-- Create ADDRESS table and sequence and seed data.
-- ------------------------------------------------------------------

CREATE TABLE address
( address_id                   NUMBER
, contact_id                   NUMBER
, address_type                 NUMBER
, city                         VARCHAR2(30)
, state_province               VARCHAR2(30)
, postal_code                  VARCHAR2(20)
, created_by                   NUMBER
```

```
,  creation_date            DATE
,  last_updated_by          NUMBER
,  last_update_date         DATE
,  CONSTRAINT pk_address_1  PRIMARY KEY(address_id)
,  CONSTRAINT nn_address_1  CHECK(contact_id IS NOT NULL)
,  CONSTRAINT nn_address_2  CHECK(address_type IS NOT NULL)
,  CONSTRAINT nn_address_3  CHECK(city IS NOT NULL)
,  CONSTRAINT nn_address_4  CHECK(state_province IS NOT NULL)
,  CONSTRAINT nn_address_5  CHECK(postal_code IS NOT NULL)
,  CONSTRAINT nn_address_6  CHECK(created_by IS NOT NULL)
,  CONSTRAINT nn_address_7  CHECK(creation_date IS NOT NULL)
,  CONSTRAINT nn_address_8  CHECK(last_updated_by IS NOT NULL)
,  CONSTRAINT nn_address_9  CHECK(last_update_date IS NOT NULL)
,  CONSTRAINT fk_address_1  FOREIGN KEY(contact_id)
   REFERENCES contact       (contact_id)
,  CONSTRAINT fk_address_2  FOREIGN KEY(address_type)
   REFERENCES common_lookup (common_lookup_id)
,  CONSTRAINT fk_address_3  FOREIGN KEY(created_by)
   REFERENCES system_user   (system_user_id)
,  CONSTRAINT fk_address_4  FOREIGN KEY(last_updated_by)
   REFERENCES system_user   (system_user_id));

CREATE INDEX address_n1 ON address(contact_id);
CREATE INDEX address_n2 ON address(address_type);
CREATE SEQUENCE address_s1 START WITH 1001;

-- Conditionally drop objects.
BEGIN
  FOR i IN (SELECT null
            FROM   user_tables
            WHERE  table_name = 'STREET_ADDRESS') LOOP
    EXECUTE IMMEDIATE 'DROP TABLE street_address CASCADE CONSTRAINTS';
  END LOOP;
  FOR i IN (SELECT null
            FROM   user_sequences
            WHERE  sequence_name = 'STREET_ADDRESS_S1') LOOP
    EXECUTE IMMEDIATE 'DROP SEQUENCE street_address_s1';
  END LOOP;
END;
/


-- ----------------------------------------------------------------
-- Create STREET_ADDRESS table and sequence and seed data.
-- ----------------------------------------------------------------

CREATE TABLE street_address
( street_address_id        NUMBER
, address_id               NUMBER
, street_address           VARCHAR2(30)
, created_by               NUMBER
```

```
, creation_date               DATE
, last_updated_by             NUMBER
, last_update_date            DATE
, CONSTRAINT pk_s_address_1   PRIMARY KEY(street_address_id)
, CONSTRAINT nn_s_address_1   CHECK(address_id IS NOT NULL)
, CONSTRAINT nn_s_address_2   CHECK(street_address IS NOT NULL)
, CONSTRAINT nn_s_address_3   CHECK(created_by IS NOT NULL)
, CONSTRAINT nn_s_address_4   CHECK(creation_date IS NOT NULL)
, CONSTRAINT nn_s_address_5   CHECK(last_updated_by IS NOT NULL)
, CONSTRAINT nn_s_address_6   CHECK(last_update_date IS NOT NULL)
, CONSTRAINT fk_s_address_1   FOREIGN KEY(address_id)
  REFERENCES address          (address_id)

, CONSTRAINT fk_s_address_3   FOREIGN KEY(created_by)
  REFERENCES system_user      (system_user_id)
, CONSTRAINT fk_s_address_4   FOREIGN KEY(last_updated_by)
  REFERENCES system_user      (system_user_id));

CREATE SEQUENCE street_address_s1 START WITH 1001;

-- Conditionally drop objects.
BEGIN
  FOR i IN (SELECT null
            FROM   user_tables
            WHERE  table_name = 'TELEPHONE') LOOP
    EXECUTE IMMEDIATE 'DROP TABLE telephone CASCADE CONSTRAINTS';
  END LOOP;
  FOR i IN (SELECT null
            FROM   user_sequences
            WHERE  sequence_name = 'TELEPHONE_S1') LOOP
    EXECUTE IMMEDIATE 'DROP SEQUENCE telephone_s1';
  END LOOP;
END;
/


-- --------------------------------------------------------------------
-- Create TELEPHONE table and sequence and seed data.
-- --------------------------------------------------------------------

CREATE TABLE telephone
( telephone_id                NUMBER
, contact_id                  NUMBER
, address_id                  NUMBER
, telephone_type              NUMBER
, country_code                VARCHAR2(3)
, area_code                   VARCHAR2(6)
, telephone_number            VARCHAR2(10)
, created_by                  NUMBER
, creation_date               DATE
, last_updated_by             NUMBER
```

```
, last_update_date              DATE
, CONSTRAINT pk_telephone_1     PRIMARY KEY(telephone_id)
, CONSTRAINT nn_telephone_1     CHECK(contact_id IS NOT NULL)
, CONSTRAINT nn_telephone_2     CHECK(address_id IS NOT NULL)
, CONSTRAINT nn_telephone_3     CHECK(telephone_type IS NOT NULL)
, CONSTRAINT nn_telephone_4     CHECK(country_code IS NOT NULL)
, CONSTRAINT nn_telephone_5     CHECK(area_code IS NOT NULL)
, CONSTRAINT nn_telephone_6     CHECK(telephone_number IS NOT NULL)
, CONSTRAINT nn_telephone_7     CHECK(created_by IS NOT NULL)
, CONSTRAINT nn_telephone_8     CHECK(creation_date IS NOT NULL)
, CONSTRAINT nn_telephone_9     CHECK(last_updated_by IS NOT NULL)
, CONSTRAINT nn_telephone_10    CHECK(last_update_date IS NOT NULL)
, CONSTRAINT fk_telephone_1     FOREIGN KEY(contact_id)
  REFERENCES contact            (contact_id)
, CONSTRAINT fk_telephone_2     FOREIGN KEY(telephone_type)
  REFERENCES common_lookup      (common_lookup_id)
, CONSTRAINT fk_telephone_3     FOREIGN KEY(created_by)
  REFERENCES system_user        (system_user_id)
, CONSTRAINT fk_telephone_4     FOREIGN KEY(last_updated_by)
  REFERENCES system_user        (system_user_id));

CREATE INDEX telephone_n1 ON telephone(contact_id,address_id);
CREATE INDEX telephone_n2 ON telephone(address_id);
CREATE INDEX telephone_n3 ON telephone(telephone_type);
CREATE SEQUENCE telephone_s1 START WITH 1001;

-- Conditionally drop objects.
BEGIN
  FOR i IN (SELECT null
            FROM   user_tables
            WHERE  table_name = 'RENTAL') LOOP
    EXECUTE IMMEDIATE 'DROP TABLE rental CASCADE CONSTRAINTS';
  END LOOP;
  FOR i IN (SELECT null
            FROM   user_sequences
            WHERE  sequence_name = 'RENTAL_S1') LOOP
    EXECUTE IMMEDIATE 'DROP SEQUENCE rental_s1';
  END LOOP;
END;
/


-- ----------------------------------------------------------------
-- Create RENTAL table and sequence and seed data.
-- ----------------------------------------------------------------

CREATE TABLE rental
( rental_id                     NUMBER
, customer_id                   NUMBER
, check_out_date                DATE
, return_date                   DATE
```

```
,  created_by                    NUMBER
,  creation_date                 DATE
,  last_updated_by               NUMBER
,  last_update_date              DATE
,  CONSTRAINT pk_rental_1        PRIMARY KEY(rental_id)
,  CONSTRAINT nn_rental_1        CHECK(customer_id IS NOT NULL)
,  CONSTRAINT nn_rental_2        CHECK(check_out_date IS NOT NULL)
,  CONSTRAINT nn_rental_3        CHECK(return_date IS NOT NULL)
,  CONSTRAINT nn_rental_4        CHECK(created_by IS NOT NULL)
,  CONSTRAINT nn_rental_5        CHECK(creation_date IS NOT NULL)
,  CONSTRAINT nn_rental_6        CHECK(last_updated_by IS NOT NULL)
,  CONSTRAINT nn_rental_7        CHECK(last_update_date IS NOT NULL)
,  CONSTRAINT fk_rental_1        FOREIGN KEY(customer_id)
   REFERENCES contact            (contact_id)
,  CONSTRAINT fk_rental_2        FOREIGN KEY(created_by)
   REFERENCES system_user        (system_user_id)
,  CONSTRAINT fk_rental_3        FOREIGN KEY(last_updated_by)
   REFERENCES system_user        (system_user_id));

CREATE SEQUENCE rental_s1 START WITH 1001;

-- Conditionally drop objects.
BEGIN
  FOR i IN (SELECT null
            FROM    user_tables
            WHERE   table_name = 'ITEM') LOOP
    EXECUTE IMMEDIATE 'DROP TABLE item CASCADE CONSTRAINTS';
  END LOOP;
  FOR i IN (SELECT null
            FROM    user_sequences
            WHERE   sequence_name = 'ITEM_S1') LOOP
    EXECUTE IMMEDIATE 'DROP SEQUENCE item_s1';
  END LOOP;
END;
/


-- ------------------------------------------------------------------
-- Create ITEM table and sequence and seed data.
-- ------------------------------------------------------------------

CREATE TABLE item
( item_id                        NUMBER
, item_barcode                   VARCHAR2(14)
, item_type                      NUMBER
, item_title                     VARCHAR2(60)
, item_subtitle                  VARCHAR2(60)
, item_rating                    VARCHAR2(8)
, item_release_date              DATE
, created_by                     NUMBER
, creation_date                  DATE
```

```
  , last_updated_by              NUMBER
  , last_update_date             DATE
  , CONSTRAINT pk_item_1         PRIMARY KEY(item_id)
  , CONSTRAINT nn_item_1         CHECK(item_barcode IS NOT NULL)
  , CONSTRAINT nn_item_2         CHECK(item_type IS NOT NULL)
  , CONSTRAINT nn_item_3         CHECK(item_title IS NOT NULL)
  , CONSTRAINT nn_item_4         CHECK(item_rating IS NOT NULL)
  , CONSTRAINT nn_item_5         CHECK(item_release_date IS NOT NULL)
  , CONSTRAINT nn_item_6         CHECK(created_by IS NOT NULL)
  , CONSTRAINT nn_item_7         CHECK(creation_date IS NOT NULL)
  , CONSTRAINT nn_item_8         CHECK(last_updated_by IS NOT NULL)
  , CONSTRAINT nn_item_9         CHECK(last_update_date IS NOT NULL)
  , CONSTRAINT fk_item_1         FOREIGN KEY(item_type)
    REFERENCES common_lookup     (common_lookup_id)
  , CONSTRAINT fk_item_2         FOREIGN KEY(created_by)
    REFERENCES system_user       (system_user_id)
  , CONSTRAINT fk_item_3         FOREIGN KEY(last_updated_by)
    REFERENCES system_user       (system_user_id));

CREATE SEQUENCE item_s1 START WITH 1001;

-- Conditionally drop objects.
BEGIN
  FOR i IN (SELECT null
            FROM   user_tables
            WHERE  table_name = 'RENTAL_ITEM') LOOP
    EXECUTE IMMEDIATE 'DROP TABLE rental_item CASCADE CONSTRAINTS';
  END LOOP;
  FOR i IN (SELECT null
            FROM   user_sequences
            WHERE  sequence_name = 'RENTAL_ITEM_S1') LOOP
    EXECUTE IMMEDIATE 'DROP SEQUENCE rental_item_s1';
  END LOOP;
END;
/


-- ----------------------------------------------------------------
-- Create RENTAL_ITEM table and sequence and seed data.
-- ----------------------------------------------------------------

CREATE TABLE rental_item
( rental_item_id               NUMBER
, rental_id                    NUMBER
, item_id                      NUMBER
, created_by                   NUMBER
, creation_date                DATE
, last_updated_by              NUMBER
, last_update_date             DATE
, CONSTRAINT pk_rental_item_1 PRIMARY KEY(rental_item_id)
, CONSTRAINT nn_rental_item_1 CHECK(rental_id IS NOT NULL)
```

```
,  CONSTRAINT nn_rental_item_2 CHECK(item_id IS NOT NULL)
,  CONSTRAINT nn_rental_item_3 CHECK(created_by IS NOT NULL)
,  CONSTRAINT nn_rental_item_4 CHECK(creation_date IS NOT NULL)
,  CONSTRAINT nn_rental_item_5 CHECK(last_updated_by IS NOT NULL)
,  CONSTRAINT nn_rental_item_6 CHECK(last_update_date IS NOT NULL)
,  CONSTRAINT fk_rental_item_1 FOREIGN KEY(rental_id)
   REFERENCES rental            (rental_id)
,  CONSTRAINT fk_rental_item_2 FOREIGN KEY(item_id)
   REFERENCES item              (item_id)
,  CONSTRAINT fk_rental_item_3 FOREIGN KEY(created_by)
   REFERENCES system_user       (system_user_id)
,  CONSTRAINT fk_rental_item_4 FOREIGN KEY(last_updated_by)
   REFERENCES system_user       (system_user_id));

CREATE SEQUENCE rental_item_s1 START WITH 1001;

-- Commit the data seeding.
COMMIT;
```

Seed Media Store Data

The seed_store.sql script adds transaction values to the tables created by the create_store.sql script, as covered in Chapter 13. This model enables you to query and transact against a small database model that illustrates transactional control issues linked to changing data in related tables.

This script contains mostly INSERT statements that use subqueries to pull correct primary key values inserted as foreign keys in the tables. They also demonstrate effective sequencing of tables from the most senior primary key to the most junior foreign key, as well as the use of the .nextval and .currval operations covered in Appendix H. The scripts also demonstrate the Oracle Proprietary and ANSI 1999 INNER JOIN syntax in one of the subqueries, and backquoting a single quote with another single quote during INSERT operations.

After populating the data in the tables, the script builds a view of current rentals. These dates should work for five days after you run the script. When you want to rerun the seed_store.sql script, you first drop and recreate the tables by running the create_store.sql script.

The script queries the CURRENT_RENTAL view before ending, as follows:

```
-- This is found in seed_store.sql on the enclosed CD.

INSERT
INTO system_user
( system_user_id,system_user_name,system_user_group_id,system_user_type
, last_name,first_name,created_by,creation_date
, last_updated_by,last_update_date)
VALUES
( 2,'DBA', 2, 1,'Adams','Samuel', 1, SYSDATE, 1, SYSDATE);

INSERT
INTO system_user
( system_user_id,system_user_name,system_user_group_id,system_user_type
```

```
, last_name,first_name,created_by,creation_date
, last_updated_by,last_update_date)
VALUES
( 3,'DBA', 2, 1,'Henry','Patrick', 1, SYSDATE, 1, SYSDATE);

INSERT
INTO system_user
( system_user_id,system_user_name,system_user_group_id,system_user_type
, last_name,first_name,created_by,creation_date
, last_updated_by,last_update_date)
VALUES
( 4,'DBA', 2, 1,'Puri','Manmohan', 1, SYSDATE, 1, SYSDATE);

INSERT INTO member VALUES
( member_s1.nextval
,'B293-71445'
,'1111-2222-3333-4444'
,(SELECT    common_lookup_id
  FROM      common_lookup
  WHERE     common_lookup_context = 'MEMBER'
  AND       common_lookup_type = 'DISCOVER_CARD')
, 2, SYSDATE, 2, SYSDATE);

INSERT INTO contact VALUES
( contact_s1.nextval
, member_s1.currval
,(SELECT    common_lookup_id
  FROM      common_lookup
  WHERE     common_lookup_context = 'CONTACT'
  AND       common_lookup_type = 'CUSTOMER')
,'Winn','Randi',''
, 2, SYSDATE, 2, SYSDATE);

INSERT INTO address VALUES
( address_s1.nextval
, contact_s1.currval
,(SELECT    common_lookup_id
  FROM      common_lookup
  WHERE     common_lookup_type = 'HOME')
,'San Jose','CA','95192'
, 2, SYSDATE, 2, SYSDATE);

INSERT INTO street_address VALUES
( street_address_s1.nextval
, address_s1.currval
,'10 El Camino Real'
, 2, SYSDATE, 2, SYSDATE);

INSERT INTO telephone VALUES
( telephone_s1.nextval
```

```
, address_s1.currval
, contact_s1.currval
,(SELECT    common_lookup_id
  FROM      common_lookup
  WHERE     common_lookup_type = 'HOME')
,'USA','408','111-1111'
, 2, SYSDATE, 2, SYSDATE);

INSERT INTO contact VALUES
( contact_s1.nextval
, member_s1.currval
,(SELECT    common_lookup_id
  FROM      common_lookup
  WHERE     common_lookup_context = 'CONTACT'
  AND       common_lookup_type = 'CUSTOMER')
,'Winn','Brian',''
, 2, SYSDATE, 2, SYSDATE);

INSERT INTO address VALUES
( address_s1.nextval
, contact_s1.currval
,(SELECT    common_lookup_id
  FROM      common_lookup
  WHERE     common_lookup_type = 'HOME')
,'San Jose','CA','95192'
, 2, SYSDATE, 2, SYSDATE);

INSERT INTO street_address VALUES
( street_address_s1.nextval
, address_s1.currval
,'10 El Camino Real'
, 2, SYSDATE, 2, SYSDATE);

INSERT INTO telephone VALUES
( telephone_s1.nextval
, address_s1.currval
, contact_s1.currval
,(SELECT    common_lookup_id
  FROM      common_lookup
  WHERE     common_lookup_type = 'HOME')
,'USA','408','111-1111'
, 2, SYSDATE, 2, SYSDATE);

INSERT INTO member VALUES
( member_s1.nextval
,'B293-71446'
,'2222-3333-4444-5555'
,(SELECT    common_lookup_id
  FROM      common_lookup
  WHERE     common_lookup_context = 'MEMBER'
```

```
    AND        common_lookup_type = 'DISCOVER_CARD')
, 2, SYSDATE, 2, SYSDATE);

INSERT INTO contact VALUES
( contact_s1.nextval
, member_s1.currval
,(SELECT   common_lookup_id
  FROM     common_lookup
  WHERE    common_lookup_context = 'CONTACT'
  AND      common_lookup_type = 'CUSTOMER')
,'Vizquel','Oscar',''
, 2, SYSDATE, 2, SYSDATE);

INSERT INTO address VALUES
( address_s1.nextval
, contact_s1.currval
,(SELECT   common_lookup_id
  FROM     common_lookup
  WHERE    common_lookup_type = 'HOME')
,'San Jose','CA','95192'
, 2, SYSDATE, 2, SYSDATE);

INSERT INTO street_address VALUES
( street_address_s1.nextval
, address_s1.currval
,'12 El Camino Real'
, 2, SYSDATE, 2, SYSDATE);

INSERT INTO telephone VALUES
( telephone_s1.nextval
, address_s1.currval
, contact_s1.currval
,(SELECT   common_lookup_id
  FROM     common_lookup
  WHERE    common_lookup_type = 'HOME')
,'USA','408','222-2222'
, 2, SYSDATE, 2, SYSDATE);

INSERT INTO contact VALUES
( contact_s1.nextval
, member_s1.currval
,(SELECT   common_lookup_id
  FROM     common_lookup
  WHERE    common_lookup_context = 'CONTACT'
  AND      common_lookup_type = 'CUSTOMER')
,'Vizquel','Doreen',''
, 2, SYSDATE, 2, SYSDATE);

INSERT INTO address VALUES
( address_s1.nextval
```

```
, contact_s1.currval
,(SELECT    common_lookup_id
  FROM      common_lookup
  WHERE     common_lookup_type = 'HOME')
,'San Jose','CA','95192'
, 2, SYSDATE, 2, SYSDATE);

INSERT INTO street_address VALUES
( street_address_s1.nextval
, address_s1.currval
,'12 El Camino Real'
, 2, SYSDATE, 2, SYSDATE);

INSERT INTO telephone VALUES
( telephone_s1.nextval
, address_s1.currval
, contact_s1.currval
,(SELECT    common_lookup_id
  FROM      common_lookup
  WHERE     common_lookup_type = 'HOME')
,'USA','408','222-2222'
, 2, SYSDATE, 2, SYSDATE);

INSERT INTO member VALUES
( member_s1.nextval
,'B293-71447'
,'3333-4444-5555-6666'
,(SELECT    common_lookup_id
  FROM      common_lookup
  WHERE     common_lookup_context = 'MEMBER'
  AND       common_lookup_type = 'DISCOVER_CARD')
, 2, SYSDATE, 2, SYSDATE);

INSERT INTO contact VALUES
( contact_s1.nextval
, member_s1.currval
,(SELECT    common_lookup_id
  FROM      common_lookup
  WHERE     common_lookup_context = 'CONTACT'
  AND       common_lookup_type = 'CUSTOMER')
,'Sweeney','Meaghan',''
, 2, SYSDATE, 2, SYSDATE);

INSERT INTO address VALUES
( address_s1.nextval
, contact_s1.currval
,(SELECT    common_lookup_id
  FROM      common_lookup
  WHERE     common_lookup_type = 'HOME')
,'San Jose','CA','95192'
, 2, SYSDATE, 2, SYSDATE);
```

```
INSERT INTO street_address VALUES
( street_address_s1.nextval
, address_s1.currval
,'14 El Camino Real'
, 2, SYSDATE, 2, SYSDATE);

INSERT INTO telephone VALUES
( telephone_s1.nextval
, address_s1.currval
, contact_s1.currval
,(SELECT   common_lookup_id
  FROM     common_lookup
  WHERE    common_lookup_type = 'HOME')
,'USA','408','333-3333'
, 2, SYSDATE, 2, SYSDATE);

INSERT INTO contact VALUES
( contact_s1.nextval
, member_s1.currval
,(SELECT   common_lookup_id
  FROM     common_lookup
  WHERE    common_lookup_context = 'CONTACT'
  AND      common_lookup_type = 'CUSTOMER')
,'Sweeney','Matthew',''
, 2, SYSDATE, 2, SYSDATE);

INSERT INTO address VALUES
( address_s1.nextval
, contact_s1.currval
,(SELECT   common_lookup_id
  FROM     common_lookup
  WHERE    common_lookup_type = 'HOME')
,'San Jose','CA','95192'
, 2, SYSDATE, 2, SYSDATE);

INSERT INTO street_address VALUES
( street_address_s1.nextval
, address_s1.currval
,'14 El Camino Real'
, 2, SYSDATE, 2, SYSDATE);

INSERT INTO telephone VALUES
( telephone_s1.nextval
, address_s1.currval
, contact_s1.currval
,(SELECT   common_lookup_id
  FROM     common_lookup
  WHERE    common_lookup_type = 'HOME')
```

```
,'USA','408','333-3333'
, 2, SYSDATE, 2, SYSDATE);

INSERT INTO contact VALUES
( contact_s1.nextval
, member_s1.currval
,(SELECT   common_lookup_id
  FROM     common_lookup
  WHERE    common_lookup_context = 'CONTACT'
  AND      common_lookup_type = 'CUSTOMER')
,'Sweeney','Ian','M'
, 2, SYSDATE, 2, SYSDATE);

INSERT INTO address VALUES
( address_s1.nextval
, contact_s1.currval
,(SELECT   common_lookup_id
  FROM     common_lookup
  WHERE    common_lookup_type = 'HOME')
,'San Jose','CA','95192'
, 2, SYSDATE, 2, SYSDATE);

INSERT INTO street_address VALUES
( street_address_s1.nextval
, address_s1.currval
,'14 El Camino Real'
, 2, SYSDATE, 2, SYSDATE);

INSERT INTO telephone VALUES
( telephone_s1.nextval
, address_s1.currval
, contact_s1.currval
,(SELECT   common_lookup_id
  FROM     common_lookup
  WHERE    common_lookup_type = 'HOME')
,'USA','408','333-3333'
, 2, SYSDATE, 2, SYSDATE);

INSERT INTO item VALUES
( item_s1.nextval
,'9736-05640-4'
,(SELECT   common_lookup_id
  FROM     common_lookup
  WHERE    common_lookup_type = 'DVD_WIDE_SCREEN')
,'The Hunt for Red October','Special Collector''s Edition','PG'
,'02-MAR-90', 3, SYSDATE, 3, SYSDATE);

INSERT INTO item VALUES
( item_s1.nextval
,'24543-02392'
```

```
,(SELECT    common_lookup_id
  FROM      common_lookup
  WHERE     common_lookup_type = 'DVD_WIDE_SCREEN')
,'Star Wars I','Phantom Menace','PG'
,'04-MAY-99', 3, SYSDATE, 3, SYSDATE);

INSERT INTO item VALUES
( item_s1.nextval
,'24543-5615'
,(SELECT    common_lookup_id
  FROM      common_lookup
  WHERE     common_lookup_type = 'DVD_FULL_SCREEN')
,'Star Wars II','Attack of the Clones','PG'
,'16-MAY-02', 3, SYSDATE, 3, SYSDATE);

INSERT INTO item VALUES
( item_s1.nextval
,'24543-05539'
,(SELECT    common_lookup_id
  FROM      common_lookup
  WHERE     common_lookup_type = 'DVD_WIDE_SCREEN')
,'Star Wars II','Attack of the Clones','PG'
,'16-MAY-02', 3, SYSDATE, 3, SYSDATE);

INSERT INTO item VALUES
( item_s1.nextval
,'24543-20309'
,(SELECT    common_lookup_id
  FROM      common_lookup
  WHERE     common_lookup_type = 'DVD_WIDE_SCREEN')
,'Star Wars III','Revenge of the Sith','PG13'
,'19-MAY-05', 3, SYSDATE, 3, SYSDATE);

INSERT INTO item VALUES
( item_s1.nextval
,'86936-70380'
,(SELECT    common_lookup_id
  FROM      common_lookup
  WHERE     common_lookup_type = 'DVD_WIDE_SCREEN')
,'The Chronicles of Narnia'
,'The Lion, the Witch and the Wardrobe','PG'
,'16-MAY-02', 3, SYSDATE, 3, SYSDATE);

INSERT INTO item VALUES
( item_s1.nextval
,'91493-06475'
,(SELECT    common_lookup_id
  FROM      common_lookup
  WHERE     common_lookup_type = 'XBOX')
,'RoboCop','','Mature','24-JUL-03', 3, SYSDATE, 3, SYSDATE);
```

```
INSERT INTO item VALUES
( item_s1.nextval
,'93155-11810'
,(SELECT   common_lookup_id
  FROM     common_lookup
  WHERE    common_lookup_type = 'XBOX')
,'Pirates of the Caribbean','','Teen','30-JUN-03', 3, SYSDATE, 3, SYSDATE);

INSERT INTO item VALUES
( item_s1.nextval
,'12725-00173'
,(SELECT   common_lookup_id
  FROM     common_lookup
  WHERE    common_lookup_type = 'XBOX')
,'The Chronicles of Narnia'
,'The Lion, the Witch and the Wardrobe','Everyone','30-JUN-03'
, 3, SYSDATE, 3, SYSDATE);

INSERT INTO item VALUES
( item_s1.nextval
,'45496-96128'
,(SELECT   common_lookup_id
  FROM     common_lookup
  WHERE    common_lookup_type = 'NINTENDO_GAMECUBE')
,'MarioKart','Double Dash','Everyone','17-NOV-03', 3, SYSDATE, 3, SYSDATE);

INSERT INTO item VALUES
( item_s1.nextval
,'08888-32214'
,(SELECT   common_lookup_id
  FROM     common_lookup
  WHERE    common_lookup_type = 'PLAYSTATION2')
,'Splinter Cell','Chaos Theory','Teen','08-APR-03', 3, SYSDATE, 3, SYSDATE);

INSERT INTO item VALUES
( item_s1.nextval
,'14633-14821'
,(SELECT   common_lookup_id
  FROM     common_lookup
  WHERE    common_lookup_type = 'PLAYSTATION2')
,'Need for Speed','Most Wanted','Everyone','15-NOV-04'
, 3, SYSDATE, 3, SYSDATE);

INSERT INTO item VALUES
( item_s1.nextval,'10425-29944'
,(SELECT   common_lookup_id
  FROM     common_lookup
  WHERE    common_lookup_type = 'XBOX')
,'The DaVinci Code','','Teen','19-MAY-06', 3, SYSDATE, 3, SYSDATE);
```

```
INSERT INTO item VALUES
( item_s1.nextval,'52919-52057'
,(SELECT    common_lookup_id
  FROM      common_lookup
  WHERE     common_lookup_type = 'XBOX')
,'Cars','','Everyone','28-APR-06', 3, SYSDATE, 3, SYSDATE);

INSERT INTO item VALUES
( item_s1.nextval,'9689-80547-3'
,(SELECT    common_lookup_id
  FROM      common_lookup
  WHERE     common_lookup_type = 'VHS_SINGLE_TAPE')
,'Beau Geste','','PG','01-MAR-92', 3, SYSDATE, 3, SYSDATE);

INSERT INTO item VALUES
( item_s1.nextval,'53939-64103'
,(SELECT    common_lookup_id
  FROM      common_lookup
  WHERE     common_lookup_type = 'VHS_SINGLE_TAPE')
,'I Remember Mama','','NR','05-JAN-98', 3, SYSDATE, 3, SYSDATE);

INSERT INTO item VALUES
( item_s1.nextval,'24543-01292'
,(SELECT    common_lookup_id
  FROM      common_lookup
  WHERE     common_lookup_type = 'VHS_SINGLE_TAPE')
,'Tora! Tora! Tora!','The Attack on Pearl Harbor','G','02-NOV-99'
, 3, SYSDATE, 3, SYSDATE);

INSERT INTO item VALUES
( item_s1.nextval,'43396-60047'
,(SELECT    common_lookup_id
  FROM      common_lookup
  WHERE     common_lookup_type = 'VHS_SINGLE_TAPE')
,'A Man for All Seasons','','G','28-JUN-94', 3, SYSDATE, 3, SYSDATE);

INSERT INTO item VALUES
( item_s1.nextval
,'43396-70603'
,(SELECT    common_lookup_id
  FROM      common_lookup
  WHERE     common_lookup_type = 'VHS_SINGLE_TAPE')
,'Hook','','PG','11-DEC-91', 3, SYSDATE, 3, SYSDATE);

INSERT INTO item VALUES
( item_s1.nextval,'85391-13213'
,(SELECT    common_lookup_id
  FROM      common_lookup
  WHERE     common_lookup_type = 'VHS_DOUBLE_TAPE')
,'Around the World in 80 Days','','G','04-DEC-92', 3, SYSDATE, 3, SYSDATE);
```

```
INSERT INTO item VALUES
( item_s1.nextval,'85391-10843'
,(SELECT   common_lookup_id
  FROM     common_lookup
  WHERE    common_lookup_type = 'VHS_DOUBLE_TAPE')
,'Camelot','','G','15-MAY-98', 3, SYSDATE, 3, SYSDATE);

INSERT INTO rental VALUES
( rental_s1.nextval
,(SELECT   contact_id
  FROM     contact
  WHERE    last_name = 'Vizquel'
  AND      first_name = 'Oscar')
, SYSDATE, SYSDATE + 5, 3, SYSDATE, 3, SYSDATE);

INSERT INTO rental VALUES
( rental_s1.nextval
,(SELECT   contact_id
  FROM     contact
  WHERE    last_name = 'Vizquel'
  AND      first_name = 'Doreen')
, SYSDATE, SYSDATE + 5, 3, SYSDATE, 3, SYSDATE);

INSERT INTO rental VALUES
( rental_s1.nextval
,(SELECT   contact_id
  FROM     contact
  WHERE    last_name = 'Sweeney'
  AND      first_name = 'Meaghan')
, SYSDATE, SYSDATE + 5, 3, SYSDATE, 3, SYSDATE);

INSERT INTO rental VALUES
( rental_s1.nextval
,(SELECT   contact_id
  FROM     contact
  WHERE    last_name = 'Sweeney'
  AND      first_name = 'Ian')
, SYSDATE, SYSDATE + 5, 3, SYSDATE, 3, SYSDATE);

INSERT INTO rental VALUES
( rental_s1.nextval
,(SELECT   contact_id
  FROM     contact
  WHERE    last_name = 'Winn'
  AND      first_name = 'Brian')
, SYSDATE, SYSDATE + 5, 3, SYSDATE, 3, SYSDATE);

INSERT INTO rental_item
( rental_item_id, rental_id, item_id
```

```
, created_by, creation_date, last_updated_by, last_update_date)
VALUES
( rental_item_s1.nextval
,(SELECT   r.rental_id
  FROM     rental r
  ,        contact c
  WHERE    r.customer_id = c.contact_id
  AND      c.last_name = 'Vizquel'
  AND      c.first_name = 'Oscar')
,(SELECT   i.item_id
  FROM     item i
  ,        common_lookup cl
  WHERE    i.item_title = 'Star Wars I'
  AND      i.item_subtitle = 'Phantom Menace'
  AND      i.item_type = cl.common_lookup_id
  AND      cl.common_lookup_type = 'DVD_WIDE_SCREEN')
, 3, SYSDATE, 3, SYSDATE);

INSERT INTO rental_item
( rental_item_id, rental_id, item_id
, created_by, creation_date, last_updated_by, last_update_date)
VALUES
( rental_item_s1.nextval
,(SELECT   r.rental_id
  FROM     rental r inner join contact c
  ON       r.customer_id = c.contact_id
  WHERE    c.last_name = 'Vizquel'
  AND      c.first_name = 'Oscar')
,(SELECT   d.item_id
  FROM     item d join common_lookup cl
  ON       d.item_title = 'Star Wars II'
  WHERE    d.item_subtitle = 'Attack of the Clones'
  AND      d.item_type = cl.common_lookup_id
  AND      cl.common_lookup_type = 'DVD_WIDE_SCREEN')
, 3, SYSDATE, 3, SYSDATE);

INSERT INTO rental_item
( rental_item_id, rental_id, item_id
, created_by, creation_date, last_updated_by, last_update_date)
VALUES
( rental_item_s1.nextval
,(SELECT   r.rental_id
  FROM     rental r
  ,        contact c
  WHERE    r.customer_id = c.contact_id
  AND      c.last_name = 'Vizquel'
  AND      c.first_name = 'Oscar')
,(SELECT   d.item_id
  FROM     item d
  ,        common_lookup cl
```

```
    WHERE     d.item_title = 'Star Wars III'
    AND       d.item_subtitle = 'Revenge of the Sith'
    AND       d.item_type = cl.common_lookup_id
    AND       cl.common_lookup_type = 'DVD_WIDE_SCREEN')
, 3, SYSDATE, 3, SYSDATE);

INSERT INTO rental_item
( rental_item_id, rental_id, item_id
, created_by, creation_date, last_updated_by, last_update_date)
VALUES
( rental_item_s1.nextval
,(SELECT    r.rental_id
  FROM      rental r
  ,         contact c
  WHERE     r.customer_id = c.contact_id
  AND       c.last_name = 'Vizquel'
  AND       c.first_name = 'Doreen')
,(SELECT    d.item_id
  FROM      item d
  ,         common_lookup cl
  WHERE     d.item_title = 'I Remember Mama'
  AND       d.item_subtitle IS NULL
  AND       d.item_type = cl.common_lookup_id
  AND       cl.common_lookup_type = 'VHS_SINGLE_TAPE')
, 3, SYSDATE, 3, SYSDATE);

INSERT INTO rental_item
( rental_item_id, rental_id, item_id
, created_by, creation_date, last_updated_by, last_update_date)
VALUES
( rental_item_s1.nextval
,(SELECT    r.rental_id
  FROM      rental r
  ,         contact c
  WHERE     r.customer_id = c.contact_id
  AND       c.last_name = 'Vizquel'
  AND       c.first_name = 'Doreen')
,(SELECT    d.item_id
  FROM      item d
  ,         common_lookup cl
  WHERE     d.item_title = 'Camelot'
  AND       d.item_subtitle IS NULL
  AND       d.item_type = cl.common_lookup_id
  AND       cl.common_lookup_type = 'VHS_DOUBLE_TAPE')
, 3, SYSDATE, 3, SYSDATE);

INSERT INTO rental_item
( rental_item_id, rental_id, item_id
, created_by, creation_date, last_updated_by, last_update_date)
VALUES
```

```
( rental_item_s1.nextval
,(SELECT    r.rental_id
  FROM      rental r
  ,         contact c
  WHERE     r.customer_id = c.contact_id
  AND       c.last_name = 'Sweeney'
  AND       c.first_name = 'Meaghan')
,(SELECT    d.item_id
  FROM      item d
  ,         common_lookup cl
  WHERE     d.item_title = 'Hook'
  AND       d.item_subtitle IS NULL
  AND       d.item_type = cl.common_lookup_id
  AND       cl.common_lookup_type = 'VHS_SINGLE_TAPE')
, 3, SYSDATE, 3, SYSDATE);

INSERT INTO rental_item
( rental_item_id, rental_id, item_id

, created_by, creation_date, last_updated_by, last_update_date)
VALUES
( rental_item_s1.nextval
,(SELECT    r.rental_id
  FROM      rental r
  ,         contact c
  WHERE     r.customer_id = c.contact_id
  AND       c.last_name = 'Sweeney'
  AND       c.first_name = 'Ian')
,(SELECT    d.item_id
  FROM      item d
  ,         common_lookup cl
  WHERE     d.item_title = 'Cars'
  AND       d.item_subtitle IS NULL
  AND       d.item_type = cl.common_lookup_id
  AND       cl.common_lookup_type = 'XBOX')
, 3, SYSDATE, 3, SYSDATE);

INSERT INTO rental_item
( rental_item_id, rental_id, item_id
, created_by, creation_date, last_updated_by, last_update_date)
VALUES
( rental_item_s1.nextval
,(SELECT    r.rental_id
  FROM      rental r
  ,         contact c
  WHERE     r.customer_id = c.contact_id
  AND       c.last_name = 'Winn'
  AND       c.first_name = 'Brian')
,(SELECT    d.item_id
  FROM      item d
```

```
           ,          common_lookup cl
   WHERE      d.item_title = 'RoboCop'
   AND        d.item_subtitle IS NULL
   AND        d.item_type = cl.common_lookup_id
   AND        cl.common_lookup_type = 'XBOX')
, 3, SYSDATE, 3, SYSDATE);

INSERT INTO rental_item
( rental_item_id, rental_id, item_id
, created_by, creation_date, last_updated_by, last_update_date)
VALUES
( rental_item_s1.nextval
,(SELECT    r.rental_id
   FROM       rental r
   ,          contact c
   WHERE      r.customer_id = c.contact_id
   AND        c.last_name = 'Winn'
   AND        c.first_name = 'Brian')
,(SELECT    d.item_id
   FROM       item d
   ,          common_lookup cl
   WHERE      d.item_title = 'The Hunt for Red October'
   AND        d.item_subtitle = 'Special Collector''s Edition'
   AND        d.item_type = cl.common_lookup_id
   AND        cl.common_lookup_type = 'DVD_WIDE_SCREEN')
, 3, SYSDATE, 3, SYSDATE);

CREATE OR REPLACE VIEW current_rental AS
   SELECT     m.account_number
   ,          c.first_name
   ||         DECODE(c.middle_initial,NULL,' ',' '||c.middle_initial||' ')
   ||         c.last_name FULL_NAME
   ,          i.item_title TITLE
   ,          i.item_subtitle SUBTITLE
   ,          SUBSTR(cl.common_lookup_meaning,1,3) PRODUCT
   ,          r.check_out_date
   ,          r.return_date
   FROM       common_lookup cl
   ,          contact c
   ,          item i
   ,          member m
   ,          rental r
   ,          rental_item ri
   WHERE      r.customer_id = c.contact_id
   AND        r.rental_id = ri.rental_id
   AND        ri.item_id = i.item_id
   AND        i.item_type = cl.common_lookup_id
   AND        c.member_id = m.member_id
   ORDER BY 1,2,3;
```

```
-- SQL*Plus formatting of view output.
COL fullname FORMAT A16
COL title    FORMAT A30
COL product  FORMAT A4

-- Query view.
SELECT   cr.full_name
,        cr.title
,        cr.product
,        cr.check_out_date
,        cr.return_date
FROM     current_rental cr;
```

Create and Seed PL/SQL Example

The `create_world_leaders.sql` script is a rerunnable example program that creates a table, sequence, and package with overloaded procedures. It also seeds data into the `PRESIDENT` table and tests the implementation of all four overloaded procedures. The package demonstrates the management of user-defined scalar variable collections, associative arrays also known as PL/SQL tables, and reference cursors.

The program is fully commented with delimited comment breaks for major sections, like seeding the 42 presidents of the United States, defining the scalar variable collections, defining the package specification and body, and testing the data and PL/SQL code. The latter section is an important tool because it enables you to know that the error is outside of the database if your PHP program fails.

The `create_world_leaders.sql` script follows:

```
-- This is found in create_world_leaders.sql on the enclosed CD.

-- Conditionally drop objects.
BEGIN
  FOR i IN (SELECT   table_name
            FROM     user_tables
            WHERE    table_name = 'PRESIDENT' ) LOOP
    EXECUTE IMMEDIATE 'DROP TABLE president';
  END LOOP;

  FOR i IN (SELECT   sequence_name
            FROM     user_sequences
            WHERE    sequence_name = 'PRESIDENT_S1' ) LOOP
    EXECUTE IMMEDIATE 'DROP SEQUENCE president_s1';
  END LOOP;
END;
/

-- Create table for dynamic web page display.
CREATE TABLE president
( president_id       NUMBER
, last_name          VARCHAR2(20 CHAR)
```

```
, first_name          VARCHAR2(20 CHAR)
, middle_name         VARCHAR2(20 CHAR)
, term_start          NUMBER
, term_end            NUMBER
, country             VARCHAR2(3 CHAR)
, party               VARCHAR2(24 CHAR)
, CONSTRAINT pk_p1  PRIMARY KEY (president_id));

-- Create sequence for primary (surrogate) key.
CREATE SEQUENCE president_s1;


-- ------------------------------------------------------------------
-- Seed data for 42 US Presidents.
-- ------------------------------------------------------------------

INSERT INTO president
VALUES ( president_s1.nextval
       ,'Washington','George',''
       , 1789,1797
       ,'USA','Federalist');

INSERT INTO president
VALUES ( president_s1.nextval
       ,'Adams','John',''
       , 1797,1801
       ,'USA','Federalist');

INSERT INTO president
VALUES ( president_s1.nextval
       ,'Jefferson','Thomas',''
       , 1801,1809
       ,'USA','Democratic-Republican');

INSERT INTO president
VALUES ( president_s1.nextval
       ,'Madison','James',''
       , 1809,1817
       ,'USA','Democratic-Republican');

INSERT INTO president
VALUES ( president_s1.nextval
       ,'Monroe','James',''
       , 1817,1825
       ,'USA','Democratic-Republican');

INSERT INTO president
VALUES ( president_s1.nextval
       ,'Adams','John','Quincy'
       , 1825,1829
       ,'USA','Democratic-Republican');
```

```
INSERT INTO president
VALUES ( president_s1.nextval
       ,'Jackson','Andrew',''
       , 1829,1837
       ,'USA','Democrat');

INSERT INTO president
VALUES ( president_s1.nextval
       ,'Van Buren','Martin',''
       , 1837,1841
       ,'USA','Democrat');

INSERT INTO president
VALUES ( president_s1.nextval
       ,'Harrison','William','Henry'
       , 1841,1841
       ,'USA','Whig');

INSERT INTO president
VALUES ( president_s1.nextval
       ,'Tyler','John',''
       , 1841,1845
       ,'USA','Whig');

INSERT INTO president
VALUES ( president_s1.nextval
       ,'Polk','James',''
       , 1845,1849
       ,'USA','Democrat');

INSERT INTO president
VALUES ( president_s1.nextval
       ,'Taylor','Zachary',''
       , 1849,1850
       ,'USA','Whig');

INSERT INTO president
VALUES ( president_s1.nextval
       ,'Fillmore','Millard',''
       , 1850,1853
       ,'USA','Whig');

INSERT INTO president
VALUES ( president_s1.nextval
       ,'Pierce','Franklin',''
       , 1853,1857
       ,'USA','Democrat');

INSERT INTO president
VALUES ( president_s1.nextval
```

```
        ,'Buchanan','James',''
        , 1857,1861
        ,'USA','Democrat');

INSERT INTO president
VALUES ( president_s1.nextval
        ,'Lincoln','Abraham',''
        , 1861,1864
        ,'USA','Republican');

INSERT INTO president
VALUES ( president_s1.nextval
        ,'Johnson','Andrew',''
        , 1865,1869
        ,'USA','Union');

INSERT INTO president
VALUES ( president_s1.nextval
        ,'Grant','Ulysses','S.'
        , 1869,1877
        ,'USA','Republican');

INSERT INTO president
VALUES ( president_s1.nextval
        ,'Hayes','Rutherford','B.'
        , 1877,1881
        ,'USA','Republican');

INSERT INTO president
VALUES ( president_s1.nextval
        ,'Garfield','James',''
        , 1881,1881
        ,'USA','Republican');

INSERT INTO president
VALUES ( president_s1.nextval
        ,'Arthur','Chester',''
        , 1881,1885
        ,'USA','Republican');

INSERT INTO president
VALUES ( president_s1.nextval
        ,'Cleveland','Grover',''
        , 1885,1889
        ,'USA','Democratic');

INSERT INTO president
VALUES ( president_s1.nextval
        ,'Harrison','Benjamin',''
        , 1889,1893
        ,'USA','Republican');
```

```
INSERT INTO president
VALUES ( president_s1.nextval
       ,'Cleveland','Grover',''
       , 1893,1897
       ,'USA','Democratic');

INSERT INTO president
VALUES ( president_s1.nextval
       ,'McKinley','William',''
       , 1897,1901
       ,'USA','Republican');

INSERT INTO president
VALUES ( president_s1.nextval
       ,'Roosevelt','Theodore',''
       , 1901,1909
       ,'USA','Republican');

INSERT INTO president
VALUES ( president_s1.nextval
       ,'Taft','William','H.'
       , 1909,1913
       ,'USA','Republican');

INSERT INTO president
VALUES ( president_s1.nextval
       ,'Wilson','Woodrow',''
       , 1913,1921
       ,'USA','Democrat');

INSERT INTO president
VALUES ( president_s1.nextval
       ,'Coolidge','Calvin',''
       , 1923,1929
       ,'USA','Republican');

INSERT INTO president
VALUES ( president_s1.nextval
       ,'Hoover','Herbert',''
       , 1929,1933
       ,'USA','Republican');

INSERT INTO president
VALUES ( president_s1.nextval
       ,'Roosevelt','Franklin','D.'
       , 1933,1945
       ,'USA','Democrat');
```

```
INSERT INTO president
VALUES ( president_s1.nextval
       ,'Truman','Harry','S.'
       , 1945,1953
       ,'USA','Democrat');

INSERT INTO president
VALUES ( president_s1.nextval
       ,'Eisenhower','Dwight','David'
       , 1953,1961
       ,'USA','Republican');

INSERT INTO president
VALUES ( president_s1.nextval
       ,'Kennedy','John','Fitzgerald'
       , 1961,1963
       ,'USA','Democrat');

INSERT INTO president
VALUES ( president_s1.nextval
       ,'Johnson','Lyndon','B.'
       , 1963,1969
       ,'USA','Democrat');

INSERT INTO president
VALUES ( president_s1.nextval
       ,'Nixon','Richard','M.'
       , 1969,1974
       ,'USA','Republican');

INSERT INTO president
VALUES ( president_s1.nextval
       ,'Ford','Gerald','R.'
       , 1974,1977
       ,'USA','Republican');

INSERT INTO president
VALUES ( president_s1.nextval
       ,'Carter','Jimmy',''
       , 1977,1981
       ,'USA','Democrat');

INSERT INTO president
VALUES ( president_s1.nextval
       ,'Reagan','Ronald',''
       , 1981,1989
       ,'USA','Republican');

INSERT INTO president
VALUES ( president_s1.nextval
```

```
        ,'Bush','George','H.W.'
        , 1989,1993
        ,'USA','Republican');

INSERT INTO president
VALUES ( president_s1.nextval
        ,'Clinton','William','Jefferson'
        , 1993,2001
        ,'USA','Democrat');

INSERT INTO president
VALUES ( president_s1.nextval
        ,'Bush','George','W.'
        , 2001,2009
        ,'USA','Republican');

-- Commit the entries to the PRESIDENT table.
COMMIT;

-- -----------------------------------------------------------------
-- User defined scalar type collections.
-- -----------------------------------------------------------------

-- Define a VARRAY of NUMBER data types.
CREATE OR REPLACE TYPE president_id_varray
  AS VARRAY(100) OF NUMBER;
/

-- Define three VARRAY of VARCHAR2 data types of varying size.
CREATE OR REPLACE TYPE president_name_varray
  AS VARRAY(100) OF VARCHAR2(60 CHAR);
/
CREATE OR REPLACE TYPE tenure_varray
  AS VARRAY(100) OF VARCHAR2(9 CHAR);
/
CREATE OR REPLACE TYPE party_varray
  AS VARRAY(100) OF VARCHAR2(24 CHAR);
/

-- Define a VARRAY of NUMBER data types.
CREATE OR REPLACE TYPE president_id_ntable
  AS TABLE OF NUMBER;
/

-- Define three VARRAY of VARCHAR2 data types of varying size.
CREATE OR REPLACE TYPE president_name_ntable
  AS TABLE OF VARCHAR2(60 CHAR);
/
CREATE OR REPLACE TYPE tenure_ntable
  AS TABLE OF VARCHAR2(9 CHAR);
```

```
/
CREATE OR REPLACE TYPE party_ntable
  AS TABLE OF VARCHAR2(24 CHAR);
/


-- ----------------------------------------------------------------------
-- Package specification with overloaded procedures.
-- ----------------------------------------------------------------------

-- Create a package specification or definition.
CREATE OR REPLACE PACKAGE world_leaders AS

  -- Define an associative array (PL/SQL Table) of numbers.
  TYPE president_id_table IS TABLE OF NUMBER
    INDEX BY BINARY_INTEGER;

  -- Define three associative arrays (PL/SQL Table) of VARCHAR2 by size.
  TYPE president_name_table IS TABLE OF VARCHAR2(60 CHAR)
    INDEX BY BINARY_INTEGER;
  TYPE tenure_table IS TABLE OF VARCHAR2(9 CHAR)
    INDEX BY BINARY_INTEGER;
  TYPE party_table IS TABLE OF VARCHAR2(24 CHAR)
    INDEX BY BINARY_INTEGER;

  -- Define procedure specification to return parallel associative arrays.
  PROCEDURE get_presidents
  ( term_start_in   IN      NUMBER
  , term_end_in     IN      NUMBER
  , country_in      IN      VARCHAR2
  , president_ids   IN OUT  PRESIDENT_ID_TABLE
  , president_names IN OUT  PRESIDENT_NAME_TABLE
  , tenures         IN OUT  TENURE_TABLE
  , parties         IN OUT  PARTY_TABLE);

  -- Define procedure specification to return VARRAYs.
  PROCEDURE get_presidents
  ( term_start_in   IN      NUMBER
  , term_end_in     IN      NUMBER
  , country_in      IN      VARCHAR2
  , president_ids   IN OUT  PRESIDENT_ID_VARRAY
  , president_names IN OUT  PRESIDENT_NAME_VARRAY
  , tenures         IN OUT  TENURE_VARRAY
  , parties         IN OUT  PARTY_VARRAY);

  -- Define procedure specification to return parallel nested_tables.
  PROCEDURE get_presidents
  ( term_start_in   IN      NUMBER
  , term_end_in     IN      NUMBER
  , country_in      IN      VARCHAR2
  , president_ids   IN OUT  PRESIDENT_ID_NTABLE
  , president_names IN OUT  PRESIDENT_NAME_NTABLE
```

```
  , tenures            IN OUT TENURE_NTABLE
  , parties            IN OUT PARTY_NTABLE);
  -- Define a PL/SQL Reference Cursor.

  TYPE president_type_cursor IS REF CURSOR;

  -- Define procedure specification to return reference cursor.
  PROCEDURE get_presidents
  ( term_start_in    IN      NUMBER
  , term_end_in      IN      NUMBER
  , country_in       IN      VARCHAR2
  , presidents       IN OUT PRESIDENT_TYPE_CURSOR);

END world_leaders;
/

-- Display any compilation errors.
SHOW ERRORS


-- ------------------------------------------------------------------
-- Package body with overloaded procedures.
-- ------------------------------------------------------------------

-- Create a package body or implementation.
CREATE OR REPLACE PACKAGE BODY world_leaders AS

  -- Implement a procedure body to return parallel associative arrays.
  PROCEDURE get_presidents
  ( term_start_in    IN      NUMBER
  , term_end_in      IN      NUMBER
  , country_in       IN      VARCHAR2
  , president_ids    IN OUT PRESIDENT_ID_TABLE
  , president_names  IN OUT PRESIDENT_NAME_TABLE
  , tenures          IN OUT TENURE_TABLE
  , parties          IN OUT PARTY_TABLE) AS

  BEGIN
    -- Define a Bulk Collect into parallel associative arrays.

    SELECT    president_id pres_number
    ,         first_name||' '||middle_name||' '||last_name pres_name
    ,         term_start||'-'||term_end tenure
    ,         party
    BULK COLLECT
    INTO      president_ids
    ,         president_names
    ,         tenures
    ,         parties
    FROM      president
```

```
    WHERE      country = country_in
    AND        term_start BETWEEN term_start_in AND term_end_in
    OR         term_end BETWEEN term_start_in AND term_end_in;

END get_presidents;

-- Implement a procedure body to return parallel VARRAYs.
PROCEDURE get_presidents
( term_start_in     IN       NUMBER
, term_end_in       IN       NUMBER
, country_in        IN       VARCHAR2
, president_ids     IN OUT PRESIDENT_ID_VARRAY
, president_names IN OUT PRESIDENT_NAME_VARRAY
, tenures           IN OUT TENURE_VARRAY
, parties           IN OUT PARTY_VARRAY) AS

BEGIN

    SELECT    president_id pres_number
    ,         first_name||' '||middle_name||' '||last_name pres_name
    ,         term_start||'-'||term_end tenure
    ,         party
    BULK COLLECT
    INTO      president_ids
    ,         president_names
    ,         tenures
    ,         parties
    FROM      president
    WHERE     country = country_in
    AND       term_start BETWEEN term_start_in AND term_end_in
    OR        term_end BETWEEN term_start_in AND term_end_in;

END get_presidents;

-- Implement a procedure body to return parallel nested tables.
PROCEDURE get_presidents
( term_start_in     IN       NUMBER
, term_end_in       IN       NUMBER
, country_in        IN       VARCHAR2
, president_ids     IN OUT PRESIDENT_ID_NTABLE
, president_names IN OUT PRESIDENT_NAME_NTABLE
, tenures           IN OUT TENURE_NTABLE
, parties           IN OUT PARTY_NTABLE) AS

BEGIN

    SELECT    president_id pres_number
    ,         first_name||' '||middle_name||' '||last_name pres_name
    ,         term_start||'-'||term_end tenure
    ,         party
    BULK COLLECT
```

```
    INTO       president_ids
    ,          president_names
    ,          tenures
    ,          parties
    FROM       president
    WHERE      country = country_in
    AND        term_start BETWEEN term_start_in AND term_end_in
    OR         term_end BETWEEN term_start_in AND term_end_in;
  END get_presidents;

  -- Implement a procedure body to return a reference cursor.
  PROCEDURE get_presidents
  ( term_start_in    IN     NUMBER
  , term_end_in      IN     NUMBER
  , country_in       IN     VARCHAR2
  , presidents       IN OUT PRESIDENT_TYPE_CURSOR ) AS

  BEGIN
    -- Collect data for the reference cursor.
    OPEN presidents FOR
      SELECT    president_id "#"
      ,         first_name||' '||middle_name||' '||last_name "Preisdent"
      ,         term_start||' '||term_end "Tenure"
      ,         party "Party"
      FROM      president
      WHERE     country = country_in
      AND       term_start BETWEEN term_start_in AND term_end_in
      OR        term_end BETWEEN term_start_in AND term_end_in;

  END get_presidents;

END world_leaders;
/

-- Display any compilation errors.
SHOW ERRORS
-- ----------------------------------------------------------------
-- Anonymous Block Testing Programs.
-- ----------------------------------------------------------------

-- Define anonymous block PL/SQL Program to test PL/SQL table  procedure.
DECLARE

  -- Declare local variables.
  t_start            NUMBER := '1914';
  t_end              NUMBER := '1943';
  t_country          VARCHAR2(3 CHAR) := 'USA';
  president_ids      WORLD_LEADERS.PRESIDENT_ID_TABLE;
  president_names    WORLD_LEADERS.PRESIDENT_NAME_TABLE;
  tenures            WORLD_LEADERS.TENURE_TABLE;
  parties            WORLD_LEADERS.PARTY_TABLE;
```

```
BEGIN

  -- Call the overloaded procedure.
  world_leaders.get_presidents
  ( t_start
  , t_end
  , t_country
  , president_ids
  , president_names
  , tenures
  , parties);

  -- Read the contents of one of the arrays.
  FOR i IN 1..president_names.COUNT LOOP
    dbms_output.put_line('Testing ['||president_names(i)||']');
  END LOOP;
END;
/

-- Define anonymous block PL/SQL Program to test Varray procedure.
DECLARE

  -- Declare local variables.
  t_start           NUMBER := '1914';
  t_end             NUMBER := '1943';
  t_country         VARCHAR2(3 CHAR) := 'USA';
  president_ids     PRESIDENT_ID_VARRAY;
  president_names   PRESIDENT_NAME_VARRAY;
  tenures           TENURE_VARRAY;
  parties           PARTY_VARRAY;

BEGIN

  -- Call the overloaded procedure.
  world_leaders.get_presidents
  ( t_start
  , t_end
  , t_country
  , president_ids
  , president_names
  , tenures
  , parties);

  -- Read the contents of one of the arrays.
  FOR i IN 1..president_names.COUNT LOOP
    dbms_output.put_line('Testing ['||president_names(i)||']');
  END LOOP;

END;
/
```

```
-- Define anonymous block PL/SQL Program to test nested table procedure.
DECLARE

  -- Declare local variables.
  t_start           NUMBER := '1914';
  t_end             NUMBER := '1943';
  t_country         VARCHAR2(3 CHAR) := 'USA';
  president_ids     PRESIDENT_ID_NTABLE;
  president_names   PRESIDENT_NAME_NTABLE;
  tenures           TENURE_NTABLE;
  parties           PARTY_NTABLE;

BEGIN

  -- Call the overloaded procedure.
  world_leaders.get_presidents
  ( t_start
  , t_end
  , t_country
  , president_ids
  , president_names
  , tenures
  , parties);

  -- Read the contents of one of the arrays.
  FOR i IN 1..president_names.COUNT LOOP
    dbms_output.put_line('Testing ['||president_names(i)||']');
  END LOOP;

END;
/

-- Define anonymous block PL/SQL Program to test PL/SQL reference cursor.
DECLARE

  -- Define local PL/SQL record type as target for reference cursor.
  TYPE president_record IS RECORD
  ( president_id   NUMBER
  , president      VARCHAR2(60 CHAR)
  , tenure         VARCHAR2(9 CHAR)
  , party          VARCHAR2(24 CHAR));

  -- Define a variable of the PL/SQL record.
  presidents PRESIDENT_RECORD;

  -- Declare local variables.
  t_start          NUMBER := '1914';
  t_end            NUMBER := '1943';
  t_country        VARCHAR2(3 CHAR) := 'USA';
  president_info   WORLD_LEADERS.PRESIDENT_TYPE_CURSOR;
```

```
BEGIN

  -- Call the overloaded procedure.
  world_leaders.get_presidents
  ( t_start
  , t_end
  , t_country
  , president_info);

  -- Explicit fetches are required for reference cursors.
  LOOP
    FETCH president_info
    INTO  presidents;
    EXIT WHEN president_info%NOTFOUND;
    dbms_output.put_line('Testing ['||presidents.president||']');
  END LOOP;

END;
/
```

Summary

This appendix has listed for your review the Oracle scripts required to set up the principal environments for Chapter 13 and 14. These scripts are also found on the enclosed CD.

Index

T

U

LICENSE AGREEMENT

THIS PRODUCT (THE "PRODUCT") CONTAINS PROPRIETARY SOFTWARE, DATA AND INFORMATION (INCLUDING DOCUMENTATION) OWNED BY THE McGRAW-HILL COMPANIES, INC. ("McGRAW-HILL") AND ITS LICENSORS. YOUR RIGHT TO USE THE PRODUCT IS GOVERNED BY THE TERMS AND CONDITIONS OF THIS AGREEMENT.

LICENSE: Throughout this License Agreement, "you" shall mean either the individual or the entity whose agent opens this package. You are granted a non-exclusive and non-transferable license to use the Product subject to the following terms:

(i) If you have licensed a single user version of the Product, the Product may only be used on a single computer (i.e., a single CPU). If you licensed and paid the fee applicable to a local area network or wide area network version of the Product, you are subject to the terms of the following subparagraph (ii).

(ii) If you have licensed a local area network version, you may use the Product on unlimited workstations located in one single building selected by you that is served by such local area network. If you have licensed a wide area network version, you may use the Product on unlimited workstations located in multiple buildings on the same site selected by you that is served by such wide area network; provided, however, that any building will not be considered located in the same site if it is more than five (5) miles away from any building included in such site. In addition, you may only use a local area or wide area network version of the Product on one single server. If you wish to use the Product on more than one server, you must obtain written authorization from McGraw-Hill and pay additional fees.

(iii) You may make one copy of the Product for back-up purposes only and you must maintain an accurate record as to the location of the back-up at all times.

COPYRIGHT; RESTRICTIONS ON USE AND TRANSFER: All rights (including copyright) in and to the Product are owned by McGraw-Hill and its licensors. You are the owner of the enclosed disc on which the Product is recorded. You may not use, copy, decompile, disassemble, reverse engineer, modify, reproduce, create derivative works, transmit, distribute, sublicense, store in a database or retrieval system of any kind, rent or transfer the Product, or any portion thereof, in any form or by any means (including electronically or otherwise) except as expressly provided for in this License Agreement. You must reproduce the copyright notices, trademark notices, legends and logos of McGraw-Hill and its licensors that appear on the Product on the back-up copy of the Product which you are permitted to make hereunder. All rights in the Product not expressly granted herein are reserved by McGraw-Hill and its licensors.

TERM: This License Agreement is effective until terminated. It will terminate if you fail to comply with any term or condition of this License Agreement. Upon termination, you are obligated to return to McGraw-Hill the Product together with all copies thereof and to purge all copies of the Product included in any and all servers and computer facilities.

DISCLAIMER OF WARRANTY: THE PRODUCT AND THE BACK-UP COPY ARE LICENSED "AS IS." McGRAW-HILL, ITS LICENSORS AND THE AUTHORS MAKE NO WARRANTIES, EXPRESS OR IMPLIED, AS TO THE RESULTS TO BE OBTAINED BY ANY PERSON OR ENTITY FROM USE OF THE PRODUCT, ANY INFORMATION OR DATA INCLUDED THEREIN AND/OR ANY TECHNICAL SUPPORT SERVICES PROVIDED HEREUNDER, IF ANY ("TECHNICAL SUPPORT SERVICES"). McGRAW-HILL, ITS LICENSORS AND THE AUTHORS MAKE NO EXPRESS OR IMPLIED WARRANTIES OF MERCHANTABILITY OR FITNESS FOR A PARTICULAR PURPOSE OR USE WITH RESPECT TO THE PRODUCT. McGRAW-HILL, ITS LICENSORS, AND THE AUTHORS MAKE NO GUARANTEE THAT YOU WILL PASS ANY CERTIFICATION EXAM WHATSOEVER BY USING THIS PRODUCT. NEITHER McGRAW-HILL, ANY OF ITS LICENSORS NOR THE AUTHORS WARRANT THAT THE FUNCTIONS CONTAINED IN THE PRODUCT WILL MEET YOUR REQUIREMENTS OR THAT THE OPERATION OF THE PRODUCT WILL BE UNINTERRUPTED OR ERROR FREE. YOU ASSUME THE ENTIRE RISK WITH RESPECT TO THE QUALITY AND PERFORMANCE OF THE PRODUCT.

LIMITED WARRANTY FOR DISC: To the original licensee only, McGraw-Hill warrants that the enclosed disc on which the Product is recorded is free from defects in materials and workmanship under normal use and service for a period of ninety (90) days from the date of purchase. In the event of a defect in the disc covered by the foregoing warranty, McGraw-Hill will replace the disc.

LIMITATION OF LIABILITY: NEITHER McGRAW-HILL, ITS LICENSORS NOR THE AUTHORS SHALL BE LIABLE FOR ANY INDIRECT, SPECIAL OR CONSEQUENTIAL DAMAGES, SUCH AS BUT NOT LIMITED TO, LOSS OF ANTICIPATED PROFITS OR BENEFITS, RESULTING FROM THE USE OR INABILITY TO USE THE PRODUCT EVEN IF ANY OF THEM HAS BEEN ADVISED OF THE POSSIBILITY OF SUCH DAMAGES. THIS LIMITATION OF LIABILITY SHALL APPLY TO ANY CLAIM OR CAUSE WHATSOEVER WHETHER SUCH CLAIM OR CAUSE ARISES IN CONTRACT, TORT, OR OTHERWISE. Some states do not allow the exclusion or limitation of indirect, special or consequential damages, so the above limitation may not apply to you.

U.S. GOVERNMENT RESTRICTED RIGHTS: Any software included in the Product is provided with restricted rights subject to subparagraphs (c), (1) and (2) of the Commercial Computer Software-Restricted Rights clause at 48 C.F.R. 52.227-19. The terms of this Agreement applicable to the use of the data in the Product are those under which the data are generally made available to the general public by McGraw-Hill. Except as provided herein, no reproduction, use, or disclosure rights are granted with respect to the data included in the Product and no right to modify or create derivative works from any such data is hereby granted.

GENERAL: This License Agreement constitutes the entire agreement between the parties relating to the Product. The terms of any Purchase Order shall have no effect on the terms of this License Agreement. Failure of McGraw-Hill to insist at any time on strict compliance with this License Agreement shall not constitute a waiver of any rights under this License Agreement. This License Agreement shall be construed and governed in accordance with the laws of the State of New York. If any provision of this License Agreement is held to be contrary to law, that provision will be enforced to the maximum extent permissible and the remaining provisions will remain in full force and effect.